Economic Psychology: An Introducti

Economic Psychology is the only up-to-date, English-language textbook that provides a comprehensive overview of theoretical topics in economic psychology and their relevance in applied fields. Written by two leading psychologists, the book looks at how people make decisions on the use of scarce resources, in particular money, from a psychological perspective. Starting with decision-making and lay theories as basic building blocks of economic behaviour, the authors go on to explore three major markets where economic behaviour occurs as an interaction between individuals and companies or institutions – consumer markets, labour markets and financial markets – before considering the challenges of collective cooperation and economic prosperity. Featuring numerous applied examples throughout, each chapter also includes an overview, a summary, figures, key terms, student questions and suggestions for further reading. This introduction is an essential resource for advanced undergraduate and postgraduate courses on economic psychology, behavioural economics and social psychology.

Erich Kirchler is Professor of Economic Psychology at the Faculty of Psychology, University of Vienna, Austria. He is the author of many papers in edited collections and journals and of *Conflict and decision making in close relationships* (2001) and *The economic psychology of tax behaviour* (2007), and was co-editor of the *Journal of Economic Psychology*, with Erik Hoelzl.

Erik Hoelzl is Professor of Economic and Social Psychology at the Faculty of Management, Economics and Social Sciences, University of Cologne, Germany. He has published many papers in edited collections and journals, for example in the *Journal of Applied Social Psychology*, the *International Journal of Psychology* and the *Journal of Applied Psychology*.

Economic Psychology: An Introduction

ERICH KIRCHLER
University of Vienna

ERIK HOELZL
University of Cologne

CAMBRIDGE
UNIVERSITY PRESS

CAMBRIDGE
UNIVERSITY PRESS

University Printing House, Cambridge CB2 8BS, United Kingdom

One Liberty Plaza, 20th Floor, New York, NY 10006, USA

477 Williamstown Road, Port Melbourne, VIC 3207, Australia

314–321, 3rd Floor, Plot 3, Splendor Forum, Jasola District Centre, New Delhi – 110025, India

79 Anson Road, #06–04/06, Singapore 079906

Cambridge University Press is part of the University of Cambridge.

It furthers the University's mission by disseminating knowledge in the pursuit of education, learning, and research at the highest international levels of excellence.

www.cambridge.org
Information on this title: www.cambridge.org/9781107040502
DOI: 10.1017/9781139629065

First published 2018
Reprinted 2018

Printed in the United Kingdom by TJ International Ltd. Padstow Cornwall

A catalogue record for this publication is available from the British Library.

ISBN 978-1-107-04050-2 Hardback
ISBN 978-1-107-66863-8 Paperback

CONTENTS

FIGURES

TABLES

PREFACE

The purpose of this book is to give an introduction to economic psychology. We are confident that the book will stimulate further interest in an emerging interdisciplinary field of research and application.

Economic psychology builds bridges between the disciplines of economics and psychology. Based on their common research focus on human behaviour, both economists and psychologists early on showed an interest in each other's fields. However, both disciplines developed their own 'languages', their specific research paradigms and methodological toolboxes, hence conducting separate research on similar topics. In the past decades, economic psychology has gained significant momentum, especially with the recognition of the research by Daniel Kahneman and Amos Tversky by the Nobel Prize Committee in 2002. At the latest since then, research in economic psychology and behavioural economics has significantly increased. It has gained visibility and relevance both in scientific discussions and in the applied fields. Specifically, economic psychology has been recognised in institutions regulating human behaviour, in applied economics, law and politics. We present an introduction to the theoretical topics of economic psychology and their relevance in applied fields.

We cover questions about how people decide over the use of scarce resources, in particular money, from a psychological perspective. After giving an overview of the field, we start out with three chapters discussing the basic building blocks of economic behaviour: decision-making from a normative and a descriptive perspective as well as lay theories. We then move on to three chapters addressing the major markets on which economic behaviour occurs as an interaction between individuals and companies or institutions: consumer markets, labour markets and financial markets. We close with three chapters focusing on society-level topics: collective cooperation, collective production and collective prosperity.

In Chapter 1, we present economic and psychological approaches towards the study of human behaviour. We also give an overview of the history and the current fields of economic psychology that we use as the guiding structure of this book.

In Chapter 2, we present normative decision-making theories, starting out with classical decision theory and empirical studies on its predictions. We give an overview on decision anomalies that arise from information processing, emotions, time and heuristics.

In Chapter 3, we present descriptive decision-making theories. First, prospect theory as a highly influential approach that can explain several systematic deviations from rationality in people's decisions is addressed. We move on to descriptive models of individual, organisational and political decisions. Finally, we discuss nudging as a strategy to regulate citizens' behaviour.

In Chapter 4, we present lay theories about economic concepts. Laypeople often have a different view from experts, and build their actions on these views. We discuss that economic knowledge, motives and behaviour develop with age, but that even adults often have limited financial literacy. We close with subjective views on money that become particularly apparent in currency reforms and in the perception of prices.

In Chapter 5, we present selected processes on consumer markets. We first cover purchase decisions by individual consumers and discuss models explaining these decisions. We move on to purchase decisions in private households, focusing on the specific challenges in these settings.

Finally, we discuss credit decisions of individuals and households, as nowadays more and more purchases involve the borrowing of money.

In Chapter 6, we present selected processes on labour markets. We start with the notion that labour markets can be viewed as an interplay of supply and demand for work power and that specific aspects of labour markets can be studied experimentally. We further discuss wages as a motivating factor as well as perceptions of wage fairness. Finally, we review entrepreneurship including relevant determinants in founding one's own company.

In Chapter 7, we present selected processes on financial markets. We discuss economic and psychological perspectives on the stock market and some common errors and biases that occur. We present findings on over- and under-reaction to news and the disposition effect. Investor decisions are influenced by heuristics, emotions and social processes. Finally, we discuss the role of trust in financial institutions.

In Chapter 8, we present collective cooperation as the question of how individuals cooperate within a large-scale economic system such as a nation. We start with a view on the shadow economy, in particular tax evasion, and move on to findings on attitudes towards taxes and on tax behaviour in general. We then present different approaches relevant in the understanding of tax behaviour and tax evasion. Finally, we discuss how the interaction climate between taxpayers and tax authorities shapes cooperation.

In Chapter 9, we present collective production as another aspect of how individuals interact within large-scale economic systems. We discuss how the meaning of work has changed over time and introduce current views on work and leisure. We present findings on unemployment, in particular psychosocial consequences and the differential impact of unemployment.

In Chapter 10, we discuss collective prosperity and the questions surrounding the connection between wealth and happiness. We start with conceptual considerations of life satisfaction, well-being and happiness. We move on to findings on the association between these concepts on the individual level and on the aggregated level within a nation. Finally, we discuss the role of economic prosperity, as for example measured by the Gross Domestic Product, regarding the happiness of citizens within a nation.

We have written this book based on our enthusiasm for the field of economic psychology, in both research and teaching. With colleagues from psychology and economics, we have ourselves published on many of the topics covered in this book. We are committed members of the International Association for Research in Economic Psychology (IAREP) and regular participants of its conferences, as well as being editors of the *Journal of Economic Psychology* (2010–15). We have taught courses in economic psychology since 1982 (Erich Kirchler) and 1996 (Erik Hoelzl) in various settings – most prominently at the universities of Vienna and Linz, Austria, and Cologne, Germany. This book builds on a successful German-language textbook by Erich Kirchler that is now in its fourth edition.

Our students only partly come with a psychology background – some have never had any psychology courses before. Therefore, our goal was to make the field accessible for non-psychologists, while at the same time providing a state-of-the-art overview. The specific features of this book are the following:

- Textbooks in economic psychology have a long tradition, but the more influential English-language textbooks now date back some decades. There are current textbooks, but those are – to our knowledge – all edited books by several contributors, whereas this book comes 'all of a piece'. We believe that our long research and teaching experience enables us to give a comprehensive

overview that ensures the linkage between theories and applications. This helps students to see the connections in a large and ever-growing field.
- We provide explanations of basic theories from social psychology, general psychology or developmental psychology as well as economics to ensure a comprehensive understanding of the thematic empirical findings.
- We provide examples and explanations of several empirical approaches in economic psychology, such as experiments (with individuals or groups), experimental markets, economic games, surveys, diary methods or analysis of spontaneous associations.
- We provide extensive and detailed references to sources, covering both classical works and recent developments, to enable students to pursue the topics in more detail.
- We start each chapter with an overview and close with a summary linking back to the overview to help students in their acquisition of a general framework for the topics presented.
- At the end of each chapter, we provide questions that allow students to check their understanding of concepts and their learning progress.
- We provide further readings at the end of each chapter, which in many cases include recent books written for a general audience.

This book is written for scholars across various disciplines, for students at different stages of their education, for practitioners interested in economic psychology and behavioural economics, for journalists and policy advisors, and for the general public with or without psychology background. It can be used for bachelor-level or master-level courses in business administration (marketing, consumer behaviour, finance or corporate development), economics (microeconomics, behavioural economics), social sciences (sociology, political science) and psychology, where students should get a basic knowledge about the foundations of economic psychology. Practitioners can benefit from insights in consumer decisions, investment decisions or taxpaying decisions.

ACKNOWLEDGMENTS

This textbook on economic psychology originated from initiatives taken by Cambridge University Press, especially from Hetty Marx in her role as commissioning editor for psychology. She encouraged us to collect our experiences as joint editors of the *Journal of Economic Psychology* from 2010 to 2015 and suggested we review economic psychological knowledge for the English-language market, starting with the collection published in the German-language volume *Wirtschaftspsychologie: Individuen, Gruppen, Märkte, Staat* by the publishing house Hogrefe in Göttingen, Germany. We analysed the contents of the *Journal of Economic Psychology*, categorised them, and developed a content structure for this book. Many of our colleagues and students helped in reorganising, selecting and updating the contents in the German textbook, corrected the text, added new literature and insights, and commented on weaknesses and shortcomings. They inspired us in many discussions about economic psychological topics: many thanks to Sebastian Beer, Michael Blens, Martina Brandtner, Linda Dezsö, Janina Enachescu, Barbara Hartl, Marc Heise, Eva Hofmann, Tobias Kapferer, Matthias Kasper, Christoph Kogler, Michail Kokkoris, Gregor Kracke, Stephan Muehlbacher, Jerome Olsen, Richard Schlicht, Jennifer Stark, Raik Thiele and Laura Winter. Without their efforts, we would not have been able to write and complete this book. We are most grateful to Elisabeth Dorfinger who with great patience drew the figures, checked the tables and completed the references list. We thank Keri Hartman for translating parts of the text from German and improving the English parts. We also thank Rosemary Crawley, Frances Brown and Maree Williams-Smith from Cambridge University Press for their support in the production of the book.

Erich Kirchler and Erik Hoelzl

1 Economic Psychology: History and Application

Overview

This chapter introduces the general theme of the book. It starts out with the presentation of different markets as an exchange of resources between households and firms (or institutions), which will serve as a framework for the following chapters. It outlines economic expectations as an example of how individual perceptions are influenced by the economy and how they influence the economy in turn. It then turns to the disciplinary perspectives: it defines economics, lists the research fields in economics, and describes economists' basic assumptions about human behaviour. The general theoretical and empirical research approaches of economics and psychology are contrasted. This section also includes a short history of economic psychology as an academic discipline and closes with an overview of current research topics in the field.

Markets are places where goods are exchanged. They are commonly defined as the intersection of supply and demand for goods and services, labour, land, capital, rights and other exchangeable resources. Actors' behaviour in the marketplace depends upon their expectations for the future, and these expectations are informed by actors' past and current experiences.

Economics and psychology as social sciences are both concerned with human behaviour. While economics concentrates on behaviour in commercial and financial contexts, psychology investigates behaviour (and experience) in a variety of life areas. There are multiple points of contact between the two disciplines; however, their scientific developments have taken different trajectories. One distinction between economics and psychology is that economics is based on a normative model of human behaviour and is concerned with behaviour in the aggregate – such as at the level of the market or of the state. Conversely, psychology concentrates on the individual, on differences between people and on (small) group dynamics.

Economic psychology attempts to build a bridge between economics and psychology. It is concerned with individual decisions, deviations from the economic (rational) model of human behaviour, with lay theories and markets, and also with welfare and well-being. The first steps towards the establishment of economic psychology as a discipline were taken at the beginning of the twentieth century but forgotten shortly thereafter. Economic psychology was briefly resuscitated in the middle of the last century before falling into obscurity once again. In the past few decades, however, especially since the awarding of the Nobel Prize to Daniel Kahneman, economic psychology has gained acceptance within the field of psychology. At the same time, behavioural economics – which shares similarities with economic psychology – has been accepted into the larger discipline of economic science.

Introduction

Various disciplines including economics and psychology attempt to understand and predict human behaviour on markets. Though there are some similarities between all these different approaches, they usually take different points of view. The focus of this chapter is to contrast the economic and psychological views on human behaviour and decision-making. It emphasises that the two approaches do not necessarily exclude each other, but can complement each other. This sets the course for an exciting research field.

1.1 Markets

An economy is determined by the activities of households, firms and the state as well as by global economic developments. While households and firms are decision-makers in the private sector, the state is a public decision-making body.

One critical state decision is whether to steer the economy by instituting central planning or to put faith in the market's self-regulation and interfere as little as possible with market forces. Fundamentally, interactions between households and firms can be regulated as either centralised or decentralised. This means that interactions between the two groups can be planned either by the state or by market participants themselves, leaving the market to its own devices. The first case is referred to as a centrally managed or a planned economy; the second defines a market economy. In planned economies, the production and distribution of goods is not left up to households and companies, but is determined by a centralised plan. In market economies, households and firms plan for themselves and try to bring these plans to fruition. Suppliers of goods and services, land, labour and capital encounter market participants who demand these goods. This meeting of supply and demand, the formation of prices for tradable goods and the exchange of them, is referred to as the market.

Economics differentiates between two groups of markets: (a) factor markets for land, labour and capital and (b) product markets for goods and services (Figure 1.1; Woll, 1981). In product markets in which suppliers encounter a high degree of competitive pressure due to a large number of competing suppliers, producers must develop strategies to market and distribute their goods widely in order to persevere in the struggle against their competitors. Similarly, households must make decisions as to how to make the best use of their available – usually limited – budgetary resources. Specifically, they need to decide how much of their income they will spend and save, which investments they will make, which goods they will purchase, and whether or not they will take out a loan to do so. In the same way, suppliers and demanders in factor markets must make decisions regarding available land, labour or capital. For example, workers make decisions about the circumstances under which they will offer up their labour, and firms make decisions about the conditions under which they will be able to employ workers.

This interaction between individuals and households on the one side and firms and institutions on the other side is reflected by economic expectations and consumer sentiment. In the marketplace, individual and household behaviour depends upon knowledge of the economy and ideas about economic relationships. Expectations about the future influence consumers' and producers' decision-making. When the assumption is that economic conditions will worsen, it seems wise to save; however, when economic prosperity is expected, it might be reasonable to take the risk of

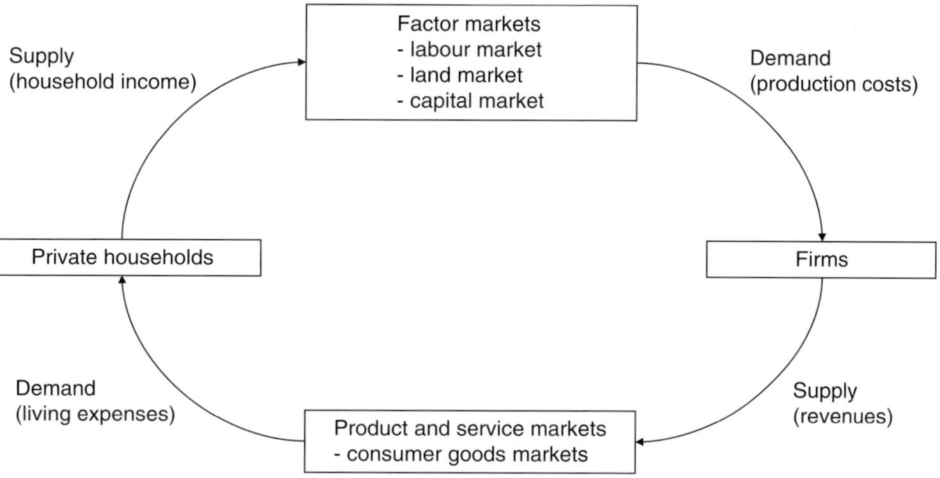

Figure 1.1 Planning in the market economy (adapted from Woll, 1981, p. 69)

buying goods on credit. Expectations about future developments in the economy determine behaviour, and behaviour determines actual economic developments.

Expectations in general were defined as 'an anticipation in the style of a daydream, and a visualisation of upcoming experiences related to the themes of our aspirations' (Lersch, 1962, p. 286). Wärneryd (2001) summarised the state of research on **economic expectations** and introduced a model integrating various theoretical currents. Economic expectations are conjectures about future economic events. They build upon forward projections of the past, meaning that attempts to predict the future are based upon extrapolations from past events. Expectations are also viewed, however, as the result of complex considerations about various possible future paths of development and of well-founded, informed decisions about the most likely path. According to Wärneryd, expectations are formed on the basis of information from three sources: (a) past experiences, (b) learning processes and (c) knowledge and opinions about new circumstances. Opinions about future events are extrapolated from past experiences. Discrepancies between expectations for past events and their actual outcomes lead to a recognition of mistakes and to learning and adjustment processes, which influence one's subjective outlook on the future. Finally, newly emerging circumstances – economic, political and social changes – can additionally influence opinions about future developments and therefore shape expectations. Kuß (1980, building on Strümpel, Schmiedeskamp & Schwartz, 1973) illustrated interactions between different variables related to sentiments and expectations, the economic context, and consumer reactions that stem from it (Figure 1.2).

In the advanced industrialised countries of the West, the proportion of private expenditures on goods and services that are not exclusively needed to satisfy basic human needs is high. Consumers have wide latitude in making decisions on how to spend their income and therefore in influencing the gross national product. For this reason, predictions and plans to take political measures related to macroeconomic processes are based on observations and analyses of consumer behaviour (Kuß, 1980). Consumers' expectations and intended actions are investigated, and built into an index of consumer sentiments upon which predictions about economic changes are based:

> Analogous to the term 'climate' in meteorology, which describes an amalgamation of seasonally and geographically specific elements of the atmospheric condition (e.g., temperature, precipitation level,

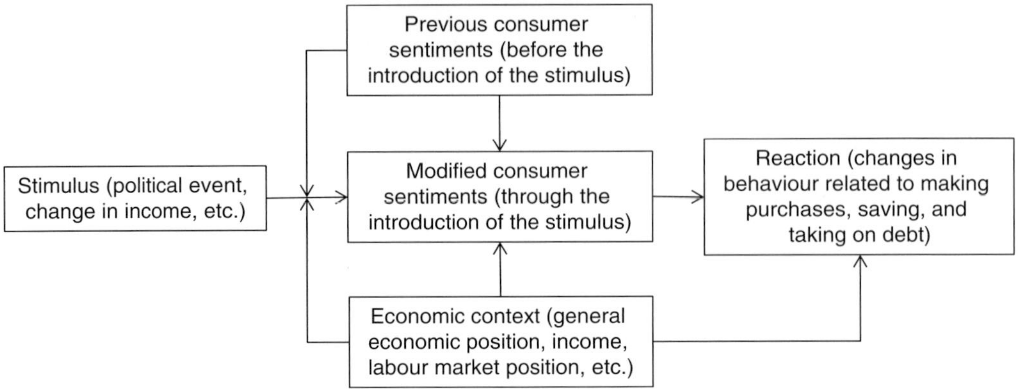

Figure 1.2 Interactions between various stimulus variables and the economic context (Kuß, 1980, p. 103)

> sunshine duration), a variety of consumer attitudes and expectations, especially those important to private consumption in a given economic sphere, can be compiled to form a 'consumer climate'. (Kuß, 1980, p. 101)

Between the two World Wars, John Maynard Keynes strove to make more realistic assertions about the behaviour of economic actors than was the case in classical economic theory. His approach placed more emphasis on consumers' and firms' attitudes and expectations. However, while Keynes limited himself to a mechanical perspective based on economic theory, George Katona (1951), working after the Second World War, attempted to connect psychology and economics. He was also the person who laid the methodological foundation for measuring consumer sentiments through his work at the University of Michigan's Survey Research Center. Since 1946, this institution has regularly conducted consumer surveys in which a few important questions have remained the same. As a result, fluctuations in consumer confidence over the course of time can be observed (Katona, Strümpel & Zahn, 1971). The **Consumer Sentiment Index** measures consumers' subjective feelings about their individual financial situation and overall economic conditions at present and in the future. The index was normalised to the value of 100 in 1964. Figure 1.3 shows the trajectory of the Consumer Sentiment Index over time. For example, the recent drop around 2007/8 coincides with the economic crisis.

Since the 1970s, the countries of the European Union have been collecting data for similar sentiment indices. Questions are asked about consumers' subjective views on the following points:

- evaluation of general economic conditions in the past year
- expectations for general economic conditions in the coming year
- expectations for changes in the unemployment rate in the coming year
- evaluation of price changes in the past year
- expectations for price developments in the coming year
- evaluation of their own household's economic position in the past year
- expectations for their household's economic position in the coming year
- evaluation of the current advisability of making larger purchases
- evaluation of whether it makes sense to save
- plans to save in the upcoming year.

The Consumer Sentiment Index reports the confidence private households have in the national economy. It is considered a leading indicator of future economic developments in a country. It has

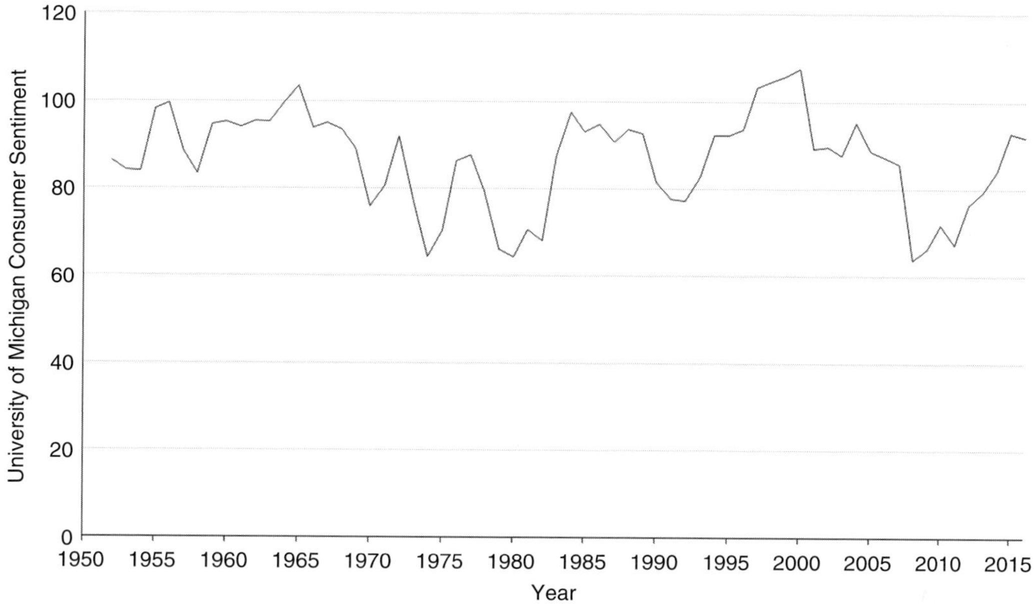

Figure 1.3 United States Consumer Sentiment Index (1952–2016, yearly average). Data from Surveys of Consumers, University of Michigan, retrieved from FRED, Federal Reserve Bank of St. Louis; http://fred.stlouisfed.org/series/UMCSENT/ and http://research.stlouisfed.org/fred2/series/UMCSENT1/ (accessed 19 July 2016)

been confirmed repeatedly that it makes sense to ask consumers questions about the future of the economy, and the Consumer Sentiment Index has proven its ability to predict economic developments (Fischer & Fischer, 1988). This is exemplified by the correlation between consumer sentiment and retail sales in the UK, found in the publications of the Office for National Statistics (Figure 1.4). Further examples providing impressive evidence for the correlation between consumer sentiment, expectations and economic changes can be found in Curtin (1979) and in Katona et al. (1971).

As a sensitive psychological indicator, the Consumer Sentiment Index has received approval. However, several points of criticism were raised as well: The index is a coarse, simplified measure of consumer sentiments. Attitudes and expectations are more complex than can be adequately captured in the few questions listed above. Changes in the economy come about as a result of complex interactions between subjective perceptions and objective economic factors, which is why changes in income and in tax revenue and changes in the tax code need to be considered in addition to sentiments.

Despite these critical limitations, it is important to emphasise that the Consumer Sentiment Index and its ability to predict further economic developments prove that changes in the economy can be based on psychological phenomena. More detailed techniques allow for an improved measurement of the subjective economic climate. By order of the European Commission, all nations of the EU periodically collect data on measures such as consumer confidence, savings climate, price and income expectations, expectations regarding the business cycle, and intentions to make major purchases in order to anticipate future economic trends. Notably, this discussion of consumer sentiment demonstrates effects in two directions: on the one hand, economic activities influence individual perceptions, and on the other hand, individual perceptions translate into economically relevant activities. Hence, psychological concepts and phenomena have an important role in both directions.

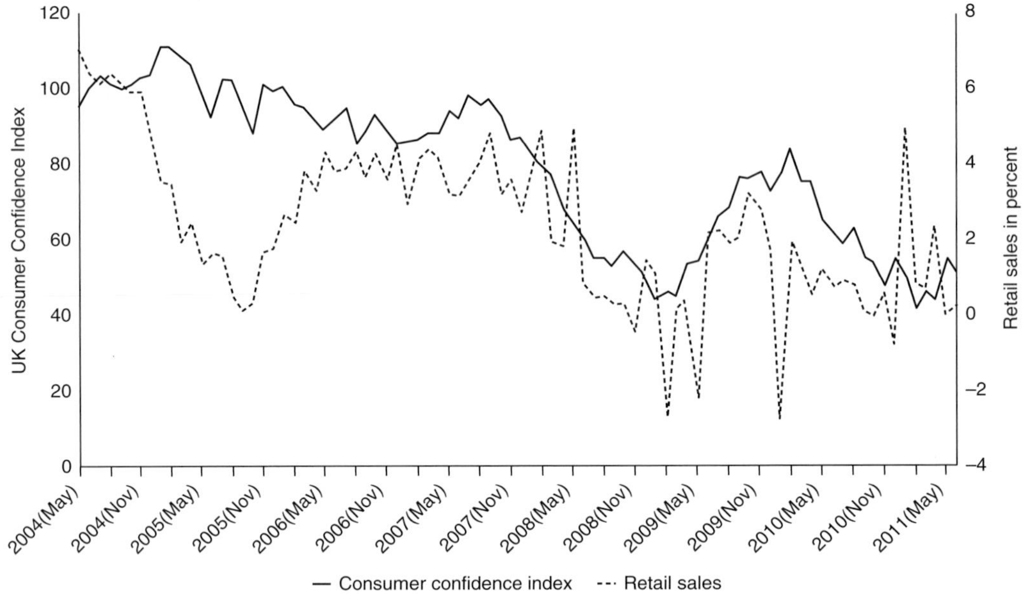

Figure 1.4 UK Consumer Confidence Index and retail sales (2004–11). Office for National Statistics, Nationwide; retrieved from www.ercouncil.org/chart-of-the-week/tag/consumer-confidence (accessed 14 July 2015)

1.2 Economics and Psychology

Like psychology, economics is concerned with behaviour, decisions, and the selection of one alternative from a set of various alternatives. In his essay on the nature and significance of economic science, Robbins (1932, p. 15) succinctly characterised the field as an academic discipline 'which studies human behaviour as a relationship between ends and scarce means which have alternative uses'. Samuelson (1980; see also Samuelson & Nordhaus, 2007) elaborated:

> Economics is the study of how men and society end up choosing, with or without the use of money, to employ scarce productive resources which could have alternative uses, to produce various commodities and distribute them for consumption, now or in the future, among various people and groups in society. (Samuelson, 1980, p. 4)

Because resources are scarce whereas wants and needs are abundant, our limited resources must be used rationally. However, it is difficult to say when a decision is rational and when it is not. Forester (1984) tells the following story by way of analogy: A man who mistakes a vending machine for a slot machine puts in one coin after another, and drinks keep falling out. His co-worker admonishes him to just drink something and stop wasting his money. Annoyed, the man tells his colleague not to bother him – he's on a winning streak! What appears irrational to one person might be considered rational and profitable by another.

Various disciplines (theology, jurisprudence, medicine, ecology, etc.) have differing perspectives as to what behaviour counts as rational or reasonable and what the goals of human action should be. Economics, however, defines goals of action from the perspective of the individual trying to reach them. Whatever persons do, they do so because it helps them reach their current specific goal, which is defined as the result of the action undertaken. This sometimes leads to situations in which, to an outside observer, rather strange goals seem to be pursued – even though they follow the rules of logic, and therefore are 'rational'!

> The standard theory of choice provides a set of conditions for rationality that may be necessary, but are hardly sufficient: they allow many foolish decisions to be called rational. (Kahneman, 1994, p. 32)

Using the metaphor of '*homo economicus*', economics as a social science focuses on the production, distribution and consumption of goods and services. While microeconomics investigates the behaviour and interactions of economic agents such as households and firms, buyers and sellers or markets, macroeconomics studies how economies work. It focuses on labour and unemployment, money, fiscal policy, inflation, economic growth, etc. This focus on decisions and on selection behaviour in a world of scarce resources and a multitude of wants and needs has generated a number of lines of research and bodies of theory within economics. The American Economic Association categorises economic research into several different fields. In the following, selected fields that are relevant for economic psychology are described according to the website of the American Economic Association (www.aeaweb.org/jel/guide/jel.php):

- 'Microeconomics' refers to the functioning of markets and the role of prices. The behaviour of individual households, firms and prices and quantities of specific products are studied. Recently, behavioural economics as the study of the cognitive and emotional dimensions of economic decisions has gained considerable momentum in microeconomics (for a detailed review of the beginning of behavioural economics in the late 1950s until the present see Angner & Loewenstein, 2012).
- 'Macroeconomics and Monetary Economics': The actions of individual agents can be summed to encompass total activity in the economy as a whole. Macroeconomics focuses on the aggregative level, the total amount of products consumed by households and firms, which must equal the total amount produced, and the total amount firms pay to workers and investors, which must equal the amount households receive in income. Economic growth, the role of money and interest rates, changes in the overall level of prices and the aggregate level of unemployment are central concerns of macroeconomics.
- 'Financial Economics' studies the process of saving and investing with a specific concern for how individuals and firms deal with risk.
- 'Public Economics' considers the role of government in the economy. It focuses on evaluating government programmes and on the design of tax systems. Issues of national security and defence appear here as well as the study of state and local governments.
- 'Labour and Demographic Economics' studies employers' decisions to hire workers and employees' decisions to work. It studies how wages are set, the nature of incentives workers face, and the role of minimum wage laws, unions, pension plans and training programmes. It is also interested in the formation of families, determinants of birth rates, migration, population change and aging.
- 'Industrial Organisation' refers to the study of individual markets, the nature of competition and the role of prices. Specific issues are anti-trust policy, advertising and pricing policies, as well as how costs vary with the scale of operations.
- 'Business Administration and Business Economics, Marketing, Accounting' refers to studies of firms' decision-making, of entrepreneurship and of leadership.

Economics uses several general principles to answer questions about the behaviour of households, firms, markets and state institutions. According to these principles, economic activity is defined as decision-making on the basis of specific criteria – in other words, as the selection of one alternative out of many. Individuals, firms and institutions engaged in economic activity (economic actors) typically cannot satisfy all of their wants and needs. They have to choose between several alternatives and are aware that selecting one of them means forgoing all the others and their respective benefits. Every choice involves **opportunity costs**, that is, the costs that arise from selecting one alternative and therefore renouncing all other alternatives and their corresponding benefits.

Opportunity costs are not exclusively relevant for individuals. Groups of people, organisations and national economies must also make decisions about which alternatives they will choose in the case when all resources are being used at full capacity, as total production cannot directly be increased. At the level of the state, it must be decided which goods out of a multitude of possible goods will be produced with the limited resources available. A graphical example from Woll's (1981) introductory economics textbook makes this clear: suppose that the so-called 'basket of goods' was reduced to two categories, private consumer goods and defence goods. With the given quantity of resources, it is possible to produce goods in one of the two categories, or in a combination of both. Therefore, it must be decided which goods will be produced in which quantities. If the production costs are exactly the same across the two categories, a production possibilities curve like the one depicted in Figure 1.5 exists. If the state selects production combination B, 'b' defence goods and 'c' consumer goods will be produced. If more consumer goods are requested, the state must forgo a specific number of defence goods. As the production combination A on the production possibilities curve shows, it is only possible to produce 'a' number of defence goods and 'd' number of consumer goods at position A. Each production combination – A ('a', 'd'), B ('b', 'c'), or any other combination – on the production possibilities curve can be attained, but only one can be attained at any one time. Hence, it must be decided which production combination will be realised. Even with complete use of all productive forces, quantity 'd' consumer goods and quantity 'b' defence goods cannot be produced at the same time. The maximum possible production combinations lie on the curve including points A and B.

The **production possibilities curve** or **production transformation curve** describes the maximum producible combinations of goods, given a specific level of resources that are used at full capacity. Production levels inside the curve are also possible (point C). When not all production possibilities are used to exhaustion, less than the maximum producible combination of goods will be produced. This occurs when some productive forces lie fallow due to unemployment or a downturn in the business cycle, but also when simply used inefficiently. Producing a combination of goods outside the production possibilities curve (for example, point D) is not possible in the short run. In the middle or long run, however, more goods can be produced with the same number of resources if they are used more efficiently – for example, through innovation and technological advance.

The production transformation curve serves to clarify challenges and problems that arise, for example, from the allocation of scarce resources to fulfil various wants and needs, or from the full use of production factors. In addition, challenges posed by an inefficient usage of production factors or changes due to economic growth can be illustrated.

Classical economic assumptions regarding the transformation curve are based on the assumption that the relevant actors will seek to deploy resources in the best possible way. According to the **profit maximisation principle**, the maximum possible result with the given quantity of resources should be achieved. At the same time, the **cost minimisation principle** dictates that resources should be deployed as economically as possible; in other words, a given result should be achieved with minimal resources.

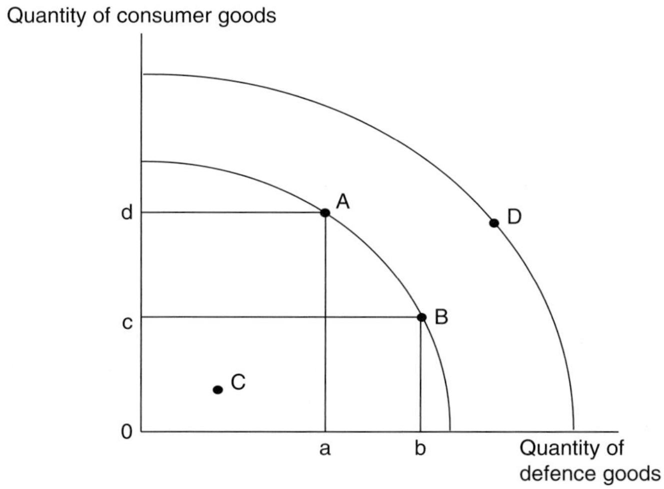

Figure 1.5 Production possibilities curve (adapted from Woll, 1981, p. 52)

The goal of economically efficient action confronts economic actors with an optimisation problem. In order to describe optimisation behaviour, economists must first attempt to understand the goals of economic actors, as optimisation can only be defined relative to the goals of an individual actor. It is assumed that, out of a bundle of possible courses of action, economic actors select the alternative that brings them maximum utility. A description of optimisation behaviour is then derived from a small number of axioms. When actors behave in accordance with these axioms, their behaviour can be described as the maximisation of a goal function. These goals can be selfish or altruistic and are commonly described using the term 'utility'. Utility does not necessarily mean profit for persons themselves. As even indirect or future harms to an actor (if these are the actor's goals) can be included in the definition of utility, the term can be confusing. Hence, instead of utility, this text will speak of goals. For the most part it is assumed not that people want to inflict harm upon themselves, but rather that they would like to optimise (that is to say, maximise) their personal utility – or, in lay terms, their goals for improving their situation.

Gravelle and Rees (1981) described several **axioms** as basic assumptions about preferences. These axioms are the point of departure for a description of optimisation behaviour and form the core of the rationality assumption:

(a) **Completeness**: If actors must choose a preferred alternative out of several alternatives, the characteristics and consequences of the various alternatives must be clear to them. These consequences must be evaluated, and all available alternatives must be compared with one another. According to the assumption of completeness, actors must be capable of ranking these alternatives in a preference order. In other words, they must be able to generate relationships between alternatives, according to which Alternative A is either better than or just as good as Alternative B ($A \succsim B$), Alternative B is just as good as or better than Alternative A ($A \precsim B$), or the two alternatives are viewed indifferently ($A \sim B$).

(b) **Transitivity**: It is further assumed that actors create consistent preference orders, and that their preferences in a decision-making scenario do not change arbitrarily. A transitive relation means that a consumer who believes that Alternative A is better than or just as good as Alternative B and that Alternative B is better than or just as good as Alternative C also believes A is better than or just as good as C (if $A \succsim B$ and $B \succsim C$, then $A \succsim C$). If Alternative A is just as good as B and B is just as good as C, the actor must also show indifference between A and C (if A ~ B and B ~ C, then A ~ C). This means that any single alternative can belong to one and only one set of alternatives to which the actor is indifferent (indifference set).

(c) **Reflexivity**: The reflexivity assumption postulates that every bundle of alternatives is just as good as itself (A ~ A). This assumption seems trivial, but it is necessary in order to guarantee that every alternative only belongs to one indifference set. This set can consist of a single alternative.

Taken together, these three axioms – the three characteristics of the preference–indifference relationship – lead to the conclusion that every alternative (completeness) belongs to one (reflexivity) and only one indifference set (transitivity).

(d) **Non-satiation**: Gravelle and Rees (1981) cite non-satiation as a further basic assumption, according to which one bundle of alternatives is preferred to another when the first bundle contains at least one good in a higher quantity than the second bundle and the same quantity of all other goods. This assumes that actors prefer to possess more of a good and not less.
(e) **Continuity**: The continuity axiom claims that it is possible to compensate for the loss of a specific quantity of Good A with a specific quantity of Good B. Accordingly, the quantity combination (a, b) is just as good as the quantity combination (a – x, b + y) to an actor viewing the two combinations indifferently.
(f) **Convexity**: Finally, it is assumed that individuals possessing a small amount of Good A and a large amount of Good B will only be indifferent to the loss of parts of A if they receive a proportionally larger quantity of B in return. The axiom of convexity corresponds to the law of diminishing marginal utility, according to which the relative increase in utility that comes from possessing more of a good decreases with increasing quantities of that good.

Based on these assumptions, economics has developed a complex system of dictates allowing the prediction of human behaviour under changing conditions (as long as people do indeed make decisions rationally and maximise their utility). According to the basic assumptions of neoclassical theory, whichever alternative an economic actor selects from a set of alternatives is the alternative that the actor prefers.

Actors seek to maximise their utility. This means that people who engage in economic activity, having full awareness of their goals, first form a consistent and stable preference order and subsequently select from all available possibilities. Under these conditions, economics speaks of rational, utility-maximising behaviour.

The basic assumptions of economics are, therefore, utility maximisation and rationality. Within this framework, economic actors are viewed in isolation from one another; they are not considered within their social context, which might determine their behaviour. Hence, economic actors are viewed as if they were in a social vacuum (Etzioni, 1988).

The neoclassical paradigm of ***homo economicus*** as a utility-maximising and rationally behaving actor has been the inspiration not only for the field of economics, but also for several branches of psychology. For example, based on this paradigm, theories of the need for achievement and of interpersonal interaction in the public sphere or in intimate relationships have been formulated. These have been celebrated as 'de-romanticised' universal theories, while at the same time being derided as techno-economic elaborations divorced from reality. Most notably, the exchange theories (Adams, 1965; Blau, 1964; Homans, 1961; Thibaut & Kelley, 1959) purporting to explain social behaviour are based on economic thought regarding rationality and utility maximisation.

As early as the beginning of the twentieth century, Simmel (1923/1996, p. 45) considered human interaction under the lens of greed and taking: 'Thus an individual, perhaps, gives "spirit," that is, intellectual values, while the other shows his gratitude by returning affective values. Another offers the aesthetic charms of his personality.' Blau (1964) and Homans (1974) later reduced the bulk of social behaviour, even behaviour between romantic partners, to the economic principle of the exchange of preferred material and immaterial resources. Taking the theory of operant conditioning as a point of departure, Homans explained human behaviour as a function of behavioural consequences: the probability of undertaking a given course of action changes according to rewards and punishments, or profit and loss. While, to Homans, there is nothing fundamentally different about social behaviour and individual behaviour in non-social contexts (both are completely determined by the behavioural consequences), Blau (1964, p. 4) made it clear that social relationships are the shared product of the individuals taking part in them, and therefore cannot be completely explained by reinforcement theory. Social behaviour is goal-oriented, which means it is also cognitively controlled. Social transactions result from strategic deliberations: interaction partners can seek to exchange material or immaterial rewards directly, but they can also allow credit by reciprocating or claiming rewards only after a certain period of time.

Thibaut and Kelley (1959) similarly argued that each interaction partner weighs the advantages and disadvantages of the contact with the other person. If both partners view the difference between these advantages and disadvantages as favourable, interactions are repeated and intensified; if the difference is unsatisfactory and alternatives that are more profitable are available, the contact is terminated. More specifically, people develop expectations about rewards in present and future interactions based on the agreeability of past interactions and the anticipated benefits that alternative relationships offer. If their expectations are not met, the current relationship is dissolved.

Out of these various exchange theories, Nye (1979) derived the following theses regarding behaviour in social interactions:

- People make rational decisions. Even social relationships are evaluated on the basis of their benefits, as well as the benefits promised by other relationships, in a manner corresponding to the individual's capacities and the available information.
- People act and react in social interactions. They make decisions and undertake actions. Their behaviour is not determined by pre-existing cultural or situational conditions alone.
- Benefits come with costs. Every behavioural act involves costs, in that it consumes time and energy that could be used for other activities.
- Behavioural patterns that have been rewarded in the past are repeated.
- If no behavioural alternative promises a profit, people will attempt to hold costs as low as possible.
- People are satisfied in their interactions when they get what they think they deserve. If they get less than that, they are disgruntled; if they get more, they can feel guilty. Benefits and costs are divided up among the partners according to specific rules (e.g., according to contribution, need or parity).
- Social contact is based on the norm of reciprocity.
- Costs are imposed upon those whose actions cause harms. Punishing hostile parties is viewed as a pleasurable, rewarding experience.
- The costs a person must bear from being punished by another person are generally higher than the benefits they gain when they inflict punishment upon someone who has hurt them.
- Different interaction partners judge the value of various objects, experiences and relationships differently.
- The more a person owns of a resource, the less value they place upon a new unit of this object or experience.

The view of humanity lying at the foundation of classical economic thought and social exchange theories within psychology is that of *homo economicus*. The basic assumptions of this view have recently come up against vehement critiques.

Although these critiques regarding utility maximisation and of the rationality assumption can in fact be justified, they often present an extreme, distorted version of the predominant view of humanity within economics. The attacks launched by psychologists are often incompetent, directed towards an inadequate, cartoonish representation of humanity that bears little resemblance to anything economists would recognise as their view of human behaviour, and are therefore largely ignored. Economists agree that humans are not exclusively

> instrumental-rational beings, slaves to their desire to acquire more possessions, following only considerations of utility maximisation, beings equipped with the capacity to adapt with infinitely quick reaction speeds to changing market constellations due to their exhaustive knowledge of market data (conditions of supply and demand) – in other words, complete information (market transparency) – who are thus able to act in order to achieve maximum possible utility. (von Rosenstiel & Ewald, 1979, p. 19)

The question that really shakes economics to the very foundations is whether human beings actually want and are able to pursue their goals in the best possible, economically rational ways. What do people want to maximise? Benefits for themselves? Profit for themselves and others? Do they seek to act according to the moral dictates of their society? What importance do considerations of fairness, trust and cooperation have? Ultimately, it is critical to consider what differences exist between isolated individuals, whose calculations are 'coldly' rational, and members of collectives, who act within normative barriers and the constraints of rules (Etzioni, 1988). The conditions under which goals can be pursued according to the rules of logic should also be scrutinised. Can the basic assumption of rationality be convincingly defended, or is it flawed as neither individuals and households nor firms and markets act according to the postulated axioms? DellaVigna (2009) reviewed research in psychology and economics and pointed to the indefensible assumptions that individuals' preferences are time-consistent, only affected by their own payoffs, and independent of the framing of a decision situation:

> Laboratory experiments in both the psychology and economics literature raise serious questions about these assumptions ... In the laboratory, individuals are time-inconsistent ... show a concern for the welfare of others ... and exhibit an attitude toward risk that depends on framing and reference points ... They violate rational expectations, for example, by overestimating their own skills ... and overprojecting from the current state ... They use heuristics to solve complex problems ... and are affected by transient emotions in their decisions. (p. 316)

Economic psychology and behavioural economics have attended to these questions and have come to the critical realisation that it is 'totally normal' to depart from the norms of the model of *homo economicus*. The assumptions of the model of *homo economicus* have fallen apart. However, the question arises as to whether these assumptions, flawed when considering the individual, continue to hold at the aggregative level, that is to say, for a hypothetical person presenting the averaged behaviour of each person in a group or a state.

Economics has developed a simple yet potent concept that purports not only to predict but also to describe human behaviour. However, the advantages of symbolic mathematical language and the precision that stems from it cannot hide the fact that people often make non-rational and irrational decisions even in economic contexts. The basic assumptions of classical economic theory are commonly violated. Decisions do not always follow the logical rules of rationality; nor is the maximisation of (selfish personal) utility the primary goal. Even the increasingly easier access to information (for example, on the internet) about each option does not lead to better decision-making;

just the opposite, too much information sometimes leads to worse decision-making. In the field of advertising communication, Kroeber-Riel (1991) stated that in the best case, people only process 2% of the glut of medial information that constantly floods into their households and businesses, and that almost all information ends up in the trash.

However, could it be possible that the model of *homo economicus* is indeed valid in situations where the decisions and actions of many different people are considered at the aggregate level (for example, at the level of the entire economy)? Following Frey (1990), there are four possible types of individual and aggregate behaviour. Individual behaviour can correspond to economic principles or deviate from them. In the same way, the economic model's dictates can hold either true or not true at the aggregate, societal level. Cell A in Figure 1.6 corresponds to cases in which both actions at the individual and aggregate level are rational and utility maximising. For adherents to the theory of rationality, this is the desired situation, as anomalies do not exist on either level. Still acceptable are those cases where individual behaviour exhibits anomalies, but these anomalies are smoothed out in the process of aggregation (Cell B). This can be the case in perfectly competitive markets, for example. On the other hand, in some cases, individual behaviour can seem completely 'normal', but behaviour at the collective level deviates from the rational model (Cell C). This exists when, for example, private goods are especially high-priced, while public goods are underpriced. This commonly leads to the emergence of phenomena known as 'free-riding' or social dilemmas, such as tax evasion, pollution or the excessive use of communal resources. A social dilemma represents a conflict situation in which people or groups have different interests. On the one hand, each person should contribute to a collective good from which all can benefit; on the other hand, selfish, utility-maximising goals discourage each individual from contributing. However, if many or all involved persons indulge their selfish goals, the desired collective good is in danger: in the final analysis, each individual's selfishness leads to a situation in which all are worse off. A real event illustrating a social dilemma was reported in the Netherlands:

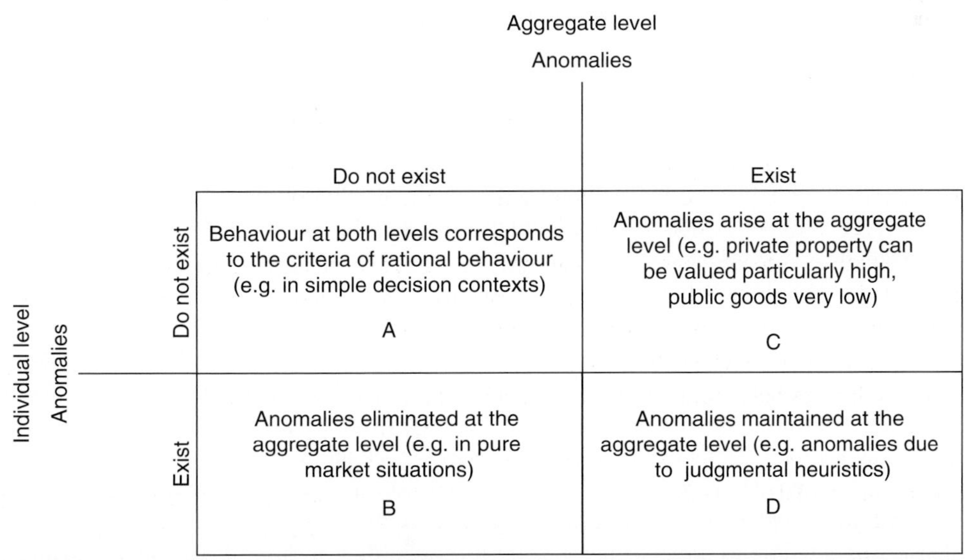

Figure 1.6 Relationships between individual and collective behaviour patterns (Frey, 1990, p. 75)

> Winter 1978/1979: Due to an unusually heavy snow, a small village in the North of the Netherlands was completely cut off from the rest of country so that there was no electricity to use for light, heating, television, etc. However, one of the 150 inhabitants owned a generator that could provide sufficient electricity to all people of this small community if and only if they exercised substantial restraint in their energy use. For example, they should use only one light, they should not use heated water, the heating should be limited to about 18°Celsius (64°Fahrenheit), and the curtains should be closed. As it turned out, the generator collapsed because most people were in fact using heated water, living comfortably at 21°Celsius (70°Fahrenheit), watching television, and burning several lights simultaneously. After being without electricity for a while, the citizens were able to repair the generator, and this time, they appointed inspectors to check whether people were using more electricity than they agreed upon. But even then, the generator eventually collapsed due to overuse of energy. And again, all inhabitants suffered from the cold and lack of light, and of course, could not watch television. (Van Lange & Joireman, 2008, p. 127–8)

Finally, in some cases, anomalies can be observed on both the individual and the collective levels (Cell D). For example, some anomalies arising from the application of judgmental heuristics, connected to risk averse, risk seeking or altruistic behaviour, can be observed on both the individual and the aggregate levels.

1.3 Economic Psychology

Economic psychology developed as an interdisciplinary field out of the shared assumptions of economics and psychology. Historically rooted in cognitive psychology (Angner & Loewenstein, 2012), it is alternatively known as socio-economics or (in economic contexts) behavioural economics.

Economic psychology concerns itself with the motives of economic actors and with the welfare of individuals, groups and entire nations. It also deals with knowledge of economic relations, causes of behaviour, decisions and economic activity. Wärneryd defined **economic psychology** as follows:

> Economic psychology studies the psychological mechanisms and processes that underlie consumption and other economic behavior. It deals with preferences, choices, decisions and factors influencing these, as well as the consequences of decisions and choices with respect to the satisfaction of needs. Furthermore, it deals with the impact of external economic phenomena upon human behavior and well-being. These studies may relate to different levels of aggregation: From the household and individual consumer to the macro level of whole nations. (Wärneryd, 1988a, p. 9)

Economic psychology is increasingly recognised as representing more than an applied field of psychology. Similarly, behavioural economics is gaining ground within the field of economics. Consequently, Brandstätter, Güth and Kliemt (2009) called for the term psychology *and* economics to replace psychology *versus* economics.

Both economics and psychology seek to understand human behaviour. At the beginning of economic science, dated from the publication of Adam Smith's *The wealth of nations* (Smith, 1776/1970), psychology was largely neglected in formal economic models. The significant and powerful concept of utility was formulated. Nineteenth-century utilitarians were of the opinion that economic actors make decisions and choose courses of action on the basis of expected utility, and that utility can be measured and analysed. Edgeworth (1881) assumed the existence of what he called cardinal utility and aimed to measure it with a conceptual 'hedonometer'. Robbins (1932) doubted that it was possible to directly measure utility. According to him, it was only possible to analyse utility indirectly, through the selection of one alternative out of a set of possible alternatives. Instead of a cardinal utility, he advocated the adoption of a concept of ordinal utility. Later, Samuelson (1938) formulated general, fundamental principles taken from behaviourism that remain the standard theory of economics today. He assumed that, for a given actor, the utility of each alternative corresponds to its place in his preference order. Utility is reflected in the behaviour of economic actors: the alternative that an actor selects out of a set of possible alternatives is the one that has the greatest utility for him- or herself at the time of the selection.

In order to be able to extrapolate the concept of utility from selection behaviour, actors must make judgments in ways that correspond to the model of *homo economicus*. They must be informed of all alternatives and their characteristics, so that they can form expectations about the consequences of the various options. These assumptions represent the foundation of the *homo economicus* model that has removed all psychological insights (Frey & Benz, 2007).

Around the end of the nineteenth century, the number of voices criticising the foundational assumptions of classical economics increased. According to its critics, the field of economics assumes that decision-making behaviour will be based on rational self-interest, and does not allow for the influence of psychological factors. Hansmeyer and Mackscheidt (1977) introduced their article on financial psychology with the following statement:

> Since Adam Smith, economic theory has been predominantly one-dimensional; the profit- or utility-maximising 'homo economicus' has remained the centre of the theoretical structure. Certainly, there has been no shortage of indications from the side of 'economic psychology' that this foundational hypothesis is incredibly narrow and does not correspond to what actually happens in the market; however, in the final analysis, the theory could always fall back on the correct observation that these hypothesised behaviours determine the market's framework for sanctioning. Even if short-term deviations are possible or conceivable, in the long run (which means, when it comes down to survival), the market only tolerates one type of behaviour. (p. 554)

Thorstein Veblen (1899), who in his studies of the behaviour of 'high society' found that some goods are in especially high demand when their prices rise, expressed his opposition to the 'inviolable' axioms of economics. He criticised the fact that economics does not take into account cultural idiosyncrasies and changes on the societal level. Wesley C. Mitchell (1914, p. 1) introduced his work on economics and human behaviour with the optimistic observation that 'a slight but significant change seems to be taking place in the attitude of economic theorists toward psychology'. He concluded the work with the prognosis that 'economics will assume a new character. It will cease to be a system of pecuniary logic, a mechanical study of static equilibria under non-existent conditions, and become a science of human behavior' (p. 47).

One line of criticism addressed a view that was an implicit part of economic theory at that time – that economic measures mutually determine one another:

> The aggregate savings ratio, for instance, is regarded as dependent upon total income, the price level is considered a function of the money supply, and the level of demand is seen as determined by the price. The human agent at the center of this dynamic is reduced to an anonymous 'black box.' A deterministic model that ignores the role of the human agent also corresponds only too neatly with the worldview to which the creators of economic policy subscribe. In actuality, however, the human person standing at the intersection of the environmental determinants and economic results of his actions is wont to obstinately do his own thing. He is governed by prejudices, temperamental, impulsive, and ill-informed. He is dominated by shifting influences, but forgets or suppresses some knowledge gained from experience, and sometimes even throws paradigms and basic principles overboard. He carries knowledge and experiences over from one area of life to the next and, when serious non-economic events come into play, even manages to change economic forecasts. He learns. (Strümpel & Katona, 1983, p. 225)

Psychology and economics have not always followed separate paths. As early as the eighteenth and nineteenth centuries, economists addressed psychological processes in their analyses of behaviour in the marketplace. In their view, these processes were decisive in understanding the mindsets and preferences of market participants. However, the science of psychology was only in its earliest stages of development at that time, meaning that the psychological suppositions of these economists were little more well grounded than folk theories (Frey & Benz, 2007).

In the past, economists who freed themselves from the rigidity of their models and incorporated psychological variables like status considerations, need for affiliation and social norms into their studies received little support from psychologists. Their psychological concepts were written off as amateurish. Psychologists' critique of economics pointed out that it is not the rate of inflation or unemployment numbers that act and influence one another, but people who undertake actions in the economic world and change it through their behaviour. However, these psychologists did not develop better psychological models that could have been incorporated into economic models. It has only been in the past few decades that a psychological sub-discipline – economic psychology – has developed, with the goal of bridging the gap between psychology and economics. At the same time, behavioural economics, which incorporates psychological concepts into economic models, has become a more and more influential movement within economics.

Gabriel Tarde (1902), who was probably the first to use the term 'economic psychology', called attention to the necessity of analysing economic behaviour from the perspective of psychology in his work *La psychologie économique*, published in France. He was most critical of Adam Smith, who did not incorporate the knowledge of human psychology into his economic concepts. In the German-speaking world, Hugo Münsterberg (1912) has been credited with setting the field in motion. Despite criticism from his teacher Wilhelm Wundt, Münsterberg emphasised the necessity of close cooperation between psychology and economic policy. He started with studies of social engineering, monotony in working life, hiring decisions, and experimental research regarding the effects of advertising. Despite this promising beginning, traces of a more or less comprehensive economic psychology soon faded into the background as fields like labour, employee, industrial and organisational psychology developed.

In the late 1940s, George Katona and his colleagues as well as Günther Schmölders, an economist at the University of Cologne, Germany, both started to write a psychology of macroeconomic processes. Schmölders, in particular, strove to incorporate the psychological perspective consistently into his economic research questions. His book *The psychology of money and public finance* (Schmölders, 1975) constitutes an important part in the foundation of economic psychology. **Financial psychology** defines itself more narrowly than economic psychology as 'the science of human experience and behaviour when dealing with money or highly liquid investments' (Schulz-Hardt, Vogelgesang & Mojzisch, 2007, p. 195).

Katona's (1951) perspective on economic psychology can be described with the following quotation:

> The basic need for psychology in economic research consists in the need to discover and analyze the forces behind economic processes, the forces responsible for economic actions, decisions and choices. Economics without psychology has not succeeded in explaining important economic processes and 'psychology without economics' has no chance of explaining some of the most common aspects of human behavior. (pp. 9–10)

The fact that economics and psychology – but also economics and sociology (Swedberg, 1991) – not only share a common border but also work on partially overlapping research questions has been acknowledged for quite a long time. Even though Mitchell's (1914) prognosis has not come fully to fruition, classical economics is falling under more and more criticism, and psychological theories are finding more and more acceptance within economics.

Little attention was paid to the interests, suggestions and admonitions of non-orthodox representatives of each discipline until the late second half of the twentieth century. During this time, a small but determined group of social and economic scientists began to advocate for the relevance of economic psychology and behavioural economics. They started to investigate the behaviour of market participants systematically. Interest and research activity in this interdisciplinary field have been growing since, developing a specialised body of knowledge.

The development of economic psychology (Kirchler & Hoelzl, 2003, 2006; Sent, 2004; Wärneryd, 1988a, 1993) was further fostered with the bestowal of the Nobel Prize in Economics (officially known as The Bank of Sweden Prize in Economic Sciences in Memory of Alfred Nobel) on the behavioural economist Vernon Smith and the psychologist Daniel Kahneman in 2002. Kahneman's long-time research partner Amos Tversky was also recognised in the announcement (more details on Daniel Kahneman's prize lecture and his biography can be found at www.nobelprize.org/nobel_prizes/economic-sciences/laureates/2002/kahneman-bio.html). A great number of economic studies (particularly within the behavioural field) have been inspired by the research of Kahneman and Tversky, who demonstrated empirically that people often behave differently in decision-making situations than economic theory would predict.

Economics ignoring behavioural insights has taken another beating in light of the worldwide financial and economic crisis that has been the subject of intense media reporting since 2008. Demands are rising that economics should become more open to psychology. For example, Sedlacek (2011) argued that economics is viewed as a predominantly value-free mathematical inquiry, but should be viewed as a cultural phenomenon. It should not exclusively focus on abstract mathematical modelling based on disputable assumptions about human behaviour but should also consider individual and societal values. Publications like *Predictably irrational: The hidden forces that shape our decisions* by Dan Ariely (2008), *Animal spirits: How human psychology drives the economy, and why it matters for global capitalism* by George A. Akerlof and Robert J. Shiller (2009) or *Phishing for phools* (2015) by the same authors, *Nudge: Improving decisions about health, wealth, and happiness* by Richard H. Thaler and Cass R. Sunstein (2008) and *Thinking, fast and slow* by Daniel Kahneman (2011) have not only impressed economic experts and other social scientists. They have also attracted the interest of a wide audience outside the authors' respective fields, as is reflected in the books' large media presence. All of these works push past the limits of traditional economics, both micro and macro, and embrace an interdisciplinary perspective, particularly considering insights of psychology.

Economic psychology seeks to explain economic behaviour as a function of people's disposition and the situational circumstances in which they find themselves at a given time. Emphasised is the fact that economics focuses its attention not on the behaviour of individuals, but on market and state behaviour. Economic variables are aggregate – which means summated, averaged or mean – quantities that arise from the behaviour of a large number of people and institutions. Every example of individual waywardness, emotionality and irrationality begs the question: 'What remains of non-rational conduct when individual actions are aggregated to macroeconomic phenomena?' Specifically, are orthodox economists validated in their argument that human behaviour is, indeed, rational in the average, even though it is too complex and irrational to predict in individual cases? The model of *homo economicus* might be a caricature of individual behaviour, but it could be viable for explaining the behaviour of a fictitious average person and a powerful model for predicting changes in the economy. However, as already argued and noted by

Table 1.1 Characteristics of economics and psychology (according to Wärneryd, 1993)

Economics	Psychology
Based on few fundamental assumptions that Becker (1976) calls 'The Economic Approach': - Utility maximisation - Stable preferences - Market equilibrium	Predominantly an inductive approach, empirical theories at low levels Explanations of individual behaviour Intensive effort to describe details
All economic laws are derived from these assumptions	
Symbolic mathematical language and models	Experimental and statistical methods, scale-building techniques
Objective data	Observational data and subjective data, including data on emotions
Interest in aggregate data (macro-level variables)	Interest in general and differential laws of behaviour
Assumptions on individual behaviour are there to assist in predicting phenomena ('as if' assumptions)	Assumptions about individual behaviour must be realistic (description and prediction)
Psychological concepts are translated into economic terminology to make them compatible with the rationality assumption	Contextual, structural and systemic variables are usually ignored

Frey (1990), deviations from the model of rationality can also be observed at the aggregate level (Figure 1.6).

The question for psychologists is how models of behaviour need to be modified when it is not individual or group behaviour that must be explained, but rather societal currents, that, despite being rooted in individual behaviour, take on a new quality as a result of aggregation. Whether or not markets – 'aggregate data' – behave rationally is especially questionable in the wake of the financial and economic crisis of 2008.

The idea that economics and psychology can learn from one another has been confirmed on multiple occasions and is considered by representatives of economic psychology to be the driving force behind their work. However, it is important not to overlook the communication difficulties between economists and psychologists that arise from the differing academic and methodological traditions in the two fields. Wärneryd (1993) summarised characteristics of economics and psychology (Table 1.1).

While the laws of economics are founded upon a few fundamental assumptions, and economists strive to incorporate as few new variables as possible into their models, psychologists primarily use an inductive approach to obtain knowledge, seeking to explain individual behaviour in all its glorious detail. Economists translate their knowledge into mathematical formulas and, in doing so, constrain themselves to clarity and consistency in their statements about human behaviour. Economists analyse objective data sets and make interpretations at the macro level, while psychologists often seek to understand subjective data on constructs that are difficult to operationalise and aspire a micro-level interpretation that closely corresponds to individual behaviour.

In both disciplines, experiments are conducted (Smith, 2008) and statistical procedures applied in order to test hypotheses. The actual practice of experimental work is comparable; nevertheless, there are also substantial differences. For example, economists take the position that participants in laboratory studies need to understand the instructions given to them and must have the opportunity to learn – for instance, by repeatedly solving the same problem. They ought not to be 'deceived' by untrue situations or research objectives. False information is a taboo, even when after the study participants are made aware of the manipulations that occurred. Participants must also be motivated to perform the tasks demanded by the experiment. It must be clear which goals they are working towards in the experiment. If financial incentives are offered, it is assumed that they will pursue the goal of earning as much money as possible. The incentives also need to be attractive, so that study participants will make an effort to obtain them (Ariely & Norton, 2007; Hertwig & Ortmann, 2001; for a review of the history of experimental economics see Svorencik, 2015).

Economic psychology is represented by various academic bodies: the International Association for Research in Economic Psychology (IAREP), founded in the 1970s primarily by European psychologists and economists, has issued the pertinent *Journal of Economic Psychology* since 1981. The goal of this journal is to publish interdisciplinary papers from the fields of economics, consumer research and marketing as well as applied psychology. It is through the *Journal of Economic Psychology* that the field has gained broad recognition and has stimulated so many research topics at the intersection of economics and psychology.

In the US, two related associations – the Society for the Advancement of Socio-Economics (SASE) and the Society for the Advancement of Behavioral Economics (SABE) – aim to interlink psychological and economic concepts and to present the results of their studies to their colleagues through the *Journal of Behavioral and Experimental Economics* (formerly the *Journal of Socio-Economics*). In addition to these research journals, economic psychology has been described in a series of introductory works (e.g., Antonides, 1991; Ferrari & Romano, 1999; Furnham & Lewis, 1986; Lassarre, 1995; Lea, Tarpy & Webley, 1987; Lewis, 2008; Ranyard, 2017; Riegel, 2007; Roland-Lévy & Adair, 1998; van Raaij, 2016; van Raaij, van Veldhoven & Wärneryd, 1988; Wiswede, 2007).

1.4 Topic Areas within Economic Psychology

Economic behaviour and decisions are influenced by conditions relating to the specific individual as well as social, cultural and macroeconomic structures. In ways corresponding to their individual dispositions, consumers and enterprises place emphasis on different things in their actions and decision-making. Traditional or progressive values prescribe people's budgeting behaviour, and cultural and religious worldviews shape business decisions, among other things. Situational circumstances like financial feasibility, responsibility for other people and market conditions are just as critical to understanding economic behaviour as characteristics of the economy as a whole, such as the country's income distribution, employment situation, rate of inflation or tax rate. Just as personal, cultural and situational conditions influence human behaviour, economic decisions, for their part, determine consumers' well-being, optimism or sentiments, their consumption behaviour and, in turn, the further development of the economy as a whole.

In the first issue of the *Journal of Economic Psychology*, W. Fred van Raaij (1981) presented a diagram that delineated relationships among the field's large number of variables, while at the same time extending what was at that time the reach of economic psychology (Figure 1.7).

This diagram suggests a number of research questions related to the interaction between these variables:

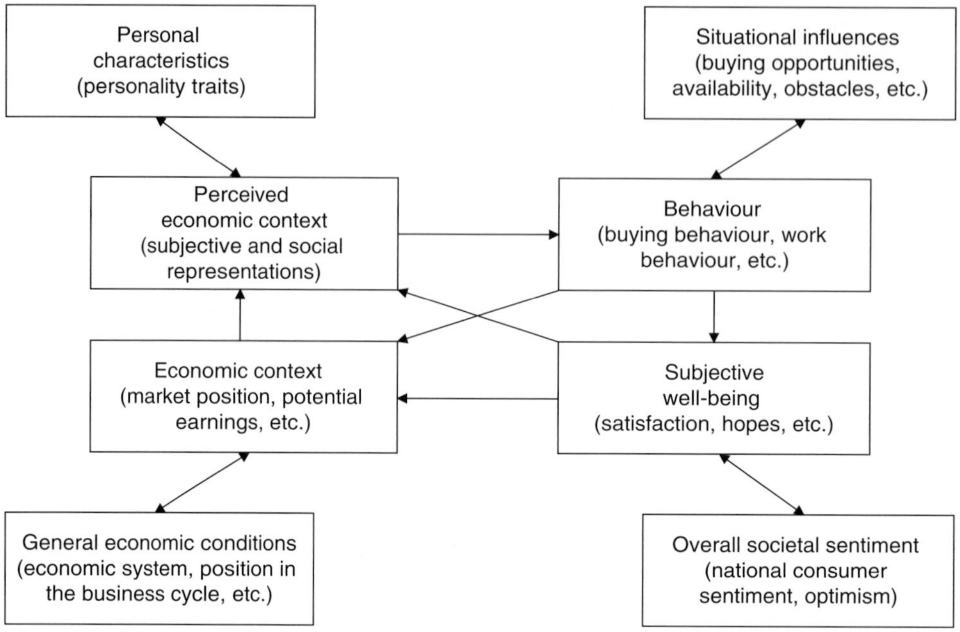

Figure 1.7 Model of economic-psychological research topics (adapted from van Raaij, 1981, p. 9)

(a) *General economic conditions and economic context.* A given household or a firm's economic context (market position, personal financial situation, type of employment, sources of income, etc.) is influenced by general economic conditions. Included in this variable are the state's economic system (e.g., a centrally managed planned economy, a market economy or a social market economy), the position in the business cycle (e.g., expansion, peak, contraction or trough), the government's economic policy, war and peace, ecological conditions, etc. According to Strzysch and Weiß (1998, p. 87), the economic system encompasses 'economic elements (natural resources, as well as people in their roles as producers and consumers), economic relationships . . . and the economic order . . . which is based on the legal and institutional rules economic processes are required to follow'. Relationships between general economic conditions and the financial opportunities of households and firms should be investigated.

(b) *Economic context, perceived economic context and personal characteristics.* Perceived economic context includes those subjective interpretations of economic conditions that are made by individuals in private households and firms according to their characteristics, values, goals, expectations and fears. These interpretations relate to aspects of the economic climate, expected price developments, the subjectively perceived income distribution and assessed level of fairness, subjectively relevant comparison groups, etc. Economic psychology investigates the importance of personality traits and their correlation with individuals' conceptions and interpretations of economic relationships.

(c) *Economic context, perceived economic context and behaviour.* The behaviour of consumers and producers predominantly depends upon perceived economic conditions. Objective economic conditions are transformed into perceived economic conditions via individual inclinations towards specific interpretations and ways of thinking. Mass media play a role in influencing subjective perceptions. For example, consumers might interpret increases in the prices of everyday consumable and durable goods as a sign that inflation is either slowly increasing or running rampant, and adjust their buying behaviour accordingly. Firms might evaluate their investment opportunities as either good or bad depending on borrowing costs. In addition, opinions and judgments about the unemployment rate, environmental pollution, inflation and energy costs are formed through conversations with other people. Studying the relationships between opinions and judgments or attitudes, decisions and behaviour, helps to understand economic structures and the ways they change.

(d) *Behaviour and situation (happenings in one's immediate surroundings).* Behavioural goals lead to actions, or, more exactly, they can lead to actions. Even if actors wish to take certain actions, situational influences can create disruptions. For example, unforeseeable events such as an illness or unemployment can force consumers to further delay the purchase of long-desired goods.

(e) *Economic behaviour, subjective well-being and perceived economic context.* According to van Raaij (1981), economic behaviour is reflected in subjective well-being. Subjective well-being is comprised of satisfaction or frustration after the purchase of a good, problems with goods and services, returns and exchanges, etc. Mental processes after a purchase – such as the reduction of cognitive dissonance or the intrinsic and symbolic value of the goods (Dittmar, 1992) – also influence one's subjective state.

(f) *Subjective well-being and overall societal sentiment.* Subjective well-being consolidates into a picture of overall societal sentiment when the experiences of all economic actors are aggregated. Individual consumers' sentiments and their satisfaction with their own health, with their relationships with their romantic partners and with their work, among other things, combine to make up their life satisfaction. Individual satisfaction scores are expressed at the aggregate level through societal satisfaction or discontent. Questions arise for economic psychology regarding the correlation between well-being in economic matters and general satisfaction, as well as between individual well-being and consumer and producer sentiment.

(g) *Subjective well-being, behaviour and economic context.* Consumers' subjective well-being determines future economic developments. This completes the circle portrayed in Figure 1.7. Marketing researchers study consumers' behaviour and satisfaction with goods and develop marketing strategies that promise to satisfy a multitude of wishes. Attempts are made to create goods that correspond to consumers' needs and desires by having producers adapt their production to match the wishes of consumers. It is not just consumers' sentiments, but also, of course, their behaviour that determine economic conditions: private households' preferences for saving or consumption as well as firms' inclinations to make investments or build up capital reserves directly influence the economy's future development.

Figure 1.7 was a first attempt at stretching the thematic reach of economic psychology, at that time still primarily from the perspective of social and consumer psychology. As is demonstrated by an analysis of the *Journal of Economic Psychology* (Kirchler & Hoelzl, 2003, 2006), research within economic psychology primarily focuses on how decisions are made, as well as how decision-making systematically deviates from the rational, neoclassical model and thereby challenges some of its basic assumptions. Cooperation and self-interest are investigated, as well as the economic knowledge of children and adults, business conduct, work and unemployment, fair compensation and commitment to one's work, budgetary decisions and sales strategies, subjective attitudes towards money and the switchover to the euro, taxpaying behaviour, the underground economy, economic development and well-being. Table 1.2 depicts a categorisation of research papers published in the *Journal of Economic Psychology* between 1981 and 2005 conducted by Kirchler and Hoelzl (2006), expanded to include publications up to 2010.

Table 1.2 Categorisation of publications in the *Journal of Economic Psychology*, 1981–2010 (updated from Kirchler & Hoelzl, 2006, to include the years 2006–10)

Category	1981–5	1986–90	1991–5	1996–2000	2001–5	2006–10	Total
1 Theory and history	6	5	8	7	23*	13	62
2 Individual decision-making	10	10	19*	26*	26*	60*	151*
3 Cooperation and competition	4	5	13	24*	20*	35*	101*
4 Socialisation and lay theories	4	16*	6	4	5	12	47
5 Money, currency and inflation	7	13*	5	13	10	25	73
6 Financial behaviour and investment	3	9	24*	26*	15	39*	116*
7 Consumer attitudes	5	4	10	10	10	3	42
8 Consumer behaviour	11*	29*	27*	20*	31*	18	136*
9 Consumer expectations	15*	13*	15*	5	7	2	57
10 Firm	1	1	7	8	4	9	30
11 Marketplace behaviour, marketing and advertising	3	3	5	15	13	15	54
12 Labour market	8	6	14	12	13	9	62
13 Tax	12*	12	14	5	16	21	80
14 Environmental behaviour	27*	0	3	2	12	3	47
15 Government and policy	9	7	10	8	6	2	42
16 Remaining categories	2	2	2	5	9	33*	53
Total	127	135	182	190	220	299	1153
Percentage contribution of top four categories	51.2%	52.6%	46.7%	50.5%	45.5%	55.9%	43.7%
Hirschman-Herfindahl index	1009.98	1056.24	864.63	896.95	813.22	1068.33	768.69

Note: The Hirschman-Herfindahl index indicates concentration of topics. It is calculated by squaring the share of each topic category in the list of topics, and then summing the resulting numbers. It can range from close to zero to 10,000. Asterisks (*) denote the top four categories.

The most common topic areas are individual decision-making and consumer behaviour. Since the beginning of the financial crisis in late 2008, however, more articles in the categories money, currency and inflation as well as financial behaviour and investment have been published. For the period between 2006 and 2010, the number of articles on well-being, life satisfaction and happiness increased; about one-third of the articles in the remaining categories focused on these topics.

A combination of van Raaij's (1981) framework and the empirical review of the publications in the *Journal of Economic Psychology* suggests three major content areas within economic psychology. The structure of this book will correspond to these three areas: basic concepts (normative and descriptive models of decision-making, lay theories), markets (consumer markets, labour markets, financial markets) and society-level issues (collective cooperation, employment and well-being).

Conclusion

This chapter indicates that economic theories and methods are not sufficient on their own to describe and predict human behaviour and decision-making. The economic approach is based on various axioms that define rational behaviour. Notably, the question arises of whether people always want to behave rationally even when they have the time and knowledge to do so. Deviations from the neoclassical model, which uses the *homo economicus* as a metaphor to describe people as rational agents maximising their utility, need to be explained. Hence, the necessity to integrate psychological knowledge into economic models becomes clear.

Summary

- Markets are places where supply meets demand and where decisions have to be made. Economics differentiates between factor and product markets.
- Expectations about future developments in the economy influence consumers' and producers' decision-making. Expectations are based on three sources: (a) past experiences, (b) learning processes and (c) knowledge and opinions about new circumstances.
- The Consumer Sentiment Index combines consumers' views about their past and future financial situation, about the past and future overall economic conditions, and about whether it makes sense to make larger purchases or rather save money.
- Economic psychology attempts to build a bridge between economics and psychology. Its goal is to apply theoretical knowledge to understand human behaviour and decision-making.
- Usually resources are limited, but needs are endless. Economic actors such as individuals, organisations and institutions have to choose between alternatives and are aware that, owing to resource scarcity, selecting one alternative means incurring opportunity costs by forgoing all other alternatives and their corresponding benefits.
- In order to deploy resources in the most efficient manner, people should behave according to the maximisation and minimisation principle. With a given quantity of resources, the maximum result should be achieved. A given result should be achieved with minimum resources.
- Economists use the metaphor of the so-called '*homo economicus*' which defines individuals as utility maximising and rationally behaving actors. Ideally, they behave in accordance with the following axioms: completeness, transitivity, reflexivity, non-satiation, continuity and convexity.
- Gabriel Tarde, Hugo Münsterberg, Georg Katona and Burkhard Strümpel are important figures in economic psychology who have argued for the need to consider psychological theories in economic research.
- Economic psychology focuses on how decisions are made, and how decision-making systematically deviates from the metaphor of the *homo economicus*.

Questions

1. Why are expectations important to understand and predict future developments in the economy?
2. What is the critique regarding the Consumer Sentiment Index?
3. What are 'opportunity costs'?
4. According to economic theory, what are the principles that determine people's behaviour?
5. What are the axioms of neoclassical economics (Gravelle & Rees, 1981)?

FURTHER READING

Akerlof, G. A., & Shiller, R. J. (2009). *Animal spirits: How human psychology drives the economy, and why it matters for global capitalism*. Princeton, NJ: Princeton University Press.

Ariely, D. (2008). *Predictably irrational: The hidden forces that shape our decisions*. New York: HarperCollins.

Lewis, A. (ed.) (2008). *The Cambridge handbook of psychology and economic behaviour.* Cambridge: Cambridge University Press.

Ranyard, R. (ed.) (2017). *Economic psychology.* Chichester: Wiley.

2 Decision-Making: Normative Models and Anomalies

Overview

Decision situations can be described by options involving consequences and probabilities, and information about these elements may be more or less available. The classical economic model of human behaviour assumes that decisions are driven by rationality and that utility maximisation is the goal. Rationality is first and foremost a formal principle of decision-making logic with a predominantly normative character. It presumes that decision-makers have preferences and that the alternative they ultimately choose is the one with the highest subjective utility. Classical decision models rely on the assumption that decision-makers have a high information processing capacity as well as the time and motivation to process such complex information.

Empirical studies have demonstrated, however, that actual behaviour diverges from the predictions of classical decision models and shows systematic 'anomalies'. Information processing capacity is limited and complex decision situations contain various sources of error. To name just a few examples, information is subjectively perceived and can be processed through different paths. The value decision-makers assign to an option changes with time, and with the associated emotions. When there is no opportunity to gather enough information, or insufficient time or motivation to do so, judgments are made on the basis of heuristics. Heuristics are decision rules that allow decision-makers to save time and energy. They can lead to suboptimal judgments in some cases because they are vulnerable to irrelevant factors. However, they can also lead to good judgments when they are used in a valid environment.

Introduction

Every day, people make a large number of decisions, important and less important ones. Some decisions are easy because their consequences are quite clear. Other decisions are hard, especially if consequences are uncertain. In some cases, people do not have the time, motivation or ability to process all information in order to analyse the entire situation. In other cases, their preferences seem to change with emotions or to change over time. People often use shortcuts, so-called heuristics, to simplify the logical and rational step-by-step process. The focus of this chapter is to show the classical, normative approach to decision-making and a number of so-called anomalies that stand in contrast to predictions from that approach.

2.1 Decisions under Uncertainty

Private households, companies and administrators all have to consider how to use their limited financial capital, energy, time and other resources sensibly. In most cases, resources are not sufficient to satisfy all of their numerous wants and needs. Decisions must be made about what is a priority and what is not. Politicians, too, make decisions about the use of state resources, about implementing some projects and postponing others. Individuals and groups in private households, in companies and in public administration are confronted with the necessity of selecting one alternative out of many: they choose one option and thereby relinquish other possible options.

Decisions are based on the evaluation of options, on assumptions about the value of various alternatives and on the probability that each option actually carries with it the features viewed as advantageous. The more valuable one option seems in comparison to the other possible options, the more preferably it is viewed in comparison to other options. In some situations, making a decision is easy. When a decision-maker has clear preferences, when only a few options are available, and when the attributes or consequences of these options and their probability of occurrence are known, the best alternative normally becomes clear quite quickly. Some decisions are easy because the consequences of a suboptimal decision are trivial. For example, the decision whether or not to bring an umbrella on days when it looks as if it may rain is generally not problematic. Decisions become more difficult when the number of options increases, when complexity increases, and when there is little time for seeking out and processing information or for evaluating options and their consequences. Decisions also become more difficult when the consequences of various alternatives are uncertain or unknown.

Depending on situational features, the topic and the personal characteristics of the decision-makers, decisions can be made either intuitively – 'from the gut' – or analytically, after explicit deliberation and the weighing of positives and negatives. Decision-makers' vision can be blurred owing to information processing limits. In addition, feelings and moods can exert great influence over decision-making, regardless of whether experts or laypeople are making the decision.

One frequently researched topic in behavioural economics and economic psychology concerns decisions under uncertainty, in which the probability that the consequences of various options will actually occur might be known to a greater or lesser degree. Risk can on the one hand be viewed as the possible emergence of an unwanted negative event, that is, as a threat in situations about which one has little knowledge. On the other hand, a decision can also be labelled risky when it is not guaranteed that certain consequences of various options will occur, but when they only have a certain probability of occurrence. Casino games, in which both winning and losing is possible, represent risky choices. While the probabilities of consequences of alternatives are known in risky decisions, in ambiguous decisions the probabilities are only vaguely known. Both risky and ambiguous decisions are termed decisions under uncertainty.

This chapter describes decision situations in which one alternative is selected out of a set of several, each of which carries positive or negative consequences with probabilities that are known to a varying degree. Risk, in the current context, is understood as these probabilities. In a different perspective, Breakwell (2007) has comprehensively summarised the literature on how people deal with risk as a threat, perceptions of risk and attitudes towards it.

2.1.1 Certainty, Risk and Ambiguity

Theoretical reflections and empirical studies about decision-making vary according to whether decisions are made under conditions of certainty, uncertainty, risk or ambiguity. **Decisions under certainty** are decisions where no probabilities are involved regarding the consequences of alternatives: decision-makers possess complete information about all possible alternatives and certainty about their consequences. However, this is rarely the case. **Decisions under uncertainty** are decisions where the consequences of alternatives only occur with some probability. In some cases, the probabilities for particular consequences can be determined. **Risky decisions** are decisions with consequences occurring with a known, specific probability (Wu, Zhang & Gonzalez, 2004). When fair dice determine the possibility of victory and only the number six signifies a win, the chance of winning is determined to be $p = 1/6$. When circumstances are more difficult, determining probabilities numerically may not be possible. **Ambiguous decisions** are decisions where the probabilities of consequences of alternatives are only vaguely known. For example, if we assume that unifying the currencies of various countries – such as was the case in the European Union – can have positive or negative consequences under certain conditions, but that the probability of these various consequences occurring cannot be known exactly, this is an example of an ambiguous decision.

In the following, an example of decision-making under risk as it is presented in empirical studies is described (Kühberger, 1994, p. 7). Study participants can participate in one of two sweepstakes. They must select either Game A or Game B. The objectively calculated expectations of winning (the expected value) in both games are equal, in both cases zero. Therefore, the choice of participating in Game A or Game B should be random.

- Alternative A provides the opportunity to win 44 monetary units with a probability of $p = 0.5$ as well as to lose 55 monetary units with a probability of $p = 0.4$. There is a probability of $p = 0.1$ that neither a win nor a loss will occur.
- With Alternative B, it is possible to win 36 monetary units with a probability of $p = 0.5$, to lose 60 units with a probability of $p = 0.3$, and to have a neutral result of zero units with a probability of $p = 0.2$.

In reality, few study participants calculate the expected value of A and B. They rather think about which alternative promises the highest payoff, which one offers the greatest likelihood of winning, or which one presents the smallest loss or the smallest chance of losing. Depending on whether participants focus on winning or losing, they select Game A or B and provide a corresponding justification for their decision. Instead of formally calculating the expected values, the tasks are simplified. Instead of all of the pieces of information available, only a few aspects of the decision are taken into account, and a decision is made on the basis of these.

People prefer decisions under certainty to risky decisions. Even more, though, they seek to avoid ambiguous decisions when it is possible to do so. If one option contains the certainty of winning 100 monetary units, a second alternative offers the possibility of winning 200 monetary units with a probability of $p = 0.5$, and a third the same prize in an ambiguous situation, then decision-makers should, from a rational perspective, be indifferent to the three options. In reality, however, certainty is preferred to risk and risk to ambiguity. Weber (1993) and Salo and Weber (1995) quote the well-known example by Ellsberg (1961), which demonstrates that individuals – as well as groups of individuals in markets – seek to avoid ambiguity and sometimes behave inconsistently. Ellsberg (1961) presented the following decision situation: Players are told that an urn contains 30 red balls and a total of 60 other balls that are either black or yellow. Players can choose Option 1a or 1b, or 2a or 2b, respectively. The options in the first game are defined as follows:

- 1a: If a red ball is drawn from the urn, the player wins.
- 1b: If a black ball is drawn from the urn, the player wins.

In the second game, the player can select among the following options:

- 2a: If a red or yellow ball is drawn, the player wins.
- 2b: If a black or yellow ball is drawn, the player wins.

Most players prefer Option 1a to 1b, but 2b to 2a, because in the first game, in 1a the probability of drawing a red ball is known ($p = 0.33$). Similarly, in the second game, in 2b the probability of drawing a black or a yellow ball is known ($p = 0.67$). Conversely, in 1b the probability of drawing a black ball cannot be calculated exactly: the urn could contain one yellow ball and 59 black balls, or two yellow and 58 black balls, etc. In 2a, the probability for drawing a red or a yellow ball is unknown. This illustrates what is known as the **Ellsberg paradox**: the possible gains in Cases 1a and 1b as well as in Cases 2a and 2b are mathematically identical. From the perspective of rational behaviour, players should not have preferences among the options. In reality, however, they are not indifferent. They behave inconsistently, contrary to axioms of classical economic theory.

In another decision situation, participants imagined that they were managers of a securities portfolio. They could choose to make a one-day investment in Security X, Y or Z. As participants themselves did not have any experience in these special types of investments, they should rely on the advice of Employees A and B. Weber (1993, p. 34 f; Salo & Weber, 1995) asked participants to state their preferences for X, Y and Z:

- Security X: Employees A and B both hold the opinion that the value of the security has a 50% chance of rising and a 50% chance of falling on the next day.
- Security Y: Employee A is certain that the value of the security will rise; Employee B is certain that the value will fall.
- Security Z: Employee A is an expert whose assessments are always correct; Employee B is not. There are memos with recommendations from both employees, but it is not clear which employee wrote which memo, and clarifying questions are not possible. One memo claims that the value of the security will rise, while the other claims that it will fall.

Even though the expected increases or decreases in value are identical for all options, participants were not indifferent. Aversion to ambiguity was also demonstrated by Pulford and Colman (2008) and Rode, Cosmides, Hell and Tooby (1999). The **ambiguity effect** states that

> when behaviour alternatives are uncertain, decision-makers' preferences are influenced by the amount of information about the distribution of probabilities upon which they are based. This means that decision-makers prefer situations in which they have a clear picture of the probabilities of occurrence for various outcomes to those in which probabilities are uncertain (ambiguous situations). This runs counter to the independence axiom of expected utility theory, as the Ellsberg paradox has shown. (Guo, 2002, p. 73)

2.1.2 Classical Decision Theory

Decisions under uncertainty are described in expected value theory, expected utility theory and subjective expected utility theory (Jungermann, Pfister & Fischer, 2010). Modern decision theory is based on the work of Blaise Pascal and Pierre Fermat, who in the seventeenth century made casino games the subject of their theoretical reflections. They came to realise that, according to profit maximisation principles, games are selected according to the size and probability of a payoff. The expected value is the product of the size of the payoff and its probability of occurrence. In order to determine the value of various decision alternatives, according to expected value theory, the values and probabilities of occurrence for the consequences of each alternative are considered.

However, a Swiss mathematician named Daniel Bernoulli put the still-nascent theory of expected value under great stress by inviting renowned academic colleagues at a conference in St Petersburg to consider the following: Let us suppose that we can choose to participate in a game and are considering how much money to invest in the game. A coin is flipped until it lands on tails. The player receives 2^n rubles, where $n = 0, 1, 2 \ldots$ and corresponds to the number of coin flips that landed on heads. If the first coin flip lands on heads, $n = 0$ and the player receives $2^n = 2^0 = 1$ ruble. If the second, third or later coin flip lands on tails, the player receives 2 rubles for one heads and one tails; 4 rubles for a series of heads, heads, tails; 8 rubles for a series of heads, heads, heads, tails; and so on. How much should a player put on the line, according to expected value theory? Since expected value is calculated by multiplying the amount of the payoff by its probability, it is extremely high in this game. A coin could land on tails for the first time after an infinite number of coin flips, making the payoff infinitely high; however, the probability is low. The **St Petersburg paradox** is that players seeking to maximise their payoff in accordance with expected value theory should be ready to invest their entire fortune in the game – most people, however, are only willing to invest a small amount of money at best.

Expected utility theory assumes that decisions are based not on the expected value, but on the expected utility an option provides. In the game described above, this means that the utility of the money is decisive. Since the marginal utility of money tends to decrease, the value of further payoffs decreases as one's wealth grows. The correlation between monetary value and utility is represented by the utility function, which is concave, not linear.

Subjective expected utility theory (SEU) was developed on the basis of expected value theory and expected utility theory. Psychological work on this topic was sparked by an overview article on decision research by Edwards (1954) and is now at a point where a clear overview is almost impossible (see, e.g., Camerer, 1995; Jungermann et al. 2010; Kühberger, 1994; Meilers, Schwartz & Cooke, 1998; Wu et al. 2004). According to the SEU model, decision-makers determine the subjective expected utility for all options in a decision situation and choose the option offering the greatest utility. Decision-makers are familiar with the associated consequences of the available options and consider how likely it is that these consequences will occur, as well as how much subjective utility these consequences provide to them. The sum of the products of the subjective probabilities and the subjective utility of the consequences results in the subjective expected utility of an option. It is assumed that an individual prefers the option with the greatest utility. Since decision-makers can be risk averse, risk neutral or risk seeking, and because some consequences mean more to one person than another, different people consistently choose different options from the same set of alternatives.

Depending on the theory, the consequences of various alternatives are assigned either objective or subjective values, and their probabilities of occurrence can likewise be either determined objectively or considered from a subjective perspective. What all three theories have in common is their implicit view of the decision-maker and the decision situation. The decision-maker is assumed to conform to the model of *homo economicus*. This model assumes that people are informed about all possible alternatives, are able to evaluate options according to their preferences and will ultimately select the option that promises maximal personal utility. *Homo economicus* weighs the pros and cons of every decision clearly, coolly and rationally – like a robot. He has neither scruples nor moral reservations, nor does he nurse any thoughts of fairness (Häring & Storbeck, 2007). The decision situation is assumed to be characterised by the following general attributes:

- There is a specific identifiable decision-maker.
- All alternatives have been laid down in advance and the decision-maker has complete information about them.
- All possible consequences can be anticipated, evaluated and put in rank order.
- Consequences are evaluated with reference to long-run goals.
- Probabilities can be assigned to all possible events.
- Judgments can be made as to the relevance of information, and relevant information can be sought out and collected. (Kühberger, 1994, p. 5, our translation)

In other words, people and groups must follow a certain protocol. Decision goals and goal criteria must be defined. Criteria have to be weighted according to their subjective relevance. After people have determined what an ideal option should look like, options have to be examined. Information about available options as well as the consequences and probabilities connected to these options needs to be compiled. Finally, the option that brings the decision-maker the greatest subjective utility has to be selected out of the set of all available options.

Subjective expected utility theory and its precursors represent maximisation models and therefore belong to the group of **normative decision models**. Normative decision models are related to optimal decisions. They specify how an (idealised) individual should make optimal decisions. Conversely, **descriptive decision models** describe how individuals actually make decisions. Normative models describe an optimum; descriptive models describe observed behaviour. In addition to normative and descriptive decision models, there are also **prescriptive decision models**, which use decision theory to offer step-by-step suggestions on how to proceed in a decision situation in order to make an optimal decision.

2.1.3 Economic Games

It is questionable whether decisions are actually made in correspondence with expected value theory or with expected utility theory, or according to subjective expected utility criteria. Economics and psychology have developed various methods for investigating choice behaviour and decision-making processes. Game theory particularly concerns itself with decisions and provides a multitude of opportunities to study the rationality and utility maximisation assumptions.

2.1.3.1 Ultimatum and Dictator Game

Within game theory, various decision situations such as the ultimatum game or the dictator game have been developed to study the behaviour of decision-makers (e.g., Diekmann, 2009; Eckel & Grossman, 1997; Fehr & Schmidt, 1999; Güth, 1994, 1999; Güth & Tietz, 1990). **Ultimatum games** investigate the choices people make when they have the opportunity to divide a good (e.g., a sum of money) between themselves and another person. Player A receives a certain good, such as a specific sum of money m and must offer their fellow player B a portion p of the sum m. If the receiver B accepts the offer, A receives the sum of money minus the amount offered to B ($m - p$), while B receives the offered amount p. If the receiver rejects the offer, both players leave empty-handed. Behavioural economics and economic psychology use different variations of this game to investigate whether people maximise their payoff, whether they consider the interests of their fellow player, and whether considerations of justice and fairness play a role. According to the rationality and utility maximisation assumptions, Player A's goal is to maximise his payoff. Therefore, he ought to offer Player B the smallest possible portion ($p > 0$) of the total sum of money m. For example, if Player A receives £100, he could offer Player B £1 and keep £99 for himself. If Player B acts according to the profit motive, he will accept the offer because £1 is better than no money at all. Since, eventually, the game will end and the players will not meet again in the future, A can assume that B will accept any amount $p > 0$. Thus, the game-theoretic solution is clear: A will retain the largest portion of the good for himself and offer B the smallest possible amount that is larger than zero.

In experiments, the players' behaviour is typically not as would be expected from this view. In most cases, the actual distribution differs dramatically. Small offers are perceived as unfair and are rejected. In order to punish unfair behaviour, many players are willing to forgo the offered sum, just so that the greedy person making the offer will not receive anything either. Many players distribute the money 50:50. Henrich, Boyd, Bowles, Camerer, Fehr, Gintis and McElreath (2001) conducted the ultimatum game on five continents among fifteen small-scale societies and tribes with different customs and cultures. Offers varied significantly among societies, ranging from 26% of the total sum among the Machiguenga in Peru to 58% among the Lamalera in Indonesia. Values corresponding to the game-theoretic predictions could not be found in any population. In industrial societies, average offers are at around 44% of the available total amount, and low offers (i.e., smaller than 30% of the available total amount) are mostly rejected (meta-analysis by Oosterbeek, Sloof & van de Kuilen, 2004). However, these figures may not be valid for much higher amounts of money. If it were possible to conduct a study dividing up sums in the millions, offers well under 44% of the total sum would most likely be accepted. Similarly, if the sum is distributed among several people, willingness to accept smaller sums generally increases.

The **dictator game** represents another version of the ultimatum game. This game leaves out the second step of the ultimatum game: Partner B has no opportunity to reject the offer. Player A receives, for example, £100 and can offer Partner B a portion p, which can be any amount from £0 to £100. The game ends for Player A with the payment of £100 minus the amount p offered to B; Player B receives the offered amount p. Since B has no opportunity to sanction offers perceived as unfair, A can – from a rational point of view – behave completely selfishly and offer £0. In dictator games, offers are smaller than in ultimatum games, but even here, 'dictators' rarely act completely selfishly, greedily keeping everything for themselves. On average, 28% of the available amount is given (meta-analysis by Engel, 2011).

Games can be played once ('one-shot' games) or more than once. Repeated games give partners the opportunity to get to know one another, to build trust and to cooperate. Finally, the ultimatum game can be played in groups, which in an appropriately described context can be used to study markets, as discussed in the chapter on experimental labour markets.

2.1.3.2 Prisoner's Dilemma

A well-known game used to investigate cooperation is the **prisoner's dilemma** (Rapoport & Chammah, 1965; Tucker, 1950, as cited by Roth, 1988). The prisoner's dilemma is a decision

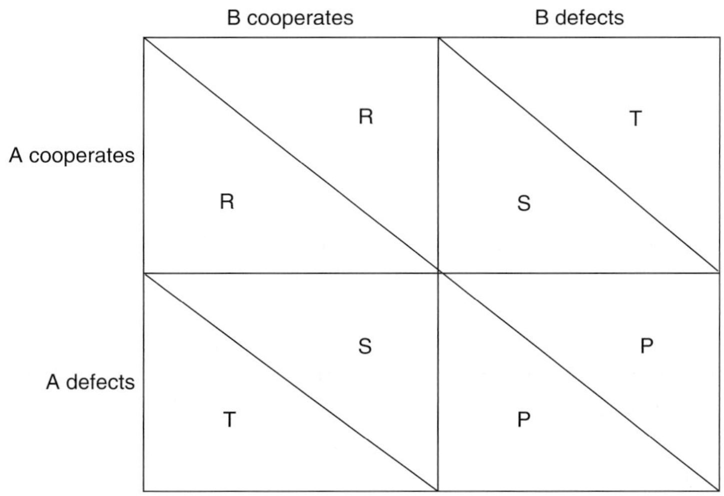

Figure 2.1 Generally formulated payoff matrix in the prisoner's dilemma (adapted from Rapoport & Chammah, 1965, p. 34)

problem where two decision-makers independently have to decide between cooperation and defection. While from an individual perspective defection is the rational solution, the overall outcome is better if both cooperate.

In the version of the game from which it draws its name, two prisoners are in pre-trial custody for a crime they committed jointly. The police already suspect both prisoners; however, they do not have enough proof to convict them. Let's say the maximum sentence for this crime is seven years in prison. If both confess or one confesses, both will be sentenced to prison for seven years. If the prisoners decide not to talk, the evidence will be insufficient to give them the maximum sentence, and they will receive a sentence of two years. In this case, it would be prudent for both to remain silent. In order to break the prisoners' silence, the police offer each of them separately a deal if they confess: if one confesses while the other remains silent, the confessor will go free; if they both confess, their sentences will be reduced to five years each. The prisoners cannot talk it over: they need to decide whether to confess without any information on the other prisoner's behaviour. The dilemma for the prisoners consists of four elements. (a) There is a temptation (T) to choose a one-sided betrayal in order to free oneself. (b) They are rewarded for cooperating with one another rather than with the police in that only a two-year sentence is imposed if neither one defects ('reward' R). (c) A sentence of five years in prison looms over them if they both betray each other ('punishment' P). (d) The prisoner who gullibly trusts the partner who betrays his confidence is sentenced to seven years in prison ('sucker's payoff' S). The general form of the payoff matrix is depicted in Figure 2.1, with $T > R > P > S$ (Rapoport & Chammah, 1965).

Each player's sentence depends not only on his own choice, but also on that of his partner. The prisoner's dilemma is based on the fact that focusing on collective utility leads to a different choice than focusing on individual utility. The total sentence is smallest when both players remain silent ($2 + 2 = 4$ years). From each individual's perspective, however, it would be advantageous to cooperate with the police rather than with his co-conspirator (dismissal of the charges versus seven years for the co-conspirator). If both cooperate with the police, the result is especially unfavourable on the collective level ($5 + 5 = 10$ years). Hence, if the co-conspirators distrust one another, their analysis leads them to cooperate with the police and betray one another, resulting in an especially disadvantageous outcome from the perspective of both players.

From a rational perspective, it makes sense according to the presented payoff matrix to maximise one's own utility and betray the co-conspirator in a one-shot game. One's own decision cannot influence the partner's behaviour; cooperation with the police always means improving one's situation. However, empirical studies show that study participants often choose to cooperate with their co-conspirator, trusting that he will also cooperate (Vogt, 2000, 2001).

When multiple rounds of the game are played, the situation changes. From previous rounds, participants learn how their co-conspirators behave and whether or not they can be trusted. One can retaliate against non-cooperative behaviour through non-cooperation ('defection'). When participants know how many rounds will be played in total, **backward induction** can be applied: by considering the rational solution in the last round, the rational solution in the previous round can be derived, and so on. Backward induction now indicates that, from a rational perspective, defection again represents the optimal strategy in iterated games (games that are played repeatedly). An analysis beginning at the end of the game goes like this: The last round is similar to a one-shot game. Because it is no longer possible to retaliate against the other person's uncooperative behaviour, a player seeking to maximise his utility will cooperate with the police. Since participants will not cooperate in the last round, it is thus also not advisable to cooperate in the second to last round, as the co-conspirator will defect to the police's side in order to minimise his sentence. If, however, players will not cooperate in the last two rounds, defection also becomes the rational strategy in the prior round. When the dilemma is analysed from the last round to the first, the arguments for cooperation start to fall like dominoes. However, when the players do not know how many rounds will be played, cooperation is likely to pay off. Betrayals are punished directly by the co-conspirator in the next round, while cooperation has a high probability of enhancing the partner's willingness to cooperate.

Numerous economic and psychological experiments have conducted game-theoretic simulations of interpersonal, economic and political conflict scenarios, studying either one-shot or repeated decisions in which the other person's behaviour is reported back at the end of each round. For example, the 'battle of the sexes' game (Wagner, Kirchler & Brandstätter, 1984) investigates how romantic partners make joint decisions.

A further cooperation game is the 'chicken' game, based on the dangerous dares teenagers use to test each other's courage. The dare is that two teenagers start driving their cars towards one another. The first person to swerve loses the game. However, too much courage on both sides has dramatic consequences. Some political conflict situations resemble the game of chicken: if two world powers arm themselves with massive amounts of nuclear weapons, the 'price of a collision' becomes enormously high. A collision would probably mean the end of everyone involved; however, a one-sided disarmament is interpreted as weakness. The Cuban Missile Crisis of 1962 is structurally comparable with the game of chicken. John F. Kennedy 'won' with his highly risky behaviour, because Nikita Sergeyevich Khrushchev ultimately called back the Soviet fleet.

2.2 Decision Anomalies

Economists argue that even though people may take many actions in their everyday lives that do not conform to the model of the *homo economicus*, economic actors are forced to behave rationally, as this is the only way to survive in the free market. The market simply does not tolerate irrational actions and hence 'cleanses' itself of decisions and actions that are not rational. In particular, the decisions of entrepreneurs are expected to be economically rational. In private households, where partners make joint decisions based on mutual feelings, critiques of rationality theory are condoned to some extent. However, psychological studies show that it is not only the decisions of private consumers, romantic partners and parents with their children that rarely proceed according to the model of *homo economicus*. Even the decisions of experts in companies, as well as political and administrative institutions, frequently do not follow this pattern of rationality. Owing to time pressure, decisions are made based on information processed inadequately. Decision-makers justify their behaviour after the fact – they 'rationalise' ex post facto. The supposition that people consistently judge options on the basis of their utility, are able to construct a stable order of preferences for all options, and select the best option based on a thorough comparison of all options, assumes an enormous capacity for calculation as well as the motivation to invest time and energy. Even if people were able to survey the available options on the market and evaluate them in detail, collecting and processing the necessary information would take too much time. Many actions would be taken too late, sometimes after a problem has lost its relevance or has 'solved itself'. Numerous judgment and decision situations show that people often forgo collecting all relevant information or do not process it adequately (e.g., Hammond, Keeney & Raiffa, 1998; Kahneman, Slovic & Tversky, 1982; Schwartz, 2008).

Laypeople and experts can make suboptimal choices regardless of whether they make decisions intuitively or proceed analytically. In complex everyday decision situations at home, at work, in the market or in political arenas, deviations from the rational model – which are labelled **decision anomalies** – are the rule. Anomalies are not the exception: they are quite normal!

Observed behaviour deviates from the postulates of the *homo economicus* theory both in research on individual decision-making stemming from statistical decision theory and in studies of group and organisational decision-making rooted in economic theories of business and game theory (March & Shapira, 1992). On the one hand, psychology has convincingly shown that people do not always perceive 'reality' as it 'objectively' is. Frequently, subjective and collective myths are 'constructed', which then govern behaviour (Moscovici, 2000). On the other hand, decision-makers often cannot evaluate every option and are neither willing nor able to collect all necessary information and process it adequately. People are frequently overwhelmed by the diversity of information available and suffer from time pressure, which makes it impossible to consider all the consequences of a decision; hence, 'shortcuts' are used. Decision-makers apply rules of thumb and rely on a few pieces of key data while disregarding other information. This means that they apply decision heuristics that are sometimes but not always optimal. Often, information is not even sought out: one simply does what has always been done in the past. Also, people can behave inconsistently with respect to their goals: when the context in which a decision is to be made has changed, attention can be directed towards different elements, such as gain or loss, and preferences can change accordingly (e.g., Kahneman & Tversky, 1979; Lichtenstein & Slovic, 1971; Slovic, 1995). In many cases, it is not the benefits offered by an option that determine conduct, but rather the regret associated with missed benefits from forgone alternatives. Anticipated emotions – disappointment and regret expected after a decision – determine which alternative is selected and whether or not a person is willing to forgo a particular option (Bell, 1982; Loomes & Sugden, 1982). A satisfactory alternative, that is, the 'first to come along', often suffices and the search does not continue after this satisfactory alternative has been found (Simon, 1957). In other decision situations, one option is implicitly favoured, and the subsequent search for information seeks to confirm the implicit choice rather than to discover a better option.

In the following section, the aforementioned sources of error are discussed as causes of systematic deviations from the rational model (cf. Jungermann et al. 2010). Information in decision situations is subjectively perceived and interpreted and human decision-making capacities are sometimes too limited to cope with the complexity of a given task. People's 'psycho-logic' can run counter to the claims of mathematical logic.

2.2.1 Information Processing

> What a piece of work is a man! How noble in Reason! How infinite in faculties! In form and moving how express and admirable! In action how like an Angel! In apprehension how like a god! The beauty of the world! (Shakespeare, *Hamlet, prince of Denmark*, Act II, Scene ii)

In economics, and not uncommonly in social psychology as well, human beings were described as 'creatures of reason', as intuitive scientists or cognitively dominated beings – until Nisbett and Ross (1980) proved that judgments in complex situations can systematically deviate from the normatively logical ones. William Shakespeare's hymn of praise to humankind – placed in Hamlet's mouth – is perhaps too optimistic. People have problems in the understanding of complex tasks and exponential growth, and problems with probability calculations. People also process information differently, leading to distorted perceptions in certain cases.

2.2.1.1 Problems in Information Processing

To start with, perceived information does not always reflect what objectively exists. Optical illusions are a good illustration of this (Figure 2.2), as are distortions of judgments in social situations (Asch, 1946; Ichheiser, 1949) and the dependency of judgments on contextual and background variables. In the financial domain, Bruner and Goodman (1947) showed that

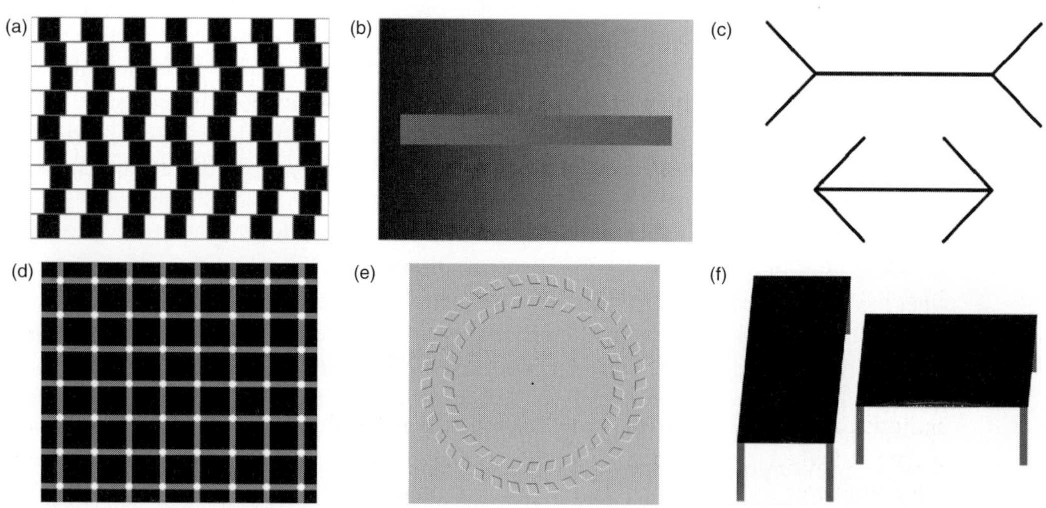

Notes:
(a) The ostensibly slanted lines are actually straight.
(b) The grey beam appears to be lighter on the left but actually has the same greyscale value over its entire length.
(c) The lines appear to have different lengths due to the angles of the fins (Müller-Lyer illusion).
(d) If you concentrate on the white intersection points, black dots seem to be flashing on and off there.
(e) If you concentrate on the black dot and move your head towards the picture and then away from it, the circles appear to be turning.
(f) The tables appear to be different, but they are the same size.

Figure 2.2 Optical illusions

1. Imagine you are participating in the lottery '6 out of 45'. Which row of numbers is more likely to be a winner? (a) 5 10 17 21 25 38 (b) 1 2 3 4 5 6
2. One hundred students are participating in a university event. Twenty of them are business students with marketing as their main subject; 80 are enrolled in the psychology programme. During the event a mobile phone rings. A student grabs her briefcase and the jacket of her stylish pantsuit and leaves the room. This is probably: (a) A business student (b) A psychology student (c) Both possibilities are equally likely
3. In Milan, there are 1,000 Ferraris and 99,000 cars of other brands. Ninety percent of the Ferraris are red, while only 30% of the other cars are red. You are standing at an intersection and see a red car go past at an excessive speed. How likely is it that this is a Ferrari? (a) About 3% (b) About 0.03% (c) About 10%
4. Check whether the following statement is true: 'When an employee works at the weekend, he gets a day off during the week.' Each of the following cards contains information about four employees. Each card represents one employee. One side states whether or not the employee worked at the weekend, while the other side states whether or not he had a day off during the week. You now have the opportunity to turn cards over in order to obtain the information on the other side. Which cards must be turned over, at minimum, in order to determine whether the statement is true? (a) worked at the weekend (b) got a day off (c) did not work at the weekend (d) didn't get a day off
5. Check whether the following statement is true: 'When there is a D on one side of a card, there is a 3 on the other side.' Each of the following cards has a letter on one side and a number on the other. Which cards must be turned over, at minimum, in order to determine whether the statement is true? (a) D (b) E (c) 3 (d) 4

Figure 2.3 Puzzles (based on Gigerenzer & Hug, 1992; Tversky & Kahneman, 1974, 1983)

children's estimates of the size of coins depended not only on their ability to make judgments, but also on their parents' financial background and therefore on the subjective value the coins represented for these children.

Decision situations are often complex. The magnitude of information frequently overwhelms human capacity to process it. Puzzles like those in Figure 2.3 show how quickly people start to have troubles in the accomplishment of a task.

Problems become particularly complex when they involve non-linear developments. People are used to projecting the development of events linearly into the future and therefore have trouble making accurate predictions about developments that proceed exponentially. The non-linear development of a variable leads to misunderstandings, erroneous interpretations and false expectations. Most people make enormously inaccurate estimations when they are asked how often a large piece of paper 0.1 millimetres thick needs to be folded in order to reach the height of a city church tower and are astonished when the solution is presented. For example, a piece of paper 0.1 millimetres thick is only 1.6 millimetres tall after it has been folded four times. However, after only folding it 22 times, it rises significantly above a 150-metre tower. In environmental politics, exponentially growing quantities represent a generally underestimated problem, as dangers are not recognised early enough. For example, air pollution due to the emission of contaminating substances, climatic changes due to logging and deforestation, and other ecological problems, do not develop linearly. Even if a lot of time passes before environmental resources are partially destroyed, it usually does not take as much time for the same amount of further damage to occur.

Problems also become complex when they involve probabilities. People are used to dealing with concrete absolute numbers, but have difficulties in understanding probability calculations. Problems that contain frequencies are easier to solve than problems that demand the calculation of probabilities (Gigerenzer & Hoffrage, 1995). It is difficult to compute compound interest as well as to understand the effects of inflation on price developments in the short and long run (Kemp, 1987). Specifically, conditional probabilities are hard to understand and are rarely adequately taken into account, as demonstrated by Gigerenzer (2004a). A famous example illustrating the difficulties in calculating probabilities is known as the **Monty Hall dilemma** or the goat problem (Granberg & Brown, 1995; Krauss & Wang, 2003; Randow, 1999). On a TV game show, candidates who have cleared every hurdle and are on the threshold of victory can choose between three or more alternatives knowing that only one alternative contains the prize they seek; the others contain nothing. For example, a candidate might get the opportunity to select one of three envelopes, only one of which holds the prize. Since only one envelope contains the prize and the others are empty, the probability of winning is $p = 0.33$. After one of the three alternatives has been selected, the host might open the other two envelopes to see if they are empty or contain the prize, and then close one of the envelopes again while showing the second one as empty to the candidate. The candidate now knows that the prize is either in his envelope or in the one that the host closed up again. Subsequently, the host might give the candidate the opportunity to amend his first choice by exchanging the envelope for the still-closed one in the host's hand. Very few candidates switch over from their first choice, believing that the chance of winning is now 50% because there are now only two closed envelopes. False assumptions about probabilities and the compulsion to be steadfast in one's decisions and behaviour convince most candidates not to switch. Particularly the anticipation of the regret one would feel after an exchange if the prize were in the envelope that was drawn first plays a role in this decision. Indeed, Gilovich and Medvec (1995) could show that people actually experience more regret and disappointment when they take action, compared to situations where they wait things out. However, in the Monty Hall dilemma this reduces their chances of winning, as switching over would actually double their chances of winning to $p = 0.67$. Suboptimal behaviour is also frequently observed when not three but many more alternatives are offered, with a single chance of winning. For example, a person can draw one of 100 envelopes, of which only one contains the prize. If the host opens all 99 envelopes in his hand, closes one of them and shows the other 98 empty envelopes to the candidate offering an exchange for the closed envelope in his hand, switching over would drastically increase the chance of winning from 1% originally to 99%. But even in this game, the majority of participants do not recognise the advantages of switching over and are not willing to exchange the envelope drawn first.

2.2.1.2 Information Processing Paths

The psychological perspective on human information processing and decision-making commonly assumes that information processing can follow two process paths. The foundations of dual-process theories lie with William James, who posited two different modes of thinking: associative and reasoning. Dual-process theories proceed from the assumption that information processing can take place through unconscious, rapid and automatic processes, through a system working at high capacity that uses information from long-term memory to make a choice or decision. An example of rapid information processing leading to immediate but wrong results is demonstrated with the cognitive reflection test by Frederick (2005, p. 27): 'A bat and a ball cost $1.10 in total. The bat costs $1.00 more than the ball. How much does the ball cost?' Most people incorrectly conclude $0.10, but feel that the result is correct and therefore avoid further inspection of the result.

Table 2.1 Two-process models (adapted from Evans, 2008, p. 257)

Authors	System 1	System 2
Chaiken (1980); Chen & Chaiken (1999)	Heuristic	Systematic
Epstein (1994); Epstein & Pacini (1999)	Experiential	Rational
Evans (1989, 2006)	Heuristic	Analytic
Fodor (1983, 2001)	Input modules	Higher cognition
Hammond (1996)	Intuitive	Analytic
Lieberman (2003)	Reflexive	Reflective
Metcalfe & Mischel (1999)	Hot	Cold
Nisbett, Peng, Choi & Norenzayan (2001)	Holistic	Analytic
Petty & Cacioppo (1986)	Peripheral	Central
Reber (1993); Evans & Over (1996)	Implicit/tacit	Explicit
Schneider & Shiffrin (1977)	Automatic	Controlled
Sloman (1996); Smith & DeCoster (2000)	Associative	Rule based
Stanovich (1999, 2004)	System 1 (TASS)	System 2 (Analytic)
Strack & Deutsch (2004)	Impulsive	Reflective
Toates (2006)	Stimulus bound	Higher order
Wilson (2002)	Adaptive unconscious	Conscious

The second processing system works more slowly. It is steered by conscious processes of appraisal and analysis, has only limited capacity, and uses working memory to process, evaluate and compare information until a choice becomes clear (Evans, 2008; Evans & Stanovich, 2013a, 2013b). In the psychological literature, various authors postulate two information processing systems; however, they differ in how these two processing systems are conceived of and labelled. Table 2.1 lists authors and their terms for the two systems.

The most commonly used terms are probably System 1 and System 2. Evans (2008, 2012) postulates that there is a tendency to perceive all dual-process theories as essentially similar. However, there are notable differences. Moreover, reducing the number of cognitive processing systems to two seems a bit premature, as multiple sub-systems could exist. An evaluation of dual-process theories of reasoning is provided by Osman (2004).

It is commonly assumed that System 1 leads to biases and errors in decision-making, while System 2 facilitates normatively correct decisions. However, this is not necessarily the case: information processing over System 2 can also lead to mistakes. Specifically, insights from System 1 are not always correspondingly audited and corrected by System 2, as this second system sometimes simply seeks justifications for intuitive insights (Kahneman, 2003, 2011; Kahneman & Frederick, 2002; Stanovich, 1999). According to Evans (2012), a few points of confusion, some misleading generalisations, and too sloppy attributions of systemically inherent functions and errors remain in the discussion of the two processing systems:

> Type 2 processing is considered to be high effort, responsive to instructions, and capable of dealing with abstraction and novelty, often allowing at least high-ability participants with appropriate instructions to solve deductive problems. Type 1 processing by contrast is rapid and low effort, and may be based on associative processing and implicit knowledge . . . It often takes the blame for cognitive biases, especially belief biases. But it is an error to think that Type 1 processing is necessarily biased or that Type 2 processing is necessarily logical and

> abstract . . . Both types of processing can lead to correct answers and both can lead to biases . . . Type 1 processing can provide intuitive feelings of confidence in conclusions that are often followed when participants are making low effort to reason analytically. (Evans, 2012, p. 16)

Over System 1, characteristics of decision alternatives are perceived spontaneously, automatically, and seen as tied to a certain stimulus and context. System 1 processes are spontaneously put in motion (Evans, 2008; Kahneman & Frederick, 2002; Morewedge & Kahneman, 2010). They activate saved schemata, generate impressions and form preliminary judgments. These can then be analysed by System 2 processes and either be adopted, obstructed or corrected (Morewedge & Kahneman, 2010). Mistakes in judgment and decision-making can occur when System 1 forms erroneous preliminary judgments and System 2 tries to rationalise these intuitive conclusions rather than analysing them properly and correcting them if necessary (Evans, 2008; Morewedge & Kahneman, 2010). According to Morewedge and Kahneman (2010), associative memory processes, which are especially attributed to System 1, can lead to systematic errors, known as 'biases'. Most of the time, the triggering stimulus automatically activates compatible associations, producing associative coherence. Often, one feature of the stimulus that is to be evaluated is unconsciously replaced by another feature that is easier to assess. Processing speed also plays a role. Compatible and coherent associations are activated quickly, and this speed increases assurance regarding the validity of the judgment. Mukherjee (2010) models

Table 2.2 Clusters of attributes associated with dual systems of thinking (adapted from Evans, 2008, p. 257)

Clusters	System 1	System 2
Consciousness	Unconscious (preconscious)	Conscious
	Implicit	Explicit
	Automatic	Controlled
	Low-effort	High-effort
	Rapid	Slow
	High-capacity	Low-capacity
	Default process	Inhibitory
	Holistic, perceptual	Analytic, reflective
Evolution	Evolutionarily old	Evolutionarily recent
	Evolutionary rationality	Individual rationality
	Shared with animals	Uniquely human
	Non-verbal	Linked to language
	Modular cognition	Fluid intelligence
Functional characteristics	Associative	Rule-based
	Domain-specific	General
	Contextualised	Abstract
	Pragmatic	Logical
	Parallel	Sequential
	Stereotypical	Egalitarian
Individual differences	Universal	Heritable
	Independent of general intelligence	Linked to general intelligence
	Independent of working memory	Limited by working memory capacity

decision-making according to the dual system and finds that the concept of two processing paths is able accurately to portray decision-making under uncertainty. Table 2.2 summarises the features of each system according to overarching categories.

The terms intuitive and analytical decision-making are closely connected to two-process theories. Intuitive decisions are attributed to System 1 and are tightly bound up with feelings. In contrast to analytical decisions, which are attributed to System 2, intuitive or instinctive decisions are not completely explicable and cannot be easily converted into a sequential algorithm (i.e., they cannot be subdivided into a series of points of consideration). Hence, these decisions are characterised as rather holistic (Epstein, 1994; Slovic, Finucane, Peters & MacGregor, 2004).

Intuitive processes are not necessarily irrational and analytical processes are not necessarily rational. In a field study, Klein (1998) investigated decision-making by experts in diverse professions. Findings indicated that experts make intuitive decisions most of the time. Notably, the intuitions upon which they base their decisions are highly reliable. Laypeople, conversely, tend to make more analytical decisions. When they do make intuitive decisions, their underlying intuitions are typically unreliable. Two different types of intuition are stipulated: intuition based on experience and knowledge and imperfect intuition based on heuristics or ignorance. Simon (1992, p. 155) defined 'skilled intuition' or intuition based on experience as follows: 'The situation has provided a cue: This cue has given the expert access to information stored in memory, and the information provides the answer. Intuition is nothing more and nothing less than recognition.'

Professional intuition is sometimes great and sometimes flawed (Kahneman & Klein, 2009). Experience alone is not necessarily a reliable indicator of judgment accuracy. It is necessary that expertise is gained in a valid environment, that is, an environment with predictable developments that allows us to learn the regularities of a phenomenon. In valid environments, cues about the current situation and cues about changes of the situation are available, and there are sufficient opportunities to recognise the relevant cues, as well as to receive accurate and timely feedback regarding the adequacy of interventions. This enables the development of skills on the base of experience. Kahneman and Klein (2009) see validity as related to the causal and statistical structure of the environment, that is, to underlying conditions and the ways they change. In other words, an environment is highly valid when stable relationships exist among objectively identifiable cues, interventions and ensuing results, or between cues and the results of actions. Doctors, firefighters and chess players, for example, operate in highly valid environments. Experienced doctors, firefighters and chess players can rely on available scripts and action programmes. They are able to diagnose situations spontaneously, pull up their automated scripts, and usually apply them correctly. Non-valid environments do not feature stable relationships between causes and effects, and the results or consequences of decisions and actions cannot be reliably predicted. Regularity in terms of change or the ways in which conditions develop does not exist or is difficult to recognise. Stock markets and political arenas represent this type of non-valid environment. Predictions about the future prices of specific stocks or long-term projections of political outcomes are not very trustworthy. Therefore, automated programmes of action do not exist and intuitive decisions are actually made 'from the gut'.

Experts make good intuitive decisions more frequently than laypeople. In situations where decisions-makers have the opportunity to master the conditions and rules governing the interplay of events and their consequences, and where reliable projections about the consequences of decisions can be made, experts are in a position to make good intuitive decisions. In rather unfamiliar situations that include new tasks to cope with and problems that cannot be solved by following old patterns, analytical processes are more expedient than intuition. 'Gut decisions' made by experienced professionals in valid environments are frequently correct, whereas 'overthinking' can cause disruptions and insecurity. On the other hand, gut decisions that are made out of ignorance and based on 'spontaneous inspiration' in invalid environments are rarely good decisions.

2.2.2 Emotions

In decision research, feelings and anticipated emotions are considered relevant – not just the expected utility of an alternative. Early on, feelings of regret stemming from the fact that all other options must be eschewed in favour of the chosen option have been integrated into decision theories. According to Bell (1982) and Loomes and Sugden (1982), the subjective value of an alternative depends not only on its own expected consequences, but also on the expected but not materialised consequences of the alternatives that are not selected. Decisions are commonly judged on the basis of what might have happened and how a decision-maker would have felt if they had selected a different option, such as a different job or a trip to a different country. According to Loomes and Sugden, decisions under uncertainty are based on anticipated feelings of rejoicing and regret. People try to avoid regret. Considering the cost of losing out on the benefits of non-selected options modifies the expected utility for the selected option with a regret–rejoice function that takes into account the non-selected option.

Psychology assumes that expectations of possible regret following a decision have a large influence on decision-making (e.g., Connolly & Butler, 2006). Zeelenberg and Pieters (2007) determined that **regret** is a negative emotion commonly connected to self-blame as well as to disappointment, vexation, guilt, grief and shame. Regret is based on the comparison of alternatives and the consequences of alternatives and can refer to decisions in the past ('retrospective regret') or the future ('anticipated regret' or 'prospective regret'): not only the results of decisions that can lead to regret, but also the decision-making process itself. Either the decision-making process is perceived to be wanting or the consequences of the decision are disappointing, even after thorough consideration. Subjectively 'bad decisions' are those that lead to worse results compared to others. The decision-making process can be experienced as inadequate if, for example, a choice is made without considering relevant information that might have been available, if judgments are made too quickly, or if advice is taken from the wrong person. However, the more easily people can justify their decisions, the less regret they feel. People are motivated to make decisions in such a way so that they have no regrets about either the consequences or the selection process.

Important decisions like the selection of a life partner, deciding whether to have children, choosing a career and buying a house are influenced by anticipated feelings. When decisions lead to the desired consequences, people are pleased. However, they react with dissatisfaction when this does not happen. The selection of an option depends not only on its expected material utility, but also on the anticipated emotions tied to the choice, such as the hope for happiness and contentment as well as the fear of frustration and regret. To avoid regret, it is important to correctly anticipate not only the expected utility but also the feelings connected to the choice.

However, predictions about the quality and intensity of feelings, and about how long they will last, can be faulty. Research on the prognosis of feelings, known as '**affective forecasting**', focuses on the prediction of emotional reactions to future events. Wilson and Gilbert (2003) differentiate among four components of affective forecasting: (1) predictions about the valence of future feelings, (2) the

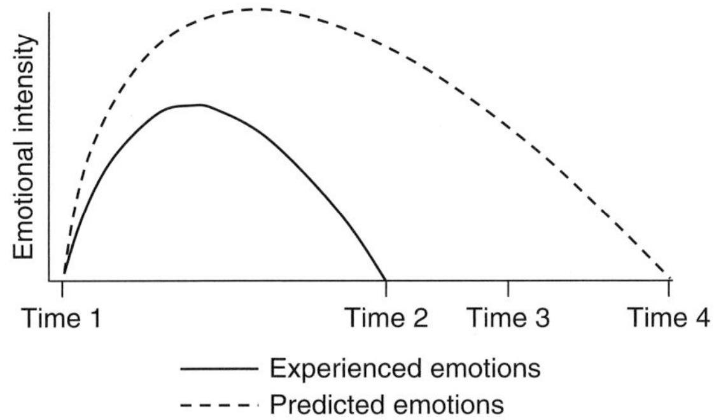

Figure 2.4 Hypothetical time progression of predicted and experienced emotions (Wilson & Gilbert, 2003, p. 350)

specific emotions that will be experienced, (3) the intensity of these feelings and (4) their duration. For the most part, people make accurate predictions about valence, about whether their feelings in response to an event will be positive or negative. This is especially true when they already have experience with this particular facet of life (Loewenstein, 2007). Predictions are also generally correct about the emotional qualities of specific situations, about whether feelings of fear or anger, disgust, happiness, joy or satisfaction will arise (Loewenstein, 2007). Robinson and Clore (2001) presented study participants with descriptions of pictures that evoke emotions. Participants were asked to predict which specific feelings they would experience when they actually had the pictures in front of them. Their predictions were actually quite accurate. They were less successful, however, in predicting their specific emotions in more complex situations involving mixed feelings (Larsen, McGraw & Cacioppo, 2001). In addition, prognoses about emotions experienced in the future became more error-prone the further the event was in the future.

The duration and intensity of one's emotional reaction are often overestimated: this most common error is known as '**impact bias**'. Jubilation over winning millions in the lottery, fans' pride after their football team has gained victory, resignation after a failed exam, grief over a shattered relationship or desperation after being diagnosed with an illness all seem substantially more intense and longer lasting in predictions than they are when experienced in real life. The hypothetical time progression of the intensity of experienced and predicted emotional reactions is depicted in Figure 2.4. As can be seen, both the peak intensity and the duration until when intensity is back to zero are overestimated. In addition, the rate of increase (acceleration) is overestimated, while the rate of decrease (deceleration) is underestimated (Wilson & Gilbert, 2003).

Wilson and Gilbert (2003) summarised various sources of errors in affective forecasts. When people think about events they have not experienced in the past, such as winning the lottery, they have to imagine these events, e.g., what they would do with this much money and how their friends would react to their winning. Representations of events depend upon the specific attributes of the event itself, which catch and hold people's attention, as well as upon situational conditions, which influence the interpretation of the anticipated event (Kahneman & Tversky, 1979). In a 'misconstrual', an event is imagined to be different than it actually is. Moreover, it must be clear to decision-makers how they will feel in certain situations. One method is to remember similar experiences. In memory, however, emotions are less intense, which can lead to faulty predictions. In another method, predictions are based on knowledge of emotional consequences. This knowledge is sometimes incorrect, as seen in the presumptions stating that material wealth is the key to permanent happiness or that a physical disability after an accident would make life no longer worth living

(Gilbert, Pinel, Wilson, Blumberg & Wheatley, 1998; Wilson & Gilbert, 2003). Predictions about feelings after a future event also depend on one's current state. People who are in a good mood at the time they predict future feelings make different prognoses than people in bad moods. Loewenstein, O'Donoghue and Rabin (2003) speak of '**projection bias**', which describes the tendency to assume that one's future feelings and preferences will be similar to the current feelings and preferences. A further prediction error can lie in the fact that an event is experienced differently depending on one's expectations. A person in an emotionally 'hot' mood often finds it hard to imagine that their feelings will cool down in the future; prognoses can be similarly faulty when a person in an emotionally 'cold' state predicts his or her feelings after a particularly moving event. When people give prognoses about their feelings on the basis of a particular event, they tend to ignore other events that could happen in the meantime. Finally, people tend to rationalise their experiences, understand their fate, find meaning and adapt themselves to whatever the current situation is (Gilbert et al., 1998; Wilson & Gilbert, 2003). In the field of consumption, however, Pollai, Hoelzl and Possas (2010) found that joy over new shoes was high at the time of purchase, but consumers did not assume their positive feelings would last all that long. They were actually more satisfied with their purchase than predicted after two and four weeks, respectively. Looking back, they were not aware of their prediction error; they claimed to have made more accurate predictions than they actually had.

2.2.3 Time

A large number of studies have investigated the selection of one alternative out of a set of possibilities in which the consequences of the decision lie in the present. Frequently, however, decisions must be made whose consequences lie in the future. A larger profit at a later time might be preferred to an immediate one. Sometimes, the total profit is composed of the individual profits of multiple decisions (distributed choices), which is difficult to get a handle on. In accordance with the maximisation principle, the time perspective needs to be taken into account in decision-making, and utility should be maximised over time.

However, it is difficult to calculate the total utility from several individual decisions as well as to muster enough patience and self-control to wait for a larger profit in the future instead of immediately enjoying a smaller one. In the following section, the patience involved in waiting for gratification, temporal discounting and melioration as well as memories of predictions are described.

2.2.3.1 Delayed Gratification

People are generally inclined to enjoy amenities immediately rather than to wait patiently for larger comforts in the future. Walter Mischel (1974) showed that people have trouble deferring rewards, even when the reward turns out to be significantly greater at a later point than in the present. In his 'marshmallow experiments', children could choose between getting one piece of candy immediately or getting twice as much at a later time. Summoning the patience to wait is often difficult. According to Metcalfe and Mischel (1999), self-control as a means of suppressing consumption impulses is especially difficult when, in the dual-processing approach, System 1, which operates emotionally, quickly and reflexively, is dominant. Notably, this system is controlled by external stimuli and typically becomes activated in stressful situations. System 2, conversely, is the one whose functioning is heavily cognitive, complex, well thought out, slow and full of self-control, typically becoming weaker in times of stress. When the 'hot' System 1 is dominant, the temptation to engage in immediate consumption is hard to resist; in the 'cool' mode of System 2, self-control and momentary sacrifices in favour of greater future rewards become easier.

2.2.3.2 Time Preferences and Discounting

Most of the time, future gains are valued less than present ones. Likewise, future costs are given a lower value than current ones. When given the choice between consuming amenities immediately or receiving comparably larger rewards in the future, most people find the decision easy: go for the immediate benefit! The choice between the enjoyment of amenities right away incurring long-run costs or the forgoing of these amenities in favour of future benefits is also generally easy: much weight is attached to current benefits, while future costs or benefits are strongly discounted. Therefore, despite its costs in the long run, immediate enjoyment is preferred to abstinence.

The preference for immediate utility vis-à-vis delayed utility is called '**time discounting**' (Frederick, Loewenstein & O'Donoghue, 2002). The discount rate of profits (and losses) over time is frequently high. However, people behave inconsistently in this regard (Ainslie & Haslam, 1992; Loewenstein & Thaler, 1989). For example, if children can choose between a large and a small bar of chocolate, they will choose the big one. If you ask them, however, if they would prefer to have the small bar of chocolate today or the large one tomorrow, they will hesitate, and many children end up choosing the small piece of chocolate right away. As the small bar of chocolate received immediately is preferred to the larger one later, it can be assumed that chocolate has a high discount factor. However, if children are offered the small bar of chocolate in 10 days' time and the large one in 11 days, the large bar of chocolate is preferred despite the fact that the same time interval of one day is at play. In this case, the value of the chocolate is not so heavily discounted after all.

2.2.3.3 Distributed Choices: Melioration

In everyday life, many decisions are repeated decisions, and the total utility results from the utility of each individual selected alternative. We make repeated decisions about what to eat, what clothes and accessories to wear, etc. According to the rational model, utility maximisation for repeated decisions would mean that the ratio of the utilities of various alternatives to one another is known and that it is possible to make the optimal sequence of choices over time. However, this optimisation of choice behaviour in every repeated decision situation would be incredibly strenuous and almost impossible in light of humans' limited information processing capacity.

In reality, it turns out that people do not follow the maximisation principle in repeated choice situations. Instead, they usually select the alternative that promises the greatest utility at the present moment, ignoring the effects of this choice on total utility over time. Although this behaviour can be economically suboptimal, classical theories of learning can explain it: it is assumed that the consequences of one's behaviour determine the probability of that behaviour occurring again in the future. Thus, on the basis of operant conditioning theory, the '**fundamental law of effect**' postulates an increase in the probability of occurrence of the behaviour that receives the most reinforcement (Thorndike, 1927). When repeated opportunities are available to choose among behavioural alternatives, the behaviour that provides a person with the most pleasurable consequences (the greatest utility) would have, after a while, to occur particularly frequently. If this were true, people would maximise their gains and act in accordance with rationality theory. To the contrary, Herrnstein (1961) found in numerous experiments on animals that deviations from the maximisation principle occurred in simple choice situations with two alternatives, each of which was reinforced to a differing degree. Sometimes one alternative was chosen, and sometimes the other one. This was even the case when the animal realised from the beginning which alternative was being reinforced more intensively. Perhaps due to satiation effects, out of curiosity or other motives, the alternative with less value was sometimes preferred to the more valuable one.

On the basis of these observations, Herrnstein (1961) expanded the fundamental law of effect by formulating the '**law of relative effect**', also known as the '**matching law**'. It states that the selection ratio of various behavioural alternatives is proportional to the subjective value of the reinforcements attached to these alternatives and inversely proportional to the time that passes between the behaviour and its reinforcement. This means that an Alternative A is selected three times more often than Alternative B when the reinforcement tied to Alternative A has a value three times higher than that of Alternative B. Conversely, it can be assumed that the subjective utility of various selected alternatives corresponds to the ratio of the frequencies with which they are selected. This behaviour, observed in animals and humans, deviates from the predictions of rationality theory.

However, if people do not maximise their utility, what are they doing instead? Herrnstein (1990) argued that people orient their behaviour on the value of contemporaneous alternatives. They compare the effects elicited by different behaviours and more frequently choose the behavioural alternative that puts them in a better position for the time being. This **melioration** principle substitutes for the principle of maximisation. Melioration is not always suboptimal: if, for example, the choice is to press one of two keys in order to win money, experimental subjects' behaviour is absolutely profit-maximising in that – after determining which key offers the larger payout – they repeatedly press that key. However, melioration can sometimes represent the strategy that reduces profits (Herrnstein, 1990, 1991; Herrnstein, Loewenstein, Prelec & Vaughan, 1993; Herrnstein & Prelec, 1991).

The difference between utility maximisation and melioration becomes clearer in the following scenario (Herrnstein & Prelec, 1991). Suppose a person visits the same restaurant every day, where two dishes are offered for the same price: pizza and sandwiches. Pizza is the person's favourite dish, whereas sandwiches are less appreciated. Both dishes have decreasing marginal utility. Since pizza is the restaurant visitor's favourite food, he eats it until he gets tired of eating the same thing all the time. At this point, he chooses a sandwich and maybe the pizza again the next time. A rational restaurant visitor needs to select the combination of pizza and sandwiches that maximises his utility over a given time, such as on workdays for four weeks. This is difficult, however, because the marginal utility of the dishes needs to be clear to him, or he must be able to judge in advance which sequence of dishes represents the best choice for him. If the restaurant visitor meliorates, he gains experience from each choice and from eating the dishes, which allows him to formulate an average utility for the pizza and the sandwich. According to the melioration principle, decisions do not proceed according to marginal utility, but according to the average utility of the pizza and sandwich. After a while, the restaurant visitor might have ordered pizza thirteen times and a sandwich seven times, meaning that he has decided upon a pizza to sandwich ratio of about 2:1. This behaviour results from melioration processes; it is difficult to determine whether it is optimal in the sense of utility maximisation. People seeking to maximise their utility must keep an account of their satisfaction with each food selection and calculate the optimal distribution of pizza and sandwiches. Figure 2.5 graphically depicts the value of pizza and sandwiches as a function of consumption over a 10-day interval as well as the average utility. The point at which the utility lines of pizza and sandwiches intersect represents the equilibrium, the 'matching point' according to the 'matching law'. The highest point on the average utility curve represents the maximum utility for the distribution of pizza and sandwiches.

Herrnstein converted these reflections on distributed choices into a simple computer game known as the 'Harvard game'. In countless experiments, he was able to show that people compare alternatives and choose the one that offers the greatest benefit at the present moment (Herrnstein, 1990, 1991; Herrnstein & Prelec, 1991; Herrnstein et al., 1993). People base their behaviour on comparisons of alternatives and choose the one which appears more profitable at present rather than

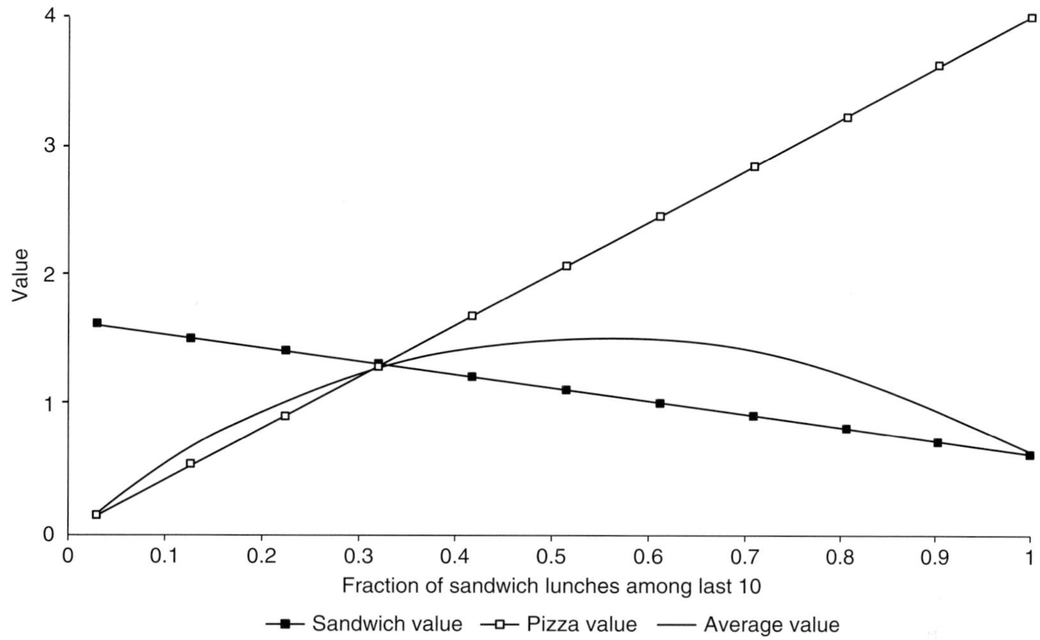

Figure 2.5 Value of pizza and sandwich lunches as a function of the last ten consumption decisions (from Herrnstein & Prelec, 1991, p. 140)

considering the future outcomes of the alternatives. The melioration principle, also known as 'short-run betterment', is also applied when, from a longer-term perspective, selecting the currently better alternative would be the worst solution over time.

In these studies, participants had the opportunity to participate in a computer game in order to win money. It is a plausible assumption that participants wanted to maximise their winnings rather than go home with less money. The game consists of a computer with a monitor and a keyboard with two keys, A and B. When either of the keys is pressed, a coin falls on-screen into a container that collects the participant's winnings. While the coin is falling, both keys are disabled. Participants are allowed to play a few hundred practice rounds before playing for real in order to familiarise themselves with the game. Finally, they are informed about the length of the game. In addition, during the game, they are constantly informed of how much time is remaining. When Key A is pressed, the coin falls in time t_A with speed v_A; when B is pressed, the coin falls in time t_B with speed v_B. The coin falls much faster when Key B is pressed than when Key A is pressed; in other words, v_B is larger than v_A and t_B is, accordingly, smaller than t_A. However, pressing Key B triggers a braking mechanism: as Key B is pressed more often, v_A and v_B become smaller and smaller, while t_A and t_B become larger and larger.

For example, the fall time for Key A might amount to $t_A = 4$ seconds, and for Key B $t_B = 2$ seconds. As keys are pressed, the fall times t_A and t_B increase at rates of $t_A = 4 + 4\ r$ and $t_B = 2 + 4$ r, respectively. Here, r refers to the relative frequency with which Key B has been selected during all previous keystrokes ($r = n_B/n = n_B/(n_A + n_B)$; n = total number of previous keystrokes; n_A = number of times Key A has been pressed and n_B = number of times Key B has been pressed). Compared to pressing Key A, the coin always falls with a higher velocity (in the example, 2 seconds faster) when Key B is pressed, but the more frequently B is pressed relative to A, the more the fall time after

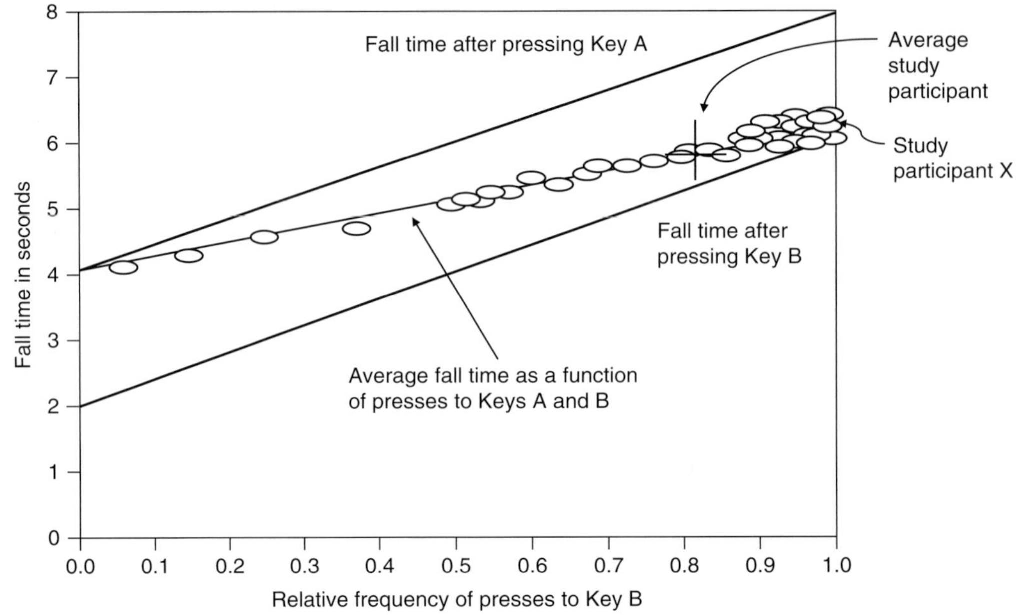

Figure 2.6 Conception and results of Herrnstein's Harvard game (Herrnstein, 1991, p. 363)

pressing both Keys A and B increases over time. If a player presses Key A first, the coin takes 4 seconds to fall into his winnings bucket on the screen. If he keeps pressing Key A, the fall time remains at 4 seconds because Key B has never been pressed (r (the relative frequency of pressing Key B) = 0; $t_A = 4$ seconds + 4 r = 4 seconds). If Key B is pressed first, the fall time is 2 seconds. If B is pressed again, $t_B = 6$ seconds, because up until this point only Key B has been pressed, meaning that $r = 1$ (2 seconds + 4 * 1 = 6 seconds). If, during some of his playing time, the player presses the keys A, A, B, A, B, B, B, B, A, B, the fall time will be $t_A = 4 + 4 * 0.6 = 6.4$ seconds the next time he presses Key A. If he presses Key B, on the other hand, the coin would now require $t_B = 2 + 4 * 0.6 =$ 4.4 seconds. If only Key B is pressed over a time span of 30 minutes, for example, the average fall time of all collected coins comes out to almost 6 seconds; if Key A had always been selected, always representing the worse alternative at the present moment, the average fall time would be only 4 seconds.

A consideration of all variants of possible keystroke sequences reveals that the greatest number of coins in the winnings bucket is achieved by pressing Key A almost exclusively from the beginning on – in other words, by choosing the profit-reducing alternative – and Key B only a scant few times shortly before the game ends. The optimal time for switching keys depends upon the length of the game and can probably only be determined for any arbitrary time with the help of a sophisticated computer program. With any playing strategy other than this optimal one, winnings will be smaller than they would have been with a rational, utility-maximising pressing of the keys. In the many experiments conducted by Herrnstein and colleagues, participants did not choose the profit-maximising keystroke combination. Figure 2.6 illustrates coin fall times after presses of Key A and Key B, respectively, and the results of one experiment. It is apparent that, if Key B has never been pressed, the coin requires 2 seconds to fall into the collection bin after Key B has been pressed and 4 seconds after Key A has been pressed. If, however, Key B is always pressed, fall times increase to 6 and 8 seconds, respectively. Which combination of Keys A and B participants actually selected is shown by the circles in Figure 2.6. The actual average fall time was over 5 seconds because alternatives were judged according to their relative benefits at the present moment, in correspondence with the melioration principle.

Suboptimal sequential decisions and their corresponding behaviour can often be observed in everyday life. Addiction is an example of this: the behaviour of smokers and drug addicts is suboptimal. Likewise, people who overindulge themselves with large quantities of rich food and who drink too much are risking their health in the long run. People who know that it would make sense to learn something new, go back to school, or go to the theatre and concerts, but instead choose to spare themselves the effort right now, are also behaving suboptimally. In some cases, people sense that they meliorate and protect themselves from long-run negative consequences by forcing themselves to do certain things to help them forgo the better alternative at the present moment. People who buy a theatre subscription tend to go to the theatre even when they are tired on the night of the performance and would prefer to stay home. People who subscribe to a newspaper are more likely to read the daily news than those who plan to buy the newspaper at a kiosk every day. People who book a stay at a wellness centre or health spa pay a lot of money so that other people will prevent them from doing what they would like to do at the present moment, but that would have harmful ramifications.

2.2.3.4 Distorted Memories

Despite their susceptibility to error and present orientation, people have quite a lot of confidence, commonly believing that they have above-average abilities or better luck than other people. If need be, they 'fix' bad decisions after the fact. In retrospect, neither their predictions about the future nor the actions they took appear so wrong as to require that they seriously consider adjusting or changing their expectations.

A common phenomenon is the '**better-than-average effect**', the effect in which people believe they are better than others (see Alicke & Govorun, 2005 for a review). Frequently, one's own positive traits are viewed as more developed and one's negative features comparatively less developed than those of other people. The 'better-than-average' or 'above-average' effect is interpreted as a motivationally distorted judgment strategy that serves to enhance one's self-worth. Kruger and Dunning (1999) had students work on various logical and linguistic tasks and then divided the sample into four groups according to their actual performance. The participants were also required to state how they would rate their performance in comparison to others. In particular, the low performers strongly overestimated their relative performance. Cross (1977) reported that more than two-thirds of professors at the University of Nebraska believe they possess superb didactic abilities and rank themselves in the top quarter of all university lecturers. The illusion that one is above average can also be found in the fields of health, romantic relations, sports, driving a car and assessing one's driving safety as well as in the financial market. For example, Svenson (1981) asked Swedish and American motorists about their driving performance and safety. Regarding driving performance, 69% of the Swedes and 93% of the Americans believed themselves to be better than average. The extent of the illusion in terms of safety was also large: 77% of the Swedes and 88% of the Americans counted themselves among those who are safer than average. Buunk (2001) determined that most people believe their romantic partnership is very good and that their own relationship is better than the already very happy average relationship. Odean (1998b) ascertained that significantly more than half of investors in financial markets believe that they are among the best as well. The better-than-average illusion, overoptimism and the illusion of control (the belief one can determine or control the outcome of uncontrollable events) can lead to suboptimal decisions and poor behaviour.

If events have taken place, people should be able to determine, in retrospect, whether their expectations were correct or whether they were too optimistic, allowing them to adjust future assessments accordingly. Kahneman (1994), however, points to the fact that people are hardly in the position to state what they have preferred in the past (or what they will prefer in the future). People have trouble maximising their utility over time; similarly, they often cannot guess or can only state with great uncertainty what they will prefer in the future. In order to be able to make rational decisions, however, they need to be able to rely on their experiences. On the basis of memories, present alternatives are evaluated with respect to future wishes. Kahneman showed that experiences are often judged according to the '**peak and end rule**'. In retrospect, an experience is often not judged by its duration and the sum of all its elements, but is strongly influenced by outstanding elements and by the elements at the end. The complete experience in its total length from beginning to end does not have an influence on judgments. If an event exhibited a few negative peaks and ended unpleasantly, it is usually remembered as a negative experience. If the end was perceived to be enjoyable relative to the rest of the time, the event is remembered as a pleasant experience. An experimental test of the peak and end rule looked like this: People had to put their arm into cold water for 60 seconds. The temperature was 14 degrees Celsius. In another condition, the experiment was elongated by 30 seconds to a total of 90 seconds; during the additional 30 seconds, the water temperature was raised to 15 degrees. Surprisingly, the experiment was evaluated as less unpleasant under the 90-second condition than in the 60-second condition, which was explained by the somewhat less unpleasant experience at the end of the experiment in the 90-second condition (Kahneman, Fredrickson, Schreiber & Redelmeier, 1993). The consequences for decisions of this kind are obvious: people prefer short but painful medical procedures with additional, less unpleasant but useless interventions at the end to short, painful procedures without additional interventions at the end. Incarcerated people will not view the entire length of their imprisonment as a punishing negative experience and possibly base their future behaviour upon it. Rather, their future behaviour will be based upon their negative experiences during and especially at the end of their imprisonment.

When looking back on an event whose subsequent course of development is known, it is not uncommon for people to claim to have always known that an event would turn out the way it actually did. After having seen how a political conflict was resolved (Fischhoff, 1975), what results the parties obtained in an election (Blank & Fischer, 2000), what economic developments occurred after the introduction of a new currency (Hoelzl & Kirchler, 2005; Hoelzl et al. 2002) and which football team won the last match, people do not remember their original predictions exactly. Instead, they correct them on the basis of this informational feedback. Fischhoff (1975) described this phenomenon as '**hindsight bias**'. This bias, also known as '**knew-it-all-along bias**', has since been investigated numerous times in diverse situations. Hoelzl et al. (2002) and Hoelzl and Kirchler (2005) asked employed people about their predictions six months before the introduction of the euro as accounting currency, and in a further study six months before the introduction of the euro in its physical form. Participants reported how likely they thought specific economic developments (e. g., increases or decreases in interest rates, increases or decreases in unemployment, increases or decreases in the export rate) would occur. Six months after the introduction of the euro as accounting currency and physical currency, respectively, they were asked to recall their earlier predictions. Participants were divided into two groups: the experimental group was informed about actual economic developments that had occurred after the introduction of the new currency; the control group was given no information. Participants in the control group remembered their predictions

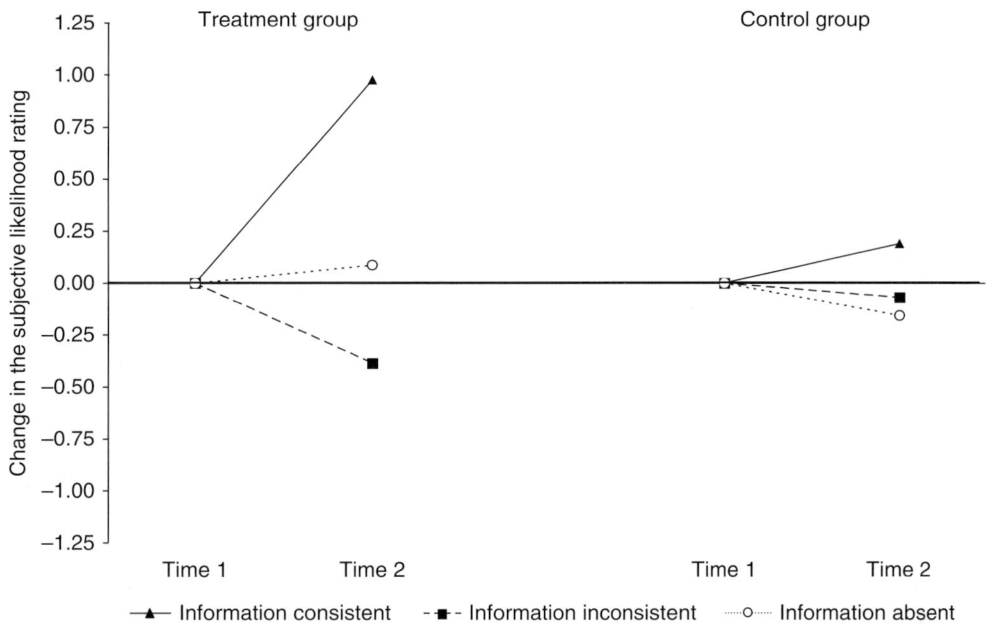

Figure 2.7 Hindsight bias as a function of time, information on economic developments, and actual economic developments that did or did not occur after the introduction of the euro in 1999. Values were standardised so that predictions always have value = 0 and can be directly compared to memories. (from Hoelzl, Kirchler & Rodler, 2002, p. 440)

from a year ago much more accurately than did those in the experimental group who were informed about economic developments. In addition, several different indices were created for memories of the predictions. In the time between prediction and recall, some developments (e.g., economic stagnation) had come to pass while others (e.g., economic growth) had not. Separate indices were created for developments that had come to pass and for those that had not. A third index was created for developments for which there were no official statistics at the time at which participants recalled their predictions. As is apparent in Figure 2.7, participants in the experimental group clearly adapted their memories of their predictions to fit the feedback they received about actual developments. When there was no information about economic developments, their memories conformed fairly closely to their predictions. In the control group that received no information about economic developments that had occurred in the meantime, there was almost no difference between predictions and memories.

In remembering the financial crises of recent years, many economic experts and laypeople purported not to be surprised that New York's economic bubble burst or that the financial crisis that started in the United States in 2007 had worldwide effects. Even though very few people had predicted these crises, in hindsight most people – even those who had lost a lot of money on the stock market – were probably 'hardly surprised' by these developments and most likely claimed to have always suspected that a crisis was coming.

Suspected causes of distorted memory are poor powers of recollection and the adaptation of memories to enhance one's self-worth. In addition, Hawkins and Hastie (1990) postulate that information about actual developments serves as an anchor for remembering predictions. At the time of remembrance, it is not one's original prediction that is remembered; instead, new prediction processes take place, with the result that 'motivated' answers are given. Hoelzl and Kirchler (2005) found empirical confirmation that hindsight bias can be traced back to several distinct motives, such as the desire to preserve self-worth and the tendency to confirm one's worldview.

2.2.4 Heuristics

In complex decision situations, neither is there sufficient time to collect and examine all relevant information, nor do people always have the motivation to weigh all facets of the decision in order to find the best option. They apply rules of thumb in order to come to a decision, base their conclusions on a few prominent pieces of information, and often make quick judgments. These judgment heuristics can lead to good results in many decision situations, but can also sometimes lead astray.

Heuristics are understood as decision-making aids that are applied when it is necessary to make judgments in especially complex situations, where there is not enough information, and neither the time nor the motivation to collect more. **Heuristics** are rules of thumb that have the advantage of making decision-making processes easier. However, they lead to systematic misjudgments in certain situations, as Kahneman and Tversky (1973) and Tversky and Kahneman (1974) most notably demonstrate. Todd and Gigerenzer (2000; Hertwig & Herzog, 2009), on the other hand, focus on the advantages of quick and economical heuristics in decision situations and argue that heuristics often do lead to correct judgments. As the environment is generally complex and our cognitive ability adequately to process all information is limited, gaining a comprehensive and accurate understanding of a decision problem is not always possible. It therefore makes sense to apply simple, contextualised decision-making aids.

The availability, representativeness, anchoring and adjustment, and affect heuristics (see Schwarz, Wänke & Bless, 1994) constitute the most well-known heuristics. This also includes the mechanisms of the 'adaptive toolbox' (Gigerenzer, Todd & ABC Research Group, 1999).

2.2.4.1 Availability Heuristic

In estimating the frequency or probability of occurrence of one or more events, judgments are often formed on the basis of the difficulty or ease with which individual pieces of information can be generated or retrieved from memory. Applying this **availability heuristic** is entirely sensible and often expedient, since common events do come to mind more easily than rare ones. The more often a person is confronted with a certain circumstance, or experiences an event, or the more frequently a subject is covered in the press, the more likely it is that a person will remember it when making a decision or judgment. The more easily a topic can be retrieved from memory, the more frequently – so the assumption of the availability heuristic – it must have been presented or experienced. In some cases, however, a one-time event might be experienced in such a lasting manner that the details are remembered quickly and accurately. 'Flashbulb events' – such as the attacks on the World Trade Center in New York City and the Pentagon in Washington, DC, on 11 September 2001 – leave behind such a deep impression that the situation in which a person found him- or herself when learning about the event is imprinted especially deeply into one's memory (Hirst et al., 2015).

Since memories of events and the availability of information depend not solely on the frequency with which they have been experienced or presented, but also on a series of other factors, the availability heuristic can lead to errors in judgment. Tversky and Kahneman (1974) tested the availability heuristic in an experiment in which they read out two lists of male and female names to participants and then asked whether the lists contained more male or female names. One group heard a list with the names of nineteen famous men and twenty non-famous women; a second group heard nineteen famous female names and twenty unknown male names. Since the names of famous people were more easily remembered and thus more quickly available than the names of non-famous people, it was expected that the percentage of men in the first list and the percentage of women in the second list would be overestimated. This is exactly what happened.

Judgments also turn out differently depending on the difficulty of the necessary cognitive operations. Tversky and Kahneman (1974) let people guess whether more sub-groups of eight people or of two people could be formed from a total group of ten people. Combinatorics teaches that an equal number of sub-groups is possible in both cases. Using the formula $n! / [k! * (n - k)!]$, with n being the total group size and k the sub-group size, it is clear that $10! / [8! * (10 - 8)!] = 10! / [2! * (10 - 2)!]$, therefore in both cases forty-five sub-groups are possible. Respondents' estimates, however, differed markedly in the two cases: the median estimate for the number of sub-groups of two was seventy, but twenty for sub-groups of eight. This bias is based on the availability heuristic to the extent that people begin mentally to group the ten elements into classes of two or eight elements each. They can quickly form many groups of two, but are not in a position to build quickly a large number of groups of eight people. Their judgment is distorted on the basis of the ease or difficulty of the mental operations.

The conspicuousness of events also leads to judgment errors, as Lichtenstein, Slovic, Fischhoff, Layman and Combs (1978) showed. Because of this, the prevalence of fatality risks that receive frequent press coverage is overestimated, while more 'banal' causes of death are underestimated. Murders and car accidents receive more attention than heart disease and cancer. For that reason, the percentage of deaths due to murder and accidents is estimated to be higher than it actually is, while the prevalence of heart attacks and fatal cancers is underestimated.

The availability of memory content depends upon, among other things, a person's mood at the time of recall. Consequently, one's current mood can be a source of error. According to Bower (1981), every affective state is saved in memory and connected in a kind of network to the circumstances that accompanied the emotional event. Activating a given affective state leads to the activation of memory content saved in close proximity to it. For this reason, people in certain moods pay more attention to some types of content than to others, store it better, are also able to retrieve it more easily when in the same mood, and tend to interpret experiences in a manner congruent with their current mood. Thus, according to the state-dependent retrieval hypothesis (Bower, 1981), people in good moods are better able to remember experiences that match their cheerful state of mind. Depending on one's mood, either negative or positive events are more easily retrievable from memory, as are events experienced in a mood that corresponds to one's mood at the time of recall. On the financial market, the availability heuristic might lead to a strengthening of current views about the market and to a consolidation of the prevailing mood. If, in times of crisis, mass media tend to publish reports that match the prevailing atmosphere, and describe and explain the current crisis as well as further disseminate the negative mood, market participants' image of a system in crisis will be strengthened. Investors evaluate the market more negatively than it actually is. Easily available information from the media, often presented in simple, eye-catching form, can lead via the availability heuristic to judgments that are not consistent with the actual state of the market.

In addition to their influence on encoding and decoding performance, current moods can also be used as information per se. In the **mood-as-information heuristic**, judgments are based on current mood (Schwarz, 1990; Wyer & Carlston, 1979). People who are in a good mood at the time they are questioned about their job satisfaction might draw the conclusion that they are highly satisfied with their job *because* they are in a good mood. Instead of remembering past events and using them to build a satisfaction judgment, their current mood is used as information.

2.2.4.2 Representativeness Heuristic

The **representativeness heuristic** is a heuristic where judgments are based on the similarity between an outcome and a model. This could be the estimated degree of correspondence or similarity between a sample and a population, an element and a class or category, an act and an agent, or an effect and a cause (Tversky & Kahneman, 1974). Representativeness is understood as the degree of congruity between prototype and element and the corresponding judgment as to whether or not a given element belongs to the category of the prototype.

In their judgment of samples, people ignore essential attributes of the population. Tversky and Kahneman described a person who had been randomly selected out of a group of one hundred people. In one case, it was stated that the group consisted of seventy solicitors and thirty engineers; in the other case, the distribution was exactly the opposite. A vague description of the randomly selected person that matched the stereotype either of a solicitor or of an engineer was then presented. Study participants formed judgments about whether the selected person belonged to the group of solicitors or engineers solely on the basis of the vague descriptions; they ignored the distribution of solicitors and engineers in the population. Interestingly, the population distribution was not even taken into account when participants were presented with a completely neutral description of the selected person: in this case, Dick was described as a 30-year-old married man with no children, highly skilled and engaged in his career, a well-liked colleague with good career prospects. Even though the probabilities that Dick was an engineer or solicitor were $p = 0.3$ and $p = 0.7$, respectively, respondents estimated that his probability of belonging to each profession was $p = 0.5$.

People also ignore sample size. Even if the theoretical probability of rolling a six on any given dice throw is 1/6, the empirically observed probability of occurrence only reaches 1/6 after a considerable number of rolls. For example, it can be assumed that each of the six numbers comes up equally often in 100,000 rolls. If the dice is only rolled ten times, the observed probabilities of occurrence for the six numbers can significantly differ from one another.

It is well known that approximately equal numbers of boys and girls are born, meaning that the probability that an equal number of boys and girls is born in a certain hospital on any given day is higher than the probability of any other combination. The distribution of combinations per day and over a certain period of time scatters more widely, statistically speaking, around the expected value of $p = 0.5$ when the number of total births is low. Hence, equal ratios of girls and boys would occur more frequently in a hospital that registers forty-five daily births than in a hospital in which approximately fifteen children come into the world each day. However, if laypeople estimate the frequency with which each hospital registers days in which over 60% of births are male, they do not give the slightest consideration to elementary laws of statistics. In Tversky and Kahneman's (1974) study, 53% of people thought a gender ratio of 6:4 would happen equally often in both hospitals, 20% thought this would be the case more often in the hospital with forty-five daily births, and only 21% judged correctly that a 6:4 ratio would be observed more frequently in the hospital with fifteen births. In a similar experiment conducted by Tversky (1973, p. 127), people were informed that N (= 10, 100 or 1,000) babies are born in a certain region every day. Study participants estimated the number of days in which equal numbers of boys and girls were born (5 boys and 5 girls; 50:50; 500:500). They also estimated the number of days in which numbers of boys and girls were imbalanced to different degrees (e.g., 0–5% boys: 0 boys and 10 girls; fewer than 5 boys and more than 95 girls; fewer than 50 boys and more than 950 girls). Subjective

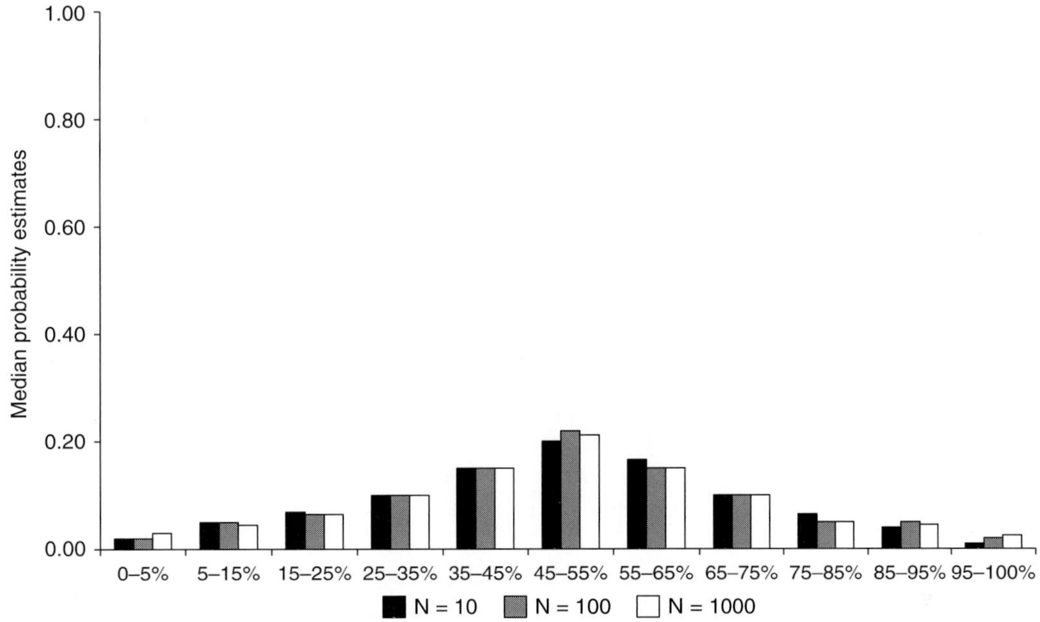

Figure 2.8a Estimated values (from Tversky, 1973, p. 128)

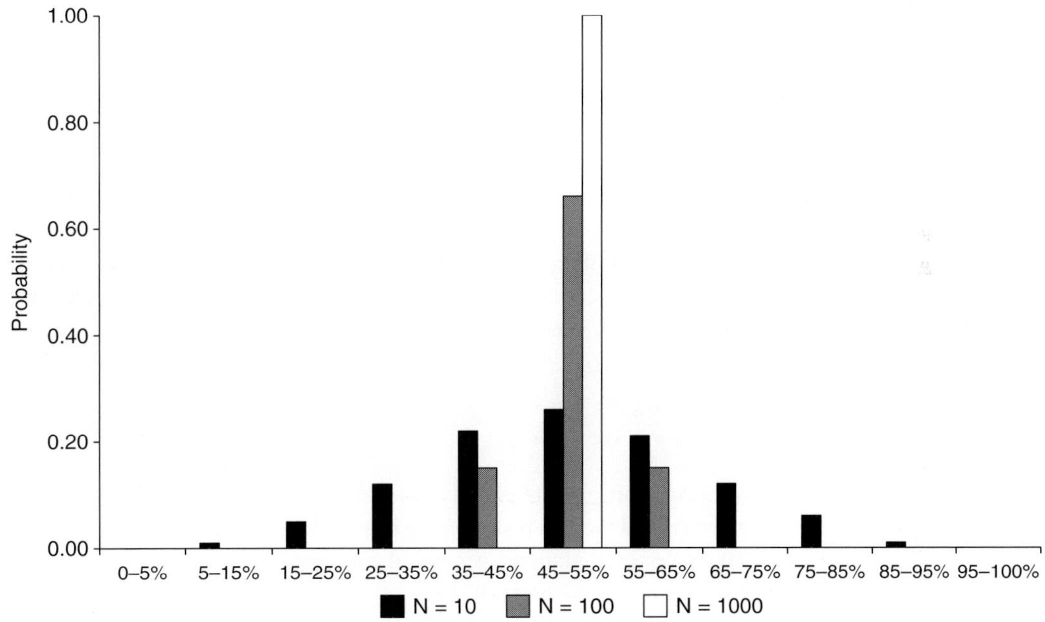

Figure 2.8b Correct values (from Tversky, 1973, p. 127)

estimates were completely independent of sample size. Figures 2.8a and 2.8b depict the estimated and the statistically correct distributions.

Inaccurate judgments are also based on misunderstandings about randomness and the typical 'pattern' of random events. For example, owing to its internal logic, the following combination of numbers does not look like a random draw from a lottery game in which six numbers out of forty-five are drawn: '1, 2, 3, 4, 5, 6'. The series '7, 13, 24, 25, 30, 41' tends to be seen as more random. For this reason, a higher probability of occurrence is ascribed to the second sequence of numbers. In reality, however, both combinations of numbers are equally likely. The belief that in roulette the probability of the ball landing on the colour 'red' increases after a long sequence of 'black' is similarly misguided. This sentiment, that the probability of hitting 'red' rises after a long sequence of 'black', has been the cause of steep financial losses for many players and is known as the '**gambler's fallacy**'. Equally false is the opposite belief according to which an athlete who has just hit his mark multiple times in a row (in a basketball game, for example) will continue to do so. The '**hot hand fallacy**' describes the belief that players can be 'hot' at a given time, increasing the probability that they will make subsequent shots.

Finally, people are not often mindful of the fact that combined events are less likely than a single event; rather, they succumb to the '**conjunction fallacy**'. Tversky and Kahneman (1983) described a woman named Linda to study participants. The provided story described Linda's engagement in the fight for women's rights. Afterwards, the subjects were asked if, after this description, it is more likely that Linda is a 'bank teller' or that she is a 'bank teller and a feminist'. The majority of participants gauged the probability of Linda being a bank teller and a feminist to be significantly higher. This view is false, because the probability of both events occurring at the same time cannot be greater than the probability that one of the events occurs in isolation. Even if all bank tellers were also feminists, the probabilities of the events 'bank teller' and 'bank teller and feminist' would only be equally high.

2.2.4.3 Anchoring and Adjustment Heuristic

Judgments are often formed on the basis of the **anchoring and adjustment heuristic**. People begin their frequency and probability estimations with an initial value drawn from the formulation of the problem or prescribed by another person. This starting value serves as an anchor, which is then (inadequately) adjusted during the course of the estimation to form judgments.

In the following arithmetic problem, the first numbers are used as an anchor or starting point, which is then adjusted during the course of the calculation in order to form an estimated result. Two groups of university students had 5 seconds to estimate the solution to the following multiplication problem:

- Problem 1: 8 * 7 * 6 * 5 * 4 * 3 * 2 * 1 = ?
- Problem 2: 1 * 2 * 3 * 4 * 5 * 6 * 7 * 8 = ?

In order to offer a solution, participants exactly calculated the first products, but when they were pressed for time, they estimated the end result on the basis of this partial result. In the first problem, a median result of 2,250 was estimated; in the second, the median estimated result was 512. The actual product is 40,320 (Tversky & Kahneman, 1974).

A further anchoring effect was demonstrated in the following experimental arrangement: Study participants should guess the percentage of African states that are members of the UN. Before beginning their estimates, a wheel of fortune was spun, and participants were then prompted to state whether the number of member states lies over or under the number shown when the wheel of fortune stopped. In one condition, this seemingly random number was ten; in another condition, it was sixty-five. In accordance with the anchoring and adjustment heuristic, the estimated percentage of member states in the first case (25%) lay far under the percentage estimated in the second case (45%) (Tversky & Kahneman, 1974).

Strack and Mussweiler (1997) were even able to demonstrate slight anchoring effects when the anchors used were completely implausible and, just as in the example above, had nothing to do with the question. If the width of Berlin's Brandenburg Gate is asked for, but the height is stated to be very large or very small, the width will be under- or overestimated on the basis of this anchor. Similarly, in inquiries about the year Aristotle was born (* 384 BC, † 322 BC), plausible anchors (220 or 490 BC) and non-plausible anchors (1832 AD or 25,000 BC) have similar effects. Nevertheless, the anchoring effect is stronger and the time spent working out an estimate lower when anchors seem plausible and correspond to the topic which is to be evaluated.

And it is not just laypeople – experts also fall prey to the anchoring and adjustment heuristic. Northcraft and Neale (1987) asked estate agents and university students to estimate the price of a residential house. Study participants could inform themselves thoroughly about the house and then estimated its value. The estate agents also had relevant experience at their disposal. The current market price of the house was US$ 74,900. In addition to a description of the object, they were given an information brochure listing either a lower (US$ 65,900) or higher anchoring price (US$ 83,900). Both students and estate agents named a lower price when a lower anchor had been presented to them (US$ 63,571 and US$ 67,811, respectively) than after being presented with a high anchor value (US$ 72,196 and US$ 75,190, respectively).

The effects of the anchoring and adjustment heuristic play a fundamental role in negotiations. The person who makes the first offer sets the anchor for all subsequent negotiations and frequently attains the better result (Galinsky & Mussweiler, 2001). Englich, Mussweiler and Strack (2006) were also able to demonstrate anchoring and adjustment effects in the legal decisions of experienced judges. Penalties were influenced by the degree of severity that had been asked for, even when an irrelevant source or a roll of a dice determined the original request.

2.2.4.4 Affect Heuristic

The **affect heuristic** is a heuristic where judgments are based on cues from positive and negative affect (Finucane, Alhakami, Slovic & Johnson, 2000). As a consequence of the affect heuristic, subjective judgments of risks and benefits are often *negatively* correlated – contrary to the real world, where risks and benefits are usually positively correlated (e.g., investments, business projects). Finuncane et al. (2000) describe the mechanism as similar to a halo effect that induces consistent perceptions: if something induces positive affect, it must be positive in having both low risks and high benefits; if something induces negative affect, it must be negative in having both high risks and low benefits. Rottenstreich and Hsee (2001) showed that in decisions with affect-rich outcomes, probabilities are treated differently than in decisions with affect-poor, neutral outcomes. When outcomes are highly emotionalising, low probabilities of occurrence are given strong weight and high probabilities are given little weight. Rottenstreich and Hsee (2001) report on an experiment in which some participants were asked to imagine that they might have to suffer a harmless, brief but painful electric shock. Other participants were told to imagine that they might have to pay a fine of US$ 20. It was assumed that imagining an electric shock is significantly more emotional than imagining paying a small monetary penalty. The probabilities for each negative event were set at two levels: either 1% or 99%. Participants were then asked how much they would be willing to pay in order to avoid receiving the shock or the fine. The results are illustrated in Figure 2.9. In the shock condition, participants were willing to

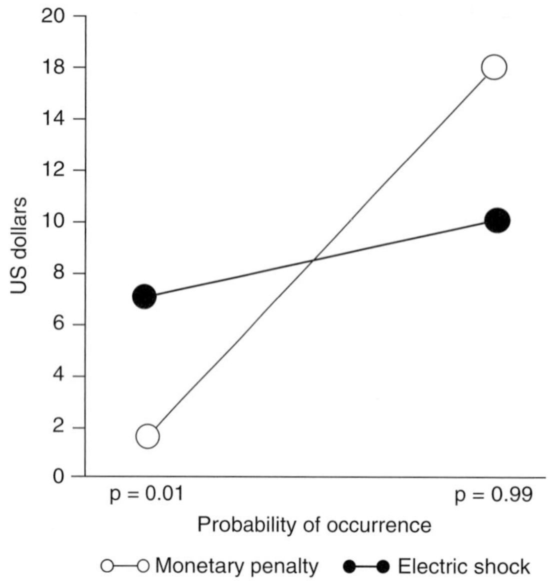

Figure 2.9 Average price participants are willing to pay to avoid a fine of US$ 20 or an electric shock, respectively, under the conditions that these negative events are almost certain not to occur (probability of $p = 0.01$) versus almost certain to occur ($p = 0.99$) (from Rottenstreich & Hsee, 2001, p. 189)

pay US$ 7 in order to avoid the shock with a 1% probability of occurrence and only US$ 10 when the probability was 99%. Participants would only pay US$ 1 to avoid the US$ 20 fine in the case with the low probability of occurrence, but in the case with the high probability they were willing to pay US$ 18. While the probability of occurrence was hardly considered in the case of the threatening shock, participants' willingness to protect themselves from the monetary penalty was thoroughly dependent on the probability of punishment.

While laypeople frequently make judgments on the basis of the affect heuristic, experts have a much lower tendency to do so. Slovic, Malmfors, Krewski, Mertz, Neil and Bartlett (1995) let laypeople and experts judge the risk of cancer stemming from exposure to high and low doses of toxic radiation. While the laypeople's judgments hardly reflected the information on the amount of the dose, experts made a clear distinction in their rulings based on the information about high or low exposure times. In a further experiment, Hsee and Rottenstreich (2004) showed that the quantity of a good remains unnoticed in conditions of affect priming. Affect priming means that people's attention is steered towards emotional aspects through unconscious pre-activation. Study participants were asked to estimate the price for a set of five CDs or ten CDs by Madonna. When participants received information to analyse the product and precisely assess its value, average prices of US$ 15.10 for the five CDs and US$ 28.81 for the ten CDs were given. Under affect priming, the five CDs were valued at US$ 22.64, while the set with ten CDs was even given a somewhat lower value, US$ 19.77.

The affect heuristic gives insurance brokers high chances of getting laypeople to sign up for an insurance policy if they vividly portray how dramatic the damage after a lightning strike and subsequent fire in the house or after a flood or another catastrophe can be. These emotionalised customers commonly do not adequately consider that the probability of these events is very small; they overestimate what are actually very low probabilities and sign up for an insurance policy.

Conversely, many people are not inclined to insure themselves against unspectacular but very probable damages.

2.2.4.5 Fast and Frugal Heuristics

Heuristics do not necessarily lead to incorrect solutions; if they fit with the decision environment, they can sometimes even be advantageous. Gigerenzer and colleagues (Gigerenzer, 2004b; Gigerenzer, Todd & ABC Research Group, 1999; Hertwig & Herzog, 2009; Todd & Gigerenzer, 2000) propose the idea of heuristics being part of an 'adaptive toolbox' developed over the course of evolution. They highlight the advantages of so-called '**fast and frugal heuristics**': Because heuristics allow a complex problem to be solved in a short period of time, they are fast, and because only a few pieces of information are needed, they are frugal. Context- and problem-specific heuristics that can be deployed in a fast, frugal and computationally cheap manner can achieve good results. Gigerenzer (2004b) emphasises that people apply heuristics in decision situations because these heuristics use abilities that developed with evolution and are learned in a social context. Most of the time, they are applied without conscious consideration of which heuristic could lead to success in a specific decision situation. Fast and frugal heuristics break the classical norms of rationality, leading to their designation as non-rational. However, if applied in the right environment, they can facilitate more correct decisions and predictions than extensive reflection.

One fast and frugal heuristic is the **recognition heuristic**. When people are familiar with only one of two objects, they often come to the conclusion that the known object is more important than the other one. Gigerenzer and colleagues (Goldstein & Gigerenzer, 2002; Hoffrage & Reimer, 2004) tested German and American university students' knowledge of American geography by asking which city is larger, San Diego or San Antonio. Sixty-two percent of American students gave the correct answer, while all of the German students knew that San Diego has more inhabitants than San Antonio. The German students had heard more about San Diego than San Antonio, leading them to conclude that the better-known object must be more important and hence larger. The American students knew too much and became uncertain. This demonstrates a counterintuitive effect, the '**less-is-more effect**': less knowledge can lead to better decisions because it allows using the recognition heuristic. In a further study, Turkish and British university students were asked to predict the result of thirty-two football games in England. Although the English students knew quite a lot about the football clubs, while the Turkish students had virtually no information, the English students' predictions, which were correct 65.6% of the time, were not much better than those of the Turkish students, who hit the mark 62.5% of the time. The Turkish students had applied the recognition heuristic. Since football clubs are often named after their home city and Turkish students were more familiar with famous cities than less-famous ones, they extrapolated the importance of the cities and therefore the quality of their football teams from their prominence. Their partial lack of knowledge led to valid information (Goldstein & Gigerenzer, 2002; Hoffrage & Reimer, 2004).

Another fast and frugal heuristic is the **'take-the-best' heuristic**. It is rare that the classical rational procedure is followed in the sense that all characteristics of available options are evaluated and that these options are compared with one another. Instead, following the take-the-best heuristic, the one characteristic that seems especially relevant is selected and the options are compared on the basis of this characteristic alone. If a decision can be made based on this characteristic, the process ends. If not, a second characteristic – the next best – is selected and options are evaluated on the basis of this characteristic. This process continues until a decision can be made. A person who would like to move to a new city and needs to choose between two cities will gather information about the cities and order it according to importance. Living in the capital city might be especially important to a given person. When one of the cities is a capital, this city is selected. If the cities do not differ in this regard, another criterion is sought out, such as the arts and cultural scene. As soon as one city can be preferred to the other based on its relevant features, the decision is made.

When a person needs to make a decision from a wide range of alternatives, the **elimination heuristic** can be applied. In this heuristic, decisions are based on sequential elimination of alternatives. Tversky (1972) described these sequential processes of elimination. Decision alternatives are viewed as sets of criteria or features. During the decision-making process, criteria are selected so that the most important ones have the highest probability of being used first to evaluate the alternatives. The alternatives are 'measured' sequentially on the basis of these criteria. When an alternative does not meet the subjective standard set by the criterion being considered, it is deemed unusable and eliminated. The next step is to select another criterion, 'filter' the alternatives according to it, and so on, until in the end only one alternative remains.

Conclusion

The aim of this chapter was to show that people rarely decide on the basis of rational, analytic and utility-oriented processing of information. Instead, their decisions are influenced by distorted information processing and different information processing paths, as well as by emotions and time factors. Often, they use heuristics that can be helpful and sometimes lead to better decisions than an analytic but time-consuming step-by-step process. However, heuristics can also be misleading. Normative models have been criticised on empirical grounds, and consequently descriptive models have been developed which will be the focus of the next chapter.

Summary

- Decisions become complex when consequences are unknown or uncertain. Decisions under uncertainty are on the one hand risky decisions – probabilities of consequences of alternatives are known – and on the other hand ambiguous decisions, where probabilities are only vaguely known. People prefer risky decisions to ambiguous ones.
- Normative models of decisions under uncertainty include expected value theory, expected utility theory and subjective expected utility theory.
- Subjective expected utility theory argues that different people consistently choose different options from the same set of alternatives because the utility of an option is subjective.
- Game theory studies the rationality and utility maximisation assumptions. Experiments show that people often do not behave according to these assumptions but instead consider factors like fairness and trust.
- Decisions are influenced by information processing. People do not always process available information in the normatively correct way. People can also reach decisions either intuitively, through unconscious, rapid, automatic processes that use information from long-term memory, or analytically, through conscious, slow processes that use information from working memory.
- Decisions are influenced by emotions such as regret, which stems from forgone benefits associated with other available options that were not chosen.
- Decisions are influenced by phenomena related to time, such as delayed gratification, time discounting, melioration and distorted memories.
- In complex decision situations, or when people do not have enough time or the motivation to examine all relevant information, people use rules of thumb – so-called heuristics. Although heuristics make the decision-making process easier, they can lead to incorrect judgments. Well-known heuristics are the availability, representativeness, anchoring and adjustment, and affect heuristic.
- Fast and frugal heuristics like the recognition, 'take-the-best' and elimination heuristics can facilitate more correct decisions and predictions than extensive reflection when applied in a valid environment.

Questions

1 What is the difference between normative and descriptive decision models?
2 What is the difference between the ultimatum game and the dictator game and how do people usually behave in these games?
3 Which attributes are associated with the two processes of thinking (Evans, 2008)?
4 What does the 'matching law' (Herrnstein, 1961) predict would happen in a decision-making situation?
5 What is the hindsight bias and what are its causes?

FURTHER READING

Evans, J. St. B. T. (2008). Dual-processing accounts of reasoning, judgment and social cognition. *Annual Review of Psychology, 59*, 255–78.

Gigerenzer, G. (2015). *Simply rational: Decision making in the real world*. Oxford: Oxford University Press.

Kahneman, D., Slovic, P., & Tversky, A. (1982). *Judgment under uncertainty: Heuristics and biases*. Cambridge: Cambridge University Press.

3 Decision-Making: Descriptive Models and Choice Architecture

Overview

The empirical study of decision-making showed systematic deviations from the predictions of normative models. Descriptive models therefore try to account for such deviations and to capture how people actually make decisions. Prospect theory was developed on the basis of models of subjective expected utility and from observations of everyday decision-making and sources of error and bias. Prospect theory postulates that decisions under uncertainty are characterised by two steps: first, the decision situation is edited, that is, complexity of information is reduced. Second, decision outcomes are evaluated relative to a reference point as gains or losses and the probability of a gain or loss is taken into consideration. When people can choose between a risky alternative and a guaranteed payoff, they tend to act risk averse, as if they were trying to safeguard their gains. When threatened with loss, however, they tend to select the riskier rather than the safer alternative, showing a tendency to try to recoup their losses. Depending on the way in which a certain issue is presented, attention can be directed to gains or to losses, and the resulting decisions diverge.

While prospect theory still contains the idea from normative models that decision-makers strive for the optimal alternative, other descriptive decision models assume that people do not necessarily seek the optimal option, just a satisfactory one. Often, choices are made implicitly. To justify an implicit choice, other available options are considered and analysed afterwards. Descriptive models illustrate how individuals and groups, organisations and politicians make decisions. They are based on the assumption that everyday decision-making is influenced by principles other than the ones postulated in classical normative models.

Descriptive models depart from the rationality and utility maximisation assumptions and accept 'very normal' anomalies, such as heuristics and biases. People often make sensible, prudent decisions, even if not always the best ones. However, weakness of will, lack of time and the inability to process all the relevant information in complex situations adequately can often block good judgment and the realisation of good intentions. For that reason, decision experts give advice on how to take good decisions, and 'decision architects' try to give citizens a 'nudge' in a desired direction. A nudge can help them behave in ways that benefit citizens themselves and/or the society, while keeping their freedom of choice.

Introduction

Decisions often do not follow the predictions from normative models, as shown by the extensive research on decision anomalies. Often, the complexity of the decision situation and the resources of the decision-maker are not matched. In decisions under uncertainty, people often try to reduce the complexity of information before evaluating possible outcomes and choosing an option. Further, people are often risk averse if an option promises a certain gain and risk seeking if the choice implies a certain loss. Prospect theory provides a framework to incorporate these behaviours, and serves as an explanation for endowment effects, sunk cost effects and mental accounting. Other descriptive models highlight that in many cases the goal may not even be to choose an optimal solution. The focus of this chapter is to show how people often 'muddle through' complex decisions and to describe decision processes in everyday life. The chapter ends with some considerations to improve decision-making and possibilities to design decision situations such that the better option is spontaneously taken.

3.1 Prospect Theory

> From tears to laughter is a happy step, which makes us forget our agonies, but when we pass from pleasure to pain the change is even yet more acutely perceptible. (Florindo in *The servant of two masters* by Carlo Goldoni)

> A man always sets a double value on what Fate has deprived him of. (*Green Henry* by Gottfried Keller)

> We suffer more . . . when we fall from a better to a worse situation, than we ever enjoy when we rise from a worse to a better. (Adam Smith, *A theory of moral sentiments*, p. 311)

Decisions, such as undertaking a challenging climb despite a bad weather forecast, investing time and money in a psychoanalytic therapy whose chances of success are uncertain, deciding to chance a bank break-in despite the possibility of getting caught, or deciding whether to attack an opponent or surrender are all decisions with uncertain outcomes. By the eighteenth century, Daniel Bernoulli had already established that people are risk averse in uncertain decision situations and prefer a certain payoff to a possible payoff of statistically equal size. A certain payoff is even preferred to an uncertain one when the alternative with the possible payoff confers more benefits, from a purely mathematical perspective, than the sure payoff. For example, people prefer a certain £8,000 to £10,000 with a probability of $p = 0.85$, even though the expected value of the riskier alternative is higher (£10,000 * 0.85 = £8,500).

The mere fact that people are risk averse is not problematic. People prefer the bird in the hand to the two in the bush and are only willing to make a risky decision when the expected reward adequately compensates for the risk. Risk aversion can be reconciled with the stipulations of the rational model. When two alternatives have equal value from a purely mathematical perspective, the more certain one is preferred. It can be further argued that the risk of losing generates costs. Hence, in order to be preferred to a certain alternative, a risky alternative needs to be mathematically more advantageous. However, people are not generally risk averse. A certain gain is preferred to a risky gain, but when threatened with loss, risk aversion is generally low and risk seeking behaviour is observed instead. Amos Tversky and Daniel Kahneman conducted a multitude of experiments showing that the risky option is often preferred to the certain one in situations containing the threat of loss. Instead of simply accepting a loss, people seize the opportunity possibly to make up for it, even when there is a danger of incurring an even larger loss.

Tversky and Kahneman (1981) invited people to imagine the following situations and to state their preferences:

- 1a: A certain payout of US$ 240 or
- 1b: A 25% chance of winning US$ 1,000 with a 75% risk of winning nothing.
- 2a: A certain loss of US$ 750 or
- 2b: A 75% risk of losing US$ 1,000 with a 25% chance of going home without a loss.

In the first case, 84% of participants selected the certain payout of US$ 240 and only 16% the risky alternative. In the second case, only 13% accepted the certain loss, while 87% chose the risky option. While risk aversion reigns in gain scenarios, loss situations create an appetite for risk. It was also emphasised, however, that risk seeking behaviour can certainly arise when profits are very small, and risk aversion when losses are very small. Kahneman and Tversky (1979) found that 84% of participants preferred a certain US$ 500 to a 50% chance of winning US$ 1,000. However, 72% of participants preferred to play a game with a $p = 0.001$ chance of winning US$ 5,000 to being given a certain US$ 5. When losses are at stake, the pattern is reversed: 69% chose the option with a $p = 0.5$ probability of losing US$ 1,000 rather than definitely having to pay US$ 500. With the options of either a small loss of US$ 5 or a $p = 0.001$ risk of losing US$ 5,000, 83% selected the certain loss of US$ 5.

A further example shows that decisions in choice scenarios are not made only on the basis of the objective features of the options. They are also influenced by the form in which the options are presented. Depending on how a situation is described, the decision-maker's attention can be directed towards gains or losses. Even when the options are equally good or equally bad, objectively speaking, people tend to practice either risk tolerance or risk aversion depending on how the options are described. Tversky and Kahneman (1981) detected a systematic reversal of preferences in what was known as the '**Asian disease problem**'. The scenario was as follows: A flu epidemic has broken out, and it is expected that 600 people will die of the disease if no action is taken to fight it. Two intervention programmes are being discussed, whose consequences are described differently in each case. In Description 1, attention is directed to the guaranteed benefit:

- 1a: 200 could be saved by Programme A.
- 1b: With Programme B, there is a one-third probability that all at-risk people will be saved and a two-thirds probability that no one will be saved.

In Description 2, attention is directed to the guaranteed loss:

- 2a: If Programme C is implemented, 400 people will definitely die.
- 2b: With the implementation of Programme D, there is a one-third probability that there will be no victims to mourn, and a two-thirds probability that everyone will die.

Description 1 points to possible damages but sets up a guaranteed benefit as an alternative. On the basis of risk aversion, the certain benefit should be preferred to the possible benefit. Out of 152 participants, 72% selected Alternative 1a, while only 28% selected Alternative 1b. However, with Description 2's suggestion of a guaranteed loss, only 22% of 155 participants proved themselves to be risk averse by selecting Alternative 2a, while 78% preferred Alternative 2b.

Attention can be directed towards either benefits or drawbacks. '**Framing effects**' show that decision-makers' preferences depend on the problem presentation. Kahneman and Tversky (1984) and Tversky and Kahneman (1981) describe a set of choice scenarios that illustrate preference reversals. Nevertheless, Kühberger (1995) points to problems in the descriptions of the decision alternatives. When, for example, measures to fight the outbreak of an Asian flu epidemic are to be considered, complete information is offered in only one case (the probability that the second measure will be effective in saving everyone or will fail is explicitly mentioned). In the other case, the information is incomplete – in the first scenario, it is only reported that a certain number of people will survive; in the second case, only that a portion of the affected people will die. Another criticism is that most study participants see the numbers of survivors and casualties not as absolute, but rather as approximate reference values. Wang (1996) found that framing effects only arise in the Asian disease example when the number of affected people is large. When there are fewer than one hundred potential victims or study participants are close to the affected people (e.g., relatives), framing effects are not detected.

Nevertheless, numerous studies document framing effects in various situations. Thaler (1985, 1992) reports experiments on fairness documenting the influence of the manner of presentation on decision-making and on perceived fairness. These experiments show similarities to Kahneman and Tversky's examples. For example, people are told that a popular car cannot be produced in sufficient numbers. Because the demand greatly exceeds the supply, the dealership decides

- in the first case, to raise the price by US$ 200
- in the second case, to stop granting the customary discount of US$ 200.

The question as to whether the dealership's reaction was fair was answered in the negative by 71% of 130 participants in the first case. In the second case, only 42% of 123 respondents considered the dealership's behaviour unfair. While the price increase in the first case creates the subjective impression of a loss for customers, the second case only gives the impression that a benefit was taken away.

A second experiment describing the situation of a firm that must absorb a large decrease in profit is similarly informative. The firm is located in an area with a high unemployment rate.

- In the first case, the management had decided to reduce pay by 7% at a time when the inflation rate was 0%.
- In the second case, the management had decided to increase pay by only 5% despite an inflation rate of 12%.

A total of 62% of participants considered the management's decision in the first case as unfair. In the second case, only 22% judged the decision as unfair.

Depending on whether attention is directed to gains or losses, information is sought out with different degrees of selectivity (Fischer, Jonas, Frey & Kastenmüller, 2008). When something is to be gained, the search for information seems to be more selective. Consistent information is sought out more frequently than when losses are at stake. Decisions about gains are also made with a greater degree of subjective certainty than decisions about losses.

In a large number of studies, Daniel Kahneman and Amos Tversky observed how people make decisions, discovering errors and distortions in decision-making, difficulties in coming to logical conclusions, the application of various heuristics, dependency on the context in which the problem is presented, and assessments of value that are not absolute but rather relative to a reference value. These psychological findings led them to formulate prospect theory, which can be seen as the most pertinent extension of subjective expected utility theory (e.g., Wakker, 2010). Just as postulated in subjective expected utility theory, Kahneman and Tversky presume that people would like to maximise their utility. Therefore, **prospect theory** also assumes that the utility of the available alternatives and the probability of occurrence of various consequences shape decision-making. Nevertheless, it is also assumed that people in complex decision situations first tend to simplify the problem, then evaluate the prospects offered by each option, and finally make a decision.

Decision-making can be divided into two phases: the editing phase and the evaluation phase. In the **editing phase**, a reference point is selected. Considerations are made as to what an event, an option and its consequences will be viewed in comparison to. In the course of this, people tend sometimes to perceive independent events as being connected to each other. On the other hand, events are perceived as being separate from one another when certain or risky consequences are probable. Similar circumstances are perceived to be much more similar, and non-similar circumstances much less similar, than they actually are. Complex circumstances are simplified and particularly prominent events are given particular weight. All of the difficulties in accurately processing information and the application of the heuristics described above can be observed in the editing phase.

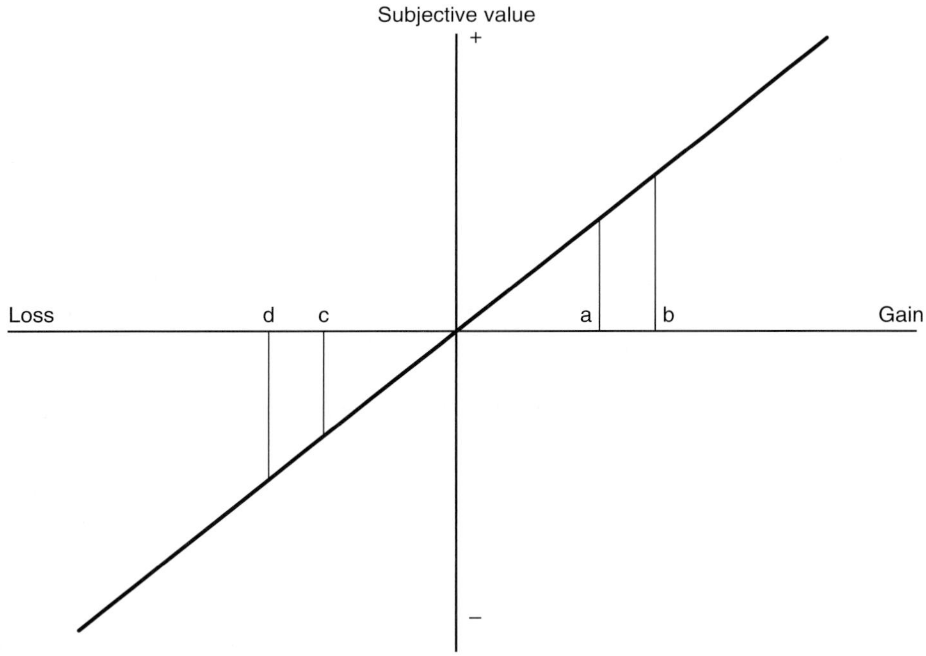

Figure 3.1 Value function with a linear relationship between objective and subjective values

In the **evaluation phase**, one considers whether the consequences of an option represent a gain or a loss relative to the reference point. The relationship between psychological value and objective results is depicted in what is called a value function. The **value function** illustrates the relationship between an objective outcome (gain or loss relative to a reference point) and the subjective value or experience of that outcome. If people experienced gains and losses in perfect correspondence to how they objectively are, a direct linear relationship would exist between objective outcomes and subjective experience. The value function would take the form depicted in Figure 3.1. If satiation effects are assumed, the relationship between objective outcomes and subjective experience would take the form depicted in Figure 3.2. Kahneman and Tversky observed, however, that behavioural patterns in gain and loss scenarios do not perfectly mirror each other; rather, losses have much more influence than gains. Prospect theory postulates a value function like the one depicted in Figure 3.3.

The value function is concave in the gains region and convex in the loss region ('S-shaped'). In addition, the value function is considerably steeper in the loss region than in the gains region. The subjective value of a gain is considered lower than a loss of the same objective size. The illustration shows that the subjective increase in value due to an objective gain (a–b) is smaller than the loss in value (c–d) experienced after a loss of the same size (from an absolute perspective).

In the evaluation phase, the events' probabilities of occurrence are also considered. The **weighting function** indicates how the objective probabilities that structure decision-making are subjectively perceived and transformed into decision weights. The weighting function in prospect theory is depicted in Figure 3.4.

The weighting function shows how objective probabilities for the consequences that might occur after choosing an option are converted into subjective ones. A gain with a probability of $p = 0.9$ is not necessarily perceived to have a probability as high as it actually does. Figure 3.4 indicates that objectively low probabilities tend to be given too much weight, while high probabilities are given too

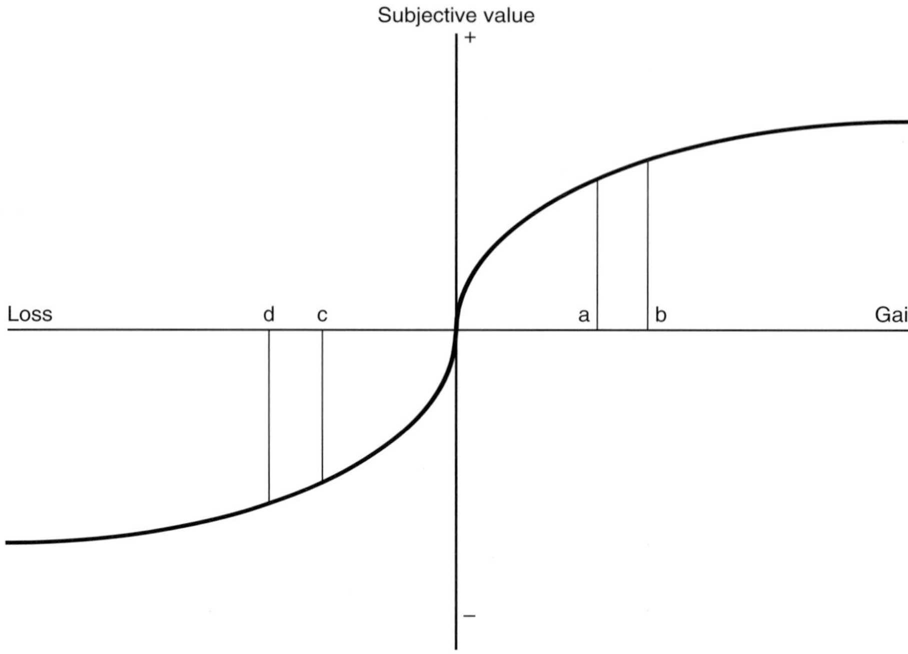

Figure 3.2 Value function with satiation effects in the relationship between objective and subjective values

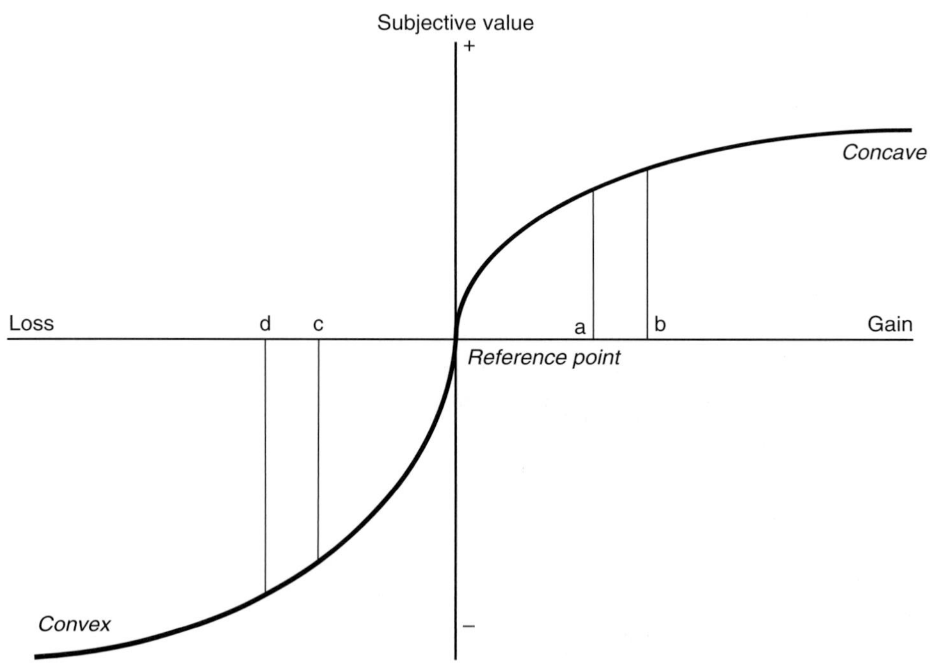

Figure 3.3 Value function according to prospect theory (adapted from Kahneman & Tversky, 1979, p. 279)

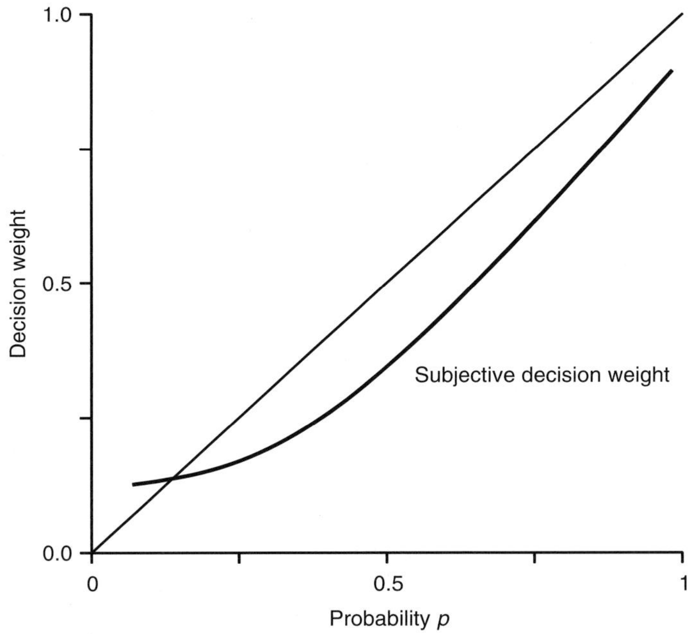

Figure 3.4 Weighting function in prospect theory (adapted from Kahneman & Tversky, 1979, p. 283)

little weight. This subjective perception of probability explains why people participate in lotteries with extraordinarily low probabilities that pay out high winnings, and why they are willing to insure themselves against damages that are extremely unlikely. On the other hand, opportunities for gain are not taken up, even when the gain has a high probability of occurrence. High probabilities are subjectively underweighted in the decision-making process. The weighting function was further developed in Tversky and Kahneman's (1992) cumulative prospect theory. Schmidt, Starmer and Sugden (2008) published an expansion of cumulative prospect theory under the name third-generation prospect theory. In this theory, uncertain reference points such as lotteries can also be included in models while keeping decision weights cumulative and specific.

Support for the postulates of prospect theory comes from neuroeconomics, among other fields. In this interdisciplinary research area, economists, neuroscientists and psychologists attempt to understand human decision behaviour by examining brain activity during decision-making. Neuroscientific methods make an analysis of the activities of the human brain possible (e.g., Prinz & Pawelzik, 2008). Not only imaging and psychophysiological methods but also single-neuron measurement, electrical brain stimulation and the shutting off of brain regions are methodological tools of the neurosciences, and as of late of neuroeconomics as well (Glimcher, Camerer, Fehr & Poldrack, 2009). Imaging methods and psychophysiological methods are primarily used, with imaging methods numbering among the most preferred (Camerer, Loewenstein & Prelec, 2005). In addition to electroencephalography (EEG), positron emission tomography (PET) is used, allowing for the generation of cross-sectional images of the human brain that depict biochemical and physiological processes. Functional magnetic resonance imaging (fMRI) allows for the depiction of metabolic activity in the brain by measuring the magnetic features of oxygenated and deoxygenated blood. Through the use of psychophysiological methods, various physiological reactions to a stimulus, such as blood pressure, pulse, perspiration, dilation of the pupils and muscle tone, are measured (Sanfey, 2007). Many studies have shown that economic decisions correlate with neurophysiological processes (e.g., Delgado, Locke, Stenger & Fiez, 2003; Knutson, Taylor, Kaufman, Peterson & Glover, 2005). Sanfey, Rilling, Aronson, Nystrom and Cohen (2003) used fMRI to examine reactions to fair and unfair offers in the ultimatum game. They demonstrated that different brain regions are activated in the case of rejected unfair offers than in accepted unfair offers. Indeed, neuroeconomics has advanced to a field of research in behavioural economics attracting much attention and fuelling high expectations. Camerer, Cohen, Fehr, Glimcher and Laibson (2015) offer an informative overview of neuroeconomics.

A study by Gehring and Willoughby (2002) testing prospect theory's assumption that losses have more weight than gains is especially interesting. Gehring and Willoughby registered physiological processes in the brain 265 milliseconds after participants were informed of a positive or negative result. Contingent negative variation, probably originating in the mediofrontal area of the cerebrum, had a higher amplitude when a loss was reported. Twelve people could choose between the numbers 5 and 25. Directly afterwards, they were told that the selected number had meant either a gain or a loss of 5 or 25 pence, respectively. When a loss was registered, electrophysiological reactions were more intensive than in the case of a gain. This result even arose when, for example, the number 5 was selected and the corresponding sum was deducted from the participant's pool of play money, rather than the number 25, which would have meant a larger loss and therefore would have been the incorrect choice. Conversely, the amplitude was smaller when gains were reported, even when 5 was selected but 25 would have offered a larger gain, meaning that the wrong choice was made. The authors argue that it is the negative result that leads to a more intensive electrophysiological correlate, rather than the correct or incorrect choice. Moreover, the study demonstrated that losses directly lead to more risky decisions: in this case, to the selection of the higher number (Figure 3.5).

3.1.1 Endowment Effect

When a gain is incurred after a decision, people quickly accept the new situation as the status quo. When a gain already realised is taken back, this retraction is not experienced as a return to the starting position, but rather as a loss. According to the value function of prospect theory, this means that the decline in value is experienced more intensively than the pleasure of gain upon receiving an object. When people buy an object, they are normally willing to spend a certain amount of money on it. Later, when the object is in their possession, they are only willing to part with it when more money is offered than they themselves were willing to pay. For example, a person might spend a certain amount of money to purchase a piece of art. When later he is offered many times the original price for the object, much more than the person himself would ever be willing to pay for it, he will nevertheless hesitate to sell the piece. Thaler (1992) speaks in this context of the '**endowment effect**' and shows that a good immediately becomes more valuable, and the loss of it immediately more painful, after a person has taken possession of it. Kahneman, Knetsch and Thaler (1990) conducted an experiment on this. They had university students sit down, put a decorated mug valued at about US$ 5 in front of some of them, and then asked them to fill out a survey. The survey given to the people with the mug (sellers) explained that they would from now on be owners of the mug. They would be able either to sell it at a price communicated later or to take it home with them. The participants were to state whether they would agree to sell the mug for prices ranging from US$ 0.5, US$ 1, US$ 1.5, etc. up to US$ 9.5. The other participants, who did not receive a mug at the beginning of the experiment, were told that they could choose between a mug or a sum of money as payment for their participation (choosers). However,

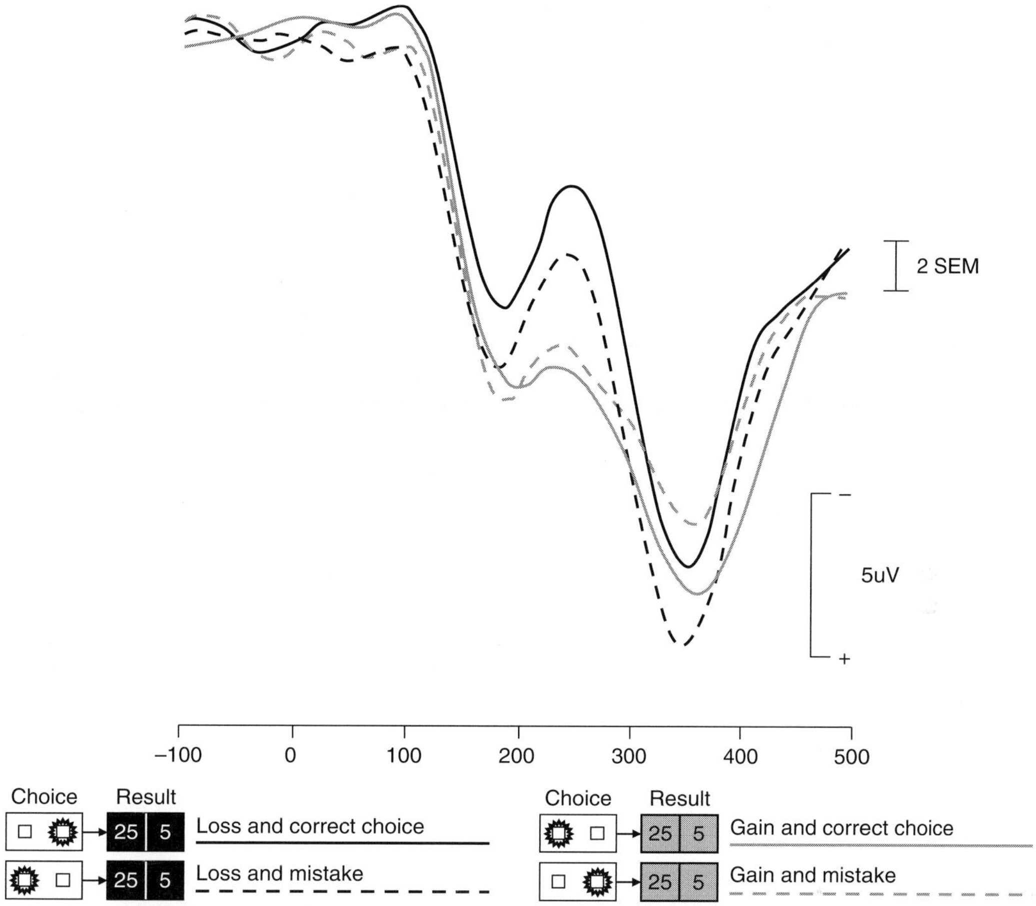

Figure 3.5 Mediofrontal activity following feedback on the accuracy of a choice (correct versus incorrect) and the direction of the result (gain versus loss) (Gehring & Willoughby, 2002, p. 2281)

before they were able to make a decision, they were asked to state their preferences between the mug and sums of money ranging from US$ 0.5 to US$ 9.5. Objectively speaking, the sellers and choosers had the same task. Yet, different reference points were set for their evaluation. While the sellers perceived giving up the mug that they already owned as a loss, the choosers viewed the mug as a gain, since they had neither the mug nor the sum of money in their possession at the present moment. In fact, the average value of the mug for the group of sellers was US$ 7.12, and in a second experiment US$ 7; for the group of choosers, amounts of US$ 3.12 and US$ 3.50 were generated. More recently, Johnson, Häubl and Keinan (2007) conducted a similar experiment on the endowment effect and confirmed Thaler's (1992) results. The selling value was twice as high or even higher than the value at which participants were willing to buy the item.

Gains are quickly taken for granted. A loss, however, even when it is smaller than the gain that directly preceded it, is registered as painful. Converted into terms of the labour market, a specific current income represents the status quo or starting point. An increase in income relative to this is positively registered as a gain, but the new salary is soon perceived as the reference point from which increases and decreases are judged. After a salary has been increased by 100 monetary units, the loss in value incurred by reducing it again by the same amount of 100 is experienced significantly more intensively and painfully than the joy over the previous increase (Tversky & Kahneman, 1991).

The endowment effect rejects the presumption that preferences are stable. Economics teaches that indifference curves never intersect. Indifference means that an individual considers one combination of goods equal in value to another combination. For example, ten units of Good A and one unit of Good B might be viewed as equal in value, or five units of A and two of B, or 3.33 units of A and three of B, etc. The indifference curve is the line connecting the combinations of goods that have the same utility or are equal in value from the individual's point of view. The form of the indifference curve depends on the subjective value assessments of the combinations of goods. It is theoretically postulated that one indifference curve cannot intersect with another because indifference curves are reversible. If an individual in possession of Object X is indifferent to the possibility of exchanging Object X for another Object Y, this individual, were he in possession of Object Y, should also be indifferent to the opportunity to exchange Y for X.

3.1.2 Sunk Cost Effect

As the endowment effect shows, gains do not only affect current decisions but have effects that are made manifest in future decisions as well. This is also true of losses. For example, if investments are made on a project, future decisions about further investments are made more readily when past investments were higher. Arkes and Blumer (1985) term this the **sunk cost effect**: it is more likely that an endeavour is continued when resources have already been invested, even when these resources are irretrievable. The irrational decision to 'throw good money after bad' is apparent in many thought experiments, has been empirically confirmed in a multitude of experiments, and is a daily reality in politics and the economy. For example, a person might plan to take a ski holiday with friends in the Rocky Mountains. The holiday costs a lot of money, approximately £4,000, and £3,000 of that needs to be paid three months before the start of the trip. It will be retained if the holiday is cancelled. Shortly before the trip, the person finds out that her friends will not be able to come along due to family problems but will instead be taking a ski holiday in the mountains nearby, which will cost £1,000. With this news, the winter holiday that has been booked loses a lot of its attractiveness for the person, while her interest in spending a few days with her friends in the mountains nearby increases. The person now stands before the following alternatives: (a) pay another £1,000 and take the ski holiday alone in the Rocky Mountains, or (b) lose the £3,000 that has already been paid and invest £1,000 in the nearby holiday with friends. In actuality, the only consideration at this time is the selection of the most enjoyable holiday for (another) £1,000. In this case, that would be the holiday in the ski area nearby. However, hardly anyone chooses the more attractive alternative in these circumstances, since the £3,000 represent sunk costs that need to be justified.

Companies do what is often enormously risky business because of their dogged adherence to decisions when costs have already been incurred. For example, a firm might create a development plan for a new product that will come onto the market in three years. A million dollars are invested in its development every year. At the end of the second year, with product development proceeding according to plan, the final million dollars needs to be budgeted for the coming year. Just before making the decision to approve the rest of the money, the decision-makers find out that a competing firm will come out with a similar product in the next year. The competitor's product will be qualitatively better and significantly cheaper than the firm's own product. What should be done at this point? Should the final million dollars be invested in developing the firm's own product in order to make it ready for market, or should the development process be stopped and the money be invested in a different project? Since 2 million dollars have already been expended, the final 1 million is often all too readily thrown after the 'sunk' money. In contrast, if the firm had not expended any capital in the past and decision-makers think about allocating a million dollars for the development of a new product that is to come out in one year, the decision would be a different one. They would certainly not be willing to invest the money after learning about the plans and anticipated success of the competing firm. Costs already incurred, though, need to be justified (Arkes & Blumer, 1985).

In the research to date, invested resources have almost exclusively been of the financial sort. Soman (2001) was able to demonstrate sunk cost effects for investments of money but not of time. In contrast, Greitemeyer, Schulz-Hardt, Popien and Frey (2005) were able to demonstrate that past investments in the form of time and considerable effort likewise produce sunk cost effects. Participants in their study, who were bank tellers, were presented with four decision scenarios, each of which consisted of two alternatives. The first alternative represented a case where investments had already been made; in the second, economically more advantageous alternative, this was not the case. In the first two scenarios, time was invested, while money was invested in the other two. In addition, a version of each scenario was created in which some generated utility could be pointed to, as well as a version in which the investments made could claim no utility. For example, in one of the four scenarios, participants were asked whether they would rather teach a very demanding statistics course for which they had already prepared intensively, or a marketing seminar with a lower time commitment. A total of 78% of respondents selected the statistics seminar despite being less interested in it.

Van Dijk and Zeelenberg (2003) were also able to show that projects tend to be carried forward when sunk costs have already been incurred. Moreover, they investigated whether sunk cost effects also arise in ambiguous situations. Participants were divided up among four experimental conditions – a control condition and conditions with low, high and ambiguous sunk costs. The participants were to imagine they owned a firm that would like to put a new drug for migraine on the market. However, one of their largest competing suppliers is pursuing the same plan. In the low sunk cost condition, investments amounting to 500,000 Dutch guilders had been made, whereas in the condition with high sunk costs, 1.5 million guilders had already been invested. In the ambiguous condition, the exact amount was not known: participants were only told that the costs ranged from a minimum of 500,000 guilders to a maximum of 1.5 million guilders. Next, participants were to choose between going forward with the project or terminating it. They advocated for continuing the project when costs of 500,000 guilders or even 1.5 million guilders had been accrued. However, in both the ambiguous condition and the control condition, the majority chose to axe the project. Ambiguity seems to obstruct the tendency to throw 'good money' after 'bad'. Ambiguous information seems to be taken less into account in decision-making than statements that are certain.

The sunk cost effect can also frequently be observed in real life. It is often difficult to advocate stopping investment in company projects that should have been given up long ago in order to avoid further costs. It is more likely that building repairs that are more expensive than knocking the structure down and rebuilding it will be authorised than it is that the property owner will acknowledge having made mistakes. The closure of nuclear power plants whose security is dubious in cases where renovations would blow past all cost projections is delayed for a long time. Deciding to pull out of a war that has long since become unwinnable is more difficult than fighting on.

As a qualification, it should be pointed out that past costs do not necessarily always lead to a higher appetite for risk: the opposite, risk aversion, is also possible. Zeelenberg and van Dijk (1997) examined risk aversion in the context of having invested time and effort into the completion of a job. The authors presented their study participants with various vignettes. For example, they were to imagine that they had performed a difficult task. Their boss then offers them US$ 50 as payment, or either US$ 100 with a probability of 0.5 or US$ 0 with the same probability. With winning or losing to be determined by a fair coin, study participants were to state whether they preferred the certain wage or the risky game. Many wanted to have the certain US$ 50, because the frustration they anticipated experiencing if they were to lose would have triggered too much regret. If, however, in addition to the agreed-upon wage, their boss offered either to pay them US$ 50 or to let them participate in a game with outcomes of US$ 100 with a probability of $p = 0.5$ and US$ 0 with a probability of $p = 0.5$, they selected the risky alternative. In addition to risk appetite, anticipated regret when one alternative and its consequences are realised while the other is forgone are relevant to decision-making (Loomes & Sugden, 1982). Moreover, it seems probable that behaviour differs by gender: women seem to be more frequently risk averse than men (Brooks & Zank, 2005).

Risk appetite and 'blindness to all reason' in loss situations is not just apparent in the behaviour of individuals and companies. Rumiati and Bonini (1996) report on total escalation in competitive situations. A standard situation for the study of escalation in competitive situations was created by Shubik (1971) and studied by Bazerman (1990). It concerns the auction for a banknote. For example, one person in a group of thirty might suggest auctioning off £100 under the following condition: each person can either participate in the auction or leave it. Everyone who participates needs to raise their offer at least £1 above the current bid. The starting price is £10. The person who makes the highest bid receives the banknote. However, the person who makes the second-highest offer also needs to pay the price they bid without receiving anything in exchange. For example, if Person A bids £35, thereby making the highest offer, and Person B had previously bid £34, A receives the £100 banknote and pays £35 for it, while Person B pays £34 and receives no money. After the auction has begun, the 'game' escalates rapidly, and participants do not recognise the trap until it is too late: the participant with the second-highest bid will offer ever-higher bids in order not to be the loser. Even when he has already bid £99 and the highest bidder is willing to pay £100, it makes sense to continue bidding and pay £101 for the banknote, and so on. In many auctions, it can be observed that competitive situations lead to escalations. Depending on the type of auction, the winner might not be at all well off. Thaler (1992) provides vivid examples of the 'winner's curse', and Foreman and Murnighan (1996) demonstrate that learning effects are rarely achieved, even when the traps built into some types of auctions are explained to the participating parties.

Ruinous escalation phenomena can also be observed in the private sector. At the time when various airlines' frequent flyer programmes were first conceived as a means of increasing customer loyalty, some airlines tried to outbid their competitors by offering credits double the number of miles flown. American experts estimated that 1.5 to 3 million dollars' worth of free flights were taken in 1987. The extreme escalation took place when Delta Airlines ultimately credited three times the number of miles (Rumiati & Bonini, 1996). It is easy to see how the spiral of escalation develops further and where it leads.

3.1.3 Mental Accounting and Hedonic Editing

The assumptions of rational profit maximisation have been called into question also by findings on event-by-event mental bookkeeping on gains and losses. The theory of **mental accounting** (Thaler, 1992) assumes that people record the costs and benefits of various operations, and remember and settle them in event-specific ways. Related to monetary expenditures, people set aside specific sums of money in their budget for specific decision categories. When the allocated budget for one area has been used up, the probability that more funds will be spent on this area sinks.

For example, most people will choose to buy a ticket to the theatre for US$ 10 despite discovering at the ticket window that they have lost US$ 10 on the way to the theatre. The same people will hesitate to buy a new ticket for US$ 10 when they had already bought a ticket a few days previously and discover in front of the theatre that it has gone missing. In the first case, 88% of a sample of 200 people chose to buy the ticket. In the second case, only 46% of respondents declared themselves willing to buy a second ticket (Kahneman & Tversky, 1984). US$ 20 is just too much money for a visit to the theatre! This behaviour is – from a purely formal perspective – inconsistent, since the same loss occurs in both cases.

If event-by-event bookkeeping is practised, it can also be assumed that people budget specific sums for specific matters (e.g., flat, recreation). For that reason, it can come to pass in purchasing decisions that a person has already spent the planned sum of money in one category but not in another. People hesitate to make further purchases and investments, even when it would be advantageous to buy a certain good, when the corresponding account is already empty. When the account for a given category is full, conversely, expenditures come easily, even when they are not very prudent (Heath & Soll, 1996).

The saving behaviour of wage earners provides a relevant practical example. When a person plans on receiving a monthly income of a certain amount, she normally considers how much money she wants to spend and what should be put aside. When a second person earns less per month but can count on definitely receiving a bonus at the end of the year, giving her the same annual income as the first person, it is frequently observed that the second person saves more money than the first. Person A, earning £1,200 per month (twelve times a year), might set aside £200 units per month. Another person B, earning £1,000 per month (twelve times a year) and receiving a bonus of £2,400, will also attempt to save a certain (smaller) amount of money each month; the end-of-year bonus is often seen as a special payment that could be saved for larger purchases. Monthly income and special payments are experienced differently and budgeted for different expenditures and savings goals. Thaler (1992) discusses the observation that income over a longer time period, such as a year, is not taken into consideration in spending decisions. This points to contradictions between empirical data and Modigliani's (1988) life cycle theory.

In addition to entering event-specific gains and losses into the books, people also file reports on their event-specific successes and failures. These reports, however, can be fashioned – with varying degrees of awareness – in such a way so that satisfaction is high (‘**hedonic framing**’ or ‘**hedonic editing**’). For example, a person has taken on the task of leading various projects in a firm. After some time, it is clear that Project A was conducted well and has yielded a profit of 100 monetary units. Project B has likewise achieved a profit of 50 monetary units. Projects C and D led to losses of 100 and 20 monetary units, respectively. At this point, it could be reported that the four projects together yielded a total profit of 30 monetary units. However, profits totalling 150 monetary units and losses totalling 120 monetary units could also be reported. A further possibility would be to report gains separately and losses jointly, namely profits of 100 and 50 monetary units and a loss totalling 120 monetary units. According to prospect theory, it is this possibility that maximises satisfaction. The sum of the separate subjective values for each of the profits is higher than the subjective value of the combined profit amount. Figure 3.6 makes clear that segregating gains and integrating losses particularly serves to create satisfaction. The sum of the subjective values G(a) and G(b) is higher than the integrated value G(a + b), and the integrated loss L(c + d) is less painful than the sum of the separated losses L(c) and L(d). Therefore, it is advisable to keep gains separate instead of combining them. However, it is advisable to combine losses into the total loss and not to focus on the individual, smaller losses (Thaler, 1999; Thaler & Johnson, 1990).

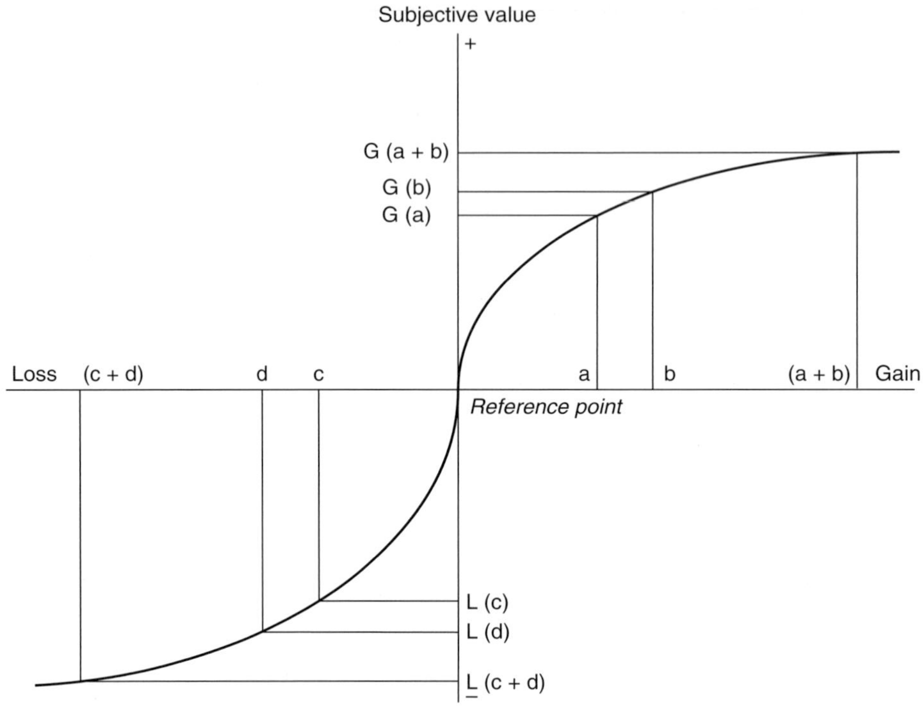

Figure 3.6 Hedonic separation of gains G(a) and G(b) and integration of losses L(c + d)

3.2 Descriptive Decision Models

Whereas prospect theory still assumes that decision-makers select the option with the higher subjective value and therefore keeps one core idea of normative decision models intact, other descriptive models have relaxed this assumption. A number of descriptive models have been proposed both for individual decisions and for decisions in organisations and in politics.

3.2.1 Individual Decisions

Normative decision models postulate that alternatives are examined and evaluated, and that the probability of preferred consequences is taken into consideration. Simon (1957) criticised the assumption of rationality, which surpasses human cognitive capacity in complex decision situations, and referred to the goal of maximising utility as a burden. The human ability to behave rationally is limited ('**bounded rationality**'). If people do not seek out the best alternative, but rather are assumed 'only' to hope to make a 'good' choice, many things become easier. Instead of the optimisation principle, the '**satisficing principle**' reigns. This postulates that people in complex decision situations act within the limits of bounded rationality: they construct simple decisions, select the most prominent characteristics or criteria of the problem and ignore or overlook a large portion of the features. Not all of the alternatives on the market can be taken into consideration, just a few. The alternatives included in the choice are judged according to their most conspicuous features. When an alternative more or less corresponds to an individual's requirements, it is selected. Decision-makers are content with an acceptable minimal level, a satisfactory alternative, not just with the maximum gain.

There are countless examples of the strategy of satisficing: a job seeker often has a clear mental image of his future position in terms of income, holiday time and social insurance contributions. He selects the first position that fulfils these requirements. The requirements can be raised for the next comparable decision when a satisfactory solution is easy to find. Conversely, the requirements can be reduced when the search for a solution proves to be difficult and fraught with problems. When a person is in the market for a new car, she might think about a discounted price at which she would be prepared to buy a specific car. In this case, she would go to car dealer after car dealer until she found one willing to give her this discount (see Roethel, 2003).

In the optimisation model, all available alternatives are evaluated and the order in which alternatives are considered is therefore not important. In contrast, decisions following the satisficing principle can depend on the order in which the alternatives under consideration are analysed. The last alternatives have a lower chance of being selected than the first ones, since the first satisfactory alternative is accepted. Figure 3.7 illustrates the decision-making process according to Simon's (1957) model.

One decision model that incorporates some unique assumptions, the '**implicit favourite model**', was introduced by Soelberg (1967) (Figure 3.8). This model assumes that decision-makers spontaneously choose one of the available solution alternatives at the start. This alternative is implicitly made the favourite, and the other alternatives are then compared to it. This comparison process mainly attempts to justify the judgment that has already been made, in that confirmation is

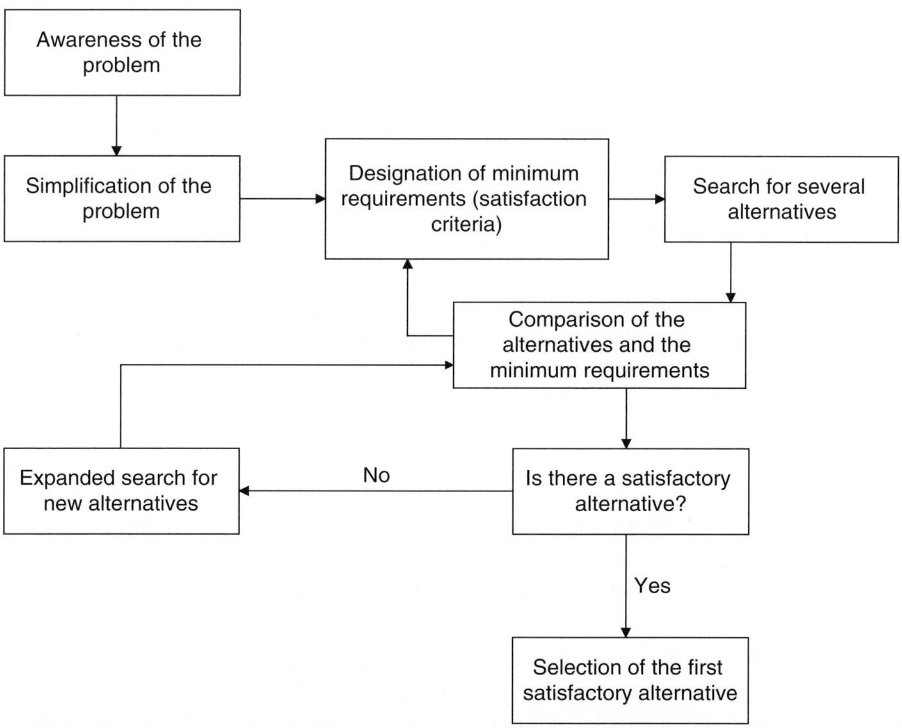

Figure 3.7 Decision model for the satisficing principle (according to Simon, 1957)

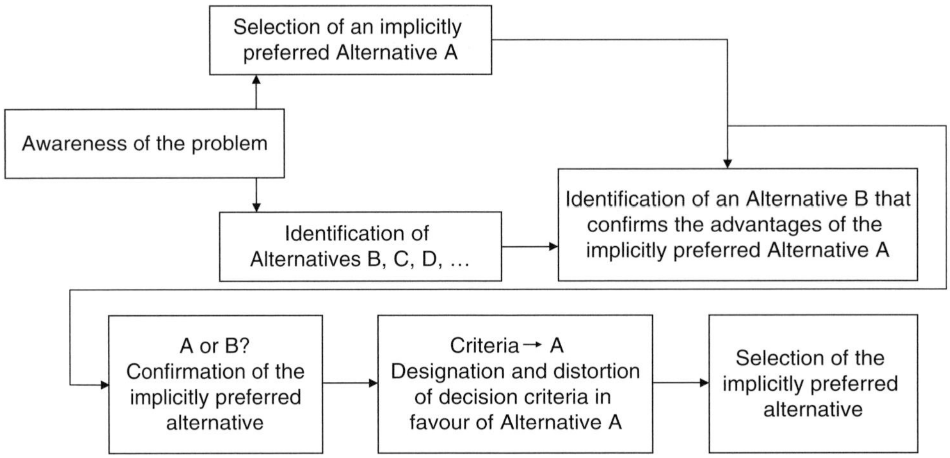

Figure 3.8 Decision model following the principle of an implicit favourite alternative (according to Soelberg, 1967)

sought out that the spontaneously preferred alternative was the correct choice. Decision-makers are often not aware that they have already selected an alternative and are undertaking deliberations after the fact to justify their choice. It is only after this implicit choice has been made that decision criteria, which are calibrated to match the selected alternative, are isolated. It seems to be easier to justify the implicitly favoured alternative after the fact than it is to make a selection out of a wider palette of options, as would be the case in a normative model.

Distortions in the way information is perceived, limited processing capacity, errors in the formation of judgments, and making hasty conclusions instead of subjecting decisions to extensive deliberation all call the rational model into question. The availability, representativeness and anchoring and adjustment heuristics, and especially fast and frugal heuristic, may contradict the model of a completely rational decision-maker, but their application is not unreasonable. When, in a complex situation under uncertainty, time pressure compels action, it is often prudent to rely on experience and to use strategies that constitute 'shortcuts'. However, it is also wise to consider whether the choice that has been made is really a good one.

3.2.2 Decisions in Organisations and in Politics

Individuals do not always choose the optimal alternative. Groups of people, as well, do not always make judgments and take action in accordance with the rational model. Reimer, Hoffrage and Katsikopoulos (2007) studied whether groups also apply the recognition heuristic. Just as in the aforementioned example, the population of two cities was to be estimated. The groups, each of which consisted of three members, were assembled so that either all group members had heard of both cities, each member had heard of only one city, or no members had heard of either city. Interestingly, it was found that in 65% of the cases in which group members disagreed on the correct answer, the recognition heuristic was applied. Reimer and Hoffrage (2006) addressed the question of to what extent the amount of information available plays a role in group decision-making. As part of this, a four-member committee was given the task of determining the best-qualified candidate for a job among three potential applicants. The committee was presented with dichotomous pieces of information, one positive and one negative characteristic for each applicant. Each committee member received information on a fixed number of characteristics of the applicants, but the amount of information varied. After individual decisions had been made, the committees were to jointly decide who the best candidate was. When there were only a few pieces of information available about the applicants, the take-the-best heuristic was applied. From the set of information on education, work experience, etc., the persons making the judgment selected the criterion they believed to be most significant and made their decision on the basis of that. The other pieces of information were ignored.

Similarly, several people working on a problem together do not always proceed rationally and analytically and sometimes make a poor choice. In social psychology, Janis (1972) used the term '**groupthink**' to describe the phenomenon that groups, even those composed of top-quality experts, make suboptimal decisions. He was able to demonstrate that highly dramatic decisions, such as those made by political and military experts, can be completely irrational in certain circumstances. Janis analysed documents on the decision to invade the Bay of Pigs in 1961. John F. Kennedy, the American president, and a group of advisors had decided upon an invasion of Cuba. It was only after everything had gone wrong that the group of experts was forced to admit that their decision had been unwise. It was puzzling how the experts could have made such an imprudent decision. Janis found that the probability of groupthink is high in highly cohesive groups that are isolated from alternative sources of information and in which a charismatic leader favours a certain solution. The danger of groupthink is high when there is high self-censorship and pressure to conform, the group's invulnerability is overestimated and collective rationalisation takes place. A failure to define goals, selective information processing, insufficient evaluation of the consequences of the alternatives and poor implementation plans can lead to highly problematic solutions.

March and colleagues (e.g., March & Shapira, 1992, p. 279) describe organisational decision-making in a way that provides little illusion of rationality, writing: 'They [organisations] gather information and don't use it. Ask for more, and ignore it. Make decisions first and look for the relevant information afterwards.' Cohen, March and Olsen (1972) formulated a '**garbage can model**' to describe decision-making in organisations. They begin by stating that organisations seldom come to decisions on their own. Instead, they copy them from somewhere else. Shortcomings, differences between actual and desired conditions and other problems are often not grasped unless a solution already exists. Organisations are chaotic arenas. In order to be able to make optimal decisions, order would need to be created and information gathered. Rituals, symbols and myths that shape collective action (and therefore decision-making as well) would need to be exposed for what they are.

March and Romelaer (1976, p. 276; as cited in March & Shapira, 1992, p. 284 f) present a bizarre image to characterise group decision-making:

> Consider a round, sloped, multi-goal soccer field on which individuals play soccer. Many different people (but not everyone) can join the game (or leave it) at different times. Some people can throw balls into the game or remove them. Individuals, while they are in the game, try to kick whatever ball comes near them in the direction of goals they like and away from goals they wish to avoid.

Constantly flowing through organisations are currents of solutions, problems and decision-makers. Decision options are viewed more as coincidental than as deliberately created connections between problems and the solutions that match them. Solutions are often discovered only coincidentally by the people responsible for decision-making. In organisations, decisions, problems, solutions and members simply 'float on through'. When the forces propelling them forward more or less align with one another, decision-makers have a correct solution for a problem ready at the correct moment. This is how a decision is made. In short, 'decision making is an arena for symbolic action, for developing and enjoying an interpretation of life and one's position in it' (March & Shapira, 1992, p. 289).

When you consider how decisions are actually made in administrative bodies, companies and other organisations, March and colleagues' model seems more sobering than comforting. How often do budgeted resources that have not yet been used by the end of a fiscal period need to be spent quickly in order to document that a budget increase is necessary for the next fiscal period? This does solve the problem of not having used all of the resources at the end of a period. However, it might result in a complicated, newly purchased gadget taking up space in the department, representing the solution to a problem that has not yet been found. In order to justify this purchase, department members will continually ask themselves if they might be able to find a use for it, for example in a prestigious project that has yet to be planned – the solution looks for an appropriate problem. If a project can be found that requires the newly purchased piece of equipment, everything works out. Spending the last of the funds during the previous fiscal year made sense, purchasing the equipment was necessary, and carrying out the project promises to be fruitful. A team of competent people, a problem and a solution came together. In hindsight, order is brought to the decision-making process: there were just enough funds available at the time to purchase an urgently needed piece of equipment that was essential for an important project. The investment was sound, and the decision itself demonstrates foresight and justifies the request for further funding increases in the future.

Even politicians, who have the fate of the country in their hands, make decisions in the same way. Braybrooke and Lindblom (1963; Lindblom, 1959, 1979) describe decision-making as a step-by-step, incremental process of '**muddling through**'. The more complex the task, the smaller is the probability that rational strategies will be used. Decisions in politics, but also in firms and in private households, do not generally match the well-defined and managed tasks with simple structures that are commonly generated in the laboratory. Because several other tasks arise in addition to the decision-making task at a given time, the decision situation is frequently complex. Unsuitable and therefore irrational coping attempts can easily arise in complex decisions where time is tight. Such coping attempts can be, for example, forgoing a judicial analysis, experimenting with unsystematic and illogical solution approaches, focusing exclusively on those subproblems with easy solutions, limiting oneself to only a few aspects of a larger task, blindly imitating previous decisions, and searching for solutions only in the usual places.

Decision-making in the political arena can be described as an incremental process and compared to walking through a swampland, with the danger that the next step might bring doom. In complex situations, small steps are taken. One step forward, and if the ground holds, another small step forward is taken. If the consequences of the action are negative, if the ground does not hold, a step is taken to the right or left. Sometimes, one's course needs to be reversed. The complex interactions of various variables, both altered and left unchanged, cannot always be predicted because consequences are frequently unpredictable. Therefore, one needs to proceed incrementally. The direction of change is maintained until a negative consequence occurs. In this way, teams of experts grope their way from one bank of the swamp to the other, and in the end they have brought about a solution to the problem step-by-step.

3.3 Designing Decision Architectures

Descriptive decision models highlight the challenges for decision-makers. The question is whether there are certain strategies that they can use or whether the decision situation can be structured in certain ways in order to increase the chances to find a 'good' solution.

3.3.1 Logic of Successful Decisions

The rational model's optimism stands in contrast to reality, as decisions made in firms, public administrative bodies and private households deviate from the rational model. Organisations are complex systems facing complex tasks in which concrete goals cannot always be identified. According to Dörner (1996), complex goals can only be realised efficiently when they are broken up into more limited subgoals. Subgoals need to be verifiable and definable in concrete terms in order to be able to be implemented. If decision-makers are expected to reach certain goals in complex situations, they often tend to solve the problems they are able to solve rather than the most relevant problems. Participants in Dörner's (1996) decision-making simulations were put in control of the fate of a city or a country (such as being the mayor of the city 'Lohhausen', with the fate of the citizens under their control; or the administrator of 'Tanaland', a fictional country which they are to lead to prosperity through their rule). Results showed that participants rarely know how to deal with these complex systems efficiently. They often begin to intervene somewhere in the mesh of interdependent variables: for example, in the simulation game, residents can be surveyed about the city's shortcomings. Measures are then often put into place to correct the deficiencies that have been detected, regardless of their importance. In doing so, it is seldom considered that solving one problem in a complex system can often create new problems. But once new problems arise, 'repair service behaviour' starts taking place. In crisis management situations, holes need to be stopped up in all the places that they apparently randomly appear. Participants hardly attend to problems not manifest at the given moment – and for this exact reason soon find themselves having to grapple with just these problems. Participants sometimes have to reach intermediate goals in order to achieve their ultimate aims. The triumph upon realising these intermediate goals beguiles many people, making them lose sight of the main goal and – distracted by the intermediate goals – try to reach goals of negligible relevance. Lapses of time, which are especially important to take into consideration in complex systems, are seldom analysed explicitly. It is not only simulated organisations that are run into the ground despite their leaders' best intentions. Dörner (1996, p. 198) concluded: 'What we did yesterday is lost in the obscurity of the past, and what we ought to do tomorrow is in utter darkness. We human beings are creatures of the present.'

What can be done to avoid poor decisions? In contrast to the 'logic of failure', Dörner (2010) emphasised in his work on the '**logic of success**' that good actors try to delineate concrete goals in complex decision situations. In doing so, they take into consideration the ways their goals interact. They select an area of emphasis without ignoring what remains in the background. The interdependency of their goals is taken into account; contradictory goals are balanced out, and goals are selected according to their importance. Good actors analyse a given situation as a network of elements dependent on one another and as a system with multiple contingencies. Additionally, they are most interested in information that contradicts their own worldview. Good actors do not believe the future can be predicted by linearly projecting forward from the present. Rather, they see the future as the effect of present causes. These causal factors, which determine changes in reality, form the primary basis of planning. Good actors make wide-ranging plans that take into account current conditions as well as long-run and side effects. They make plans that match the current situation and causal factors and test whether current conditions meet the requirements for successful action, even if this has always been the case up until now. In carrying out decisions and actions, they monitor the effects of their own actions, analyse failures, and alter their behaviour in accordance with its causes and effects. Good actors are willing to analyse failures with an eye to their own responsibility and do not rashly seek out 'scapegoats'. This willingness to conduct intensive self-reflection on the failures and shortcomings of one's own thinking, planning and formation of hypotheses helps good actors transform their thinking instead of clinging to habitual analyses.

Reflexivity can increase team performance (Gurtner, Tschan, Semmer & Nägele, 2007). Reflexivity means that people are capable of connecting new knowledge to the knowledge they already possess. Group reflexivity inhibits 'commander behaviour' and places more emphasis on strategies, allowing those that are too general to be helpful to be identified as such. Reflexivity is useful in developing new strategies that are more efficient in finding solutions.

What can be done in unclear situations? Lipshitz and Strauss (1997) analysed several concepts of uncertainty and risk and described various tactics used by people in risky situations, including tactics for making risky decisions efficiently. Risk is described as a feeling of doubt that leads one to hesitate to take action. To arrive at a decision, attempts can be made to (1) reduce uncertainty by, for example, looking for new information, waiting until new knowledge is attained, etc. People also can try to (2) accept uncertainty, and to use it as a basis for making their decisions while at the same time considering which consequences have potential risks and how these should be handled. Finally, people can try to (3) suppress uncertainty. In order to decide on a course of action, people sometimes ignore uncertainty, give in to a false sense of security, and assume that certain developments do not pertain to them. They can suppress information or change its weight, tune out sets of facts and circumstances, and seek out symbols that are only ostensibly related to the decision but provide a path out of paralysis. Lipshitz and Strauss (1997) instructed over one hundred officers in the Israeli military to sketch out a situation from their personal experience that contained uncertainty and to describe how they had arrived at a decision. The officials had experienced uncertainty primarily when they completely lacked information or had only partial or unreliable information. In addition, uncertainty also arose when the circumstances were new or not clearly and completely understood, or a conflict was experienced because several alternatives appeared to be just as attractive. The causes of uncertainty could be traced back to a lack of clarity about the decision situation, about possible results of the decision or about the role of the decision-maker. A total of twelve tactics for dealing with uncertainty were discovered:

1. Tactics for reducing uncertainty consisted of (a) seeking out new information; (b) delaying the decision until new information arrives; (c) soliciting expert opinions; (d) following normative guidelines to make a decision; and (e) developing opinions and using them to construct a mental model of the decision situation, then performing mental tests of the model and further modifying it as necessary to make a decision on the basis of this model.
2. Tactics for accepting uncertainty involved (f) planning one's reaction to unintended consequences of the decision; (g) setting resources aside in order to compensate for negative events; (h) planning reversible actions and avoiding irreversible actions and their consequences; and (i) weighing the advantages and disadvantages of the available alternatives.
3. Tactics for suppressing uncertainty were (j) remaining ignorant of uncertainty; (k) trusting one's own intuition; and (l) leaving things to chance, such as flipping a coin to make a decision.

Further analyses of situationally dependent tactics ultimately led to a conceptual model of decision-making processes in uncertain decision situations. In this model, the **RAWFS model**, eleven of the twelve tactics are combined into five clusters. Cluster R ('reduction') consists of tactics (a), (b), (c) and (d); Cluster A ('assumption-based reasoning') encompasses tactic (e); Cluster W ('weighing pros and cons') contains tactic (i); Cluster F ('forestalling') includes tactics (f), (g) and (h); and Cluster S ('suppression') incorporates the tactics (j), (k) and (l). The situational dependent choice of

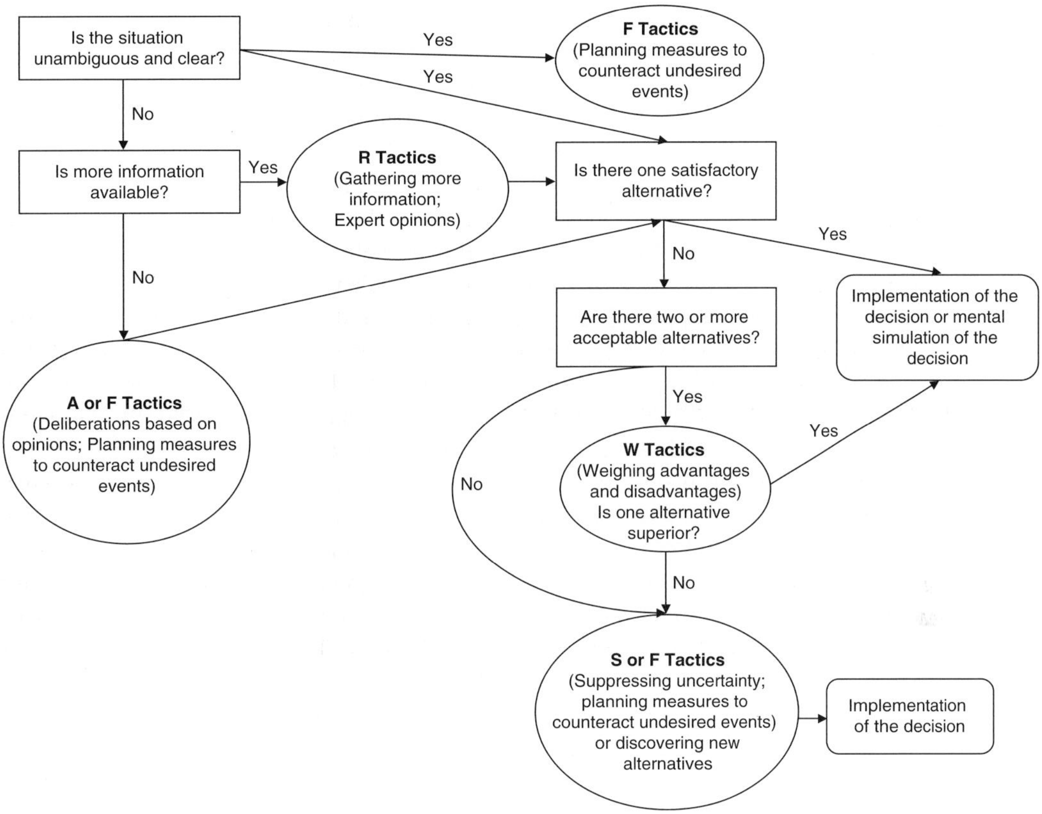

Figure 3.9 RAWFS model for dealing with uncertainty (Lipshitz & Strauss, 1997, p. 159)

a tactic is depicted in Figure 3.9. Decision-making begins with an attempt to gain clarity about the situation. If this is achieved, alternatives and consequences are considered. If there is sufficient time, mental simulations of the decision are carried out. If clarity cannot be successfully achieved, considerations are made as to how unwanted developments might possibly be impeded or what countermeasures might be taken. If there is a lack of information and more information cannot be gathered, opinions are formed upon which the eventual decision can be based. If two or more satisfactory options are found, a decision conflict is at hand, which is handled by weighing advantages and disadvantages. If no alternative can be selected successfully, information is suppressed, consequences and countermeasures are considered, or new alternatives are sought out until ultimately a decision can be made.

In risky decisions that could have an undesired outcome, there is an opportunity to consider which measures might be taken in a crisis. A holiday in a tropical land seems attractive because it provides the opportunity to explore an exotic country with strange customs but also perilous because of the risk of possibly contracting diseases that are difficult to diagnose and treat. With this in mind, a tourist could consider whether to embark on the holiday, select another destination or stay at home. If he chooses to take the holiday in the tropics, he could further consider what he might do to reduce the risk of illness. For example, he could get vaccinated against tropical diseases, or make arrangements to have the appropriate medicines immediately available in case of illness. Oswald Huber (e.g.,

Huber, 2007, 2012; Huber & Huber, 2003; Huber & Macho, 2001; Ranyard, Hinkley & Williamson, 2001; Shiloh, Gerad & Goldman, 2006; Tyszka & Zaleskiewicz, 2006; Williamson, Ranyard & Cuthbert, 2000) terms these arrangements for mitigating menacing negative consequences '**risk defusing operators**'. A risk defusing operator is an action aimed at reducing the risk that negative consequences will occur after a certain option has been selected. Risk defusing operators are commonly applied in everyday life, such as when people sign up for insurance policies against hazards (Huber & Huber, 2008). As a general concept, risk defusing operators seek to keep danger in check. Huber and Huber (2003) differentiate between risk defusing operators that are applied before a negative consequence arises and those that are applied afterwards. In the example of the holiday in the tropics, vaccination represents an operator applied before negative consequences occur, while buying medications is an operator for after negative events have already taken place. In the first case, costs need to be borne (the costs of the vaccine, pain, etc.) even if no illness ultimately occurs; in the second case, costs only arise if the negative event actually occurs. Decision-makers weigh the costs of risk defusing operators and the probability of negative events before choosing to take measures before or after the occurrence of negative events. If a negative event is certain to be discovered and there is a possibility of fixing it, people select operators applied after negative consequences have occurred. If the probability of discovery is low and a fix would be difficult, they tend to select operators applied before undesired consequences occur (2003).

Deviations from the rational model create costs. In order to increase their chances of receiving benefits, people can attempt consciously to counteract irrational behaviour. This can happen by, for example, fighting their obsessions and addictions, repressing their compulsions, or guarding against the traps represented by love and hate. They can attempt to apply tactics to deal with risk and consider risk defusing operators.

3.3.2 Nudging towards Desirable Behaviour

More and more institutions aim to design choice situations according to insights into human behaviour. Behavioural sciences, economic psychology and behavioural economics inform about decision dynamics and deviations from assumptions of the neoclassical model. As Sunstein (2016a) points out, the insights from behavioural economics and psychology are more and more applied by policymakers to design initiatives in savings, finance, highway safety, consumer protection, health, education, poverty, development, crime, corruption and tax compliance, energy consumption, climate change and the environment. Default rules, simplification, focusing attention to desirable goals, communication of social norms and the right timing of initiatives have sometimes even larger effects on behaviour than economic incentives (e.g., monetary incentives to shape desired behaviour or taxing undesired behaviour).

People make a vast number of choices and decisions every day, and many are barely registered. Design changes can markedly affect individual behaviour. As one example, the Paris Metro system provides an example of clever architecture: passengers validating their tickets can stick them into the machine facing any direction. The machine can read them and releases the entrance to the Metro. In other cities, tickets must be inserted in a certain direction in order to be read, which delays some passengers and leads to unnecessary congestion and bottlenecking during peak hours. As another example, cashpoint machines in Europe do not disburse the desired amount of money until after the bankcard is removed from the machine. In some countries, conversely, the cash is disbursed first, leading to a situation where many people forget their bankcards.

The findings from behavioural economics and economic psychology have made it necessary to adapt classical economic assumptions. They have also shown that apparently non-rational decisions are not always poor ones. Nevertheless, there are situations where it seems advisable to motivate people to behave rationally. Thaler and Sunstein (2008) write that human behaviour is not innately rational: people are easily influenced, quickly lose sight of the bigger picture, and are inclined to take the path of least resistance. The authors use insights from behavioural economics and economic psychology to develop suggestions for politicians and business leaders. They provide the motivation for 'decision architects' to give small **nudges** that induce rational behaviour without curtailing individual freedom. Halpern (2015, p. 22) defines a nudge as a 'means of encouraging or guiding behaviour, but without mandating or instructing, and ideally without the need for heavy financial incentives or sanctions'.

More and more institutions are offering services to support people in their attempts to avoid irrational, costly and payoff-reducing behaviour by providing advice on monetary matters, nutrition counselling or fitness training to help reduce the stress of everyday life. A decision architect can attempt to determine which small nudges provide people with support in their decision-making by creating incentives for desirable behaviour. Owing to weakness of will, many people have trouble rationally directing their behaviour on their own. One thing that can be done in many spheres of life where people tend towards inertia is to use opt-out provision: options are fashioned in such a way that rational action becomes the default, but free choice to do the opposite is retained. If offering a company retirement savings plan is considered sensible and a firm matches the amounts employees regularly contribute, a standard savings amount could be automatically deducted from all employees' pay packets. People against this would still be able to decide against it and people behaving in a thoroughly rational way would not be affected at all by nudges. Because people often tend to take the path of least resistance, more employees would save in this case rather than in a case where the standard procedure is an opt-in provision – which, of course, requires actively deciding to save for retirement. In countries where according to standard procedure every citizen is registered as an organ donor (but individuals still have the freedom to refuse being a donor), there are significantly more organ donors than in countries in which standard procedure is that citizens themselves need to register for organ donation. Many people have the best intentions of registering, but do not get around to it because of a lack of time, absentmindedness or taking the path of least resistance.

'Libertarian paternalism' is the term used by Thaler and Sunstein (2008) to describe the general idea – do provide paternalistic guidance, but still allow every individual to choose as they want. Decision architects who understand how to structure decision situations can use small nudges to prompt people to behave rationally without placing restrictions on their freedom of choice. People with positions of authority in business and in politics have the opportunity to apply insights from behavioural economics and economic psychology in order to structure decision and action situations in such a way that they bring benefits to all. Governments in several countries – for instance, in the UK – have set up organisations, so-called 'nudging units' (e.g., the Behavioural Insights Team in the UK), with the task of developing ideas and providing advice to improve government policy by nudging citizens, rather than by issuing binding laws.

Halpern describes in his book *Inside the nudge unit* (2015) the birth of the British Behavioural Insights Team. The British prime minister, David Cameron, set up in 2010 a team of behavioural scientists with the objective to 'inject a new and more realistic understanding of human behaviour across UK government' (p. 8). The team browsed through the literature with the aim of identifying determinants of decision-making and classifying robust effects. The team conducted dozens of experiments across a variety of subjects, such as, e.g., healthcare, tax compliance, energy conservation and crime reduction, and showed that small changes can have large effects. In 2010, the Behavioural Insights Team published a report proposing the framework '**MINDSPACE**' as a summary of effects that might influence people's behaviour in a specific context and as a memory aid for policymakers. The framework summarises nine robust effects:

Messenger:	We are heavily influenced by who communicates information.
Incentives:	Our responses to incentives are shaped by predictable mental shortcuts such as strongly avoiding losses.
Norms:	We are strongly influenced by what others do.
Defaults:	We 'go with the flow' of pre-set options.
Salience:	Our attention is drawn to what is novel and seems relevant to us.
Priming:	Our acts are often influenced by subconscious cues.
Affect:	Our emotional associations can powerfully shape our actions.
Commitments:	We seek to be consistent with our public promises, and we reciprocate acts.
Ego:	We act in ways that make us feel better about ourselves. (Institute for Government & Cabinet Office, 2010, p. 18)

In this framework, 'Messenger' points out that the source of information is sometimes more important than the information itself. Perceived expertise of the communicator, similarity and sympathy influence the interpretation of information. 'Incentives' refers to key aspects from prospect theory such that losses loom larger than gains, that the reference point matters whether outcomes are evaluated as loss or gain, and that small probabilities are given stronger weight. Money is allocated to different mental accounts. Future losses and gains are discounted and people often tend to live for today at the expense of tomorrow. 'Norms' refers to the fact that social and cultural norms guide behaviour through expectations and rules. Norms are especially binding the more an individual identifies with the group or society that established the norm. Social norms often act as automatic guidance of individuals' behaviour. 'Defaults' refers to findings that pre-selected options are often perceived as advice or as the norm. Defaults are powerful regulators of behaviour because changing a default option can be perceived as a loss or enhance feelings of anticipated regret, or as costly with regard to energy and time. 'Salience' highlights that much of the information encountered is filtered out, and only a few messages which attract people's attention are registered. Simplicity and immediate understanding of what should be done are important. 'Priming' refers to findings that certain words, labels, pictures and smells serve as cues that influence the focus and interpretation of information and situations. These cues consequently shape behaviour. 'Affect' highlights that emotions and mood are strong forces in judgments and decision-making. Fear, anger, greed, pride, anticipated regret, etc. can influence financial decisions and health behaviour. 'Commitments' refers to the fact that willpower is often weak and procrastination is a well-known phenomenon when difficult or boring tasks should be accomplished. Knowing that smoking causes health problems, that overeating and overspending should be avoided, is often not enough to change one's behaviour. Commitments can help us to do what is considered the better behaviour. Especially costly commitments, such as public promises, contracts involving financial costs in case of breaking a commitment, or concrete planning of behaviour to reach a long-term goal are robust strategies to improve one's behaviour. Finally, 'ego' highlights that people tend to invest in impression management and in a positive self-image. They attribute success internally and failure to bad luck. They also like to appear consistent in beliefs and behaviour. The advertising industry and marketing have long known the strengths of sales strategies that address consumers' positive self-image (Institute for Government & Cabinet Office, 2010).

Recently, the framework has been simplified and become widely known under the acronym **EAST**. If a certain behaviour is to be encouraged, than it should be made Easy, Attractive and Social, and the nudges should be provided Timely. Halpern (2015, p. 149) summarises the insights and describes successful nudging examples.

'Easy': People are more likely to do low-hassle activities as compared to time and energy consuming activities. Therefore, a form should be simple to complete. For instance, simplifying tax rules and declaration forms makes filing easier and fewer unintended errors are made. Defaults should be set as a path to healthy, safe, environmentally friendly behaviour, and obstacles to reach a desired goal must be removed. In the case that a behaviour is undesired, frictions should make the behaviour costly. Examples of successful defaults are organ donation regulations in various countries or automatic enrolment in pension programmes. Brown, Johnstone, Hascic, Vong and Barascud (2013) tested the effect of defaults on the thermostat settings of OECD employees by manipulating the office thermostats during the winter heating season. A one-degree decrease of the temperature caused a significant reduction of heating costs. However, a decrease of two degrees had no effect. People perceived the change of temperature and reset the thermostat to the initial temperature. A convincing example of the effect of frictions was observed in Germany in 1980. When fines were introduced on motorcyclists not wearing helmets with the goal of reducing head injuries, unexpectedly thefts of motorcycles fell by 60%. Indeed, somebody intending to steal a motorbike had to bring a helmet along. The requirement of a helmet created an obstacle to stealing a motorbike. Hansen, Jespersen and Skov (2015) examined how the size of plates at a standing lunch at the Danish Opera House affected food waste: those guests who had a smaller plate left much less food over than guests with standard-sized plates. The size of the plate introduced a friction to take too much food. Consider, however, that guests with the small plate did not need to starve; they could go back to the buffet as often as they wanted.

'Attractive': People are guided by what catches their attention and what appears attractive. Halpern (2015) reports on a study conducted in Copenhagen. Caramels were handed out to pedestrians and the number of wrappers on the streets and in the garbage cans were counted afterwards. Then, green footprints that led to litter bins were placed on the street. Again, caramels were distributed and wrappers counted. The attention caused by the green footprints led to an increase of 45% of wrappers ending up in the litter bins. Another successful example of nudging is the 'piano stairway' that was installed in a subway station in Stockholm: stairways designed like a piano and producing sounds at each step stimulated pedestrians to use the stairways rather than the escalator. Finally, personalised letters catch more attention than direct mails. The impact of personalised letters has been shown in experiments on tax compliance and the likelihood of paying fines on time. Often people do not even open 'official looking envelopes'.

Experts and named individuals are conceived as more reliable messengers than anonymous sources, salient goals are more likely to be pursued than other goals, and feelings and emotions play an important role in decisions. For instance, people donate more to emergency appeals with stories of one child as compared to information about millions of affected individuals. Halpern (2015) reports a study conducted by HMRC, the British tax and revenue service, which confirmed the effect of attracting attention. Doctors receiving their salary from their hospital or practice often receive extra money for working privately. While tax is deducted from the regular income on source, extra income needs to be declared for taxes. HMRC sent letters to doctors in three versions: a generic version reminding them to declare their extra income; a version that made reference to doctors specifically and their frequent extra earnings which need to be declared; or a version in which omission of declaring extra money was mentioned and that ignoring the reminder would be taken as an active choice of the addressee not to declare the extra income. Depending on the version of the letters, responses and declaration of extra income increased from 4% to 21% up to 35%.

'Social': People follow the herd. What others are actually doing is strongly determining what we are doing. So are recommendations from friends, reminders from others and active commitment. Reciprocity has long been acknowledged as a norm that people follow universally. Important field experiments conducted by the Behavioural Insights Team provide evidence about the impact of social norms (Hallsworth, 2014). Hallsworth, List, Metcalfe and Vlaev (2014) used administrative data from more than 200,000 UK taxpayers who received a reminder letter to pay their taxes on time. Besides noting that recipients had not yet correctly paid their taxes, a sentence was included in the letter, informing the recipient about timely tax payments by the majority of taxpayers. The sentence either informed about how many people out of ten pay their taxes on time, or it informed about the general practices in the country; some letters referred to the local descriptive norm. At almost no cost, the sentences were exceedingly effective in combatting delayed payments and producing higher revenue. Norm messages have a strong impact on tax compliance as they appeal to moral behaviour, make due dates salient and act against procrastination.

In his book on influence and persuasion, Cialdini (2001) defined six key principles of influence: reciprocity, commitment, social proof, authority, liking and scarcity. Goldstein, Cialdini and Griskevicius (2008) have shown the effectiveness of social norms and reciprocity in affecting behaviour. For the benefit of the environment and for reducing laundry expenses, hotel managers encourage their guests to reuse their bath towels. Typically, information cards in the washrooms appeal to guests to reuse towels. Goldstein et al. (2008) used different messages to encourage people to reuse their towels: environmental protection, social responsibility, social norms, environmental cooperation and benefits to the hotel. The environmental protection appeal read as follows: 'Help save the environment. You can show your respect for nature and help save the environment by reusing your towels during your stay.' The social responsibility appeal pointed to saving resources for future generations, whereas the social norms appeal informed about other guests having reused their towels. Frequency of towel reuse increased especially when people were informed about others' cooperative behaviour. The descriptive norm – the information about what people are actually doing – proved to be more effective in shaping peoples' behaviour than prescriptive norms – the information about what people should do.

Studies on energy saving showed that individual behaviour can be influenced by providing feedback about the behaviour of others. Ayres, Raseman and Shih (2013) provided feedback to customers on home electricity and gas consumption. In their field experiment, they drew attention to the behaviour of peers as a reference point and found that the information served to regulate the customers' energy consumption. Graffeo, Ritov, Bonini and Hadjichristidis (2015) conducted experiments in a similar way and concluded: to make people save energy tell them what others do.

'Timely': When is the right moment to nudge? Nudging is more effective at certain moments and less at other points of time. Interventions are more likely to influence behaviour before habits have been formed or when undesired behaviour has been disrupted. For instance, taxpayers are twice less likely to respond to nudges if they were paying late the previous year. Smart tax authorities know that it is advisable to provide service and support to self-employed taxpayers and small businesses the first year of filing to help them complete tax forms correctly and pay on time. Shu, Mazar, Gino, Ariely and Bazerman (2012) investigated how to discourage dishonesty in reports on taxable income. Tax authorities and insurances rely on honest reporting. Usually, the identity of the person filling out the form, the consent to what is on the form and confirmation of honest reporting are proofed by signing a form at the end. Still, people sometimes cheat for their financial self-interests. In laboratory and field experiments, the team of researchers found that signing a form at the beginning rather than at the end makes ethic norms salient and reduces dishonesty.

Biases and heuristics research in the arena of tax behaviour has shown that framing effects and shift of reference points are relevant to understand whether taxpayers perceive taxes as a loss, as a forgone gain or a gain. If losses are experienced or expected, taxpayers are likely to take risks to repair or prevent the loss. On the other hand, in gain situations they act risk averse. Often taxpayers pay a lump sum of income tax in advance, and when filing their taxes at the end of the year they have paid either too much or not enough tax and have either a refund or a balance due. Those taxpayers who have a refund due might perceive their tax refund as a gain. Those whose tax liability actually paid is lower than the liability determined at the end of the year are requested to pay additional taxes. In this case, taxpayers may perceive the taxes due as a loss and try to repair it by not reporting income or overstating expenditures. Evidence shows that compliance increases if taxpayers pay sufficiently high amounts in advance and receive a tax refund at the time of filing. Deliberate overwithholding of income taxes might increase compliance and substitute for costly detection efforts in enhancing compliance (Kirchler, 2007). Shift of reference point and consequently risk averse or risk seeking behaviour is also related to 'out of pocket' tax payments. In many countries, income tax is deducted at source. Employees receive their net income and may perceive taxes as a forgone gain rather than as a loss. The self-employed, on the other hand, collect all income, and often also value added tax, and need to pay taxes 'out of their pocket'. When evaluating tax payments, their reference point is likely to be the gross income. Taxes are then perceived as loss, which triggers risk seeking. In conclusion, it is worthwhile to consider how taxpayers perceive their payments, as loss or forgone gain, and to design the decision situation such that risk aversion and compliance increase.

Halpern (2015) summarises also priming and anchoring effects, time inconsistency, and discounting future gains and losses under the label 'timing'. The price of a product appears smaller if sellers show to their customers products at higher prices before presenting the demanded product. In negotiations, clever negotiating partners set a high price first followed by concessions. They, thus, exploit anchoring and reciprocity effects. With regard to time inconsistency and discounting of future losses, the lesson learned is that people make better choices for future behaviour (e.g., healthy nutrition, reading a good book rather than watching TV, engaging in sports) in comparison to decisions and choices regarding their actual behaviour. People also are more likely to realise their purposes if they develop concrete plans in advance.

Decision architects, such as policymakers or managers in organisations, harnessing the insights of psychology and behavioural economics can steer people towards certain decisions. Nudging has an ethical component and nudging 'for the good' is guided by three principles (Thaler, 2015):

- Nudging should be transparent and not misleading.
- Nudging should allow to easily opt out.
- Nudging should ground on good reasons to assume that the encouraged behaviour will improve welfare of the society and of the people being nudged.

While nudging is widely recognised as successful regulatory intervention (Halpern, 2015; Sunstein, 2016a, 2016b), there is also sharp criticism pointing at often missing transparency and non-conscious manipulation of citizens and consumers (Jung & Mellers, 2016; van der Heijden & Kosters, 2015). Indeed, the three mentioned principles are formulated as a plea rather than a command, and not every decision architecture provides benefits to consumers – nudging also can serve the interests of sellers. Ariely (2008) reported on the following promotional offer from the magazine *The Economist*. In advertisements for subscriptions, an internet subscription for US$ 59 was offered. There was another option of buying a subscription to the printed edition for US$ 125. Assuming that many readers would want the quick access offered by the online edition and find the additional charge for the print edition unattractive, it could be predicted that most readers would select the first option. For these reasons, a third option was offered: both the internet subscription and the print edition for a combined total of US$ 125. Who would turn down an offer that good for both editions, in which you essentially get the internet version for free?

Missing transparency, misleading offers and difficulties in opting out are cumbersome forms of nudges. Yet, they can be observed in the field of subscription offers of magazines, insurances sold with flight tickets, and other 'fishing' attempts by various suppliers on the market. Akerlof and Shiller (2015) provide a number of cases of 'phishing for phools'. Despite the keen interest of many governments in nudging, support for steering citizens in the described 'libertarian paternalistic' way is mixed. Reisch and Sunstein (2016) report results of representative surveys in Denmark, France, Germany, Hungary, Italy and the UK. While people generally support nudging in some topics (e.g., aiming to reduce childhood obesity, distracted driving, green energy or healthy food placement), support in other topics is high in some countries but low in others (e.g., smoking, carbon emission charge, organ donation).

Behavioural insights and nudging can be successfully used to develop strategies and to apply programmes to steer people's behaviour. However, not all nudging projects have been effective. Before applying nudging strategies, it is necessary to define the goals clearly and to set concrete criteria to evaluate the effectiveness of nudging. It is important to understand the context people are living in, to develop interventions, to run experiments with randomised control groups and to measure the impact on behaviour, as well as to control whether nudges remain powerful in the course of time.

Conclusion

Descriptive models of decision-making aim at capturing actual decisions and accommodating deviations from the predictions of normative models. Prospect theory assumes that in decision situations under uncertainty people first reduce the complexity of information. Second, they evaluate options relative to a reference point as gains and losses. Finally, they choose the option promising the highest benefit or lowest loss, depending on the probability of the expected outcome. More general descriptive decision models assume that rationality and utility maximisation are the exception rather than the norm. Learning from a variety of insights in behavioural science, conclusions about how to improve decisions and how to design decision architectures to nudge people 'for the good' can be drawn.

Summary

- People are risk averse in uncertain decision situations and prefer a certain payoff to a possible payoff of statistically equal size. However, prospect theory indicates that people are not generally risk averse: when threatened with loss, risk aversion is low and risk seeking behaviour can be observed.
- Prospect theory assumes that the utility of the available alternatives and the probability of occurrence of various consequences shape decision-making. The theory proposes a two-phase decision process. In the editing phase, complexity is reduced and a reference point is set. In the evaluation phase, outcomes are evaluated as either gains or losses, relative to this set reference point. The presentation of a decision problem ('framing') can systematically influence whether the outcome is viewed as a gain or loss.
- In prospect theory, the relationship between an objectively occurring gain or loss and the experience of it is depicted in the value function. It is concave in the domain of gains and convex in the domain of losses, and steeper for losses than for gains. How the objective probabilities are subjectively perceived is depicted in the weighting function. It shows that objectively low probabilities tend to be given too much weight, while high probabilities are given too little weight.
- Prospect theory explains that people intending to buy an object are normally willing to spend a certain amount of money on it. Later, when the object is in their possession, they are only willing to part with it when more money is offered than they themselves were willing to pay. This effect – the endowment effect – can be explained by prospect theory and loss aversion.
- Loss aversion also accounts for the sunk costs effect. Sunk costs are costs that have already been incurred and cannot be recovered. Individuals and groups are often reluctant to admit having wasted resources on past decisions. Even if costs cannot be recovered, people tend to continue 'throwing good money after bad money' and to spend energy or time to fix what was not working with the risk of losing more.
- The theory of mental accounting assumes that people record the costs and benefits, losses and gains of various operations, and remember and settle them in event-specific ways. In this context, hedonic editing explains how multiple losses and gains compared to a reference point need to be combined in order to increase satisfaction.
- It is not only individuals who do not always decide rationally; groups of people, for example in organisations and in the political arena, also use non-rational decision-making strategies.
- The human ability to behave rationally is limited. Instead of searching for the optimal option, individuals search for a satisficing option. Sometimes, decision-makers spontaneously choose one of the available solution alternatives at the start and collect further information to justify their implicit favourite. In group settings, 'groupthink' sometimes accounts for suboptimal decisions. Decisions in organisations have been described in the 'garbage can model' and experts in public administration often 'muddle through' decision processes rather than deciding rationally how to maximise the country's welfare.
- Decision-making simulations reveal shortcomings in complex situations such as 'repair service behaviour' and allow drawing conclusions about how to improve decision-making. Complex

goals can be realised efficiently when they are broken up into more limited subgoals and when the interaction between goals is taken into consideration.

- In risky decisions that could have an undesired outcome, it can be helpful to consider which measures might be taken in a crisis. 'Risk defusing operators' are actions aimed at reducing the risk that negative consequences will occur after a certain option has been selected or at fixing costs caused by a suboptimal decision.
- The insights from behavioural economics and psychology are applied by policymakers to design initiatives to guide people's behaviour, but without mandating or instructing. Small nudges provide people with support in their decision-making by creating incentives for desirable behaviour.
- Decision architects can structure decision situations by making desired behaviour easy, attractive and social, as well as by setting nudges in a timely way.

Questions

1 What form has the value function in gain and loss situations according to prospect theory?
2 How can the endowment effect be explained?
3 What is an example of the 'sunk cost effect' in product development?
4 How can negative consequences of risky choices be reduced?
5 What are 'nudges' and what does EAST stand for?

FURTHER READING

Akerlof, G. A., & Shiller, R. J. (2015). *Phishing for phools: The economics of manipulation and deception*. Princeton, NJ: Princeton University Press.

Halpern, D. (2015). *Inside the nudge unit: How small changes can make a big difference*. London: Allen.

Kahneman, D. (2011). *Thinking, fast and slow*. New York: Farrar, Straus and Giroux.

Sunstein, C. R. (2014). *Why nudge: The politics of libertarian paternalism*. New Haven, CT: Yale University Press.

Thaler, R. H., & Sunstein, C. R. (2008). *Nudge: Improving decisions about health, wealth, and happiness*. New Haven, CT: Yale University Press.

4 Lay Theories: Knowledge and Money

Overview

This chapter introduces the notion that people act more upon their subjective interpretation of the situation than on its objective characteristics. One major feature of this notion is the concept of lay theories as opposed to expert theories. Laypeople without training in economics still form an understanding of economic topics and act upon that understanding. Lay theories have often been studied using the theory of social representations. This theory explains how new ideas and concepts are integrated into existing knowledge and identifies important elements of lay theories. Empirical studies on lay theories pertain to the economic system as a whole and to specific economic phenomena such as poverty, unemployment or money.

A second feature is that people differ in their economic knowledge. This can best be understood by studying children growing up. The ability to grasp economic concepts is tied to cognitive development. In addition to knowledge, cooperation and the ability to take other people's perspective change with age. This means that economic motives such as egoism and altruism are evolving over time. Children and adolescents are also economic actors, both by spending money on their own and by influencing decisions within the household. In all these three areas, abilities improve with age. However, adults earning and spending their own money still may show gaps in economic understanding. The degree of economic sophistication can be captured by the concept of financial literacy.

A third feature is that money, as the resource at the core of many economic activities, is not only the functional medium of exchange as described in economics. Money takes on subjective meanings that differ between individuals, and is valued differently depending on circumstances. The subjective sides of money become particularly prevalent during currency reforms or changeovers. An important event was the introduction of the euro in many European countries in 2002 when citizens had to learn to deal with a new currency. Finally, prices are perceived and interpreted subjectively. Consumers often assume that higher prices indicate higher quality although correlations between price and product test results are mostly low.

Introduction

In many areas of life, most of us are not experts but laypeople. Still, we make decisions using what we know. Few of us have studied to be dieticians, but still we manage to decide that the lovely chocolate cake may not be the best choice if we want to lose weight. Few of us are trained economists, but still we manage to decide which products to buy, how much money to save or which job to take. We make decisions on our subjective understanding of the economy and the economic concepts at hand. These subjective bases of economic behaviour are the focus of this chapter. The goal is to understand economic behaviour by understanding the lay theories of people – for example, understanding why consumers do not use a new form of payment although objectively it seems to offer many advantages.

4.1 Lay Theories

People strive for an understanding of their environment. They want to understand mundane and exceptional events, and to identify cause and effect. Based on personal experiences, on communication with other people and on media reports, people form subjective theories, also called lay theories. These theories, in turn, often are the basis for decisions and actions.

Theories can be more or less complex. The economy is an example of a relevant area of knowledge and behaviour that allows a wide range of complexity in the related theories. The knowledge of economic experts can be assumed to form a complex picture of the interplay of economic phenomena. The knowledge of laypeople can be assumed not only to be less complete, but also to be structured differently. Expert theories can be assumed to be formed on logical structuring of data collected systematically. Lay theories – in contrast – can be assumed to be formed on the basis of everyday experiences and fragmented facts. In consequence, lay theories are often simplified and schematic, while at the same time being focused on explanation and action orientation. For example, in a study by Haferkamp, Fetchenhauer, Belschak and Enste (2009), 380 laypersons and 80 economists were surveyed on labour market regulations (e.g., minimal wage, maximum wages, lay-off protection). Economists – as experts – mostly rejected regulations, whereas laypersons supported these regulations. Economists also used different criteria for their evaluation. They focused mainly on efficiency criteria, whereas laypersons instead focused mainly on fairness criteria.

Based on more or less detailed theories, decisions are made, actions are planned, and new information is integrated into the existing knowledge (Bastounis, Leiser & Roland-Lévy, 2004). Media reports are relevant for the development of lay theories. Doms and Morin (2004) showed that the frequency of terms with a negative connotation (e.g., 'recession' or 'layoff') in the reporting about the business cycle in US daily newspapers is correlated with consumer sentiment. With media reports, consumer sentiment and the assessment of the economic situation also vary. Even when – based on actual economic data – no reason for pessimism exists, consumer sentiment decreases when the media transfers negative information. This highlights the importance of understanding how lay theories of the economic system are composed.

4.1.1 Theory of Social Representations

Lay theories about economic phenomena have most often been studied based on the **theory of social representations** (e.g., Moscovici, 1981). According to this theory, people's opinions are a complex result of experiences, emotionally loaded judgments, and information that is subjectively experienced, transformed and cognitively available. This view can be extended to economic phenomena, such as economic crises, unemployment and poverty. The theory combines psychological and sociological elements and partly goes back to Durkheim's idea of collectively constructed and shared realities (see, e.g., Durkheim, 1898). Moscovici and Hewstone (1983) describe social representations as '**common-sense**' theories about fundamental questions of a collective or a community. Common sense is the sum of knowledge, being composed of images and opinions and forming the basis for decisions and actions (see also Purkhardt, 2015).

The term 'social representations' is not simply a synonym for attitudes. **Attitudes** are usually defined as summary evaluations of objects (e.g., Petty, Wegener & Fabrigar, 1997). Attitudes can refer to all kinds of objects (e.g., ideas, topics, physical items, people, etc.) and evaluate such objects from negative to positive. Social representations are a much broader concept that aims at capturing a social reality. As such, they have similarity with belief systems in a society (Moscovici, 1981). Social representations are related to concepts as ideology or conviction since these concepts are reflecting social relationships as well as constructing them. Wagner, Duveen, Farr, Jovchelovitch, Lorenzi-Cioldi, Marková and Rose (1999, p. 96) wrote: 'A social representation is a collective phenomenon pertaining to a community which is co-constructed by individuals in their daily talk and action ... a social representation is the ensemble of thoughts and feelings being expressed in verbal and overt behaviour of actors which constitutes an object for a social group.' Social representations are characterised by several aspects that are here described according to el Sehity and Kirchler (2006). The main function of social representations is to make unfamiliar phenomena familiar and thereby providing a homogeneous setting for everyday discourse. It is assumed that this transformation occurs on the individual cognitive level. However, the elements that enter the transformation process are provided by the society, via the existing available representations. Such contents or theories that are not consensual within a society, or are too complex for everyday discourse, are selectively discarded. For example, in his study about the social representations about psychoanalysis, Moscovici (1961) could show that the central thesis of psychoanalysis – the sexual drive – became marginal in the social representations due to social taboos. In a sense, social representations take a buffering function: Unknown contents undergo a transformation process that makes them compatible with the existing stock of societally accepted representations. This function becomes clear in the structure of social representations, which can be differentiated into core elements and peripheral elements.

The **core elements** of social representations have two functions. First, they define the meaning of a social representation. Second, they organise the social representation (Abric, 1994). The core elements explicitly or implicitly form the basis in everyday discourse. They are an explicit basis when they themselves are in the focus of discourse (e.g., when people try to clarify specific aspects of 'democracy'). They are an implicit basis when the discourse is about specific occurrences related to the core elements (e.g., when people discuss privacy rights on the background of democratic ideas).

The **peripheral elements** of social representations have three functions, all serving the stability of the social representation's core. First, depending on the context, the core of a social representation is made more concrete and thereby more understandable. Second, by adapting to the temporal development in context, the peripheral elements avoid that the social representation becomes outdated. Third, both of these aspects indirectly have a protecting function for the stable core of a social representation by moderating between the core and the ever-changing context (el Sehity & Kirchler, 2006).

When unknown contents enter everyday discourse, individuals experience a confrontation between the unknown and the available stock of knowledge. Existing representations are compared with the new, unknown content. These comparisons are based on individual memory, but also on the societal

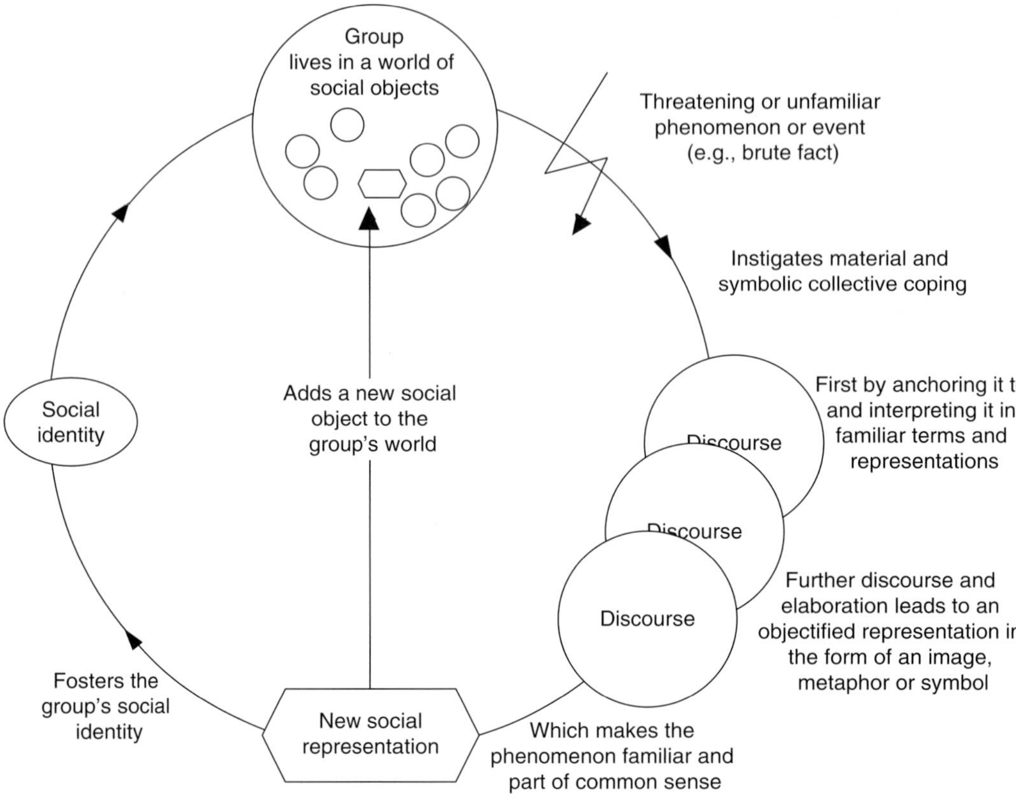

Figure 4.1 Sociogenesis of social representations (Wagner et al., 1999, p. 98)

motive of consensus. The development of a new social representation can be described as a sociogenesis (Wagner et al., 1999) and is depicted in Figure 4.1. Two cognitive processes occur in the development of new social representations, called anchoring and objectification.

Anchoring describes an organisation process in which memory is searched for existing representations. The unknown, unfamiliar or threatening phenomenon is then classified according to categories already known. During this process, the existing categories and the established representations also change. For example, when the free associations of psychoanalysis are anchored in the established representation of confession in the Catholic Church, not only does the concept of free association become closer to confession, but the representation of confession also becomes broader. This illustrates the dynamic change that the established social representations also face.

Objectification describes the process responsible for the vividness of social representations. Representations require 'drawing a picture'. Unknown phenomena by definition are abstract and therefore difficult to picture. The objectification process is the basis for making representations of the unknown possible: abstract concepts are represented as quasi-physical objects. Such objectified representations can be an image, a symbol or a metaphor. For example, Moscovici (2000) illustrated that an abstract concept such as courage is made concrete by personification in heroes (el Sehity & Kirchler, 2006).

Besides their main function of making new phenomena understandable and usable in everyday discourse, social representations fulfil a number of other functions. These functions are closely interwoven with their production. Social representations are developed by individuals within a group. They serve the needs of the collective and the requirements that society puts on their members. They guarantee, via moral standards, keeping to the existing norms. Social representations have a 'selective' function: they distinguish between the own social group and other groups or subcultures. Often members of the ingroup are viewed positively, while members of other groups are viewed negatively (Doise, 1978; Tajfel, 1981). Another function is the 'justificatory' function that becomes apparent in stereotypes about social classes. These stereotypes serve to regulate the distance between the social classes, which in turn maintain and justify economic differentiation. According to Doise (1978), social representations also have an 'anticipatory' function, because certain interaction patterns between groups can be anticipated. Hewstone, Jaspars and Lalljee (1982) mention two more functions. On the one hand, social representations have an 'attributional' function, in the sense that they provide explanations of social behaviour. On the other hand, they have a 'social identity' function in the sense that they provide social identity – how persons see themselves as members of a group, a social class or category, or a society. These five functions together make social representations important for the organisation and interpretation of the individual environment and for social interaction with others (el Sehity & Kirchler, 2006).

Existing studies on lay theories and social representations of the economy explore either the economic system in general or specific aspects of the economy (e.g., unemployment, money). Most studies examine elements of lay theories (Which elements do people see as particularly prominent, which elements do they neglect? Which elements are seen as positive, which as negative?) and connections between elements (Which elements do people see as connected or isolated? How do people see the causal mechanisms?) (e.g., Vergès, 1987). Research methods span ethnography, focus groups, content analyses, analyses of free associations, interviews and questionnaires. Experiments have even been used. However, in most cases non-directive interviews are conducted, open-format texts are analysed, or free associations to a stimulus are collected and analysed (de Rosa, 1995).

4.1.2 Social Representations about the Economic System

As one example of a study about lay theories on the economic system in general, Williamson and Wearing (1996) surveyed ninety-five adults using both questionnaires and interviews. The results from the questionnaires showed that respondents had rather little objective knowledge about the economy. However, the interviews revealed some 'inner logic' in respondents' thinking regarding important elements and their interconnection. These results were condensed into 'cognitive models' of the economy that showed two major characteristics. First, economic concepts were often based on stereotypes – excluding the respondent him/herself, however (e.g., 'Australians are lazy' but 'I myself am hard-working'). Second, economic concepts were often intertwined and integrated with psychological, social and moral variables. Figure 4.2 shows a part of the cognitive model Williamson and Wearing (1996) described. For example, respondents linked welfare/unemployment benefits (as economic concepts) to unwillingness to work (as a psychological concept), to the need for better education (a social concept), and to government benefits going to undeserving people (a moral concept).

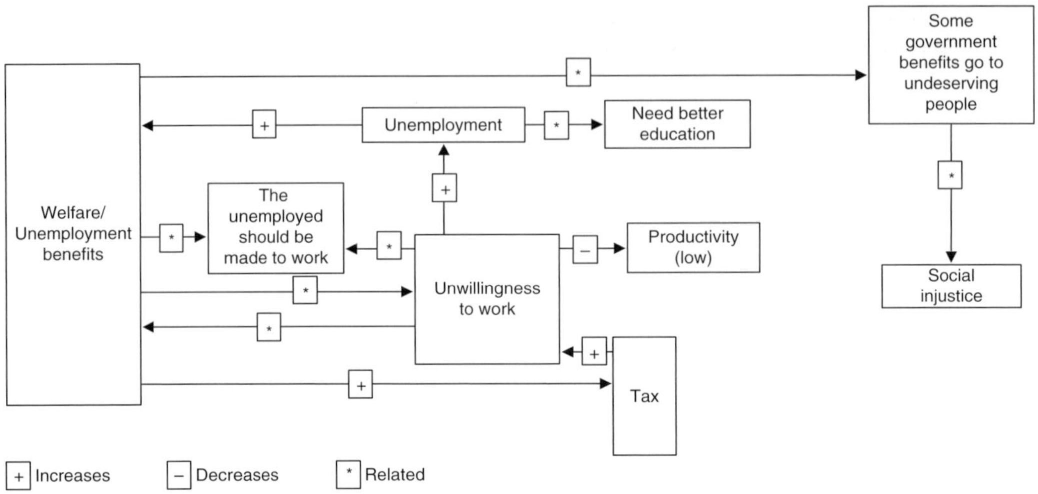

Figure 4.2 Part of the 'composite cognitive model of the economy' (adapted from Williamson & Wearing, 1996, p. 26)

A similar idea is illustrated by the findings of Antonides, Farago, Ranyard and Tyszka (1997). They asked 800 participants in four different countries (Poland, Hungary, the UK and the Netherlands) to evaluate forty different economic activities according to several dimensions. These activities included, for example, job change, saving, taxpaying or buying a car. The authors found that – independent of the country in which data were collected – laypeople seem to judge economic activities primarily according to two basic dimensions. On the one hand, activities were judged by their economic value (e.g., by cost-benefit analyses, gainfulness or effort). On the other hand, activities were judged according to their social value (e.g., by moral standards, security for others or attractiveness).

Other studies highlight the relevance of the societal environment for social representations. For example, Tyszka and Sokolowska (1992) explored lay theories about economic topics in Poland, shortly after the political and economic change to a market system. They found that laypeople group economic topics mostly according to their everyday experience, and do not necessarily search for logical connections. Often, inconsistent wishes were expressed: for example, social welfare programmes from the state were demanded, but at the same time taxes were seen as unjustified. Lay theories of groups with lower income and lower education seem mostly to be based on personal experiences, whereas lay theories of groups with higher income and education were more logically organised. In an unpublished study, Vergès, Tyszka and Vergès (1994) compared social representations about the economy between students from Poland and France. First, participants were asked to name three to eight economic topics that they consider important. Then, they were confronted with a list of eleven economic concepts (e. g., firms, state, profit, taxes or unemployment), and asked to draw connections between concepts that they see as closely related. Then, they were given twenty-seven words such as welfare, competition, inflation or risk and asked to group these as they wished. Finally, they had to mark in a list of twelve potential goals of entrepreneurs three important and typical goals. Results indicated that in both the French and the Polish samples the economy was primarily distinguished into the state sector and the company sector. In the French sample, in addition the private household as a consumption unit was important. Regarding the structure of social representation, the French students reported more and presumably more complex connections between the economic concepts. This was interpreted with the limited experience of the market system among the Polish students at the time of study.

4.1.3 Social Representations about Poverty and Unemployment

Lay theories about economic phenomena in general, and particularly about individual wealth, poverty and job loss, are often intertwined with a belief in a just world. According to the theory on **belief in a just world** (Lerner, 1980), people have a need to assume they live in a world that is just and where outcomes are not determined by random events. The world is seen as 'just' when there is a connection between the actions of persons and the fate they encounter. A just world is one where people get what they deserve, and where they deserve what they get (Montada & Lerner, 1998).

Bénabou and Tirole (2006) modelled the connection between a belief in a just world and the support for different redistribution politics and the perception of the poor. Bastounis et al. (2004) collected data in eight nations and found a positive correlation between belief in a just world, internal locus of control and satisfaction with the economy. In a follow-up study (Allen, Ng & Leiser, 2005), a positive correlation between belief in a just world, satisfaction with the economy and the level of modernisation in the respective country was found. In each of these studies, furthermore, a negative correlation between just-world beliefs and the support for social security was found. The negative attitude towards social welfare from the state seems to be based on attributions. The need for support is attributed to individuals' inability to improve their situation on their own. Consequently, disadvantaged groups and people with lower abilities are particularly stigmatised.

Research on laypeople's explanations of poverty goes back a long time. Already in 1945, in a study by the US Opinion Research Survey, respondents were asked about the sources of poverty. The majority thought that poverty had internal causes: poor people would lack initiative and engagement, and they would have a weak character or little endurance. External causes, such as economic, political or educational differences were mentioned less often. In 1977, the European Community commissioned a study in different countries about the perceived causes of poverty. In that study again, poverty was mostly attributed to individualistic causes (e.g., laziness, lack of motivation) and fatalistic causes (e.g., bad luck), but less to societal and structural causes (Furnham, 1988). However, a more recent study conducted in the USA found different patterns: Hunt (2004) showed that laypeople attribute wealth to individualistic causes, but poverty to structural causes. This is interpreted against the background of the 'American Dream' where it is assumed that competent and motivated people are able to improve their economic standing, and poverty is attributed to the social system. In general, attributions seem to be heterogeneous between population groups: Feagin (1975) and Hunt (2004) reported differences between ethnic groups, religions, age groups, income groups and education groups.

Lay explanations of economic welfare and poverty also seem to depend on the respective economic and political situation of the country, the religion and the prevailing ideology. In a study by Hayati and Karami (2005) conducted in Iran, farmers mostly reported structural aspects such as a negligent government, too few opportunities for work, discrimination, etc. as causes for poverty. Similarly, in a study with students from Lebanon, structural attributions were in the majority. This was explained by political and economic crises and social change in these countries (Abouchedid & Nasser, 2001). Finally, changes in the general economic situation influence lay explanations, as shown for example by Roland-Lévy, Pappalardo Boumelki and Guillet (2010) in their study on social representations of credit and debt in the financial crisis of 2008.

When studies examine lay theories about unemployment, they mostly focus on subjective causes of unemployment. For example, in one study conducted in Austria (Kirchler, 1993a), participants were asked what they see as the most important reasons for unemployment. Among the 234 named reasons, a large portion (overall 37.3%) concerned personal characteristics of the unemployed person. One part of these reasons concerned missing work motivation, lack of interest, missing endurance, negative work attitudes, dissatisfaction, alcoholism, illness or being too old (18.9%). A second part concerned missing mobility, narrow job aspirations or missing flexibility (6.3%). A third part concerned insufficient training (2.6%) and lacking the willingness to be retrained to counter problems arising from too many academics or too few skilled workers in the job market (9.5%). All these answers indicate internal attributions and a belief in a just world. In contrast, only 26.8% of the named reasons for unemployment concerned the management and restructuring projects within companies. Also, only 23% concerned the economic and political situation, such as inflation, reduction in demand or working hours regulations.

A related study conducted with experts – employees in the Public Employment Service who often have direct contact with unemployed persons – showed similar results (Kirchler, 1993a). The fifty-seven respondents named 537 reasons. A large proportion of 66% of reasons concerned personal problems (mental or cognitive disabilities, age, physical disabilities, motivational problems, etc.). Between 10% and 13%, respectively, concerned problems with social integration, problems within the company or problems with the economic and political situation. On the one hand, it is not surprising that these employees primarily named personal problems as the reasons for unemployment, given that in their daily work they are confronted with individual unemployed persons and not with the general economic situation. On the other hand, it can be problematic that the picture of individual responsibility becomes reinforced this way.

Unemployed people can be a source of unease. On the one hand, their situation demands empathy and help; on the other hand, there may be doubt about individual or collective reasons for being unemployed. One possible reason to distance oneself from the adverse fate of the unemployed, and to escape their demands for help, is to attribute the reasons to the unemployed person (instead of to the economic or societal situation). Through individualising the problem, blame for being unemployed can be put on the victims. Unemployment becomes a self-inflicted problem, and the responsibility for its consequences and its solution is put on the unemployed themselves. In one study, such mechanisms were found very clearly: Kirchler (1993a) asked respondents from seven different occupations about their social representations of unemployment and unemployed persons. Entrepreneurs, blue-collar workers, white-collar workers, public servants, students, housewives and unemployed persons were asked to describe a typical representative of their own group and of each of the other groups. It is well established from work in social identity research (Tajfel, 1981) that members of a group (or social category) attribute more positive characteristics to members of their own group than to members of other groups. They usually also see their own group more positively than the group is seen by outsiders. Accordingly, it can be assumed that respondents describe a typical representative of their own group positively, and representatives of other groups more negatively. Following this hypothesis, entrepreneurs should describe the typical entrepreneur as positive, workers the typical worker, and unemployed persons the typical unemployed.

However, results indicate worrying differences between the unemployed and the other groups. First, in line with previous research (e.g., Jahoda, 1982; Wacker, 1983), unemployed persons were described more negatively than other groups. Second, the typical unemployed was described negatively by all groups, even by the unemployed themselves. In spite of being affected by unemployment themselves, unemployed people devalued the social category of the unemployed. Entrepreneurs, blue- and white-collar workers and public servants each described a typical representative of their own group better than it was described by all others. While students and housewives at least described a typical representative of their own group positively, the unemployed described the typical unemployed person particularly negatively. These results suggest that the unemployed cannot identify with their situation and with their companions in misfortune. In contrast, they differentiate between themselves and other unemployed persons – they experience their own unemployment as being externally caused, but blame other unemployed persons for having caused their situation themselves (e.g., by having too high demands, by being not flexible enough or by not being willing to work; Kirchler, 1993a). Such low identification with one's own social category is likely to hinder solidarity and effective representation of the interests of unemployed groups.

A theoretical explanation why the unemployed rarely form groups to advocate their interests can be found in social identity theory and in social categorisation theory (Tajfel, 1978, 1981; Tajfel & Turner, 1979; Turner, Hogg, Oakes, Reicher & Wetherell, 1987; for short summaries see e.g., Petersen & Six, 2008). **Social categorisation theory** builds on findings from cognitive psychology that information about persons and objects is organised in knowledge structures, and cognitively represented in schemata. For forming such schemata, categorisation is important. For example, people can be categorised as good or bad, friendly or unfriendly, etc. Processes of social categorisation help to structure social events and therefore offer a basis for actions. Research has shown that, under certain circumstances, similarities within a category (**assimilation effects**) and differences between categories (**contrast effects**) are perceived as more pronounced than they actually are. For example, members of a social group or social category often overestimate similarities among group members and the differences from other groups. In particular, members of positively evaluated groups (e.g., groups with high social status) identify with their group and tend towards devaluation of other groups.

According to **social identity theory**, people strive for a satisfactory self-concept and high self-esteem. One part of the self-concept is determined by membership in groups – this part is called social identity. Social identity therefore arises from categorisation processes in which the social environment is divided into 'own' and 'other' environment. A positive social identity arises when individuals identify with their own group and this group fares positively on relevant dimensions compared to other groups. In contrast, a negative social identity arises if one's own group is evaluated negatively in these comparison processes. Accordingly, groups or social classes with low status – those being subordinated to other groups in a social system (e.g., unemployed in society) – cannot provide their members with positive social identity. In such cases, an individual can try to achieve change through social mobility or social change, by reducing identification with their group, or by trying to move to a positively evaluated group. Specifically, Brown (1988) listed the following opportunities: (a) leaving the group (e.g., members of an ethnic group who want to be seen as members of another group); (b) limiting comparisons to other subordinate groups (e.g., blue-collar workers comparing themselves with unskilled workers); (c) changing the meaning of comparison dimensions (e.g., introducing new values, rituals or norms such as in punk subculture); (d) directly attacking the dominant group (e.g., feminist activists). In the case of unemployed persons, one way to protect social identity is by not identifying with the category of 'unemployed' in the first place.

4.1.4 Social Representations about Money and Currency

Studies on lay theories about money and currency were predominantly conducted in connection with the introduction of the euro in the countries of the European Union, 1 January 1999 virtually, and 1 January 2002 as cash. As an example, some findings from a Europe-wide study by Kirchler, el Sehity and Kulich (2004) are described here. In 2001 and 2002, over 2,700 participants reported free associations to their previous national currency and to the euro. Social representations of the euro were examined in both structure and content. In terms of structure, in all countries these associations became considerably more compact over time – fewer distinct associations were reported as the euro became more familiar. Also, the distinction between the core elements of the social representation ('new currency', 'European currency') and the peripheral elements became more pronounced (el Sehity, Kirchler & Muehlbacher, 2003). In terms of content, the results nicely illustrate the two processes in the development of a new social representation. Anchoring processes of the social representation were found in comparison to another currency, the US dollar. In 2002, some of the attributes of that global currency became available for the euro (e.g., international competition, globalisation, capitalism). This indicates that respondents were able to imagine the euro in analogy to the dollar. In addition, associations to the euro (e.g., new, modern, future, European) were contrasted with the previous national currencies (e.g., old, traditional, history, cultural). Objectification processes were found in the appearance of neologisms. In German-speaking countries, the term 'Teuro' appeared, being a combination of 'teuer' (German for 'expensive') and 'euro'. This term appeared in the media as early as 2000, but since 2002 has symbolised the societal consensus that the introduction of the euro brought price increases. What was first an unclear economic meaning of a new currency was reduced to a more clear – if negative – meaning.

Social representations of money can contribute to a better understanding of people's attitudes towards innovations, such as the introduction of a new currency or new payment methods. In one study conducted in Austria before the euro introduction, respondents reported their attitudes towards the euro and provided free associations. The results indicate that euro opponents and euro supporters had qualitatively different social representations. Supporters primarily named economic and political advantages (e.g., stability, transparency, stimulating the economy and political union). Opponents primarily named negative and more emotional concepts (e.g., unfairness, economic disadvantages and loss of national autonomy). The findings also showed that social identity was important: those respondents who strongly saw themselves as 'Austrians' particularly saw the euro as a threat to identity (Meier & Kirchler, 1998). Another study examined why consumers may be hesitant to accept the technical possibility of having a budget stored on the chip of their ATM card (also termed 'electronic purse'). In that survey, respondents were asked to draw connections between different payment methods (e.g., cash, electronic purse) and political, economic and psychological concepts (e.g., taxes, government, work, risk, trust, control). The results, illustrated in Figure 4.3, showed that the 'electronic purse' was mainly connected to mistrust and loss of control. This was interpreted as partly explaining consumers' resistance to using this new payment method (Penz, Meier-Pesti & Kirchler, 2004).

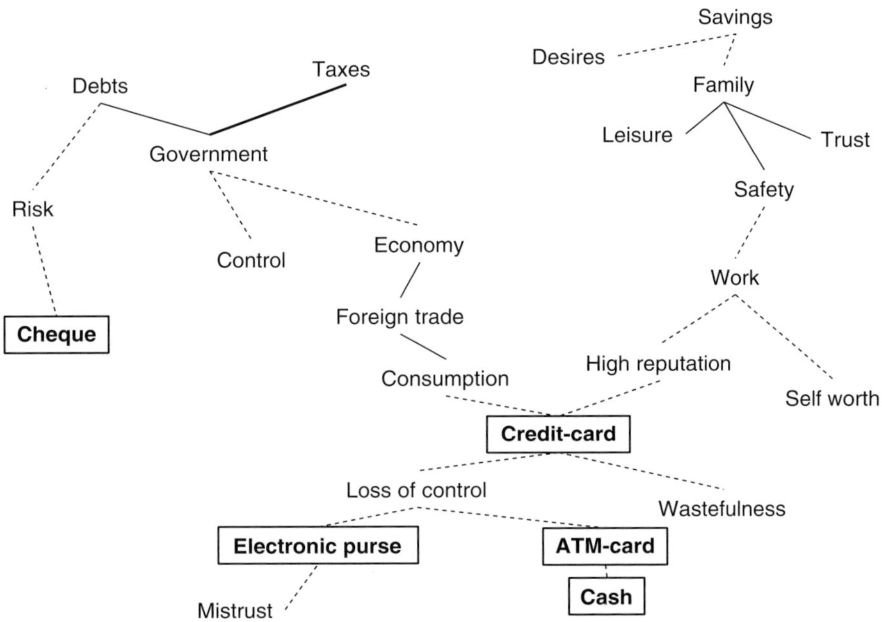

Figure 4.3 Conceptual network of associations (Penz, Meier-Pesti & Kirchler, 2004, p. 783)

4.2 Economic Knowledge

When making economic decisions, people rely partly on their lay theories and partly on their knowledge. As shown above, lay theories structure people's views and consequently highlight which elements are considered relevant and how they are seen as related. Clearly, it is relevant to have knowledge and understanding of these elements. Such an understanding is linked with cognitive prerequisites that develop with age, such as abstract thinking or considering another person's perspective.

4.2.1 Development of Economic Understanding

Knowledge about the economy and an understanding of economic topics are based on development processes and socialisation. Pre-school children know very little about production and distribution of goods, about demand and supply, or about other economic activities. With an increase in age, understanding develops slowly. By age 14, children begin to have a differentiated knowledge of the economy.

Jean Piaget (1896–1980) proposed a theory about human cognitive development. This theory is also very useful to describe the development of economic understanding. A summary about the theory by Jean Piaget is given here following Montada (1995) and Gillibrand, Lam and O'Donnell (2011). Piaget assumed that cognitive development is a process serving to establish and to maintain a balance between individual and environment. Knowledge can only be gained through the interaction with an object. These interactions can be either concrete or imagined and lead to mental transformations. Each interaction is an act of adaptation, understood as a fluid state of equilibrium between the adaptation of the environment to the individual (termed **assimilation**) and the adaptation of the individual to the environment (termed **accommodation**). As an example, consider a situation when a person encounters a new, unknown object. Assimilation means that the person tries to fit the new object into the available cognitive schemata. Through the interaction with the object, the person develops a deeper understanding and a differentiated view. Accommodation refers to these changes in the cognitive schemata.

Cognitive development in the sense of Piaget is an increasing balance between assimilation and accommodation between individual and environment. It goes along with generalisation, differentiation and coordination of the corresponding cognitive schemata and structures. Cognitive development progresses from a global state to a cognitive structure that is organised in a differentiated way, is flexible, is consistent over time, and allows logical thinking. Starting from the structure of cognitive schemata, Piaget proposed a **cognitive-developmental theory** with four developmental phases:

1 **Sensorimotor intelligence**. This phase (from birth to approximately 2 years of age) is characterised by first reflexive reactions shortly after birth, by first motoric habits, by the linking of means and ends, and by active experimenting. Children in this age group make their first spontaneous 'inventions' and they internalise sensorimotor schemata. Children develop a differentiation between causes and consequences, ideas of experimentation, and mental representations about results of own actions.

2 **Preoperational thought**. This phase (between 2 and 7 years) is characterised by the development of internalisation – the ability to copy objects and actions in the environment to a mental representation and to develop symbols. Language is an important prerequisite for this. Thinking during this phase is characterised by egocentrism, by focusing, by rigidity, by realism and by irreversibility. During this phase, higher cognitive performance is limited by two factors. On the one hand, the internalisation of objects is comparable to a copy process where only the concrete aspects remain. On the other hand, mental operations on different aspects cannot be made simultaneously (or quickly sequentially). The following task illustrates the limits of thinking during this phase. Children were shown a string with a total of twenty wooden beads – seventeen black and three white. To make sure that the children were able to distinguish between the different beads, they had to show to the researchers, by turns, the black beads, the white beads and all wood beads. In a next step, the children were asked whether the string contains more black beads or more wood beads (black and white). Most children answered that there were more black beads. This is explained by the process they used: They start with the black beads and compare them with the remaining white beads. The term 'wood beads' changes its meaning and is used for the remaining white beads, resulting in contradictions. Children in this phase are not able to abstract to a more general level, remember the number of black beads and compare it mentally to the number of all beads. Thinking is limited in flexibility and focused on the concrete situation. It also is not possible to understand classes of objects that are nested, such as sets and subsets.

3 **Concrete operational thought**. This phase (between 7 and 11 years) is characterised by the loss of egocentrism. Thinking reaches a system of coordinated and reversible transformations. Mental operations in this phase are still bound to concrete actions. However, they are less a copy of real objects because they are represented more abstractly. Different operations can now be conducted simultaneously, or at least sequentially and linked. As an example, the task with the wood beads can now be solved.

4 **Formal operations**. This phase (between 11 years and adulthood) is characterised by the independence of mental operations of the concrete object. Children develop the ability to

reason formally, based on hypothetical assumptions. At this phase, rational decisions become possible. Thinking is no longer limited to the information given – it is possible to go beyond it.

The economic socialisation of children seems to fit well with Piaget's theory. Burris (1983) interviewed children in three age groups (4–5, 7–8 and 10–12 years) about their knowledge on goods, values and prices, work and property. Regarding goods, children in the youngest age group showed only a very limited understanding. For example, a baby would be a good, whereas a cow would not be a good because it is too large and cannot be taken along in the car. In this age group, buying and selling were understood as physical actions – goods are owned and transferred in a physical sense. In the middle age group, children were reasoning with social norms: for example, a baby would not be a good because it cannot be bought or because buying would violate existing laws. Regarding value and price, children in the youngest age group answered that larger goods would cost more than smaller goods – for example, a watch would cost more than a diamond. Children in the middle age group answered that the price depends on the usefulness of the good: a watch would cost more than a diamond or a book because a watch tells the time, whereas a book can only be read and there are very few uses for a diamond. They also used other concrete aspects as criteria for price, such as the durability, or how much fun the goods are. Children in the oldest group, in contrast, considered how much effort is needed to produce the goods, and answered that price depends on the material used (e.g., glass, metal, wood) and the necessary steps in production. Based on these findings, Burris (1983) concluded that children's understanding develops from a diffuse and global knowledge to a differentiated knowledge about economic institutions and processes.

Very detailed explorations about the development of economic knowledge were conducted by Bombi, Berti and colleagues (e.g., Berti & Bombi, 1981; Berti, Bombi & De Beni, 1986). To summarise, they support the assumption that there are stages in knowledge acquisition that clearly correlate with children's age:

(a) Children of pre-school age know only diffuse terms that they cannot connect. For example, they do not know about the production of goods and see goods as something that is bought in a shop, and the shop owners previously bought it from other shops. Children know that money is needed to buy goods, but they see this as a ritual of the grown-ups. Money is seen as coming from the banks or from rich people who give it to others to perform these rituals. Their view of the economy distinguishes only between consumers on one side and sellers on the other side; transactions are an exchange of goods and money. Children in this stage showed an important characteristic of Piaget's preoperational thought by being unable to quantify and therefore not being able to set prices for goods.

(b) Children aged 6–7 understand that shop owners get their goods from producers. However, they mostly see producers as craftsmen who make new products from old ones – for example, children answered that new coffee cups were made from fragments of old cups, or new clothes from old rags. Regarding money, children in this age group understand that different banknotes have different values. However, they do not understand why customers receive change – often they assume this is so that people still have some money after a purchase. Children understand that most money comes from paid work. Children in this stage therefore have new elements in their knowledge (e.g., production, relation between money and work) and understand some rules about monetary transactions.

(c) Children aged 7–10 begin to draw a clear line between sellers and producers, and understand that these are linked through sales agents, wholesalers and shipping businesses.

Children know money and its value rather well and understand its meanings in buying and selling. However, they do not understand the concept of profit. They know that some goods are more expensive than others, but they assume that the price is exactly what the seller has paid for the good previously. They know that workers have bosses and that some people are entrepreneurs, but do not understand how bosses and entrepreneurs earn their money. In sum, children in this age group have a more complex and differentiated view of the economic system, but still seem to think in two distinct spheres – one including bosses, workers and wages, the other including buyers, sellers and producers. The connections between the two spheres are still unclear. This can be seen as a consequence of the concrete operational thought at this stage: abstracting beyond the immediate experience and connecting different spheres is not possible.

(d) Children aged 10–14 start to develop a clear and complete picture of basic economic concepts. Prices are now seen as depending on production effort, and it is understood that sellers need to claim higher prices than what they paid themselves. It also is now clearer how entrepreneurs earn money – by selling goods and services. Public institutions receive money from fees or taxes. Children now also understand that different occupations earn differently. In this stage, the most important development is the integration of the knowledge into a complex network. Even previously contradictory and heterogeneous information is connected and integrated (Berti & Bombi, 1981; Berti, et al. 1986).

Other work has highlighted asymmetries in understanding demand and supply in children aged 6–12 (Leiser & Halachmi, 2006). Children seem better to understand demand for goods than their supply and production. Leiser and Halachmi (2006) offer the following explanation. Children see the seller as the person who sets the price for a good. They know from experience that a customer asks how much something is and that the seller names the price. If demand increases, the seller can exploit the situation and raise the price; if demand decreases, the seller can lower the price. In other words, children see the reasons for price changes in a change in demand and a corresponding, well-considered decision by the seller. In contrast, if a change in supply occurs, customers cannot simply offer a different price, because – in the children's view – it is the seller who sets the price. Customers can only refrain from purchasing the good, or go to another store. Maybe the seller can reduce the price to win the customers back. This form of aggregated causality is more complex and more difficult to understand for children than a change in demand (Leiser, 1983).

Results as reported by Bombi, Berti and colleagues were confirmed in several studies in different countries (see *Journal of Economic Psychology, 4*, 1990). In Hong Kong, in several countries in Europe and North Africa, in Australia and in the USA, different stages of economic understanding were found, with fragmented knowledge becoming more detailed and correct with increasing age. However, these studies suggest that children in developing countries and economically deprived areas, and children from poorer families, seem to be quicker to reach a differentiated knowledge than children who do not know financial difficulties. This is particularly the case for handling of money and for trading. In a similar vein, children from rich families know little about poverty and economic problems in their countries. Johnson and Hagerman (2006) reported that these children mostly associate poverty with desolate living conditions or homelessness, but do not understand that there are 'working poor', that is, people being poor despite paid work.

Children who pursue economy-related activities (e.g., playing and trading with marbles, having to make do with their pocket money over a certain period of time) seem to have an advantage.

Cram and Ng (1994) showed that children who have opportunities to speak with others (e.g., the owner of a bus) about economic topics tend to have more differentiated knowledge. Some studies showed that trainings can be efficient to improve economic understanding in children. For example, Roos, Chiroro, van Coppenhagen and Smith (2005) conducted a study in Pretoria, South Africa, to determine the effectiveness of a one-week training programme. The goal was to improve children's knowledge and understanding of economic concepts such as money, income, saving and costs. Among other things, the programme included making collages with coins or role-plays where children had to buy something. A group of thirty-seven children, aged 4.5–6.5 years, participated in the programme. Economic knowledge and understanding were measured before and immediately after the programme, and one month later. Results indicated that younger children had poorer understanding than older children at all times, but that the understanding of economic concepts was improved considerably through the training. This and other studies suggest that it would be important to teach economic knowledge early on. However, as will be discussed later, the results on interventions for improving economic knowledge are mixed (e.g., Fernandes, Lynch & Netemeyer, 2014).

4.2.2 Development of Economic Motives

As shown above, knowledge and understanding of economic topics develops with age, from concrete to abstract concepts. Another ability that develops with age is to see situations from the perspective of other people. Accordingly, with age, children's thinking becomes less egocentric. More and more, motives develop from pure selfishness towards altruistic cooperation. Fehr, Bernhard and Rockenbach (2008) studied children aged 3–8 years regarding their altruistic and egoistic preferences in the distribution of resources. In several economic games, children had the opportunity to anonymously distribute sweets between themselves and another child. They could either give themselves and the other child equal amounts of sweets, or they could choose an unequal distribution. Each child participated in three experimental conditions and played with an anonymous partner from the same or a different kindergarten or school. The first condition studied a prosocial motive. Children could choose between an egalitarian distribution (1:1) where both received sweets, and an unequal distribution where only they themselves received a sweet (1:0). Prosocial behaviour would be indicated by the egalitarian distribution; choosing the unequal distribution would not bring a benefit for oneself. Egoistic children would not benefit from disadvantaging their partner. Even when everyone would be egoistic an equal split between the choices could be expected, with 50% choosing 1:1 and 50% choosing 1:0. The second condition studied an envy motive. Children could choose between an egalitarian distribution (1:1) and an unequal distribution favouring the partner without costs for oneself (1:2). Here, if children choose the egalitarian distribution, they enviously ensure that their partner has no advantage. The third condition studied an equality motive. Children could choose between an egalitarian distribution (1:1) and a situation where they keep everything for themselves and give nothing to the partner (2:0). Egoistic children would not share the sweets, but keep them. The results, shown in Figure 4.4, indicate that younger children acted more egoistically than older children. Among the children aged 3 and 4, egoism was the dominant motive – they maximised their own advantage and did not seem to care about their partners' well-being. Also, children aged 5–6 predominantly behaved egoistically. However, children aged 7–8 showed a different pattern: a clear majority chose an egalitarian distribution and therefore showed a care about their partners' well-being. In addition, Fehr et al. (2008) could show that children favoured their ingroup: they gave more to children from

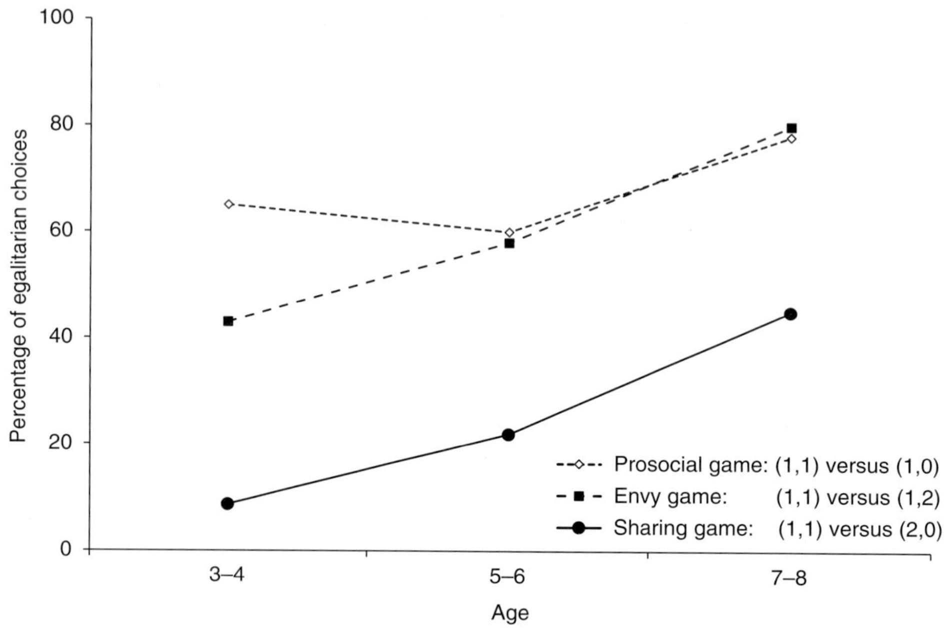

Figure 4.4 Relative frequency of egalitarian choices in three games (Fehr, Bernhard & Rockenbach, 2008, p. 1080)

their own kindergarten or school than to children from a different institution. Similar results were reported by Gummerum, Hanoch, Keller, Parsons and Hummel (2010): with increasing age, children preferred an equal distribution of resources. In addition, girls gave more than boys and therefore were less egoistic.

It seems that prosocial behaviour needs to be learned. Sutter and Kocher (2007) conducted trust games with participants ranging in age between 8 and 80 years, and found that trust and trustworthiness increase with age in a rather exact linear relation. Trust may only pay off among adults. In the trust game, one participant receives a budget and can decide to give a part to their partner. That part is multiplied by some factor and given to the other person, who then can decide whether to return something or not. Sutter and Kocher found that younger children act rather egoistically, in line with the model of *homo economicus*, and therefore trust is not rewarded. However, it may be that the reason is not intentional egoism, but more an inability to understand the complex interplay of cooperation. Only with increasing age may children understand moral values and the value of cooperation.

4.2.3 Development of Economic Behaviour

Children and adolescents are important economic actors. Consequently, industry has a strong interest in guiding and influencing their preferences. This becomes apparent in TV-spots specifically designed to attract children's attention as potential buyers or in the fact that all large banks offer specific accounts for adolescents. Videogames, just as one example, bring in enormous profits for producers. Other examples are the toy and fashion industries that clearly target and shape trends in the consumer culture of children and adolescents. In a classical statement, children and adolescents were described as important for marketing in three ways: 'all children are considered a current market, a market of influencers, and all certainly are viewed as future consumers' (McNeal, 1992, p. 15).

First, children form a 'current market' according to McNeal because they are potential buyers with financial opportunities. Children often receive regular pocket money. In addition, they receive extra financial rewards on birthdays, for good school grades or for helping in the household. From this budget, children save a part and spend the other part. Regarding the prevalence of pocket money, Furnham (2001) surveyed British parents about their attitudes towards pocket money. About 90% of respondents said that they think that children should receive pocket money already at an age of 6.5 years. Similar results were found by Furnham and Kirkcaldy (2000) for Germany. A majority of respondents (80%) also asserted that pocket money should be given on a regular basis, whereas only 10% suggested that pocket money should only be given when currently needed. These findings indicate that a large proportion of children have at least some money at their disposal for potential spending.

However, in the surveys by Furnham and colleagues, many parents (75%) also stated that children should be encouraged to save. Otto, Schots, Westerman and Webley (2006) explored saving strategies used by children aged 6, 9 and 12 years. Results showed that the older children are not necessarily better savers, but they use different strategies. In the study, children first selected a toy they would want to have. They then played a board game with the goal of saving up a certain number of bonus points for this toy. The game consisted of six sections. In each section, children received some pocket money in the form of bonus points. During the game, they should consider income and expenses. They had opportunities to spend bonus points in shops offering tempting sweets and toys. They also had the opportunity to deposit bonus points in a bank. In one variant, the children did not know exactly how long the game would last. Results here showed that 6-year-old children spent more on toys than 12-year-olds, and that 12-year-olds put more points in the bank than younger children. However, contrary to expectations, no differences between 6-year-olds and 9-year-olds were found in saving success: both were successful in reaching the goal. In another variant, children did know the exact duration of the game, and additionally there were either low or high variations in income over the rounds. Results here showed that older children were not much more successful in saving than younger children. Differences were only found in the strategies used. Whereas older children saved up a buffer against potential losses, younger children were particularly careful not to spend their bonus points.

Second, children form a 'market of influencers' according to McNeal (1992) because they are an active part in purchase decision processes within the family. They directly and indirectly influence their parents' decisions. On a methodological note, it is important to see that existing studies – if they considered children at all – mostly aimed at studying the relative influence of children on decisions of their parents. Usually, the mothers were interviewed. Only rarely, the triads of mother, father and child are interviewed (e.g., Tansuhaj & Foxman, 1990), although it is acknowledged that this would give a more detailed picture of decision-making in the family than by interviewing just one person. The main reasons are the high effort and difficulties in data analysis when information from three persons is available. In addition, when interviewing younger children, specific methods are necessary that are suited to their cognitive development. Findings from the existing studies showed that the relative influence of children depended on product category, age of children, family structure and educational style.

In classical studies, Ward and Wackman (1973) used questionnaires in which mothers of 5–12-year-old children reported how often their children influenced a decision and what they did to get their way. They found that when children wish for something, the product category is an important factor in whether these wishes are followed. For example, when deciding on cereals, snacks, sweets or juices, 55% of mothers followed their children's wishes. However, when deciding on other food, such as bread or coffee, only 9% did so. For durables that directly concern the children, such as bicycles, toys or clothes, 29% of mothers reported following the wishes of their children. Szybillo and colleagues (Szybillo & Sosanie, 1977; Szybillo, Sosanie & Tenenbein, 1977) studied the influence of children above 5 years of age on decisions about restaurant type (fast-food or conventional) and family outings. They found that often these decisions were made jointly between parents and children, but also found dyadic coalitions (e. g., mother–child or father–child). Children had most influence in the choice of fast-food restaurants.

Older children are given more influence than younger children, and have influence also in areas that go beyond their direct interest sphere (e.g., Frideres, 1973). Ebster, Wagner and Neumüller (2009) studied the influence of children and adolescents on the purchases of their parents directly in the store. They corroborated the finding that age of children and their influence is strongly correlated. In addition, they showed that placement of product in the store is important: if products were placed at eye level of the children and children had high freedom of movement, they more often asked for a specific product. Adolescents are assumed to have a larger area of influence (Burns & Gentry, 1990). These opportunities are used differently depending on interest and involvement (Beatty & Talpade, 1994).

While most studies implicitly assume a 'traditional family' consisting of father, mother and children, Foxman, Tansuhaj and Ekstrom (1989a) highlight the family structure as an important determinant of children's influence. Ahuja and Stinson (1993) show that children's influence in single-parent families is not generally higher, but that there are huge differences within this family form. They found differences in influence depending on product type, decision stage, age of oldest child or sex role orientation of the mother. Regarding educational style, adolescents profit from a style that aims at fostering children's independence (Foxman, Tansuhaj & Ekstrom, 1989b).

Which strategies do children and adolescents use to reach their goals? In a classical study reported here to demonstrate the research approach, Atkin (1978) observed children aged 3–12 years and their parents when buying breakfast cereals in a supermarket. Although younger children were not yet allowed to decide on their own, they still influenced their parents' purchases. In 66% of cases, children took the initiative and begged or demanded the preferred cornflakes. In 42% of cases, parents obliged.

Age is an important determinant of influence strategies. Buijzen and Valkenburg (2008) observed the communication between parents and children (up to 12 years) in supermarkets and toy stores in the Netherlands. They found that influence attempts and insisting increased to early school age and decreased afterwards. Isler, Popper and Ward (1987) found that children between 3 and 11 years of age tend simply to ask for products they want. Adolescents, on the other hand, seem to use a whole repertoire of influence tactics. Based on in-depth interviews with one hundred families, Palan and Wilkes (1997) developed a comprehensive classification system for adolescents' influence tactics and parents' responses. This system contains bargaining, persuasion, emotional and request tactics mentioned by both the adolescents and the parents. In addition, parents mentioned expert strategies (i.e., informing the child about certain customer-relevant aspects), legitimation strategies (i.e., a purchase is not possible due to financial restrictions) and directive strategies (i.e., pointing out the price–performance relation, or sending the child to the other parent for permission). Regarding the effectiveness of strategies, adolescents saw 'money deals' (offering to take over part of the costs), reasoning and direct asking as effective. Begging, referring to other children and anger were seen as

Table 4.1 Adolescent influence strategy effectiveness (percentages for sample size $n = 100$) (Palan & Wilkes, 1997, p. 167)

	Informant		
	Adolescent	Mother	Father
Most effective strategies	Money deals (20%), reasoning (17%), direct ask (15%)	Reasoning (18%), reasonable request (14%), other deals (11%)	Reasoning (13%), other deals (12%), direct ask (10%)
Least effective strategies	Begging (19%), everyone else (13%), anger (12%)	Whining (19%), everyone else (15%), anger (14%)	Begging (18%), anger (17%), whining (13%), demands (13%)

ineffective. This view was rather consistent with that of their parents. Table 4.1 shows examples for the most effective and ineffective strategies as seen by the adolescents, mothers and fathers.

The studies above referred to direct influence. However, children's views are not always heard. It might be that their direct influence is limited to certain decisions and overall small (Filiatrault & Ritchie, 1980). However, children can influence decisions indirectly. For example, when the parents disagree, the child's opinion can tip the scales one way or the other. In conflicts between parents, direct or indirect coalitions with children are frequent influence tactics used (Kirchler, 1993b). In particular, mothers win influence through coalitions: in the studies by Kirchler (1989), children form coalitions with the mother about three times as often as with the father.

To summarise, children play a relevant role as influencers in purchase decisions in the family. Their influence can be direct or indirect, and varies with age, product type and family characteristics. A better understanding of the interaction between parents and children in purchase decisions therefore seems of great importance for consumer research.

4.2.4 Financial Literacy

Knowing about economic concepts and the subjective understanding of economic phenomena provide an important basis for financial decisions. In the previous sections, we showed that economic knowledge is closely linked to cognitive development and age. In this section, we will examine concepts and findings on financial literacy of adults.

Financial literacy is the ability to understand and use financial concepts (e.g., Servon & Kaestner, 2008). These concepts include, for example, percentage calculation, interest rates or inflation. The main idea is that people need to be able to understand the basic building blocks behind economic phenomena, similar to knowing the letters and meanings of words for being able to read. One of the challenges to the study of financial literacy is, however, the broad range of conceptualisations and measures used in different studies: Huston (2010) found that 72% of the studies examined did not give a definition of financial literacy, and 47% equated financial literacy with financial knowledge.

Studies on financial literacy often find very low levels of financial literacy in the general population (for overviews see, e.g., Lusardi & Mitchell, 2007a). For example, in a large-scale survey in the USA among adults aged 51–56 years, only about 18% were able to calculate compound interest correctly (see Table 4.2). For that age group, the results can be considered troublesome because they are rather close to their retirement age and soon will have to rely on what saving choices they made (Lusardi & Mitchell, 2007a). In other countries, similar findings are reported. For

Table 4.2 Financial literacy among early baby boomers (adapted from Lusardi & Mitchell, 2007a, p. 37)

	Correct	Incorrect	Do not know
'If the chance of getting a disease is 10%, how many people out of 1,000 would be expected to get the disease?'	83.5%	13.2%	2.8%
'If 5 people all have the winning number in the lottery and the prize is 2 million dollars, how much will each of them get?'	55.9%	34.4%	8.7%
'Let's say you have 200 dollars in a savings account. The account earns 10% interest per year. How much would you have in the account at the end of two years?'	17.8%	78.5%	3.2%

example, in a large-scale household survey in the Netherlands, Van Rooij, Lusardi and Alessie (2011) found that levels of basic and sophisticated financial literacy are rather low.

The level of financial literacy is related to socio-economic factors. Less knowledge in financial matters was found to be related to being underprivileged (e.g., low education), to being female and to belonging to a minority group. On the other hand, low financial literacy is linked with unfavourable economic outcomes (e.g., less saving, poor retirement arrangements). This can be considered as a potential vicious circle because underprivileged groups start from a disadvantaged economic situation and may also make poor decisions (Lusardi & Mitchell, 2007a).

Financial literacy has been found to be correlated with several relevant economic behaviours. For example, Lusardi and Mitchell (2007b) found that financial literacy is related to retirement planning. Van Rooij et al. (2011) also found that levels of financial knowledge had a robust relationship with retirement planning, even after controlling for a number of potential other explanations. People with higher financial literacy were more likely to plan for retirement. In addition, when considering economic education in their socialisation, the authors suggest that more financial literacy leads to more planning and not vice versa. Financial literacy was also found to be related to credit card debt among students (Norvilitis et al., 2006), consumer debt (Gathergood, 2012), and incurring higher costs on credit card borrowing and mortgage (Huston, 2012).

Financial literacy can come from different sources. Shim, Barber, Card, Xiao and Serido (2010) found that financial knowledge of first-year students was related to direct teaching by their parents, financial education in high school and work experience during high school. In many countries, explicit financial education programmes have been established over the last decades. However, evidence on their effectiveness is mixed: while programmes with specific goals (e.g., matched-savings programmes) show positive effects, programmes intended to enhance general financial literacy show less clear effects (see Braunstein & Welch, 2002 for a review). As a recent meta-analysis (Fernandes et al. 2014) shows, the average effect of interventions to improve financial literacy is significant but extremely small, explaining only 0.1% of variance in financial behaviours. At the same time, the findings confirm that measured financial literacy and financial behaviours are connected relatively strongly. Fernandes et al. (2014) suggest that 'just-in-time' education that is linked to specific behaviours could be more efficient.

Because financial literacy focuses mostly on knowledge, in recent years the concept of financial capability was introduced. **Financial capability** extends the focus and highlights behaviour, taking into consideration institutions and regulations (e.g., Johnson & Sherraden, 2007). It is argued that financial behaviour is influenced by three areas of financial capability: (1) knowledge and understanding, (2) skills and (3) confidence and attitudes (Kempson, Collard & Moore, 2005). Financial capability consists of financial knowledge and five further domains: (1) managing money – making ends meet: having little problem dealing with financial obligations; (2) managing money – keeping track: having an overview of expenses; (3) planning ahead: being future oriented; (4) choosing products: deciding reasonably in financial matters; and (5) staying informed: seeking information on financial products and changes in the economy (Atkinson, McKay, Kempson & Collard, 2006). As becomes clear from these domains, financial capability has a more skill-oriented view.

Even if consumers have sufficient information, they do not necessarily act on their knowledge. De Meza, Irlenbusch and Reyniers (2008) argued that variations in financial capability are less a matter of information, but more a matter of psychological differences. In their report, the authors identify several biases hindering the transformation of knowledge into goal-directed behaviour: mental accounting, information overload, status quo bias, procrastination, regret and loss aversion. Consequently, De Meza et al. (2008) argue that financial capability programmes should go beyond education and take into account such biases. For example, Antonides, de Groot and van Raaij (2011) examined the relationship between mental accounting and financial management in the household. Results from a large survey conducted in the Netherlands indicated that financial management and having an overview of one's finances were positively related to mental budgeting (e.g., separate different categories of expenditure). Taking into account the concept of mental budgeting could therefore improve financial capability programmes. On the one hand, education in financial knowledge could be beneficial when behaviour is under cognitive control. On the other hand, it may be less efficient for behaviour that is limited by external circumstances or for more habitual or automatic behaviour (Fernandes et al. 2014; Lynch & Wood, 2006).

4.3 Money

Money has a central position in the economy. From an economic point of view, money has a number of functions: (a) it is a medium of exchange and avoids the problems of a barter economy such as finding a willing transaction partner; (b) it is a unit of account to summarise and to simplify the value of goods; (c) it is a standard of deferred payment and allows us to transfer goods now and pay for them in the future; and (d) it is a store of value and allows us to receive payment now but to postpone purchase (Lewis, Webley & Furnham, 1995). Consequently, money is assumed to be desired for three reasons: (a) transactional motives (e.g., planned purchases); (b) precautionary motives (e.g., being prepared for unplanned circumstances); and (c) speculative motives (e.g., buying stocks to make profit; Lewis et al., 1995).

4.3.1 Subjective Meanings of Money

Besides the objective functions of money in an economy, individuals have subjective views on money. This starts with the understanding of the concept. Snelders, Hussein, Lea and Webley (1992) highlight that 'money' is a polymorphous concept, i.e., a concept that is not clearly defined and distinguishable. Money as a concept is understood through social exchange and through experience. It is described by different terms and is made vivid through examples. Snelders et al. (1992) found that UK participants reported 1 and 20 pound notes and 5 pence coins as typical examples for 'money'; 90% saw a cheque as typical, 72% a savings book and 68% a diamond. Coins and banknotes were prototypical for the concept of money. Credit cards, cheques or foreign currencies were seen as further away from the definitional core. In an Italian study by Rumiati and Lotto (1996), similar results were found: banknotes were seen as typical for money, as well as coins, cheques or credit cards. Vouchers or phone cards were seen as less typical. The authors conclude that payment forms that are available immediately ('ready money') are prototypical for money. Payment forms where the bank is involved ('bank money') are less typical, and payment forms that replace money in some way ('money substitutes') are least typical. Lotto, Rubaltelli, Rumiati and Savadori (2006) studied social representations about money shortly after the changeover from the Italian lira to the euro. They assumed that those payment forms that are most often used are experienced as prototypical. The lira had a very different value scale than the euro, with 1 euro corresponding to approximately 2,000 lire. Previously, lira coins were not used, and banknotes were typical for money. With the changeover, the 1-euro coin became used more often. In this study, three different groups (students, bank employees and retailers) were asked to report how typical different coins, banknotes, cheques, stamps and vouchers are for the concept 'money'. In general, 1- and 2-euro coins and 10-euro, 20-euro and 50-euro banknotes were seen as typical, whereas other payment forms were seen as less typical. Differences between the three groups indicated that experts have a different representation of money than laypeople.

From a psychological perspective, money has several important functions. The available budget is an indicator of purchasing power and symbolises individual success, power and independence, and brings social respect and reputation. It brings opportunities to act. As the identity of people is tied to their actions and their possessions, the self is also defined over the money available. Belk (1988) and Dittmar (1992) see material possessions as 'extensions of the self' and money as a means to buy things or do something that is an expression of the self.

Money has different meanings for different people, and money attitudes can be measured in several ways. Furnham (1984) developed a questionnaire to measure the subjective meaning of money and discovered several psychological functions of money. Money is a form of power, it serves to win the affection of other people, and it gives security. Money is a way of gratification for success, but can also lead to excessive control, thriftiness and stinginess. Money can also be a source of envy. Yamauchi and Templer (1982) distinguished between three dimensions that describe how people think about money and how they manage it: security, retention and power/prestige. The security dimension describes being good at managing money versus the anxiety about having too few resources. Retention describes how easy it is to spend money. Power/prestige describes the degree to which money is associated with power, influence and prestige. In these dimensions, some gender differences were found. Men reported seeing money more as an expression of power and prestige than women did. Women, on the other hand, reported that they see money as less functional and less connected to their sense of self, but more important in comparison with other people. For women, money seems more relevant for the fulfilment of hedonic needs and pragmatic necessities. It is also a source of envy when relevant other persons have more financial resources than they themselves have (Dittmar, 1992; Prince, 1993). Tang, Tang and Luna-Arocas (2005) identified four different groups, so-called 'money profiles', based on participants' answers on the 'love for money' scale developed by the authors.

(a) Money-repellent individuals (15.5%) had a negative attitude towards money and in general thought of money as evil. This group showed low intrinsic and extrinsic satisfaction with their job, low self-esteem from their job and low levels of needs satisfaction.

(b) Apathetic money managers (31.1%) do not think that money can adequately represent their success and their self-esteem. This group strived to manage their (usually low) income reasonably and thought that they could achieve an appropriate living standard; they were satisfied in their needs and described themselves as happy.
(c) Careless money admirers (30.2%) had a positive attitude towards money, strived to earn a lot of money, but managed their money rather carelessly. Their satisfaction was average.
(d) Achieving money worshipers (23.2%) appreciated money and had very positive attitudes to it. They also strived to earn a lot and managed their money carefully. Their satisfaction, job-related self-esteem and self-actualisation motives were high.

These findings show that money can acquire very different meanings for individuals. These meanings vary across groups and are related to other aspects of life.

The meanings of money clearly change with context. Heyman and Ariely (2004) differentiated between 'monetary markets' and 'social markets'. Monetary markets are situations based on economic exchanges in which money is suitable as a medium of exchange. Here, effort (e.g., willingness to help lifting a sofa) is low when compensation is low and high when compensation is high. Social markets are situations based on social exchanges in which money is unsuitable. Here, effort is high irrespective of compensation. The use of money is also restricted in certain situations. Among these situations are neighbourly help (Webley & Lea, 1993) or gifts to parents (Webley, Lea & Portalska, 1983). For some situations, people find it morally offensive even to consider putting a financial value to an exchange. These situations were labelled 'taboo trade-offs' (Fiske & Tetlock, 1997) and include selling human organs or selling one's loyalty to the home country. In specific cases, money is loaded with a moral connotation (e.g., money used for charitable donations versus money used for bribes) and treated with near-religious respect. Belk and Wallendorf (1990) used the term 'sacred usage' for such cases.

Money can also acquire symbolic values. Triggering these values can lead to changes in people's attitudes and behaviour. In a recent review, Vohs (2015) discusses existing work on money priming and suggests two major effects of being reminded of money in more or less obvious ways. On the one hand, money-related thoughts seem to make people less prosocial and interdependent. On the other hand, money-related thoughts seem to make people more performance-oriented.

4.3.2 Subjective Value of Money

How does money acquire a subjective value? Several theoretical approaches have been proposed (see, e.g., Lea & Webley, 2006 for an overview). One explanation comes from developmental theories. As shown above, these approaches highlight that the understanding of money and other economic concepts is linked to the cognitive development of children and adolescents. A second explanation comes from social-psychological theories. For example, in the **resource theory** by Foa and Foa (1974), money is one among several resources that people exchange in their interaction. Besides money, people exchange information, goods, services, status and love. A third explanation comes from learning theories. According to **operant conditioning theory** (Skinner, 1953), reinforcers are stimuli that increase the probability that a certain behaviour that was performed before the stimulus is performed again. Some stimuli can directly satisfy needs and are experienced positively; these are called primary reinforcers. Other stimuli are in the beginning experienced neutrally. However, through learning processes they can acquire a reinforcing quality and become secondary reinforcers. Money is one example of a secondary reinforcer. An initially neutral stimulus such as money can become a reinforcer in the following way. If a neutral stimulus is repeatedly followed by a primary reinforcer within a short time span, it becomes a secondary reinforcer. It now can be used in operant learning processes without a primary reinforcer (Herkner, 1993). Money is a generalised secondary reinforcer because it can cover different needs. Money can cover basic needs such as buying food against hunger and clothes against the cold. Money also can cover higher needs such as the desire for power, respect or success, or the possibility of controlling one's environment. The more acquiring and keeping of money have been rewarded in the past, the more an individual would value money. With an increase in wealth, one could assume that satiation effects occur: if people have fulfilled their deficit needs and move towards self-actualisation, people would see money as less important. However, expansion effects often occur: money can lose its function as a means to an end, and can become a motive of its own. Money can become an independent and intrinsic motive where more money strives for even more (Wiswede, 1991).

In a classical study by Bruner and Goodman (1947), the subjective value of money was measured via estimation of the size of coins. Children from poorer and richer families were first asked to estimate the diameter of cardboard circles (which had the same size as coins) and then the diameter of the respective coins. When estimating the size of the (worthless) cardboard circles, both children from poorer and richer families were equally good. However, when estimating the size of the coins, children from poorer families overestimated size much more than children from rich families. These results indicate that, for poorer children, the coins appeared more valuable and therefore were perceived as larger.

Not only the financial situation of a person, but also perceived inflation can influence the subjective value of money. For example, Lea (1981) found that coin sizes in the UK after the change to the decimal system were underestimated and they interpreted this as a consequence of high inflation. Leiser and Izak (1987) report an impressive study from Israel. In 1980, the Israeli currency was changed from the Israeli pound (IL) to the Israeli scheqel (IS = 10 IL). After a period of extremely high inflation rates, the currency was changed again in 1985 to new scheqel (NS, 1 NS = 1,000 IS). Participants were shown the current and the previous, now substituted, coins in a standardised size, and were asked to estimate the size of the real coins. Findings showed that the real size was significantly underestimated. Findings also suggested that it was not inflation as such that led to a loss in subjective value, but that inflation undermined the trust in the economy and the currency. Such a connection between inflation and trust of consumers was also documented in Strümpel and Katona (1983). Ostaszewski, Green and Myerson (1998) conducted a study in Poland on the subjective value of a future reward, expressed in either old zloty, new zloty or dollars. Keeping the objective value constant, the subjective value was smaller with old zloty because this currency was associated with high inflation.

Is all money treated equally? According to economic theory, it should be irrelevant from which source money or income is generated. Several studies, however, showed otherwise. Monetary rewards were valued more highly when they were ascribed to internal causes, such as own performance, than when ascribed to external causes such as luck or chance (Loewenstein & Issacharoff, 1994). Unexpected gains or '**windfall gains**' – for example money won in gambling – are spent more easily and invested more riskily than money earned through work (Arkes, Joyner, Pezzo, Nash, Siegel-Jacobs & Stone, 1994). Money earned through hard work as opposed to easy work is more likely to be kept for oneself: in a study by Muehlbacher and Kirchler (2009), participants contributed less to a public-good game when they received their budget through higher effort. One consequence of treating money differently depending on the source could be differences in tax evasion. According to prospect theory (Kahneman & Tversky, 1979), people become more risk seeking when they experience a loss situation. Do people who earned their money through hard work experience even more loss? Do they become more risk seeking when it comes to evading taxes? Following prospect theory and findings on sunk cost effects (Arkes & Blumer, 1985; Thaler, 1980), it can be assumed that hard work increases the value of money. Therefore, people in loss situations become more likely to take the risky decision to evade taxes. However, the opposite effect is also possible: if one has earned one's income through hard work, one expects at least a modest financial compensation. Such an aspiration level can serve as a criterion to simplify the decision for or against tax evasion. If the net income (after taxes) is equal or higher than that aspiration level, a person will pay their taxes honestly. Tax evasion could possibly bring more money, but also the risk of detection and fines, consequently falling below the aspiration level. Kirchler, Muehlbacher, Hoelzl and Webley (2009) examined whether high effort in earning the income leads to higher or lower tax evasion than earning the income effortlessly. Results indicated that hard-earned income was more likely to be declared honestly in order to secure at least the net income, whereas easily earned income was more often put at risk by attempted tax evasion. These findings were corroborated by surveys in several countries (Muehlbacher et al., 2008). As shown in Figure 4.5, in a majority of the countries included in this study, tax evasion was lower in the conditions of high effort.

Another aspect of subjective valuation of money is knowledge of prices, especially in times of inflation. One side effect of high inflation is that consumers do not know the current prices of goods. Shamir (1985) reported that during a period of inflation rates of more than 130%, consumers were only able to give correct prices of groceries in about one-third of cases. In contrast, in a study conducted in the UK during an inflation rate of 0%, Gabor and Granger (1961) found that about three-quarters (73%) of consumers knew the correct prices. If prices change very quickly due to inflation, consumers are likely to be unsettled because they experience a loss in price knowledge.

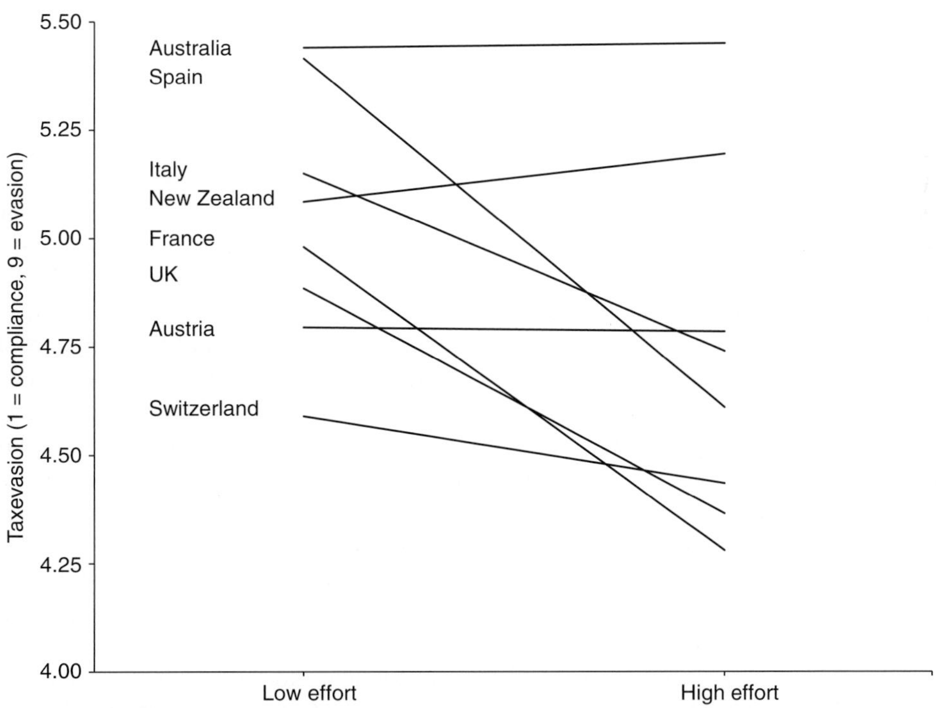

Figure 4.5 Tax evasion tendency in different countries by low and high work effort (adapted from Muehlbacher et al., 2008, p. 302)

They also have difficulties in remembering or predicting price changes. One challenge is that price changes from inflation imply an exponential change over time, and people often have difficulties when estimating such non-linear effects. Regarding past prices, Bates and Gabor (1986) asked consumers how strongly the prices of selected groceries have changed over the last month. The actual inflation rate was minus 0.61%. However, 57% of respondents said that prices have increased considerably, 36% said that prices have remained stable and only 1% said that prices have decreased. Correspondingly, the estimated inflation rate was 4.5%, much higher than the actual rate. Kemp (1987) asked consumers to report how much they had paid one year ago for a product that today costs NZ$ 10. Prices one year ago were underestimated, in line with an overestimation of the inflation rate. Regarding future prices, Bates and Gabor (1986) also asked how many years it would take until the prices of selected products would be twice as high as today, assuming an inflation rate of either 4% or 10%. For both cases, participants gave very similar estimates that were below the correct answers. These findings indicate that the future growth of prices is underestimated, in contrast to the overestimation of the past growth.

Lay beliefs about the reasons and consequences of inflation are diverse. Leiser and Drori (2005) asked psychology students, pupils in a technical school, merchants and teachers to freely associate to the term ‘inflation’. All groups associated higher prices, higher costs of living and a value loss of money. However, associations concerning income, unemployment or the general economy were surprisingly rare. Svenson and Nilsson (1986) studied ‘cognitive maps’ of causes and consequences of inflation among Swedish students from psychology and economics. Economics students had better knowledge of actual inflation rates, and also gave different explanations. They indicated that the main causes for inflation are expectations, wage levels and international developments. The main consequences were seen in changes in wages and adaptation of expectations.

The above findings show that the subjective value of money depends on learning and development, on the source of money and on changes in the economic environment such as inflation. Knowledge about current, past and future prices is often limited, especially in times of high inflation.

4.3.3 Currency Reforms and Currency Changeovers

The currency of a country is the money that is accepted as a payment method during a specific time and in a localised area. In times of economic crises, when inflation rises uncontrollably, often currency reforms are proposed to counteract the loss of trust in the currency. There are several historical examples of such reforms. In Germany, after the two World Wars, in 1923 and 1948 large reforms were conducted. In France, in 1960, 100 old francs were changed to 1 new franc. In Turkey, in 2004, 1 million old lira were changed to 1 new lira. Currency reforms introduce new coins or banknotes and new prices, and may introduce different exchange rates for cash, savings or liabilities. When all old prices and values are simply transformed with the same exchange rate, the precise term is a currency changeover. In this respect, the introduction of the euro was a currency changeover.

The introduction of the euro in eleven member states of the European Union – 1999 as book money and 2002 as cash – was an extraordinary political, economic and social-psychological event. The introduction did not occur for reasons of high inflation, but economic and political considerations made many nations give up their national currencies and introduce a common currency. This situation provided a unique opportunity for social science to study expectations, hopes and fears concerning the changeover, the formation of social representations of a new currency, and the strategies used to adapt to a new currency, to understand its value and to manage new prices of goods and services (see, e.g., Müller-Peters, Pepermans, Kiell & Farhangmehr, 2001). Economic psychologists from several European countries conducted research projects on (a) representations about the logistics of the changeover, attitudes, and the formation of social representations of the euro and (b) strategies to adapt to the new currency and development of an intuition for euro prices. Because the euro changeover represents such a unique 'experiment', a number of studies will be presented in more detail here.

4.3.3.1 Lay Beliefs and Representations about a Currency Changeover

A large-scale project such as the euro introduction has a very long preparation stage. Political and economic institutions discussed scenarios of the changeover long before the actual introduction. Along with these discussions, research projects were initiated. As one example, the Austrian National Bank commissioned a research project on the logistics of the changeover (Kirchler & Meier, 1998). The goal was to analyse how laypeople think about the changeover, which problems they anticipate and which scenarios gain acceptance in the population. Based on focus groups, a survey was developed that was completed by a representative sample of 1,550 respondents. It contained eighty statements on the changeover, as well as a list of twenty-eight institutions or groups to be judged in terms of responsibility and competence. It also contained measures on attitudes to the euro and the European Union, and identification with one's nation and the EU. The results showed that in 1998 a high degree of mistrust was prevalent and respondents feared that they would be taken advantage of. They feared that merchants would round prices to their own advantage, goods would become more expensive and money would lose value. In particular, these fears were expressed by euro opponents, women, and groups with low income and education. Respondents were also pessimistic about the logistics, and expressed concerns that vending machines (e.g., cigarettes, drinks) would not be ready in time, or that small change would be missing in shops. In particular, euro opponents made clear that they would not cooperate (e.g., by using cashless payment methods), and were rather demanding of shop owners, banks and the government to make the changeover convenient (e.g., by accepting both the old and the new currency, by advertising prices in both currencies, or by training employees). The National Bank was seen as the core player in the euro changeover, in terms of both responsibility and competence. It was also seen as responsible for protecting consumers from arbitrary price changes by merchants. From a psychological perspective, the attitude towards the euro proved to be the most relevant moderator variable. Respondents with more positive attitudes expressed less fear of the changeover and more willingness to cooperate. They also were more optimistic about the speed of adaptation: euro supporters estimated that within two months people would have adapted to the new currency, whereas euro opponents estimated that five months would be needed.

The introduction of the euro was discussed among experts and among laypeople. Arguments for and against the introduction were in the media for months at a time and were the topic of everyday conversation. This situation – of a new event that is relevant – was particularly suited for studying the development of social representations. In several research projects in the member states, such social representations were studied primarily by eliciting associations to the term 'euro' and examining changes in these associations over time. In Germany, Dehm and Müller-Peters (2001) found before the introduction as cash that the German mark was seen as an important symbol of the national identity. In France, studies on adults and adolescents showed that the euro was mostly associated with terms like 'Europe' and 'Union' (Nivoix & Roland-Lévy, 2002; Roland-Lévy, 2002). These findings indicate that the euro also was seen as a symbol of community and connection between nations.

While most studies examined social representations in one or a few countries in the EU, el Sehity et al. (2003) compared developments in ten nations (Belgium, Germany, Finland, France, Greece, Ireland, Italy, Austria, Portugal and Spain). Results show that before the introduction of the euro as cash in winter 2001, social representations about the euro were clearly different from those of the national currencies. The euro was associated with the European Union, whereas the national currencies were associated with the respective country and other payment means. The euro also elicited more and more diverse associations, which indicates that the social representations of the national currencies were clearer and more homogeneous. One year later, in winter 2002, the number of diverse associations to the euro was considerably lower. Social representations of the euro and the national currencies became more similar, and social representations of the euro became more homogeneous. These results indicate that before the introduction, 'euro' was a diffuse term. Over time, this unknown but relevant object was integrated into everyday discourse.

In a related line of research, attitudes to the euro were studied. Classical theories in social psychology examine attitudes as potential determinants for behaviour. For example, the theory of reasoned action by Fishbein and Ajzen (1975) described how behavioural intentions – as precursors for behaviour – are influenced by subjective norms regarding the behaviour on the one hand and attitudes towards the behaviour on the other hand. Consequently, several studies were conducted on the attitudes towards the euro with the goal of understanding how people would manage the new currency. Another goal was to describe changes in attitudes over time and differences in attitudes across countries. The European Commission conducted surveys on the attitudes of citizens towards the European Union and the euro on a regular basis. In 1998, in all countries the attitude to the euro improved; in 2000, it deteriorated, remained constant (or improved slightly) until 2003, and it deteriorated again in 2004. Those citizens with negative attitudes to the European Union also had negative attitudes towards the euro. Banducci, Karp and Loedel (2003) came to similar conclusions in their analysis of the Eurobarometer data between 1992 and 2000. In addition, the national economic situation was relevant for attitudes towards the euro. Kaltenthaler and Anderson (2001) also highlight the financial benefits that a country gained from being a European Union member and how accepted the national governments were.

Attitudes and expectations regarding the euro were examined in a joint project between economists and psychologists from the fifteen European Union states in summer 1997 (see Müller-Peters, Pepermans & Kiell, 1998, and the Special Issue of the *Journal of Economic Psychology, 19*(6), 1998). Over 15,000 European Union citizens were surveyed on a variety of concepts, including (a) attitudes towards the euro, (b) fairness considerations, and (c) national identity as related to the euro.

(a) Regarding attitudes, support for the euro differed across countries. In 1997, respondents in some countries were enthusiastic about the euro (Italy, Spain, Ireland, Belgium, France, Luxembourg) or very positive (Portugal, Greece). On the other hand, respondents in some countries (the Netherlands, Denmark, Germany, Sweden and the UK) on average were against the euro. In all countries, respondents who supported the idea of European integration and the European Union also supported the currency changeover. In general, respondents who were more interested and involved in the changeover and felt subjectively well informed also had more positive euro attitudes. Interestingly, attitudes were more closely related to the subjective feeling of knowledge than to the objective knowledge. An interpretation could be that fears and negative stances come from the subjective impression of not knowing what will happen. It could have been assumed that, with more knowledge about the planned changes and potential consequences, attitudes would become more extreme (positive and negative), while little knowledge would result in an indifferent attitude. However, this was not the case: Knowledge was the basis for support of the changeover and for cooperation.

(b) Regarding fairness considerations, in many countries respondents assumed that national welfare programmes need to be reduced in order to fulfil the criteria for participating in the currency union (e.g., a low inflation rate and a low degree of debt). Respondents were rather well informed whether their own country profited financially and whether it was a net payer or a net receiver within the European Union (i.e., whether it paid more than it received in support). The degree of these fairness perceptions correlated with the attitude to the euro. Interestingly, respondents in larger countries thought that the smaller countries would profit from the currency union, whereas respondents in smaller countries thought that the larger countries would benefit. Similarly, respondents in poorer countries feared that the richer countries would claim the largest part of the joint resources. Respondents in richer countries assumed that they need to support the poorer countries to reach European standards.

(c) Regarding national identity, identification with one's own country and the European Union was found to be a particularly relevant determinant of attitudes towards the euro. For Germany, the changes in attitudes towards the euro between 1997 and 2002 were attributed mainly to individual-level factors such as general life satisfaction, the perception of national identity, pride in national symbols and the perceived financial benefits of the euro (Kiell, Müller-Peters & Fischer, 2002). Jonas, Fritsche and Greenberg (2005) showed in two experiments with German participants that the attitude towards the euro can be influenced by national identity. Shortly before measuring attitudes, some participants were given material to ensure that they identify with the social category 'own nation' and feel empowered and secure. These participants judged the euro as worse than participants in a control group. This suggests that national identity and the threat of identity loss are important factors. The identification with own nation, together with economic considerations, was also found to be related to attitudes towards the euro in Austria (Meier & Kirchler, 1998) and the Netherlands (van Everdingen & van Raaij, 1998). Similarly, the negative attitude to a euro introduction in the UK was based in a strong national identity (Routh & Burgoyne, 1998). A study conducted in Austria looked at national identity in a more fine-grained way. It highlighted that national identity can have two different sources: (a) economic and political achievements and (b) culture and history. Meier-Pesti and Kirchler (2003a) showed that nationalistic identification with one's own country correlated negatively with the identification with the European Union, whereas patriotic identification correlated positively. Respondents with a nationalistic identification took a competitive stance towards other countries and glorified Austria in comparison, whereas respondents with a patriotic identification were proud to be Austrian without demoting others. For an identification with the European Union, a nationalistic identification is detrimental. Instead, a dual identification – both with one's country and with the more general European Union – is necessary. In a second project, Meier-Pesti and Kirchler (2003b) examined the connection between national identification and the economic and political status of one's own country. Respondents with a strong identification with their country who also thought that their country had equal status with other countries had positive attitudes to the euro. However, respondents with a strong identification who thought their country had lower status than others had negative attitudes to the euro. This was interpreted as a protection mechanism: those who doubt the economic stability and strength of their country fear that other countries take control and protect themselves by rejecting the euro that symbolises the European Union.

4.3.3.2 New Money and New Prices

The euro changeover required consumers not only to learn how to handle unknown coins and banknotes, but also to learn a new price scale and to develop a feeling for prices expressed in euros. Across most countries, one problem was that coins had rather little value and banknotes high value. However, with the euro changeover, coins suddenly represented a much higher value. For example, in Italy 2-euro coins equalled approximately 4,000 lire, while the smallest banknote in Italy had a value of 1,000 lire. Kollmann, Simperl and Huber (2003) reported that, in the beginning, Austrian consumers had difficulties in coming to terms with the euro coins. In January 2002, 33% of respondents claimed to have difficulties; this number dropped to 25% in January 2003, but still a quarter of respondents saw problems one year after the introduction. Similar problems were found in Ireland where respondents noted that the unfamiliar money was seen as the biggest problem in the changeover (Ranyard, Burgoyne, Saldanha & Routh, 2003).

Another problem was the new scaling of value. In all member states except Ireland, the nominal amounts in euros were smaller than the nominal amounts in the respective national currency. In Ireland, 1 euro equalled 0.79 pound; in France, 1 euro equalled 6.56 francs and in Italy 1,936 lire. Researchers assumed that with the changeover the phenomenon of money illusion might become relevant. **Money illusion** (Fisher, 1928; Shafir, Diamond & Tversky, 1997) occurs when the perceived economic value of money amounts is influenced by the units in which they are represented. In many cases, people give too much weight to the nominal values, and consider too little the real values. For example, people prefer a nominally higher income, even when the purchasing power of the income remains the same due to concurrent inflation.

In the context of the euro introduction, the term '**euro illusion**' was used. It describes the phenomenon that the perception of prices in euros is influenced by the respective original currency and the corresponding exchange rates. Euro illusion (Burgoyne, Routh & Ellis, 1999; Gamble, Gärling, Västfjäll & Marell, 2003) was assumed to increase unwanted consumer spending because the resulting small nominal prices would be perceived as good deals. In Germany, Fischer, Katzer and Kiell (2002) asked consumers directly about their experiences: 50% of respondents agreed that, at least sometimes, they had thought products to be cheaper than they actually were. On the other hand, Jonas, Greitemeyer, Frey and Schulz-Hardt (2002) could not find direct evidence. For Ireland, the only country where the euro resulted in higher nominal prices, Ranyard et al. (2003) could find some support in interviews: the majority reported that at least sometimes they intuitively thought of euro prices as too high because they used the nominally smaller pound prices as reference.

Money illusion studies were also conducted in other European countries that did not join the currency union. Gamble, Gärling, Charlton and Ranyard (2002) found support for money illusion in Sweden, but not in the UK: prices expressed in British pounds were experienced as higher than prices in euros although the pound resulted in smaller nominal prices. In a follow-up study, the results for Sweden could be corroborated: when participants could choose between prices and wages in Swedish crowns or in euros, a majority chose wages in the nominally higher crowns and prices in the nominally smaller euros (Gamble et al. 2003). Overall, the results on euro illusion are mixed.

Attitudes towards the euro as well as familiarity seem to moderate the size of euro illusion. It was smaller among euro opponents than among supporters, and smaller for products bought on a daily basis than for products bought rarely (Gamble et al. 2002). On the other hand, euro illusion was higher when participants had limited cognitive processing capability because of a positive mood and low activation (Gamble et al., 2003).

In many countries, the euro introduction has evoked expectations and perceptions of higher costs of living (European Opinion Research Group, 2001, 2002). Most European Union citizens in 2002 held the opinion that the prices would be rounded up to their disadvantage when exchanged into euros. Additionally, media coverage suggested that, across Europe, the euro has led to price increases. For Austria, in early 2003 nearly 90% perceived price increases and attributed them to the euro (Spectra, 2003). At first glance, this seems to contradict the euro illusion. However, this apparent contradiction is easily solved: a perception of smaller prices when expressed in euros can lead to less control over one's spending and, in turn, to higher expenses overall. Such factual increases in spending, combined with apparently smaller wages, can foster the perception of price increases. Van Raaij and van Rijen (2003) also hypothesised that euro illusion makes the difference between cheap and expensive products appear smaller and therefore makes taking the expensive product easier. Some support for this idea was reported by Gamble et al. (2003). They asked consumers to choose between a technical product with or without any special features. When the price for the product was expressed in euros, the product with the special features was chosen significantly more often than when it was expressed in crowns. Both the apparently smaller price in euros and the apparently smaller differences between products can contribute to higher expenses. Not surprising for psychologists, consumers prefer to attribute the unwanted expenses not to their own mistakes, but to the euro.

Experimental studies on the attribution of price increases to the euro were conducted for example by Jonas et al. (2002). They asked consumers to estimate prices of products in German marks and in euros. The resulting real prices were higher in euros than in marks. This was explained by anchoring on the nominally higher prices in marks. When estimating prices in euros, respondents took the known but nominally higher prices in marks as an anchor, which led to an upward bias in the estimates for euro prices. In several studies with restaurant prices, Traut-Mattausch, Schulz-Hardt, Greitemeyer and Frey (2004) asked participants to examine the menu of an Italian restaurant. They first saw the menu with prices in German marks and then the same menu with prices in euros. Depending on the experimental condition, euro prices were 15% lower, equal or 15% higher. Participants had to choose dishes from both menus, and afterwards to estimate the price difference between the two menus. Results showed that prices in euros were always perceived as higher than prices in marks, even when participants could directly compare the menus and when they had financial incentives to be correct. These perceptions also translated into behaviour: participants chose more and costlier dishes from the menu with the prices in marks (Greitemeyer, Schulz-Hardt, Traut-Mattausch & Frey, 2002; see also Greitemeyer, Traut-Mattausch & Frey, 2008).

Even years after the euro changeover, similar effects were found by Hofmann, Kamleitner, Kirchler and Schulz-Hardt (2006). In their study, not only prices for Italian dishes but also wages for usual student jobs (e.g., secretarial support, babysitting) were estimated. As shown in Figure 4.6, euro prices in general were overestimated, even when they factually were 15% lower than the prices in schillings. However, the perceptual bias did not extend to wages. It seems that the perception of changes in monetary amounts expressed in euros leads to perceived increases in prices, but not in wages.

The magnitude of the perceptual bias is linked with the availability of cognitive resources. Traut-Mattausch et al. (2004) showed that, with less concentration on converting the prices, fewer errors were detected. This also results in detecting fewer cases of errors not conforming to expectations. In another study, a close connection between expectations of price increases and perception of price increases was found (Greitemeyer et al., 2002). Greitemeyer, Schulz-Hardt, Traut-Mattausch and Frey (2005) provided even clearer evidence on the importance of expectations by experimentally manipulating the expectations. When expectations of increased prices were induced, participants perceived increased prices even when the prices remained stable. When expectations of stable prices were induced, a factual price increase was significantly underestimated.

A theoretical framework is provided by a '**selective outcome correction process**'. It is assumed that participants hold expectations about outcomes, and these expectations guide whether errors in calculations are detected or not. Those errors that support the own expectations are less likely to be

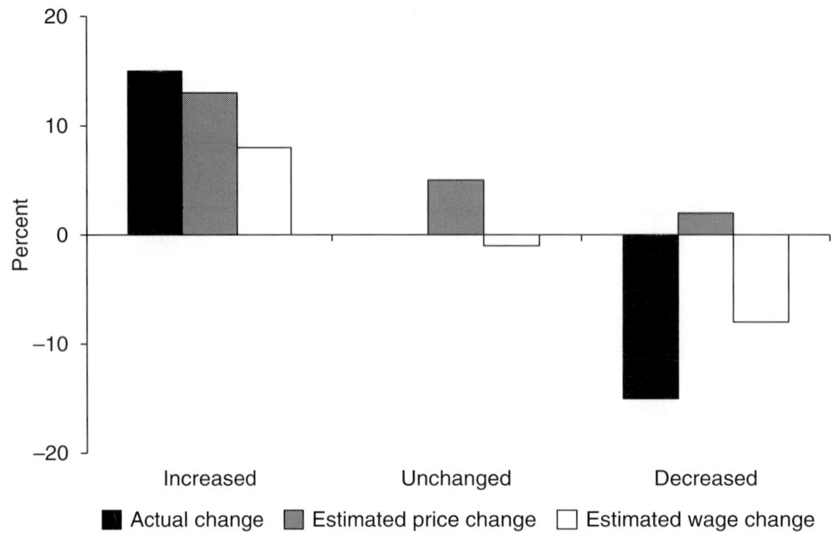

Figure 4.6 Actual and estimated changes in prices and wages (Hofmann et al., 2006, p. 104)

detected than those that contradict the expectations. Figure 4.7 shows the postulated process (Traut-Mattausch, Greitemeyer, Frey & Schulz-Hardt, 2007).

Not only consumers but also investors were confused by the euro. Jonas and Frey (2003) showed that investors search for other information when making investments in euros than when making investments in German marks. In particular, those investors who assumed that the euro would make the stock markets more risky searched more for information on the alleged advantages of the investment. Jonas and Frey (2003) explain this increased search for pro-arguments with cognitive dissonance (Festinger, 1957): searching for advantages can balance out the fears of the expected euro risk.

One particular form of nominal values are 9-ending prices. In the context of the euro changeover, previous price endings in the national currencies changed due to the exact transformation into euro. Before the changeover, prices often ended in 9 or in 'round prices' such as 0 or 5. These endings were replaced in the first phase of the changeover (Deutsche Bundesbank, 2004; el Sehity, Hoelzl & Kirchler, 2005). For example, in Germany, before the introduction more than 50% of prices ended in 9 and 30% in 5 or 0. Two years later, in September 2003, approximately 40% ended in 9 and 35% in 5 or 0 (Deutsche Bundesbank, 2004). 'Round prices' were more frequent than before the euro introduction. Similar results were found in studies by el Sehity et al. (2005) conducted in ten countries of the currency union (Austria, Belgium, Germany, Finland, France, Greece, Ireland, Italy, Portugal and Spain). In each country, selected prices for products in two supermarkets were collected over three time points: shortly before the introduction (winter 2001), and half a year (summer 2002) and one year (winter 2002) after the introduction. In winter 2001, prices were already advertised both in the national currencies and in euro to make the transition easier for consumers. In 42% of the cases, prices in national currencies ended in 9, while only 14% of prices in euro did. Half a year later, in most cases prices were only advertised in euro and the price ending 9 was already more frequent (23%). One year later, price endings with 9 were already the most frequent (32%). Besides the frequency of price endings, the subjective perception of prices ending in 9 after the euro introduction was examined. Van Raaij and van Rijen (2003) concluded that 9-ending prices had little influence on consumer behaviour as long as there was no sufficient intuition

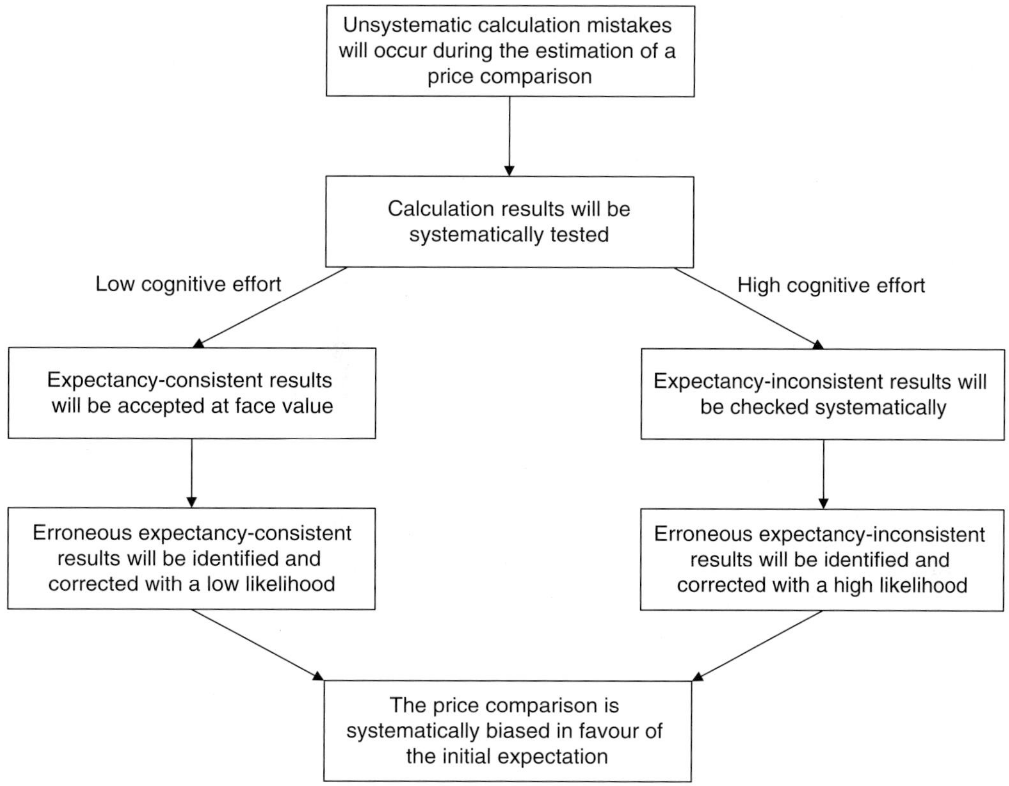

Figure 4.7 Selective outcome correction process (Traut-Mattausch et al., 2007, p. 427)

for the value of euro prices. Prices such as 0.99 euro were mostly rounded to 1 euro to make comparisons with the original currency easier. Consequently, consumers did not see differences between prices of 0.99 and 1.01 euro.

The subjective perception of widespread price increases seems to be in contradiction with the objective numbers for inflation rates during the time of the euro changeover. In all European Union countries, inflation is measured by examining the prices for selected goods. In addition, surveys ask for subjective inflation by asking consumers whether, in their opinion, prices have increased, stayed the same or decreased over the last few months. Integrating ideas from prospect theory (Kahneman & Tversky, 1979), Brachinger (2005) suggested a more detailed analysis: his index of perceived inflation focuses on loss/gain asymmetries and the frequency of purchases for selected products. Because losses are perceived more strongly than gains, price increases are perceived as more intense than price decreases (Brachinger, 2005). The index for perceived inflation during the changeover was considerably higher than the official inflation index and seems to capture adequately the subjective feelings of price increases. As shown in Figure 4.8, the index of perceived inflation before, during and after the changeover (January 2001 to June 2002) was above the inflation index, and converged afterwards (Jungermann, Brachinger, Belting, Grinberg & Zacharias, 2007). Vogel, Menz and Fritsche (2009) examined perceived inflation in twelve European Union member states and found that during the changeover indeed those products that became more expensive received more weight

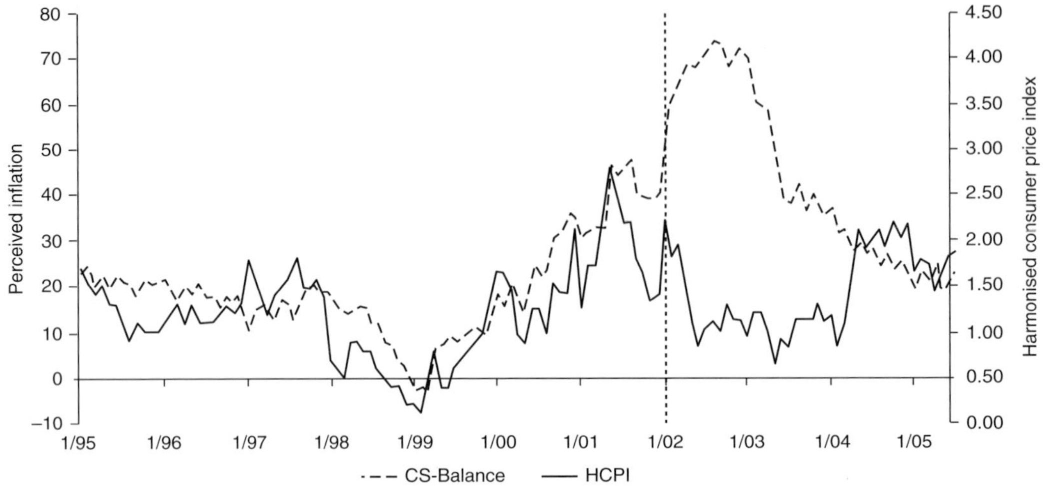

Figure 4.8 Harmonised consumer price index ('HCPI', right scale) and perceived inflation ('CS-Balance', left scale) (Jungermann et al., 2007, p. 406)

than those that became cheaper or remained at the same price level. Furthermore, in line with an availability heuristic, products bought frequently received more weight than products bought rarely.

The introduction of the euro posed considerable adaptation challenges for consumers. The new price scale was still unknown and consumers lacked immediately available standards. Consequently, judgments about offers being 'expensive' or 'cheap' were not spontaneously possible. Accordingly, in the transition phase consumers planned to spend less money until they developed an intuition of the euro (Meier-Pesti & Kirchler, 2001). But how do consumers develop such intuition? Meier-Pesti and Kirchler identified four major strategies to adapt to the new currency: (a) exact calculation, (b) forgoing calculation, (c) learning of selected prices (so-called anchor prices or reference prices) to quantify other prices, and (d) learning selected euro amounts (e.g., 100 schillings = 7 euro; 5 euro = 70 schillings); these serve to estimate other amounts. The first strategy, exact calculation, is the most precise one, but it also delays the adaption to the new currency. Studies showed that exact calculation was used primarily for expensive products. For everyday purchases, exact calculation increased with age and was more frequent in groups with lower education and income (Meier-Pesti & Kirchler, 2003c). In most cases, however, consumers did forgo calculations or used selected prices or amounts as orientation. Marques and Dehaene (2004) examined the adaption to the euro and the development of price intuition by asking whether (a) prices are learned completely from scratch or (b) the scaling of prices is adapted. In the first case, one would expect that price intuition develops in particular for products bought frequently. In the second case, price intuition should develop independent of purchase frequency. Results for Portugal and Austria indicate differences between countries. In Austria, learning processes were more prominent and an intuition was developed more quickly for frequently bought products. In Portugal, mixed results were found.

The initial difficulties with the new currency became smaller over time. European Union citizens adapted to the euro and developed price intuition. Mussweiler and Englich (2003), for example, showed that in Germany in summer 2002 price estimates were already independent of external anchors, which suggests an internalisation of euro prices. While in winter 2001, price estimates for a car in euros were strongly influenced by external random values, half a year later this influence disappeared. Subjective confidence in judgments in the handling of the euro increased strongly within months after the changeover (Mussweiler & Englich, 2004). A similar finding was reported by Jonas, Greitemeyer, Graupmann and Frey (2002), who showed that the orientation on prices in German marks disappeared within the first year of the euro. This also corroborates the development of a price intuition for prices in euros.

However, not all consumers adapted to the euro equally quickly. Witte and Raphael (2004) found that euro opponents still reported adaptation difficulties. From a psychological perspective, such connection with attitudes is not surprising. Euro opponents predicted more difficulties and in retrospect selectively focus on problems to confirm their expectations. Hoelzl, Kirchler and Rodler (2002) and Hoelzl and Kirchler (2005) examined a hindsight bias in connection with the euro changeover. Six months before the introduction, participants were asked to predict the influence of the euro introduction on the economy six months after. For example, participants predicted how imports and exports, the employment situation or prices would develop. In a second survey, participants were asked to reproduce these predictions. One half of the participants were given information about the actual developments, and in line with the hindsight bias their answers were biased towards the information. However, the effect was moderated by attitudes: euro supporters said in retrospect they had foreseen the positive developments; euro opponents said they had foreseen the negative developments. Consequently, the hindsight bias supported and stabilised the worldview of respondents concerning the euro.

4.3.4 Subjective Interpretation of Prices

In general, price and demand for goods are negatively related, so that with price increases fewer consumers are willing to buy a product. However, in some cases this relationship can be less clear-cut or even reversed (von Rosenstiel & Ewald, 1979; Winkelmann, 2008):

- Consumers may not react to price changes because they do not realise them. For example, Dickson and Sawyer (1990) found that only 47.1% of respondents in a supermarket were able to give the correct price of a product they had just bought, and only 49.7% were able to recognise correctly whether an item was on sale or not.
- Consumers may find some products more attractive after a price increase. Conspicuous consumption (Veblen, 1899) can be used to signal to others that one is able to afford luxury, and a corresponding 'snob appeal' or 'Veblen effect' can increase demand after a price increase.
- Consumers may fear further price increases or delivery problems and react with panic purchases.
- Consumers may infer changes in quality from price changes.

In the next sections, findings on the connections between price, perceived quality and objective quality are reviewed, following Kirchler, Fischer and Hoelzl (2010).

4.3.4.1 Price and Quality

As shown above, consumers often have limited price knowledge. In addition, they often follow heuristics when interpreting price. In particular, consumers assume that price can be used as a cue for product quality. In a classical study, Leavitt (1954) demonstrated that consumers use prices to infer quality. In his study, consumers were asked to decide between two offers from the same product category, one with a lower and one with a higher price. When participants assumed very small quality differences, nearly all of them chose the cheaper product; but when they assumed large quality differences, a majority chose the more expensive product.

The '**expensive = good heuristic**' (Cialdini, 2001) or '**price–quality heuristic**' (e.g., Gneezy, Gneezy & Lauga, 2014) describes the belief that there is a positive correlation between price and quality. Consumers often perceive more expensive products as better. In surveys, consumers directly express the belief that the price of a product is positively linked to its quality, and more so for durable goods (Boyle & Lathrop, 2009; Lichtenstein & Burton, 1989). In experiments where the price is manipulated, the same product is judged better when it appears to be more expensive. For example, Plassmann, O'Doherty, Shiv and Rangel (2008) found that the pleasantness of the same wine varied with its manipulated price label, and Gneezy et al. (2014) showed that higher prices raise expectations that serve as reference points. Not only judgments, but also more tangible aspects are influenced by price: Shiv, Carmon and Ariely (2005) found that participants who consumed energy drinks that were ostensibly on sale subsequently had lower performance in solving puzzles than participants who consumed energy drinks with the regular price.

The positive correlation between price and perceived quality was confirmed in meta-analyses. Rao and Monroe (1989) reported an average correlation of $r = 0.34$. Völckner and Hofmann (2007) confirmed a positive, moderately strong relation ($r = 0.27$) between price and perceived quality, and found that this correlation was stronger for durable goods, for more expensive goods and for goods consumers were less familiar with. This last point also suggests that, for complex products, consumers will be more likely to rely on the price–quality heuristic.

Besides the correlation between price and perceived quality, there is research on the correlation between price and more objective measures of quality. Product tests that compare products from different brands can be found in consumer magazines such as 'Consumer Reports'. These tests are usually conducted by independent experts who are blind to the specific brands tested and can be viewed as a measure of objective product quality. In many of these tests, quality ratings and average market prices are reported, allowing a test of whether these are correlated.

Empirical studies often find that correlations between prices and objective quality ratings are low. In one of the first studies, Oxenfeldt (1950) reported that the median correlation between the quality of products tested in Consumer Union reports and their price was positive ($r = 0.35$) – however, the correlations for different products showed extremely high variation between $r = -0.81$ and $r = 0.82$. A meta-analysis of several similar studies reported an average correlation of $r = 0.16$ (Hanf & von Wersebe, 1994). The overall picture of low correlations was found in several countries (Imkamp, 2004). For example, the average correlation was $r = 0.17$ in Canada (Bodell, Kerton & Schuster, 1986), $r = 0.29$ in the Netherlands (Steenkamp, 1988) and $r = 0.13$ in Germany (Fürst, Heil & Daniel, 2004). In a study conducted in Austria, the average correlation was $r = 0.30$ (Kirchler et al. 2010). As shown in Figure 4.9, the correlation varied considerably across individual product tests (circles) and across product categories (line).

Not only is the average correlation quite low, there is also considerable variation across product categories. In some categories, the average correlation was even found to be negative – for example, for the German food sector (Schulze, Spiller, Böhm & de Witte, 2008). Meta-analyses showed that the correlation between price and quality is stronger for those products for which consumers have more information (Tellis & Wernerfelt, 1987), for example when products induce more search behaviour because the price range is larger. Similarly, the correlation is stronger for those products for which it is easier for consumers to recognise quality (Hanf & von Wersebe, 1994). Overall, these studies demonstrate a weak correlation between price and 'objective' product quality: High-priced products do not always receive the highest rankings in independent consumer tests, and conversely high-quality products can be available for low prices. As a consequence of the low correlation, consumers using price as a cue to product quality are likely

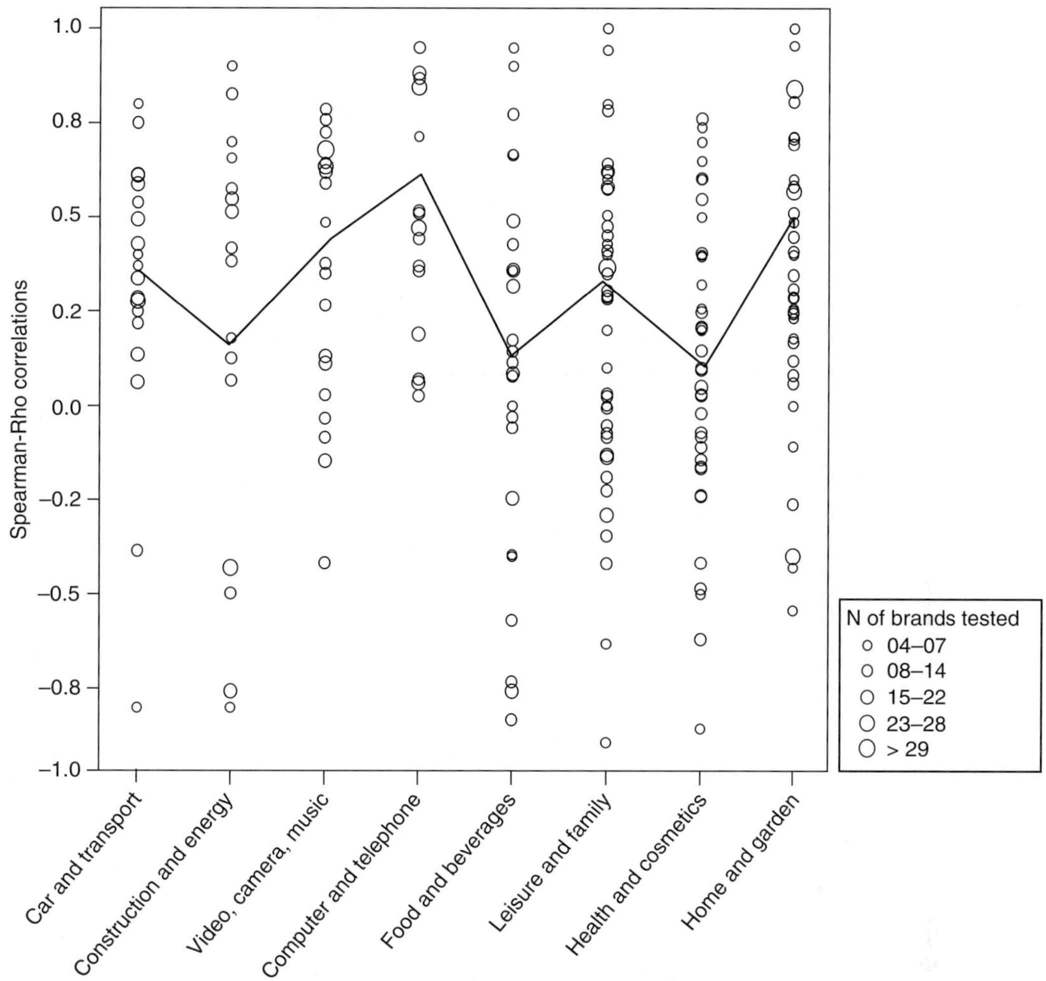

Figure 4.9 Price–quality correlations in the Austrian market, by product category (Kirchler et al., 2010, p. 281)

to make mistakes: selecting a high-price product does not reduce the risk of getting a low-quality product (Hjorth-Andersen, 1992).

However, consumer tests mostly focus on measurable, objective characteristics and therefore only capture some facets of product quality (Hjorth-Andersen, 1992; Imkamp, 2004). Subjective aspects (e.g., design) are not contained, and search costs and product image are not considered. Some authors have therefore suggested that the correlation between price and subjective quality may be considerably higher than suggested by these studies (Imkamp, 2008).

From a consumer policy perspective, it would be desirable if, at least for expensive products, price would be a reliable indicator for quality. However, the magnitude of the price–quality correlation is only weakly related to price level (Hanf & von Wersebe, 1994). It would also be desirable if consumers could be well calibrated in the sense that they can correctly identify those product categories with a higher magnitude of the price–quality correlation. Studies on calibration found that the correspondence between the price–quality correlation in product tests and the subjective beliefs of respondents is on average positive, but not particularly strong (Boyle & Lathrop, 2009; Lichtenstein & Burton, 1989). Kirchler et al. (2010) found a positive but moderate correlation between subjective beliefs about the price–quality link and consumer test results on the price–quality correlation ($r = 0.23$). These findings indicate that consumers are not very good at identifying product categories where price would be a better cue to product quality.

4.3.4.2 Price Perception

Finally, the subjective interpretation of prices concerns the perception of a given price. Prices are perceived not in absolute terms, but relative to other prices: they are compared to reference prices (el Sehity, Kirchler & Brandstätter, 2005; Winer, 1986). These reference prices may come from personal experience (internal reference prices), for example what one has paid for a similar product in the recent past. Reference prices may also come from the current price context (external reference price; Briesch, Krishnamurthi, Mazumdar & Raj, 1997), for example by seeing the previous price advertised.

On a theoretical level, internal reference prices have been explained by adaptation level theory (Helson, 1964). It states that the weighted average of the strength of previous stimuli forms the reference value for the evaluation of new stimuli. In a price context, the reference price would then be formed by previously experienced and remembered prices. Another theoretical approach to explain reactions to prices is in terms of assimilation and contrast effects as formulated by Sherif and Hovland (1961). This approach suggests that within a certain price interval, a new price is assimilated to the reference price and perceived as being the same. Outside the price interval, contrast effects set in and a new price is perceived as considerably higher (or lower). In consequence, price differences that occur close to the reference price are underestimated or not even perceived, whereas price differences further away from the reference price are overestimated. This explains why consumers often do not pay attention to small differences between real prices and subjective reference prices (Tybout & Artz, 1994). As shown above, memory for prices is rather poor, so that the reference prices formed from experience may be vague.

If external reference prices are available, exact memory is not necessary, and current prices can be compared. Janiszewski and Lichtenstein (1999) built on range theory (Volkmann, 1951), which suggests that the endpoints of a scale are essential for the evaluation of a stimulus. The evaluation of a specific price therefore depends on its relative distance to the endpoints of the range of external reference prices. In their study, Janiszewski and Lichtenstein (1999) presented the same price in different ways – once in the middle of a price range, once in the upper and once in the lower part of the price range. The same price was perceived as fair, expensive or cheap, respectively.

A specific form of prices are '**psychological prices**'. These are prices that try to evoke the impression that they are considerably below a round number (e.g., Foxall & Goldsmith, 1994). Other terms used are 'just-below-pricing' or 'oddpricing.' (e.g., Knauth, 1949). In many cases, this is done by making the last digit of a price the number 9. Most research focuses on these **9-ending prices**. In the market, 9-ending prices are rather prevalent, next to prices ending in 'round' digits (0 and 5). In a study analysing newspaper price advertisements, 31% of prices ended in 9, 27% ended in 0, and 19% ended in 5 (Schindler & Kirby, 1997). In a study analysing scanner panel data for tuna and yoghurt, between 36% and 50% of prices ended in 9 (Stiving & Winer, 1997). After the euro transformation, price endings that changed through the exact conversion reverted to previous distributions quickly (el Sehity et al. 2005).

Why would 9-ending prices work? The mechanisms were classified into image effects and level effects (see Stiving & Winer, 1997 for a review).

(a) **Image effects** operate when the advertised price changes the perception of the good (for example, being of lower quality) or the perception of the relation between the good and the price (for example, being on sale). In one study, products with 99-ending prices were more likely to be perceived as being on sale than products with 00-ending prices (Schindler & Kibarian, 2001).
(b) **Level effects** operate when the advertised price is cognitively transformed (for example, through rounding down, left-to-right comparison or memory effects). These level effects are intuitively plausible, but found rather little empirical support. One study, using scanner data, suggested that both image effects and level effects operate (Stiving & Winer, 1997).

The actual effects of 9-ending prices on sales are disputed. Empirical evidence is mixed (see Gedenk & Sattler, 1999 for a review). Some studies documented a clear advantage of 9-ending prices (e.g., Anderson & Simester, 2003; Schindler & Kibarian, 1996), whereas other studies found negative effects, no effects or mixed effects (e.g., Wedel & Leeflang, 1998).

Conclusion

The topics presented in this chapter highlight that people base decisions on subjective understanding and subjective knowledge which may substantially differ from objective factors or expert views. Since most people are laypeople with respect to economic topics, a clearer insight into the structure and the limitations of these subjective bases is important. Examples include policy considerations when it comes to currency reforms, marketing considerations when it comes to the perception of price changes in times of inflation, or compensation in companies when it comes to subjective meanings of money.

Summary

- The theory of social representations is often used to study lay theories of economic phenomena. The theory focuses on how a new concept is integrated in everyday discourse, in particular through anchoring and objectification.
- Social representations about economic systems often include not only economic concepts, but also psychological, moral and social concepts. Social representations about unemployment and poverty often focus on individualistic causes, and less on structural causes. Social representations of money and currency show that money is also linked to non-economic aspects such as trust and identity.
- Economic understanding in children develops in parallel to their cognitive development, from diffuse and experience-based concepts to more differentiated and abstract concepts. Economic motives such as altruism also develop with age. Children and adolescents are important economic actors, both through direct spending and through influencing their parents' decisions.
- Financial literacy is often generally low even among adults. Levels of financial literacy are related to economic outcomes such as consumer debt or retirement saving. Results on the effects of financial literacy trainings are mixed.
- Money has subjective meanings and people differ in money attitudes. The subjective value of money depends among other factors on the source of money which has practical consequences (e.g., for spending and tax compliance).
- Changes in currency systems are often challenging due to psychological processes. In the context of the euro introduction, factors like national identity, money illusion or distorted perception of price developments have been identified.
- Prices are often perceived as a signal about product quality, and consumers assume a positive correlation between price and quality. However, the correlation with quality as measured in product tests is often low and varies considerably. Consumers have difficulties identifying product categories where the correlation is higher.
- Prices are perceived relative to internal or external reference prices. 'Psychological prices' influence price perception through image effects and level effects.

Questions

1. What is 'anchoring' in the theory of social representations?
2. What is 'money illusion'?
3. What is 'selective outcome correction' in price perception?
4. Define windfall gains. How and why do people treat them differently from hard-earned money?
5. Which phases are distinguished in the cognitive-developmental theory of Piaget and how do they relate to children's economic understanding?

FURTHER READING

Furnham, A. (2014). *The new psychology of money.* London: Routledge.

Mitchell, O. S., & Lusardi, A. (2012). *Financial literacy: Implications for retirement security and the financial marketplace*. Oxford: Oxford University Press.

Purkhardt, S. C. (2015). *Transforming social representations: A social psychology of common sense and science*. London: Psychology Press.

5 Consumer Markets: Purchasing and Credit Use

Overview

Economic decisions in private households are made by individuals, usually in collaboration with others. For instance, couples make economic decisions when they plan their next holiday, gather information about different ways to save money, or compare different credit opportunities.

Economic decisions therefore are relevant tasks that can create problems for couples. It is not only because private households control the bulk of every country's total economic budget that these problems are of interest to the social and economic sciences. Economic decisions are simultaneously the cause of conflicts between partners, which can pose a threat to the quality of the relationship. Additionally, economic decisions are reflecting the quality of the relationship between partners.

When 'private households', 'romantic partners', 'married couples' or 'the family' are mentioned, a decision-making unit consisting of two or more people is generally meant. These terms, of course, are not perfectly interchangeable. In its narrow sense, 'the family' is generally understood to mean a unit consisting of parents and their children. In its wider meaning, grandparents and other relatives can be added to this group. Decisions between partners relate to how two people think about deploying their financial resources. These partners are living together (whether with or without a marriage certificate) and have an intimate relationship with one another. Finally, a 'private household' refers to a group of people running a joint household who do not necessarily need to have an intimate relationship with one other. However, in this book these four terms are used rather indiscriminately: what is essential is that they refer to a decision-making unit consisting of two or more people who have a close relationship to one another and make joint decisions on the use of financial resources.

After introducing a taxonomy of economic decision-making in private households, this chapter will turn to a discussion of models of individual decision-making before moving to a process model of purchasing decisions in those households. When partners have differing opinions, decisional conflicts can arise which need to be resolved. The conflict resolution process depends not only on the type of conflict but also on the harmony of the relationship and existing power relations between the partners. In a complex process model, the progression from the beginning of a purchasing decision up to its conclusion is outlined. Furthermore, differential influence patterns of men and women as well as determinants of each partner's influence will be examined. In addition to each partner's expertise and interest in the decision, the couple's decision-making history turns out to be

---

Parts of this chapter have been taken from Kirchler, E., Rodler, C., Hoelzl, E., & Meier, K. (2001). *Conflict and decision making in close relationships: Love, money and daily routine.* Hove: Psychology Press. and from Hoelzl, E. (2015). *Consumer credit decisions in a dual-process perspective. DFG-Grant HO 4767/2–1 proposal within the research unit FOR 1882: Psychoeconomics*. University of Cologne.

particularly important. Finally, tactics used by each partner to reach their goals as well as the results of decision-making processes will be described.

The final part of this chapter will cover psychological perspectives on credit use. Individuals and households can purchase goods from the available budget, but increasingly often they use credit in different forms – for example, credit cards or consumer credit. After outlining recent developments and potentially negative consequences of credit use, a process model of credit use will be introduced. This model views credit use as extending over time and consisting of three phases that involve different decisions by consumers. In a final part, this chapter covers mental accounting as related to credit use.

Introduction

Making decisions can be a complex process. Considering that most decisions are not made in a social vacuum, but instead in a dynamic social context, further complicates the issue. Private households represent an important social context. That is why this chapter focuses on how families and especially couples handle complex decision-making situations. We will show that various factors influence decisions associated with purchases. Those factors can be found primarily in the aspects of the product itself and in the quality and history of the partnership. To get a deeper understanding of the decision-making process between partners, we will first examine purchase decisions made by individual consumers.

5.1 Purchase Decisions by Individual Consumers

In households, both financial and non-financial decisions are made. Non-financial decisions are those topics where money does not play a role, for example whether to watch movie A or movie B. Financial decisions concern all monetary matters. The bulk of studies in economic psychology examine purchasing decisions (Kirchler, Rodler, Hoelzl & Meier, 2001). Only as late as the 1990s, an increasing number of works were published in economic psychology regarding savings, credit or debt among individuals, couples and groups in private households (e.g., Breuer, Hens, Salzmann & Wang, 2015; Brown, Garino & Taylor, 2012; Brown, Taylor & Wheatley Price, 2005; Burgoyne, 1995; Cosma & Pattarin, 2011; Davies & Lea, 1995; Donkers & Van Soest, 1999; Goode, 2010; Groenland & Wahlund, 1996; Groenland, Bloem & Kuylen, 1996; Gunnarsson & Wahlund, 1997; Kamleitner, Hoelzl & Kirchler, 2012; Lea, Webley & Levine, 1993; Lea, Webley & Walker, 1995; Lunt, 1996; Lunt & Livingstone, 1992; Navarro-Martinez et al., 2011; Ottaviani & Vandone, 2011; Sweet, Nandi, Adam & McDade, 2013; Walker, 1996; Wärneryd, 1999; see also Earl & Kemp, 1999).

5.1.1 Typologies of Purchase Decisions

Financial decisions made by individuals, couples, and traditional and non-traditional families with children – in general, by households encompassing one or more persons – entail:

(a) money management, such as budgeting or allocating disposable income into various spending categories, conducting explicit or mental accounting of expenditures on various necessities like housing, food, recreation, etc., and dealing with bills;

(b) asset and investment management, such as, for example, decisions to invest in real estate or the stock market;
(c) expenditures – in other words, decisions about whether or not to buy a certain good;
(d) savings decisions, such as decisions about setting up reserve funds for major purchases or retirement;
(e) credit use, that is, decisions to take on loans that must be paid back later.

Purchasing decisions are differentiated into purchases of short-lived and long-lasting products and services based on the type of good being purchased. Kotler (1982) distinguished between durable consumer goods, non-durable consumer goods and services – as well as between goods for daily use, goods to satisfy sophisticated needs and specialty goods – primarily on the basis of the length of time the goods in question can be used and on consumers' shopping habits. Decisions about non-durable goods or goods for daily use concern material goods that tend to be bought frequently and consumed in the short run (e.g., groceries). Similarly, durable goods or goods designed to meet sophisticated needs are also material goods, but they can be used more than once, tend to be expensive, and for that reason are bought only infrequently (e.g., electronic appliances, flats and flat furnishings, cars). In contrast to decisions about non-durable goods, which are bought spontaneously or habitually, cognitive routines that lay out a programme to steer decision-making are rarely available for goods purchased infrequently. Long drawn-out decision-making processes often take place with the goal of making an optimal choice. If several people in a household are involved in a decision and have differing opinions, it is also important to make decisions in a way that resolves these differences in a manner that spares the relationships involved.

Purchasing decisions can be made by one person alone, by couples with or without children or by a group of people who share a household. They can be categorised according to whether: (a) cognitive scripts are available to steer the decision-making process, (b) large or small amounts of financial capital are involved, (c) a good has symbolic value and a high social visibility or (d) purchasing a good affects only one person or several persons (Kirchler et al., 2001).

Depending on the expression of various characteristics of a certain good, different forms of decisions are likely. On the one hand, purchases can be made spontaneously or out of habit. On the other hand, purchases can be made after **extensive decisions**, which are decisions that involve complex information processing. Decisions are termed '**syncratic decisions**' when more than one person is involved and decisions are made jointly by two or more persons in the household. The more often the purchase of a certain product or service is repeated and with decreasing quantity of information necessary to be processed for achieving a satisfactory choice, the more likely it is that cognitive decision-making scripts will be available. Consequently, the likelihood that household members will reach decisions autonomously increases. Syncratic decisions become more likely if such decision-making scripts are not available. Syncratic decisions also are more likely for purchases of expensive goods and goods with high social visibility. When multiple persons will be affected by a purchase, usually it is not just one person who extensively deliberates about which option promises to be the most advantageous. Instead, syncratic decisions will be made.

When several people participate in a decision, conflicts of opinion are often reported (Spiro, 1983). Here, a **conflict** is understood as a difference of opinion among the people concerned, the severity of which might be large or small. A debate ensues, and the involved parties try to get their own way or find a compromise. In traditional partnerships, in which a man and a woman allocate responsibility for goods in various areas on the basis of gender roles, syncratic decisions and conflicts are rare because the distribution of power is already established; in egalitarian relationships, conversely, conflicts and conflict resolution processes can be frequently observed.

Syncratic decisions can represent conflicts of various degrees about each partner's desires and goals. When partners have similar desires and ideas about goods, no conflict exists. However, when partners perceive the characteristics of various goods differently, judgments will differ, and a dispute over the facts arises that must be resolved. A real conflict arises when the partners differ in their ideas about what goals should be worked towards. The severity of the conflict depends on whether the differences of opinion are limited to subgoals or concern fundamental values (see Madden, 1982; March & Simon, 1958). In a similar manner, Brandstätter (1987) differentiated between probability conflicts, value conflicts and distribution conflicts:

(a) **Probability conflicts** arise when partners agree about the goal, but disagree about the best way to reach the goal. For example, they agree about the social significance of being well dressed for an important business dinner. However, making a decision about which specific suit or dress to buy can be difficult because their assessments of the various options may differ qualitatively or they may have different estimates of the price–performance ratio.
(b) **Value conflicts** arise when fundamental differences between the partners' goals exist. These conflicts are not primarily a matter of solving factual problems; rather, they concern differing understandings of values. For example, one partner might want a certain fashion item, while the other objects to the purchase. The second person might agree that the price and quality of the article are acceptable, but doubts the necessity of the purchase or considers the methods used to produce the article ethically dubious.
(c) **Distribution conflicts** arise when the distribution of resources is at stake. Even if the partners are both convinced that a certain product represents the optimal alternative on the market, one partner might be against the purchase because the product does not benefit him and therefore the distribution of utility between the partners is perceived as unfair.

Financial decisions in general, and decisions about expenses in households with one or more persons in particular, can be classified as illustrated in Figure 5.1. The areas highlighted in grey concern decisions involving more than one person.

5.1.2 Stage and Process Models of Purchase Decisions

From early on, researchers tried to understand purchase decisions in terms of models, finding some common framework to understand these decisions and – of particular interest to marketing – to identify those aspects that can be influenced.

A classical stage model of purchase decisions goes back to the beginning of the twentieth century (Dewey, 1910, as cited in Bruner & Pomazal, 1988) and is still part of many major textbooks on consumer behaviour (e.g., Solomon, 2011). It consists of five stages: (a) problem recognition, (b) information search, (c) evaluation of alternatives, (d) product choice, and (e) evaluation of outcomes. For the problem recognition stage, Bruner and Pomazal (1988) highlighted that a discrepancy between an actual state and a desired state first must be recognised by consumers. The desired state can be influenced by factors such as reference groups or novelty seeking. The actual state can be influenced by assortment deficiencies or arousal of needs. Both states can be influenced by financial considerations, the current situation or marketing efforts. Importantly, also, post-purchase evaluations can influence the actual state, thereby providing a link between the last of the five stages to the first in a

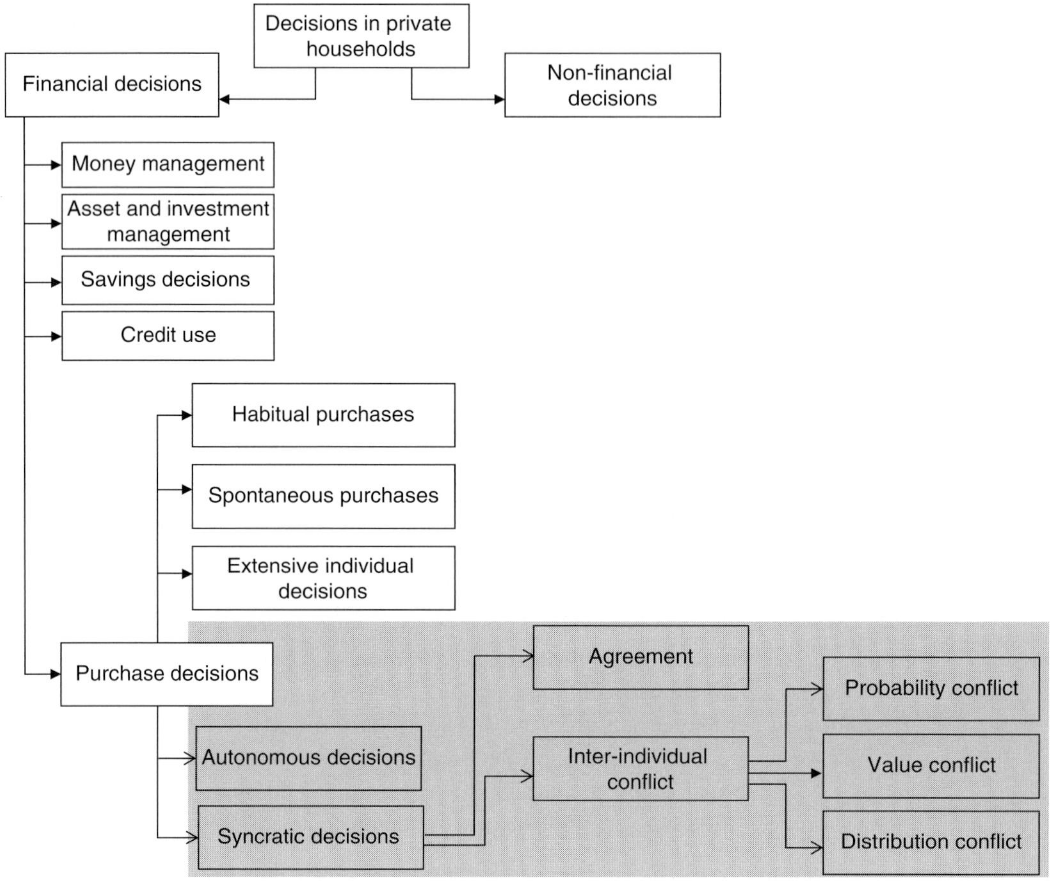

Figure 5.1 Classification of financial decisions in households with one or more persons (adapted from Kirchler et al., 2001, p. 77)

feedback loop. Bruner and Pomazal (1988) also distinguished between need recognition (mostly triggered through changes in the actual state) and opportunity recognition (mostly triggered through changes in the desired state). For the information search stage, Solomon (2011) points out that search is not always continued until enough information is acquired, and that it can take different forms. Bloch, Sherrell and Ridgway (1986) distinguished between prepurchase search and ongoing search. Prepurchase search means search that is driven by involvement in the purchase, and motivated by the wish to make better purchase decisions. Ongoing search, on the other hand, is driven by involvement in the product or product category, and motivated either by wishing to build up information for future use or by experiencing fun and pleasure. A potential pitfall of ongoing search is that it can contribute to impulse buying. Either way, the amount of information search can vary, from superficial and incidental scanning to deliberate search efforts. For the evaluation of alternatives stage and the product choice stage, Solomon (2011) highlights that actual consumer behaviour can deviate from what would be considered 'rational behaviour' and is influenced by heuristics (e.g., the price–quality heuristic), mental accounting, loss aversion or inertia.

Models of consumer behaviour are particularly developed in marketing contexts to explain effects of advertising. Fennis and Stroebe (2016) give an excellent overview of these models, grouping them into hierarchy-of-effects models and information processing models.

Hierarchy-of-effects models assume mediating processes between the advertisement and the desired outcome on the part of the consumer. These processes are cognitive, affective and conative (behavioural) – in other words, consumers are assumed first to think about the ad, then to form some emotional response and then to act (e.g., purchase the product in the ad). One of the earliest models in this domain was the **AIDA model**, named as the acronym of its four components: attention, interest, desire, action. According to Fennis and Stroebe (2016), this model dates back at least to the end of the nineteenth century. Later variations of this idea include the model by Lavidge and Steiner (1961), who suggested a sequence of awareness, knowledge, liking, preference, conviction and purchase. In this model, awareness and knowledge refer to the cognitive aspect, focusing on information. Liking and preference, the second two stages, refer to the affective aspects, focusing on favourable attitudes or feelings about the product. Conviction and purchase refer to the conative aspect, focusing on action. Later models questioned the assumption of a fixed sequence of 'think–feel–do': while this sequence may hold for some purchases, in other cases the order may be different. As one example of a more detailed approach, Vaughn (1980) suggested differentiating purchase situations along two dimensions: high involvement versus low involvement, and thinking versus feeling. He suggested that in each of the four resulting quadrants, a different sequence is relevant. (1) In the quadrant combining high involvement and thinking, comprising purchases such as cars, houses or new products, a 'learn–feel–do' sequence would apply, similar to the one described above. (2) In the quadrant of low involvement and thinking, comprising food or household items, a 'do–learn–feel' sequence would apply, for example through habit formation. (3) In the quadrant of high involvement and feeling, comprising cosmetics, fashion or jewellery, a 'feel–learn–do' sequence would apply. (4) Finally, in the quadrant of low involvement and feeling, comprising liquor, cigarettes or candy, a 'do–feel–learn' sequence would apply. Despite the intuitive appeal of these models, Fennis and Stroebe (2016) point out that several critical points have been raised – among others, that empirical support is weak, and that these models have a simplistic view of consumer behaviour without concern about moderators or mediating processes (Weilbacher, 2001). The limitations of hierarchy-of-effects models have led to moving away from trying to capture consumer behaviour in a single model, instead pinpointing specific processes, in particular attitude change and information processing (Fennis & Stroebe, 2016).

Among **information processing models**, the cognitive response model by Greenwald (1968, as cited in Fennis & Stroebe, 2016) introduced the idea that consumers not only passively react to a message, but also cognitively transform it – for example, by producing counterarguments or supportive arguments – and that this is more likely to occur with higher involvement. Dual-process models of persuasion, such as the **elaboration likelihood model** (ELM; Petty & Cacioppo, 1986) have refined this idea by distinguishing two different paths of persuasion: a central route and a peripheral route. The model describes that, when consumers are highly involved in a topic, they will follow the central route. They will carefully consider the arguments for and against the topic, evaluate whether these arguments are strong or weak, and change their attitudes accordingly. For example, they will be influenced by an ad that convincingly demonstrates that a new brand has better performance than the previous brands. Conversely, when consumers are not involved, or if they lack the capacity to process information, they will follow the peripheral route. They will more readily react to heuristic cues and their valence – for example, whether a liked celebrity is advertising a product.

Strack, Werth and Deutsch (2006) provide an integrative view on consumer behaviour based on the **reflective–impulsive model** (RIM; Strack & Deutsch, 2004). In particular, they view a specific behaviour not as either impulsive or reflective, but often as comprising components of both processes in different strengths. The strength of the reflective component will be higher when the topic is more important or when consumers are held accountable for their actions (e.g., by their spouses). The strength of the impulsive component will be higher, for example, when consumers have a strong habit in a certain consumption domain.

5.1.3 Goals and Motives in Purchase Decisions

According to the rational choice model, consumers objectively weigh the advantages and disadvantages of various alternatives and select the most beneficial one. In reality, however, decisions are also shaped by emotions. Consumers sometimes gain more enjoyment from the act of purchasing itself than from the product they finally decide to buy, and let themselves be influenced by sales offers even when they do not really need a given product.

The pleasure of buying and consuming is a decisive factor in many purchasing decisions. 'Enjoying life means consuming for pleasure, not consuming for survival or for need' (Gabriel & Lang, 1995, p. 100). Bell (1976) underscored the contradiction of rationality and discipline on the one hand and hedonism and wasteful extravagance on the other. Consumers with a hedonic orientation are viewed as irrational because the costs of hedonic behaviour accumulate in the long run.

Hedonism describes the search for pleasure and increased gratification. Pleasure is felt when bodily needs are satisfied. However, pleasure also changes with experience and adaptation. Campbell (1987) discussed luxury as experiences beyond the bounds of the familiar. Luxury and pleasure are linked to extraordinary experiences because experiences are only perceived as pleasurable when they are given mental attention. As the frequency of certain experiences rises, however, the amount of attention paid to them drops. For example, hunger can be assuaged by any number of foods. A feeling of pleasure, then, as opposed to merely a satisfaction of needs, emerges when this ordinary hunger is assuaged by extraordinary delicacies. However, the more frequently these delicacies are eaten, the more mundane they become, and their hedonic value sinks.

Consumers with a hedonic orientation pursue other goals in purchasing decisions beyond merely the basic use value of a good (Hirschman & Holbrook, 1982; Holbrook & Hirschman, 1982; Lunt & Livingstone, 1992). Accordingly, Babin, Darden and Griffin (1994) made a distinction between the utility aspects and the hedonic values of shopping. Consumers doing their shopping are described as people in search of something. They may seek out needed goods with the best price–performance ratio. They may strive for hedonic experiences. They may look for goods that symbolically correspond with their self-image, particularly accentuate it, and communicate who they are or how they would like to present themselves to their social environment (Reekie, 1992).

Besides the basic use value of a good, the added value arising from the symbolic benefits offered by a good (beyond instrumental opportunities to satisfy needs and wants) plays an important role (Vershofen, 1940). The experience of gaining attention in one's social environment, winning status and recognition, or looking attractive and desirable due to the purchase and consumption of specific goods lends these commodities a value in addition to their basic use value. According to Bourdieu (1984), the importance of additional value in affluent societies far exceeds that of basic use value. Consumption is described nearly exclusively as a function of aesthetics and personal style: 'everyday reality . . . becomes aestheticized, with objects and activities assuming the qualities of art and losing their functional and material bearings. Style becomes more important than utility, which acquires a vulgar, common hue' (Gabriel & Lang, 1995, p. 116). The extent to which symbols determine decision-making is made clear when the effect of promotional activities is investigated, through which very specific feelings are fused with the purchase of certain goods, and 'lifestyles' are created.

While hedonic-oriented consumers primarily seek out emotions, other people often look for symbols that define and symbolically extend their self-image. Holt (1995) introduced a typology of four consumer practices:

(a) 'Consuming as experience' refers to consumption that is driven by a search for emotional states and feelings.
(b) 'Consuming as integration' refers to consumption that serves to extend the self: consumers seek out symbols and buy them in order to be similar to their idols, to communicate with their idols through specific metaphors, or to help shape the world of their idols.
(c) 'Consuming as play' refers to consumption behaviour that is driven by a desire for socialising: consumers buy things enabling them to talk about their purchase, to entertain others and to put themselves in the spotlight.
(d) 'Consuming as classification' refers to the idea that consumption also serves as a means of differentiation and of identification with a social group (Holt, 1995). In some cases, consumers buy things in order to distance themselves from certain social groups and to demonstrate belonging to other groups (Kirchler & Pießlinger, 1992). Gasana (2009) reported that primarily clothes, cars and certain brands are used to compare oneself to other people.

Goods serve to satisfy basic needs, generate emotions, emphasise one's own identity or communicate with one's social environment. However, 'shopping' can also be perceived as a goal in itself and not just a means of reaching a goal. Since the middle of the 1980s, reports about two worrying developments can be found: **shopping addiction** and **compulsive buying** (e.g., O'Guinn & Faber, 1989; Raab, Neuner, Reisch & Scherhorn, 2005; Scherhorn, 1990). These two terms reflect a different view on the feelings during the act of buying. Scherhorn (1990) argued that the act of buying itself unleashes intense positive feelings that are sought out again and again. The costs and negative consequences, such as going into debt and overextending one's resources or feelings of guilt, are superseded by the positive experiences of buying. This picture is similar to other forms of addiction. O'Guinn and Faber (1989) argued that a purchase is made in reaction to negative feelings such as anxiety or tension, with the goal of calming down. This description is similar to other compulsions (e.g., compulsive hand-washing). A recent review (Müller, Mitchell & de Zwaan, 2015) argues that neither view fully captures the phenomenon and suggests the term **'pathological buying'**. The general characteristics are that the act of buying is no longer the means to an end, but is itself perceived as pleasurable and valuable. The possession of the purchased goods can lose so much importance as a motivator that affected consumers no longer even take their purchased products out of the packaging, but immediately dispose of them upon arriving home. Major characteristics are a preoccupation with shopping, strong urges to shop, and guilt after the frequent shopping episodes. Pathological buying is often accompanied by distress, marital conflicts and financial problems (Müller et al., 2015).

A combination of biological, social and psychological factors is suspected of causing this behaviour. Biological factors are made manifest in the diminished serotonin level of affected people, which has been observed with the phenomenon of compulsive buying (Faber & O'Guinn, 1992). Raab, Elger, Neuner and Weber (2011) were able to find differences in brain activity using functional magnetic resonance imaging (fMRI). Social factors can be seen in the increasing symbolic importance of consumer goods. Buying things demonstrates that one has money, success and power. The positive psychological experiences while shopping – such as the attention, recognition and social confirmation given to buyers in shops – encourage further acts of buying (O'Guinn & Faber, 1989). Psychological factors can be found in the initially positive reinforcement of shopping episodes and their use as escape from depression or anxiety, in failures of self-regulation, in materialism and in low self-esteem (Müller et al., 2015). Scherhorn, Reisch and Raab (1990) argued that buying things increases self-esteem. After making the purchase, however, negative feelings in the form of anger and guilt reduce self-esteem. In this way, a negative feedback loop arises between low self-esteem, going shopping to increase self-esteem, and negative consequences that reduce self-esteem. Dittmar, Beattie and Friese (1996) empirically confirmed pathological shoppers' attempts to increase their self-esteem: the surveyed shopping addicts exhibited a significantly lower self-esteem than unproblematic shoppers did, and the act of purchasing specific products served to bridge the perceived discrepancies between the current and the ideal self.

Although the physical ownership of a good is not seen as a motive for buying it, pathological buying usually involves a preference for specific classes of products. Evidence on potential gender effects in the magnitude of pathological buying is mixed – some studies find no gender differences, others report that women more often show pathological buying (Müller et al., 2015). Gender differences occur in the specific products bought: men prefer to buy high-tech products and sporting goods, while women tend to buy clothing and shoes, jewellery and cosmetic products (Dittmar, 1992). The aforementioned product categories are fraught with symbolism and therefore have a positive effect on self-esteem. Dittmar et al. (1996) concluded that low self-esteem in the form of discrepancies between the current and ideal self, which are perceived as unpleasant, only leads a person to develop shopping addiction when goods are awarded a high symbolic value and purchasing goods is therefore seen as an effective means of increasing one's self-esteem.

5.2 Purchase Decisions in Private Households

Financial matters are important in partnerships, whether with or without children, and are a common cause of differences of opinion. Studies of money and how it is handled concern themselves with the income of the husband and the wife, whether they feel that the distribution of money is fair and that each person's influence on decision-making is balanced, with their satisfaction with the relationship, and with the significance of the money earned by the husband and the wife, respectively (Burgoyne & Kirchler, 2008).

Particularly in relationships in which money represents a part of the 'emotional economy' (Goode, 2010), the importance of money can extend far beyond its mere material value. Due to shared experiences dealing with money, the topic becomes laden with meanings (Nyman, Reinikainen & Stocks, 2013) that contain expectations about future behaviour. Halleröd, Díaz-Martínez and Stocks (2007) speak of a personalisation of money. According to a recent study by de Henau and Himmelweit (2013) focusing on satisfaction with household income, men's full-time employment – in contrast to women's employment – has a significant positive influence on both partners' satisfaction with household income. Kan and Laurie (2011) found that men's well-being was influenced solely by their own money management, whereas women's well-being was determined partly by their own and partly by their partner's behaviour.

In the family, the man is traditionally the breadwinner and therefore plays the decisive role in financial decision-making (Pahl, 1995; Vogler & Pahl, 1994). The woman's income is considered 'extra money'. In the United States – where, in contrast to Europe, there is little political intervention in family matters – a higher income awards a man not only the title of breadwinner but also a higher status (Nyman et al. 2013; Wilson & Stocks, 2007). When the wife earns more than the husband, however, this represents such an irritating state of affairs that attempts are actively made to neutralise the imbalance caused by the differences in income and to restore the classic image of the male breadwinner. This also happens in couples in which the woman has higher status and is the main provider (Tichenor, 1999). In the literature, this phenomenon is called '**doing gender**' (West & Zimmerman, 1987; for a review see Bennett, 2013). One's income level is not uncommonly equated with one's level of personal success. Within this context, Ratliff and Oishi (2013) examined the influence of a romantic partner's success or failure on one's own self-esteem. It turns out that men's implicit self-esteem is lower when their partner succeeds than when their partner fails, whereas women's implicit self-esteem is not. Men had lower self-esteem when their partner did well at a social intelligence task than when their partner did poorly. Women's self-esteem was unaffected by partner performance. Doing gender refers to a gender norm violation, as is the case when a woman's earnings rise and her share of housework decreases (Rizavi & Sofer, 2010). The situation becomes especially critical when her income rises beyond the point where it equals her husband's income (Sevilla-Sanz, Gimenez-Nadal & Fernandez, 2010).

Men and women typically have different levels of financial resources at their disposal. Daly and Rake (2003) collected data from European Union countries as well as from the United States and found that women, on average, had direct control of less than one-third of household income. According to data collected via the British Household Panel Survey, women's proportion of private household expenditures is not half of the family's total financial resources but only 40% on average (Couprie, 2007). Similar results were reported by Kalugina, Radtchenko and Sofer (2009).

Women have fewer resources at their disposal for personal expenditures than men (Cantillon, 2013). This disparity can be offset in that the man supports the woman financially; bills are not paid together, but exclusively or primarily by him. When expenditures exceed the income of the partner with the lower income and the other person pays the bills, the first partner loses status and autonomy. In order to preserve their own autonomy, women in Sweden were willing to give up the higher standard of living that would be possible by accessing their partner's money (Nyman & Reinikainen, 2007). Contributing equally to paying the bills is especially important, according to Ashby and Burgoyne (2008), in order to avoid differences in status and the loss of autonomy.

How household income is dealt with varies in different partnerships. Pahl (1995) distinguished joint money management, in which the partners have equal command of the money, from joint funds that are managed by either the husband or the wife. In an international study encompassing data from thirty-one nations, Lauer and Yodanis (2011) found that most married couples tend to manage their money jointly. The authors see the increase in efficiency stemming from being able to avoid constant negotiations between partners as the reason for this, while Pahl (2008) assumed that it is primarily the couple's needs that are at the fore in choosing this system. Studies by Díaz-Martínez, Dema and Ibánez (2007), Pahl (1989) and Vogler, Brockmann and Wiggins (2006) produced similar results.

In relationships where the partners have low income, the woman often manages the joint income, while the man keeps the accounts in high-income households (Vogler, 1998). Sung and Bennett (2007) show with qualitative data that the 'all in one pot' method is typically practised in relationships with low or middle income. According to Sonnenberg (2008), however, it should be noted that 'putting everything in one pot' subsumes not just practices of joint money management, but also money-related actions taken separately. In some partnerships, the man or the woman has autonomous command of the money. In other cases, separate funds for different areas of expenditure, segregated by gender, are reported. In a few households, partners keep completely separate accounts.

Studies of household financial matters usually related to married couples and their money management. Recently, 'couples with marriage licences' have lost their exclusive status as a unit of investigation due to an increase in life partnerships of various other types (Burgoyne, 2008). Accordingly, there is steadily growing interest within the current research in relationships beyond the traditional family, such as young cohabiting parents, childless cohabiting partners, same-sex couples and couples living separately. Due to societal changes, it seems reasonable to investigate money management in private households as a function of the quality of the relationship of the people living under one roof. Elizabeth (2001) was able to detect a trend towards more autonomy and separate finances among life partners, for example (see also Burns, Burgoyne & Clarke, 2008; Evertsson & Nyman, 2012). Addabbo, Emilia, Arrizabalaga, Borderias and Owens (2010) consider whether this is a manifestation of a life cycle stage or an enduring trend resulting from the rejection of the male breadwinner ideology and other societal developments. Vogler, Brockmann and Wiggins (2008) argue that whether or not the partners are married is not the most critical factor – rather, it is the joint obligations that the partners enter into. Money management in life partnerships where the partners have children is similar to that of married parents, for example, and different from the money management of married couples without children. According to Burgoyne, Clarke and Burns (2011), same-sex couples (without children) also tend to manage their finances separately, similarly to married couples without children. Regarding partners' influence, Schneider, Schöneberg and Ferié (2013) found that homosexual couples tend to use highly egalitarian processes in purchase decisions.

5.2.1 Models for Describing Purchase Decisions in the Household

Purchasing decisions among members of private households are complex. Everyday life under a shared roof does not just consist of a sum of actions and reactions, but rather represents a social system whose dynamics are influenced by the structure of the relationships, the characteristics of the individuals and the general social and physical surroundings.

In economics, purchasing decisions in multi-person households are frequently described on the basis of the rational choice model (Himmelweit, Santos, Sevilla & Sofer, 2013). What are known as 'unitary models' are based upon the assumption that the family acts as a single decision-making unit. One person, usually the breadwinner, makes decisions in the name of everyone. Other models, known as 'bargaining models', use either cooperative or non-cooperative game theory to describe decisions as bargaining between individuals whose preferences differ. Still other models, 'collective models', are a generalisation of cooperative bargaining models that integrate more complex interaction processes among household members. According to Antonides (2011), these more complex models describe financial matters in the home much better than simple normative models.

Economics typically makes use of normative models, while psychology attempts to describe the complex events in the household in a way that is as true to life as possible. Normative models postulate that decision-making processes are characterised by an unambiguously defined beginning and a clearly perceivable end. According to this, partners consistently pass through various phases until they are able to make a subjectively optimal decision after having weighed all available alternatives. However, when households made up of multiple people are accepted to be complex, dynamic systems, it cannot be assumed that decision-making processes follow normative models. Economic decisions are generally embedded in the household's daily routine, in which numerous tasks and problems are dealt with that do not follow after one another in an orderly fashion, but frequently take place simultaneously.

The attempt to describe how partners make decisions as precisely as necessary, yet at the same time as simply as possible, has led to the development of structural models, particularly in consumer research. The bulk of these **total models** – those models, according to Kroeber-Riel (1992), that attempt to depict all purchasing and decision-making behaviour – concern individual decision-making (e.g., Engel, Blackwell & Miniard, 2007; Howard & Sheth, 1969; Nicosia, 1966). Decisions in private households have been described by Corfman (1987), Pollay (1968), Sheth (1974) and Scanzoni and Polonko (1980) and were summarised in a **model of purchase decisions in private households** by Kirchler (1989). This model describes decisions as influenced by product type, power and harmony in the relationship and the resulting interaction principles, and conflict type, as well as regulation of benefits such as utility debts or influence debts. The model, shown in Figure 5.2, will now be introduced in more detail.

Market events are the starting point for purchase decisions. On the basis of individual needs and desires, information about available goods is obtained, or targeted information can produce new needs that demand satisfaction. Depending on the severity of the desire for a good or the frequency with which it is needed, goods can be bought as immediate gratification (spontaneous purchase), or the good can be bought as part of a routine (habitual purchase). However, when the desire for a good arises that is infrequently purchased, a genuine, extensive decision-making process begins. The wish for a certain good can be immediately shared with one's partner in order to learn his or her position and to prompt him or her to collect information and make a selection. The wish can also be shared only after information about the various product alternatives has been obtained and an individual preference has been developed. The active partner – the one who harbours the wish to make the purchase – can obtain information about various options and either share the intention to make the purchase with the other person or make an autonomous decision without discussing it with the other person beforehand.

Autonomous decisions do not take place completely independently of the passive partner – the partner who does not have a wish to buy the relevant product. The active partner estimates the other partner's utility from the available product alternatives as well as approval of the purchase and takes these estimates into account.

Whether a spontaneous, habitual, autonomous or joint decision evolves depends primarily on the clarity and strength of the desire, on the type of product, on the power structure within the relationship and on the relationship quality. The cheaper, the more socially inconspicuous, the simpler and the more banal the product palette, the lower the likelihood of a joint decision. This likelihood is also lowered when the active partner has more power in the relationship or when the relationship harmony is generally low. Finally, in relationships with a traditional role orientation, where gender roles are strictly divided, some decisions clearly fall within the area of responsibility of exclusively one partner. Despite these boundary conditions, a large portion of purchasing decisions in households are not made by one person acting alone (Kirchler et al., 2001). Couples also report higher satisfaction when they make decisions together rather than autonomously (Vogler, Lyonette & Wiggins, 2008).

When neither a spontaneous, a habitual nor an autonomous individual decision is made, a decision-making process begins between the partners. After one or both partners have collected information about possible options, the available alternatives are evaluated according to costs and quality. Analysing the available alternatives and comparing them with one's ideal leads to the development of preferences. The preference for one alternative is based on the extent to which it satisfies one's own needs and on the value it has for the other partner. These simultaneously occurring goals – to satisfy one's own needs and desires while not jeopardising the relationship – are frequently in competition with one another and are considered more or less important depending on the quality of the relationship. In harmonious relationships, especially, partners do not make their 'calculations' without taking the other person into account. In their deliberations, they consider the consequences for the other person and seek to maximise joint utility. Their own subjective order of preferences, therefore, depends to a varying degree upon what they presume their partner's preferences to be. These ideas can be expressed as a general formula:

$$P_{ik} = f(b_{ik} * S_{ik,} b_{jk} * S_{jk})$$

This formula states that the preference of a Person i for a Product k (P_{ik}) is a function of that person's own anticipated satisfaction with the product (S_{ik}) and the anticipated satisfaction of the partner (S_{jk}). These two elements are given variable weight (b_{ik}, b_{jk}). The better the quality of the relationship, the more a person tends to place just as much or even more weight on the partner's anticipated satisfaction as on their own ($b_{ik} \leq b_{jk}$). In egoistic relationships, the person primarily considers his or her own anticipated satisfaction, but not that of the partner ($b_{ik} > b_{jk}$ or even $b_{jk} = 0$).

At the beginning of a joint decision, the partners develop preferences for the purchase of one alternative or about forgoing the purchase altogether. In order to learn about each other's preferences they need to talk about them, and if their preferences are different a conflict arises. In what are often long drawn-out discussions, the partners attempt to exert influence on one another in order to bring their standpoints closer together. Depending on the conflict type (probability conflict, value conflict, distribution conflict), the partners will try to influence the other person's position using factual, emotional or bargaining tactics. The partners seek to both (a) maximise their utility from the purchase and (b) minimise the costs that an overly harsh discussion style would have on the relationship. Depending on power and harmony in the relationship, one goal or the other can seem more important to them, and correspondingly the partners will apply various tactics in order to resolve the conflict.

Even after agreement is reached, the decision-making process still proceeds. First, intra-individual conflicts can arise (having 'second thoughts' about a decision) and lead back to earlier stages of information search. Second, it still remains to be considered whether one partner will benefit more from the purchase than the other, and, if so, how the regulation of benefits occurs. Potential asymmetries in utility and influence are considered. If one partner profits significantly more than the other, **utility debts** arise that need to be settled over the short or long term, depending on the quality of the relationship. In addition to utility debts, the partners can also consider **influence debts** that result from a potentially lop-sided distribution of influence in the decision. When, for example, a woman wants to buy an expensive article of clothing, she also wants her husband to approve of it. If her selection strikes his fancy, leading him to approve of the purchase, the product is bought. Even though both partners selected the same alternative from the available selection of clothes, the wife accrues utility debts as a result of the purchase. This means that the husband, depending on the intra-familial arrangement regarding utility differences, has the right to her approval in the next purchases he intends to make. Utility debts and influence debts frequently show up in lines of argument: when one of the partners would like one good, but the other partner prefers a different one, the first partner can either point out that it's currently his turn to make a purchase, or that it's his turn to make the decision because the other person called the shots in previous decisions.

Relationships differ in terms of power structure and harmony, and specific modes of interaction follow from these differences. Kirchler (1989) distinguished four **interaction principles**: love principle, credit principle, equity principle and egoism principle. These interaction principles also concern the regulation of utility debts and influence debts. In an egalitarian and satisfying partnership, the distributions of utility as well as influence between partners should be balanced over the course of time. The way in which debts of utility and influence are kept tabs on and eventually called in depends on the interaction principle:

(a) If the relationship resembles one between acquaintances and an imbalance of power in favour of either the man or the woman is present, meaning that the relationship can be described on the basis of the egoism principle, the partner with more power decides how and when utility debts need to be settled.
(b) If the quality of the relationship is low but power is distributed in a more egalitarian manner, interactions between the partners will be perceived as a deal of give and take as between business partners (equity principle). Restitution for the utility that arises for the other person in the purchase situation needs to be made immediately.
(c) If the relationship resembles one between good friends, the partners act according to the credit principle. Since the partners trust one another, utility differences can remain in place over long periods of time. In the long run, however, balance is aimed for.
(d) The more harmonious the relationship, the more the partners act according to the love principle. They are altruistic and each person seeks to bestow favours on the other without expecting repayment. Partners do not keep tabs on the loss of utility in a conflict situation because the partner's pleasure has more weight than the satisfaction that would result from consuming or using the product alone. A benefit for one partner means a benefit for the other partner as well. Asymmetrical distributions of utility become meaningless.

When the partners are in agreement about the regulation of utility debts and influence debts, nothing more stands in the way of a final syncratic decision, and the decision-making process is finished (Figure 5.2).

5.2.2 Methods of Studying Purchase Decisions in the Household

A variety of social scientific methods is used to study decision-making dynamics in purchase decisions and the distribution of influence among household members. Commonly, either surveys are conducted or interaction dynamics are observed. Couples and their children can be observed in their natural life context or be invited into the laboratory.

It is extraordinarily difficult to persuade household members to come into the laboratory to conduct an argument about how an imaginary sum of money is to be spent or to have a serious disagreement about some other financial matter. In addition, when partners are asked to reproduce natural everyday family life in their home in front of the cameras, the data recorded are often unproductively 'smooth' and incident-free. Therefore, the question arises as to whether findings from small group research or from '**synthetic families**', consisting of a male and female participant of about equal age plus another younger person, can be extrapolated to cover intimate relationships. However, efforts to draw parallels between ad hoc small groups and partners in intimate relationships have proven unsuccessful. Unique processes develop within intimate relationships. Hence, family members' behaviour must be observed in its natural setting, which is difficult, especially since the act of observation cannot be allowed to disrupt and therefore distort the relevant behaviour.

While adequately observing behaviour is difficult, it is easy to make use of interviews and surveys. These methods have found particularly frequent application in studies of purchasing behaviour in private households, most of which have been conducted by market research institutes. Interviews and surveys often are focused on a specific area of expenditure and are mainly conducted with one partner, occasionally with both, and rarely with children as well.

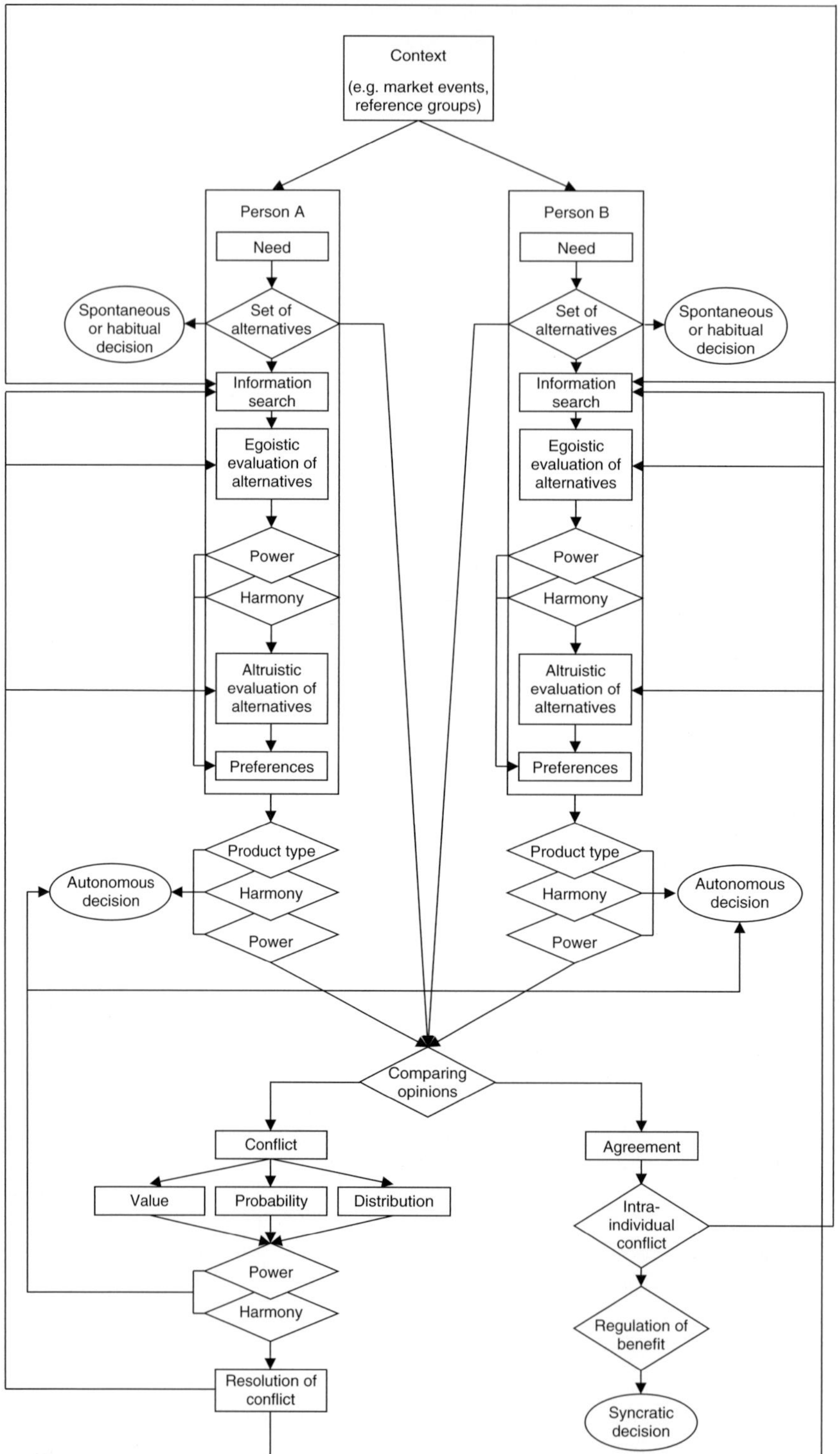

Figure 5.2 Model of purchase decisions in private households (Kirchler et al., 2001, p. 82)

If partners are asked to recount their shared experiences, their accounts often differ markedly. These differences are partly caused by the difficulty people have in recalling and 'reconstructing' mundane events and partly because people distort their accounts to bolster their own self-esteem. Smith, Leffingwell and Ptacek (1999) argued that the information recalled by people about their experiences lacks validity because experiences are encoded in an incomplete or distorted fashion, and details are forgotten. Answers are affected by social stereotypes, a tendency to portray oneself in a better light, and the tendency to conform to notions of social desirability. Schütz (1999) interviewed couples separately about joint conflicts and found that in each case the other partner was blamed for initiating the conflict. Respondents claimed that it was the other one who began the argument and behaved in a negative manner, not themselves.

When devising sets of questions to be asked about the private household, consideration must be given as to who will be asked to provide information, and which experiences should be reported; and the formulation of the questions and the suggested answers may influence the data obtained. These problems will now be discussed in turn.

In earlier studies, it was common to ask only one person to provide information about everyday events, and for interviews conducted at home this was usually the woman. Her interpretation of shared activities was taken to be valid and reliable, based on the assumption either that both partners shared the same views on an issue, or that one partner knows and is able to report accurately on the views of the other partner. However, a series of studies have shown that individual reconstructions of a shared reality vary considerably, both between adults and between adults and children. One partner can only offer their version of shared experiences, not reality as perceived and reconstructed by all. Kirchler (1989) summarised the results of sixteen studies looking at influence patterns in relationships, as reported by both partners, and found that reports were congruent in about 60% of all cases. However, in over a third of cases the reports differed.

When complex information needs to be processed with little time available, or when events were originally perceived and processed without being paid much attention and are therefore recalled poorly, interviewees will often resort to stereotypes, prejudices or schematised images in the hope that reality will correspond to these to some degree (Hastie, 1982). If complex scenarios need to be recalled, these are subjectively modified in such a way as to make sense in the current situation, regardless of the actual events in the past. For these reasons, the answer to the question as to who should be asked to provide information is clear: in order to record a shared reality, it is necessary to ask all those involved in sharing it.

Cognitive psychology has collected a large amount of findings pointing to various systematic errors (e.g., Ross & Nisbett, 1991; Schwarz, 1999). Everyday life at home is marked by a variety of mundane, routine events that are seldom paid any attention. Because attention is directed elsewhere, the reliability of one's memory of those events is questionable. Research into judgment heuristics (Tversky & Kahneman, 1974) offers an explanation for this. When judgments build on the availability heuristic, they are formed on the basis of the difficulty or ease with which individual pieces of information can be recalled from memory. Since memory is dependent not only on the frequency of presentation but also on various other factors, such as the attention paid to events while perceiving them and the degree of reflection about them, the availability heuristic can lead to misjudgments and overestimation of the frequency of notable events.

If difficulties occur in recalling events and in providing an account of them, interviewees could be inclined to give answers that conform to social stereotypes. People are not always interested in completing lengthy questionnaires. It is not surprising that, when asked about the distribution of influence in joint decisions, their answers tend to reflect traditional models of gender roles.

A further fact challenging traditional questionnaire-based studies is that experiences in the private sphere are often accompanied by intense emotions. However, these emotions usually have faded again by the time the questionnaire is completed. The intensity of the situation is forgotten, and the thoughts that were once wholly concentrated on the situation at hand are now given over to other things. Moreover, everyday life is complex, and intimate partners cognitively structure this complex reality in their own subjective manner. The private language of partners is an indication of their subjective organisation of shared events. In a questionnaire, however, opportunities for subjectively structuring one's experienced reality are severely limited.

The fact that memories and reports about past events as recounted in a questionnaire are not free of distortions has been demonstrated repeatedly (e.g., Fiedler, 1991; Forgas, 1991; Schwarz, Strack, Kommer & Wagner, 1987). The current mood can influence whether positive or negative events come to mind more easily (Bower, 1981), or mood can be used as a piece of information in itself (Schwarz, 1987). Reports in questionnaires also depend on the order of specific and general questions (Strack, Martin & Schwarz, 1988) or the degree of differentiation in answer scales (Schwarz & Scheuring, 1988).

It is not only errors in memory that speak against the use of questionnaires. In a questionnaire, it is hardly possible to represent the dynamics of everyday life. Processes that extend over time become compressed into a single point of reporting. What is reported is that which appears – in retrospect – to be relatively unchanging. In taking these reports at face value, it is implicitly assumed that rigid action–reaction sequences exist and are recognised as such. However, it is precisely in everyday life that completely different courses of action can be found (Pulver, 1991).

Traditional social scientific methods were commonly criticised as not accurately capturing the full complexity of household situations (e.g., Clark & Reis, 1988; Miller & Boster, 1988). There seems to be consensus that a variety of methods and longitudinal studies including all members of the household are necessary to capture adequately the dynamics of everyday events (Burns & Gentry, 1990; Kirchler et al., 2001). In order to investigate complex decision-making processes in private households and their results, research techniques that capture the entire social system are necessary. **Diary methods** are measures (usually short questionnaires) that are repeatedly completed in a real-life situation, either at a specific time or at a specific event. They lend themselves well to capturing sequences of decision-making episodes and the interconnectedness of various tasks (Duck, 1991; Kirchler et al., 2001). Most notably, diaries offer the advantage of being able to capture immediately the real behaviour of individuals during the decision-making process, making them less biased by problems that couples have recalling what are often mundane events (e.g., Belch & Willis, 2002; Muehlbacher, Hofmann, Kirchler & Roland-Lévy, 2009). Therefore, diary methods have a high degree of what is termed 'ecological validity' (Brunswick, 1949).

Hektner, Schmidt and Csikszentmihalyi (2007) provided an overview of diary procedures. In household studies, diaries have long been deployed to examine partners' time use (Hornik, 1982; Robinson, Yerby, Fieweger & Somerick, 1977; Vanek, 1974). Using diaries to capture interaction processes between partners has also been attempted (Auhagen, 1987; Duck, 1991; Feger & Auhagen, 1987; Kirchler, 1988a; Kirchler et al., 2001).

Kirchler (1996) developed the **decision diary**, an events diary for partners that enables researchers to capture not only economic decision-making but also non-economic decision-making processes running in parallel over long sequences of time. The diary is filled in every evening by both partners separately, after they have agreed upon which topics of conversation led to differences of opinion during the current day. The partners report on whether they spoke to one another on the given day, how long they talked and about what topics, whether they had disparate opinions, and how they felt during their conversations. In the daily entries, they are also asked to describe how good their relationship to one another is, how free and strong they feel in the relationship, and how strong they feel in comparison to the other partner. If one or more differences of opinion are reported, further questions on this topic have to be answered. The participants indicate what the difference of opinion or conflict consisted of, where the conversation took place, what else they were doing simultaneously, and who else was present. It is also noted how long the conversation lasted, how often this topic had already been discussed, who initiated the conversation, who had more expertise on the topic, how important this topic was to the partners, to what extent the conversation proceeded factually or emotionally, how much influence each person exerted on the outcome of the conversation, whether or not a decision was made, how high each partner's subjective benefit was, how fair the decision-making process and the outcome of the conversation were, which tactics each person used to convince the other, if it concerned a value conflict, probability conflict or distribution conflict, and how satisfied they were with the outcome of the conversation. When the difference of opinion concerned economic issues, the partners also estimated the amount of money concerned. An example page from the diary and the instructions can be found in Figures 5.3a, 5.3b and 5.3c. This diary was kept by a group of forty married couples for a year (Kirchler et al., 2001).

5.2.3 Influence Distribution between Spouses

Who has how much influence in syncratic purchasing decisions in households with or without children, and what are the causes of this? It makes sense that the probability that several people will take part in a purchase decision is high in the case of expensive, long-lasting goods for which no distinct cognitive decision-making scripts exist, that concern multiple people in the household, and that are important for the household's social standing. What remains in question is why in some partnerships the man has more say than the woman regarding the purchase of certain goods, while the woman has more say in other areas.

Studies on influence distribution between partners go back several decades. Some had a more applied focus, mainly wanting to determine who is responsible for the bulk of the family budget. Others had a more academic focus, trying to understand the specific determinants of influence in household decisions. Averaged across several studies, findings show that men and women claim to make more than half of decisions together. The remaining decisions are made approximately equally often by men and women acting autonomously. Both partners have about equal say (Kirchler et al., 2001).

However, these averages may mask important variations. Davis (1976) emphasised that whether the husband or wife dominates the decision depends on the category of the product. He pointed out that, at that time, the woman most frequently handled purchases made in the supermarket and made decisions about non-durable consumer goods such as groceries and food, cleaning products and other goods that are needed daily. The woman also decided how the residence will be furnished; not only was she responsible for the kitchen and for procuring and preparing food, she also maintained the residence and made decisions about personal care products, called the doctor when necessary and bought medicine. She bought her own and the children's clothes, and often those for her husband as well. In matters related to durable consumer goods, however, the man stepped into action as a decision-maker significantly more frequently than the woman. He was in charge of matters concerning the purchase of a car, a camera, a television and stereo equipment, a refrigerator or a dishwasher. Aside from these areas of expenditure, the man seemed to control the money management (insurance, loans and bills) and savings behaviour in the household. The purchase of

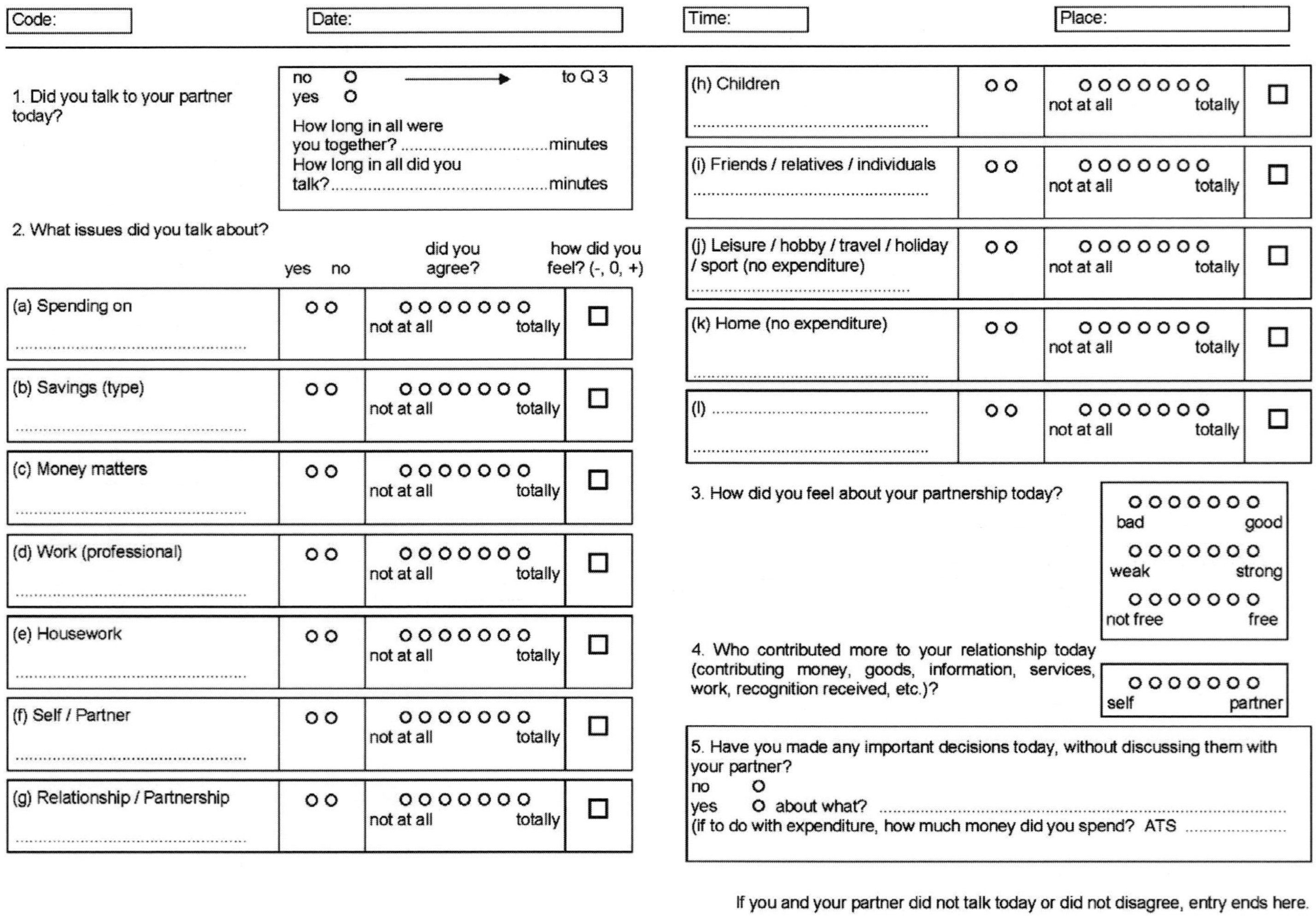

Code: | Date: | Time: | Place:

1. Did you talk to your partner today?

no O → to Q 3
yes O
How long in all were you together? ....minutes
How long in all did you talk? ....minutes

2. What issues did you talk about?

	yes no	did you agree?	how did you feel? (-, 0, +)
(a) Spending on	O O	O O O O O O O not at all … totally	☐
(b) Savings (type)	O O	O O O O O O O not at all … totally	☐
(c) Money matters	O O	O O O O O O O not at all … totally	☐
(d) Work (professional)	O O	O O O O O O O not at all … totally	☐
(e) Housework	O O	O O O O O O O not at all … totally	☐
(f) Self / Partner	O O	O O O O O O O not at all … totally	☐
(g) Relationship / Partnership	O O	O O O O O O O not at all … totally	☐
(h) Children	O O	O O O O O O O not at all … totally	☐
(i) Friends / relatives / individuals	O O	O O O O O O O not at all … totally	☐
(j) Leisure / hobby / travel / holiday / sport (no expenditure)	O O	O O O O O O O not at all … totally	☐
(k) Home (no expenditure)	O O	O O O O O O O not at all … totally	☐
(l)	O O	O O O O O O O not at all … totally	☐

3. How did you feel about your partnership today?

O O O O O O O bad … good
O O O O O O O weak … strong
O O O O O O O not free … free

4. Who contributed more to your relationship today (contributing money, goods, information, services, work, recognition received, etc.)?

O O O O O O O self … partner

5. Have you made any important decisions today, without discussing them with your partner?
no O
yes O about what? ....
(if to do with expenditure, how much money did you spend? ATS ....

If you and your partner did not talk today or did not disagree, entry ends here.

Figure 5.3a Decision diary (first page; Kirchler et al., 2001, pp. 116–17)

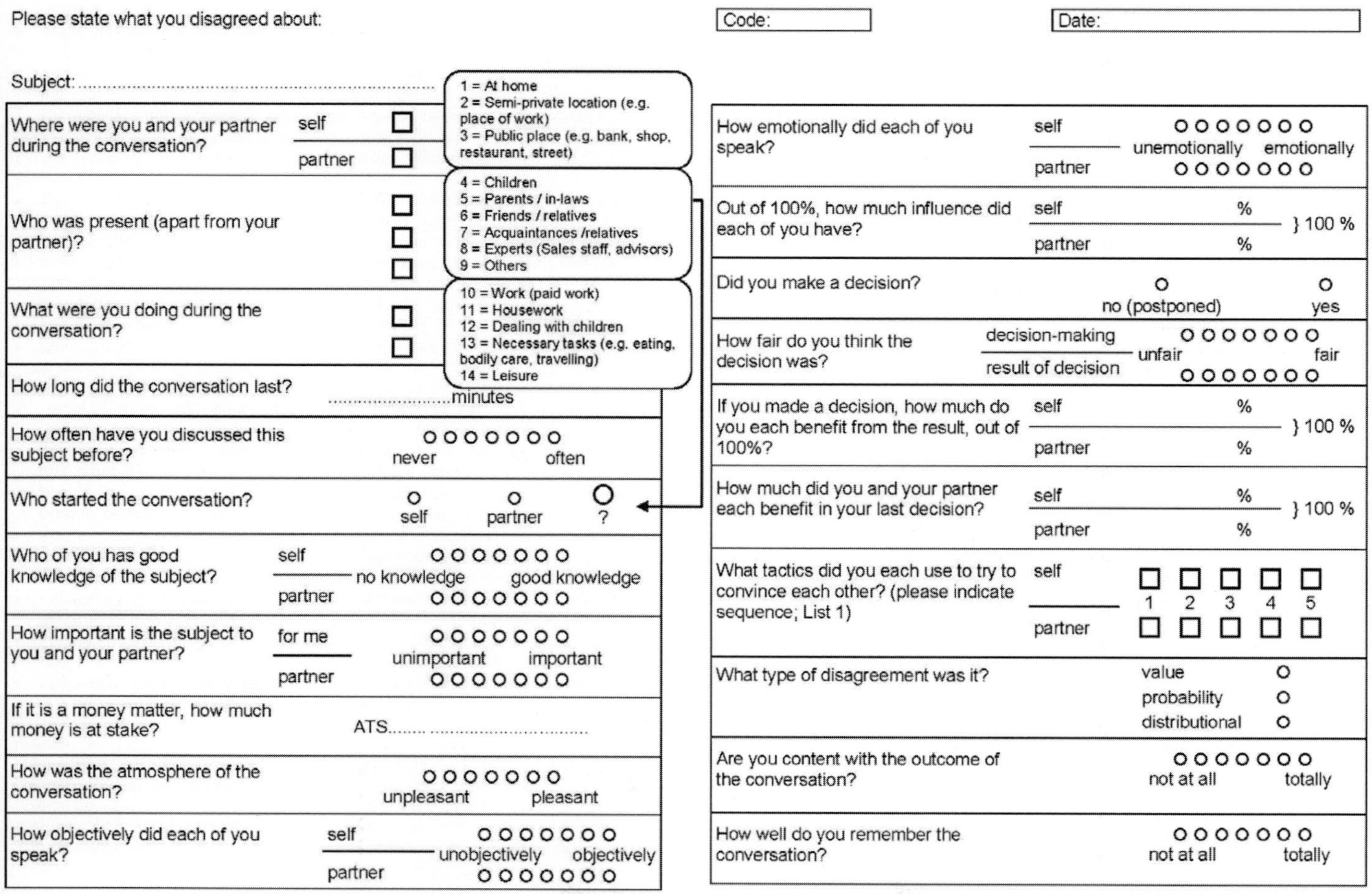

Please state what you disagreed about:

Code:

Date:

Subject: ....

Where were you and your partner during the conversation?	self ☐ / partner ☐
Who was present (apart from your partner)?	☐ ☐ ☐
What were you doing during the conversation?	☐ ☐
How long did the conversation last?	........................minutes
How often have you discussed this subject before?	O O O O O O O never … often
Who started the conversation?	O self O partner O ?
Who of you has good knowledge of the subject?	self / partner: O O O O O O O no knowledge … good knowledge
How important is the subject to you and your partner?	for me / partner: O O O O O O O unimportant … important
If it is a money matter, how much money is at stake?	ATS....... ....
How was the atmosphere of the conversation?	O O O O O O O unpleasant … pleasant
How objectively did each of you speak?	self / partner: O O O O O O O unobjectively … objectively

1 = At home
2 = Semi-private location (e.g. place of work)
3 = Public place (e.g. bank, shop, restaurant, street)

4 = Children
5 = Parents / in-laws
6 = Friends / relatives
7 = Acquaintances /relatives
8 = Experts (Sales staff, advisors)
9 = Others

10 = Work (paid work)
11 = Housework
12 = Dealing with children
13 = Necessary tasks (e.g. eating, bodily care, travelling)
14 = Leisure

How emotionally did each of you speak?	self / partner: O O O O O O O unemotionally … emotionally
Out of 100%, how much influence did each of you have?	self % / partner % } 100 %
Did you make a decision?	O no (postponed) O yes
How fair do you think the decision was?	decision-making / result of decision: O O O O O O O unfair … fair
If you made a decision, how much do you each benefit from the result, out of 100%?	self % / partner % } 100 %
How much did you and your partner each benefit in your last decision?	self % / partner % } 100 %
What tactics did you each use to try to convince each other? (please indicate sequence; List 1)	self ☐ ☐ ☐ ☐ ☐ / 1 2 3 4 5 / partner ☐ ☐ ☐ ☐ ☐
What type of disagreement was it?	value O / probability O / distributional O
Are you content with the outcome of the conversation?	O O O O O O O not at all … totally
How well do you remember the conversation?	O O O O O O O not at all … totally

Figure 5.3b Decision diary (second page; Kirchler et al., 2001, pp. 118–19)

Instructions for completing the diary

Together with your partner, recall all the conversations you have had together today, and what topics were discussed in these conversations. Try to remember the conversations accurately, and recall any differences of opinion between you and your partner at the beginning, during, or at the end of the conversation. When you have decided together what it was you talked about, and which matters you disagreed about – even if the difference of opinion was only slight – please fill in the diary on your own. Begin by stating what you talked about. Then answer in detail about the conversations which represented a difference of opinion between you and your partner.

Here is some information that you will find useful in completing the diary question sheet:

- In general, a box is completed by filling in a number or symbol, and a circle by putting a cross in the relevant one.
- On the first page of the diary, you will find some possible topics of conversation listed, as well as some statements about feelings.
- Question 1: This asks whether you and your partner have had a conversation. If you have not talked, go straight to question 3; if you did talk to each other, please answer the questions in the order that they appear.
- Question 2: Here you will find a series of conversation topics. The first three relate to economic matters. The first is about expenditure on a product or service, whether expensive or inexpensive. Please specify which product or service it was. The second relates to savings, either methods of saving or actual funds. Again, please state exactly what type of savings you discussed. Your answer on the third topic is the place to mention all the money matters that do not come under the heading of the first or the second topic. Question 2 then continues with other subject areas. At the end, there is space for subject areas that do not feature in the list. These are for you to fill in yourself as required.
- Record your feelings during the conversation by putting a '+' in the relevant box if you felt definitely good, and a '-' if you felt definitely bad. If, exceptionally, you cannot decide whether your feelings were good or bad, or if you were entirely indifferent, enter the symbol '0'.
- If you did not talk to your partner on a particular day, or did not disagree, then your entry will end at the bottom of the first page. Otherwise, turn to the next page.
- All the questions on the next page relate to a single conversation with your partner. Please answer all the questions. There are lists associated with some of the questions. Wherever this is the case, please refer to the relevant list. Sometimes just one answer is required; in other cases, you can give more than one answer.
- If you talked about several subjects on a given day, or if you discussed one topic several times, please complete a separate copy of the second page for each conversation.
- Finally, if you happen to be on holiday or away on business at the time, please state this on your answer sheet.

On the second page, you are asked what type of disagreement you had. You need to state which category the issue mainly belongs in: probability, value, or distributional.

- Probability: It is a probability issue if you and your partner are of different opinions, but still both want the same ultimate goal. This usually arises if you have different information available, or if you see the importance of certain information differently. The discussion is therefore about the usefulness of different solutions to a problem.
- Value: It is a value issue when a difference of opinion arises from a difference in values. Based on different desires, one partner wants this, the other something fundamentally different. The sticking point of the problem is usually the difference between the desires of the partners.
- Distributional: A distributional issue is one about something that needs to be shared between two or more parties, and the wishes of everyone concerned add up to more than the total that is actually available.

List 1: Tactics

1. Positive emotions
   (flattery; being nice; behaving seductively)
2. Negative emotions
   (threats; shouting; cynicism; ridicule)
3. Helplessness
   (tears; showing weakness; pretending to be ill)
4. Physical force
   (forcing; injuring; violent or aggressive behaviour)
5. Offering resources
   (performing a service; being attentive)
6. Withdrawing resources
   (withdrawing financial contributions; punishing the other by no longer doing something)
7. Insistence
   (nagging; constantly returning to the subject; conversations designed to wear down opposition)
8. Withdrawal
   (refusing to share responsibility; changing subject; going away; leaving the scene)
9. Open presentation of facts
   (making suggestions; asking for co-operation; presenting own needs/subjective importance/own interest)
10. Presenting false facts
    (suppressing important information; distortion)
11. Indirect coalition
    (referring to other people; emphasizing utility of the decision for others)
12. Direct coalition
    (discussion in the presence of others, hoping for their support)
13. Trade-offs
    (book-keeping; reminders of past favours)
14. Integrative bargaining
    (search for the best solution for all concerned)
15. Reasoned argument
    (presenting factual arguments; arguing logically)

Figure 5.3c Instructions for completion of the decision diary (Kirchler et al., 2001, pp. 120–1)

a house or flat was discussed and decided upon jointly. Similarly, partners decided jointly where they will go on holiday, whether they will go out in the evening, and in which restaurant they will eat. Partners also jointly discussed questions related to raising the children or the type of school their children will attend.

Gender role specialisation in private households seems to be primarily determined by social norms and the partners' values. In the last few decades, a shift in roles within the family seems to have taken place. Shifts from traditional patriarchal relationships over the moderately changed conceptions of gender roles labelled 'modern' towards truly egalitarian partnerships were identified (Peplau, 1983; Scanzoni, 1972; Scanzoni & Fox, 1980). Traditional families who favour a strict division of roles are less common in Western industrialised countries than egalitarian partnerships. As stereotypes about gender roles fade away, partners are obtaining increasingly equal rights in what were formerly separate spheres of activity. More democracy and the shift in conventional roles should lead to more joint decision-making. Children also appear to have more influence in decision-making processes than before. A study of Finnish families found that decision-making in families with children happens quite democratically (Raijas, 2007).

However, some argue that a dramatic shift from autonomous to syncratic decision-making has nowhere near been reached. On the basis of a suggestion by Davis and Rigaux (1974), Muehlbacher et al. (2009) surveyed over 800 men and women living in close relationships. Participants were asked about decision-making influence for what were formerly typical female-dominated products (cleaning products, kitchen utensils), typical male-dominated products (cars, computers), and products where both partners had made joint decisions (living room furniture, holidays). Participants were asked who typically is in charge of purchase decisions: the man, the woman or both. In addition, three phases of the decision-making process were considered: the initiation, information-gathering and purchasing. Muehlbacher et al. (2008) differentiated between three age groups: up to 30 years, between 30 and 50 years, and over 50 years. For each age group, for each product and for each of the three phases of decision-making, the data were analysed according to Davis and Rigaux's (1974) **role triangle**. This method illustrates product-specific influence in purchase decisions and how influence is distributed between men and women in close relationships. In the role triangle, two values are calculated: (a) the partners' average influence for each product and (b) the percentage of joint decisions. While the first value indicates the distribution of influence between husband and wife, the second value reflects the level of joint decision-making. Using both values, the role triangle can be developed. It can be broken up into four areas of control:

(a) When over 50% of respondents state that they and their partner have equal influence in matters concerning a specific product, the term 'syncratic decision' is used. When the value lies under 50%, three cases are distinguished.
(b) If the average influence clearly favours the wife, a decision is termed 'female-dominated decision'.
(c) In analogy, if the average influence clearly favours the husband, it is termed 'male-dominated decision'.
(d) If the average influence lies in between, meaning that this decision is not primarily controlled by one partner or the other, the term 'balanced decisions' is used.

The study by Muehlbacher et al. (2009) delivered sobering results: as shown in Figure 5.4, the same gender-specific patterns of influence were reported as in Davis and Rigaux's (1974) study, and there were hardly any differences between the three age groups. These results are also supported by the findings of Ganesh (1997), Harcar and Spillan (2006), Na, Son and Marshall (1998, 2003), Penz and Kirchler (2012), Yang et al. (2006) and Yavas, Babakus and Delener (1994), resulting from

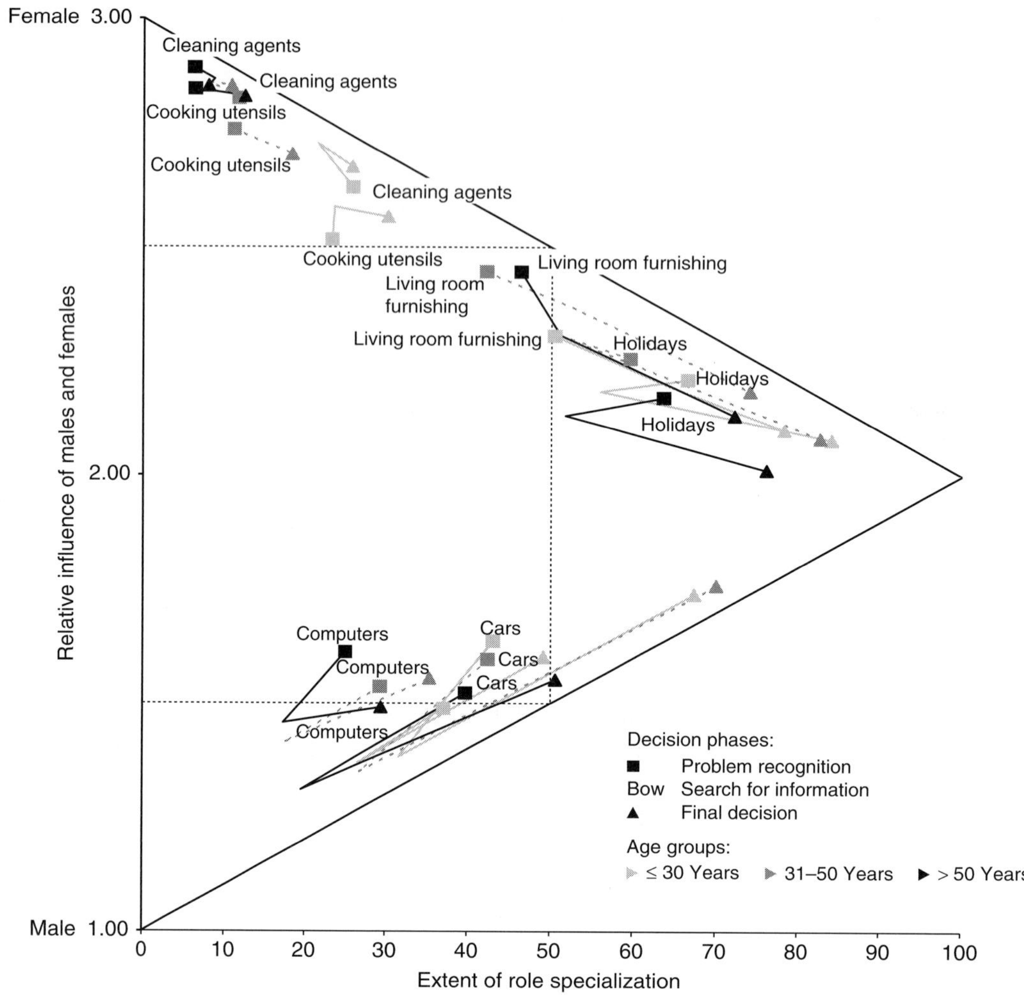

Figure 5.4 Variation in decision-making roles during the desire, information-gathering and buying phases in six selected product categories, separated for age groups (according to Muehlbacher et al., 2009, p. 30)

numerous studies in Saudi Arabia, Singapore, India, Korea, Latin America and Central Africa. Nevertheless, it should be noted that cross-cultural studies and the interpretation of similar or different findings can be problematic: as Hantrais (1999) points out, sociocultural, economic and political contexts are important for cross-national comparative research. A difficulty lies in the fact that the same concept, term or question can be interpreted differently in different countries. Culture-specific social dynamics, different meanings of concepts, and cultural understandings of social roles, terms and symbols can lead to misunderstandings in the interpretation of seemingly objective data (e.g., Nyman et al. 2013; Ponthieux, 2012).

A re-analysis of studies from the 1960s to the 1980s did not indicate an increase in joint decision-making over time, either (Kirchler, 1989). Bisdee, Daly and Price (2013) come to a similar insight, but add that shifts in gender-specific patterns of behaviour and money management can come about due to fundamental lifestyle changes, such as those after a severe illness. Although it can be concluded from longitudinal studies that money management systems are very stable (Laurie & Gershuny, 2000),

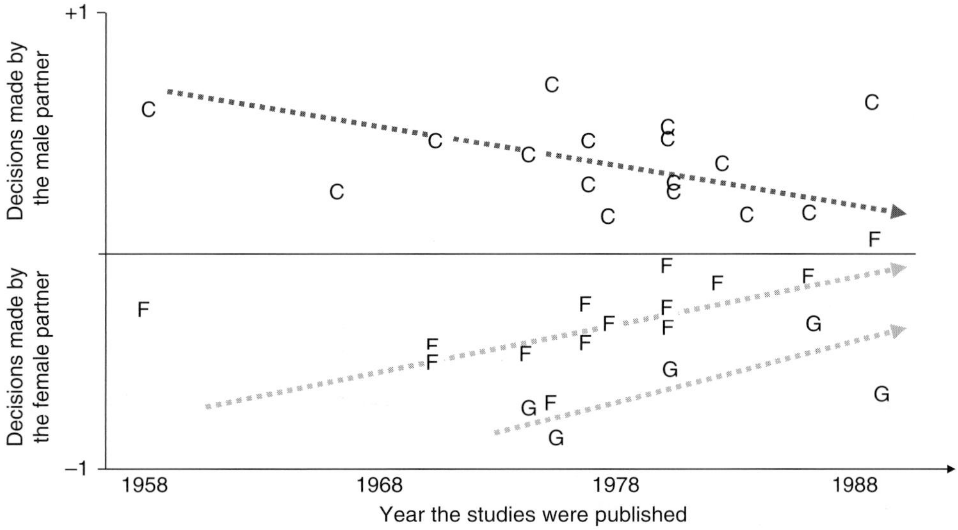

Figure 5.5 Male and female influence in decisions to buy furniture (F), groceries (G) and cars (C) during 1958–88 (from Kirchler, 1989, p. 194)

critical life events such as the birth of a child can induce changes (Fleming, 1997). Further factors that can induce a change, according to Goode, Callender and Lister (1998), are capacity for change and the ability to learn from experience, including learning from previous relationships.

Unlike in the past, however, the near total dominance of one partner in some product areas can no longer be observed, which means it can be assumed that the perceived shift in gender roles has led not to an increase in joint decision-making, but rather to more autonomous decisions. Today, both men and women make decisions alone that used to be reserved for one gender. Figure 5.5 shows the average influence of men and women in three product areas over thirty years of research in this field (Kirchler, 1989).

What does the distribution of influence between partners depend upon? According to **relative resources theory** (Blood & Wolfe, 1960), the prevailing social norms and the partners' relative contributions of resources are important determinants of each partner's influence. Since this theory was formulated, influence in joint decisions has almost exclusively been attributed to the partner with more education, with a higher-paid and more prestigious career, and who, in general, possesses more material and immaterial resources than the other person. The importance of relative resource contributions was frequently confirmed in the past, but since the 1980s, studies have failed in their attempts to demonstrate that relative resources theory is still valid in Western industrialised countries. Szinovacz (1987) argued that the validity of relative resources theory has been called into question because it is not the difference in objective resource contributions that counts, but rather the difference as subjectively perceived by the partners (in male homosexual partnerships, however, relative resource contribution still seems to play a role; Schneider et al., 2013). Furthermore, the types of resources enumerated by Blood and Wolfe (1960), namely education, income and career status, only represent a small proportion of the resources that matter in a partnership.

Another important determinant of influence in decision-making is informational pressure. The partner who knows more about a product than the other partner, has good arguments and is adamant about them is more likely to get their own way than the other person. The partners' knowledge and competence are what counts (Burns, 1976; Burns & Granbois, 1977; Davis, 1972; Seymour & Lessne, 1984). In addition to competence, interest in the decision matters as well. Burns (1976) asked each partner how interested they were in a decision and confirmed that a partner's influence increases as their interest rises. Corfman and Lehmann (1987; Corfman, 1987) asked couples about the probability that they would buy various products in the future, how much money they would spend, how much they cared about the purchase, how much expertise they had about each of the specific products, and their estimate of how much influence they would have when making a decision with their partner. The couples then discussed various products about which their attitudes differed. Relative interest in a product and expertise were positively correlated with influence. The more important it was for one of the partners to get their way, the more likely they were to do so. Similarly, the more knowledge a partner considered they had about the product alternatives, the more say they had in decision-making. When one of the partners sought to improve the quality of the relationship or at least to avoid jeopardising it, that partner tended to give in more often and let the other partner's influence increase. The partners' relative resource contributions were of no importance. The partner who chips in more resources may very well possess more potential power than the other, but the actual power exercised does not appear to depend on this.

The partners' decision-making history also proved to be significant in Corfman's studies. Since decisions about various products were made in succession, the authors were able to investigate whether patterns of influence remained constant or varied over a series of decisions. Corfman and Lehmann (1987) proceeded from the assumption that an unwritten law calls for balance between each partner's influence and hypothesised that partners strive to achieve a balance of influence over the course of various decisions, meaning that first one person makes the decision and then the other. The probability of exerting influence did actually increase when one's partner had called the shots in previous discussions. Calculated across multiple decisions, influence is evenly distributed between the partners. Basically, 'influence gains' in the past compel concessions in the future. Corfman and Lehmann (1987) argued that the degree of influence matters less than whether one partner or the other dominates decision-making. The magnitude of influence is forgotten; what is not forgotten, however, is who dominated.

Kirchler (1989) used the diary method to search for determinants of influence in purchasing decisions. It was found that for both men and women, and for happy and unhappy couples, what counts is primarily the relative competence of each partner, as subjectively perceived by the partners themselves. The higher the competence of one partner in a certain product area was perceived to be, the more that partner tended to get their way. In happy relationships, the partners' relative interest in the product, the urgency of their wish for the product and the objectivity of their arguments mattered as well. While competence, needs and wishes mattered in happy relationships, the intensity of the partner's wish was only of little importance in unhappy relationships.

It was surprising that decision-making history – the distribution of influence in the past – did not have an effect on the distribution of influence in current decisions. In reality, partners could 'pay back' their influence debts not only in a future purchasing decision, but also in non-economic decisions. However, partners could also strive for a middle- or long-term balance of influence. Diary entries made on the days in which a joint purchasing decision took place were singled out for analysis, separately for each couple. Details on the distribution of influence between husband and wife over the entire period of data collection were plotted graphically. In Figure 5.6, variations in influence pulled from the entries of two couples are depicted. Similar trends were recorded for the remaining relationships in the study. The influence of the husband and wife, respectively, is not stable. Autocorrelations of the influence values, with (a) the influence index from the current

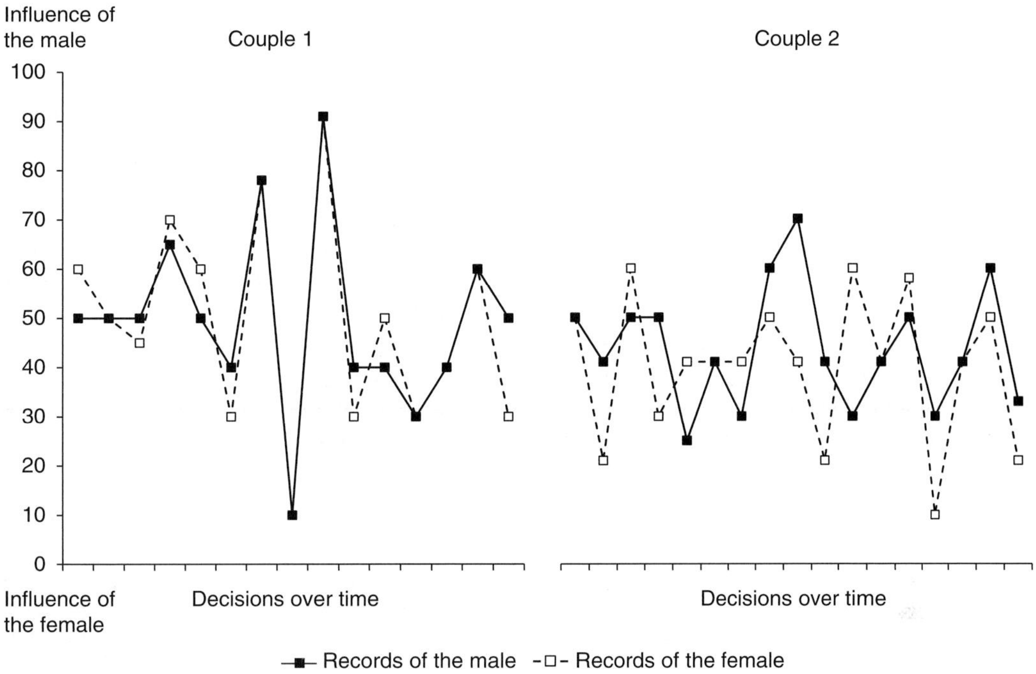

Figure 5.6 Male and female influence on the purchase decisions of two randomly selected couples over the course of four weeks (according to Kirchler, 1989, p. 214 f)

decision and (b) values from previous decisions, reveal that current influence is dependent upon the distribution of influence in previous purchase decisions. Influence debts appear to determine influence in later decision-making situations. The more often one partner has had their way in previous decisions, the higher the probability that the other partner will have their way in the future. In the long run, the distribution of influence between husband and wife balances out.

The **Vienna Diary Study** (Kirchler et al., 2001) was an extensive study on household decision-making using the decision diary described above. It confirmed that the distribution of influence between partners appears to depend upon their relative interest in the product, relative competence and influence debts. The findings support the assumption that mental accounts of each partner's influence are kept and that balancing-out effects are present, especially in economic matters. The utility that each partner derives from the decision also appears to be entered into a mental account, remembered and balanced out over time.

A study analogous to the Vienna Diary Study was conducted by Peterlik (2009) in Vietnam. Couples kept a diary for a period of three months. The findings with respect to decision-making history contradicted those of the Vienna Diary Study. It was found that, in all topic areas, the partner who had called the shots in one decision-making situation also dominated in the future. Not only did a balancing of influence debts fail to materialise – even a stabilisation of influence took place. These results indicate that a segmentation of gender roles exists in Vietnam, according to which the wife is responsible for some areas while the husband dominates others.

Summarising these findings (Burns, 1976; Burns & Granbois; 1977; Corfman, 1987; Corfman & Lehmann, 1987; Davis, 1972; Hubel, 1986; Kirchler, 1989; Kirchler et al., 2001; Seymour & Lessne, 1984), the relevant predictors of the influence distribution between partners are interest, competence and – in Western societies – decision-making history. The relative resource contributions of the partners explain hardly any part of the influence distribution.

In conclusion, it may be said of partners' influence in decision-making – especially in purchasing decisions – that studies from the 1960s onwards indicate a fairly even distribution of influence. One partner or the other will have greater influence depending on the issue to be decided (product type, for example) and on which aspects of the various alternatives are discussed. Further determinants of influence are cultural values and, linked with these, sex role orientation. Depending on cultural context, the partners' relative contribution of resources, their relative subject-related knowledge and interest in the decision, and the distribution of utility debt from past decisions may also have an effect.

5.2.4 Process Analysis of Decisions in the Household

Once differences of opinion between partners have been established, attempts are made to resolve them using various tactics. Seeking to avoid escalation while also pursuing their own preferences, the partners move through various decision-making phases: from the desire phase to information-gathering and sometimes back again in erratic leaps, attempting to win the other person's agreement using factual arguments, manipulation, flattery, threats or a tit-for-tat deal. One's own preferences can change as a result of conversations with one's partner or due to new information. If one's partner cannot be persuaded to give up their perspective but the product is still desired, other tactics are tried out until an agreement is reached. If the conflict threatens to escalate, the partners will either steer away from it by backing down and jumping to other issues or, depending on the relationship's structure, steer right into a negative conflict.

Partners apply various tactics to convince the other person of the accuracy of their own perspective and the advantages of their own preferences. Kirchler (1990) isolated a total of eighteen different **influence tactics** that partners can deploy in probability, value and distribution conflicts. These tactics are summarised in Table 5.1. The first twelve represent tactics of persuasion; Tactics 16 and 17 are negotiation tactics. Tactic 18 represents factual, rational argumentation. Tactics 14 and 15 are more conducive to avoiding conflicts than resolving them. Tactic 13 ends disagreement over the purchase decision, but might start a conflict concerning the partner's behaviour. In addition to listing their names, the tactics are briefly defined in Table 5.1 by means of examples.

In various studies (Barlés-Arizón, Fraj-Andrés & Martínez-Salinas, 2008; Kirchler, 1993b, 1993c), these tactics have been corroborated and were found to depend on type of conflict, relationship quality, length of partnership and gender. The relationship power structure and the partners' personality structures did not matter in the selection of tactics. In summary, it has been shown that partners are more likely to put forward logical, rational arguments in conflicts over facts than in value and distribution conflicts. Bargains are made in distribution conflicts, whereas persuasive tactics are applied in value conflicts. Happy and young couples behave differently than unhappy and older couples. In contrast to unhappy couples, happy ones exhibit emotionally positive behaviour towards one another. Gender differences were also observed: women are more likely to seek out integrative solutions, but they are not more emotional than men.

5.2.5 Outcomes of Decisions: Fairness and Satisfaction

Conflicts about economic matters can be evaluated on the basis of whether the handling of scarce resources is rational or whether the partners are wasteful in deploying their resources. In intimate

Table 5.1 Classification of tactics (from Kirchler, 1990)

Tactic content		Tactic label	Examples
Emotion	1.	Positive emotions	Manipulation, flattery, smiling, humour, seductive behaviour
	2.	Negative emotions	Threats, cynicism, ridicule, shouting
Physical force	3.	Helplessness	Crying, showing weaknesses, pretending to be ill
	4.	Physical force	Coercing, injuring, violence, aggression
Resources	5.	Offers of resources	Performing services, being attentive
	6.	Withdrawal of resources	Withdrawing financial contributions, punishing
Presence	7.	Insisting	Nagging, constantly returning to the subject, conversations designed to wear down opposition
	8.	Withdrawal	Refusing to share responsibility, changing the subject, going away, leaving the scene
Information	9.	Open presentation of facts	Asking for cooperation, presenting one's own needs, talking openly about importance/interest to self
	10.	Presenting false facts	Suppressing relevant information, distorting information
Coalition	11.	Indirect coalition	Referring to other people, emphasising utility of purchase to children
	12.	Direct coalition	Discussing in the presence of others
Fact	13.	Fait accompli	Buying autonomously, deciding without consulting partner
Role segmentation	14.	Deciding according to roles	Deciding autonomously according to established role segmentation
	15.	Yielding according to roles	Autonomous decision by partner according to role
Bargaining	16.	Trade-offs	Offers of 'trade-offs', book-keeping, reminders of past favours
	17.	Integrative bargaining	Search for the best solution to satisfy all concerned
Reason	18.	Reasoned argument	Presenting factual arguments; logical argumentation

relationships, the economically rational deployment of resources is not always possible, particularly in cases where nurturing the relationship is considered something to strive for alongside economic goals. In these situations, goal conflicts can arise, and partners may place caring for the relationship above economic goals. In happy relationships, expenditures may be made in order to fulfil the partner's wishes. Someone who loves their partner, can anticipate their partner's every wish and thinks only of fulfilling them can easily lose sight of economic goals. Conversely, someone who is currently in conflict with their partner might think about spending joint funds for their own purposes before the other person can claim them for themselves. Happy and unhappy couples spend approximately equal amounts of money, but they spend it in different ways and with different objectives. Schaninger and Buss (1986) showed that, beyond fulfilling egoistic or altruistic wishes, happy couples buy fewer objects than unhappy ones with the same level of total expenditures. While happy couples buy more expensive and indivisible objects, unhappy couples – as if anticipating a separation and the need to split up the household effects – prefer divisible goods.

Even if decision-making in intimate relationships is described as an incremental, gradual process of feeling one's way to a solution, joint decisions are not necessarily always economically unsound. Quite the contrary: Lindblom (1979) determined that decision-makers need to deviate from a completely rational model of action if they want to make any decision at all in complex situations. Partners in intimate relationships hardly have the time at their disposal that would be necessary to conduct a proper syncratic decision-making process. In order to avoid steering into overly 'hot' relationship conflicts, feeling one's way step-by-step is often the only possibility.

The assertion that incremental decisions are more prudent than economically rational ones notwithstanding, optimism that partners in intimate relationships may represent a good problem-solving unit is not justified. Hill (1972) radically pulls the rug out from under this hope. In his opinion, intimate relationships, especially the family, are 'a poor planning committee, an unwieldy play group and a group of uncertain congeniality. Its leadership is shared by two relatively inexperienced amateurs for most of their incumbency, new to the rules of spouse and parent' (p. 14). In private households, because decision-making processes related to purchases do not exist in isolation from other decision-making tasks, the partners' attention is never fully concentrated on any one problem. Economic decisions can mutate into power struggles. Instead of looking for a good solution, the partners may seek to settle utility debts that arose in completely different situations or try to balance out the distribution of influence by giving in to the other person because the other person did so in the past, not because the other person is currently proposing the better alternative. Finally, suboptimal decisions can be made deliberately for the sake of the quality of the relationship. Decision-making under one roof frequently comes down to acquiescing to the other person's wishes as a favour and not out of conviction that fulfilling their wishes would be prudent. In the case of purchase decisions, Granbois and Summers (1975) demonstrated that couples plan and realise a greater number of distinct purchases than men and women separately. If it is considered prudent to forgo goods that are not absolutely necessary and save the money that would have been spent, individual decision-making can be considered more 'cost-effective' than decision-making by couples. In this study, partners probably acquiesced to the other person's wishes in order to avoid conflicts and preserve the existing harmony. Uneconomical actions often pay off in emotional terms – an obstacle to economic problem-solving. Aside from limited cognitive capacity, 'poor' decisions can also be traced back to the fact that many marginal problems and marginal goals affect the decision-making process.

Necessary preconditions for achieving an economically rational decision and minimising costs for the relationship are the following: high interdependency between partners, consideration of the wishes of the other person, fact-based communication in which all parties participate and can express their ideas without being criticised, an egalitarian distribution of influence, open communication of one's goals, a ban on strategies of indirect persuasion, and sufficient time (Klein & Hill, 1979). Economic efficiency and satisfaction could be thought of as opposites, but Kourilsky and Murray (1981) confirmed that they are actually positively correlated.

In financial decisions, partners in intimate relationships seek not only to implement the economically superior alternative but also to work out conflicts in a fair manner (Su, Zhou, Zhou & Li, 2008). Acceptance of decisions was investigated in the Vienna Diary Study (Kirchler et al., 2001) with regard to the perceived fairness of the decision-making process and its result as well as satisfaction with the outcome of the decision. Each day when they experienced a conflict with their partner, participants indicated in their diaries how fairly the process of resolving the differences of opinion had transpired and how fair the result was. They also indicated their satisfaction with the outcome of the conversation. Their answers were analysed for correlates of fairness and satisfaction, focusing on the tactics selected by the partners to settle their differences, the relative influence of each partner, and the utility distribution.

Regarding the tactics used, analyses revealed that one's own choice of tactics explained about 10% of the variance in perceived fairness; the tactics perceived to be used by one's partner explained an additional 9% in the sample of women and 4% in the sample of men. Satisfaction with the outcome of the conversation was likewise determined to a considerable extent by the tactics selected (11–12% of variance was determined by one's own choice of tactics and approximately 4% by the tactics of one's partner). That the choice of tactics is especially pertinent for coming to a decision and the quality of the relationship can also be seen in the fact that partners evaluate and adapt their tactics according to their efficiency and fairness (Su, Fern & Ye, 2003). In the Vienna Diary Study, the outcome of a decision was more likely to be judged as fair and satisfactory when one person offered resources (Tactic 5, Table 5.1) or made factual, rational arguments (Tactic 18). The other person should also use factual arguments (Tactic 18) and should most importantly make integrative proposals (Tactic 17). Conversely, the result tended to be perceived as unfair when one expressed negative emotions (Tactic 2) oneself, acted helplessly (Tactic 3), became adamant (Tactic 7) or withdrew from the scene (Tactic 8), or when one's partner employed these tactics. In addition, the other person should not present false facts (Tactic 10) or achieve a good result for themselves using flattery (Tactic 1). Contented couples, in particular, considered flattery (Tactic 1) and insistence (Tactic 7) to be unfair methods of winning influence when used by the other person. Unhappy couples, especially women in unhappy relationships, considered threats by the other person and the withdrawal of resources (Tactic 6) to be unfair. Openly stating one's own desires and preferences (Tactic 9) was perceived to be a fair tactic for one's partner primarily in unhappy relationships.

Regarding the utility distribution, a major question concerns the appropriate fairness rule. In the literature on justice, the question is often posed as to which rules for the distribution of resources are considered fair. Hereby, distinctions are usually made among (a) equity rules (the distribution of resources based on contributions), (b) parity or equality rules (resources are divided up equally among everyone), and (c) needs rules (resources are distributed according to the severity of each person's need). Clark and Chrisman (1994) provided an overview of the research and concluded that there is empirical support for the utilisation of the equity, equality and needs rules in intimate relationships. Equity theorists (Hatfield & Traupmann, 1981; Hatfield, Traupmann, Sprecher, Utne & Hay, 1985; Hatfield, Utne & Traupmann, 1979; Walster [Hatfield], Walster & Berscheid, 1978) made the case that resource distribution proceeds proportionately to contributions even in intimate relationships and that this determines satisfaction. Other authors, conversely, have found less support for the assumptions of justice theories and argued that the equity rule is not optimal in romantic relationships (Michaels, Acock & Edwards, 1986; Michaels, Edwards & Acock, 1984; Lujansky & Mikula, 1983; Clark & Mills, 1979). A number of studies have shown that the equality rule is often followed in intimate relationships (Greenberg, 1983; Pataki, Shapiro & Clark, 1992; Steil, 1994). With respect to influence in decision-making, Gray-Little and Burks (1983) demonstrated in a comparison of twelve studies that the perception that influence is distributed equally between partners is correlated with high relationship satisfaction. Conversely, other authors argued that the distribution of resources in intimate relationships proceeds in accordance with the partners' needs (Clark, Mills & Powell, 1986; Deutsch, 1975, 1985; Lamm & Schwinger, 1983; Mills & Clark, 1982). Finally, the literature points to the importance of entitlements – notions of what is owed to oneself and to one's partner in the relationship (Attridge & Berscheid, 1994; Desmarais & Lerner, 1994). As a consequence of societal norms, the 'just' distribution can therefore deviate from the three aforementioned rules, with more influence in certain areas conceded to one partner, for example. Consequently, even a one-sided distribution might be perceived as fair. Because of these inconsistent results and the lack of studies on how utility distributions are evaluated, the Vienna Diary Study (Kirchler et al., 2001) considered three possibilities:

(a) Pure egoism could dominate: the more utility an actor derives from a decision, the more fair he or she will perceive it to be.
(b) The balance of utility between both partners could determine the perceived fairness: decisions that equally benefit both partners should then be perceived to be fairest.
(c) A utility distribution corresponding to the partners' needs could be perceived as fair.

The results show that both egoistic motives and the desire for balance influence the perception of fairness with respect to decision-making in intimate relationships. For example, this balance can be achieved when one partner compensates for a lower contribution to the family's finances (on account of a lower income) by taking on a greater share of the housework or by being frugal with shared funds (Stocks, Díaz-Martínez & Halleröd, 2007). Extreme imbalances in utility distribution, even to one's own benefit, were found to be perceived as unfair; however, the decisions judged to be fairest are not those that bring both partners equal utility, but rather those in which one's own utility gain is somewhat higher than that of the other person. At least in economic decisions, the strength of one's partner's need seems to have no effect on the perceived fairness (Kirchler et al., 2001).

Regarding the outcome of the decision, partners in intimate relationships keep at least two goals in mind during differences of opinion: on the one hand, the desire to get their way; on the other hand, the desire not to jeopardise the harmony in the relationship (Ben-Yoav & Pruitt, 1984; Filley, 1975; Kirchler, 1989). Seen in this light, it can be assumed that both of these components are considered in evaluating one's satisfaction with the outcome of a decision. Thus, it is plausible that a positive discussion climate and high distributive fairness contribute to maintaining and rebuilding harmony, thereby leading to relationship satisfaction. High utility and influence help to achieve the goal of getting one's way in a decision. Nevertheless, it can be assumed that an overly one-sided distribution of utility or influence upsets harmony – therefore, there is probably a reversed U-shape relationship between satisfaction on the one hand and influence or utility on the other. Findings show that satisfaction with a decision increases when the process of coming to a decision and the result of the decision are perceived as fair, when the discussion climate was good, when the benefit to oneself is high but not overly high, and as one's own influence on the decision-making process increases. Perceived fairness and an equal distribution of utility and influence, in particular, seem to be important determinants of satisfaction with a decision in egalitarian partnerships. These results should be interpreted with caution due to the small number of couples with different types of power relations in the diary study (Kirchler et al., 2001). At the same time, they seem exceedingly plausible in cases where the definition of egalitarianism goes beyond equal rights for both partners to encompass utility as well, and decisions that put both partners in an equally good position are considered fair.

5.3 Credit Decisions of Individuals and Households

When individuals and households decide to spend money for purchases, they can either use available funds (from current income or savings) or borrow money. Consumer credit has risen in many countries over the last decades and is now a widespread phenomenon. For example, during 2013 in Germany 7.7 million new credits were opened, and the total number of open credits was 17.7 million (SCHUFA, 2014). While during and after the financial crisis of 2007/8, consumers' demand for credit has decreased in some European countries, it increased again in 2014 in Germany, Spain and France (European Central Bank, 2014).

These developments are disconcerting because research has found consumer credit to be related to financial and psychological problems. For example, credit use was found to be connected to compulsive buying (e.g., Norum, 2008) and overextension of credit can be a route into problem debt (Canner & Luckett, 1991). In a comparison of fifteen EU countries, on average 16% of households were classified as over-indebted (1996 data; Betti, Dourmashkin, Rossi & Yin, 2007). Debt and unsecured credit were linked to reduced psychological wellbeing (Brown, Taylor & Wheatley Price, 2005), increased depression (Bridges & Disney, 2010) and increased criminal behaviour among adolescents and young adults (Hoeve et al., 2014). Over the last years, new forms of consumer credit have developed. In many cases, access to credit is now far easier and the money itself is almost instantly available. Applying for credit can nowadays be done via the internet or even via SMS. There is also a rising market for peer-to-peer lending, that is, borrowing money from other consumers via an internet platform. Many stores now offer financing in the form of in-store credit for a purchase. From a policy perspective, there is some concern that in particular the new forms of credit may further disadvantage vulnerable consumer groups. Availability of credit differs between consumers, and credit conditions are influenced by available collaterals or credit history. Several researchers have highlighted that when consumers have no access to mainstream credit from banks, they encounter high costs on the alternative credit market (e.g., Lawrence & Elliehausen, 2008). This is the case for moneylenders or pawnshops, but also for the more recent forms of instant credit. For example, small instant loans via SMS were found to be used often by consumers with low incomes or no regular credit cards (Autio, Wilska, Kaartinen & Lähteenmaa, 2009).

On the one hand, taking up a credit – for example to finance living space – is reasonable and desirable from a macroeconomic view. On the other hand, credit is nothing else than indebtedness which can lead to severe problems for consumers. In surveys, respondents stated that the easy access to credit can also tempt one to buy products that are not needed (Berthoud & Kempson, 1992). In particular, this can become a problem for consumers with a tendency towards compulsive shopping (Wang & Xiao, 2009). Using credit via credit cards can lead to imprudent purchases and can increase the danger of over-indebtedness (Canner & Luckett, 1991). Credit card users sometimes have difficulties in remembering how much they have just spent shortly after the purchase (Srivastava & Raghubir, 2002). According to Christen and Morgan (2005), credit card debts in 2000 accounted for slightly less than 10% of the overall indebtedness of households.

What are other important factors for over-indebtedness? In a large study by Lea, Webley and Levine (1993), three groups were compared – one without debt, one with mild debt and one with severe debt. The results indicated that indebtedness was mostly correlated with financial poverty – people with low income were more likely to be in severe debt than people with higher income. In contrast, irresponsible spending, careless budgeting or other personal variables were less often found as reasons for indebtedness. Livingstone and Lunt (1992) compared persons with and without credit debt and found that young people, people with positive credit attitudes and people who experience consumption as rewarding were more likely to be indebted. The level of debts was partly related to socio-demographic and psychological variables, but mostly with income. These findings highlight the importance of economic factors. Also, data from German debt counsellors highlight that the most frequent causes of over-indebtedness are job loss and unemployment (26%), whereas overspending is less frequently the cause (11%) (Liersch, 2013). In contrast, lay theories about debt are mostly dominated by individual attributions, that is, making the indebted persons themselves responsible for their situation (e.g., Viaud & Roland-Lévy, 2000).

5.3.1 Credit Use as a Process

Kamleitner and Kirchler (2007) suggested that credit use is not a one-time decision, but that it extends over time. In their **integrative process model of consumer credit** they suggest a view of credit use as a process starting with a purchase consideration and ending after payback. Specifically, three phases are distinguished: (a) before credit take up, (b) during credit take up and (c) during the repayment period. In the first phase, consumers decide that they want to buy a good and they decide on credit use as the financing method. In the second phase, consumers decide on a specific credit offer. This phase ends with the implicit or explicit signing of a credit contract. The third phase covers all activities and psychological processes that follow during the payback phase. It ends when, with the final repayment, the debt is settled (Figure 5.7).

Phase 1: Similar to the model of purchase decisions in private households, this model assumes that consumers have different needs. For example, depending on the life cycle stage, individuals or families want to invest in education, need an apartment or want a car. These needs interact with market information that can shape needs and provide specific opportunities (point 1 in Figure 5.7). As a result, a desire for a good develops (point 2). Depending on the type of good (point 3), a spontaneous purchase or a habitual purchase will occur, or an extensive decision process will be triggered (point 4). In the first two cases, consumers can use credit cards and this spontaneous decision for credit use links directly to point 7. After an extensive decision process about advantages and disadvantages of the good, consumers can reach different conclusions (point 5) – for example, that they do not really need the good and therefore abandon the purchase or that they do not need to buy it right now and can delay the purchase. A third outcome is that they reach the conclusion that they want to purchase the good now, and then need to decide whether to finance it from available funds or whether to use credit (point 6).

For this first stage, different situational and personal factors are likely to matter. Credit is used (a) to maintain a living standard (e.g., after a loss in income) and (b) to improve the living standard (e.g., to buy a larger apartment) (Norton, 1993). Whereas families with small income sometimes use credit as a substitute for insufficient income, families with higher income see credit as an economically feasible alternative to using own funds (e.g., Croden, 2000). Status concerns also play an important role. Years ago, Duesenberry (1949) argued that consumers compare themselves with others and adjust their consumption accordingly. If available income and savings are not sufficient, this may induce credit use. Indeed, indebted persons reported comparing with others and valuing material possessions as important (e.g., Bernthal, Crockett & Rose, 2005), and rising income inequality has been linked with debt, assuming that consumers want to 'keep up with the Joneses' (Christen & Morgan, 2005).

Phase 2: If the decision for credit in principle is made, consumers can take two routes (point 7). On the one hand, they can spontaneously choose a credit, for example by using a credit card for purchasing or by accepting an in-store financing offer. On the other hand, they can make an extensive decision about which credit to take by searching for information about available offers and their conditions. In that case, one possible outcome is that the purchase decision is revised. In the process model, this is illustrated by an arrow leading back to points 4 and 5.

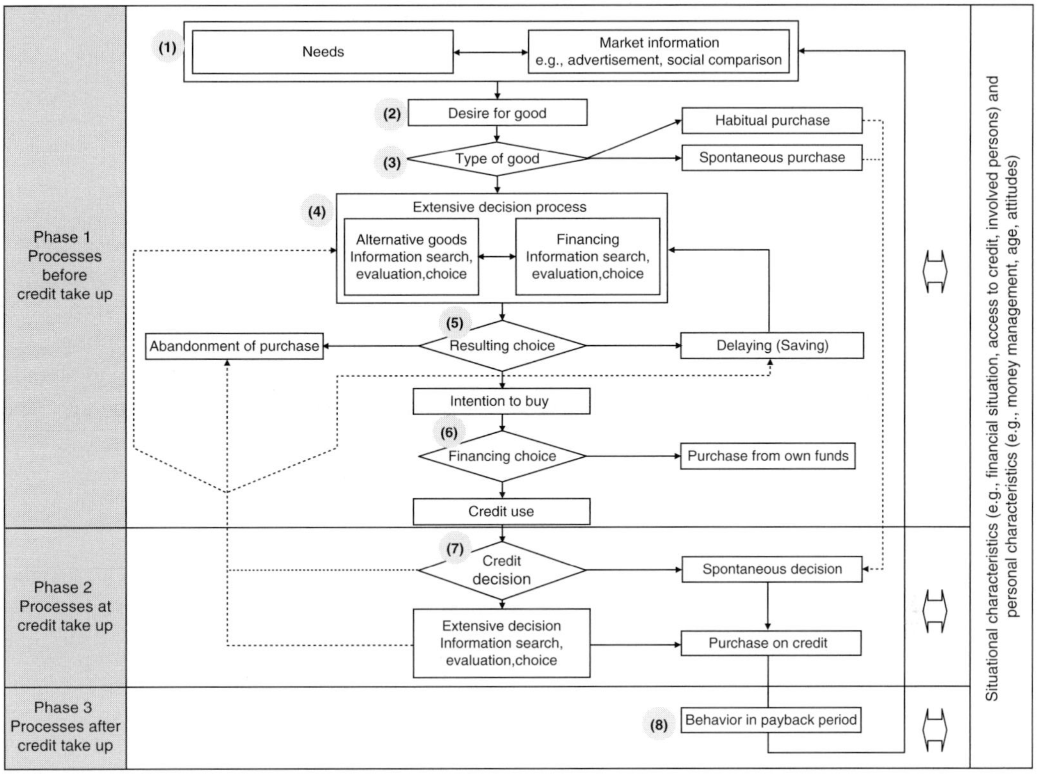

Figure 5.7 Integrative process model of consumer credit (adapted from Kamleitner & Kirchler, 2007, p. 269)

Extensive decisions about credit offers are complex and require effort: consumers need to search for information, and compare conditions such as interest rates, instalments and fees to make a good decision. In many cases, credit contracts are signed without thinking much about the consequences (Berthoud & Kempson, 1992) and without much information search or comparison (Hilgert, Hogart & Beverly, 2003). If information is collected, it is most often done through acquaintances or the house bank (Kaynak & Harcar, 2001). Decisions are made frequently using heuristics, and in many cases consumers are overly optimistic and too careless about credit (Perry, 2008). Katona (1975) argued that consumers often are not interested in detailed credit information and may not have the relevant knowledge to calculate correctly the costs of interest, periodical instalments and total costs. If consumers have to estimate how long it takes to repay a credit, they usually underestimate this duration. One reason seems to be the strong discounting of future costs (Ranyard & Craig, 1993). Discounting of future costs means that their magnitude is estimated smaller the later they occur. The same holds for benefits. At the time of their actual occurrence, both costs and benefits are experienced as more intense than forecasted (Ainslie & Haslam, 1992).

The decision to take up a credit and to repay it in instalments is an intertemporal choice between immediate pleasure of consumption and delayed burden of repeated repaying. It may be the case that this burden is seen as small in comparison to the benefits of the newly acquired good. Consumers who think about purchasing a good now may be blinded by the pleasure it promises, and may disregard the instalments that are far in the future – the benefits of the desired good outweigh the later costs. When consumers consider an immediate purchase, it can be

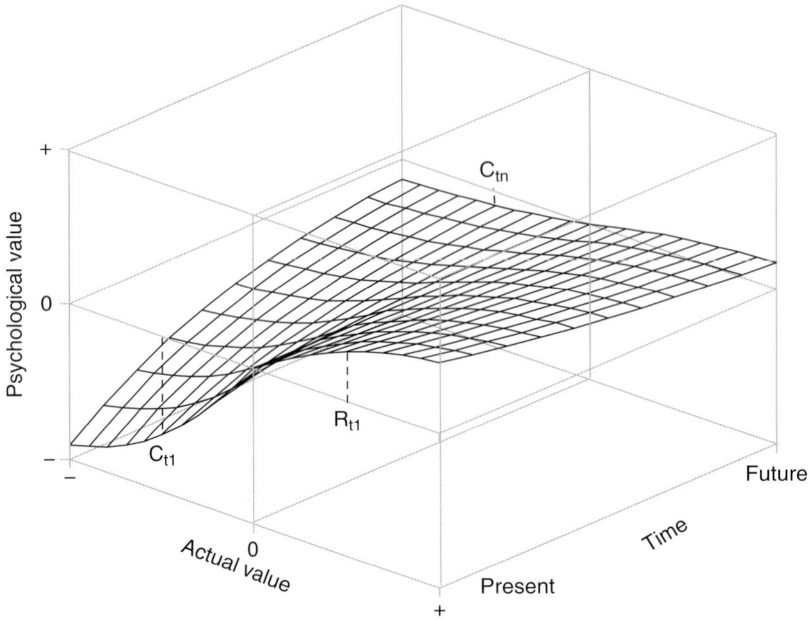

Figure 5.8 Time and outcome valuation model (adapted from Mowen & Mowen, 1991, p. 56)

assumed that the psychological value of ownership is high. Based on prospect theory (Kahneman & Tversky, 1979), one can assume also that the costs are experienced as high. As shown in Figure 5.8, the value of a currently purchased good R at the time of purchase t_1 is high. However, the price C, which objectively corresponds with the value of the good, is perceived even more intensely at the current time t_1, so that the perceived costs are higher than the perceived value of the good ($R_{t1} < C_{t1}$). In this case, consumers may abandon the purchase. If, however, satisfaction through the immediate ownership of a desired good can be reached now (R_{t1}) while the price for it is to be paid later (C_{tn}), the pattern changes. According to the **time and outcome valuation model** by Mowen and Mowen (1991), the value function in prospect theory becomes more flat for outcomes occuring in the future as compared to outcomes in the present. Future costs are discounted and the difference between R_{t1} and C_{tn} is likely to become positive ($R_{t1} > C_{tn}$), making the purchase seem attractive – even more so when the possibility exists to pay the price in instalments and therefore only small amounts occur in the future. The costs C_{t2}, C_{t3}, C_{t4} etc., not only are in the future and therefore are discounted, they also appear very small. The total sum of the amount to be paid in instalments (also taking into account the difficulties in calculating it) most likely will appear attractive, making the benefits of the purchase outweigh the costs by far ($R_{t1} > \Sigma\ (C_{t2}, C_{t3}, C_{t4} \ldots)$). Indeed, studies confirm that present orientation and high discounting factors correlate with credit use (Fehr, 2002; Laibson, 1997).

The decision to take up a credit is risky and often consumers shy away from risky choices. One way to reduce risk is to search for so-called risk defusing operators (Huber, 2007; Huber & Huber, 2008). Risk defusing operators can be either a preventive action or a consideration about action in the 'worst case'. RDOs at least to some extent allow people to control the risk (e.g., Vlek & Stallen, 1981; Weinstein, 1984). For example, the risk of over-indebtedness through credit could be defused by buying a credit repayment insurance. Ranyard, Hinkley and Williamson (2001) and Ranyard and

McHugh (2012) examined risk management strategies in consumers with different credit experience. If the risk exceeded a certain threshold and a person had already had some negative experience with credit, consumers thought about loss scenarios and RDOs. On the other hand, when the credit sum was low and the repayment duration short, consumers neglected the risk of possibly not being able to repay.

Phase 3: From a theoretical perspective, it can be assumed that at the time of signing the credit contract, the subjective pleasure outweighs the burden of future payments. However, do consumers take into account that both the pleasure and the burden may change over time, and are they able to forecast these developments correctly? Research on affective forecasting in general highlights that in many cases people are not very accurate in forecasting future feelings (see, e.g., Wilson & Gilbert, 2003 for a review) and that these forecasts often do not match with actual experience. A particularly problematic case would be if consumers forecast the pleasure of their new good to be stable over time, but then the curve for experienced pleasure with the good drops fast. On the other side, the experienced burden of payments, which seemed negligible at the outset, may even increase over time. Such comparisons between experienced benefits and costs are likely to matter for behaviour in the payback period (point 8).

Related to this idea, a quasi-experimental field study (Hoelzl, Pollai & Kamleitner, 2009) examined how consumers anticipate the future burden of a credit. Home owners reported how burdensome they currently perceived the credit for their home to be. Based on the time since taking up the credit, they were segmented into three groups (up to 5 years; 5.1–10 years; 10.1–15 years). The first group was asked to predict how they would perceive their credit 5 and 10 years from now; the second group was asked to predict how they would perceive their credit 5 years from now. All groups reported that they either remembered or expected that credit burden would decrease over time. However, results showed that the current experience of credit burden did not differ between groups. For group 1, the group who just started to repay, predicted future credit burden was lower than the corresponding currently experienced credit burden in groups 2 and 3, resulting in a potential underestimation of future burden of a credit (Figure 5.9).

In a recent review, Kamleitner, Hoelzl and Kirchler (2012) distinguished between four perspectives on credit use that can be identified in the literature: (1) credit use as a reflection of the situation, (2) credit use as a reflection of the person, (3) credit use as a cognitive process and (4) credit use as a social practice. In combination with the three phases of the process model by Kamleitner and Kirchler (2007), these perspectives help to organise the extant literature on credit use in psychology and behavioural economics. Another review article (Kirchler, Hoelzl & Kamleitner, 2008) focused on credit use within households and the interaction processes between partners.

5.3.2 Mental Accounting in Credit Use

Mental accounting is helpful to understand some of the cognitive processes involved in credit use. Mental accounting (see also Chapter 3) is a broad concept that describes several cognitive aspects of money management. It was defined as a 'set of cognitive operations used by individuals and households to organise, evaluate, and keep track of financial activities' (Thaler, 1999, p. 183). Two aspects of mental accounting are particularly relevant for credit decisions:

(a) Grouping of outcomes and decisions. The concept of **choice bracketing** (Read, Loewenstein & Rabin, 1999) distinguishes between broad and narrow bracketing, which refers to considering several decisions jointly or in isolation. Narrow bracketing has been shown to lead to suboptimal outcomes, for example when taxi drivers set a target earning for a day at a time (Camerer,

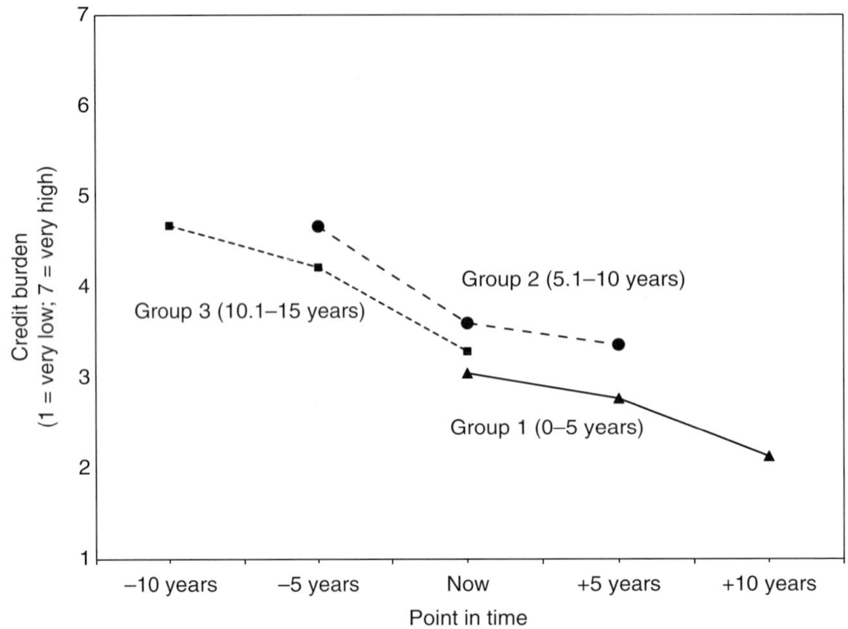

Figure 5.9 Currently experienced, remembered and predicted credit burden for three groups of home owners (data from Hoelzl et al., 2009, p. 449, Table 1)

Babcock, Loewenstein & Thaler, 1997). Recent research suggests that overspending on exceptional expenses is partly driven by narrow bracketing (Sussman & Alter, 2012). Since consumer credits are more likely to be used for exceptional purchases, narrow bracketing can contribute to credit use.

(b) Grouping of money into accounts. When consumers think about financial issues, they often group these issues in separate 'accounts'. These accounts can refer to incomes (e.g., current income, future income) and to expenditures (e.g., health, leisure). While these accounts can be helpful for organising and keeping an overview of financial activities (Antonides, de Groot & van Raaij, 2011), they can be disadvantageous in terms of over- and underconsumption. For example, when a purchase was categorised as matching with a certain category where previous expenses have occurred, participants were less willing to spend money on it (Heath & Soll, 1996).

Mental accounts can cover several related transactions (e.g., a budget for all leisure activities) or they can focus on a specific transaction. The **double-entry mental accounting model** (Prelec & Loewenstein, 1998) provides an elaborate framework for specific transactions that involve intertemporal trade-offs, such as the case of purchasing a good on credit. This framework suggests that consumers anticipate streams of future pleasure of consumption and pain of payment. These streams can be linked in the mental account. Coupling is the degree to which thoughts of payment arouse thoughts of consumption and vice versa. If consumers strongly couple payment and consumption, every consumption episode is attenuated by the disutility of the outstanding debt. Because of the negative effect of instalments on consumption pleasure, the model predicts strong overall debt aversion, despite temporal discounting. Mental accounting is relevant for consumer credit in three ways:

(a) Mental accounting influences credit decisions in the processes of the second phase described in the process model above. For example, consumers try to match the credit duration with usage time of the good (Hirst, Joyce & Schadewald, 1994) and match the source of money with hedonic or utilitarian products (O'Curry & Strahilevitz, 2001). In line with debt aversion, consumers were found to prefer lower instalments in the end when instalments change over time (Hoelzl, Kamleitner & Kirchler, 2011). In that study, participants were presented with scenarios describing a purchase situation (e.g., car, apartment) and a credit offer by their bank. Credit offers were systematically varied to show different repayment profiles. Rising profiles consisted of low instalments in the beginning and higher instalments later on; falling profiles consisted of high instalments in the beginning and lower instalments later on, thereby providing a 'happy ending'. Constant profiles were used as control. In line with preference for improvement (Loewenstein & Prelec, 1991) and with debt aversion (Prelec & Loewenstein, 1998), results showed robust preferences for falling over rising profiles, even when financially disadvantageous. An additional mechanism relevant for credit use is the phenomenon that exhausting the available financial resources increases the pain of payment and reduces product satisfaction ('bottom dollar effect', Soster, Gershoff & Bearden, 2014). Credit use may be seen as overcoming the problem of exhausting the available budget.

(b) Mental accounting influences experience and behaviour during the repaying phase. Experience of consumption depends on payment timing: Advance payment can make consumption feel 'free' (Gourville & Soman, 1998); conversely, payment that is still open can decrease enjoyment of the product (Prelec & Loewenstein, 1998). In one study, participants reported enjoying a gift basket less when they obtained it on 'credit', that is, when they knew that they still needed to pay for it later on (Hahn, Hoelzl & Pollai, 2013). Behaviour such as the repaying of instalments also depends on mental accounting. This is particularly relevant when consumers have several open credits. Although the closing of debt accounts can be motivating for the pursuit of the overall goal of debt elimination ('small victories', Gal & McShane, 2012), mental accounting can backfire. In one study (Amar, Ariely, Ayal, Cryder & Rick, 2011), participants had to manage multiple debts simultaneously. They focused primarily on reducing the number of open accounts and less on repaying the debts with the highest interest rates, a phenomenon termed 'debt account aversion'. In addition, this effect was found to be stronger for hedonic purchases and linked to the perception of goal progress (Besharat, Carrillat & Ladik, 2014).

(c) Mental accounting can serve as a self-control measure by mimicking a commitment mechanism. Self-control has so far been studied mostly in terms of individual differences. The ability to delay gratification was quite consistently found to be linked to credit use and the risk for indebtedness (e.g., Norvilitis et al., 2006). Consumers' underestimation of their future desire for immediate gratification may become problematic for repaying a credit (Heidhues & Kőszegi, 2010). Ottaviani and Vandone (2011) report a positive correlation between impulsivity and consumer credit. Another study measured individual differences in elaborating on possible outcomes of one's decision and found correlations with credit card debt (Nenkov, Inman & Hulland, 2008). Closely related are economic concepts like present bias and myopia. For example, present bias as measured in choice experiments was found to be related to having credit card debt (Meier & Sprenger, 2010) and a lower credit score rating (Meier & Sprenger, 2012). On a more general level, trait self-control was found to correlate with the propensity to incur credit card debt for purchases (Haws, Bearden & Nenkov, 2012). Mental accounting can help self-control, for example by setting budgets which are deliberately too low in specific accounts (e.g., wine, expensive hobbies) or by allocating money to accounts that are considered 'off-limits' (Thaler, 1999). The explanation of attempted self-control through mental accounting has been evoked for the otherwise puzzling finding of consumers holding debts and savings (with lower interest rates) at the same time. For example, Gathergood and Weber (2014) report that 12% of households co-hold consumer credit and liquid saving, and that co-holding is related to impulsive spending. Bertaut, Haliassos and Reiter (2009) use a dual-selves model ('accountant' and 'shopper') in their analysis of credit card debt. These considerations highlight the connection between mental accounting and self-control in credit use.

Conclusion

In private households, various economic decisions are made. On the one hand, some of them are made autonomously – although often not independently, because people in harmonious partnerships try to anticipate the needs and preferences of the partner. On the other hand, decisions are made jointly. Such syncratic decisions are more likely with higher relationship quality and with higher expensiveness and social visibility of the product. However, they do not always lead to economically sound decisions. Partners often give priority to other factors than purely logical thinking and arguing. They consider utility debts and perceived fairness. Conflicts can arise, and partners resort to persuasion tactics and other tactics to reach their goals. Spending and borrowing money can be sensitive topics in households.

Summary

- Purchase decisions can be categorised according to whether cognitive scripts are available, the amount of money involved, the symbolic value and social visibility of the product, and the number of people affected by the purchase. Depending on these factors, spontaneous purchases, habitual purchases or purchases after extensive decision procedures are made individually or jointly (syncratic decisions).
- The classical stage model of purchase decisions consists of five stages: problem recognition, information search, evaluation of alternatives, product choice and evaluation of outcomes.
- Models of consumer behaviour can be grouped in hierarchy-of-effects models and information processing models.
- Purchase decisions are based not only on the basic use value of a good, but also on the hedonic experience they provide as well as their social and symbolic features. In extreme cases such as pathological buying, purchasing is no longer a means to an end, but rewarding in itself.
- Purchase decisions in households can be described along a model that incorporates individual and joint decisions, conflict types, interaction principles and regulation of utility debts.
- Different methods to study decision-making in households are used. Interviews and surveys have severe limitations in this area. Diary-based methods are better able to capture interaction processes between partners.
- Influence in decisions partly depends on gender and product category. Recent studies still show gender-specific influence domains and suggest that, instead of more syncratic decisions, more decisions are made autonomously.
- Partners use different tactics to convince the other person in household decisions. Tactics used depend on the relationship quality, length of partnership, type of conflict and gender.
- Couples are satisfied with a decision when the process of coming to a decision and the result are perceived as fair, when the discussion climate was good, when the benefit to oneself is high but not too high, and as one's own influence increases.
- The decision to take credit is the choice between immediate pleasure of consumption and delayed burden of repaying. Credit use is not a one-time decision, but a process over time in which three phases can be differentiated: (a) before credit take up, (b) during credit take up, and (c) during repayment period.
- The concept of mental accounting is useful in understanding and describing credit use. Mental accounting influences the specific credit taken up, experience and behaviour in repayment, and can serve as a self-control measure.

Questions

1 Which models of consumer behaviour have been proposed?
2 Depending on the relationship quality, how do couples settle 'utility debts'?

3 Which methods are used to study decisions in the household and what are their advantages and disadvantages?
4 What is the 'role triangle' and in which context is it used?
5 How can mental accounting influence credit decisions?

FURTHER READING

Kamleitner, B., Hoelzl, E., & Kirchler, E. (2012). Credit use: Psychological perspectives on a multifaceted phenomenon. *International Journal of Psychology*, *47*, 1–27.

Kirchler, E., Rodler, C., Hoelzl, E., & Meier, K. (2001). *Conflict and decision making in close relationships: Love, money and daily routine*. Hove: Psychology Press.

Tichenor, V. J. (2005). *Earning more and getting less: Why successful wives can't buy equality*. New Brunswick, NJ: Rutgers University Press.

van Raaij, F. (2016). *Understanding consumer financial behavior*. Basingstoke: Palgrave Macmillan.

6 Labour Markets: Wages and Entrepreneurship

Overview

From an economic perspective, the same laws are valid in the labour market as in markets for consumer goods: demand and supply determine the price. Employers have a demand for workers and workers supply their labour. The combination of demand and supply is assumed to determine the wages. These assumptions can be tested in experimental labour markets. The setup of these labour markets can mimic different aspects of real-life labour markets, in particular by allowing reciprocity. Findings indicate that higher wages are reciprocated by higher effort.

Wages are often discussed as a tool to increase motivation. However, the connection is not always straightforward. Several theories of motivation have highlighted the importance of subjective perceptions of values and probabilities as well as social comparisons. An important aspect of wages is whether they are perceived as fair or unfair. Equity theory offers an explanation of these subjective fairness perceptions: importantly, fairness perceptions are influenced not only by own input and output, but also by the comparison with other people.

Entrepreneurs run companies or found new companies and thereby provide job opportunities in labour markets. They seek to make a profit through participation in the market but run the risk of possibly losing their invested capital. On the one hand, established entrepreneurs have been found to show characteristic personality traits and motivations. On the other hand, the process of successfully founding a company is a complex interplay between personal characteristics and situational conditions. Female entrepreneurs face specific challenges due to stereotypes.

Introduction

Labour occupies a major part of life for most of us. In this chapter, the goal is to understand how labour markets work. Do they work on the basis of supply and demand or is this approach alone too simplistic? What motivates people to seek employment and to provide effort? What are the psychological processes through which wages can improve motivation and performance? What is considered a fair wage? Finally, who are the people that create jobs for themselves and others?

6.1 Supply and Demand for Labour

In markets, selling and buying takes place. Just as consumer goods and services are supplied and demanded in markets, labour power is supplied by workers on the one hand and demanded by employers on the other. Labour markets arise when workers are matched with open positions and hiring decisions are made. Every day, thousands of career decisions are made. New hires are secured, and notices of termination release workers onto local and national labour markets.

How do labour markets work from an economic point of view? Since markets in general are defined by the coming together of supply and demand, labour markets should also be understood as the interplay between the behaviour of employers and employees. In economics, it is assumed that under perfect competition – when there are no government regulations and neither labour unions nor employers' associations intervene in wage negotiations – what happens in the market follows certain laws, which in classical economic theory are precisely formulated. In fact, there are few markets in the real world in which the conditions of perfect competition are met. There are labour unions that represent workers' interests and occupy powerful positions in wage negotiations. There are employers' associations that represent employers' interests, and there are governmental regulations that intervene in the labour market by, for example, stipulating minimum wages. Nevertheless, this chapter will describe classical economic assumptions about market dynamics under perfect competition and primarily present studies that empirically test these assumptions.

In classical economic theory, the labour market is considered a market governed by principles of trade; however, it is one in which units of labour rather than physical goods are traded (Woll, 1981). Workers supply their working capacity, which is demanded by employers. Since employees create costs, it is to be assumed that employers carefully consider how many workers they need to hire at what cost. No more workers are hired than is absolutely necessary. As wages increase, employers can hire and pay fewer workers. If demand for goods remains the same, demand for labour sinks as wages increase (Figure 6.1(a)). If demand for goods rises, so that production can be increased, the number of workers can remain the same or even increase despite an increase in wages. The demand curve shifts horizontally from T to T' (Figure 6.1(b)).

Workers also make decisions. They decide whether it would be worth taking a job at a certain pay level. Since work is understood as a burden in economics, getting to work and buying work clothes generates financial costs. In addition, the strain at work generates health costs, and time spent at work comes at the cost of free time. For these reasons, wage offers cannot fall below a certain level. The higher the wage, the more likely it is that a worker will accept a position. The relationship between wage levels and labour supply is positive (Figure 6.1(c)).

The wage level that takes hold in free markets depends on the supply and demand for labour. While the demand curve shows the wage levels at which employers are willing to hire workers, the supply curve represents workers' willingness to work at specific wage levels. As wages increase, more and more workers take jobs but fewer and fewer employers are willing to hire more employees, which generates conflict. The point of intersection between the demand and supply curves reveals the level at which wages will settle at a given point in time (Figure 6.1(d)). The **equilibrium wage** on the labour market is determined by employers' demand for labour and workers' supply of it. At this wage, the market is 'cleared', meaning that supply corresponds to demand. The **market-clearing wage** corresponds to the equilibrium wage. In other words, market interaction dynamics lead to a situation where all employers who are willing to pay a given wage hire those workers who accept this offer. Employers who will not or cannot pay a given wage and workers who cannot or will not accept a job offer at this wage do not enter into a labour contract. When all workers who want to accept a job offer have done so and all employers wishing to do so have hired employees under conditions acceptable to both parties, market equilibrium is reached.

According to the definition of the labour supply function, at the equilibrium wage rate, '**full employment**' for the economy as a whole is obtained. Full employment is understood as the condition where all workers who want to work at a given wage level find a job. Wage offers above the market-clearing wage lead to involuntary unemployment, because more workers push

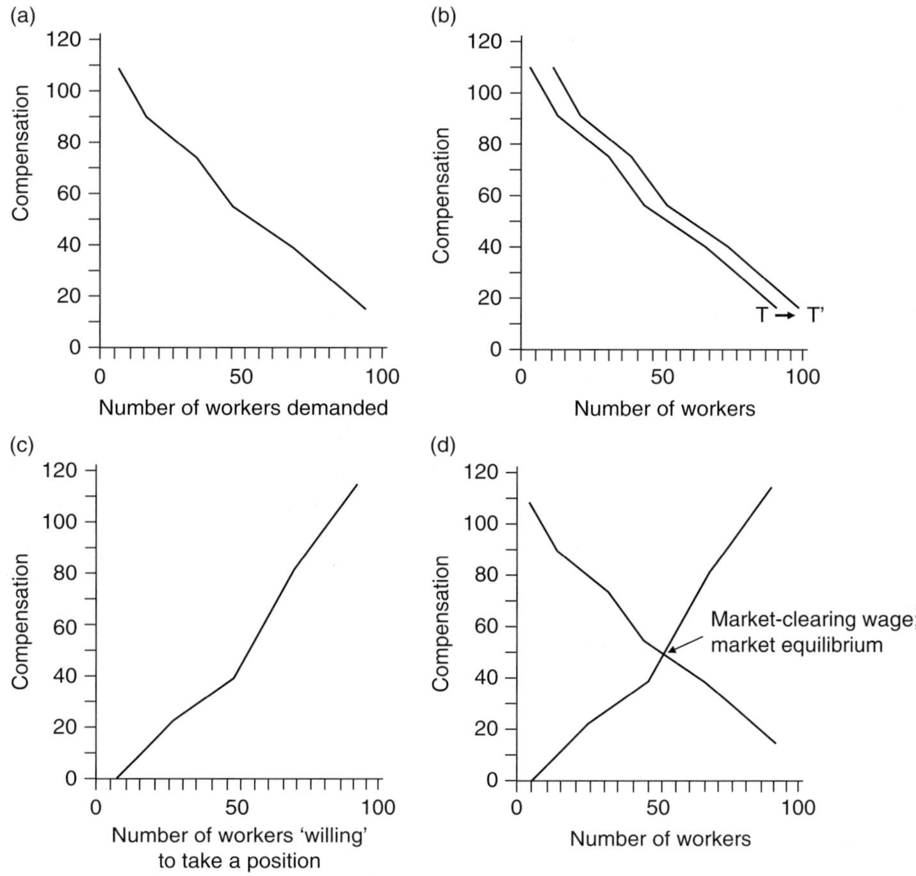

Figure 6.1 Demand and supply for labour

in to the labour market than are hired by employers. In Figure 6.1(d), the market-clearing wage amounts to 50 money units. Every worker who wants to work at this wage level finds a job. In the example depicted here, out of 100 workers, 55 are employed – namely, those 55 who want to work for a wage of 50 money units. The others, who are not willing to accept the market-clearing wage, are by definition in a situation of '**voluntary unemployment**'. When the wage is 100 money units, more than 80 workers are looking for work, but employers are only willing to hire approximately 10 of them; the others are unemployed. If wages would sink below the market-clearing wage of 50 units, employers would demand more workers than there are workers who are actually willing to enter the market. According to the model depicted here, wages in markets under perfect competition settle at the market-clearing wage.

From the perspective of psychology, the economic notions about employment and unemployment appear abstract. Can unemployment really be explained by the prevailing wage level? The definition of full employment is also disconcerting: people who do not want to work for a certain wage are labelled voluntarily unemployed. In order for workers to be able to take a job offer, it is often necessary for them to be willing to accept a long commute or to move to another city. Travel costs, a second residence or moving to another area represent not just financial costs but also social ones. For that reason, moving from a structurally weak area to a more economically hopeful one is not always tolerable. The costs associated with retraining, a career change or taking a job below one's qualification level are often unacceptable. In economics, however, workers have the opportunity to choose between alternatives and take a job even if the associated financial and social costs exceed the wage. Someone who receives a job offer under such conditions but rejects it is defined as voluntarily unemployed. When the fate of workers is considered rather than theoretical notions, the contention that choices exist and people select the best available alternative starts to sound cynical.

The theoretical assumptions about markets under perfect competition are brilliantly formalised. They are nonetheless suspect, as they do not consider that involuntary unemployment can also exist under conditions of perfect competition. For example, employers often voluntarily set their employees' wages over the market-clearing equilibrium because they fear that their employees will reduce their performance if wages fall. Fehr (2001) reports that workers in labour market experiments who indicate a willingness to work for a low wage in the hope of finding a job are often not hired for exactly that reason. In such cases, employers suspect that their performance would also be low. Falk, Fehr and Zehnder (2006) illustrate the effects of a minimum wage. Study participants were prompted to name their reservation wage, the lowest wage level at which they would still be willing to take a job. If a wage offer amounted to less than the reservation wage, the worker would reject it. The study occurred under two separate conditions: in the first condition, a minimum wage was imposed, but not in the other. When no minimum wage was specified, low wages resulted. However, when a minimum wage was introduced, the market wage settled at a level considerably above the minimum wage. The same was true of the reservation wage: in that regard, workers' perception of fair wages played an important role. Receiving minimum wage was seen as unfair because employers were legally required to pay it. If a minimum wage is introduced in experimental studies and then removed again, it becomes apparent that the temporary adoption of a minimum wage has a lasting effect on the actual wages workers earn in the experiment as well as on their reservation wages. Workers become habituated to the higher pay and are no longer willing to work for lower wages at a later time. The '**fair wage-fair effort hypothesis**' (Akerlof & Yellen, 1988) builds on equity theory (Adams, 1963, 1965) from social psychology, and assumes that workers' behaviour on the labour market is governed by considerations of fairness: they respond to higher wages with higher effort and to lower wages with lower effort. Companies anticipate this and are aware that wage reductions will be answered with reduced performance. In the following section, the usefulness of experimental economics and game theory in testing the assumptions of economics regarding labour markets will be illustrated.

6.1.1 Experimental Economics and Game Theory

Hey (1991) argued that as long as the bulk of economists accept neoclassical theory and use theories based on mathematical logic, experiments should be conducted to test economic hypotheses. Experiments are considered as a particularly rigorous method of scientific research. Specifically, investigators are able to control for all variables relevant in testing a hypothesis, as well as being able to manipulate the testing conditions systematically to determine their influence on the dependent variable of interest. This allows the determination of causal effects (Friedrichs, 1982). In experiments on labour markets, some study participants take on the role of employers and offer wages. The others take on the role of workers and can either ask for specific wages or accept wages offered to them.

Game theory is concerned with strategic behaviour in social interactions (e.g., Diekmann, 2009; Rieck, 2008). While decision theory primarily investigates the conditions under which individuals make rational decisions, game theory describes tasks in which an individual's success depends not only on his or her own actions, but also on the actions of one or more partners. When applied to economics and the social sciences, game theory seeks to explain which strategies people use to achieve their goals (Owen, 2001). In 1944, von Neumann and Morgenstern published their influential book *Theory of games and economic behavior*, which marks the beginning of game theory. Game theory has become of interest to economic psychology because certain 'games' allow testing the rationality criteria of economics (Diekmann, 2009). If the assumptions of the *homo economicus* model are correct, 'players' in social interactions ought to behave selfishly and attempt to maximise their own benefits. Thus, they should look for the 'optimal strategy' serving themselves. Various types of games were developed in order to investigate in which cases participants adhere to rationality criteria and under which conditions they deviate from them. The dictator game, the ultimatum game, the trust game and repeated games that require backward induction (e.g., centipede game, beauty contest) are especially relevant to the labour market experiment described later.

As described in Chapter 2, the dictator game involves a Player A who receives a certain divisible good, such as a specific sum of money, from the experimenter. Player A must decide whether to turn over a portion to Player B, and if so, how much. Player A can give away nothing and keep everything for herself. Alternatively, Player A can allocate some amount to Player B, which diminishes her own result by the corresponding amount. Player B has no opportunity to react to the offer in a way that would affect Player A. In the ultimatum game, Player A receives a certain divisible good and can determine how much of it to hand over to Player B. Player B can decide whether to accept the offered amount or to reject it. If B accepts, A receives the good minus the amount offered to B, and B receives the amount offered by Player A. If Player B rejects the offer, both players go away empty-handed, and the good is returned to the experimenter.

A further extension is the **trust game**. Here, the first Player A decides whether or not to give part of a divisible good to Player B. Player B can then react like the dictator in the dictator game by keeping everything or giving part of the amount received back to A. Then the game ends. In most trust games, the amount that A gives to B is multiplied by a specific factor. Player A can hope to get back more than he offered – if he trusts B to act cooperatively and give something back. When both partners act as trusting and trustworthy, they can earn higher profits. However, Player A might worry that Player B will not give anything back, since the game ends after his action and A has no opportunity to react to B. For example, A could give all of the initial 100 money units to B. If the multiplicative factor is four, Player B now has 400 money units. Player B can now either keep everything or give, say, 200 money units back to A. Why should A trust B to share, when B can keep the entire amount without having to fear any repercussions? Johnson and Mislin (2011) analysed data from 162 replications of the trust game including more than 23,000 participants. They found that behaviour clearly deviates from neoclassical predictions. On average, 50% of the endowed amount was transferred from Player A to Player B, with means varying from a minimum of 22% to a maximum of 89% among the 162 studies. After multiplication by the experimenter, Player B on average passed back 37% to Player A, with means ranging from 11% to 81%.

The **centipede game** represents a sequential game played repeatedly with two or more players. Player A receives an amount of money and can either keep it and end the game, or pass it on to Player B. This amount of money is then multiplied by a certain factor, and B can now either keep everything or give everything back to A. If B gives the money back to A, it is again multiplied by the given factor and now A gets to decide whether to take the money or to pass it back to B so that the amount increases further. Each player can decide whether to end the game and win a sum of money or to pass the money on to the other player. Every time someone decides to keep playing, the amount of money grows. If one of the players ends the game, the person who gave the money away gets nothing. What should the players do? Should they keep the money or pass it on so that the amount increases, despite the risk that the other player will not act cooperatively? If the players are told at the beginning how many rounds are going to be played, from an economic perspective they should not start to play at all: Player A should simply keep everything for himself. This assumption arises from backward induction (Heifetz & Pauzner, 2005), which was already discussed in Chapter 2: considering that in the last round one player, for example A, is supposed to transfer the total amount of money accrued to B and then the game ends, A would come up empty-handed and B would win everything. For this reason, A will terminate the game in the second-to-last round. Since B suspects this, he will keep everything for himself in the round before that. Because A knows this, however, he will terminate the game even earlier and so on. When considering which strategy will result in the greatest profit, by reasoning backwards from the last round it quickly becomes apparent that Player A needs to end the game in the first round and keep the amount of money issued to her right away. In a literature review on game-theoretic settings, Güth and Kocher (2014) summarise that observed behaviour in experimental settings cannot be explained by backward induction in most cases. Thus, players usually do not end the game in the first round. Johnson, Camerer, Sen and Rymon (2002) stated that 'backward induction is a neat trick that is not computationally hard to execute (at least in these simple games) once it is taught, but it seems to be difficult to induce from raw experience' (p. 40).

How difficult it is and how much motivation is necessary to conduct a backward induction analysis for a simple task can be shown via the example of a group sweepstake. Imagine a group of people who are each instructed to write a number from zero to 100 on a piece of paper. Afterwards, all the numbers written down are added up and the arithmetic mean is calculated. The person who has written down the number corresponding to two-thirds of the mean wins the game. What number should be written down if all players acted rationally and know that all of the other players are acting rationally too? The following backward induction analysis must be employed. If all participants write down 100, the mean is 100 and the winning number would be 2/3 * 100 = 66.7. Since all participants know this, none of them will write down a number over 66. Thus, the average cannot amount to more than 66 and the winning number would be 44. Since everyone knows this, no one will write a number above 44, and the mean sinks to a maximum of 44. The winning number can thus be no higher than approximately 30, and so on. The analysis continues until no one will write down a number higher than zero, meaning that the mean of all the numbers is also zero. Since 2/3 of the average of zero is also zero, the winning number can only be zero. When this game is actually played, however, it turns out that most participants begin a backward analysis but give up after a few steps, adjust their estimate according to the value they calculated for these few steps, and ultimately write down a number far higher than zero (e.g., Nagel, 1995; Yavas, Sefton & Katok, 2002). Nagel (1995) reports that in her studies, in which players were tasked to estimate two-thirds of the average or half of the average, no one wrote down zero and only 6% of players invoked a number under 10. Montier (2010, p. 281) reports on a study in which people were invited to estimate two-thirds of the mean of the numbers from zero to 100 that had been written down by all participants. Approximately 9% indicated the number zero; more than 5% wrote down numbers over 67. Figure 6.2 depicts the distribution of the numbers that were written down.

What could the winning number be when the players know that their rationality is limited, and that no one or only a few players will write down the number zero? In this case, the game is related to Keynes' (1936/1997) **beauty contest**: players need to put themselves in the position of the other players, take their limited rationality into account when making their own estimate, and consequently anticipate the others' estimates. In the real world, the investors who are most likely to profit from the stock market are those who align their actions with the suspected behaviour of other market participants rather than allowing their actions to be dictated by strictly rational considerations. The following quote from Keynes nicely illustrates this idea:

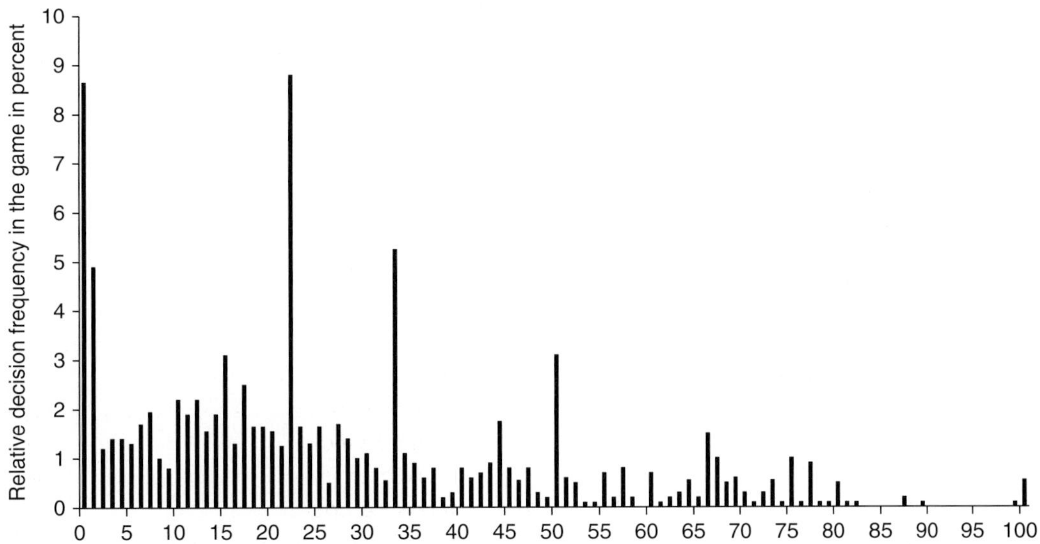

Figure 6.2 Distribution of estimates of two-thirds of the mean of numbers written down from zero to 100 (Montier, 2010, p. 283)

> Professional investment may be likened to those newspaper competitions in which the competitors have to pick out the six prettiest faces from a hundred photographs, the prize being awarded to the competitor whose choice most nearly corresponds to the average preferences of the competitors as a whole; so that each competitor has to pick, not those faces which he himself finds prettiest, but those which he thinks likeliest to catch the fancy of the other competitors, all of whom are looking at the problem from the same point of view. It is not a case of choosing those which, to the best of one's judgment, are really the prettiest, nor even those which average opinion genuinely thinks the prettiest. We have reached the third degree where we devote our intelligences to anticipating what average opinion expects the average opinion to be. (Keynes, 1936/1997, p. 156)

Elements of these games and their analysis can be used to design a labour market and conduct experimental investigations (e.g., Davis & Holt, 1993; Fehr, Kirchler, Weichbold & Gächter, 1998). A group of 15–20 people could be invited to participate in an experiment. A small portion of participants could play the role of employers, who receive a certain sum of money and can hire employees during a market period by offering them a portion of their money. The remaining participants are workers who can either accept or reject jobs. If an employment contract between employer and worker is agreed upon, the employer receives his money minus the amount offered to the corresponding employee. The worker receives the agreed-upon amount. If no contract is agreed upon, neither the employer nor the worker receives any money. The amount of money issued to the employer at the beginning of the game needs to be returned to the experimenter. The market game can be played once or repeatedly. It can take several forms: instead of a market in which employers can enter into contracts with different workers in each round, a situation can be designed in which either the same partners negotiate wages in each round or the partners change every time.

6.1.2 Labour Market Experiments

According to Davis and Holt (1993), instructions for a market experiment under perfect competition in which a group of employers and a numerically larger group of workers participate could read like

Table 6.1 Instruction for participants in the role of workers and employers in a labour market experiment (adapted from Davis & Holt, 1993, p. 47)

You are participating in a market experiment. Your task is to take on the role of an employer or a worker. Workers can offer their labour power to employers for a certain wage; employers can either accept a worker's offer or present their own wage offers to employees and try to persuade them to work for that wage. The experiment is divided into a series of market periods. During each market period, you have the opportunity to enter into a contract with a worker or employer. You can only enter into one contract during each period. The total profit paid out to you at the end of the experiment will be determined by the wages you receive as a worker or pay out as an employer over all of the periods put together. You can calculate your profit for each market period.

Employer

Your decision to pay a certain wage to a worker will be booked on a piece of paper, the employer's sheet. Each column on the employer's sheet represents one market period. During each period, you can enter into an employment contract, thus hiring a worker for a certain wage. In each market period, you have a certain amount of money available, which is listed in the first row of the employer's sheet. This value represents the sum of money that you have available to you when you make a wage offer. For example, your initial sum in Market Period 0 amounts to US$ 210. Should a worker be willing to enter into an employment contract with you during this period for, say, US$ 160, your profit for this period amounts to US$ 210 – US$ 160 = US$ 50. Your profit is calculated as the difference between the initial amount and the wage offer. Write down the wage in the second row and the result of the profit calculation in the third row of the employer's sheet. Should you not enter into an employment contract during a given market period, your initial sum is forfeited and you have no profit.

Period	0	1	2	3	4	5	6	7	8	9	10
Initial value	210										
Wage paid											
Profit											

Worker

Your decision to accept a wage offer will be booked on a piece of paper, the worker's sheet. Each column on the worker's sheet represents one market period. During each period, you can enter into an employment contract, thus selling your labour power for a certain wage. Accepting a job creates certain costs (e.g., travel costs, loss of unemployment compensation), which are listed in the second row of the worker's sheet. For example, the costs of working in Market Period 0 amount to a total of US$ 130. Should an employer be willing to enter into an employment contract with you during this market period, offering you US$ 190, your profit during this period would amount to US$ 190 – US$ 130 = US$ 60. Your profit is calculated as the difference between the offered wage and your costs. Write down the wage you accept in the first row of the worker's sheet and the result of the profit calculation in the third row. If you do not enter into a work contract during a given market period, you do not have to bear any costs, but you do not receive any profit either.

Period	0	1	2	3	4	5	6	7	8	9	10
Wage											
Expenses	130										
Profit											

those shown in Table 6.1. These instructions are intended to make the costs and benefits of entering a work contract very clear. Hence, participants in the role of employees should be motivated to consider carefully the wages they offer, whereas participants in the role of workers should consider carefully which wages they accept.

The experimental labour market is conducted over several market periods, in the current example ten rounds, with a limited time per period. In each period, contracts are determined in a double auction: employers can make wage offers that workers can accept, or workers can make wage

Table 6.2 Initial sums of money for seven employers and expenses for ten workers

Employers' initial sums of money		Workers' expenses	
B1	US$ 150	S1	US$ 80
B2	US$ 140	S2	US$ 90
B3	US$ 130	S3	US$ 100
B4	US$ 120	S4	US$ 110
B5	US$ 110	S5	US$ 120
B6	US$ 100	S6	US$ 130
B7	US$ 90	S7	US$ 140
		S8	US$ 150
		S9	US$ 160
		S10	US$ 170

demands that employers can accept. When offers or demands are not accepted, they can be improved. There is competition for contracts among both the employers and the workers, because if they do not manage to enter a contract by the end of the period, their payoff for this period is zero. Every participant only has information about his or her own role and the corresponding initial sums or expenses. In an experiment with seven employers and ten workers, values could be distributed as in Table 6.2.

What results can be expected from a market experiment designed in this way? Based on the sums of money they have been issued, all seven employers could enter into contracts with employees. In this case, the maximum possible number of workers would have a job. For example, the employer who has US$ 150 at his disposal could hire the worker with costs of US$ 140. The employer with US$ 140 could hire the worker who faces costs of US$ 130, and so on, until the employer with US$ 90 enters into a contract with the worker whose costs are lowest. In reality, this result rarely occurs: it turns out that accepted wages settle at around US$ 120 within a few trading periods, meaning that four workers with correspondingly lower costs accept jobs and four of the seven employers enter into contracts with these workers.

The workers' expenses and employers' resources can be represented in the form of a supply and demand curve. The theoretically justifiable market-clearing wage and the number of employment contracts can be demonstrated on this curve (Figure 6.3). Assuming perfect competition, a wage between US$ 110 and US$ 120 can be predicted and four contracts between employers and workers will be concluded in each round. A wage between US$ 110 and US$ 120 also corresponds to maximal profit opportunities for workers and employers and thus represents a utility maximum for the economy as a whole. Numerous market and auction experiments have demonstrated the robustness of the assertions of economic theory, as the market-clearing wage is indeed achieved in such experiments designed as double auctions after only a few rounds of playing (see Davis & Holt, 1993; Lopes, 1994). In one-sided auctions, in which only one party is able to make an offer and the other party must either accept or reject it, prices or wages lie slightly under the predicted wage (Lopes, 1994).

Why does the equilibrium wage represent the maximum exhaustion of profits from the perspective of the economy as a whole? Looking at Figure 6.3, it is clear that under full employment, that is, with four contracts between workers and employers, profits for the group of workers and employers as a whole are greatest (Table 6.3). A total profit of US$ 160 is available. If the wage level is at US$ 110,

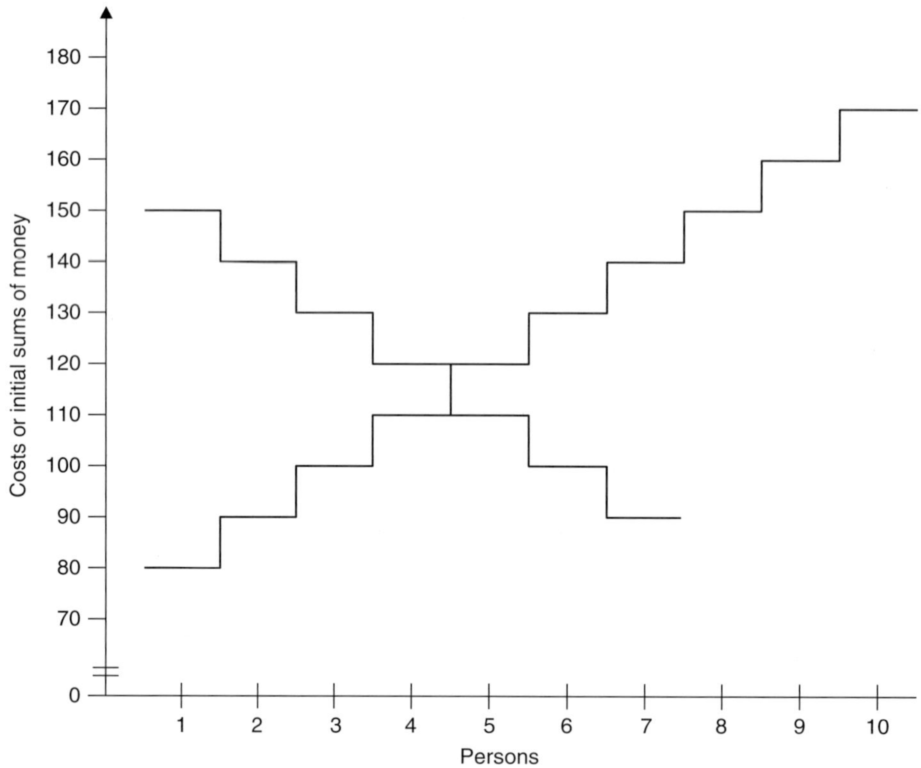

Figure 6.3 Supply and demand curve for the seven employers and ten workers

employers obtain a total of US$ 100 and workers a total of US$ 60. If all seven possible contracts were concluded, the total profit of US$ 70 (Employer B7 trades with Worker S1, B6 with S2, etc.; each profit amounts to US$ 10) would lie far under the maximum of US$ 160. From an economic perspective, it would therefore be more advantageous if only four workers were hired and thus only four employers went into business, while the others remained out of work. In order to avoid disadvantaging and discriminating against those who are without work, the benefit of the economy as a whole would need to be redistributed accordingly – for example, through taxation – so that those without employment contracts and without an income could also share in the prosperity.

Depending on the parameters chosen for the numbers of employers and workers and their initial values and costs, payoffs can be dramatically different for employers and workers. When, for example, more workers participate in an experiment than employers and all workers accrue costs of 50 money units when they enter into an employment contract, while all employers have 500 money units available, the equilibrium wage amounts to 50 or approximately one money unit higher. According to the assertions of classical economics, employers only need to cover the costs of their workers' labour power because competition between workers for scarce jobs pushes wages down to about 50. Workers will accept a position even when taking the job puts them in only a marginally better financial position than forgoing work. With wages at 50 + 1 = 51 money units, minus expenses of 50 units, workers would have a profit of one money unit (wage – expenses = profit). Employers would generate a profit of 500 – 51 = 449 money units (initial sum – wage costs = profit). Even though the distribution of profits between employers and workers is completely unequal and would be frequently criticised as

Table 6.3 Profit calculations for employers and workers

Aggregate profit calculation from the employers' perspective				Aggregate profit calculation from the workers' perspective			
B7	does not trade	=	0	S10	does not trade	=	0
B6	does not trade	=	0	S9	does not trade	=	0
B5	does not trade	=	0	S8	does not trade	=	0
B4 (S4)	US$ 120 – 110	=	10	S7	does not trade	=	0
B3 (S3)	US$ 130 – 100	=	30	S6	does not trade	=	0
B2 (S2)	US$ 140 – 90	=	50	S5	does not trade	=	0
B1 (S1)	US$ 150 – 80	=	70	S4	US$ –110 + 120	=	10
	SUM		160	S3	US$ –100 + 130	=	30
				S2	US$ –90 + 140	=	50
				S1	US$ –80 + 150	=	70
					SUM		160

unfair, workers would accept the exchange because – according to theory – a profit of one unit is better than no profit at all. From the perspective of psychology, these assumptions do not appear very credible, because norms of fairness and reciprocity regulate behaviour in social relationships and thus also in markets. However, considerations of fairness can only be expected to determine the behaviour of market participants when they have complete information about the resource distribution and everyone else's profit opportunities. When the initial sums issued to employers and employees' costs after accepting a contract remain unknown, it is impossible to judge which offers are fair. When market participants possess no information about other participants' resources and costs, the prognoses of economics are confirmed after only a few market periods (Davis & Holt, 1993, p. 142).

In the market experiment just described, participants have no possible actions other than making offers and accepting or rejecting them. However, real labour markets are more complex, a fact that should be better accounted for in the laboratory. In labour markets, workers are able to do more than just accept or reject an open position. They are also able to respond to the fairness of a wage offer by putting a corresponding amount of effort into their work. Moreover, employers are likely to be aware of this, to take reciprocity of favours into account and to offer wages higher than the low market-clearing wage in real-world contexts, regardless of what classical economic market theories say. The reason for this could be the pursuit of selfish profit maximisation, but it could also be the result of altruistic motives. Among others, Kirchler, Fehr and Evans (1996) and Fehr et al. (1998) conducted experiments in which workers had the opportunity to respond to fair wage offers with fair effort at work. These experiments showed that norms of reciprocity and perceptions of fairness are relevant to understand the behaviour on the market.

6.1.3 Reciprocity on the Labour Market

In a market experiment designed as a one-sided auction, employers dictate wages to workers. If seven employers can enter into contracts with any of ten workers and have, for example, 120 money units available, market theory dictates that they will offer just enough for workers to cover their costs and earn a minimal profit. If costs are set at 20 money units, roughly 20–21 money units will be offered and accepted. It is questionable as to whether the low market-clearing wage also arises in market situations in which workers can react to an offer after having accepted it by adjusting their work performance. If commitment to one's work generates costs to workers but results in higher revenue for employers, workers could answer generous wage offers from employers with higher commitment. They could do so for reasons of fairness. They could also follow the **norm of reciprocity** that prescribes that behaviours of others should be returned in kind. If workers are able to respond to generous offers with more effort and higher performance, and thus with more revenue for their employers, employers would be able to offer a higher wage than the theoretically predicted equilibrium wage, which would then stabilise in the course of repeated market periods.

In a bilateral interaction, not only does the opportunity exist to pay back a favour in the form of a fair wage offer, there is also social pressure to achieve an equal or at least balanced distribution of resources among participants. In an experiment designed not as a market situation but rather as a bilateral interaction, employers might be willing to pay a higher wage than the market-clearing price. This is even more likely to be the case when each employer repeatedly interacts with the same worker. From the perspective of psychology, it is understandable that the theoretically postulated wage emerges in pure market experiments under perfect competition. However, in market experiments with opportunities for reciprocity, utility maximisation tendencies seem less likely. The market-clearing wage is especially unlikely to emerge when an employer repeatedly interacts with a certain worker. In repeated games, actors' reputations can also have an effect on outcomes. If employers have information that a certain worker accepted a relatively low wage offer in the past or that a certain worker did not fairly reciprocate a generous offer with high effort, employers might offer him lower wages on account of his reputation (Nowak, Page & Sigmund, 2000).

In a pure market situation, it is probable that average wages turn out to be lower and come closer to the market-clearing wage postulated in market theory. However, in a market situation with opportunities to answer wage offers by putting greater effort into work, this seems less likely. Average wages are probably also lower in bilateral interactions between two people conducted only once compared to repeated bilateral interactions. There are two reasons for this: first, fairness is seen as a morally correct and socially desirable behaviour, and second, employers trust in workers' tendencies towards reciprocity. They are likely to believe that a high wage offer will lead to higher work performance, meaning that higher wages lead to higher profits. When individuals and groups interact with one another repeatedly, relationship structures characterised by a growing ability to anticipate one's partner's behaviour as well as an increasing tolerance for risks due to trust in one's partner's cooperation can be established (e.g., Bazerman, 1994; Mannix, Tinsley & Bazerman, 1995). When interactions are repeated, when cooperation is advantageous for both partners and when partners can trust one another, cooperative behaviour pays off. Indeed, Cochard, Nguyen Van and Willinger (2004) experimentally demonstrated that higher sums are exchanged in repeated games. They compared offers in market experiments with seven rounds to offers in experiments with only one round. When several iterations of the game took place, higher amounts were offered at the beginning. However, offers in the last round did not differ from those of the experiments with only one round.

If employers and workers know that ten market or interaction periods are scheduled in the experiment, employers could employ the following logic of backward induction when choosing the size of their wage offers. Since workers are likely to maximise their profits in the last round by putting in only low effort after receiving a high wage, employers can pre-empt this behaviour by offering a low wage. Since nothing will be left for either partner to gain in the last round, workers will similarly put in the lowest amount of effort in the second-to-last round. Of course, these rational considerations on the workers' side are also clear to employers, meaning that a high wage offer in the

Table 6.4 Representation of assumptions on wages and effort in the market experiment by Kirchler, Fehr and Evans (1996, p. 322)

Condition	Economic hypotheses	Psychological hypotheses
(a) One-shot bilateral interaction (wage offer with opportunity for reciprocity, interaction partner changes from one interaction period to the next)	Achieved wage = market-clearing wage Workers' effort = minimal	Achieved wage > market-clearing wage Workers' performance correlates positively with wage level
(b) Repeated bilateral interaction (wage offer with opportunity for reciprocity; a certain employer interacts with the same worker during every interaction period)	Achieved wage = market-clearing wage Workers' effort = minimal	Achieved wage > market-clearing wage Workers' performance correlates positively with wage level
(c) Competitive market with reciprocity (wage offer with opportunity for reciprocity)	Achieved wage = market-clearing wage Workers' effort = minimal	Achieved wage > market-clearing wage Workers' performance correlates positively with wage level
(d) Competitive market without reciprocity (wage offers from employers but no opportunities for reciprocity from workers)	Achieved wage = market-clearing wage	Achieved wage = market-clearing wage

second-to-last round would be irrational (i.e., it would reduce their profits). Thus, the argumentation for the last round is also valid for the second-to-last round. Backward induction is thus presumed to spell doom for all cooperation and reciprocity hypotheses: reasoning from the last interaction period to the first, it pays to maximise one's own profit and always offer the minimum wage. This also means that employees will put in the lowest possible effort. The theoretical assumptions resulting from backward induction are clear. Nevertheless, as already mentioned, higher sums are exchanged in repeated games than in games with only one round (Cochard et al., 2004), even if sums in the last round no longer differ from games that are played only once. Although utility-maximising tendencies do play a role in later rounds of the game, backward induction is not fully applied all the way back to the first round. As mentioned earlier, Güth and Kocher (2014) argue that observed behaviour in experimental settings cannot be explained by backward induction in most cases. Furthermore, Johnson et al. (2002) claim that information search is characterised by limited look ahead rather than by backward induction. Thus, people focus on current rounds when making decisions in market experiments. In centipede games, Bornstein, Kugler and Ziegelmeyer (2004) found that people either find it difficult or simply have little motivation to think through the exchange process from the last round back to the first.

It is thus clear that from the perspective of economics, all market conditions – with or without opportunities to answer an offer with higher or lower effort, as well as one-time and repeated bilateral interactions – result in employers offering the market-clearing wage and workers putting in only minimal effort. These assumptions are shown in Table 6.4.

Does cooperation develop in the labour markets conditions described above or not? If cooperation does develop, does the behaviour of workers and employers stabilise, or does the cooperation built

Table 6.5 Profit calculation for employers and workers in the market experiment by Kirchler, Fehr and Evans (1996)

Market condition with no opportunity for reciprocity (condition d):		
	Worker:	Profit = Wage – travel costs
	Employer:	Profit = Starting sum – wage
Bilateral conditions and market condition with opportunity for reciprocity (conditions a, b, c):		
	Worker:	Profit = Wage – travel costs – performance costs
	Employer:	Profit = (Starting sum – wage) * performance level

up at the beginning of the game fall apart at the end because at that point it is anticipated that cooperation in the last round would be costly? To test these conjectures, experiments (Fehr et al., 1998; Kirchler et al. 1996) were conducted with soldiers undergoing mandatory military service using four experimental conditions: (a) a one-shot bilateral interaction, (b) a repeated bilateral interaction, (c) a competitive market with reciprocity (gift exchange market), and (d) a competitive market without reciprocity (pure market). In conditions (a) and (b), participants were randomly assigned to act either as workers or employers, comprising two groups of ten participants. In conditions (c) and (d), competitive experimental labour markets were implemented by assigning a larger group of participants to be workers than employers, specifically entailing 50% more workers than employers. In the first two conditions employers offered a wage to one worker they interacted with. In the last two conditions, they publicly set wages that individual workers could choose to either take or reject.

The bilateral interaction conditions (a) and (b) only differed with regard to one's interaction partner in consecutive rounds, with the same pairs of workers and employers interacting over the course of ten rounds in condition (b), while new pairs of different partners were matched in each round in condition (a). Thus, only the repeated bilateral interaction condition (b) allowed one to build up a reputation. In both conditions, workers who had decided to accept a wage offer were asked to indicate a work effort level, enabling workers to reciprocate high wage offers with high effort.

The competitive market conditions (c) and (d) differed in the opportunities for reciprocity. While in condition (c) workers could indicate their work effort after accepting a wage offer, in condition (d) the market situation was characterised by complete contracts, meaning that once an offer was accepted, the worker did not have the opportunity to choose an effort level.

Thus, in conditions (a), (b) and (c), giving workers the chance to indicate their effort level after accepting a wage offer implied that reciprocity was possible. Each employer received 120 money units at the beginning of each round and each worker had to bear travel costs of 20 money units. Additional costs for each worker were a function of the amount of work effort. With increasing effort, workers' costs increased, as did their employers' profits. Table 6.5 shows the profit calculations.

The experiment lasted an average of two hours. Since workers' and employers' profits formed the basis for calculating their payment for participation in the experiment, there was great interest in generating a large profit. This was especially true because participants in the experiment could earn up to €10, which was a considerable sum of money compared to the monthly pay of soldiers completing their compulsory military service at that time.

Standard economic theory predicts wages of 20 money units or one unit above as well as the lowest possible effort level in all conditions. However, the results of the study clearly demonstrated that the predicted market-clearing wage of approximately 20 money units did not

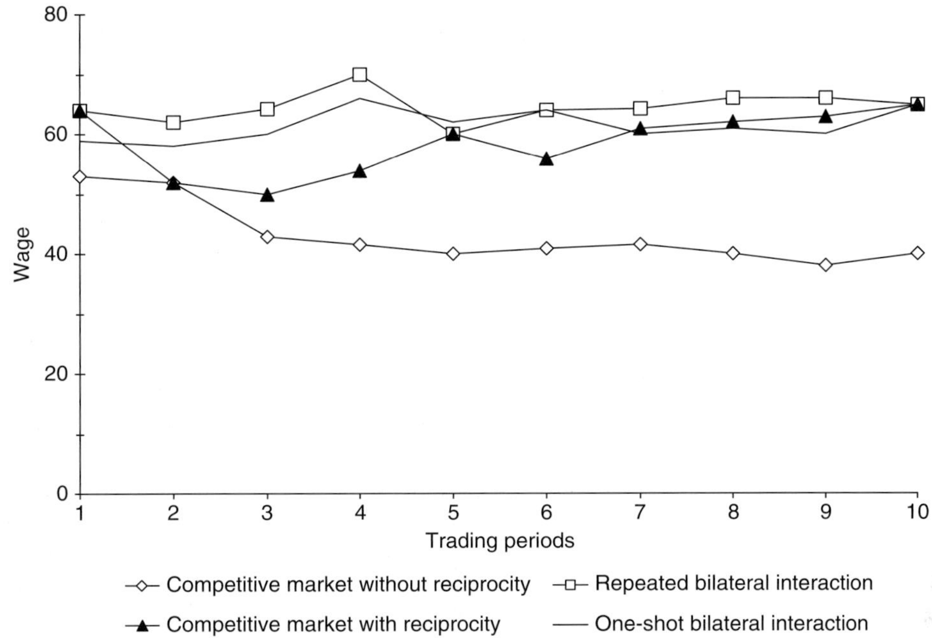

Figure 6.4 Average wages in four interaction conditions over the course of ten trading periods (Kirchler, Fehr & Evans, 1996, p. 326)

arise under any of the four conditions. Employers' wage offers did sink over the course of the ten trading periods in the condition with no opportunity for reciprocity and workers were willing to accept lower wages. However, even in this condition the expected wage of 20 money units was not reached either. Figure 6.4 shows that, except for the pure market condition, wages remained at the same level over all ten periods and thus did not converge towards the theoretically postulated market equilibrium.

The results cited here demonstrate that the equilibrium wage postulated by market theory does not arise in market situations in which workers can react to wage offers. Employers and workers appear to be bound by the norm of reciprocity. Employers offer higher wages and hope for a profitable reaction from workers; workers fulfil these expectations. The correlation between wage level and performance level amounted to an average of $r = 0.54$. In the condition with repeated bilateral interactions and the condition representing a gift exchange market, the average correlations amounted to $r = 0.64$ and 0.61, respectively; in the one-shot bilateral interaction condition, the correlation was $r = 0.25$. High wage offers thus increase the chances of high profits. Many participants did not apply the only justifiably 'rational' strategy of always offering the market-clearing wage. 'The heart appears to have a strategy that reason cannot know', argued Lopes (1994, p. 220), and this strategy appears to be more profitable for all participants than the economically 'rational' one.

In summary, this experiment (Fehr et al., 1998; Kirchler et al. 1996) demonstrates that classical economic assertions about wage developments in competitive markets are not always confirmed empirically. Fairness plays an important role in such situations. Even though some people did exploit their partner's trust and willingness to cooperate in order to maximise their own profits, the fact that norms of reciprocity determine what happens on the market is indisputable.

A wage that is perceived as fair and satisfactory boosts one's willingness to cooperate by exerting more effort. The highest wage offers occurred in the three conditions with incomplete work contracts in which workers had to indicate their work effort individually. Fehr, Goette and Zehnder (2009) argue that in the real world contracts are rarely complete. Tasks are complex and multidimensional, and relevant problems that may arise over the course of time cannot be foreseen at the point in time at which an agreement is signed. According to the authors, 'the employer faces a fundamental problem: If duties and obligations are only vaguely specified, how can the employer motivate the worker to provide more than minimal effort?' (p. 362). The question is why workers should put a great deal of effort into their work if there is no contract to enforce this behaviour. The answer seems to lie in the norm of reciprocity, as shown in the experimental study described earlier. Dohmen, Falk, Huffman and Sunde (2009) asked the same question for real-world labour market behaviour. They measured reciprocal inclinations in a representative survey study with more than 20,000 participants using a six-item questionnaire (e.g., 'If someone does me a favour, I am prepared to return it') and correlated these with work effort, which was operationalised as overtime hours worked. The results show that workers with high reciprocal inclinations are more likely to work overtime, especially if they regard their wages as fair. Furthermore, the authors found evidence that reciprocally inclined people are more satisfied with their lives, interpreting this as a measure of success. In this domain, Dohmen et al. (2009) speak of the *homo reciprocans* as a response to the *homo economicus*.

In a widely acclaimed study, Fehr and Gächter (2002) demonstrated that fairness plays an important role in human interaction. They were able to show that people react angrily to unfair behaviour and are willing to punish unfair people. They even punish free-riders, strike-breakers, etc. when they do not profit from this punishment and even when they incur costs by doing so. Unselfish punishments – Fehr and Gächter (2002) speak of '**altruistic punishment**' – ensure cooperation in a community. In a public goods game, participants punished players who did not behave cooperatively, which fostered a sense of community and thus ultimately led to an increase in total cooperation. A subsequent neuropsychological study on altruistic punishment revealed that the punishment of free-riders causes reward-related neural activities, even if the punishing person suffers a monetary loss (de Quervain et al., 2004).

The **public goods game** is commonly applied in order to study cooperation. In this game, players receive a sum of money at the beginning of the game. They can choose to invest a portion of this or even the total sum in a community fund. The amount invested in the community fund is designated as a public good and is then typically multiplied by the experimenter (e.g., doubled) and distributed equally among all players. The players as a group would earn the largest profit if they all deposited their entire initial sum. However, the dominant strategy in this game is free-riding, in that each player's profit is highest when he deposits zero into the joint fund and thus receives his initial sum plus his portion of the public good. If all players choose the dominant strategy, however, no public good comes into being (Diekmann, 2009).

Fehr and Gächter (2002) conducted a public goods game among 240 university students playing in groups of four, where complete anonymity was established. Players received an initial sum of 20 money units each and could deposit as much as they wanted into a community fund. In the last round, the fund was distributed equally among the players in such a way that each player received 0.4 money units for each money unit that had been paid into the fund. This corresponds to a multiplication of the fund by a factor of 1.6. If each player were to invest all 20 money units in their possession, 80 units would be in the fund and each player would receive $80 * 0.4 = 32$ money units. The group would thus earn the most money if everyone invested their entire initial sum. However, if only one of the four players paid in, that player would receive only $20 * 0.4 = 8$ money units; the others would receive another 8 in addition to their initial sum of $20 = 28$ money units. As

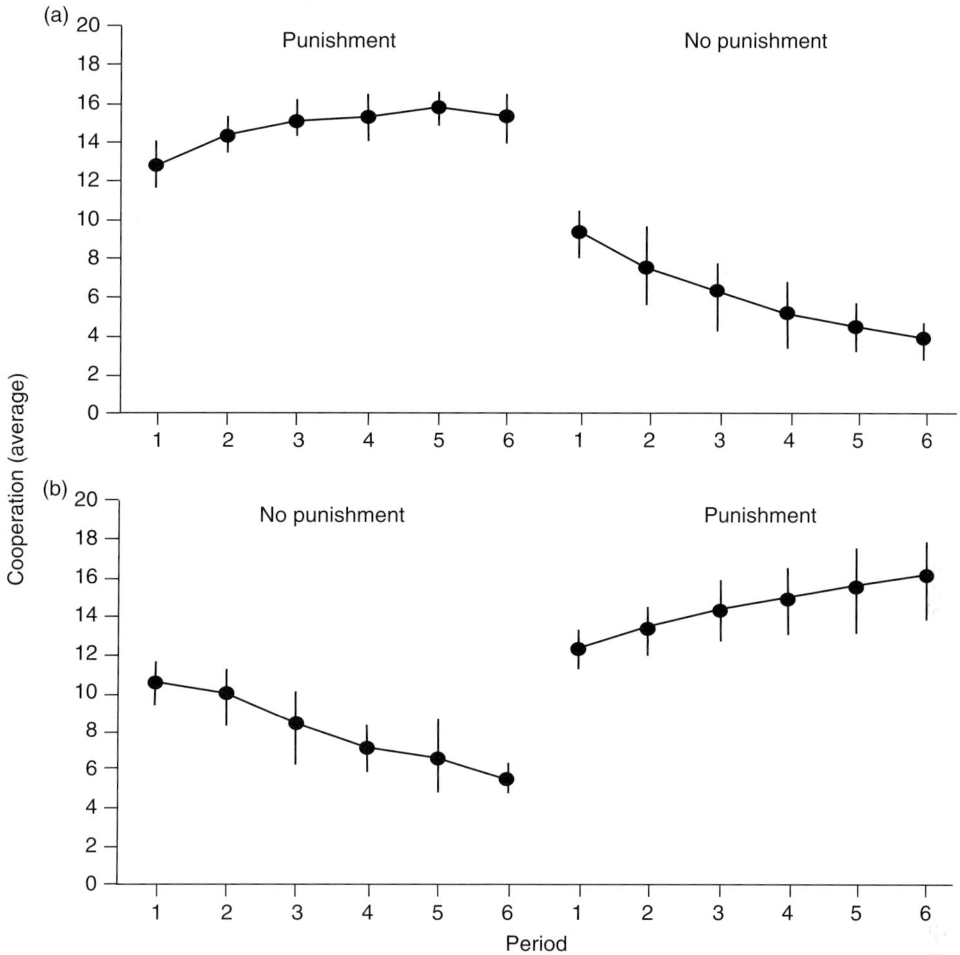

Figure 6.5 Average cooperation in public goods games with (a) punishment opportunity in the first six rounds, but no punishment opportunity in the next six rounds; (b) no punishment opportunity in the first six rounds, but punishment opportunity in the next six rounds (Fehr & Gächter, 2002, p. 138)

described in the tragedy of the commons, community goods are quickly drawn down to nothing if everyone thinks exclusively about their individual utility.

Fehr and Gächter (2002) introduced an intermediate stage to the game in which they announced each player's contributions. After that, the players could take away portions of each other's profits (i.e., punish one another). However, getting worked up about another player's unfair behaviour and punishing him for it cost players a portion of their own profits. If a player wanted to punish a fellow player who behaved unfairly, he could either do it himself at his own expense or allow other players to punish the non-cooperating player. Punishments were costly for both the punished and the punisher and had no financial value to the punisher. Nevertheless, many players punished those who contributed little to the community fund. These 'altruistic punishments' caused cooperation to remain at a high level and re-established it when it was low. Figure 6.5(a) shows cooperation levels in six rounds when 'altruistic punishment' is possible and sinking cooperation in the following six rounds when no punishments are possible. Figure 6.5(b) shows cooperation levels when no punishments are possible in the first rounds, but are allowed in the next six (Fehr & Gächter, 2002).

The significance of 'altruistic punishment' has been demonstrated in various cultures (Fehr & Fischbacher, 2003) and is considered as evolutionarily advantageous behaviour that was necessary for the survival of humanity. Masclet, Noussair and Tucker (2003) investigated the effects of non-monetary punishments. A player could express the degree of his displeasure with another person's behaviour by giving him a certain number of 'disapproval points'. These expressions of displeasure had no effect on the amount of money won. Findings showed that this kind of punishment also had an effect on the willingness to cooperate. However, the effect of non-monetary punishments was smaller compared to monetary punishments.

6.2 Wages

A working relationship is only established between an employer and an employee when both contractual parties expect to benefit from it. A person only commits to render labour services for a certain amount of time when the compensation they receive at least covers the costs of working. When an employment contract is concluded between an employer and an employee, typically a compensation is stipulated. This refers to the payment that the employer owes the employee for performing the work. Compensation, remuneration, salaries and wages are typically understood as monetary sums. Thus, a salary is defined as compensation that remains the same every month, whereas a wage is understood as a payment that is disbursed hourly, daily, weekly or monthly and that can vary from month to month. Compensation is generally paid in the form of money, but 'in-kind' payments such as non-cash benefits can also be offered as remuneration. When employed people compare their compensation with one another, they usually refer to nominal wages. Nominal wages correspond to the sum of money paid as compensation for work, expressed in a certain currency. Real wages, in contrast, refer to the relationship between nominal wages and a current price index.

If workers render their services for a certain wage and seek to maximise their own pay in opposition to their employers' interests, they need to have precise knowledge of their compensation. However, in answering the question of how much they earn, Thierry (1992) finds that most workers will admit after a short period of embarrassment that they do not know the exact amount of their monthly compensation. Nevertheless, wage is an important variable that not only allows covering the costs of working, but also ostensibly determines a person's self-worth and their 'value' in society. In social scientific studies, questions about one's compensation or about one's income are usually considered to be problematic because they require a person to disclose information about a particularly private issue. In a society that elevates 'consumption potency' to a personal characteristic worth striving for, the value of a person in society can indeed be measured by their income and wealth. Alongside other variables, financial opportunities help to determine a person's self-worth.

Why is income so important? Thierry (1992) gives the following reasons for the significance of compensation for workers:

(a) Satisfaction of needs. Wages are particularly important from an instrumental point of view because money provides an opportunity to satisfy an array of needs. The need for security and feelings of personal competence, in particular, but also the need for self-actualisation can be perceived to be satisfied through money. Wages can thus have a motivating effect because they satisfy needs.

(b) Relative status. Wages provide information about the quality and quantity of the performance rendered. Wage earners can compare their performance with those of other people on the basis of their wage and thus define their status in the workplace.

(c) Opportunities for control. Salary negotiations require skills and persuasive abilities. Thus, one's wage level can be seen as an expression of the scope of one's influence or one's control over other people.

(d) Consumption possibilities. The financial resources persons have available determine their spending behaviour. The more opportunities a person has to choose between various products and services, the higher this individual's prosperity.

Compensation is important not only for employees, but for employers as well. The attractiveness of a given workplace is determined by the wages paid. High wages are instrumentally deployed to recruit and retain qualified workers and to encourage high-quality work. Wage supplements can be paid as compensation for stressful and particularly taxing work. Finally, wages are frequently the cause of conflicts in the workplace and at the same time contain the key to solve such conflicts (Thierry, 1992).

6.2.1 Wages and Motivation

Wages are given particular importance as a motivating factor and – with respect to considerations of fairness and justice – also as a determinant of job satisfaction. In this regard, it should be noted that various payment systems have been developed, each of which has advantages and disadvantages as well as different effects on performance motivation (Fischer & Fischer, 2010; Rost & Osterloh, 2008; Rynes, Gerhart & Parks, 2005). The assertions of wage as a motivating factor are based on the assumption that monetary compensation is a highly valued reward among workers. Since people learn early that money can buy things that serve the satisfaction of needs, money represents an important secondary reinforcer from the perspective of the theory of operant conditioning. Just like people, animals can learn that certain neutral objects, like coins, can be deployed as a medium of exchange (Lea, Tarpy & Webley, 1987, p. 319 f).

If money is valuable, it is worthwhile to bear certain costs, such as the effort put into work or the sacrifice of free time, to obtain it. Workers will thus be motivated to perform work in order to receive compensation. From the perspective of **valence-instrumentality-expectancy theory** (V-I-E theory, Vroom, 1964), money can be considered as the final result and performance can be seen as a significant intermediate result that has a high probability of leading to the desired compensation. According to this theory, motivation is based on cognitive processes: people evaluate various goals and attempt to reach the most highly valued goals that also appear to be attainable. The concepts of valence, instrumentality and expectancy form the essence of V-I-E theory:

(a) Valence is the subjective intrinsic value or appeal of a certain action, or of the results of certain actions. For example, the value of the result 'wage' or 'money' could be high or low for a given person. A distinction is made between first-order and second-order valences. A certain result, such as a particular amount of work, might appear valuable because another result, such as a pay raise, praise or a career bump, depends upon it. It is thus necessary to make a distinction between the valence of an action and the valences of the outcomes of further actions that result from carrying out the first action (Nerdinger, 1995).

(b) Instrumentality is the subjective connection between an action and more or less valuable outcomes. For example, a person could assume that qualitatively outstanding performance will definitely lead to a high wage. Certain actions can have unpleasant consequences – for example, qualitatively poor performance can lead to a loss of status. Therefore, the instrumentality of actions ranges from –1 to +1, where –1 means that an action will definitely prevent a person from reaching the goal, while +1 means that an action will definitely lead to the goal.
(c) Expectancy is the subjective belief about the feasibility of an action. People might be of the opinion that a certain action (e.g., performing well at work) will lead to a valuable goal (e.g., a pay rise or promotion). However, they might fear that they will be unable to perform well enough or that current circumstances might prevent them from successfully accomplishing a given task. Expectancy varies from 0 to +1. Unattainable accomplishments are given a rating of 0; the more feasible an accomplishment appears to be, the higher its expectancy value.

If wages are used to motivate better work performance, it must first be ensured that workers place a particularly high value on monetary compensation. According to Vroom (1964), a motivation process would then need to take place, which can be described by the following formulas (from von Rosenstiel, 1992, p. 382):

$$V_j = f\left[\sum\nolimits_{k=1}^{n} (V_k * I_{jk})\right]; (j = 1 \ldots n)$$

The valence of the action outcome V_j (e.g., performance) is a function of the value of the end goals V_k (e.g., pay rise, recognition, a higher position) multiplied by the perceived instrumentality (I_{jk}) of the action outcome V_j for the realisation of the end goals V_k. The more likely performance leads to a pay rise, praise, etc., and the more valuable this higher wage or praise is, the more valuable high performance will appear to be. However, high performance could be difficult to achieve and might depend not only upon effort or motivation, but also upon specific abilities and circumstances. The effort or motivation F_i to achieve high performance increases with the value of the action outcome V_j (e.g., the value of the accomplishment as a means of achieving a higher wage, as was calculated in the previous formula) and the subjective expectancy E_{ij} that one will actually be able to achieve the performance j by means of action i:

$$F_i = f\left[\sum\nolimits_{j=1}^{m} (E_{ij} * V_j)\right]; (i = 1 \ldots m)$$

In terms of limitations, it must be noted that this theory only describes the selection of a goal and the renunciation of alternative goals, not the entire process from the intention to carry out an action to realisation and evaluation. For this reason, Heckhausen (1989) further developed Vroom's (1964) model by taking into account the situation in which a decision is made. In some situations, the outcome can be determined by the situation itself. If this is not the case, it is considered whether the targeted result can be brought about. However, if the outcome is determined by the situation itself, the question arises as to whether the possible consequences of the outcome are important enough to take action. If the consequences are important enough, it must be considered whether an action will lead to the desired series of results – whether it can serve as an instrument for reaching the end goal (see Nerdinger, 1995). Figure 6.6 graphically integrates Vroom's (1964) and Heckhausen's (1989) theories of goal selection.

On the basis of Vroom's (1964) model, Porter and Lawler (1968) developed a differentiated motivation-satisfaction model. They also assume that wages, as an extrinsic remuneration, have an effect on performance effort. Furthermore, wages perceived to be fair should contribute to job

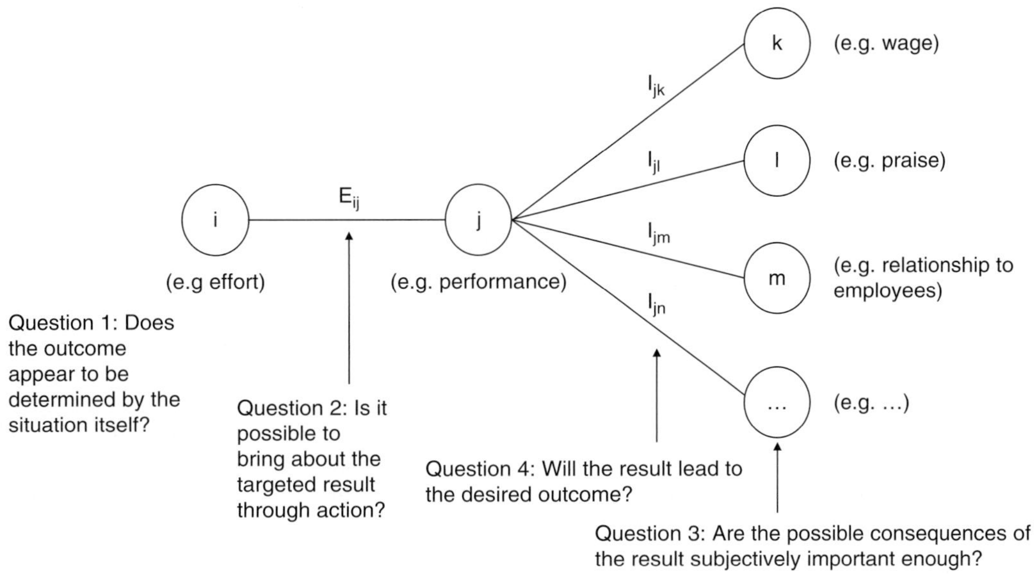

Figure 6.6 Graphical representation of Vroom's (1964) motivation model and questions that a person asks before carrying out a goal-directed action, from Heckhausen's (1989, p. 185) expanded model

satisfaction. The degree of effort put in depends on the subjective value of a given result (e.g., a career advancement, receiving a bonus, praise or recognition), the presumed probability of actually achieving the result, and past experiences showing that a certain intensity of effort leads to the desired result. Effort, abilities and skills as well as supply and demand in the labour market, norms and role constraints determine performance. Performance can either have an intrinsic remunerative value and/or serve to reach extrinsic remuneration (e.g., praise, recognition or a bonus). Employees' level of satisfaction with their performance and ultimately their job satisfaction depend on the size of their compensation and their subjective perceptions of fair compensation.

Wiswede (2007) criticised theories of work motivation for their overly individualistic approach and integrated social norms and peer pressure into Porter and Lawler's (1968) model. Work behaviour depends upon numerous expectations in addition to the valence of a result: internal expectations of efficiency, expectations regarding consequences, perceived norms and role constraints and the tendency to conform to these social expectations. People consider whether they are able to accomplish something (efficiency expectation), how the accomplishment will benefit them (consequence expectation), and what other people in the current situation and position expect (social expectations). Moreover, work behaviour and performance also depend upon individual abilities and on the situation. Wiswede (2007) linked efficiency expectations and consequence expectations multiplicatively. Since norms can compensate for valence, valence and norms are linked by addition. Wiswede's (2007) model is depicted in Figure 6.7.

Wages are understood as an extrinsic form of compensation in both Porter and Lawler's and Wiswede's models. Wages underlie the concept of performance as a goal worth striving for. When a pay rise is possible and appears to be desirable and when high work performance will result in a pay rise, it is expected that people will make an effort to perform well.

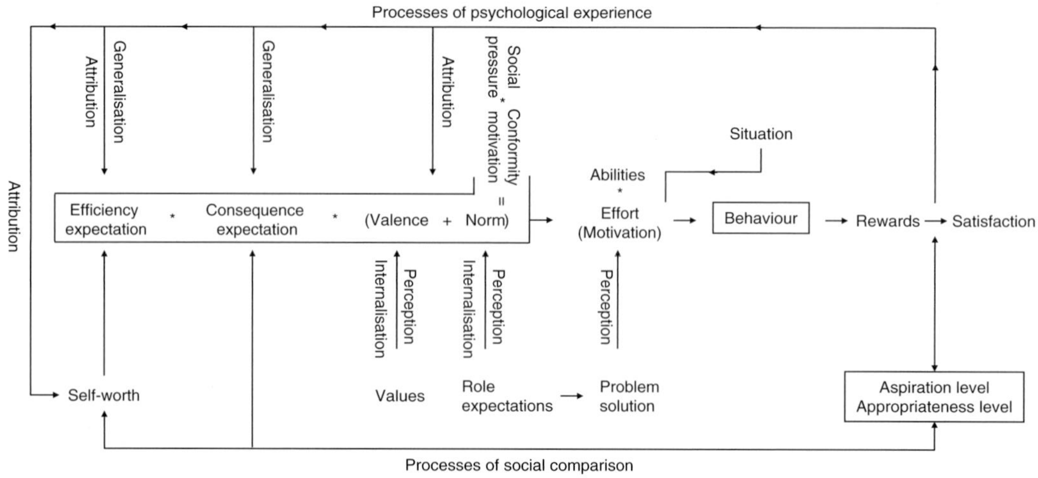

Figure 6.7 Expectancy model of motivation according to Wiswede (2007, p. 210)

Both models also take job satisfaction into consideration. The more closely one's compensation for performance corresponds to individual benchmarks, the more satisfied a person should be with their job. Individual benchmarks determine whether compensation is perceived as fair and thus satisfactory.

6.2.2 Wage Fairness

As a caveat, it should be emphasised that the result of work – that is, the wage – can be perceived as fair, but the process of assessing wage levels is also important (Hegtvedt, 1989). Wage satisfaction depends not only on wage levels and thus on the fairness of the distribution, but also on a variety of other variables (Miceli, 1993). Greenberg (1990), for instance, investigated employee theft as a reaction to underpayment inequity and found significantly higher theft rates for the group of workers whose pay was reduced temporarily by 15%, unless pay cuts were thoroughly and sensitively explained.

People are anxious to evaluate their attitudes, actions and action outcomes. In the absence of objective standards of evaluation, they tend to compare themselves with others in similar situations. Comparative processes can result in either concordance or discordance between one's own qualities and those of others. Discordance can trigger contentment or discontent. In **equity theory**, Adams (1963, 1965) described comparative processes between one's own contributions and results and the contributions of others and their results. With regard to the issue of wage fairness, comparisons are made between one's own performance (Inputs; I_p) and wages (Outcomes; O_p) and others' performance (I_a) and their wages (O_a). The basic message of equity theory is that people perceive things to be fair when the ratio between their own outputs and inputs corresponds to the ratio between the outputs and inputs of other people. Feelings of inequity, discordance or injustice are experienced when the comparison with others reveals disproportionality (Table 6.6).

Table 6.6 Key messages of equity theory (adapted from Adams, 1965, pp. 280–1)

Formula	Equity/ Inequity	Perception	Example
$\frac{O_p}{I_p} = \frac{O_a}{I_a}$	Equity	The relation of one's own outcomes to one's inputs is equal to those of others	Fair payment
$\frac{O_p}{I_p} < \frac{O_a}{I_a}$	Inequity	Compared to others, one's own outcomes are small in relation to one's inputs	Underpayment
$\frac{O_p}{I_p} > \frac{O_a}{I_a}$	Inequity	Compared to others, one's own outcomes are large in relation to one's inputs	Overpayment

Hence, discordance, unfairness and ultimately discontent can even be perceived when a person receives higher wages than other workers do. Although it can be assumed that relative disadvantage leads to more negative feelings than overpayment, in general, various studies seem to indicate that a proportional distribution of profits or payment in accordance with one's own input and the comparative inputs of other people is preferred to all other distributions of results. Overpayment seems to lead to lower satisfaction than fair compensation; underpayment leads without a doubt to feelings of anger and frustration and thus to dissatisfaction (e.g., De Dreu, Lualhati & McCusker, 1994; Mikula, 1991).

In order to determine whether wages are fair, people compare their own wages with the wages of other people and with comparison groups. Without any changes to performance or wage level, workers can become convinced that their wages are fair given the work performed or that they are being over- or underpaid, depending on the person they are comparing themselves with. Robbins (1993) cited four possible points of comparison and argued that people choose different points of comparison depending on their level of education, job tenure and wage level. Persons can compare their input and output (a) with their input and output in another position at the same company or (b) at a different company. However, persons can also compare their input and output (c) with those of a person or group within the company or (d) outside the company. Robbins (1993) reported that employees with high salaries and levels of education have more information about the world of work at their disposal and thus choose standards of comparison outside the organisation in which they work. Employees who have been working at a company for a long time compare their wages with those of their co-workers. Employees who have only been working at a company for a short time seek out points of comparisons from their own work history.

Shore and Tashchian (2006) investigated internal wage comparisons with people from the same organisation and external comparisons with people from other companies. The higher an employee's wages in comparison to other people, the greater was his satisfaction with his wages, the amount of support he feels he receives from the organisation, and his work motivation. Wage fairness is greatest when compensation is equal. However, when people receive lower wages than employees of another organisation do, they argue that overpayment for workers in their own organisation would be fairer than equal pay, as a compensatory measure for their current underpayment. This study also revealed that comparing oneself to a peer group has a greater effect on work attitudes than comparisons with individuals: it bothers a worker more to realise that he is underpaid in comparison to most other people in the company than in comparison to just one other person.

When an imbalance is perceived between performance and wage, a person can raise or lower her input (e.g., her performance) accordingly; she can also try to change her output. In a piece rate system, workers can try to produce a greater number of pieces. A person can also increase or decrease the value of her own performance or the value of other people's performance or earnings. Further, a person can take a point of comparison different from the previous one, such as comparing oneself to former schoolmates or colleagues at another company. Final actions include a 'retreat from the field' by terminating one's employment contract, looking for a new employer or reacting to perceived injustice by means of absenteeism, taking sick leave, etc. (Adams, 1963, 1965).

People's reactions to experiences of unfairness in the workplace have been investigated from many sides. In particular, discordant associations between wages and performance in both time rate and piece rate systems have been analysed experimentally. The assertions of equity theory could often be confirmed. According to equity theory, workers in a piece rate system who feel underpaid and possibly angry strive to increase the number of pieces produced at the expense of quality. Workers who feel overpaid and possibly guilty reduce the quantity in favour of quality. In time rate systems, underpaid people cut down on the quality and/or quantity of their performance; overpaid people will try to justify the wage difference with increased performance (Goodman & Friedman, 1971; Greenberg, 1982).

In the literature on social and organisational psychology, studies have primarily focused on what levels of wages are perceived as fair. Of course, work experiences are not evaluated only on the basis of the performance that must be delivered and the monetary compensation. In addition to wages, factors such as the organisation's image, work climate and relative status characteristics (e.g., a company car, an appropriate office set-up, etc.) should also be taken into account in performance versus compensation comparisons (Greenberg, 1988). These factors influence people's decisions about whether to remain with a company or to terminate an employment contract. The decision to terminate one's contract also depends on the perceived chances of finding another, more satisfactory job in the labour market.

The question of fair compensation has primarily revolved around the appropriate compensation ratio between the lowest and highest wage earners. In many countries, the salaries of top executives were disclosed as part of the implementation of transparency regulations and guidelines for corporate governance. These figures stoked public debates about whether large wage differences within companies are justifiable. In 1970, the ratio between an average executive salary and the average salary for an industrial worker in the USA was 26:1. This ratio had risen to 302:1 by 2003. Income discrepancies in Europe have widened as well, though to a lesser extent (Weibel & Bernard, 2006).

These glaring differences in income can be justified with the argument that they encourage higher performance, thus increasing a company's success. In economics, tournament theory assumes that differences in income motivate better performance and encourage maximal achievement. The focus is on the individual who prevails in the competition with his rivals. Psychology concerns itself not just with the 'victor', but also with the losers of the tournament and surmises that the losers are demotivated by the expanding pay gap and prime salaries of top executives: the differences in salary are perceived as unfair, allegiance to the organisation falls, and trust and the willingness voluntarily to deliver high performance decrease.

The question of fair wages also leads to a consideration of gender differences in income. Despite the political acknowledgment of gender equality and legal frameworks stipulating equal treatment, differences in income between men and women still persist. Women earn less money than men in the same occupations and less frequently climb to high positions, including top management, than men (e.g., Winder, 2009). Jann (2008) conducted a study on acceptance of differences in income in

Switzerland. He constructed eight vignettes describing either a woman or a man who either is or is not in great financial need, delivers either high or low performance at work and earns 4,000 CHF per month. More than 1,600 people were asked whether this income was too low, too high or an appropriate amount. The majority of respondents found this income too low; 27% considered it to be just right and 17% as too high. Independently of age, family status, occupation and their own income situation, respondents particularly judged the income as too low in cases when a man was described, when financial need was high and when performance was high. Even women discriminated against the women described in the vignettes and saw their salary levels as more appropriate than when a man earned the same salary. Gender discrimination decreased as participants' level of education increased.

Finally, social scientific studies have determined that differences in income do not just differ by gender, but also depend upon workers' physical attractiveness. In an economic study, Hamermesh and Biddle (1994) demonstrated that people perceived as particularly attractive earned 10% more than people of average beauty did. Aside from an attractiveness bonus, an ugliness malus of between 5 and 10% was also detected (see also Hamermesh, 2011). Andreoni and Petrie (2008) invited people to play a public goods game and had participants interact with various fellow players over the course of forty rounds. In one experimental condition, participants were shown photos of their fellow players; in another, both photos and the players' contributions to the public good were revealed. Indeed, it turned out that participants were more cooperative with fellow players judged as attractive. Berggren, Jordahl and Poutvaara (2010) found a relationship of beauty with electoral success. Sierminska (2015) reported that physically attractive people earn more and get higher rewards than less attractive people do, and that this is particularly the case for men. Mobius and Rosenblat (2006) further investigated this beauty premium and found that physically attractive people are on average more confident and have better communication and social skills, both of which increase wages. This can be regarded as a halo effect of physical attractiveness on employers' evaluations of workers' abilities and skills.

6.3 Entrepreneurship

In public opinion, the prevailing view is that entrepreneurship is essential to economic growth and social prosperity. In line with the perception that start-ups and self-employment are the driving force of innovation, jobs and economic growth, measures are frequently taken to support entrepreneurs in starting companies (e.g., De, 2005). In the USA, more than a million people are employed by companies founded by former students of MIT in Boston alone. Their turnover amounts to hundreds of billions of dollars, and if these companies formed their own country it would be the twenty-fourth largest economy in the world (Franke & Lüthje, 2002). Similar success stories are reported for Stanford University and the Silicon Valley. In Germany, self-employed people with university degrees on average employ more workers than self-employed people with a lower level of education (Franke & Lüthje, 2002). Particularly university graduates appear to have good chances of successfully starting companies. Accordingly, university students' entrepreneurial spirit has been frequently investigated (Frank, Korunka & Lueger, 2002; Franke & Lüthje, 2002). In a lecture at an economic psychology conference in 1988, Brandstätter (1988a) accused both psychologists and economists of neglecting one of the most dazzling figures in economic life, the entrepreneur. The economist Joseph A. Schumpeter (1883–1950) is reported to have noted even decades ago that 'the theorists have just about managed to overlook this, the most richly coloured figure of contemporary economic life' (see also Schmölders, 1978, p. 43).

Commonly characterised as far-sighted, sensitive to economic and social phenomena and willing to take risks, entrepreneurs and their activities play an important role in introducing innovations and shaping the economy. What are companies or enterprises and how can the people who found and lead companies be defined? The challenge of coming up with a definition stems from the relevance of two distinct factors: the business opportunity as a necessary condition, and the presence of a person who can successfully execute essential entrepreneurial actions (Shane & Venkataraman, 2000; Venkataraman, 1997). Martinelli (2001) used the metaphor of a seed (a person) finding the right ground (market conditions) for the emergence of an entrepreneur. Staying with this metaphor, economic psychology tends to focus more on the seed than on the ground. Cuervo, Ribeiro and Roig (2007, p. 1) defined the individual **entrepreneur** as a person who 'detects or creates business opportunities that he or she then exploits through small and medium-sized firms, normally participating in funding the capital for that firm, carries out the role of arbitrator, or simply "sells the idea" of the business project'. Martinelli (2001) provided the following definition:

> The entrepreneur is the head of the firm and coordinates the factors of production; introduces new methods, processes, and products and creates opportunities for economic growth; bears the risks connected with his or her activities; and enjoys power and high status in capitalist market societies. (Martinelli, 2001, p. 4545)

The common usage of the term entrepreneur includes executives, company or department leaders, company founders without managerial responsibilities, pure investors, and so on. It is difficult to make strict distinctions among these terms (Steyrer, 1995). Cuervo et al. (2007) differentiated between (a) entrepreneurs, who discover and exploit opportunities, (b) capitalists, who are the capital owners and thus shareholders, and (c) managers, who take on administrative functions and manage resources. One major difference lies in risk aversion: while entrepreneurs accept risks and introduce new modes of action, capitalists and managers are described as risk averse. On the basis of an analysis of various definition attempts and the results of surveys conducted among workers and industrialists, Brandstätter (1988a) defined self-employed entrepreneurs as people who run a business, retain the profits generated and bear the capital risks.

From an economic perspective, the role of entrepreneurs emerges inevitably from market transactions. Since behaviour in markets is determined by market happenings, entrepreneurs have little latitude to develop their individual idiosyncrasies. From a psychological perspective, entrepreneurs' unique tasks and activities suggest that certain characteristics ought to be relevant in taking initiative and performing executive functions in a company. Consequently, it must be possible to differentiate between entrepreneurs and other market participants. In particular, personality and motivational structures of entrepreneurs are investigated.

6.3.1 Characteristics of Entrepreneurs

What conditions does an entrepreneur face when taking action? One aspect is independence from other people. An entrepreneur acts autonomously, makes decisions and tries to turn (innovative) ideas into reality. Brandstätter (1988a, 1997) argues that people who are more independent of others are more likely to possess the disposition for entrepreneurial behaviour than people who are more dependent on their social surroundings. Entrepreneurs try to turn innovative ideas, the success of which is not always certain, into reality. Therefore, they must be willing to take risks but not be blind to them. Emotional stability should also be a significant factor, since entrepreneurs need to make social contacts, conduct business and demonstrate leadership skills. Socially extraverted people tend to show more talent for this than introverts.

In a meta-analysis, Stewart and Roth (2001) determined that entrepreneurs exhibit a higher tendency to take risks than managers do. Moreover, entrepreneurs whose main goal is to increase profits and grow their business appear to be willing to take more risks than entrepreneurs who are more focused on income. Zhao and Seibert (2006) conducted a meta-analysis of twenty-three studies investigating the relationship between personality characteristics and entrepreneurial status as well as the differences between entrepreneurs and managers. Zhao and Seibert (2006) defined entrepreneurs as company founders or owners whose goal is business growth. Managers, on the other hand, work at various levels in a company and hold manifold executive positions. In line with the five-factor model, personality was described by the dimensions neuroticism, extraversion, openness to experience, agreeableness and conscientiousness. Results showed significant differences between entrepreneurs and managers on four personality dimensions, although effect sizes were low. Compared to managers, entrepreneurs displayed higher values in conscientiousness and openness to experience, as well as lower values in neuroticism and agreeableness. No differences were found in extraversion. Ciavarella, Buchholtz, Riordan, Gatewood and Stokes (2004) also investigated emotional stability, extraversion, openness to experience, agreeableness and conscientiousness in connection with business success. Business success was defined as the length of time a business had been in existence. They found that conscientiousness alone correlated positively with a business' time of existence. Notably, in the long run, openness to experience appeared to have a negative influence on success. In the early phases of starting a company, openness, innovation and creativity might well be important. However, after the company has been launched and is beginning to become established, these traits steadily lose importance or even have a negative effect on business success.

Langan-Fox and Roth (1995) investigated female entrepreneurs' personality characteristics and found several different factor profiles. Female entrepreneurs could be categorised into three groups according to their personality traits. The group of 'leaders' was primarily distinguished by their efforts to exert power and influence, their resistance to domination attempts by others, an internal locus of control, deliberate career planning and low social trust. 'Performance-oriented entrepreneurs' could be described based on their high performance motivation and trust, as well as by their smaller efforts to gain influence and power. 'Pragmatic entrepreneurs' were characterised by average values on nearly all of the personality traits investigated.

Independence and stability seem to be crucial personality characteristics in the population of entrepreneurs. In order to carry out innovation and at the same time achieve monetary success, entrepreneurs not only need to be independent and emotionally stable, but also need to possess a high achievement motivation. It is crucial that they do not shy away from contact with other people; however, they also need to preserve their independence. Consequently, they should display a low need for affiliation, but at the same time want to take the lead in group interactions, thus having power motivation. Achievement motivation has been frequently studied as a source of entrepreneurial talent. Although the association between achievement motivation and business success is consistently positive, the correlation is typically low (Davidsson, 1987; Wärneryd, 1988b). Several studies suggest that a specific combination of motivations might be relevant for success: high power motivation and high achievement motivation, combined with a low need for affiliation, should lead to higher success (Heckhausen, 1989; McClelland, 1975; McClelland & Boyatzis, 1982). For example, Wainer and Rubin (1969) collected data from fifty-one entrepreneurs of small and recently founded companies in the technology sector regarding their need for power, achievement and affiliation. The companies' economic success was measured by the growth rate in

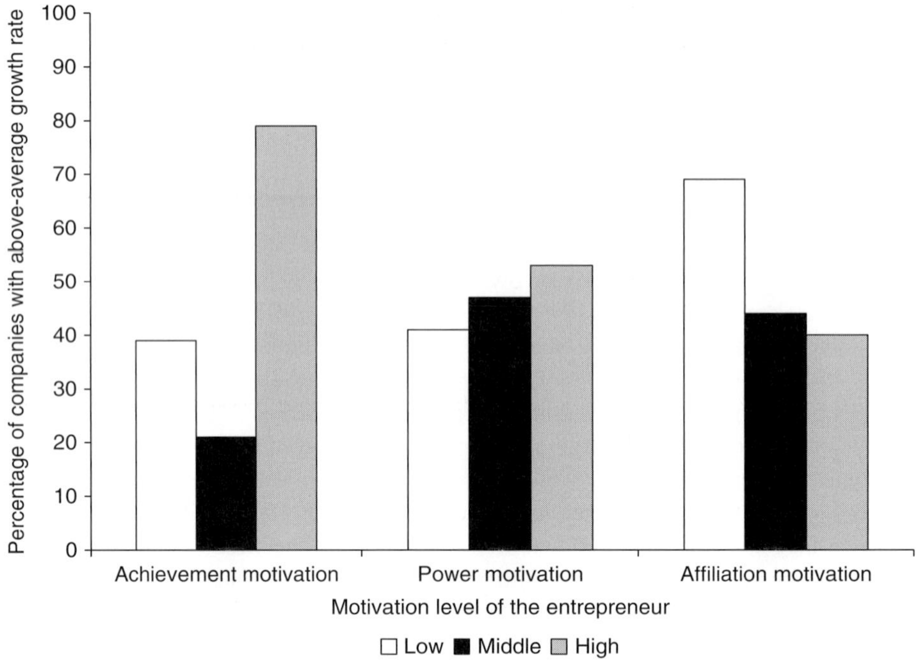

Figure 6.8 Percentage of companies with an above-average growth rate by entrepreneur's level of achievement, power or affiliation motivation (Wainer & Rubin, 1969, p.182)

the last year. As shown in Figure 6.8, the entrepreneurs who displayed higher values in achievement motivation were more often found to be leaders of companies with above-average growth rates, compared to their counterparts who were low in achievement motivation. The results with respect to the need for affiliation showed the exact opposite: the higher the motivation to connect with people, the more likely a person was to lead a company where growth rates were not above average. In terms of power motivation, a positive correlation with company growth rates tended to occur.

Entrepreneurial personalities are also described as self-confident and unafraid of risks. Aside from achievement motivation, locus of control and risk behaviour have been investigated most frequently (e.g., Brockhaus, 1982). When put together, the data from various studies support the conclusion that successful entrepreneurs have a stronger internal locus of control than those who are only moderately successful. Not only do they score higher on achievement motivation, entrepreneurs are also more likely to be convinced that they themselves are in control of their performance outcomes. Rauch and Frese (2007) confirm high correlations between self-efficacy and business creation and performance. However, results in terms of risk appetite are ambiguous (Wärneryd, 1988b). The fact that entrepreneurs have been described as achievement-oriented people with both a great thirst for power and a low need for affiliation whose goal is material profit makes it clear that a high appetite for risk might push entrepreneurs to put their ideas into action too hastily. The entrepreneur's role as initiator and the striving to reach economic goals force them to gather information about possible business activities and their chances of success as well as to consider various options carefully. However, business decisions are frequently complex. In particular, addressing the question of whether to start a company or to postpone is difficult. In addition to that, risks are often unknown. The more complex the situation, the more difficult it is to estimate the risk of success or failure, and it is thus hardly surprising when mistakes are made. For this reason, entrepreneurs who found a company or apply new strategies often fail. As 'pre-testers', they open themselves up to unknown risks and are subject to failure, while those who learn from the mistakes of these pre-testers are often the ones who prevail (Fenzl & Brudermann, 2008). It only pays off to take a certain risk when a given action's chances of success are satisfactorily high. Accordingly, Wärneryd (1988b) suggested a three-dimensional factor system spanning the dimensions of pursuit of innovation, a level-headed firmness of purpose and risk appetite. In this system, entrepreneurs are located at the point where the tendency to break the mould and the desire for success are particularly high and where an above-average willingness exists to take on a certain amount of risk in carrying out an action with promising chances of success. Actions with little chance of success are avoided. Moreover, the decision to take on risks is considered particularly carefully.

People differ with regard to their regulatory focus (Higgins, 1997, 1998) and can find themselves in a motivational state of prevention focus or promotion focus. A **prevention focus** concentrates on protection, security and safety. It causes individuals to avoid losses and setbacks, and increases sensitivity to negative outcomes. In contrast, a **promotion focus** concentrates on growth and accomplishment. It causes individuals to be motivated by the prospect of gains and achievements, and increases sensitivity to positive outcomes. In the field of entrepreneurship, Hmieleski and Baron (2008) investigated the fit between entrepreneurs' regulatory focus (promotion versus prevention focus) and their decision context (stable versus dynamic industry environment). Stable industry environments are characterised by risk. Entrepreneurs can gather information relevant for decisions regarding potential opportunities and the probabilities of various outcomes associated with them. In contrast, dynamic environments are characterised by uncertainty. In this case, entrepreneurs are unable to gather relevant information because such information on probabilities of events or outcomes does not exist. This situation requires a tolerance of ambiguity and an understanding that business concepts will probably need to be adjusted in order to respond to unpredictable changes in the market. The authors argue that stable industry environments are well suited for entrepreneurs with a prevention focus, since they tend to self-regulate their behaviour towards making the right decisions by avoiding wrong ones. Additionally, they should have high risk reducing tendencies, leading them to conduct sophisticated planning before making decisions. This is likely to be helpful in a stable environment where predictions are possible. Promotion focus is characterised by opportunity-seeking, which can lead to deviations from an initial business plan and is thus expected to be less effective in stable environments. Conversely, in dynamic industry environments characterised by uncertainty, entrepreneurs with a promotion focus should be most successful. Their focus on emerging opportunities allows them to adapt quickly to the changes that are taking place. A prevention focus is expected to lead to more rigid behaviour in conditions of uncertainty. These assumptions were tested among a random sample of 201 US entrepreneurs using a questionnaire. In stable industry environments, the assumptions could not be confirmed. There was no relationship between entrepreneurs' regulatory focus and business performance. Hmieleski and Baron (2008) argued that this might be the case because in stable environments successful strategies and actions are equally apparent to both regulatory focus groups. However, in dynamic environments the results showed that regulatory focus does correlate with business performance. Promotion focus was positively related to business performance, while prevention focus correlated negatively with business performance under conditions of uncertainty. These findings indicate that, in unpredictable environments, a focus on achieving gains and maintaining flexibility (promotion focus) is most effective. Similarly, in a theoretical paper, Trevelyan (2011) argued that a promotion orientation should lead to high work effort in explorative tasks (i.e., tasks characterised by information search, risk taking and thus the search for new possibilities), while a prevention focus should increase the effort in exploitative tasks (i.e., tasks relating to the improvement of existing components of the business). However, these assumptions have not yet been tested empirically.

More generally, Brandstätter (2011) concluded on the basis of five meta-analyses that personality traits play at least a moderate role in business success. However, several caveats apply: in most cases, respondents' own descriptions of their personalities were collected. These reports might be both cause and effect of the entrepreneurs' previous experiences. It also needs to be considered that the entrepreneurial activities under investigation, such as the intention to start a company, actually founding the company and subsequently managing it, differ from study to study. Notably, the significance of personality probably differs over the course of this process. Frese and Gielnik (2014) emphasise that correlations between personality constructs and business performance are nearly always heterogeneous and call upon further research to investigate moderators of these relationships.

6.3.2 Founding a Company

Whereas most of the studies discussed above examined people who were already established as entrepreneurs, other studies have focused on the process of successfully founding a company. Many of these studies have pointed out that the combination of person and situation is crucial for success. Since it is the prevailing opinion that entrepreneurs are particularly important in creating a prosperous economy, it is not surprising that the personal and situational conditions relevant to founding a company have been a frequent subject of investigation. Korunka, Frank and Becker (1993) particularly emphasised the striving for autonomy as a relevant personality dimension. Similarly, Frese (1998) characterised successful company founders by their high values in independence. In a meta-analysis of 104 studies on the relationship between entrepreneurs' personality traits and the actual founding of companies as well as their success, Rauch and Frese (2007) concluded that striving for achievement, the pursuit of innovation, stress tolerance, the need for autonomy and proactive behaviour are important. Consequently, people with these characteristics are more likely to have the intention of starting a company and actually to do so.

A study by Frank and Korunka (1996) provides relevant findings on entrepreneurs' risk appetite, decisiveness and proactiveness. The authors investigated 106 company founders and assessed the success of their companies some time after they had been founded. Success was measured by turnover as well as by growth in the number of employees. Afterwards, they connected these success criteria to action control as a significant characteristic of company founders' individual information processing and decision behaviour. Action control is frequently assessed by means of a person's action and state orientation (Kuhl & Goschke, 1994). While **action orientation** refers to a person's tendency to convert their intentions into actions, **state orientation** refers to a person's tendency to be bound up in thoughts that relate to current, past or future states and that impede the systematic implementation of an action. Both personal dispositions and situational stimuli can influence action and state orientation and can lead to thoughts and emotions that either are conducive to action or keep one stuck in one's current position. Frank and Korunka (1996, p. 950) write:

> Action control is determined not just by personal factors, but rather – in the sense of an interactional conceptualisation – by a differentiated interplay between situational and dispositional factors. In situations in which failure is feared ('failure situations'), state-oriented people stand out for their excessive absorption with the problem ('preoccupation'), while action-oriented people are able to quickly detach themselves from it ('disengagement'). In situations characterised by the need to make decisions quickly ('decision situations'), state-oriented people draw out the decision-making process

('hesitation'), while action-oriented people quickly and actively proceed through the decision-making process. These people proceed from the maxim that 'quick decisions are good decisions,' which means that they ultimately attribute a higher net utility to quick decisions compared to more drawn-out ones. In 'success situations,' action-oriented people stand out for their stubbornness in maintaining the status quo, while state-oriented people are characterised here by their independence.

Frank and Korunka (1996) were able to show that successful entrepreneurs exhibited a greater degree of action orientation than less successful entrepreneurs in those situations that involve a great risk of failure or heightened decision-making pressure. In success situations, however, successful entrepreneurs were more state-oriented than less successful entrepreneurs. These findings suggest that, instead of a general risk appetite, a situationally specific willingness to take risks matters for success.

In their study investigating the foundation of companies, Tang, Tang and Lohrke (2008) differentiated between higher or lower entrepreneurial alertness as well as between internal and external attributional styles. The authors build on Kirzner (1979) and refer to **entrepreneurial alertness** as the ability to discern entrepreneurial and business opportunities precisely and quickly and to have a 'feel' for them. People with high entrepreneurial alertness can thus quickly recognise opportunities for action in the economy, before these opportunities are discovered by others. However, Tang et al. (2008) argued that entrepreneurial alertness alone is insufficient to explain why some entrepreneurs found companies or recognise opportunities for economic advancement. For this reason, they introduced entrepreneurs' attributional style as an additional factor, and argued that individuals with high entrepreneurial alertness found companies when they also exhibit an internal attributional style. This attributional style is characterised by the individuals' belief that skills and effort are the key resources for business success and that they themselves possess these attributes. On the basis of the two dimensions of entrepreneurial alertness and attributional style, four types of entrepreneurs can be identified as 'true believers', 'clueless entrepreneurs', 'practical entrepreneurs' and 'reluctant entrepreneurs':

(a) True believers are characterised by high entrepreneurial alertness and an internal attributional style, and represent the typical entrepreneur in traditional studies. They would like to bring about change and believe they have the ability to redeploy available resources in order to meet situational requirements. They have a great deal of potential and are highly dedicated to founding companies and leading them to success.
(b) Clueless entrepreneurs exhibit low entrepreneurial alertness paired with an internal attributional style. They feel spurred to found companies less frequently than others and have little knowledge of the market. When they go into business, it is because they are convinced that success is possible with hard work and the capability to deliver high performance, never mind the obstacles.
(c) Practical entrepreneurs are characterised by high entrepreneurial alertness and an external attributional style. They are quick to notice new opportunities in the market; however, they tend to overlook these potential opportunities because their attributional style makes them sceptical. They take action when they are expressly encouraged to do so and often do not have enough confidence to be successful.
(d) Reluctant entrepreneurs are characterised by low entrepreneurial alertness and an external attributional style. In most cases, they go into business for specific reasons. For example, losing a job could lead them to become self-employed. They are not very motivated to gather new market information because their attributional style is not conducive to seek out changes actively.

The authors investigated these four types of entrepreneurs with regard to the characteristics of risk appetite, achievement striving and attachment to the company, which had been identified as important for entrepreneurship in previous studies. True believers exhibited the highest values in all three dimensions, followed by the clueless, the practical and the reluctant.

In their configurational approach, Korunka, Frank, Lueger and Mugler (2003) considered contextual factors in addition to personality traits. They addressed the influence of personality characteristics, resources, environmental conditions and organising activities during the process of founding a company. Young entrepreneurs were surveyed on these dimensions and divided into the following three types on the basis of their answers using a cluster analysis as 'entrepreneurs against their will', '"would-be" entrepreneurs' and 'networking entrepreneurs with risk avoidance patterns':

(a) Entrepreneurs against their will are primarily characterised by low values in achievement motivation, an internal locus of control and low initiative. They have poor social support, a small social network and insufficient resources. So-called 'push factors' (i.e., external circumstances such as unemployment that push them into self-employment) are high. When entrepreneurs conform to this pattern, founding a company is often problematic.
(b) 'Would-be' entrepreneurs commonly feel a great drive for self-actualisation. They are additionally characterised by a high internal locus of control and have positive role models. Their financial starting position is often problematic.
(c) Networking entrepreneurs with risk avoidance patterns possess good prerequisites for founding a successful company, including security, a large number of relevant resources and little external pressure. Risk appetite is low, social support is high and the social networks at their disposal are dense. People in this group possess information relevant to starting a company and have a detailed understanding of the obstacles they face and of the potential for failure.

The personal characteristics and situational circumstances of these three classes of company founders were compared with the average characteristics and situational conditions of a sample of successful entrepreneurs. As seen in Figure 6.9, there are significant differences between the profiles of the three classes of founders as well as when comparing them to successful entrepreneurs. The greatest differences appear between successful entrepreneurs and founders who start companies against their will.

In their work, Korunka, Frank and Lueger (2004) and Frank, Lueger and Korunka (2007) stress the fact that the significance of personality characteristics and situational conditions might differ according to phase. They studied need for achievement, locus of control and risk appetite at different points in the process of starting a company. Their results suggest that personality only plays a role in the intention to found a company, explaining 20% of the variance in intention. In the realisation and success phases, personality plays only a minor role. Figure 6.10 depicts the proportion of variance explained by personality and environment in different phases of the entrepreneurial process. On the basis of their findings, the authors suggest that measures promoting the development of personality characteristics relevant for founding intentions should be included in school and university curricula (see also Korunka & Frank, 2005).

The interest in entrepreneurially oriented employees, so-called '**intrapreneurs**', is growing among both researchers and practitioners. Ebner, Korunka, Frank and Lueger (2008) developed and tested a model for intrapreneurship using a survey design. Their results support the assumption that the dimensions proactive behaviour, innovation orientation, need for achievement, social competency, field-specific professional skills and field-specific self-reliance are important to an entrepreneurial orientation. By re-analysing an American study spanning sixty years, Schmitt-Rodermund (2005) was able to show that personality (achievement motivation, extraversion,

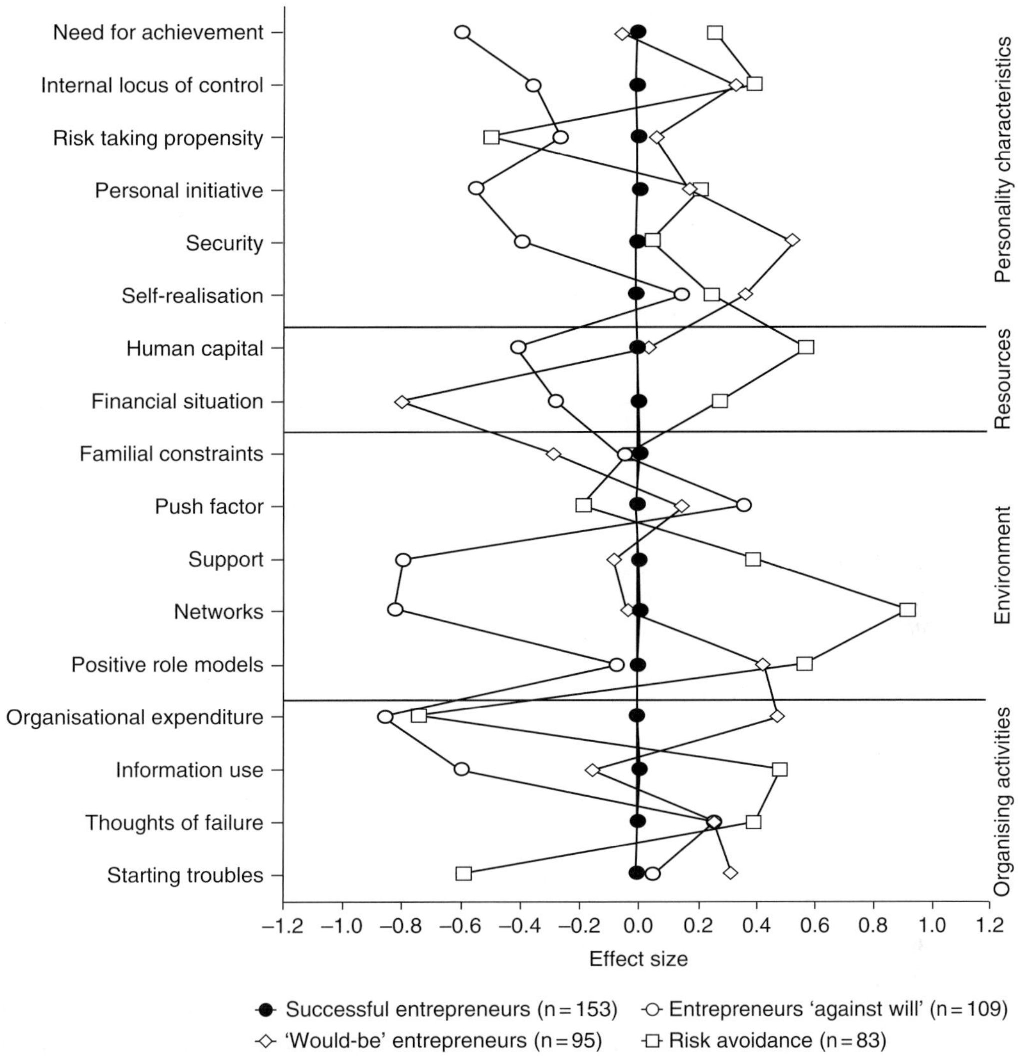

Figure 6.9 Configuration of personality characteristics, resources, environmental conditions and organising activities in the three classes of company founders compared to successful entrepreneurs (Korunka et al., 2003, p. 33)

stability, etc.) and a supportive parenting style, as well as early interest and abilities, were predictors of entrepreneurial activities in adulthood. Jacob and Richter (2005) developed and tested an instrument to measure students' motivation to found businesses (IMMES) based on an extension of the theory of planned behaviour (Ajzen, 1985, 1987). The authors described four principal factors that predicted the intention to found a company with high accuracy: attitude towards entrepreneurial behaviour, subjective norms, perceived behavioural control and entrepreneurial identity.

Athayde (2009) also constructed a survey to measure young people's entrepreneurial potential as well as the effectiveness of the Young Enterprise Company Programme, which was implemented in six London middle schools as an initiative to promote entrepreneurial skills. Entrepreneurial skills are assumed to build on the dimensions achievement, control, creativity, leadership ability and

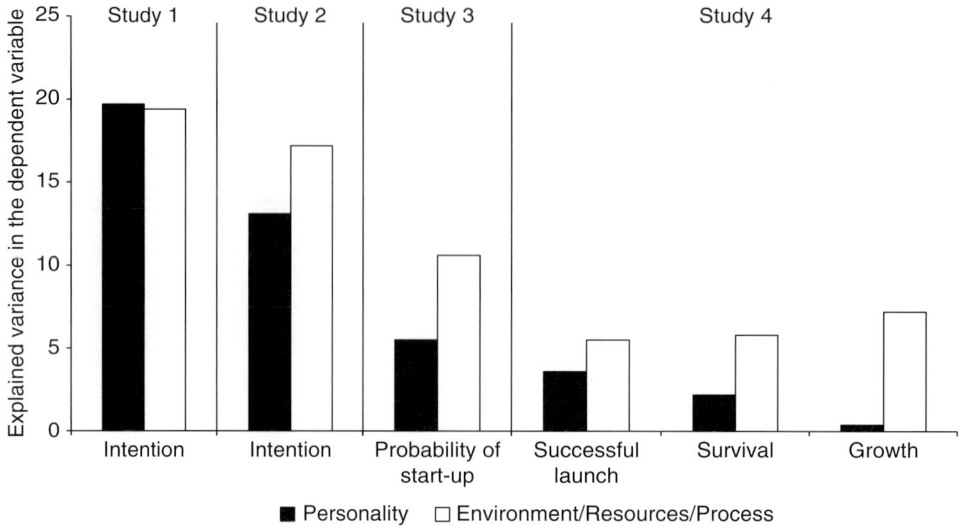

Figure 6.10 Proportion of variance explained by personality and environment from the intention to found a company to business growth (Frank et al., 2007, p. 245)

intuition. The study of the effectiveness of the training programme showed that participation led to a positive attitude towards self-employment as well as enhancing students' entrepreneurial potential. It also became clear that self-employment in the family has a positive influence on encouraging students to run their own businesses. This has been additionally shown by Schmitt-Rodermund (2005). Soutaris, Zerbinati and Al-Laham (2007) conducted a further investigation of the effectiveness of training programmes. Similarly, this study supported the notion that the intention to become self-employed can be developed through training.

6.3.3 Gender Differences in Entrepreneurship

The search for typical personality characteristics leading to entrepreneurial success went on for a long time. However, the rigid stance that there is one most successful personality profile is increasingly being abandoned in favour of diversity and a recognition of its advantages for organisations (e.g., Cheung & Halpern, 2010; Chin, 2010; Eagly & Chin, 2010; Fassinger, Shullman & Stevenson, 2010). Regarding diversity, the question arises of the extent to which female and male entrepreneurs exhibit similarities in characteristics. It is additionally interesting to investigate why men more frequently run companies than women, as well as why in general they can be found more frequently in positions of leadership.

One approach examines the preconditions of becoming an entrepreneur. Niederle and Vesterlund (2007) speculated that women and men react differently to competitive situations. They investigated gender-related preferences for competitive situations in an experimental setting. Although men's and women's performance on the task did not differ, men showed higher preferences for competitive situations compared to women: in the study, 73% of men but only 35% of women preferred to compete with others. This gender difference was explained by men's high self-confidence, while women seemed to be more self-critical and tended to shy away from competition. Runyan, Huddleston and Swinney (2006) investigated gender-specific differences in personality traits as well as with regard to male and female entrepreneurs' social capital. Bourdieu (1983) described social capital as current and potential resources that can be linked to participation in a network of social relationships of mutual acquaintance. The network gives access to the resources of social life, such as support and assistance, recognition, knowledge and mutual promotion. Social capital arises from social network members' willingness to cooperate with one another. Thus, social trust, which allows for the development of cooperation and mutual support, is necessary. Social capital refers to interpersonal relationships and is thus more broadly conceived than human capital, which relates to the natural person (Coleman, 1988). Runyan et al. (2006) investigated 209 female and 242 male small business owners. They found that women had lower values than men with regard to innovation, taking initiative and risk appetite. Both men and women possessed social capital (helpful relationships, opportunities for reciprocity and joint visions) that is important for a company to survive and thrive, although women had significantly higher values in the dimensions of reciprocity and joint visions. The authors concluded that women are often disadvantaged when it comes to financial issues. However, the personal resources necessary to run a company successfully are present at least to an equal extent in women as in men.

Another approach examines gender stereotypes and stereotypes about entrepreneurs. Entrepreneurs are commonly described as self-reliant, emotionally stable, independent, power-conscious and willing to take risks. These characteristics are frequently labelled as typically masculine traits. In an investigation of stereotypes, Passauer (1992) surveyed thirty female entrepreneurs, thirty male entrepreneurs, thirty female employees, thirty male employees and thirty executives on the typical characteristics of male and female entrepreneurs using the 16 PA-Test (Brandstätter, 1988b). Results showed that, independent of entrepreneur's gender, all groups described the entrepreneurial personality as high in emotional resilience and independence, and as average in openness, resolve and deference to norms. Participants were also asked to describe successful female and male entrepreneurs in their own words (Passauer, 1992). They had to imagine a successful female entrepreneur and a successful male entrepreneur and make free associations with respect to their characteristics. In order to prevent serial effects, one half of the sample first had to think about a male entrepreneur and then about a female entrepreneur; the other half first thought about a female entrepreneur and then about a male entrepreneur. After completing the first association task (description of either a male or a female), some of the participants remarked that the characteristics from the first task similarly apply to the second person. Notably, an interesting asymmetry arose in terms of these responses. When respondents noted the characteristics of a male entrepreneur first, 30.6% of participants claimed that the female entrepreneur had the same traits as the male. However, when the characteristics of a female entrepreneur were reported first, only 12% were still of the opinion that the man was the same as the woman. An even more distinct asymmetry was apparent in the group of male respondents: 73.3% of men said that the female entrepreneur was the same as the male, but only 15.5% claimed that the male was the same as the female. In contrast, asymmetry was low in the group of female respondents (43.3% versus 36.7%).

This asymmetry corresponds to Tversky's (1977) treatise on the asymmetry of similarity (see also Codol, 1986; Hurtig & Pichevin, 1990; Pichevin, Hurtig & Piolat, 1993): the similarity of A to B is not necessarily equal to the similarity of B to A. Prototypes are significantly less similar to their derivatives than derivatives are similar to their prototypes. For example, a picture is more similar to the person depicted than the person is to the picture, a son is more similar to his father than the father to the son, and an ellipse is more similar to a circle than a circle is to an ellipse. Returning to gender stereotypes, Passauer's (1992) findings indicate that men represent the prototypical entrepreneurs. Women can also have a knack for entrepreneurship; however, according to the prevailing societal understanding, this is not as obligatory among them as it is for men. Further studies showed that, in

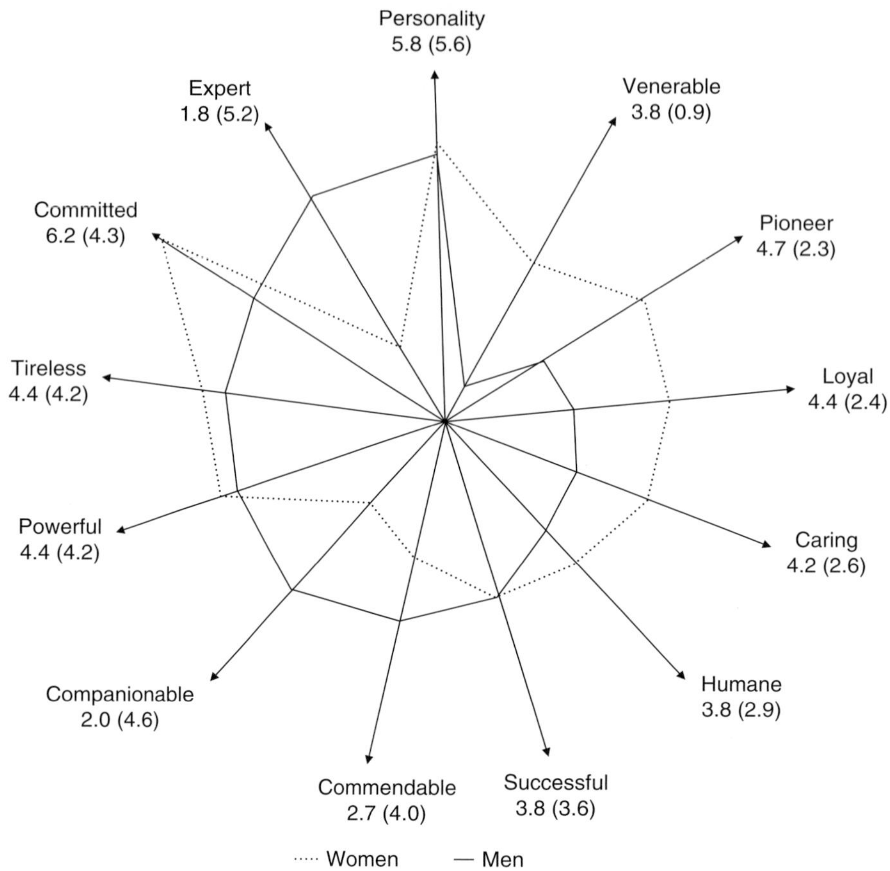

Note: Percent of the attributes of female and male (in parentheses) executives

Figure 6.11 Traits commonly attributed to executives as a function of gender (Walenta & Kirchler, 2011, p. 112)

fact, in accordance with social stereotypes, men are more likely than women to be credited with entrepreneurial skills and particularly with successful leadership (Kirchler, 1997c; Kirchler, Wagner & Buchleitner, 1996). The fact that Passauer (1992) found no differences in explicit descriptions of successful female and male entrepreneurs may be due to the tendency to provide socially desirable answers.

One way of avoiding problems of social desirability which may arise from direct surveys about stereotypes are indirect methods. Rodler, Kirchler and Hoelzl (2001; see also Hartl, Kirchler & Muehlbacher, 2013; Kirchler, 1992) analysed obituaries for women and men who had been active as executives. These obituaries were written by the companies and organisations for which the deceased had worked. The assumption was that the descriptions in these obituaries reflect stereotypes about male and female executives. The following description of this study is taken from Rodler and Kirchler (2002) and Walenta and Kirchler (2011).

Obituaries from four major newspapers from the years 1974, 1980, 1986, 1992 and 1998 were collected. In a first step of the analysis, a total of 4,057 words used to describe executives were identified. These words were classified by independent raters into a system of fifty-eight content categories. Figure 6.11 depicts the most frequently mentioned attribute categories for female and male

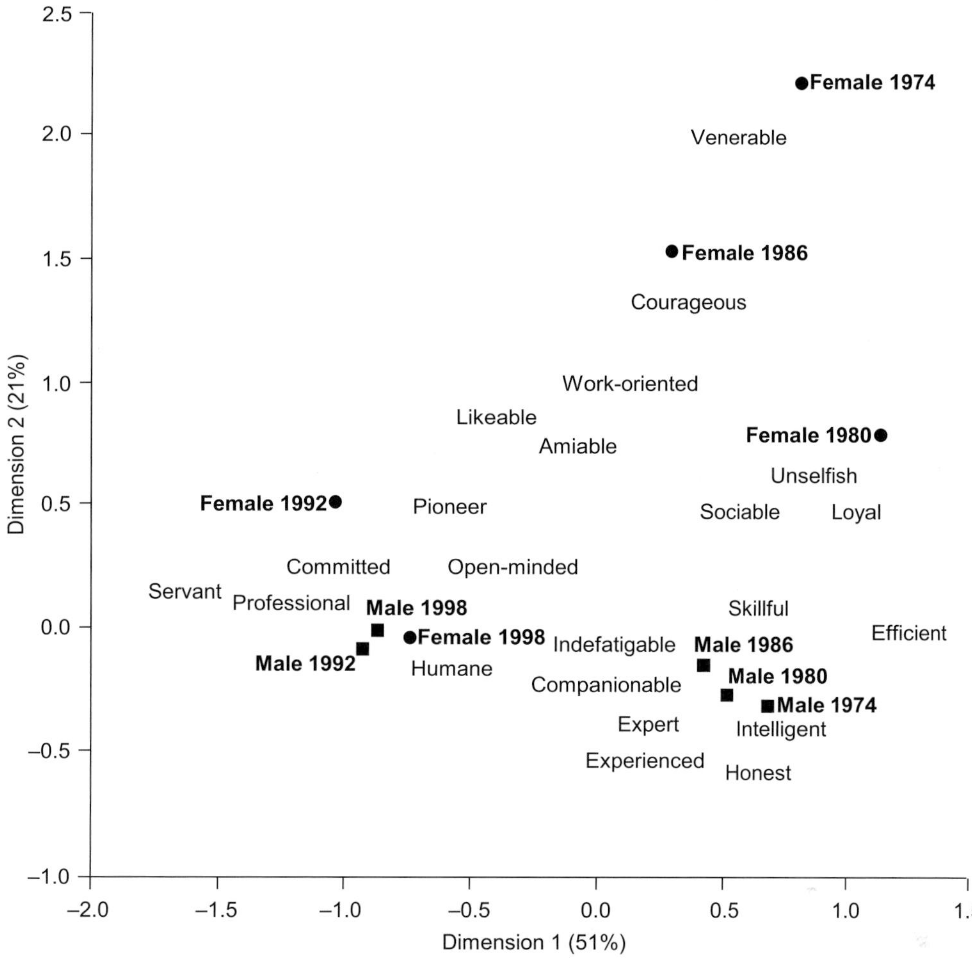

Figure 6.12 Two-dimensional solution of the correspondence analysis (with 51% and 21% explained variance, respectively) of traits associated with deceased men and women in executive positions (Rodler et al., 2001, p. 834)

executives by percentage. Executives were frequently described as people with personality, as experts, as committed, as tireless, etc. In terms of gender, clear differences in the frequencies can be observed.

In a second step, a correspondence analysis was conducted, taking into account the attribute categories on the one hand and the year of the obituary and the executive's gender on the other. The results reveal changes in the descriptions of male and female executives over time. While men and women were described very differently from 1974 to 1986, a clear convergence in the descriptions becomes apparent in 1992 and 1998. The results of the correspondence analysis with the characteristics that make the largest explanatory contributions are depicted in Figure 6.12.

Finally, the attributes were judged according to whether they rather referred to the leadership styles task orientation or person orientation. Afterwards, the proportion of attributes classified as task-oriented was compared to the proportion categorised as person-oriented for both men and women. An increase in person-oriented attributes can be seen starting in 1992. Among women, first an increase in the proportion of task-oriented attributes took place. Subsequently, in 1998, a further hike in the proportion of attributes classified as person-oriented was observed (Figure 6.13).

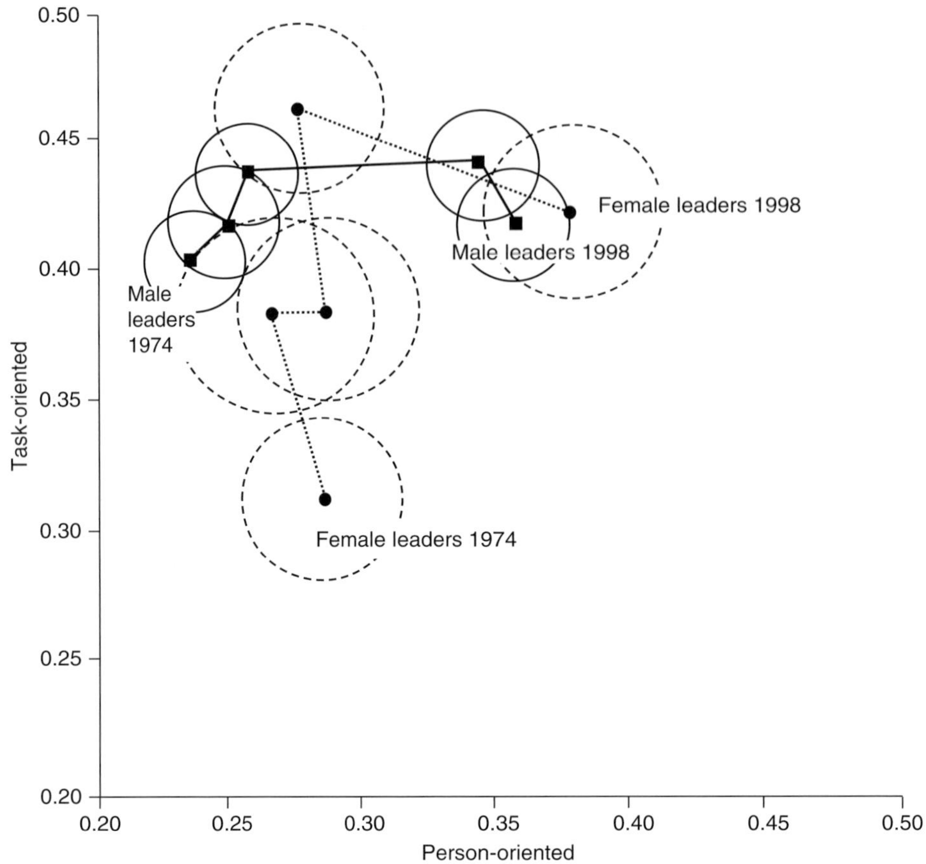

Figure 6.13 Change in the proportions of task-oriented and person-oriented attributes from 1974 to 1998 (circles correspond to 95% confidence intervals; Rodler et al., 2001, p. 837)

The results clearly show a change in the description of female executives over the past few decades. The correspondence analysis illustrates how the image of women changed compared to 1974. Back then, female executives were primarily described as venerable, likeable and loyal. Over the years, the image changed, including attributes such as courageous and work-oriented. Ultimately, female executives were described as committed and professional in 1998. The male stereotype remained relatively stable from 1974 to 1986. While in the 1970s women's obituaries hardly mentioned any attributes suggesting leadership skills, they were at least credited with high commitment in the 1980s. In contrast, men were regarded as competent, intelligent and far-sighted in all periods under investigation. The gender stereotypes detected here are especially relevant with regard to subordinates' trust in an executive and his or her effectiveness and competence. While women were at best seen as committed, which represents an unstable attribute, stable attributes were accredited to men. It is thus hardly surprising that women in top management had to work especially hard to convince employees of their competency and gain their trust. When men are viewed as competent on the basis of their gender, business success is subjectively attributed to their characteristics and skills, while failures can be perceived as resulting from situational factors. The foundation of trust that women needed to generate themselves through successful leadership appears to have come to men simply on the basis of their gender. In the 1990s, a shift towards greater person orientation, represented by attributes such as humane or open-minded, became apparent. Moreover, in 1992 and 1998, a convergence in the descriptions of male and female executives took place. This indicates that female and male leadership roles were viewed more similarly in the 1990s than in the 1970s and 1980s.

Further research on gender stereotypes and the characteristics of women and men in positions of leadership can be found in Eagly, Johannesen-Schmidt and van Engen (2003) and Rosette and Tost (2010). Particularly relevant studies on prevailing gender stereotypes and context dependency, as well as women's roles in leading unsuccessful companies by being nurturing, creative and intuitive leaders, have been conducted by Alexander Haslam and Michelle Ryan and collaborators (e.g., Ryan, Haslam, Hersby & Bongiorno, 2011).

Gender stereotypes were also studied in connection with founding a company. Gupta, Turban, Wasti and Sikdar (2009) studied the role of gender stereotypes and their influence on women's and men's intention to found companies. Data were collected at two points in time, investigating economics students in the USA, India and Turkey ranging from 18 to 41 years of age. At the first measurement point, participants provided self-descriptions and descriptions of entrepreneurs. At the second measurement point, approximately four to six weeks later, the participants were randomly assigned to one of two conditions, in which they answered a questionnaire describing either women or men. In addition, all participants answered questions about their intentions to found a company. The authors were able to show that gender role stereotypes and identification with one's gender were significantly related to perceptions of entrepreneurs and the intention to become an entrepreneur. Both young men and young women linked the term entrepreneur with stereotypically male characteristics. However, the intention to found a company could not be traced back to biological sex; it was the identification with male traits that positively correlated with the intention to found a company. People who identified more strongly with men showed a greater intention to found a company than those who identified less strongly. This differentiation did not hold true for people who identified more or less strongly with women. Thus, among both men and women, becoming an entrepreneur depended on one's similarity to male attributes. These results arose in all three countries. Mueller and Conway Dato-On (2008) studied gender stereotypes and entrepreneurial self-efficacy. Entrepreneurial self-efficacy is typically taken into consideration in models predicting intentions to start companies. The sample comprised MBA students who had founded a company, who were working as entrepreneurs or who originated from families of entrepreneurs. Men and women did not differ with regard to their self-efficacy. However, the associations between self-efficacy, gender roles and entrepreneurial activities proved to be complex. In the process of founding a company, which requires creativity and innovation, both male as well as female and androgynous characteristics seemed to be relevant. Nevertheless, over the further course of running the company, a masculine orientation combined with persuasion and leadership activities seemed to be important for both men and women.

Conclusion

In the context of the labour market, classic economic theory offers a reasonable framework with the concept of supply and demand. However, when tested in experiments, this approach often lacks validity. The incorporation of psychological concepts, such as reciprocity, can improve the quality of prediction.

The relevance of wages for motivation is part of several psychological theories that highlight the importance of subjective perceptions. In particular, the perceived connections between effort, performance and wages are relevant. Perceptions also play a role for whether people judge their wages as fair. In these judgments, comparisons with others are key. Perceived unfairness can have severe consequences.

Entrepreneurs have been found to show characteristic personality traits and motivational structures. Given that successful entrepreneurs are creating job opportunities on the labour market, the interplay between these personal characteristics and situational aspects is an important topic with consequences for both education and policy.

Summary

- In classical economic theory, the labour market is described as a market governed by principles of trade between employers' demand for labour and households' supply of it. When supply corresponds to demand, an equilibrium is reached.
- Yet the equilibrium wage postulated by market theory does not arise in market situations in which workers can react to wage offers. Employers and workers appear to be bound by the norm of reciprocity.
- In experimental markets, employers and employees interact over several rounds. The strategic challenges in such markets (for example, backward induction) can be studied through concepts originating from game theory, such as the dictator game, the ultimatum game, the trust game or the centipede game.
- The income level is important to workers because it serves the satisfaction of needs, and provides information about relative status, as well as opening opportunities for control and consumption possibilities.
- From a psychological perspective, wages do not directly transform into effort or performance. Motivation theories such as V-I-E theory or expectancy models clarify that motivation is a function of subjective perceptions of values and of probability links between effort, performance and wages.
- People perceive fairness when the relationship between their own performance and their wages corresponds to the relationship between others' performance and wages. When unfairness is perceived, different elements of this comparison can be influenced, or the comparison can be avoided.
- Entrepreneurs play a critical role in the economy for creating jobs. Independence and stability seem to be crucial personality characteristics. Entrepreneurs score higher on achievement motivation and are more likely to see themselves in control of their performance outcomes. They are willing to take risks when chances look promising, but consider them carefully.
- Successful company founders can be differentiated by several personal characteristics. For long-term success, however, situational characteristics are even more relevant.
- Gender stereotypes influence the perception of entrepreneurs and executives. However, in recent years the female and male stereotypes seem to converge on characteristics formerly accredited only to men.

Questions

1. What is 'market clearing' in the context of the labour market?
2. What are the psychological hypotheses for a competitive market with reciprocity?
3. What is 'instrumentality' in V-I-E theory in the context of wages?
4. What are the key elements of equity theory?
5. What differences in personality characteristics between entrepreneurs and managers have been found (Zhao & Seibert, 2006)?

FURTHER READING

Akerlof, G. A., & Yellen, J. L. (1988). Fairness and unemployment. *American Economic Review, 78*, 44–9.

Axelrod, R. (1984). *The evolution of cooperation*. New York: Basic Books.

Eagly, A. H., & Chin, J. L. (2010). Diversity and leadership in a changing world. *American Psychologist, 65*, 216–24.

Gintis, H. (2000). *Game theory evolving: A problem centered introduction to modeling strategic interaction*. Princeton, NJ: Princeton University Press.

Hey, J. D. (1991). *Experiments in economics*. Oxford: Blackwell.

7 Financial Markets: Risk and Investment

Overview

Financial markets worldwide conduct transactions running into billions, making them particularly important for individuals as well as national economies. Since financial markets, particularly stock exchanges, represent ideal markets, it can be assumed that decision-making there follows the laws of *homo economicus*, at least at the aggregate level. However, behavioural economics and financial psychology – particularly the psychology of the stock exchange – have substantiated that financial markets are also subject to psychological influences. Decision-making anomalies lead to outcomes diverging from those postulated by the *homo economicus* model, even at the aggregate level. For example, actors' current moods are relevant in determining their expectations with regard to market trends; conversely, stock prices are also a reflection of current moods of actors on the market. Actors' convictions with regard to their ability to control events are also often massively overblown. People frequently do not behave as the available factual information would suggest, but rather follow the crowd in a form of herding behaviour.

This chapter provides an overview of psychological and behavioural-economical approaches to describe financial markets. It starts out with reactions to news, and information use by investors. It then moves to a systematic pattern of how investors treat stocks that have lost or gained in value, the disposition effect. Heuristics used by investors and financial managers will be discussed, using examples from both real-life financial markets and experiments. A particularly important part is heuristic risk diversification in investors' portfolios. Emotions and mood also influence decision-making on financial markets. Of particular relevance are social influences, such as the herd behaviour that can frequently be observed in financial markets and that can lead to speculative bubbles. Finally, the role of trust in financial institutions will be discussed.

Introduction

The *homo economicus* is a rational thinking and self-interested human intent on maximising utility or profit. But is this idea applicable to humans in the context of financial markets? The goal is to understand how the seemingly irrational movements and fluctuations in the financial markets come to be – for example, the creation of speculative bubbles. These observations are hard to explain by rationality alone. For this reason, we expand our view to behavioural economics and psychology. Making the right decision is a difficult task, yet some traders are more successful than others. What are the mistakes traders make? People over- and under-react to news, have distorted memories of past events, treat stocks differently because of past events, use heuristics to make decisions, and are affected by emotions and by the trading behaviour of other investors.

7.1 The Exchange

Financial markets are markets where capital is traded: money, foreign currencies, credit, etc. One typical financial market is the stock exchange. However, commodities, grain and other products are also traded on exchanges. Half a millennium ago, in 1531, the first stock exchange was founded in Antwerp, Belgium.

7.1.1 Economic Perspectives on the Exchange

The term 'exchange' refers to a market in which goods are traded by brokers. Prices and rates are developed under regulated conditions and at designated times, according to supply and demand. What is meant here is an organised market for securities (e.g., stocks, bonds), foreign currency, goods (e.g., commodities, metals), or rights derived from them. Wiendieck (1990, p. 48 f; as cited in Fischer & Mörsch, 1999, p. 35 f) described the exchange as follows:

> At first glance, the exchange represents a market, but one with the peculiarity of double abstractedness or anonymity. The traded goods and securities are not physically exchanged there, nor do buyers and sellers encounter each other personally. Moreover, it is not individual items, but rather mass goods that can be divided almost completely arbitrarily (or rather the rights to them) that are traded. Viewed thusly, it is logical to assume that specific features of the good at hand or characteristics of individual market participants are irrelevant, that they are levelled out by the large numbers at play. Considered in this way, the exchange could be viewed as the parade ground of the pure market economy. Various specimens of the 'homo economicus' encounter each other and exchange with a great deal of rationality something that they don't care about at all, simply in order to have more money afterwards than they did before.

The term 'exchange' is often used synonymously with securities and foreign currency exchanges. As pure financial markets, exchanges should be 'efficient', meaning that all of the information available at a given time should be reflected in the price of the traded securities. Capital markets are consistent with the ideal of the efficient market according to the **efficient markets hypothesis** (Fama, 1965, 1970): Many market participants are immediately aware of all freely available, relevant information; process it quickly and fully; and behave in a rational, goal-oriented manner, buying and selling according to price without any noteworthy transaction costs. As Schulz-Hardt, Vogelgesang and Mojzisch (2007, p. 206) noted, according to the efficient markets hypothesis, the price formation for securities such as stocks proceeds 'with no time lost and having taken into account all pieces of information. The exact price level at any given time is solely the consequence of expected dividend payments as well as expected increases in value and accurately reflects both.'

It is clear that people participating in financial markets are not able to process all available information immediately and correctly. Nor are they able instantly to adapt their operations to the most current information and adjust prices and rates accordingly. Nevertheless, it is still assumed that individual failings balance each other out, that deviations from the rational model vary in unsystematic ways, and that they thus have no effect at the aggregate level. According to the '**random walk hypothesis**', at the aggregate level, the prices of securities represent their fundamental values. Owing to the market's ability to self-regulate, prices only vary unsystematically, that is, completely at random.

If the economic value of a stock is the sum of its future (discounted) dividend payouts, traders on the stock market need to try to identify the true value of stocks and react to new information. They should buy when prices lie below the future value and sell when they are above this value. The daily price fluctuations of stocks make it difficult to calculate their true values. It is important to consider future changes in value and not to allow decisions to be influenced by past values, so that speculation on profits is always forward-looking, taking the current price level as its starting point. This advice holds true because current prices are formed in a rational process, and thus contain all currently available information. Price changes can thus only arise as a result of new information. If traders make rational decisions, they sell and buy as soon as they need cash or would like to invest. New information cannot be predicted – or else it would already be taken into account in the purchase price. This means that nothing about future price movements can be learned from previous ones.

However, current prices do not always behave according to the efficient markets hypothesis, and do not vary completely at random. Instead, many actors on the stock market allow themselves to be guided by how high prices were at the time they bought a given security. Past information influences their decisions to sell or keep securities. There are traders who behave rationally or at least attempt to do so. However, there are also so-called '**noise traders**', who do not take some information into account, who place too much value on certain rumours, and make many more trades than would be the case among rational traders. Other investors, known as '**passive investors**', make many fewer trades than rational traders would: they make purchases and then do not trade again for a long time (Kelly, 1997). Behavioural finance has identified a number of phenomena that illustrate deviations from the efficient markets hypothesis. These deviations include systematic differences in returns at specific times (calendar effects, weekly effects, intraday effects, holiday effects) or for specific stocks (initial public offerings effects, price earnings effects). In particular, these deviations are excessive trading volume and market volatility that cannot be explained by rational market forces (Duggan, 1999; Wärneryd, 2001).

The reason for systematic deviations from the rational model lies in the fact that traders and investors do not behave in a purely rational way. Predictions about economic developments are important for the stock exchange, but market participants' moods affect their hopes and fears about future developments. The available information does not always adequately reflect the economic situation: companies have nuanced information policies, and not all relevant information is always available. Actors on the financial market are often not able, or lack the motivation, to process complex information in a sufficiently detailed way. They apply heuristics, fall prey to judgment errors, and are drawn to making riskier or more cautious decisions depending on the way an issue is presented. Moreover, information is frequently not sought out at all; rather, people align their behaviour with that of other market participants (e.g., DeBondt, 2008; Odean, 1999; Pitters & Oberlechner, 2014; Shleifer & Vishny, 1997).

7.1.2 Psychological Perspectives on the Exchange

In 2007, a wave of foreclosures on the US real estate market sent shock waves through the entire financial market. The financial crisis of 2008 followed and the fundamental assumptions of financial economics came under sharp criticism. Belief in market self-regulation and the efficient markets hypothesis was permanently shaken. Markets are supposed to be efficient when a large number of participants in a market with negligible entry costs are aware of all available information and are able to process it adequately. As a result, prices should reflect both the current situation – due to market participants' rational expectations – and the future proceeds of a given security. Even if some market participants mistakenly assess the value of a security as too low, while others put it too high, the average of these individual assessments and thus the price of the security should be correct.

While the fundamental assumptions of financial economics are criticised by some, they are also tenaciously defended by those who point out that it was practice, not theory, that failed. Nevertheless, the financial crisis of 2007/8 – whose intensity is frequently compared to that of the 1920s – has made it clear that a fair amount of psychology is at play on the financial market. Behavioural economists, particularly Robert Shiller (2000, 2008, 2015), have launched direct attacks on the efficient markets hypothesis by referring to the influence of psychology.

Speculative bubbles prove that price movements on international financial markets cannot be explained solely by means of the rational model. Information processing on financial markets does not correspond to the assumptions of the rational model either, even at the aggregate level. The 'fair' value of a security is not necessarily generated by market participants' processing of the available information, at least not in the short or medium term. Relevant pieces of information are ignored, while too much attention is paid to irrelevant pieces of information.

As an example of inadequate information processing, Oberlechner (2004) cites the effect of a *New York Times* report on a potential breakthrough in cancer research. This report led to a massive increase in the stock price of the pharmaceutical company associated with the development. On the day after the report was published, stocks of EntreMed rose to seven times that of the closing price on the previous trading day. However, the newspaper article did not contain any new information. The 'news' had already been published several months earlier, also in the *New York Times*.

How does inefficient information processing like this come about? To answer this, Oberlechner (2004) surveyed currency traders and financial journalists about the bases of their decision-making on the financial market. Currency traders were asked to name the information that had been decisive in their best and worst trading decisions. Figure 7.1 illustrates the factors that were considered relevant in good and bad decisions. Decisions were sometimes made as a result of analytical thinking; however, more often they were made on the basis of feelings, spontaneously, or as a result of experience. Traders considered their gut feelings to be the most important factor in both their best and their worst decisions. Less significance was attributed to rational considerations, analytical thinking, the analysis of fundamental data and computer-assisted decision-making programmes.

The following section describes some of the psychological phenomena that can lead to suboptimal decision-making on the financial market. Such behaviour can elicit price fluctuations that do not reflect the fundamental values of the traded securities. These phenomena are primarily known as cognitive fallacies. They include excessive certainty (overconfidence), excessive optimism, asymmetric risk behaviour, loss aversion, mental accounting habits, and heuristics that make quick decisions possible but sometimes lead one astray. Emotions also play an important role in decision-making, and individuals typically base their behaviour on what the 'herd' of other investors is doing. Montier (2007, 2010) summarised the many sources of error in a diagram, which is reproduced in Figure 7.2. Many sources of error have already been described in Chapter 2, while a few which relate specifically to financial markets are discussed here.

In addition to cognitive fallacies and distortions, the influence of emotions, and herd behaviour, the presentation of the information on which investment decisions are based also determines preferences and perceptions of risk. Diacon and Hasseldine (2007) investigated the effect of different ways of presenting information on past stock developments. Study participants were

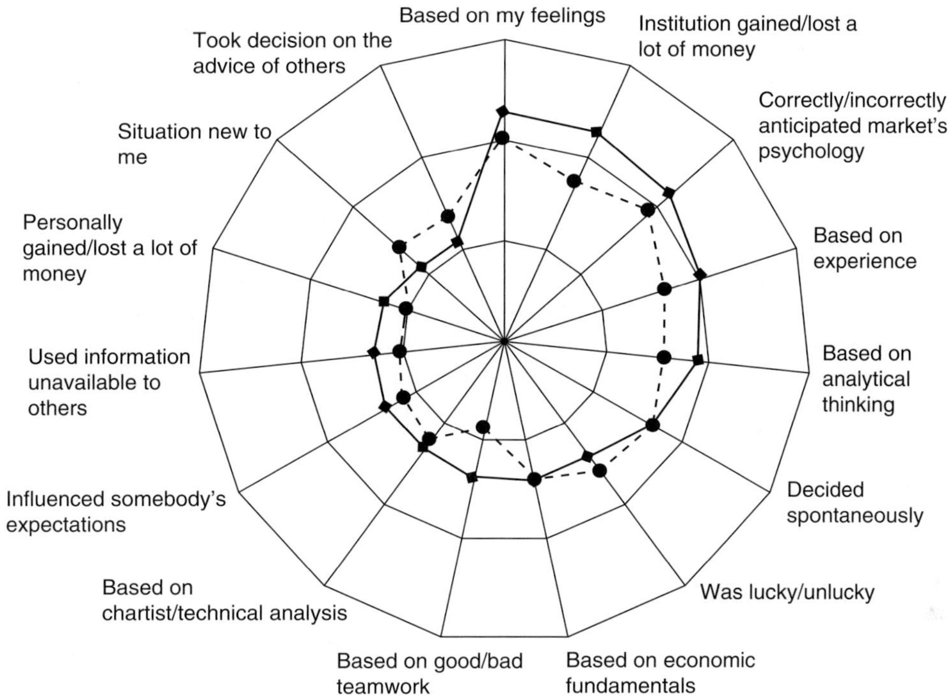

Figure 7.1 Bases of the best (solid line) and worst (dashed line) trading decisions. Ratings range from 'strongly disagree' in the centre of the figure to 'strongly agree' in the outermost circle (Oberlechner, 2004, p. 24)

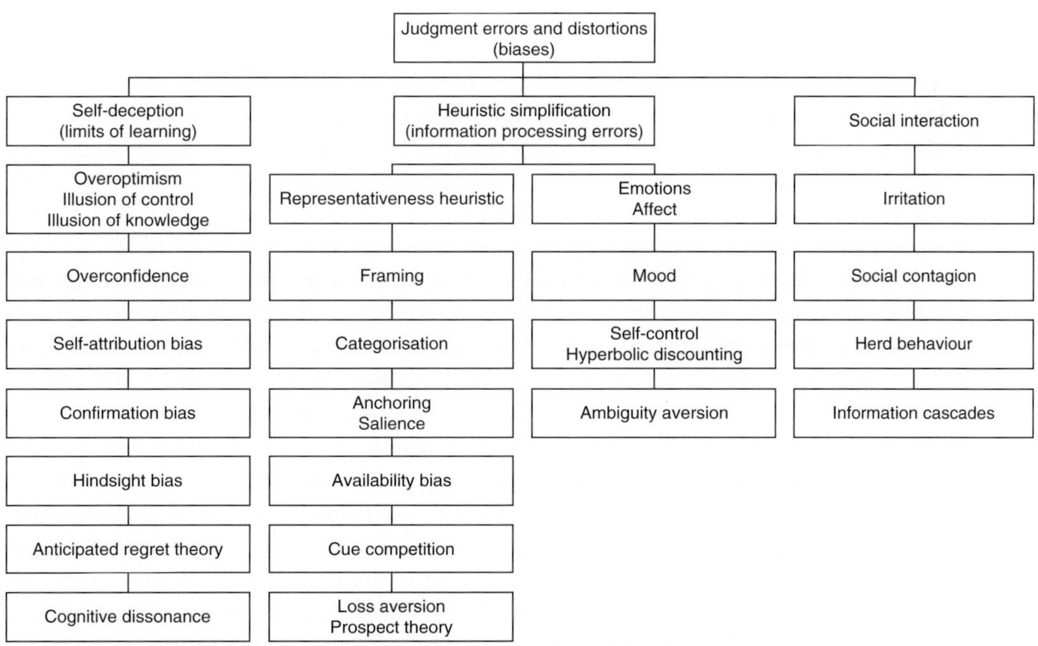

Figure 7.2 Sources of error in financial decision-making (Montier, 2010, p. 57)

given pitches on equity funds and fixed-interest funds, and were shown either a line graph of share values or a bar chart depicting the percent yield. In addition, the time scales of the diagrams were varied to show either short-term or long-term developments. Before being presented with information on the funds' developments, participants read brief vignettes stating that they were supposed to provide advice to a friend in choosing the most profitable fund. Afterwards, the perceived risk of each fund was measured using a questionnaire. The presentation format proved to be highly relevant in determining preference for a fund as well as perceived risk. An equity fund had a low probability of being chosen when the information was presented in the form of percent yield. In addition, more than 50% of participants who had originally recommended an equity fund when presented with the share value graph switched over to a fixed-interest fund when the information was presented in the form of percent yield. Surprisingly, the time scale had no influence on fund selection or perceived risk. Interestingly, around half of study participants stated that their selection process was influenced by the past development of the securities. In a similar vein, Mussweiler and Schneller (2003) reported that investors are influenced by charts of previous performance.

7.1.3 Investors' Mistakes

What distinguishes particularly successful traders on financial markets? Oberlechner (2004) conducted a survey of European currency traders with the goal of discovering what characteristics traders themselves viewed as critical to success as a currency trader. The survey covered personality characteristics, professional competences, cognitive abilities and other factors. The currency traders were asked to provide their views on twenty-five statements regarding the characteristics of traders. According to the study, the most important characteristic of a successful currency trader was the ability to react quickly to new information. Discipline, experience, stress resistance and concentration were discovered to be further characteristics of success. At the rear were social skills. Factor analysis allowed eight factors to be extracted from the statements: the first factor, 'disciplined cooperation', consists of discipline and the ability to work in teams. Discipline is one of only a few characteristics under one's own control. That makes it important in complex situations in which conditions can change quickly and unpredictably. Traits such as aggressiveness, stress resistance, willingness to take risks, concentration and the ability to react quickly load onto the second factor, 'tackling decisions'. All of these characteristics are critical for decision-making in a risky market environment. The third factor, 'market meaning-making', consists of the ability to evaluate information appropriately and create meaning from it. The two key elements of this factor are the accurate assessment of complex situations and the investment in lucrative stocks. The experience and intuition that successful traders develop over the course of time is also critical. The fourth factor, 'emotional stability', refers to the ability to keep a cool head. In the interviews with currency traders, one trader emphasised that a professional, level-headed demeanour is important for success. When emotions gain the upper hand, concentration on the task at hand suffers. The fifth factor, 'information processing', comprises analytical thinking, the ability to learn, and the ability to process multiple pieces of information simultaneously. Three further factors were also identified; however, in contrast to the first five, these were considered of little relevance to successful trading. The sixth factor, 'interested integrity', consists of curiosity and integrity: the seventh factor, 'autonomous organisation', of autonomy, organisational abilities and optimism; and the eighth factor, 'information handling', of mathematical, social and communicative abilities.

Discipline, concentration on the issue at hand and appropriate meaning-making were characteristics discovered to be relevant to currency traders' success according to the traders themselves. However, 'sins' are also committed on the financial market, often with a detrimental impact on returns. These sins can be explained by psychology. Montier (2005) provided a compilation of mistakes on financial markets, calling them the 'Seven Deadly Sins of Fund Management'. The following section provides a brief description of the seven deadly sins – which represent a summary of the psychology of financial markets according to Montier (2005, 2010, p. 181 f):

- *Pride: the sin of overconfidence in one's forecasts.* Good forecasts are extremely difficult and are often only possible with a lot of luck. We are often too optimistic and too confident in our abilities. This is why 75% of fund managers believe they are better than average at their job. Why is forecasting nevertheless a core part of the investment process? Possibly because our evaluations and forecasts give us an anchor on which to orient ourselves. The content of this anchor can be completely irrelevant to the assessment or prediction and still influence it.
- *Gluttony: the sin of accumulating information and the illusion of knowledge.* Fund managers and investors appear to believe that one needs to be in possession of as much information as possible in order to be able to outwit other people in the market. However, our cognitive capacity to process information is limited. We eventually reach a point after which more information will only overwhelm us rather than improve our decision-making. Decisions made in this condition do not differ from those based on less information. Rather, additional pieces of information serve to increase our (unrealistic) self-confidence.
- *Lust: the sin of believing information from company executives or fund managers.* Conversations with company executives are an important virtue in the investment process. In these conversations, they hope to gain objective insights into companies' plans for the future in order to make better investment decisions. Five points call the usefulness of this approach into question: (a) More information is not necessarily better information. (b) Company executives can also succumb to cognitive illusions and sometimes see things from a distorted perspective. (c) We tend to look for information that confirms our beliefs. Rather than asking critical questions and amending our opinions on the basis of the answers, we tend to ask questions that lead to the answers we want to hear. (d) We fall under the spell of authority figures and frequently react uncritically to the numerical data presented to us by company heads. (e) Finally, we often do not realise when tactically astute executives are trying to mislead us, even though we think we're incredibly good at separating lies from the truth.
- *Envy: the sin of excessive self-confidence.* When a specific piece of information points to an increase in the price of a stock, many traders are convinced that they are the ones who will be able to process and deploy it most quickly. However, the short time horizon on the stock market greatly hinders any attempt to outwit the rest of the market. In reality, traders often only consider their next one to two moves in strategic decisions. They do not think further ahead.
- *Greed: the sin of hyperactivity.* Fund managers are relying more and more on short-term trading for their success. For example, the average holding period for stocks on the New York Stock Exchange (NYSE) is around eleven months. One's return on investment over such a short time period is based solely on price fluctuations, not on changes to the fundamental value of the stock. This is speculation, not investing, and the associated transaction costs are quite substantial.
- *Sloth: the sin of credulity.* Stock traders are often quick to accept rumours as hard facts without sufficient reflection because they find it so hard to resist the seductive prospect of a profit.

Heuristics frequently play an important role in decision-making. For example, Langer, Blank and Chanowitz (1978) demonstrated that we often do not hear rationales, but only signals that there is a rationale. When waiting in line, it is often enough to say that you would like to skip ahead because you want to reach the front more quickly for people to let you cut ahead of them. A rationale for why you would like to skip ahead is not necessary. In many cases, the signal 'because' appears to be sufficient.

- *Wrath: the sin of group decision-making.* Ideally, group decision-making involves an exchange of ideas among group members where others' opinions are heard, one's own misconceptions are corrected and the situation is considered objectively. However, group dynamics can often lead to a strengthening of misconceptions; the diversity of opinions is restricted, as those differing from that of the group leader for the most part remain unexpressed or are quickly dismissed as incorrect. The group members who are perceived to be especially competent are the ones who agree with the general opinion of the group rather than the ones with differing opinions that the group has to deal with (Montier, 2005, 2010).

The list above gives a vivid impression of the psychological processes that can interfere with the goal of successful actions on the stock market. In the following sections, some of these processes are explored in more detail.

7.2 Over- and Under-reactions to News

New information on the financial market leads to the purchase or sale of securities and to changes in price. Bad news induces a decline in prices: reports about companies' difficulties, losses or lower-than-expected profits mean that a company's fundamental value has changed and that its stock now has a lower value than before. Information about the results of political elections, political crises, war or natural disasters also affects price developments on the stock market. Investors often react unduly strongly to such reports (Kaplanski & Levy, 2010). Volatility in prices partially arises from the fact that older information is given too little weight and new information too much. Volatility as a result of media reports is particularly high on destabilised stock markets (Andreassen, 1990; Jebabli, Arouri & Teulon, 2014; Schachter, Hood, Gerin, Andreassen & Rennert, 1985).

Political, social and other non-economic events can have a strong effect on stock markets. Schachter et al. (1985) provide a few examples of this. They show how stock market fluctuations are influenced by events such as political elections, airplane crashes, etc. Uncertainty about the credibility of the available information and turbulent political, social and economic situations affect stock brokers' decisions: they allow their actions to be guided by external events, such as disasters. This leads, in turn, to higher price fluctuations on the stock market. The sales volume of two large department stores in New York City was demonstrated to correlate with newspaper reports of violence. When a murder was reported on the first page of the *New York Times*, sales volume fell by an average of 6%. When several murders were depicted, even more potential customers stayed away: revenue would sink 19% on that day. This correlation occurred independently of season, day of the week and other factors. A similar pattern holds true for the stock market. Doing business on the stock exchange requires careful consideration of economic conditions and possible changes to them, and most market participants try to make rational decisions. However, the stock exchange is also in large part 'psychology'. The stock exchange guru André Kostolany (1997, p. XII) emphasised: 'The role of psychology on the stock market cannot be overstated. In the short and middle term, it represents – on the stock market and in the economy – 90%.' However, Kostolany qualified this statement by arguing that psychology has little significance for long-term developments, which depend on economic performance.

Reports on non-economic events are interpreted, arouse emotions and lead to expectations about future developments. These expectations tend to be overly dependent on the most recent events, leading to behaviour that exhibits a similar dependence. Stock market developments are partially determined by feelings rather than cold calculations, the illusion of understanding the mechanisms that lead to price changes and of the ability to control future developments, stereotypical interpretative concepts and decision-making heuristics rather than extensive data analysis, norms of social behaviour and group influences, shifting moods and personal motives. Even stockbrokers are not consistently rational in their decision-making, but rather apply judgment heuristics that sometimes lead them astray (Stephan & Kiell, 1998). The influence of psychological phenomena has been demonstrated both in observational analyses of stock market activity (e.g., Jünemann & Schellenberger, 1997; Maas & Weibler, 1990; Pinner, 1997) and in experimental simulations staging market situations. On these markets, which conduct trade in labour, stocks and even political parties, trends can be observed that lead to typical market overheating and even to crashes (e.g., Smith & Williams, 1993).

The influence of external factors such as reports about disasters and acts of violence on stock market activity varies, and depends partially on the past experiences of market participants. Schachter, Hood, Andreassen and Gerin (1986) argued that investors on the stock market learn from previous developments. When a stable upward trend prevails on stock markets for years at a time, investors have faith in further positive activity and conduct their business independently of daily events. When conditions are unstable, however, external factors become more relevant in trading decisions. The Dow Jones Industrial Average from 1950 to 1966 and onwards provides an example of this. From 1950 to 1966, the American stock market index rose by 600%. Investors could be confident that the index would continue to rise regardless of daily events of both economic and non-economic nature. Starting in February 1966, the situation changed dramatically: the direction of stock market developments became unclear; there were some winners, but also many losers. If the assumption of Schachter and colleagues is correct, daily events before 1966 should have had little influence on stock market behaviour, but events after this date should have been quite significant. Indeed, the authors were able to prove that the market reacted more sensitively to plane crashes and political elections after February 1966 than it did before. While investors in times of stable development tend to have their own hypotheses and opinions, they more frequently seek out the opinions of others in times of unstable developments. These opinions, in turn, influence investor behaviour and therefore stock market happenings.

At the beginning of the 1990s, Italy's political and economic scene provided an impressive example of the influence of external events on stock market activity. It is presented here for purposes of illustration, rather than in a way that seeks to satisfy strict academic criteria of analysis. In the late summer of 1992, Italy's currency was disincorporated from the European Monetary System with its stabilised exchange rates. The lira then sharply devalued. But even before, there were a few political events that shook the country's stock exchange. The assassinations of Italy's best-protected judicial officers in the war against the Mafia – Giovanni Falcone on 25 May 1992 and Paolo Borsellino on 20 July 1992 – crippled public life. It destroyed all belief in the security of the republic as well as the success of the war against organised crime. While the first assassination barely affected the economy, the second was the straw that broke the camel's

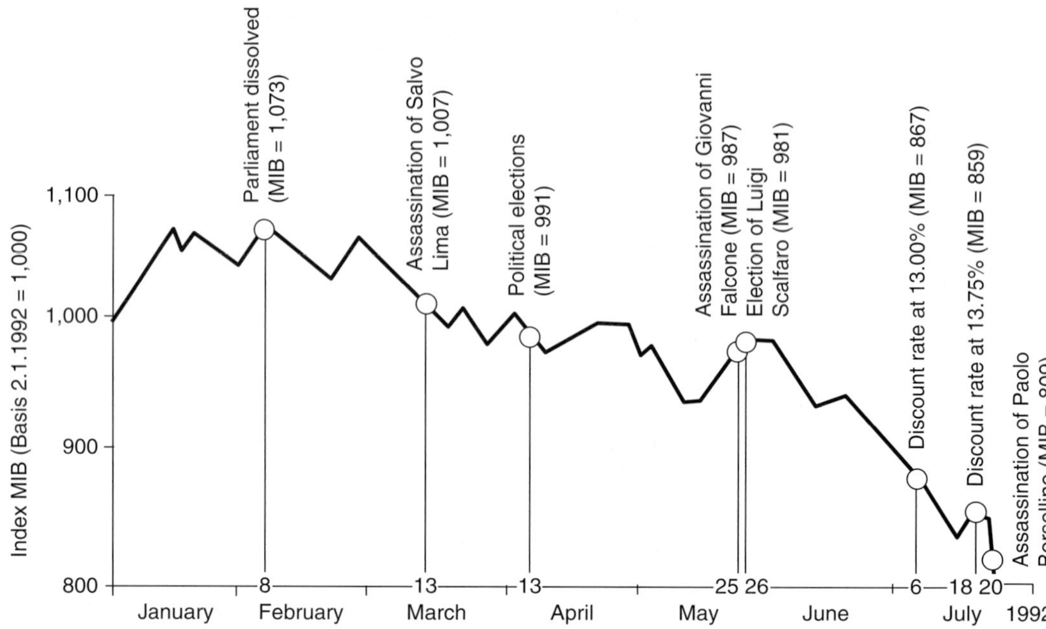

Figure 7.3 The Italian stock exchange under the blows of the political and economic crisis (from the newspaper *Corriere della Sera*, 21 July 1992, p. 10)

back. The resulting panic on financial markets was described in *Corriere della Sera* on 21 July 1992 (p. 1) as follows:

> Another black day for the Italian economy: the massacre feeds the distrust of foreign investors. / Prices crash on the stock exchange (-5.82%), lira collapses. / Market at a historic record [low] . . . / From Palermo to financial markets: The Mafia's new massacre shocks the stock exchange and the lira as well, in a last, ferocious blow to the credibility of the state system. On financial markets, the emotions led to moments of panic.

The newspaper (p. 10) also described the progression of the Milan Stock Exchange Index in 1992, putting price developments in the context of political events. The chart is reproduced in Figure 7.3.

Negative socio-political events can influence financial activity just as much as positive ones can. In a referendum on 18 and 19 April 1993, Italians expressed their opinions on eight groups of socially and politically significant topics. They voted by an overwhelming majority (82% of eligible voters) for a change in the existing electoral law and therefore to the political power structure. The enormous proportion of votes in favour of change was seen as the dawn of a new age for the Italian republic, as the impetus for a new beginning in general. The newspaper *La Repubblica* (20 April 1993, p. 10) commented on the current economic situation on the day after the referendum as follows:

> Revolution of 'Yes' / Euphoria on the markets / 'Yes' wins and markets gain strength. The lira rises to the psychologically significant mark of 950 compared to a German mark . . . the stock exchange closes having risen 2.38%. In summary, the stock exchange puts on its rose-coloured glasses and sees the future as riddled with positive news.

The Italian lira had already been steadily recovering against the German mark in the days leading up to the referendum in the expectation of a positive outcome, while the stock exchange also reacted positively. Nevertheless, the unexpectedly high outcome was decisive in leading to a noticeable upward surge in the lira and the stock market. The Italian stock market index MIB rose by 2.38% to a value of 1,160.

Stock prices are more than an 'objective' number; they are a kind of aggregate opinion (Frey & Stahlberg, 1990). The moods, and especially the expectations, of investors, consumers and producers, coloured by their personal experiences as well as public events, have a significant influence on the economy.

Over-reactions are also possible as a result of money illusion. Svedsäter, Gamble and Gärling (2007) showed that students in possession of stocks with a high nominal value expected greater fluctuations in prices following positive or negative media reports than those whose stocks had a lower nominal value. Expectations about percentage changes varied depending on whether stock values are given in euros or Swedish krona. Splitting stocks also leads to changes in investors' behaviour. When a split is conducted, stocks are divided according to a certain ratio. When the split ratio is 1:2, an investor will own two shares after the split, for example, each with a value of $50, rather than one share with a value of $100. The total value of a person's shares does not change. Nevertheless, stock prices tend to rise after a split. Conversely, when several shares are aggregated into one, prices frequently fall (Ikenberry, Rankine & Stice, 1996). The change in nominal value and the impression that shares have become cheaper are seen as reasons for these outcomes following a stock split.

Economic variables can also be responsible for volatility. Investors' projections of price developments usually represent an over-reaction, as price developments typically demonstrate a tendency to return to the centre; prices that have just risen tend to sink, while a stock often recovers again after having fallen. For example, DeBondt and Thaler (1985, 1987) found that the future price development of stocks that have lost value will be positive. According to Odean (1999), investors make projections with regard to price developments and buy winning stocks, while selling losing ones. However, it should be emphasised that the disposition effect shows that stocks tend not to be sold when the price at which a stock was bought is lower than the current market price, as the sale would bring about a loss.

Self-fulfilling prophecies can sustain a price trend for some time. It is difficult to predict how long a trend will hold. Beliefs cause people to overestimate their own capacities and to make optimistic predictions about the price developments of the securities they own. This includes the belief that negative effects are more likely to happen to other people than to oneself (overoptimism), the belief that one can influence random events (illusion of control) and an exaggerated sense of certainty with regard to the accuracy of one's own judgments (overconfidence) (Moore, Kurtzberg, Fox & Bazerman, 1999). When over-reactions are recognised, under-reactions frequently follow, with the result that the correct price is eventually reached (Shleifer, 2000).

Not only news and expectations about future developments, but also memory errors and the reconstruction of past developments can influence decision-making on financial markets. In hindsight, events are often perceived in a distorted way, and the illusion arises that one always suspected that past events would turn out the way they did. Hindsight bias (Fischhoff & Beyth, 1975) refers to the tendency to remember previous predictions accurately after the fact and to believe one provided forecasts corresponding to actual developments. Kahneman, Higgins, Hall and Riepe (1998) designated hindsight bias as a cognitive illusion. The literature points to three possible causes of hindsight bias: first, simple memory errors; second, the belief that one 'knew it all along' (Hoelzl, Kirchler & Rodler, 2002; Wood, 1978); and third, the belief 'that it had to turn out that way', also known as '**creeping determinism**' (Nestler, Blank & von Collani, 2008). Financial markets provide frequent opportunities to observe hindsight bias. Kahneman et al. (1998) found that at the end of a trading day, experts frequently portray price developments as self-evident, even when their own predictions the day before were completely different. Biais and Weber (2009) investigated whether investors suffering from hindsight bias over-react to information signals, draw false conclusions, and make worse investment decisions than others. In order to test these hypotheses empirically, traders at large European banks in Frankfurt and London were studied. The traders were tasked with structuring portfolios and with making trading and investing decisions. They also had to provide opinions on how economic data would develop, for example on changes to the price of gold over the course of one year. After being given feedback on the actual developments of the economic data, many participants believed that they had predicted that the developments would occur in that way. Traders with high earnings on the financial market were much less likely to succumb to hindsight bias than those whose earnings were lower. On financial markets, there is a danger of overestimating one's own abilities by assuming that future developments are easier to predict than they actually are. Furthermore, many investors do not understand why they were not alerted much earlier, for example by their financial advisor, about a drop in prices. After all, the development was foreseeable! The tendency towards hindsight bias hinders people's ability to question critically the deliberations that led to their predictions and to make any necessary corrections; in short, it prevents them from learning. Biais and Weber (2009) also point to the potential for hindsight bias to inhibit learning processes with regard to future decision-making.

7.3 Disposition Effect

Imagine that you have two sets of stocks. Set A was bought for a price of \$500, has just gained value and is now worth \$1,000. Set B was purchased for \$1,500, has just lost value and is now also worth \$1,000. If you now need to sell one set of stocks, which do you sell? Most investors sell the set that has gained value, refusing to take a loss of \$500 by selling the losing stocks. The same is true on the stock exchange, where investors hold on to losing stocks for too long and sell winning stocks too quickly. This effect is known as the **disposition effect** (Shefrin & Statman, 1985).

Odean (1998a) investigated securities transactions registered between 1987 and 1993 at 10,000 randomly selected depots of an American discount broker, comparing the proportion of realised losses with the proportion of realised gains. Odean calculated the percentage of winning stocks sold compared to all winning stocks and the percentage of losing stocks sold compared to all losing stocks. While roughly 15% of winning stocks were sold, just 10% of losing stocks were sold. Moreover, these results held true even when the investigation was narrowed to just those transactions conducted by the 10% of investors who traded most frequently – nearly all of whom were likely to be experts (see also Barber, Odean & Zheng, 2005).

Kahneman and Tversky's (1979) prospect theory is commonly cited as an explanation for the disposition effect. Since losses have greater psychological weight than gains, people put more effort into avoiding losses. A loss is perceived to be about twice as large on average as a gain. For this reason, risky actions are sometimes taken when there is a chance to make up for a loss. When the buying price of a stock is taken as the reference point for determining whether it has gained or lost value, stocks that can be sold for more than they were purchased for are considered winning stocks. Conversely, losing stocks are those that would need to be disposed of at a value below the price at which they were bought. Losing stocks are kept, because there is a chance that their price could rise, even when further losses threaten. Conversely, winning stocks are sold because there is a chance that their price could fall again, making all one's profit go up in smoke, even when further increases in price are possible.

The disposition effect has also been demonstrated experimentally. In a study by Kirchler, Maciejovsky and Weber (2005), participants in a laboratory stock market sold winning stocks earlier than losing stocks. Chen, Kim, Nofsinger and Rui (2007) analysed the behaviour of traders at a Chinese stock trading company and determined that the stocks that were sold had a higher return than the ones that were bought. In a study by Lee, Park, Lee and Wyer (2008), Korean students traded stocks in an e-trading situation, and here again losing stocks were held on to longer than winning stocks. Weber and Camerer (1998) found that the disposition effect is suppressed when participants in an experimental stock market are instructed to sell their securities at the end of each trading period but also have the opportunity to buy them back at the same price. This would indicate that the effect is particularly linked to investors' difficulty selling losing stocks. It is not caused by greater demand among investors for losing stocks, pushing them to encourage other investors to sell their losing stocks.

Linnainmaa (2005) investigated stock market activity among Finnish day traders, who attempt to accrue profits through short-term speculation. Day traders buy securities at the beginning of the day with the purpose of selling them with profit at the end of the same trading day. He found that traders showed an aversion to taking losses at the end of the day. Instead of selling stocks that had fallen, investment costs were financed by selling stocks that had risen. That led to changes in the make-up of traders' portfolios that would otherwise be considered undesirable, such as owning securities that were too high risk. In fact, day traders' short-term daily profits and long-term returns tended to be negatively correlated. Day-trading businesses that are profitable at the beginning and the trader behaviour generated by this lead to portfolios that exhibit poor returns in the long term. This is especially true for more active day traders, whose new portfolios yield returns that are 6% lower on average than their original portfolios. Among less active day traders, the difference is only 2%. This can also be traced back to the fact that fees and transaction costs rise with the number of market transactions, which is typically not sufficiently taken into account in decisions to buy and sell stocks.

The **house money effect** (Thaler & Johnson, 1990) describes the fact that previous gains can lead to greater risk appetite. The term derives from casino gamblers, who perceive recently acquired winnings as 'house money' as opposed to their own money. Applied to the stock market, Oberlechner (2004) describes how stock traders also sometimes do not yet consider the recently earned profits from stock sales to be their own money. This perception makes it easier for both casino gamblers and traders on financial markets to take greater risks following a profit on the previous day, and not to take potential losses too seriously. A survey conducted by Oberlechner (2004) on a European sample confirmed the house money effect. When the most recent trading days had been successful, foreign exchange market traders were more willing to make risky decisions than in the case of price declines. Looking more closely at traders' statements, Oberlechner (2004) was able to determine that the house money effect was apparent among currency traders working for commercial and investment banks, but not among those who conducted trades on behalf of central banks. Different trading goals were cited as the reason for this. Traders working for commercial and investment banks are primarily interested in accruing profits. Traders for central banks, on the other hand, appear to be less profit-oriented. Their primary aim is to represent the goals of the central bank, such as bringing stability to a currency, for example.

The use of prospect theory to explain the disposition effect could be challenged by arguing that investors keep their losing stocks because these could very well be the future winners. When over- and under-reactions are observed on the market, there is a large chance that losing stocks recover. This argument sounds quite reasonable, but cannot explain why investors avoid selling losing stocks even when they could use this to their advantage in the form of a '**tax swap**'. Losing stocks could be exchanged for stocks with similar risks and return prospects. The realised loss could be deducted from the investor's taxes, while making the exchange ensures that the return prospects are preserved. According to Shefrin and Statman (1985), people have a general aversion to tax swaps, which can be explained with reference to mental accounting (Thaler, 1985). When the losing stocks are sold, the corresponding mental account is closed and a new account is opened for the stocks that have just been bought. Closing the old account leads to the perception of a loss, which investors react sensitively to.

Dhar and Zhu (2006) determined that wealthy investors and professional stock traders exhibit a lower than average disposition effect. According to Grinblatt, Keloharju and Linnainmaa (2012), more intelligent people are less susceptible to the disposition effect than less intelligent people. Experienced traders are less likely to succumb than investors with less experience. The disposition effect can also be resisted through a deliberate exertion of self-control (Thaler & Shefrin, 1981). However, one's reason and feelings are often in competition. Since there is often no room for rational considerations when negative feelings such as regret or fear of losing face arise, self-control techniques must be deployed. For example, one possibility would be to enlist the services of a financial advisor to monitor the development of one's stocks and offer them up for sale when the price falls below a certain value without asking for confirmation.

Learning about other people's outcomes can also reduce the disposition effect. Fox and Dayan (2004) presented study participants with a scenario showing the results of investments in an oil business. Half of participants gained a profit of 50%, while the other half lost 50% of their investment. The results of other people (close friends of the participants with similar investments) varied in the scenarios from much better to much worse. After being presented with this information, study participants were to indicate whether they wanted to continue investing in the same stocks or sell them. They were also to report how sure they felt about their decision and whether they perceived the situation as a gain or a loss. Not surprisingly, participants who had earned a profit were more likely to assess the situation as a gain than participants who had taken a loss. However, friends' results also had an influence on further investment behaviour. When a person's friends had earned a larger profit than they had, the situation was more likely to be viewed as a loss than when the friends achieved the same results or realised a loss. Conversely, when one's friends realised a loss or had similar results to oneself, a gain was perceived. The strongest curtailment of the disposition effect arose when one's own outcome corresponded to those of one's friends. When this was the case, study participants behaved in a manner contrary to the disposition effect: they held on to investments that made a profit and sold stocks whose price had fallen. Fox and Dayan (2004) explain these results by arguing that participants used their friends' results as a source of information on the future development of the investment.

A further limitation on the disposition effect can be observed among people who have been induced with a positive mood. In an experiment by Piñón and Gärling (2004), a photo was used to put one test group in a positive mood. A negative mood was induced in the other test group. Results showed that the group in a positive mood tended to ignore a stock's previous losses and sold it. The group in a negative mood held on to the losing stocks, acting according to the disposition effect.

7.4 Heuristics

In certain situations, laypeople and experts alike make decisions on the basis of heuristics. This includes decision-making situations when time is rare, when the information is highly complex, or when there is little motivation to take all relevant pieces of information into account. There are hardly any industries in which information is more complex or the time pressure for decision-making greater than on the financial market. Thus, it is hardly surprising that traders on international financial markets also apply heuristics. Since most heuristics have already been described in Chapter 2, only examples of their application to the financial market will be presented here.

7.4.1 Representativeness Heuristic and Anchoring and Adjustment Heuristic

The representativeness heuristic, on the one hand, involves base rates being neglected – the 'baseline fallacy'. On the other hand, it involves logical violations known as the 'conjunction fallacy'. Oberlechner (2004) conducted a study with a European sample in which both foreign exchange market traders and financial journalists were to sort the following statements according to their probability of occurrence:

(a) The US dollar will rise compared to the German mark.
(b) The Swiss franc will be stronger in December than in July.
(c) The US dollar will rise compared to the German mark and the Swiss franc will be stronger in December than in July.
(d) The US dollar will rise compared to the German mark or the Swiss franc will be stronger in December than in July.

A total of 75% of the foreign exchange market traders surveyed regarded the composite and thus more detailed Statement (c) as particularly likely. The same error was found among 74% of financial journalists. These results show that even foreign exchange market traders and financial journalists ignore essential characteristics of statistical reasoning. The probability that a single event will occur, as in Statement (a) or Statement (b), is necessarily higher than the probability of an event that is defined as the combination (i.e., conjunction) of two individual events in Statement (c).

Research on judgments and decision-making has repeatedly shown the anchoring and adjustment effect to be particularly relevant (Tversky & Kahneman, 1974). When people are asked to make numerical judgments, they tend to use them as a basis for subsequent prognoses, regardless of whether or not the two figures have any substantive connections to one another. When people calculate a number or are given a predefined one, they base subsequent judgments or estimates on this value. The calculated or predefined number serves as an anchor.

Which anchors play a role in financial markets? Baker and Nofsinger (2002) summarised various studies on this topic. Decision-makers on financial markets typically make judgments by proceeding from a given reference point. Benartzi and Thaler (1995) postulated that the selection of a reference point is unconscious in most cases, and is crucial in determining whether an investor considers the transaction a loss or a gain. When stocks were bought not too long ago, their purchase price represents an important point of reference. A further reference point is the highest price that an investor would have been able to receive for the stocks in the past. Heath, Huddart and Lang (1999) investigated reference points in exercising the stock options that company employees received as part of their salary. Stock options refer to the right to buy or sell a certain stock at a later point at an agreed-upon price. At some point, employees could decide to exercise their options and sell the stock, which meant that they would receive the difference between the current price and the base price. The authors found that the highest price of the stock in the past year was the most commonly applied reference point. An analysis of data from more than 50,000 employees in seven companies revealed that the exercise of stock options doubled when the price of the stock exceeded the 52-week high at the time of the potential sale. The highest price achieved in the past was considered a reference point in determining whether exercising stock options at the present time should be considered a gain or a loss.

High starting values are not always necessary for high final values. Ku, Galinsky and Murnighan (2006) reported an opposite effect to the anchoring effect, which they called the '**starting low but ending high effect**'. In auctions, low starting prices can lead to high final prices. The effect described by Ku et al. (2006) could be the reason why stocks issued at low values usually reach high closing values at the end of their first day of trading. Three fundamental processes appear to be responsible for the effect. First, low starting prices encourage participation in auctions and stock purchasing, as the barriers to entry are reduced. However, prices tend to rise as more people participate in an auction or a market. Second, low starting prices entice bidders to invest time and energy in the auction or market. These investments, in turn, represent sunk costs, which make it more difficult for participants to withdraw. Finally, brisk participation might lead bidders to conclude that particularly valuable goods are at stake, which makes them willing to pay a higher price. In reality, the outcomes of auctions for Persian rugs and photo cameras on eBay do support the assumptions of Ku et al. (2006). The starting price, final price and progression of each auction were recorded and analysed. Auctions with lower starting prices saw higher participation and were more likely to result in a transaction and in high final prices than auctions with higher starting prices.

7.4.2 Recognition Heuristic

A further heuristic is the recognition heuristic, as already described in Chapter 2. An experiment by Borges, Goldstein, Ortmann and Gigerenzer (1999) applied the recognition heuristic to the financial market. The authors sought to answer the question of whether the price development of stock portfolios compiled on the basis of the recognition heuristic could compete with stock market investment funds created by experts. The recognition heuristic can be applied by laypeople who have partial but not complete knowledge of companies in the stock market. German and American study participants were asked to indicate which of 798 companies listed on the New York Stock Exchange or on German stock exchanges were familiar to them. Four groups of people were investigated: American and German laypeople versus American and German experts. Laypeople were passers-by in Chicago and Munich; experts were economics and finance students at the universities of Chicago and Munich. The groups of American and German laypeople were both unanimously familiar with a total of eight companies. There were twenty-one companies known to all of the American experts; sixteen companies were known to all of the German experts. American participants were primarily familiar with American companies, while German participants were largely familiar with German firms. In order to test the recognition heuristic, two investment portfolios were subsequently generated for each of the four samples. One of the portfolios contained stocks from well-known companies in the group's own country of origin ('domestic recognition'; the portfolio consisted of stocks of companies that more than 90% of participants had indicated that they were familiar with). The other contained stocks of the ten most well-known companies from the other country ('international recognition'). A total of eight portfolios were assembled: stocks of well-known companies from the group's own country as well as the foreign country for American and German laypeople and experts. Next, each portfolio's development was monitored over a period of six months and compared to the price developments of the following sets of stocks, investment funds and indices:

(a) portfolios consisting of stocks of unknown companies (companies that were familiar to fewer than ten members of each sample were categorised as unknown)
(b) market indices (the DAX 30 index for German companies and the Dow Jones 30 index for American companies)
(c) investment funds (the Hypobank Investment Capital Fund for German companies and the Fidelity Blue Chip Growth Fund for American companies)
(d) random selection (average performance of 5,000 randomly selected portfolios).

The results were surprising. The stock portfolios of domestic companies selected using the recognition heuristic earned consistently better returns than those containing stocks of less well-known companies or stocks selected randomly. In the German samples, the recognition portfolios achieved the highest returns; in the American samples, their returns were somewhat lower than conventional market indices and investment funds' returns. The fact that the domestic recognition portfolios of American laypeople and experts yielded lower profits than the market indices and investment funds may stem from the fact that Americans already knew 'too much' about companies listed on the stock exchange. The recognition heuristic was also confirmed in the 'international recognition' condition. In both the American and the German samples, recognition portfolios achieved the highest returns with stocks of well-known companies from the respective foreign country. A potential explanation for the success of the recognition heuristics is that market share and profitability are often connected, and market share also contributes to a company name being more well known. As a caveat, the authors noted that the study was conducted at a time in which stock markets were rising in general. It is unclear whether the same results would arise when stock markets are generally moving sideways or downward.

7.4.3 Heuristic Risk Diversification

People who are interested in investing their assets will probably make a selection from various alternatives in the form of stocks and other securities. Diversification appears to be a good strategy for reducing risk. If, for example, the value of one stock falls, only a part of the invested money has been lost. Risk is a given due to the volatility of profits from stocks. When stocks' volatility is high, it is possible to earn large profits; however, there is also a great danger of incurring a loss. An optimal portfolio should promise high returns with a fixed level of risk (Markowitz, 1959). For this reason, it is important to assess the risk of stocks and to own various types of securities whose price developments are not correlated with one another.

However, many investors diversify without giving it too much thought. Achieving an optimal distribution of risk requires adequate processing of complex information. However, there is a limit to how much information people can absorb and process. Instead, decision-making rules are applied in order to come to a result quickly. When in doubt, and given the choice of distributing their money across various forms of investments, investors tend to distribute their assets equally among all available alternatives. This represents a solution that is simple and easy to calculate, but not necessarily the most profitable one. Benartzi and Thaler (2001) were able to prove that laypeople do distribute their assets equally among several options. Given the opportunity to invest one's assets in relatively riskless bonds and in more risky stocks, people often buy one with half of their assets and the other with the other half. This approach is called the **1/n heuristic** and is based on naive diversification. Investors believe that it will minimise their risk; however, they often do not pay attention to the risks of each individual security and the correlations between their price developments.

Insufficient diversification also exists with regard to stocks of domestic and international companies. French and Poterba (1991) were able to demonstrate a '**home bias**' among investors, which was also more recently corroborated by Ke, Ng and Wang (2009): for the most part, investors select stocks from their own country. In doing so, they ignore the fact that the values of these stocks correlate more closely with one another than do the values of stocks from different countries. Kroll, Levy and Rapoport (1988) were able to show that laypeople typically completely disregard the correlation among stocks. In an experiment by Hedesström, Svedsäter and Gärling (2007), laypeople were able to diversify more effectively when the significance of the correlation between stocks was pointed out to them.

On the stock market, optimal diversification and therefore distribution of risk seldom occurs. People also seem to have problems with optimal diversification in other areas of life. Sometimes they strive for diversification, but not in ways that maximise satisfaction. People tend towards variation when they have several options for nourishment, structuring their free time, etc. at their disposal. However, in their prognoses, they tend to assume that they prefer a much higher degree of variation than they actually do. Simonson (1990) let study participants choose from a selection of sweets. One group was allowed to choose at the beginning the sweets they would like to have during the entire study period (simultaneous choice), while another group made a selection each week (sequential choice). When choices were made simultaneously, a significantly greater variety of sweets was selected than was the case with sequential choice. Read and Loewenstein (1995) suspect that the tendency towards diversification exists to stave off potential saturation. However, people frequently underestimate the time lapses between consumption events and overestimate the saturation effect. Moreover, during a simultaneous choice, decision-makers use their current wants and needs and the current situation as a starting point. With sequential decisions, each choice is embedded in a different situational context. In each decision-making situation, people choose the option that they currently prefer, and different preferences can arise in different situations. Satisfaction with the chosen alternatives was also higher in the experimental condition of sequential choice than in the simultaneous choice condition.

7.5 Emotions

Discussions of 'the psychology of the exchange' are frequently centred on emotions that shape market happenings. Media reports often ascribe feelings to the financial market itself by way of illustration: on some days, an euphoric exchange is spoken of, while on other days the exchange is described as ill-humoured or depressed. However, emotions do not necessarily need to be seen as adversarial to rationality. In interviews with stock traders, Mayall (2010) found that feelings were an integral part of their deliberations and actions. Their emotional connection to analytical instruments, such as chart analyses, gave them security and a feeling of control. They tended to cling to trusted instruments and made intuitive decisions, even when this reduced their profits. A sense of security and trust in analytical techniques is critical on the stock market if one wants to be able to make decisions at all in the dense jungle of information.

Moods and emotions can influence decision-making in several ways (see, e.g., Loewenstein, Weber, Hsee & Welch, 2001; Peters, Västfjäll, Gärling & Slovic, 2006). On the one hand, some emotions and moods are experienced at the time of decision-making but have no connection to the task at hand (**incidental affect**). On the other hand, some emotions and moods are directly linked to the decision itself (**integral affect**). They can occur in the form of either '**anticipated emotions**' concerning the consequences (e.g., delight, disappointment) or '**anticipatory emotions**' concerning the immediate visceral reactions to risk (e.g., dread, anxiety).

The influence of one's current mood – classified as positive or negative, intense or not intense – on decision-making has been well documented empirically (e.g., Isen, 2000). When in a good mood and in a state of low emotional arousal, people tend to make decisions after deliberating less intensely than when in an intense, negative mood. A positive mood leads to more surface-level thinking processes compared to a neutral or negative mood (Schwarz, 2001). When intensive information processing is necessary to make a good choice, this means that worse outcomes will be obtained when one is in a good mood. Au, Chan, Wang and Vertinsky (2003) had their study participants – who were put in a positive, neutral or negative mood using music – trade foreign currencies in an internet-based trading system. It turned out that participants in a neutral mood had the highest profits, while those in a positive mood were least successful.

Other studies have also explored the influence of potentially mood-inducing variables such as temperature, sunshine or rain (Dowling & Lucey, 2005; Nofsinger, 2005). For example, stock market returns were found to be lower on cloudy days (Saunders, 1993) and stock returns tend to rise on sunny days (Hirshleifer & Shumway, 2003). As already described, after Piñón and Gärling (2004) induced study participants with positive or negative moods, they found that the group in a positive mood ignored declines in value and sold losing securities, effectively disregarding the disposition effect. The group in a negative mood held on to the losing stocks.

The spectrum of anticipated feelings due to the outcome of a decision ranges from joy and pride to disappointment and regret. While a negative outcome evokes disappointment, a positive outcome will elicit feelings of regret when the corresponding alternative has not been chosen (Zeelenberg, 1999). Västfjäll et al. (2004) highlighted that anticipated feelings are also significant in decisions about participating in lotteries with opportunities for financial gain. When the chance of a profit rises, anticipated joy and pride gain in intensity, while anticipated regret and disappointment rise in cases where a loss becomes more probable. MacGregor, Slovic, Dreman and Berry (2000) instructed a group of students to describe industrial companies that were connected with positive or negative feelings (e.g., biotechnology, logistics). Some sectors elicited strong positive feelings, while others elicited negative feelings. Afterwards, the students were more willing to purchase stocks from companies associated with positive feelings. They also thought that these securities would exhibit better performance than those from the sectors perceived negatively. However, these expectations were not confirmed by stock market developments.

7.6 Social Influences

When investors increase their purchases of stocks from a specific company or specific sector, other investors can observe their behaviour, discuss it with others and perhaps conclude that these stocks will increase in value. Media outlets can report on specific industries or on increasing purchases of specific stocks, also leading to a situation where investors see good return prospects and buy the stock. The opinions of influential people such as former US Federal Reserve Chairman Alan Greenspan, known as 'opinion leaders', are often accepted at face value. '**Herd behaviour**' on the financial market refers to situations in which some investors buy specific stocks and others follow them. Sias (2004) defines herd behaviour as a tendency among investors to follow the behaviour of other investors blindly, as buying and selling stocks along with the crowd. Herd behaviour is a behavioural tendency towards conformity, which can arise even when the actual state of the facts does not give a good reason for the purchase or sale of a stock.

Schulz-Hardt et al. (2007) identify three kinds of social influence: influence via interpersonal communication and group processes, influence via media information, and influence by way of observing other investors' behaviour. Rumours can form and spread in conversations about the state of financial markets, and some investors will act in accordance with these rumours. Even when a piece of information is known to be untrustworthy, investors seem to give it just as much weight as reliable news (DiFonzo & Bordia, 1997). Price changes are communicated in the media, and attempts are often made to find explanations for them. Even when price changes are random, patterns and tendencies are often identified and described. When investors hear about reasons for price changes in the media, they may conclude that a given trend will hold at least temporarily. They then make decisions to buy and sell in accordance with this, strengthening the (alleged) trend. 'Swimming against the tide' takes effort, and should it turn out that one's unconventional behaviour led to a loss, one can expect to experience great disappointment and regret at having passed up a potential profit (Loomes & Sugden, 1982). As early as the middle of the twentieth century, Keynes (1936/1997) noted that it is less damaging to one's reputation to make conventional mistakes, that is, to make the same mistakes as many other people, than to unconventionally swim against the tide and possibly be proved wrong. According to Scharfstein and Stein (1990), unfavourable investments are less damaging to traders' reputation when many people made the same investments; for this reason, private information is often ignored in order to 'swim with the tide'.

The processes through which information is passed on and accepted are known as **information cascades**. Information cascades begin when investors ignore their private information and imitate others (Banerjee, 1992; Shiller, 2000). An illustration of this can be found in Schulz-Hardt et al. (2007; see also Anderson & Holt, 1997):

> Let's assume that 100 people hold Stock A. Out of this group, 49 people have a signal (= private information) that Stock A will fall, 1 person has a signal that it will rise, and 50 people have no signal at all with regard to Stock 1. For whatever reason (e.g., because he is impatient), the person with the signal that the price will rise is the first to make his decision, which is to buy further shares of Stock A, commensurate with his signal. This is observed by a person who has no signal. He deduces from the first person's behaviour that they probably have received a signal that the price will rise, and also decides to buy. A third person, who has a signal that the price will fall, is now conflicted. She has a signal to sell, but has observed two people who have bought. She knows that not everyone on the market has signals at their disposal. If she (correctly) assumes that every other person has a signal, she should realise that one of the two buyers has a signal to buy – which balances out her own signal. Thus, she decides to wait (just like everyone else with a sell signal). After two more people without a signal decide to buy, however, the same person calculates that there are now probably two people with a buy signal, and also decides to buy. In this way, a kind of self-reinforcing herd behaviour arises in which each person's decision to join the herd makes further entries more likely. This herd behaviour also

> leads to a 'bubble', an overly high stock price given that 49 out of 50 signals indicated that one should sell. (Schulz-Hardt et al., 2007, p. 211, our translation)

By definition, a **speculative bubble** refers to the difference between the market price of an investment and its fundamental value. This means that the book value of an asset at any given time can deviate sharply from the long-term price trend (Cornicello, 2003). Long-term price trends are determined by the discounted future expected profits and expected dividends of an investment. A speculative price bubble arises when the actual price of an investment moves away from its fundamental value and becomes much higher than objectively justifiable. Such deviations can also arise when fundamental values fall. The prices of assets can shoot up immensely and become inflated on the basis of objectively non-justifiable beliefs that their value will increase further in the future. Since these increases in value cannot go on forever, the bubble will burst at some point. However, the difficulty of distinguishing between a price bubble and an actual increase in the value of an investment also makes it hard to predict when a bubble will burst. When investors finally realise that prices are too high, massive, panicked selling of investments can occur, triggering extreme price crashes (Genze, 2006). One classic historical example of a speculative bubble was 'tulip mania' in Holland in the sixteenth and seventeenth centuries. Prices for tulips, even ordinary ones without exceptional patterns, reached absurd heights. At the peak of the bubble, some investors sold all of their belongings and invested the proceeds in tulip bulbs, hoping that they would further increase in value. However, the bubble burst: the market price had reached its peak, and the tulips that just recently were being bought and sold for thousands of dollars were suddenly worthless (Cornicello, 2003). A more recent example of speculative bubbles was the so-called 'dotcom bubble'. For purposes of illustration, the chart in Figure 7.4 depicts the index of the National Association of Securities Dealers Automated Quotation (NASDAQ), the NASDAQ 100. The stocks of the hundred largest technology companies in the United States by market capitalisation are listed on the NASDAQ 100. In May 2016, companies such as Apple, Google, Facebook, eBay and Microsoft were all included on the index. The chart shows a rapid increase in the price of stocks listed on the index from Fall 1998 to March 2000. This rapid rise was triggered by excessively high profit expectations, particularly for companies operating in the internet, mobile communications and computer sectors. Spurred by extremely positive media coverage, more and more investors jumped on the bandwagon and bought stocks. With a bit of luck, they thought, the value of their invested capital would double or even triple or quadruple in only a short amount of time. The speculative bubble reached its peak in March 2000, and then burst. The initial euphoria was followed by a downward trend that lasted for several years and did not end until summer 2002, when the index stood at less than 1,000 points. This downward trend was also overstated; market participants' panic that they would lose their money pushed prices down. The most recent financial crisis, which was first felt in 2007 but entered general consciousness in Fall 2008 with the bankruptcy of the American investment bank Lehman Brothers Inc., had its roots in investments in subprime mortgages. Credit to purchase real estate was extended to people who would not have received loans at typical market rates. This pushed up demand and prices for real estate, with the result that even more loans were given out in the belief that prices would continue rising forever. At some point, however, the mortgage debts became unpayable. As a result, a liquidity shortage posed major problems for many financial institutions, and stock prices crashed. The financial crisis spread from the USA to global financial markets and to the real economy due to the interdependence of the global financial system. This crash was surprising to

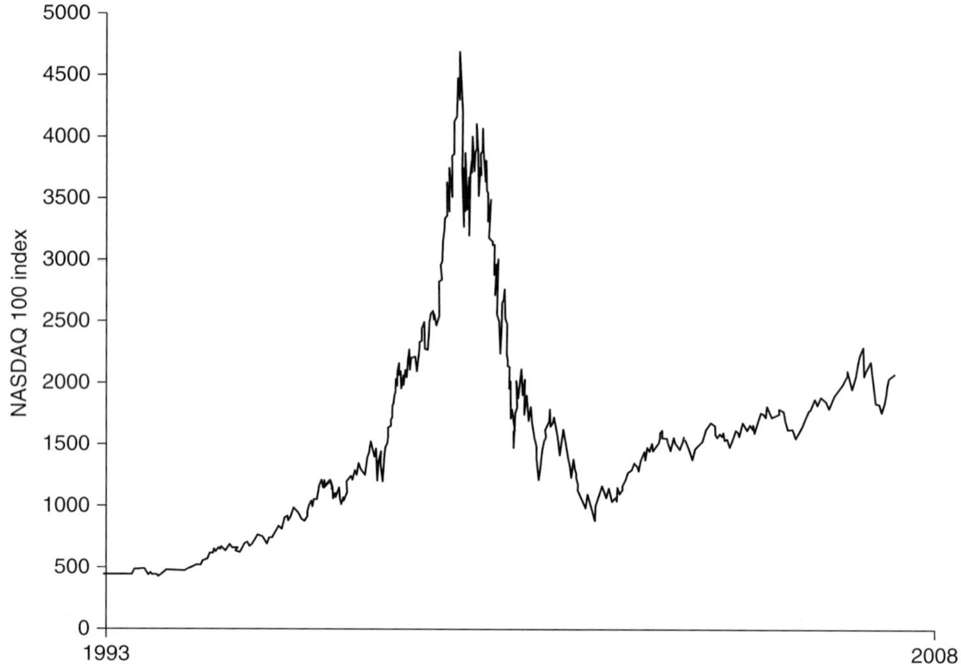

Figure 7.4 NASDAQ 100 index from 1993 to June 2008 (Montier, 2010, p. 759)

many economists, few of whom had been able to predict it (e.g., Shiller, 2000). Thaler and Sunstein (2008) hold a lack of self-control among investors, and particularly their susceptibility to social influences, responsible for the mortgage crisis. Analyses of the credit and financial crisis from a psychological perspective can be found in the second issue of the *Journal of Socio-Economics*, 2010 (e.g., Leiser & Rötheli, 2010; Lewis, 2010; Rötheli, 2010).

Given that studying speculative bubbles on real financial markets is possible only with great difficulty, the development of bubbles is frequently investigated under controlled conditions in experimental stock markets (Caginalp, Porter & Smith, 2000).

One proposed experimental design was developed by Smith, Suchanek and Williams (1988). At the beginning of their experiments, participants received a certain amount of money as well as stocks that could be traded over fifteen trading periods. Before each market period, the expected dividend of each stock was calculated and the results were shared with all participants. The stocks could be traded in auctions that were similar to an exchange. At the end, participants were paid the sum of all dividends, their starting capital and capital gains minus capital losses in the form of US dollars (Smith et al., 1988). According to rational expectations, prices should have developed in accordance with fundamental values. In reality, inexperienced traders produced long-lasting bubbles with high amplitudes, up to three times higher than the fundamental value of the stock. Prices almost always fell back to the fundamental value in the last market period. As market experience increased, price bubbles became less likely and prices moved more in accordance with fundamental values. Caginalp et al. (2000) summarised the results of more than 150 experiments in which inexperienced investors produced a speculative bubble relative to fundamental values but returned to fundamental values at the end of the trading periods. The authors reported that the formation of bubbles was reduced when participants were more experienced and/or more educated. University graduates in economics, with general knowledge about the economy as well as specific knowledge of game theory, but with little experience in experimental stock trading, kept their trading at prices close to the fundamental values.

The work of Averbeck (2010) focuses on speculative bubbles and the contributions of behavioural economics to understanding the development of stock prices. Various mechanisms have been made responsible for the development of speculative bubbles (Fenzl, 2009; Shiller, 2000; Wärneryd, 2001): financial contagion, mutual psychological contagion and psychological escalation. Financial contagion refers to the spread of speculative bubbles (and also crises) via physical cash flows in the international and global trade of goods. Mutual psychological contagion proceeds similarly to the way an infectious disease spreads by way of a virus. The 'virus' here refers to investors' emotions, attitudes and expectations. Investors develop hopes with regard to a stock, a company or an industry either via direct communication, indirectly by means by media information or by observing other investors. Some investors allow themselves to be infected by this information, increasing their demand for securities that promise high profits, while others are resistant and do not alter their trading behaviour. According to Fenzl (2009), psychological escalation can be compared to feedback on a microphone: an external trigger, such as a media report about the future success of a new technology or the curative power of a new drug, generates euphoria among investors. They seek to purchase the corresponding stock, which leads to an uptick in the price. This, in turn, results in renewed euphoria and even greater demand for the stock, leading to a massive escalation in prices.

Herd behaviour on financial markets implies that investors in the 'herd' allow themselves to be infected again and again. At times, it might be sensible to join the herd – for example, when everyone is trying to access their savings, and the proverbial last person who tries to withdraw their money from the bank discovers that it has gone bankrupt. Arguments for the '**wisdom of the crowd**' (Surowiecki, 2004) point to the statistical effect according to which, under the condition of independent random selection, an aggregate collective judgment is more accurate than individual judgments. In an experiment, Treynor (1987) had fifty-six people estimate how many beans were in a jar. The jar held 850 beans and the aggregate estimate amounted to 871 beans. Only one study participant provided a better estimate; the rest were outdone by the collective judgment.

Mistakes in judgment can certainly arise when investors in a complex market look for signals to help in decision-making situations but do not know all fundamental data and orient themselves on price developments or the behaviour of other investors (Andersson, Hedesström & Gärling, 2014).

The process of 'herding' is usually initialised by influential people, institutions and media outlets. Once the process has started, it can keep going in a manner similar to the snowball effects that lead to avalanches (Oberlechner, 2004). At the beginning of the herding process, there is a phase in which it is important for traders to position themselves correctly. When prices rise, it makes sense to buy stocks. In the opinion of many currency traders, it is better to follow a trend in the beginning rather than to run the risk of positioning oneself in opposition to the crowd. In the next phase, when prices have already risen (or fallen) and mass media continue to speak of enormous price gains, but the reports upon which they are based are not actual news, the point has been reached at which it is advisable to sell one's stocks. Professional traders become cautious at this point and start to offer their stocks up for sale. It is at this point that the market typically begins to correct course from its previous extremes.

7.7 Trust in Financial Institutions

Depositors' and investors' trust in banks and institutions is of critical importance to the financial market. Trust serves to reduce complexity in social interactions and in interactions with institutions that bear the risk of being hurt or exploited by another party. **Trust** is the acceptance of vulnerability to the actions of another party. Acceptance can originate from experience of benevolence of the other party in the past, and can be either reason-based or implicit. Mayer, Davis and Schoorman (1995, p. 712) defined trust as 'the expectation that the other party will perform a particular action important to the trustor, irrespectively of the ability to monitor or control the other party'.

Interestingly, trust cannot be viewed from a consequentialist perspective alone. Compelling evidence from trust games shows that interpersonal trust decisions are different from risky decisions (e.g., Eckel & Wilson, 2004; Fetchenhauer & Dunning, 2012) and that people trust others even though they hold rather cynical views about the likelihood that their interaction partner will prove trustworthy (Fetchenhauer & Dunning, 2010). Instead, trust also has other components that are more situated in the act of trusting itself. On the one hand, these are emotional components such as positive feelings when trusting and negative feelings when not. On the other hand, these are social components such as moral norms, in particular respect (Dunning, Anderson, Schlösser, Ehlebracht & Fetchenhauer, 2014; Dunning, Fetchenhauer & Schlösser, 2012).

A number of authors have suggested that trust can build on different sources and have distinguished between reason-based and implicit trust. Kirchler and Gangl (2015) highlighted that:

> reason-based trust origins from (a) the perception to depend on another party to achieve a specific goal, (b) the trustor's evaluation of the trustee's willingness and ability to achieve the specific goal, that is, the trustee's motivation and competence as well as benevolence in taking actions which are not to the disadvantage of the trustor. Additionally, situational conditions such as specific opportunities or hindrances to achieve the goal are evaluated. Based on reflective processes the trustor decides whether or not to trust the other party. In contrast, implicit trust results from automatic and unintentional processes and is based on the perception of similarity between the trustor and trustee, shared social identity, and shared values (Castelfranchi & Falcone, 2010). (Kirchler & Gangl, 2015, p. 442)

Both reason-based trust and implicit trust are relevant for financial institutions. While trust can easily be destroyed, establishing or re-establishing trust is difficult. How can trust be built, and how can it be restored following a case in which trust is lost? Gärling, Kirchler, Lewis and van Raaij (2009) identified seven criteria upon which trust in financial institutions is based and which can serve to build, maintain and restore trust:

- Actors' competence is of significance. Representatives of financial institutions and banks active on the financial market need to have a sound factual grasp of financial products and be able to accurately convey this information to their clients. Knowledge of their clients' risk appetite and desire for security is also part of actors' competence. Actors need to provide honest information about risks and the potential for both profits and losses. When financial products are so complex that even experts have difficulty evaluating them, it is not to be expected that customers will be able to accurately assess the risks of their investments.
- Integrity means that all clients are advised honestly and with care, and that actors' behaviour is genuine. Institutions need to not only develop a code of honour for their work, but also adhere to

it and allow it to guide their behaviour. For institutions active in the sector, integrity can be assured via the imposition and monitoring of adherence to an honour code or via political authorities.

- Transparency refers to openness as well as the use of clear terminology and language clients can understand. Transparency also means that rules and procedures are communicated and that clients are informed about rates of return and fees for the financial institution's services as well as how changes in the wider economy will affect their costs.
- Benevolence on the part of financial institutions means that representatives of these institutions are able to view things from their clients' perspective. They should consider their clients' interests rather than only looking out for their own self-interest. Long-term client relationships and loyalty are more important than and more profitable in the long run than the short-time maximisation of profits. It is also important that clients are notified about changes to the market, so that they can find out when it would be beneficial to alter the positioning of their assets in accordance with the latest considerations.
- **Value congruence** refers to a fit between the values held by financial institutions and their clients. The norms and values of all parties in the interaction should be congruent. Congruence is a necessary precondition for building clients' identification with their financial institution as well as for client retention. Financial institutions interested in investing in ecologically sustainable projects and ethically sound industries – that do not invest in the war industry or in companies that do not shy away from child labour, despite the prospect of lucrative returns – are attracting more and more clients with similar values.
- Stability for financial institutions and insurance companies means that they work to ensure continuous and long-term returns. A sustainable business model is based on the assumption that the interests of stakeholders come before the interests of shareholders, rather than on trying to maximise short-term profits for the companies' stockholders. Thus, it needs to be ensured that interest groups across the board are taken into account and that the sustainability of the company's activities is considered a matter of prime importance. Many investments are the result of long-term planning, and pension insurance is taken out in order to provide financial security in one's old age. For this reason, it needs to be ensured that the institutions entrusted with these investments are able to keep their 'promises' through professional, competent work.
- Finally, reputation refers to a financial institution's positive image, which is critical for trust. Previous achievements and the communication of these achievements as well as a financial institution's values form the basis of its reputation. Positive associations with a financial institution's 'brand' and corresponding marketing activities top off this 'catalogue' of requirements for trust in financial institutions.

Conclusion

Making the right decision in a financial market is a truly difficult task. First, the exact value of a security is often unknowable, making way for far more ambiguity and uncertainty than an investment in future developments already has. Secondly, traders do not only act on behalf of conclusions of rational thinking but use heuristics as well. While heuristics certainly speed up the process of finding a decision, this decision may not be the best. Furthermore, traders are prone to certain fallacies and base their decisions on factors they clearly should not – for example the date in the calendar, their emotional state, the fact whether they recently made a profit or not and general non-economic events. They over- and under-react to news, sell profitable securities too early and keep bad ones too long. This is especially the case in market environments with high uncertainty and negative outlook. Traders watch influential people and the media and follow them, sometimes even blindly so. As a result, successful traders need to be well informed and restrain themselves with discipline. Both education and experience have a positive effect on the success in financial markets. Considering the growing importance of private retirement provision, it becomes clear that not only financial literacy itself, but also the knowledge about how to make good financial decisions, avoiding fallacies and pitfalls, should be a major educational goal of societies.

Summary

- Prices do not always behave according to the efficient markets hypothesis, and do not vary completely randomly. They show some systematic deviations and both market volume and volatility are often higher than expected.
- Traders and investors do not behave in a purely rational way, due to judgment errors, self-deception, heuristic simplifications, emotions and social interaction. They over-react and under-react to news and even non-economic events can have a strong effect on stock markets.
- Investors hold on to losing stocks for too long and sell winning stocks too quickly. This effect is known as the disposition effect. Several moderating variables (e.g., intelligence and experience) were identified.
- Heuristics influence decisions of investors. Besides the representativeness heuristic and the anchoring and adjustment heuristic, the recognition heuristic was also studied in stock market contexts.
- Heuristic diversification can become problematic when investors split their portfolio inadequately or when they favour domestic companies.
- Mood and emotions influence investment decisions. Positive mood can lead to more surface-level thinking.
- The opinions of influential people are often accepted as true. This contributes to 'herd behaviour' when some investors buy specific stocks and others follow them.
- Speculative bubbles develop by mechanisms of financial contagion, mutual psychological contagion and psychological escalation. The basis of the latter two are the emotional responses of investors and self-reinforcing feedback loops.
- Discipline, concentration on the issue at hand and appropriate meaning-making are characteristics relevant to a trader's success. Albeit, there are severe mistakes a trader can make, summarised as the seven deadly sins – for example overconfidence in one's forecasts, labelled as pride.
- Trust in financial institutions is based on the perceived competence, integrity, transparency, benevolence, value congruence, stability and reputation.

Questions

1. What is the 'disposition effect' and how can it be explained?
2. What role does the 'house money effect' play in financial markets?
3. What are the common heuristic simplifications that investors use for decision-making?
4. How will investors evaluate the performance of a security that elicits strong positive feelings?
5. What is 'value congruence' in the context of trust in institutions and banks?

FURTHER READING

Gärling, T., Kirchler, E., Lewis, A., & van Raaij, W. F. (2009). Psychology, financial decision making, and financial crises. *Psychological Science in the Public Interest, 10*, 1–47.

Montier, J. (2003). *Behavioral finance: Insights into irrational minds and markets*. New York: Wiley.

Shiller, R. J. (2015). *Irrational exuberance* (3rd revised edn). Princeton, NJ: Princeton University Press.

Shleifer, A. (2000). *Inefficient markets: An introduction to behavioral finance*. Oxford: Oxford University Press.

Wärneryd, K.-E. (2001). *Stock-market psychology: How people value and trade stocks*. Cheltenham: Edward Elgar.

8 Collective Cooperation: Shadow Economy and Tax Paying

Overview

In the official economy, economic success is achieved within the framework of regulatory laws. Labour and capital income, consumption, etc. are taxed to provide public goods, to balance income differences in the society, and to regulate the behaviour of individuals and firms. However, money is also made in the shadows of the official economy, and some citizens do not pay taxes as prescribed by law.

This chapter starts out with a discussion of the shadow economy. In the narrowest sense, the shadow economy comprises work on the black market and the exchange of goods there. In a broader sense, housework and helping one's neighbours also count – as do illegal activities like drug dealing, smuggling and dealing in stolen goods. In general, those activities are discussed that would otherwise be included in official calculations of the gross national product, but are concealed through the circumvention of regulations and the evasion of social contributions in general, and of taxes in particular.

One particular problem analysed by economic psychology concerns the willingness to pay taxes and fees. This can be partly described through attitudes towards taxes and tax morale. However, taxpayer behaviour can range from deliberate tax evasion to voluntary cooperation and needs to be examined more closely. Different actors can be distinguished in the field of taxation (government, tax authorities, tax accountants, taxpayers) and they interact in complex ways. Various research methods are applied in studying taxpayer behaviour and these sometimes produce inconsistent findings.

Taxpaying can be researched within different paradigms. There has been a shift from investigations of the effect of tax authorities' enforcement on taxpayer compliance towards investigations of trust-building measures that encourage cooperation for the welfare of the community. Perspectives range from the effectiveness of audits and fines, social norms and fairness considerations in social contribution dilemmas and the 'psychological contract' to the interactional climate where actors mutually influence each other. Over the past few decades, the predominant view of taxpayers has shifted from an authoritarian perspective, where authorities compel citizens to pay their taxes, to a view where authorities are encouraged to provide the necessary services to promote compliance, and, more recently, to a view where authorities and citizens cooperate with one another. The slippery slope framework is presented as a theoretical concept, integrating economic and psychological approaches to compliance and cooperation. Finally, some recommendations for developing and maintaining a climate of mutual cooperation are discussed.

Parts of this chapter have been taken from Kirchler, E. (2007). *The economic psychology of tax behaviour* Cambridge: Cambridge University Press and from Alm, J., Kirchler, E., and Muehlbacher, S. (2012).Combining psychology and economics in the analysis of compliance: From enforcement to cooperation. *Economic Analysis and Policy, 42* 133–51.

Introduction

Paying taxes is not fun. Yet it is necessary to finance many services provided by society – such as education, healthcare or public security. In addition to that, taxes can be a tool to incentivise desirable behaviour in a community. However, at best we think of paying taxes as a moral obligation and contribution to society. At worst, taxes feel like legal theft by the government. So, how should taxpayers be viewed by the tax authorities? As potential criminals who will try to increase their profits at the cost of the society? Or as partners willing to comply out of intrinsic motivation? We will investigate the reasons for carrying out one's business in the shadow economy, the nature of tax morale and determinants of tax compliance, as well as the environment in which authorities and taxpayers interact.

8.1 In the Shadow of the Official Economy

The officially calculated gross domestic product (GDP) is an indicator of the 'formal economy' and encompasses the total value of all goods and services sold on the market as well as public services (Skolka, 1985). Parallel to the formal economy, there are also informal and hidden sites of economic activity comprised of legal but also illegal enterprises. The shadow economy can be viewed in a broad sense and a narrow sense.

In the broad sense, the **shadow economy** is defined as 'those economic activities and the income derived from them that circumvent or avoid government regulation, taxation or observation' (Schneider, 2012, p. 3). Activities outside official statistics can be differentiated into the following categories:

(a) Services within private households and their values are not captured by macroeconomic figures, nor are they easily included in conventional statistical measures (Gershuny & Pahl, 1981). Not only does the private household fulfil economic functions, partners also provide each other with emotional refuge. As the household lost its economic functions, more space was opened up for privacy and intimacy within the family, which MacIver (1949, p. 154) expressed several decades ago with the often-quoted statement: 'As the family lost function after function, it found its own.' Despite this, household work represents an important yet largely undocumented economic measure. Adults in industrialised countries spend approximately just as much time providing services to themselves, chiefly within the household, as they spend at their official jobs. According to Oakley (1980), approximately 40% of production in (British) society as a whole takes place within the household. Typical housework, such as washing, cooking and cleaning, is for the most part performed by the members of the household themselves. Service providers on the market carry out the rest. Not only does housework represent an important economic variable, the gender role division that goes along with it has also made an important contribution to the development of the economy as a whole. Douglas and Isherwood (1979) argued that the division of labour within the household is a sensible strategy for propelling economic growth, particularly in less developed countries. Leaving aside questions of justice, oppression and emancipation, while it is true that this gender role division forces one person to perform menial, repetitive domestic work, it also provides the other person with the opportunity to specialise and to concentrate on socially recognised work outside the home. The unbalanced division of household labour and childcare between the genders and the resulting dependence, usually of women on men, is a frequent subject of political discussions. It is also a topic of investigation within the social sciences, where it is characterised as unjust. Women take on the bulk of household work and are responsible for childcare. This changes only slightly when they also work outside the home. It is notable that women do not inevitably experience the unequal burden placed upon them at home as unjust. Whether women view the division of labour within the household as fair or unfair depends on whether they compare their responsibilities to those of their husband or to those of other women (Bodi, Mikula & Riederer, 2010; Kluwer & Mikula, 2002; Mikula, 2006; Mikula, Schoebi, Jagoditsch & Macher, 2009).

(b) Income from legal sources within alternative economies like agricultural and industrial communes is also not officially declared and can only be estimated.

(c) Parallel to the official economy, a unique 'service sector' is blooming without anyone taking notice: an economy of 'friends of friends'. Boissevain (1974) analysed complex networks of acquaintances and their 'economic' function. As an example, he reported the following story. A student from a small town in Sicily wants to write his dissertation on a certain topic, which could be supervised by a professor at the University of Palermo. According to the prevailing social norms, he cannot cold call this professor, but must find a way to be recommended to him. The student knows a lawyer from his hometown for whom he did a favour a while ago. The lawyer thus 'owes' the student a favour. The student knows that the lawyer has friends in Palermo and suspects that one of them might in turn know people who have friends at the University of Palermo. The student contacts the lawyer, politely refuses to accept a prefabricated dissertation that the lawyer pulls out of his desk drawer, and travels to Palermo with a letter of introduction for the lawyer's cousin that names him as the lawyer's best friend. The cousin, the secretary of an important local official in Palermo, refers him to a friend who knows people at the university. The cousin's friend then introduces the student to the professor's assistant. Finally, the assistant sets up an appointment with the professor, but he doesn't forget to mention that the professor will be a candidate in the upcoming elections in Sicily and needs volunteers for his campaign. After the professor has finally heard the dissertation proposal, the student mentions where he is from and that he worked for one of the candidates during the last election cycle. Full of interest, the professor asks whether it would be possible for the student to canvass for him in his hometown. He is now obviously interested in the dissertation topic as well and is ready to advise the student. The lawyer, who served as the 'communication agent' in the student's social network, made his circle of acquaintances available. He thereby returned the previous favour paid to him by the student and balanced the 'account of reciprocal claims and liabilities'. In order to preserve this network of mutual favours, it is important to have 'friends' who are indebted to one (Boissevain, 1974).

(d) Substantial amounts of income also arise from illegal businesses like drug dealing, prostitution and selling stolen goods, which do not appear in national account systems. The economy includes not only goods exchanged with money, but also 'trafficking in gifts', in stolen goods, etc. Businesses dealing with stolen goods are able not only to make money but also, as is the case with economic dealing among friends and acquaintances, build and maintain a 'unique' kind of social network. Henry (1978, p. 84) argued, 'Exchanges are managed so that the accounts are kept unbalanced, with one party always in credit and the other always in debt. In this way there is always a need to continue with the relationship.' Debt and credit accounts can remain out of balance over long periods of time and might even persist over generations, creating particular dependencies among 'special friends', as anthropological studies of the mafia indicate (Boissevain, 1974).

In a narrow sense, the shadow economy consists of the market-based legal production of goods and services that is deliberately concealed from public authorities for the following reasons:

(a) to avoid payment of income, value added or other taxes
(b) to avoid payment of social security contributions
(c) to avoid compliance with certain legal labour market standards, such as minimum wages, maximum working hours, safety standards, etc., and
(d) to avoid compliance with certain administrative obligations, such as completing statistical questionnaires or other administrative forms (Schneider, 2012, p. 3).

Illegal activity is excluded from this narrow definition of the shadow economy. However, illegal operations, especially white-collar crime, ought to be assigned great importance. Braithwaite (2008) described white-collar crime as illegal and prosecutable behaviour by organisations or their members. Criminal offences are considered white-collar crimes when they are committed as part of actual or sham business activities, and do not just result in injury to a given individual but rather interfere with economic life in the community as a whole. These include, for example, misrepresentations in corporation documents, bankruptcy fraud, false accounting, embezzlement, fraud, product piracy, bribery, corruption, computer crimes, insider trading, subsidy fraud, money laundering and tax evasion. These illegal activities are used not primarily to enrich individuals but rather to serve the goals of organisations. Driven by greed and the desire for profit, firms commit white-collar crimes to cut costs and maintain a black market, thus harming their competitors. The auditing firm PricewaterhouseCoopers conducted surveys with authorities responsible for preventing and investigating crimes in collaboration with a German university. Nearly half of companies worldwide were victims of white-collar crime between 2003 and 2005. Simpson (2002, p. 14) characterised white-collar crime as perhaps the 'most dangerous crime in the world'.

Although economic transgressions are certainly viewed as criminal in the society as a whole, in the business world smaller offences are commonly written off as minor infractions (Kirchler & Pitters, 2007). Black market labour and tax evasion, especially, are seen as petty offences. According to Schneider (2007), even expert opinions on the problem posed by black market labour vary. On the one hand, black market labour is considered at least partially responsible for economic problems like rising public debt, and the growing deficits of social insurance systems. On the other hand, it is argued that black market labour allows individuals to create an area free from the paternalism imposed by the government, giving them the opportunity to 'conduct their economic activities in peace'. Schneider (2007) argued that at least part of economic prosperity stems from the underground economy, and that the bulk of the funds generated there flow back into the official economy.

More or less exact numbers exist concerning the productivity of the official economy; no reliable data, however, exists on the various areas of economic activity in the shadow of the official economy (Schneider, 2012; Weck, Pommerehne & Frey, 1984). If participants seek to conceal their dealings, how can the magnitude of the underground economy be measured? Schneider (2003, 2012) and Schneider and Klinglmair (2004) claim that only estimates can be provided, but the validity of estimation models is highly controversial (Feige, 2016). Schneider (2012) made a fundamental distinction between:

(a) direct procedures at the micro-level (e.g., surveys) for measuring the magnitude of the shadow economy at a specific point in time,
(b) indirect methods that seek to identify micro-level indicators of developments in the shadow economy over time, and

(c) modelling approaches that attempt to discern the size of the shadow economy, considering it as an 'unobservable' variable in statistical estimation procedures.

Weck et al. (1984) likewise made a distinction between direct and indirect methods of estimation. Direct methods include audits from tax authorities and other institutions with sanctioning power as well as interviews and written surveys based on voluntary participation and more or less reliable statements from respondents. Since the shadow economy leaves 'traces' in various officially accessible areas of economic activity, indirect estimation methods can also be applied. For example, differences between household revenue and expenses can be interpreted as indicators of underground economic activity. When statistical bureaus determine the official national product, they can collect data on expenditures for products and services, and can gain information on household incomes. The size of the difference can serve as an estimate for the amount of black market labour. Another estimation procedure is based on official employment figures. When official numbers show a drop in employment, but the population's actual amount of time spent at work remains constant, it can be inferred that more income is being hidden. Finally, changes in cash circulation can be investigated. Since cash payments are customary in the underground economy and this typically incolves a circulation of large bills, an increase in the amount of cash could also be an indication of hidden activity.

Schneider (2012) estimated the magnitude of the shadow economy as a percentage of the official GDP in various countries on the basis of a simulation model (MIMIC). Table 8.1 shows estimates for the years 2005 to 2015 (Schneider, 2015; Schneider & Buehn, 2013).

Just as it is difficult to measure the shadow economy, it is also difficult to ascertain its root causes. Weck et al. (1984) posited that the size of the shadow economy increases when the taxation rate rises, but the probability of audits and the severity of penalties decrease. Black market labour and the tax evasion that goes along with it are primarily correlated with moral attitudes towards paying taxes, known as tax morale. Torgler (2007) defined **tax morale** as an intrinsic motivation arising from the moral obligation to pay taxes correctly. Figure 8.1 shows the correlation between the magnitude of the shadow economy and the predominant tax morale for fifteen European countries and the United States. When tax morale is highly developed in a given country, the black market for labour is smaller (Alm & Torgler, 2006) and cooperation with the authorities is more common (Frey & Torgler, 2007; see also Torgler & Schneider, 2009).

8.2 Taxes and Contributions

The relationship between the individual, the society and the state is a particularly important field of research within economic psychology. Questions arise with respect to the acceptability of contributions to local and state authorities and to the legitimacy of tax collection (which is commonly taken for granted). In addition, questions regarding taxpayers' behaviour and the establishment and management of public goods, community facilities and resources like water, air and energy are discussed.

The state can only fulfil its responsibility to serve its citizens when it has economic resources. Fulfilling these responsibilities creates costs. The resources to cover these costs are secured through public sources of revenue based on the state's authority to raise financial contributions from its citizens, revenue obtained from the private sector in exchange for services rendered, revenue from bonds sold on financial markets at home and abroad, and other miscellaneous revenue streams. In addition to fees, duties and tariffs, taxes are also included among these contributions. Taxes are fees

Table 8.1 Size of the shadow economy as a percentage of official GDP in thirty-five countries in the years 2000, 2005, 2010 and 2015 (adapted from Schneider & Buehn, 2013, p. 18, for the year 2000 and from Schneider, 2015, for the following years)

Countries	2000	2005	2010	2015
1. Australia	14.30	10.30	8.20	8.20
2. Austria	9.80	12.60	10.30	10.30
3. Belgium	22.20	20.10	17.40	16.20
4. Bulgaria	36.90	34.40	32.60	30.60
5. Canada	16.00	14.30	12.20	10.30
6. Czech Rep.	19.10	18.50	16.70	15.10
7. Denmark	18.00	16.50	14.00	12.00
8. Estonia	25.60	30.20	29.30	26.20
9. Finland	18.10	16.60	14.00	12.40
10. France	15.20	13.80	11.30	12.30
11. Germany	16.00	15.40	13.90	12.20
12. Greece	28.70	27.60	25.40	22.40
13. Hungary	25.10	24.50	23.30	21.90
14. Ireland	15.90	14.80	13.00	11.30
15. Italy	27.10	24.40	21.80	20.60
16. Japan	11.20	10.30	9.20	8.40
17. Latvia	23.60	29.50	27.30	23.60
18. Lithuania	27.10	31.10	29.70	25.80
19. Luxembourg	9.80	9.90	8.40	8.30
20. Malta	27.10	26.90	26.00	24.30
21. Netherlands	13.10	12.00	10.00	9.00
22. New Zealand	12.80	11.70	9.60	8.00
23. Norway	19.10	17.60	15.10	13.00
24. Poland	27.60	27.10	25.40	23.30
25. Portugal	22.70	21.20	19.20	17.60
26. Romania	34.40	32.20	29.80	28.00
27. Slovakia	28.90	17.60	16.40	14.10
28. Slovenia	27.10	26.00	24.30	23.30
29. South-Cyprus	28.70	28.10	26.20	24.80
30. Spain	22.70	21.30	19.40	18.20
31. Sweden	19.20	17.50	15.00	13.20
32. Switzerland	8.60	9.00	8.10	6.50
33. Turkey	32.10	30.70	28.30	27.80
34. United Kingdom	12.70	12.00	10.70	9.40
35. United States	8.70	8.20	7.20	5.90

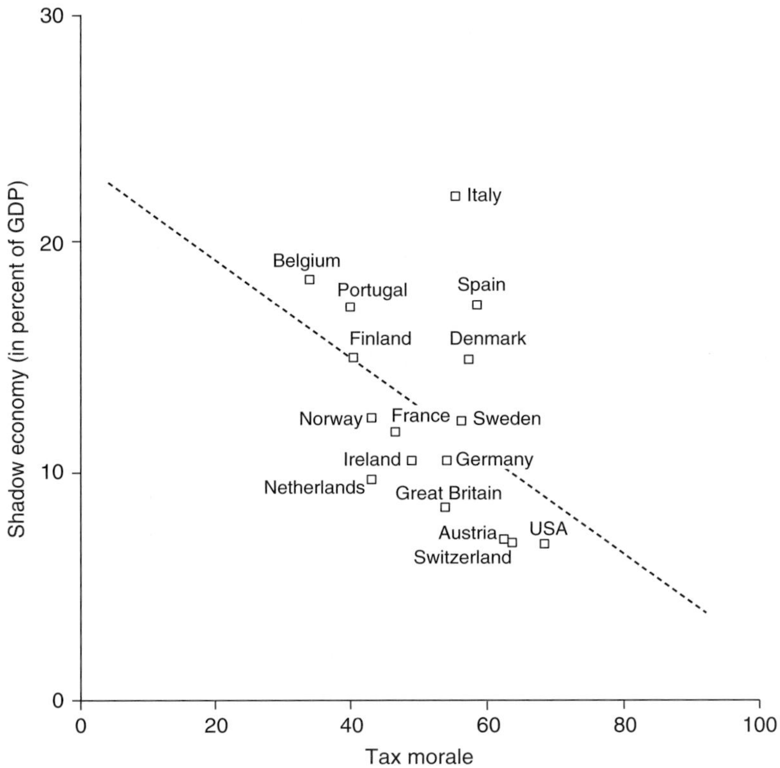

Figure 8.1 Correlation between the estimated shadow economy and tax morale (adapted from Alm & Torgler, 2006, p. 243)

that are imposed upon natural and legal persons by the public laws of the commonwealth. The payment of these fees is compulsory and does not entitle a person to any special services in return.

Revenues are not exclusively collected to fund public goods. Taxes, charges and levies also serve to regulate the behaviour of citizens and organisations, and to influence markets. For example, they are used as incentives for the consumption of healthy food and for environmentally friendly activities, or as disincentives against undesirable behaviour such as the excessive consumption of energy (Freiberg, 2010). Taxes are also applied as a policy instrument to redistribute wealth in society.

The state's body of financial laws regulates the levying of taxes, which includes the rights and responsibilities of taxation authorities and the distribution of tax revenues. In the ancient world, collecting fees to meet the financial requirements of the state was considered an extraordinary measure for times of emergency; it primarily affected social groups with low prestige. In ancient Rome, financial problems were offset by the spoils of war and by tribute payments from conquered peoples. In the Middle Ages, tax-like contributions on property holdings were calculated and duties collected. Complex systems of direct and indirect taxation were finally developed in the seventeenth century as part of the emergence of the money economy in England and France and later throughout the Western world. Typical direct taxes include income taxes, corporate taxes and wealth taxes. In contrast, value-added taxes, vehicle taxes and beverage taxes are indirect taxes. In the former case, the people from whom the tax is collected are the same people who are supposed to be paying the tax;

in the latter cause, taxes are collected from people who are not themselves required to pay the tax (Henrichsmeyer, Gans & Evers, 1982).

Various reasons are given to justify the collection of taxes: for one thing, emphasis is placed on the fact that public goods are made available through tax revenues, which serve the common good; for another thing, taxes regulate economic processes and level out an unfair distribution of resources (Henrichsmeyer et al., 1982). The field of public finance teaches that taxes are justified because

(a) private taxes equal the amount of services provided by the state (equivalence or interests theory),
(b) private tax payments are a fee collected for the public protection of one's property and person (insurance theory), and
(c) every citizen contributes to the fulfilment of community endeavours by making a sacrifice corresponding to his or her productive capacity, thus ensuring the existence and development of the state (sacrifice theory).

Taxes are necessary

(a) because certain deficiencies which emerge in a free market system in certain economic sectors can be remedied through taxation,
(b) because they can correct injustices in the distribution of resources between a society's richer and poorer members, and
(c) because they allow for at least the partial steering of economic activities and processes as a whole (Lea et al., 1987).

Levies and taxes on income, consumption, capital and property have sustained effects on consumer behaviour and the demand for labour. They serve as a governmental tool for the regulation of consumer and labour markets. In addition, taxes are considered a mechanism for levelling out differences in income and wealth that are perceived as unfair. With increasing international interconnectivity on both the economic and the political level, the effects of various taxation systems on national economic competitiveness are becoming increasingly important. In integrated economic areas, such as the European Union, the competitive disadvantages posed by taxes can be reduced through the harmonisation of tax systems. This means that income tax bases and rates are adjusted to match one another, and a net value-added tax is introduced in all member states.

What effects do taxes have on income and the demand for labour? Does the reduction in income represented by levies and taxes boost motivation, with people working more hours and more intensively in order to compensate for the lost income? Or do workers react to this reduction in income with frustration and resignation? When the tax burden is too high, taxpayers may indulge themselves with more leisure time than they did in the past because the rewards of work are lower. Sweden provides an example of high tax pressure and its unintended effects, as during the 1970s and 1980s the government imposed the industrialised world's most steeply progressive income tax schedule. The marginal tax rates for several broad categories of employees reached 80 to 90%. The strain of high taxes led to high levels of tax avoidance and a lack of interest in working more to increase one's income (Agnell & Persson, 2000). The idea that too high a tax rate can lead to a reduction in productivity is expressed in the so-called Laffer curve. The Laffer curve – showing the relationship between tax rates and tax revenue collected by the government – suggests that, as tax rates increase from low levels, the tax revenue collected by the government also increases. However, it also shows that increases in tax rates beyond a certain point might cause people to work less or not at all, thus leading to a reduction in tax revenue. Garboua, Masclet and Montmarquette (2009) experimentally tested whether people's work habits change with increases in their tax burden. They found that a tax rate of more than about 50% is considered unfair and causes a drop in productivity.

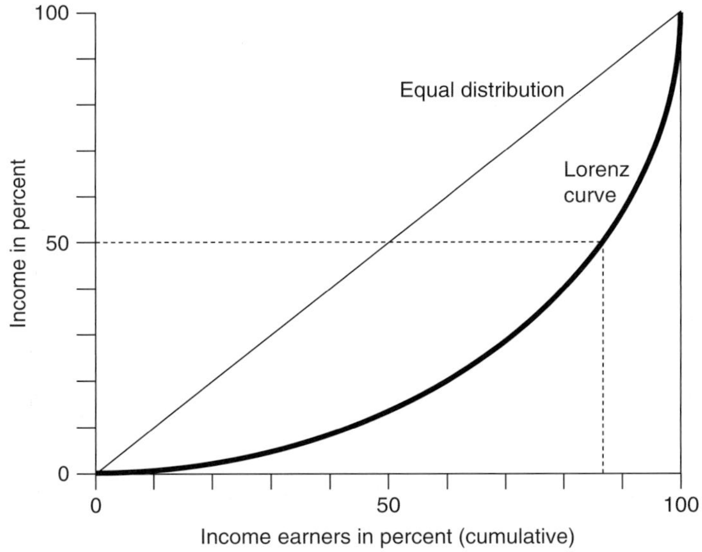

Figure 8.2 Example of a Lorenz curve

Swenson (1988), Sillamaa (1999) and Sutter and Weck-Hannemann (2003) reported similar results. However, changes in income might affect work behaviour of men and women differently: women work more when their own income rises and less when the income of their husband rises. Tax increases seem to increase the amount of work men do outside the home, while leading to decreases in paid work among women; women then do more household work, receiving less help from men (Aschenfelter & Heckman, 1974; Leuthold, 1983; James, 1992). Nevertheless, survey studies have established that, although respondents are aware of changes in the tax rate, their willingness to work largely depends upon factors other than the reduction in income represented by tax increases (Calderwood & Webley, 1992; Lea et al., 1987; Wiswede, 1991).

How effective are taxes and social contributions in regulating disparities in income and wealth? One method of determining the distribution of income and wealth was developed by the American statistician Max O. Lorenz, and is known as the Lorenz curve (Woll, 1981). The **Lorenz curve** shows the distribution of income within a country. It consists of a series of points reflecting the relation between the cumulative percentage of the population (x-axis) and the cumulative percentage of the population's total income. The Lorenz curve demonstrates to what extent the total income of a society is allotted to a specific proportion of the population. In a society with a perfectly equal income distribution, the curve would form a diagonal line. The more unequal a society's income distribution, the more the Lorenz curve deviates from the diagonal. This discrepancy can form the basis of a strategic restructuring of tax law with the goal of decreasing income disparities through targeted taxation. Figure 8.2 shows an example of a Lorenz curve for a fictional society. In this example, about 87% of income earners receive 50% of the total income; conversely, about 13% of income earners receive the other 50% of the population's total income.

The area between the diagonal line (equal distribution) and the Lorenz curve, relative to the total area under the diagonal, represents the extent to which the distribution is unequal. This measure, known as the **Gini coefficient**, measures the degree of concentration in a country's income distribution. The Gini coefficient provides a summary measure of income inequality using a scale from 0 to 1, where 0 represents perfect equality, indicating that everyone has the same income, and 1

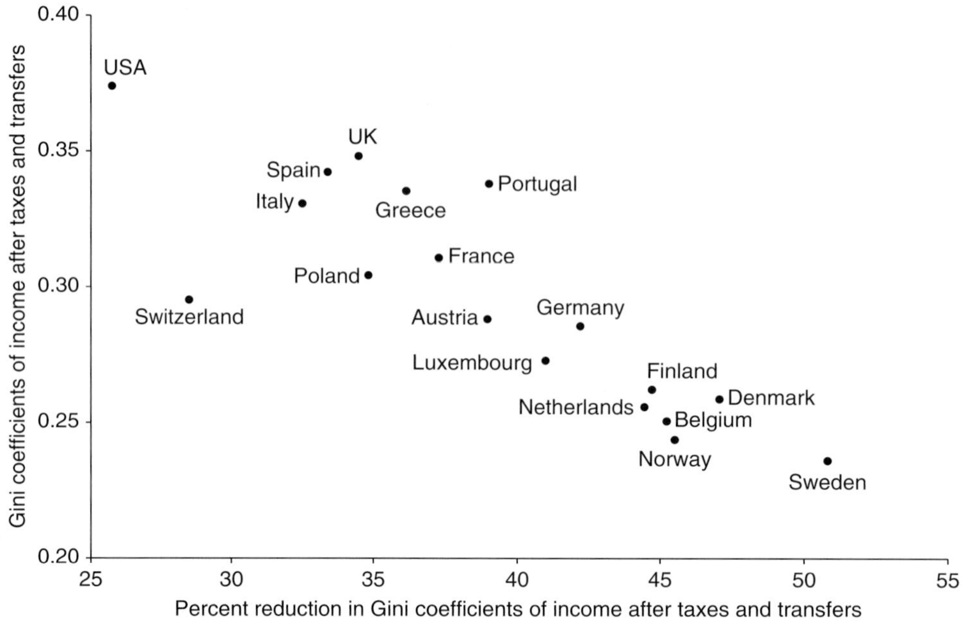

Figure 8.3 Effects of taxes and transfers on Gini coefficients of income in selected OECD countries in 2012 (Sachverständigenrat, 2015, p. 371)

represents perfect inequality, indicating that one person earns everything. Changes of the coefficient after a tax reform show the effectiveness of the reform.

Taxes and transfers can be appropriate regulatory tools aiding in the creation of a more just income distribution. Data show that the changes in income distribution vary widely across countries depending on the tax system (flat or progressive, and steepness of progressive taxation). The average Gini coefficient in OECD countries in the 2000s was 0.45 before taxes, and 0.31 after taxes and transfers. In the USA, the respective numbers were 0.46 and 0.38 and in the UK 0.46 and 0.34. In contrast, the numbers in Sweden were 0.43 and 0.24 (Sachverständigenrat, 2009). The effectiveness of taxes and transfers in different countries is illustrated in Figure 8.3, building on 2012 data (Sachverständigenrat, 2015). While in the USA the Gini coefficient of income after taxes and transfers was still 0.37, with a reduction by taxes and transfers of only 26%, the Gini coefficient in Sweden was 0.24 after taxes and transfers, yielding a reduction by taxes and transfers of about 51%. In other words, the Swedish tax system is more effective in reducing income inequality.

In the OECD countries, a majority of the population considers the income distribution to be unjust. Presumably, many people would consider it fair if rich people would have to pay higher taxes. Conversely, people at lower income levels should receive more public goods. The introduction of progressive taxation instead of a flat tax can correct for unevenness in the income distribution. However, do taxpayers prefer a progressive taxation scheme to a flat tax, and does progressive taxation lead to higher levels of subjective well-being in a nation? This question is not easy to answer. First, many citizens do not feel competent to make decisions about taxation models. Second, different preference data arise from different survey methods and types. A summary of empirical findings related to preferences for progressive versus flat taxes can be found in Kirchler (2007).

Public opinion polls and surveys are used to gain insights into citizens' preferences and acceptance of flat tax rates as opposed to progressive tax rates and the related issue of fairness (e.g., Lenartova, 2003). However, Roberts, Hite and Bradley (1994) convincingly demonstrated how problematic the results of opinion polls can be if respondents do not have a thorough understanding of the concepts involved. They examined knowledge of progressive taxation by comparing participants' choice of a fair tax rate structure in response to questions framed in either abstract or concrete terms. Participants were presented with either abstract or concrete questions asking for their opinions about differences between types of income tax rates. Examples of abstract questions included the following (p. 187; with answer scales ranging from 1 to 9, 'much less fair' to 'much more fair'):

A Are progressive tax rates (where the tax rate increases as income increases) more or less fair than flat tax rates (where the tax rate is the same at all income levels)?
B Are progressive tax rates more or less fair than regressive tax rates (where the tax rate decreases as income increases)?

Examples of concrete questions (p. 187; with answer scales ranging from 1 to 9, 'the same' to 'five times') included the following:

C Andy and Bob are the same age. Andy has taxable income of $40,000 per year. Bob has taxable income of $20,000 per year. In terms of fairness, how much more income tax do you think Andy should pay than Bob?
D Frank had taxable income of $16,000 last year. This year, Frank has changed jobs and his taxable income has increased to $24,000. In terms of fairness, how much more income tax do you think Frank should pay this year as compared to last year?

In surveys of the general public using abstract questions, Roberts et al. (1994) found that a majority of participants preferred progressive taxation. More than 75% preferred progressive tax rates when progressive rates were compared to both flat taxes and regressive taxes (items A and B). This preference, however, was reversed in the situation with concrete questions, where participants favoured a flat tax, that is, tax rates that are the same at all income levels. When considering item C, only 12% assigned progressive taxes to the higher income of Andy, while a majority of 61% found it fair for Andy to be paid twice as much as Bob; 27% preferred a regressive tax by indicating that Andy should pay more than Bob but less than twice as much. Answers to item D were similar: only 18% selected progressive tax rates, while a two-thirds majority favoured a proportional tax rate. This preference reversal is hypothesised to be associated with participants' lack of understanding of progressive taxation. A majority of participants interpreted a tax rate as progressive when a higher-income taxpayer paid a higher amount of money than a lower-income taxpayer, but not a higher percentage of their income. Similar results of preference reversals are reported in studies by McCaffery and Baron (2003, 2004). However, in Sweden, Edlund (2003) found that, irrespective of whether abstract or concrete measures were applied, progressive taxation was favoured.

A low understanding of flat taxes and progressive taxation was also confirmed in a study on New Zealanders' preferences with regard to fair tax structures. Although Kemp (2004) presented detailed explanations of flat, progressive and regressive tax structures, respondents' preferences for flat and progressive taxes, suitable for the provision of various services, varied substantially. Many responses were given at the midpoint of the answering scales, indicating a lack of pronounced preferences and indecision. This was probably due to a lack of knowledge, which made it difficult for respondents to indicate clear preferences. Using a German sample, Seidl and Traub (2001, 2002)

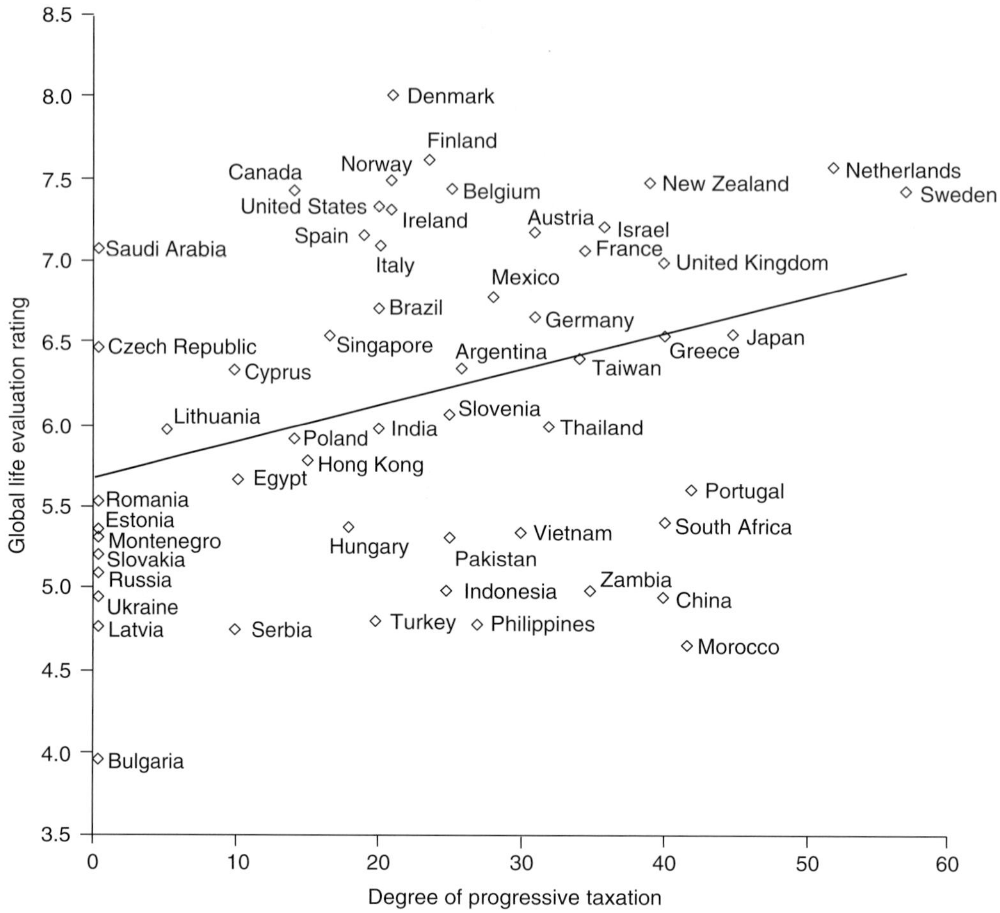

Figure 8.4 Global life evaluation rating as a function of progressive taxation in various nations (adapted from Oishi et al., 2012, p. 88)

found that respondents' preferences for different forms of taxation are inconsistent. However, in general, flat-rate taxation and lump sum taxes did not receive much support.

In summary, the majority of survey respondents seem to prefer a progressive taxation scheme to the flat tax and also tend to rate the former as fairer. Oishi, Kesebir and Diener (2011) analysed General Social Survey data from 1972 to 2008 and found an inverse correlation between income inequality and happiness, as well as a higher perceived fairness and general trust in other people, when income inequality was low. Lower-income Americans, especially, were on average happier in years with less national income inequality than in years with more national income inequality. Oishi, Schimmack and Diener (2012) examined whether progressive taxation is associated with subjective well-being of nations and found that nations with higher progressive taxation and high satisfaction with the provision of public goods do indeed report higher national well-being. Figure 8.4 shows the scatter plot of global life evaluation ratings in different countries as a function of progressive taxation (adapted from Oishi et al., 2012, p. 88).

The levelling out of incomes leads to more social contentment, but the question of whether or not it promotes a country's long-term productivity remains open. A wide gap between the lowest and highest income categories could have positive effects on achievement motivation, heightened performance and productivity leading to higher levels of prosperity for everyone.

High tax rates that seek to create a more just income distribution can be subjectively experienced as an enormous burden and interpreted as capriciousness on the side of the state. It is seldom that the value of the public goods received in return is perceived as fair recompensation. Despite the nobility of the effort to create prosperity and justice through taxes and other contributions, attitudes towards taxes are often negative, leading to a negative tax morale.

8.3 Attitudes towards Taxes

With the state taking over many activities in an attempt to regulate the economy at least rudimentarily, the scope of taxation has increased enormously. The tax burden (including social insurance) stands at 40% in many OECD countries. This means that, on average, about half of the total amount of work per year is solely dedicated to paying taxes and other contributions. Paraphrasing Sloterdijk (2010), governments have been taking money out of the pockets of working people for thousands of years. With impressive resourcefulness, politicians have inundated their subjects with taxation. Taxes are 'legal theft', as Thomas Aquinas (1225–74) is reported to have said in the Middle Ages. The current fiscal system has been degraded to an ignoble relic of the late absolutist state kleptocracy, as Peter Sloterdijk (2010) concludes: the state takes a cut of all transactions undertaken by its citizens and residents. The worries of Queen Victoria from a long time ago now appear almost heart-warming in light of the current situation: in 1850, upon the introduction of an income tax of 5%, she expressed the worry that the measure might have gone too far (Sloterdijk, 2010).

Nobody likes paying taxes. Many people have such an aversion to the payment of taxes that they are even willing to take on additional costs in order to avoid doing so. Sussman and Olivola (2011) investigated the phenomenon of tax aversion, the desire to avoid taxes per se that exceeds the rational economic motivation to avoid a monetary cost. People were shown to have a stronger preference for avoiding tax-related costs than for avoiding equal-sized or even larger monetary costs unrelated to taxes. Consumers considered goods advertised as 'tax-free' to be more attractive than goods whose price was reduced by a larger amount, but where a reduction in sales tax was not mentioned.

Nevertheless, the question arises if it is not sensible for citizens to invest part of their income into public goods in the form of healthcare institutions, educational and cultural institutions, research and innovation, traffic and public safety? After all, these services exist for the common good and contribute to the economic stability of the country. There is hardly any doubt about the value of the public goods financed by tax revenues (Kirchler, 1997a, 1997b). However, questions remain as to whether the tax budget is administered frugally and for the general welfare, and whether the projects favoured by policymakers are also desired by taxpayers. It also remains open whether an individual's tax burden seems fair in relation to the tax burdens of other individuals and in relation to one's own opportunities to take advantage of public goods. Some taxpayers may conclude that they are best off by withholding their own contribution to the public good, while the overwhelming majority of productive society pays their legally prescribed contribution.

Since taxes are viewed as a burden, direct repayment in the form of public goods is often not apparent. Considering media reports on the squandering of public funds, ill-considered investments and purchases abound, it is no surprise that the disinclination to pay taxes is high. In addition, for the majority of the taxpaying public the tax law is extraordinarily difficult to understand. A half century ago, in 1959, Schmölders tested politicians in the German parliament and members of its finance committee on their economic knowledge and found that they had a poor understanding of fiscal policy. Tax authorities face problems related to the complexities of public finance and tax law, as well as ambiguities in interpreting and executing it. For ordinary taxpayers, complex tax law is even more difficult to understand. Moser (1994) undertook a linguistic analysis of tax laws and identified several problems that make it difficult for ordinary taxpayers to understand the law. Examples of unnecessary complexity include the high level of abstraction in the language, long and complex sentences, the use of abbreviations, and a general writing style directed at experts rather than ordinary readers. Measured on the basis of a formula used to determine reading level, which takes such factors as the length of sentences and the number of syllables into consideration, it was calculated that standard texts in British tax law required a reading age of 13. Similarly, the US tax code required a reading age of 12.5. On average, however, the British population had a reading age of only 9 years. In Australia, only those who have reached a reading age of 17 would have been able to understand the tax code. Reading a high-brow, quality magazine is much less demanding. In general, people do not understand tax guidelines and do not know much about their own tax rates either (Lewis, 1978). People blame the complexity of tax law for their feelings of tax incompetence and lack of interest in the system (McKerchar, 2001). Lewis (1982) found that, for most people, fiscal policy is not an important issue, and Furnham (2005) wrote that young people seem most ignorant with regard to fiscal policy. The adult population also lacks understanding (e. g., McKerchar, 1995). Sakurai and Braithwaite (2003) surveyed Australian taxpayers and found that a relatively small percentage of respondents described themselves as fully competent. It is not surprising that more than three-quarters of taxpayers rely on tax agents (Sakurai & Braithwaite, 2003). Close to 60% of individual income tax returns in the USA in 2001 were signed by a preparer.

The complexity of tax laws and the trends towards increasing complexity in the past fifty years are well illustrated by Owens and Hamilton (2004), who reported a considerable increase in the number of words used in the US IRS Code. In response to this increasing complexity, many countries have endeavoured to simplify the law, unfortunately without much success. ‘I hold in my hand 1,379 pages of tax simplification’, said US Congressman Delbert L. Latta (*US News & World Report*, 23 December 1985), expressing with this ‘bon mot’ experiences and feelings towards tax complexity as well as ongoing endeavours to reduce complexity on the part of tax administers and politicians.

Uncertainty in the tax law makes it difficult both for taxpayers to follow the law and for tax authorities to decide unequivocally what is legal and what is not. There is a grey area between tax avoidance and tax evasion, for which Seldon (1979) coined the term ‘tax avoision’. In this grey area, it would be important the taxpayers comply not only with the letter but also with the spirit of the law. When tax law is too complex for ordinary taxpayers to comprehend, and when this complexity offers high-income earners the opportunity to hire creative experts to find loopholes to reduce their tax liability, it is not surprising that ordinary taxpayers perceive the tax law as unjust and therefore devaluate it. Poor understanding or misunderstanding breeds distrust. Consequently, negative attitudes towards taxes and their legitimacy may result in low tax morale, in the perception that the correspondence between one’s contributions to and benefits from the community is unfair, and in reduced participation in the contribution to public goods.

According to surveys, most people consistently support reductions in taxes; conversely, however, they also support increasing government investment in nearly all branches of the state at the same time. Tyszka (1994) collected data on French and Polish students’ preferences with regard to the administration of public funds for social issues, tax policy, state interference in economic dynamics, welfare programmes, privatisation, the legal regulation of private property, etc. Both Polish and French students were unanimously of the opinion that taxes need to be reduced, but that state expenditures on

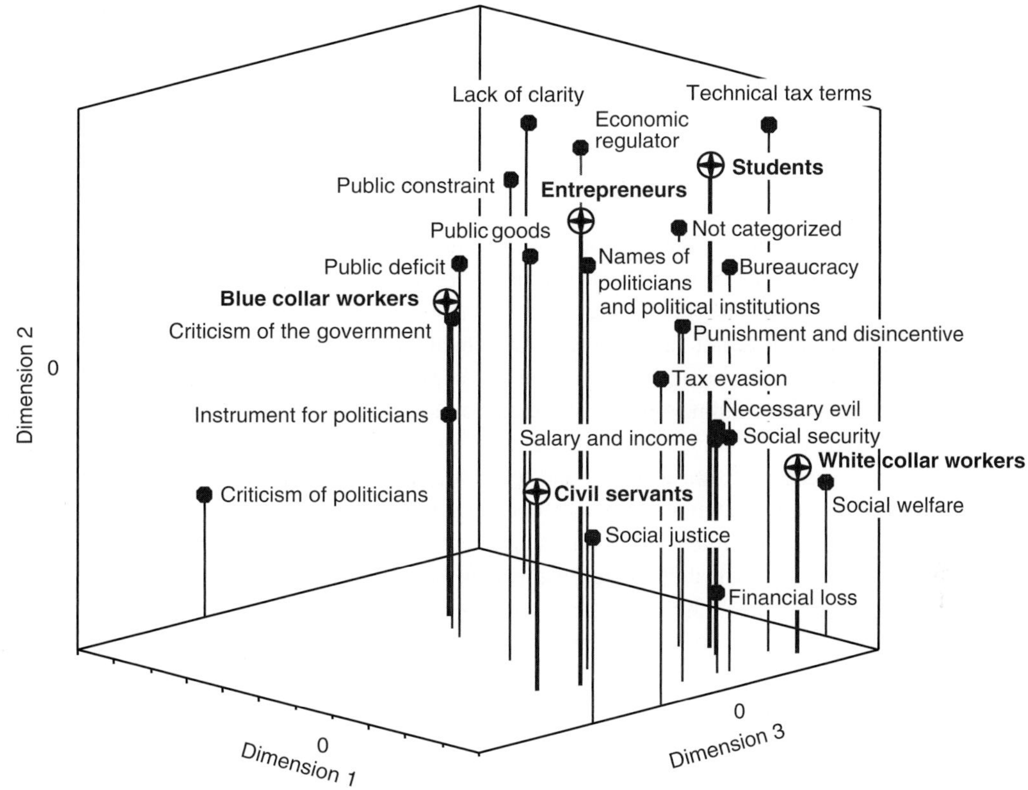

Figure 8.5 Semantic space of associations to 'taxes' by entrepreneurs, blue- and white-collar workers, civil servants and students (Kirchler, 1998, 2007, p. 44)

public goods need to increase at the same time. Schmölders (1975) reported similar results in Germany: when interviewees were asked about possibilities for lowering the state's budget deficit, the majority believed that expenditures should be reduced. At the same time, however, they demanded that the state should invest more in practically all government programmes. Kirchler (1997b) asked taxpayers how high they estimated public expenditures to be, as well as how high they ought to be. They were also asked how much utility they themselves obtained from each category of expenditure and how much they should be getting. Respondents wanted expenditures in several areas to be reduced, but believed that the benefits they personally obtained from state investments in each of these areas ought to be increased.

People are keen to profit from public goods, but reluctant to pay for this privilege (van de Braak, 1983; Williamson & Wearing, 1996). Kirchler (1998) investigated attitudes towards taxes, the state, tax offences, tax evaders and penalties, all of which determine tax morale. On the level of behaviour, tax morale finds expression in various levels of tax compliance and tax evasion (Strümpel & Katona, 1983). Tax morale means conscientiously complying with one's tax obligations, which appears to be an 'absolute, inherent ingredient of the complex of obligations demanded of citizens', as Otto Veit wrote in 1927 (p. 323). Kirchler (1998) measured attitudes and the resulting tax morale for entrepreneurs, civil servants, students and blue- and white-collar workers. Study participants were instructed to think about taxes and to write down everything that spontaneously came to mind. Over 540 different associations were mentioned, which were then sorted into twenty-five categories. The frequencies of twenty categories of associations differed significantly among the occupational groups. These categories were further investigated using correspondence analysis. The results of the three-dimensional solution are depicted in Figure 8.5.

Compared to other groups, freelancers and entrepreneurs more commonly thought about the collection of taxes as a punishment and a demotivator, about the lack of transparency, the coercive force of the law, and tax evasion. Civil servants emphasised opportunities for creating social justice. White-collar workers associated taxes with income and salaries, social security and welfare, and thought of taxes as a necessary evil. In contrast to that, blue-collar workers criticised politicians and the government, and were of the opinion that taxes are a ‘tool’ that politicians make use of to serve their own selfish ends. University students mostly referred to legal jargon. Group-specific analyses revealed that freelancers and entrepreneurs associated taxes with a contribution that can be legally coerced, perceiving this as a demotivating factor and probably as a reduction in freedom. Losing the freedom to invest money that one already possesses for one’s own purposes can lead to reactance. Possibly for this reason, associations falling under the categories of ‘resistance and evasion’ were more commonly invoked among these groups. White-collar workers and civil servants commonly associated taxes with terms that correspond to social justice and social welfare. Their attitudes towards taxes may be primarily influenced through what they perceive as exchange relationships between the individual and the state. In contrast, blue-collar workers personalised taxes in the sense that they thought about politicians and their machinations, criticising individual persons and the government as a whole. According to this view, taxes rather serve to enrich individuals than to secure the prosperity of the citizenry.

Kirchler (1998) also collected data on participants’ judgments of typical taxpayers (i.e., people who are somewhat lenient about tax rules), honest taxpayers and tax evaders. It is probably no surprise that honest taxpayers were evaluated more positively than tax evaders. However, it was unexpected that people who evade taxes were evaluated more positively than typical taxpayers. The descriptions of typical, honest and dishonest taxpayers also differed: while honest taxpayers were described as hardworking, intelligent people, typical taxpayers were viewed as lazy. All five occupational groups characterised tax evaders with diligence and intelligence. According to these results, tax morale cannot be especially high.

From a psychological perspective, it is hardly surprising that citizens have developed a negative orientation towards taxes and that tax morale is low. Schmölders (1966) operationalised tax morale as attitudes to tax-based crimes, tax evaders and penalties for tax offences. In a study on self-employed persons’ tax morale, seven cases of tax evasion were offered up for judgment. Tax offences were commonly assessed by participants as petty infractions and only rarely seen as theft. Moreover, in most cases, participants decided against imposing sanctions. Tax morale was correlated with the perception that the tax burden was unjustly distributed as well as with negative attitudes towards the state. Schmölders (1966) also found that personal characteristics are connected with poor tax morale: ambitious people who preferred high income and opportunities for career advancement over other advantages of an occupation, as well as people less engaged in religious activities, exhibited a lower tax morale than others. The influence of religiosity on tax morale was also supported by Prinz (2004).

Schmölders (1966) emphasised that tax morale has less to do with rational arguments than with personal attitudes:

> It is much more that . . . individual attitudes and personal circumstances, such as age, attitudes toward making money, and religious engagement determine the extent to which irrational, defensive reactions against paying taxes can be held in check by citizenly discipline and one’s better judgment; resistance to paying taxes and the inner process of overcoming it is primarily a problem of personality. (Schmölders, 1966, p. 90)

In addition, it can be argued, in line with Strümpel (1969), that tax morale or the willingness to pay taxes also depends upon the perceived rigidity of the state, the harshness of the statute, and the inquisition-like character of prosecution. When the state is perceived as an opponent, as is sometimes the case in southern European countries, tax morale is poor. In an empirical study, Dornstein (1987) confirmed that people with a negative disposition towards the state are much less satisfied with their tax bill as well as perceiving taxes as more burdensome and more unjustly distributed than people with a positive disposition towards the state.

Webley, Robben, Elffers and Hessing (1991, p. 1) pointed out that taxes have always been viewed negatively and that paying taxes was perceived as unjust even when taxation was minimal relative to today's rates: 'Ironically, even though tax rates in Victorian England were set at levels that now seem unbelievably low . . . there were complaints about evasion from the outset. In 1866 it was estimated that the average taxable income declared was less than half what it should have been.' Moreover, de Kam (1992) determined that changes in tax law have only minimal effects on taxpayers' (negative) attitudes and behaviour.

8.4 Tax Behaviour: Definitions, Relevant Actors and Research Methods

According to economic theory, rationally acting taxpayers seek to keep their taxes and other contributions as low as possible and only contribute when audits are both common and efficient and the punishments for tax offences are high. If citizens view their government as an opponent and view the 'smart' handling of taxes as a trivial offence, they will need to be forced to fulfil their obligations. If, however, a climate of cooperation exists between citizens and the state, tax honesty can become the rule and not the exception. The upcoming section will first provide definitions on taxpayer behaviour before launching into a discussion of its determinants. Actors will be described in contexts related to the design of taxation systems and the payment of taxes, and research methods for the study of taxpayer behaviour will be introduced.

8.4.1 Definitions of Tax Behaviour

Research on tax behaviour in the social sciences uses terms such as intended or observed tax honesty, tax compliance, tax flight, avoidance, evasion, cheating, etc. **Tax compliance** is probably the most neutral term to describe taxpayers' willingness to pay their taxes. Non-compliance represents the most inclusive conceptualisation of the failure to meet tax obligations, regardless of whether that failure was intentional. The degree of compliance varies, however, and non-compliance does not necessarily imply a violation of the law. James and Alley (2002) view compliance as a continuum of definitions, ranging from the narrow law enforcement approach to wider economic definitions, on to versions where taxpayers make the decision to conform to the objectives of tax policy and to cooperate with social measures. While at one end of the continuum non-compliance is illegal, at the other end, non-compliance can conform to the law.

McBarnet (2001) distinguished between three different forms of compliance: (a) committed compliance is taxpayers' willingness to pay their taxes without complaint, (b) capitulative compliance refers to reluctantly giving in and paying taxes, whereas (c) creative compliance is characterised by efforts to reduce taxes by taking advantage of possibilities to redefine income and deduct expenditures while remaining within the letter of the law. Kirchler (2007) and Kirchler, Hoelzl and Wahl (2008) distinguished between taxpayers who voluntarily comply with the tax law and taxpayers who comply as a result of enforcement activities. Kirchler and Wahl (2010) developed a questionnaire assessing voluntary compliance, enforced compliance, tax avoidance and tax evasion as distinct concepts.

In most countries, there is a legal distinction between tax avoidance and tax evasion. As Webley (2004) states, **tax avoidance** is not illegal, as attempts are made to reduce tax liability by legal means, taking advantage of loopholes in the law and 'creatively' configuring one's own income and deductions. On the other hand, **tax evasion** is illegal, as it involves deliberately breaking the law in order to reduce the amount of taxes due. Evasion can involve acts of omission (e.g., failing to report certain assets) or commission (e.g., falsely reporting personal expenses as business expenses). Similarly, Elffers, Weigel and Hessing (1987) describe 'tax evasion behaviour' or 'tax cheating' as deliberate acts of non-compliance that result in the payment of less tax than actually owed, whether or not this behaviour results in a subsequent conviction for tax fraud. Tax evasion excludes inadvertent non-compliance resulting from memory lapses, calculation errors, inadequate knowledge of tax laws, etc. With respect to income tax, evasion behaviour usually takes the form of deliberately under-reporting income or claiming unwarranted deductions. King and Sheffrin (2002) quote the US IRS Code, Section 7201: 'Tax evasion occurs when an individual knowingly and willfully fails to declare taxable income' (p. 505). Sandmo (2003) defined tax evasion as a

> violation of the law: When the taxpayer refrains from reporting income from labour or capital which is in principle taxable, he engages in an illegal activity that makes him liable to administrative or legal actions from the authorities. In evading taxes, he worries about the possibility of his actions being detected. Tax avoidance, on the other hand, is within the legal framework of the tax law. It consists in exploiting loopholes in the tax law in order to reduce one's tax liability . . . In engaging in tax avoidance, the taxpayer has no reason to worry about possible detection. (p. 4)

However, he added that many people might have difficulty seeing the difference between tax evasion and tax avoidance from a moral perspective. He argued:

> The house painter who does a bit of extra work in the black economy violates the law, while the wealthy investor who engages a tax lawyer to look for tax havens does not. From a moral point of view their behaviour may not seem to be all that different. Clearly, the borderline between what seems morally right and wrong does not always coincide with the border between what is legal and illegal. (p. 5)

According to Gassner (1983), tax law distinguishes between tax avoidance, **tax circumvention** and tax evasion. Generally, taxpayers are not deterred from designing their income in order to pay a minimal amount of taxes. The freedom to present one's income within the legal range in such a form so as to pay the least amount of tax is defined as tax avoidance. The principle of freedom of income presentation ends where taxes are circumvented, that is, where this 'creativity' in designing tax reports is against the spirit and purpose of the law. While tax circumvention is not fined, taxpayers are obliged to modify their tax filings and pay the additional tax due. Tax evasion results when tax law is deliberately violated. Evasion involves a deliberately illegal form of tax reduction, which is liable for prosecution. Penalties can range from financial sanctions, which can frequently entail up to double the evaded sum, to prison sentences.

Within James and Alley's (2002) continuum concept, one pole would be defined as committed, voluntary compliance, followed by capitulative compliance or compliance due to threats and harassment. Creative compliance would be positioned one step further. Cases where taxable income is presented against the spirit and purpose of the law would represent tax circumvention and tax flight. Deliberately illegal actions – that is, tax evasion – represent the other pole of the continuum. Within this definition, compliance is described as taxpaying behaviour that follows both the letter and the spirit of the law (James & Alley, 2002).

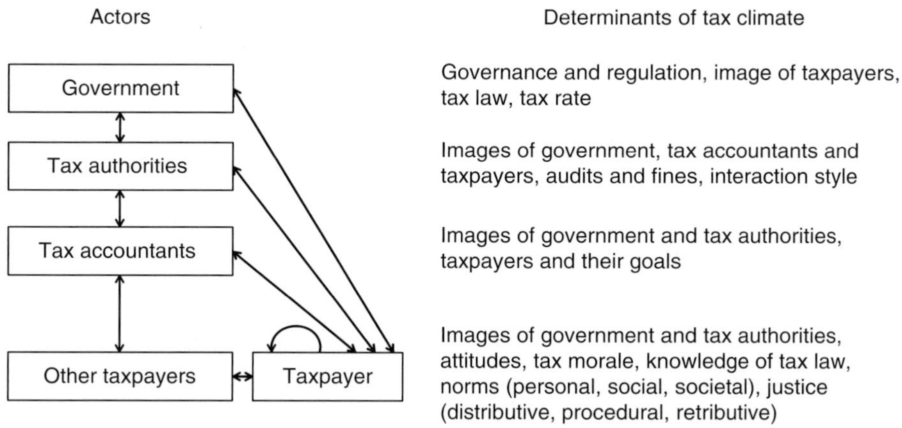

Figure 8.6 Structuring the field: actors and determinants of tax climate (Alm, Kirchler & Muehlbacher, 2012, p. 136)

8.4.2 Actors in the Field

In the arena of tax collection and tax payment, various actors are involved who are more or less likely to cooperate with one another depending on the interaction climate. Figure 8.6 shows actors and paths of interaction. Relationships exist among political authorities (here labelled 'government'), tax authorities, tax accountants and taxpayers that can be aggregated to form a system of concepts, judgments and interactions. When political authorities pass legislation, their ideas about tax rates and the acceptance of those ideas among members of the taxpaying public are relevant. Tax authorities act under a state mandate. Their actions are based on conceptions and judgments about the government, tax accountants and taxpayers. Tax accountants base their efforts on their own conceptions of the tax authorities and of taxpayers. Finally, taxpayers' cooperation depends on their conceptions and judgments about the government, authorities, tax accountants and the activities of other taxpayers. Ultimately, the behaviour of each individual taxpayer is also dependent on that individual's own values, personal norms, other personality characteristics and situational factors. Personal norms and ethical values also affect companies' tax planning, avoidance and evasion strategies. According to Gribnau (2015a, p. 225) firms who endorse corporate social responsibility 'accept ethical obligations beyond compliance with the law'.

Clearly, the state and its institutions are legitimated to raise taxes. The executive, the legislature and bureaucratic authorities draft, enact and enforce laws. Yet there is the question of how much reflection goes into the limitation of rights and the imposition of duties and how clearly and comprehensibly laws are formulated and communicated. Undoubtedly, in many modern states legislation suffers not only from an excessively burdensome framework of rules and exceptions, but also from language that is almost impossible for the general public to understand. This creates room for the subjective interpretation of taxes and often turns negotiations over the actual contributions owed into something of a horse trade, while at the same time obfuscating the moral issues involved for even the most conscientious citizens. Simplification of the law is urgently necessary (Manhire, 2016), and endeavours in this direction are currently undertaken in many industrialised countries. However, efforts to reduce complexity by reformulating tax laws are rarely successful. Thus, the debate is shifting from a reformulation of the specific, complex rules that often lead to ambiguity, to an establishment of general principles to serve as guidelines for tax behaviour. Instead of a jungle of regulations, John Braithwaite (2005) suggests that principles of behaviour should be formulated to clarify what the law actually *intends*. In contrast to principles of behaviour, a body of rules, however dense it may be, offers loopholes for inventive minds to act according to the letter of the law, rather than according to its spirit.

A special focus needs to be placed on tax authorities, as they are the ones who maintain direct contact with taxpayers, offer services, implement controls and impose punishments according to their conceptions of the motives driving taxpayers' behaviour. Depending on their view of humanity in general and of taxpayers in particular, tax authorities approach taxpayers either as selfish, non-cooperative profit maximisers or as sovereign citizens with a clear understanding of the benefits of taxation. Taxpayers belonging to the latter group are expected to delegate power to the authorities who invest public revenues to the benefit of the community.

Until now, neither tax authorities nor tax accountants – who act as intermediaries between authorities and taxpayers – have been studied in any detail. Tax accountants often assume that their clients' goal is to exhaust all available means to reduce their tax burden. Yet Sakurai and Braithwaite (2003) have established that taxpayers actually expect accountants to fill out their tax declarations correctly and simply seek to pay their taxes properly, in order to diminish their concerns regarding unintentional mistakes in their tax declarations and subsequent audits from the fiscal authorities.

Until now, taxpayers have been the centre of attention in research on tax compliance. With evidence growing that not all taxpayers rationally strive to maximise their selfish gains, it has been established that willingness to pay taxes increases with increasing awareness of tax laws and clarity about the rules. In addition, it is acknowledged that social norms are strong regulators of behaviour, that citizens generally have a pronounced sense of justice, and that they respond to violations of the principles of justice accordingly (Tyler, Goff & MacCoun, 2015). The motivations for cooperation or tax evasion vary among taxpayers: whereas a large proportion of the population acknowledges the necessity and benefits of taxes, it would be naive to believe that this sense of community responsibility is shared by all. The 'black sheep' cannot be efficiently dealt with by the 'carrot' of incentives, but rather needs to be confronted with the 'stick' of fines. This ensures that a few evaders cannot selfishly take advantage of the majority's cooperating behaviour. Table 8.2 summarises determinants of tax compliance. Besides economic determinants, psychological phenomena also undoubtedly affect tax behaviour.

8.4.3 Research Methods

Studies on tax behaviour have employed various definitions of tax compliance, focused almost exclusively on individual taxpayers, and have applied various research methods. Results depend on the definitions of concepts, their operationalisation, and the methods applied. Not surprisingly, the plethora of methods, sampling techniques and operationalisations of variables as well as the uneven use of self-reported and observed tax non-compliance have been extensively discussed (e.g., Alm, Bloomquist & McKee, 2015; Fischer, Wartick & Mark, 1992; Groenland, 1992; Hallsworth, 2014; Kirchler, 2007; Torgler, 2002; Webley et al., 1991). In their review of the literature on compliance and the probability of detection, Fischer et al. (1992) summarised insights stemming from analytic studies in the field of microeconomic decision theory. These studies predominantly developed mathematical models of tax evasion to examine the impact of income, audit probability, fines in

Table 8.2 Determinants of tax compliance (adapted from Alm, Kirchler & Muehlbacher, 2012, p. 138)

Economic determinants	Frequency of audits	Probability of audits (subjective probability appears to have a higher impact on compliance than objective probability)
	Fines	High fines appear to have deterrent effects
	Marginal tax rate	Tax rate effects are not unequivocally confirmed empirically
	Income size	Empirical results reveal an unclear pattern on the effects of income on tax compliance
	Opportunity to avoid or to evade taxes	The self-employed with ample opportunities to evade taxes are more likely to be non-compliant than taxpayers with limited opportunities
Psychological determinants	Complexity of tax law	For the average individual, tax law is too complicated and compliance is thus difficult, even if strived for
	Attitudes	Opinions and judgments on the criminality of tax fraud, on tax evasion, the tax authorities, etc.; attitudes are often treated as the source of tax morale
	Personal norms	Internalised values or the personal tendency to obey laws
	Social norms	The norms and values in a social setting
	Societal norms	The norms and values of a society as a whole
	Distributive justice	Distinction made between horizontal fairness (an individual's tax burden in comparison to others), vertical fairness (individual tax burden in comparison to those capable of contributing more or less) and exchange fairness (tax burden relative to the provision of public goods financed by tax revenues)
	Procedural justice	The fairness of tax-related decision-making procedures: having a voice in policy making, transparency, consistency, neutrality, etc., and fairness of interaction between authorities and taxpayers
	Retributive justice	The fairness of the form and severity of the punishment imposed on tax offenders

cases of evasion and marginal tax rates. However, these models typically fail to incorporate all relevant facets of taxpayers' realities. For instance, psychological variables, such as fairness considerations, social norms, attitudes, etc., are hardly considered in the economic income function. Moreover, taxpaying is considered as an act that occurs at a single point in time; neither experience with past audits nor the relationship between taxpayers and tax authorities are considered. Although mathematical models provide valuable insights into compliance behaviour, they reduce taxpayers' goals to purely financial profit maximisation and consider only parts of the taxpayers' reality, which results in predictions of tax compliance that are almost never sufficiently accurate to guide policy (Fischer et al., 1992).

Microeconomic models are frequently tested with data taken from the US IRS 'Taxpayer Compliance Measurement Program' data pool. This data pool, described as 'the best data set in the world' (Slemrod, 1992, p. 3) and 'among the best available for studying tax non-compliance' (Andreoni, Erard & Feinstein, 1998, p. 836), includes estimates of voluntary compliance rates of audit classes and aggregate data on numerous taxpayer characteristics.

The difficulty of obtaining 'hard' empirical data on tax compliance has led researchers to generate their own data via surveys and experimental simulations (Baldry, 1987). Economic psychological approaches rely heavily on surveys. In surveys, taxpayers are asked to self-report their evasion activities. Although surveys are usually an economical way to collect data, they have several shortcomings that limit the generalisability of findings (e.g., Wilson & Sheffrin, 2005). The reliability and validity of measurements, especially construct validity, are major problems for this approach. For instance, honesty and perfect recall are required if answers to survey questions are expected to represent accurate reflections of tax compliance. Researchers in the Netherlands conducted studies on the methodologies used in tax evasion research (e.g., Antonides & Robben, 1995; Elffers et al., 1987, 1991, 1992; Hessing, Elffers & Weigel, 1988; Hessing, Kinsey, Elffers & Weigel, 1988) in which they compared self-reports to behavioural data obtained from tax authorities. Hessing et al. (1988) explored the limitations of self-reports as substitutes for the observation of tax evasion behaviour and found negligible correspondence between respondents' self-reports of tax evasion and officially documented behaviour. Non-significant correlations were obtained despite the fact that all government claims against the respondents had been settled before the start of the study, and that respondents were aware that the accuracy of their self-reports might be checked against their tax records. The results of the study suggest that different explanatory variables may be correlated with each type of behavioural measure. Measures of attitudes towards tax non-compliance and of subjective norms exhibited significant correlations with the self-report data but not with officially documented behaviour. In contrast, measures of broader personal dispositions predicted actual behaviour but not self-reports. To gain further insights into the observed lack of association between self-reported tax evasion behaviour and official designations, Elffers et al. (1987) studied data generated from self-reports and reports from tax authorities, as well as from experimental methods on the same sample of taxpayers (see Table 8.3). Not only was the lack of association between self-reported behaviour and official classifications replicated; nor did evasion in the experimental setting correlate with either of these measures. The authors concluded that tax evasion consists of several conceptually independent elements that need to be assessed with independent measures.

While the Dutch studies identify causes for serious concern, Hite (1988) reported a positive relationship between results obtained from different measures. She determined whether self-reported taxpayer compliance rates and hypothetical reporting decisions corresponded to government-reported compliance rates, as well as whether self-reported compliance rates corresponded to hypothetical reporting decisions. The relationships were low, but positive. In their study on 3.6 million Swedish taxpayers' loss aversion, Engström, Nordblom, Ohlsson and Persson (2011) also concluded that a quasi-experimental field study yielded similar results to those obtained in the laboratory; thus, different methods do not necessarily lead to different results.

Measurement problems originate from different sources. First, it is not always clear how non-compliance, evasion or avoidance is defined. Ordinary taxpayers participating in a survey may also have problems understanding tax issues, as was found in studies on taxpayers' preferences for progressive or flat tax systems (e.g., Roberts et al., 1994; Seidl & Traub, 2002). In addition, they may just not be interested in the issue and therefore lack the motivation or ability to recall their experiences correctly. Moreover, wording is of eminent

Table 8.3 Correlation between tax evasion and psychological variables (Elffers, Weigel & Hessing, 1987, p. 328)

	Behavioural outcome measures		
Psychological variables	2-year self-report	Documented status	Documented amount of tax evaded
Personal instigators			
Malcontents			
1. Dissatisfaction with tax authorities	0.05	0.21**	0.22**
2. Comprehensibility of rules and information	0.10	0.20**	0.28**
Personality orientation			
1. Competitiveness	0.05	0.17*	0.20**
2. Alienation	0.10	0.22**	0.29***
3. Tolerance of deviance	–0.01	0.18*	0.22**
Personal constraints			
Fear of punishment			
1. Perceived certainty	–0.27***	–0.03	–0.01
2. Perceived severity	–0.07	0.09	0.13
3. Perceived risk index	–0.30***	0.02	–0.03
Social controls			
1. Perceived frequency	0.22**	–0.09	0.00
2. Perceived social support	0.22**	–0.01	0.07
Personal controls			
1. Attitude towards under-reporting	–0.25***	0.04	0.07
2. Attitude towards false deductions	–0.19**	0.10	0.12

Note: * $p < 0.05$; ** $p < 0.01$; *** $p < 0.001$.

importance in surveys and experimental settings. For instance, Green, Kahneman and Kunreuther (1994) investigated the sensitivity of survey measures for the willingness to pay for public goods. Visitors to a science museum were asked about funding two projects either by donations or by means of a tax increase. Willingness to pay was substantially reduced by a seemingly innocuous reminder about how many individuals would be affected by a tax or would be asked to contribute to a given cause. Subtle changes in question order and wording can affect the nature of the responses. Moreover, the perspective taken by respondents seems to play a role in their attribution of the causes of non-compliance. If respondents are asked about their own tax behaviour, they commonly attribute evasion to external factors, whereas they attribute evasion to internal factors when asked about the behaviour of other taxpayers (Hite, 1987).

Second, tax officials may not always be able to detect intentional and non-intentional acts correctly and thus remain unable to distinguish between fraud and taxpayers' errors. In his studies on the value added tax, Webley (2004) confirmed that objective and self-reported measures do not line up. He concludes that self-reported measures are an indication of who has committed or is likely to commit deliberate acts of non-compliance. Thus, self-reports are useful in assessing actual and potential tax evasion. Objective measures are an indicator of who has been detected for non-compliance by inspectors. Clever evaders may avoid being defined as non-compliant, while some unintentionally careless taxpayers may be defined as evaders. Indeed, Elffers, Robben and Hessing (1991) studied tax officials' processing of tax returns, which were subsequently reassessed by independent tax officers. When independent tax officers and teams of three officers judged tax returns independently, they only reached an agreement rate of approximately 50%.

Third, variables that influence intentional evasion behaviour may differ from those explaining inadvertent non-compliance. With respect to income taxes, evasion in the form of deliberately under-reporting income may depend on different variables than those that determine the claiming of unwarranted deductions.

In economics and economic psychology, experiments are becoming increasingly accepted methods for testing theoretical predictions in a controlled field (Davis & Holt, 1993). Experiments can be seen as a link between models and the 'real world' (Guala & Mittone, 2005) and are frequently applied in tax behaviour research (e.g., Alm, 1991; Webley et al., 1991). Experimental analysis of taxpayers' reporting behaviour gives researchers control over a complex environment and allows the isolation of several aspects of taxpayers' behaviour, which are manipulated to test specific predictions derived from a theoretical model. The value of inferences that can be drawn from experiments depends on how the individual interprets the experimental situation as well as on what goals he or she tries to achieve (Alm, 1991). Participants must have a positive preference for the rewards provided in experiments. Their decisions and behaviour must be related to those rewards – specifically, participants have to recognise that their actions affect the outcomes they experience. Moreover, rewards must be large enough to offset any subjective costs that participants place on a participation in the experiment. However, the magnitude of the gains and losses that participants face are often too small, and thus irrelevant to them, creating the perception that experimental studies are 'games'. Experiments have to be administered in a uniform and consistent manner to allow replicability. They should not be excessively long and instructions should be easy to understand, ensuring that participants fully comprehend the experimental scenario and do not lose motivation. Moreover, instructions should be phrased in a neutral way, excluding examples that may cause anchoring effects. Researchers must also ensure that participants believe that the instructions and procedures described to them are indeed veridical. All these criteria are important to ensure that the experimenter has control over participants' preferences and to prevent participants from developing different mental representations of the experimental conditions or different mental scripts (Alm, 1991).

In summary, experimental approaches are a major source of knowledge (Falk & Heckman, 2009) and have the potential to address some of the weaknesses of other methods. However, experimental situations often appear artificial and lack ecological validity. In contrast to this critique, Alm et al. (2015) found that the behaviour of participants – even of students – demonstrated in laboratory experiments conforms to the behaviour of individuals in natural settings who are confronted with similar decisions. Nevertheless, natural field experiments have more advantages than laboratory experiments and yield results that are more convincing for policymakers (Hallsworth, 2014).

8.5 Paradigms of Tax Behaviour Research

The decision about whether to pay taxes in compliance with the law, to use legal loopholes or to engage in illegal tax reduction is a complex one. To date, there has not been sufficient research on this question for academics and practitioners to develop a consensus about the impact of various regulation measures. Nevertheless, one trend seems to be clearly established in both theoretical research and the practice of tax authorities: in the 1970s, tax behaviour research primarily focused on the efficiency of controls in cases of tax evasion and the deterrent effect of negative sanctions. Later, finding explanations for the behaviour of individuals and the collective played a central role in the 'social dilemma of tax honesty'. Currently, a differentiated understanding of taxpayers is gaining ground. This view not only acknowledges the existence of an intrinsic motivation to cooperate, but also recognises the danger of measures that overemphasise surveillance. In addition, the focus on taxpayers is being expanded to include all actors in the system. It is becoming the accepted consensus that the interaction climate among all actors in a state is decisive for whether individuals maximise their personal gains or whether cooperation takes place voluntarily.

8.5.1 Decisions under Risk

Even several decades ago, economists were pointing to the significance of taxpayers' attitudes towards the state, the government and taxes in order to explain tax behaviour (Schmölders, 1959; Veit, 1927). However, the real breakthrough in tax research took place when scholars looked at the decision of tax compliance or evasion as a decision taken under risk, where the consequences are not entirely certain. Taxpayers either decide to declare their taxes honestly, so that the remaining sum remains safely at their disposal, or they choose the risky option and engage in tax evasion. If no tax audit takes place, those individuals acting riskily possess a higher income than their honest counterparts. With efficient auditing and the establishment of proof of incorrect behaviour, tax debt has to be paid. However, this also includes a fine, so that the tax evader ultimately has less money at his disposal compared to the honest taxpayer. Under what conditions does an individual act honestly and which factors lead to an increase in the tendency to engage in tax fraud?

Gary S. Becker (1968) formulated an **economic theory of criminal behaviour** that assumes that criminal behaviour can be understood as considerations of costs and benefits. The threat of punishment has a deterrent effect if crimes are discovered and punished. Therefore, the level of punishment and the probability of discovery are relevant in determining behaviour. In two different articles published during the early 1970s, Allingham and Sandmo (1972) and Srinivasan (1973) presented a model of tax behaviour postulating that tax honesty increases with the probability of an audit and the level of fines. Income level and tax rate may also have an effect on taxpayers' honesty. Although the effect of audits and negative sanctions can be shown in lab experiments (Alm, Sanchez & de Juan, 1995; for a meta-analysis see Blackwell, 2007), even in the artificial laboratory situation – where morality plays a subordinate role – the effect is less than expected. Kirchler, Muehlbacher, Kastlunger and Wahl (2010) summarised the results of various studies on the effect of tax audits, fines, marginal tax rates and income effects; the results are shown in Table 8.4. Audits and fines seem to have a clear deterrent effect, albeit only a slight one. Moreover, audit probability seems to be more relevant than fines, whereas results are inconclusive when it comes to tax rate and income.

Similarly, Andreoni et al. (1998) concluded that audits have little specific deterrent value and speculated about possible reasons for this:

> One possible explanation is that audits may not turn out as badly as taxpayers initially fear. For example, if an audit fails to uncover non-compliance that is present or if a substantial penalty is not applied to discovered non-compliance, a taxpayer may conclude that it pays to cheat. Alternatively, perhaps taxpayers do find audits to be a negative experience, but the impact of this experience is to make them want to evade by more in the future in an attempt to 'get back' at the tax agency. (Andreoni et al., 1998, p. 844)

Table 8.4 Review of effects of income level, tax rate, audit probability, and fines on tax compliance (adapted from Kirchler, Muehlbacher, Kastlunger & Wahl, 2010, pp. 26–7)

		Effect of determinants of tax compliance			
Publication	Method	Level of income	Tax rate	Audit probability	Fines
Ali, Cecil & Knoblett (2001)	Aggregate data	–	–	+	0/+**
Alm, Jackson & McKee (1992)	Experiment	+	–	+	+
Alm, McClelland & Schulze (1992)	Experiment			+	
Alm, Sanchez & de Juan (1995)	Experiment		+	+	+**
Anderhub, Giese, Guth, Hoffmann & Otto (2001)	Experiment	–			
Baldry (1987)	Experiment	–	0		
Christian (1994)	Aggregate data	+			
Clotfelter (1983)	Aggregate data	+	–	+	
Collins & Plumlee (1991)	Experiment		–		0
Dubin, Graetz & Wilde (1990)	Aggregate data	+	–	+	
Feinstein (1991)	Aggregate data	0	+		
Fishlow & Friedman (1994)	Aggregate data	+			
Friedland (1982)	Experiment			+	+
Friedland, Maital & Rutenberg (1978)	Experiment		–		~**
Gerxhani & Schram (2006)	Experiment				
	Dutch sample			+	
	Albanian sample			0	
Lang, Nohrbaft & Stahl (1997)	Survey*	–	–		
Mason & Calvin (1978)	Survey*	+		+	
Moser, Evans III & Kim (1995)	Experiment		0/–**		
Park & Hyun (2003)	Experiment	0	–	+	+
Pommerehne & Weck-Hannemann (1996)	Aggregate data	–	–	+	0
Porcano (1988)	Survey*	0	0		
Schwartz & Orleans (1967)	Experiment				0**
Slemrod (1985)	Aggregate data	–	–		
Slemrod, Blumenthal & Christian (2001)	Experiment			+**	
Spicer & Lundstedt (1976)	Survey*	0		0	0
Spicer & Thomas (1982)	Experiment			+**	
Trivedi, Shehata & Lynn (2003); Trivedi, Shehata & Mestelman (2005)	Experiment			+	
Vogel (1974)	Survey*	–			
Wärneryd & Walerud (1982)	Survey*	0		0	
Webley, Robben, Elffers & Hessing (1991)	Experiment			+	0
Weck-Hannemann & Pommerehne (1989)	Aggregate data	–	–	+	

Note: + = positive effect; – = negative effect; 0 = no effect; ~ = ambiguous effect on tax compliance. * In surveys, fines and audit probabilities are sometimes measured by subjectively perceived audit and fine rates; ** Interactions with other variables.

Audits and fines do not have a long-lasting effect. Guala and Mittone (2005) studied tax behaviour in laboratory experiments by simulating tax filings over a '60-period taxpaying life span' and found a strong decrease in taxpayers' compliance immediately after an audit. This finding – called the '**bomb crater effect**' – has proven to be quite robust in various experimental studies (e.g., Kastlunger, Kirchler, Mittone & Pitters, 2009). Maciejovsky, Kirchler and Schwarzenberger (2007) conducted a laboratory study in which participants earned money over several rounds, which was subsequently taxed. On average, with an audit likelihood of 30%, 58% of income was honestly reported. Immediately following a tax audit, honesty sank to 35%, and remained low for two rounds at 45%. It took up to four rounds after an audit for compliance to reach the level of 55% again. It seems that after an audit, taxpayers consider themselves safe from another one; hence, they think tactically and tend towards risky behaviour. Only when confronted with repeated rounds do they begin to suspect that audit likelihood is increasing again and return to more caution. It can also be assumed that those taxpayers who were punished due to incorrect tax declarations will strive to regain that lost money in future filing periods.

Audits and the threat of negative sanctions can be perceived as a signal of a lack of trust, not only contributing to mistrust on the part of the taxpayer, but also promoting deliberate decision-making, where selfish cost and benefit considerations dominate behaviour. Deliberate decision-making can crowd out the intrinsic motivation to cooperate and can undermine an unsolicited willingness to comply. In addition, punishments that are considered disproportionate lead to negative attitudes about the authorities and taxes in general. Thus, not only do questions regarding the deterrent effects of audits and fines arise, but it is not clear what form of sanction is considered appropriate and effective in the case of tax evasion. In a study of Austrian taxpayers, a total of 86% said that they consider a fine to be a fair sanction for tax evasion, while considering a prison sentence as inappropriate. The offender's ability to pay should be considered as an alternative to current sentencing practices, according to which punishments are based on the extent of the tax evasion committed. Since the current system might encourage the notion that fines are 'affordable', an alignment of penalties with the offender's income might increase the deterrent effect of punishments (Muehlbacher, Hoelzl & Kirchler, 2007).

Studies on tax behaviour as decision-making under risk place their focus on individual taxpayers. In comparison with Figure 8.6, government, authorities, tax accountants and the psychological or social aspects of interaction dynamics between these agents are neglected. All taxpayers are considered as decision-makers with the same dominant motive. Fundamentally, it is assumed not only that they are all striving for the greatest individual gain according to rational criteria, but also that the use of controls and sanctions sufficiently high is enough to ensure compliance. Subsequently, authorities' views of taxpayers are highly authoritarian, shaped by the presumption that coercive power is necessary to prevent taxpayers from maximising their own profit.

8.5.2 The Social Contribution Dilemma

Empirical findings about the impact of audits and fines on taxpayer behaviour are sobering, as is the image of humanity inherent in the dominant theories that see selfish gain maximisation as the primary determinant of human behaviour. However, the public goods financed by tax revenues benefit both the community and the individual. Taxpayers acknowledge that their contributions support the community welfare and react with the understanding that taxes need to be paid. While on the one hand it might be doubted that all collected tax revenues are spent efficiently in ways that serve the public good, there is also the suspicion that some people might use the uncertainty of the situation to their own benefit and avoid paying taxes. Taxes raise a social contribution dilemma, where individual profit motives run contrary to the collective good, and – despite acknowledging the importance of taxation – some members of the community might seek to minimise their contributions to public coffers.

A **social dilemma** (Dawes, 1980) is a decision problem in which individual interests are opposed to the goals of the community, creating a situation where an individual can gain by acting selfishly. However, if the majority of citizens maximise their own individual profits, the collective and ultimately the individuals themselves are harmed because the financing of public goods is not secured. In experiments, a social dilemma can be set up with the following simple rules. Participants are given a starting capital from which they can contribute a freely chosen proportion – from everything to nothing at all – to a collective account. The experimenter promises to multiply the sum which was contributed (for example, to double it) and then to divide the multiplied amount of money equally among all players. If all players contribute their entire starting capital, they will each end up with double their starting capital. However, each individual can try to exploit the situation for themselves by paying nothing, hoping that the other players contribute large sums. Those who do not cooperate hold on to their starting capital and receive a payment from the community account on top of it. If all players are uncooperative, however, nothing can be paid out from the collective account and each person only retains his or her starting capital. Notably, the individual earning is significantly less than when all cooperate.

Under what conditions does readiness to cooperate increase in public contribution scenarios? In the laboratory, there is little reason to doubt the experimenter's promise that the amount collected will be multiplied and equally shared with all participants. In other words, in the laboratory, the 'government' is reliable and acts in the interests of the public – it is whether or not the other players can be trusted that is dubious. However, if cooperation can be made a binding social norm so that others can be trusted, the cooperation of the majority is assured. Willingness to cooperate increases in small groups where players can communicate with one another and set the rules of the game, and when defection is made public. In fact, parallels between experimental results and actual tax contributions can be drawn with regard to the higher tax morale and tax honesty in those regions with direct democracy. In particular, those cantons in Switzerland with a higher degree of direct democracy showed higher levels of tax morale (Frey, 1997a, 1997b).

Rothstein (2000) wrote that, without norms of trust, the social dilemma leads to the 'tragedy of the commons'. He describes an encounter with a Russian tax official who argued that most Russians do not want to pay taxes. Even though they prize the public goods financed by tax payments, they face a social dilemma due to high corruption and weak social norms of cooperation. To change this, two conditions would need to be fulfilled: taxpayers would need to trust other taxpayers to pay their fair share, and tax authorities would have to ensure that the money was being invested in public welfare rather than simply lining the pockets of tax bureaucrats. In other words, interpersonal trust leading to binding social norms, as well as institutional trust, is of paramount importance to ensure cooperation.

Besides acknowledging the effects of audits and fines, social dilemma research also acknowledges the value of social norms. However, the individual is still assumed to be primarily motivated by rational gain maximisation, and the suspicion is that an individual would not behave cooperatively in the anonymity of the crowd. The focus of behavioural research in social dilemma situations lies on the individual taxpayers and the group, whereas the behaviour of authorities in institutions is kept constant; the experimenter acts in an expected, reliable way. Looking at Figure 8.6, in this tradition of research, the government, authorities and tax accountants are left out of the analysis, while the taxpayer is considered as a decision-maker with utilitarian and social-normative motivations. This research still takes an authoritarian view of taxpayers. Taxpayers are supposed to act according to the law, are subject to controls and are punished in cases of violation. Nevertheless, it is not only audits and fines that affect taxpayer behaviour – the behaviour of others (i.e., social norms) needs to be accounted for as well.

8.5.3 Differences among Taxpayers

Taxpayers should not all be lumped together and perceived as a homogeneous group: they find themselves in various situations, have developed different personal values, often prove generous when there are calls for donations to the socially disadvantaged or to those affected by catastrophes, and frequently have a strong sense of community. That individuals differ in terms of their morality was shown by Pruckner and Sausgruber (2013) in a natural field experiment on honesty in newspaper purchasing. In Austria, newspapers are often sold on an honour system, where customers are theoretically required to pay, but can also pay less than the requested amount or nothing at all. Especially at weekends, newspapers are placed in plastic bags attached to street lights outfitted with a cashbox. Customers are informed of the price of the newspaper and are asked to deposit the appropriate amount in the cashbox. Pruckner and Sausgruber (2013) found that approximately one-third of observed customers paid at least part of the price, whereas two-thirds did not pay anything at all for the newspaper. Moreover, when a message was placed on the plastic bag thanking customers for being honest, hence appealing to internalised norms of honesty, they found that cooperation increased. In contrast, a statement emphasising that stealing was illegal had no effect on cooperation.

Schmölders (1966) and later Kirchler (1997a, 1997b, 2007), Kirchler and Berger (1998), Lewis (1982), Groenland and van Veldhoven (1983) and others have called attention to the importance of socio-demographic, cultural and personality-specific variables. Various studies have reported that women are more honest than men and that older taxpayers are less inclined to commit tax evasion than younger ones (Kastlunger, Dressler, Kirchler, Mittone & Voracek, 2010; Kirchler, 2007). Personal characteristics like religion, political ideology, personal moral attitudes, norm adherence, Machiavellianism and competitiveness should be just as relevant as cultural and situational contexts.

Opportunity makes the thief. In particular, the self-employed are considered a high-risk group for tax evasion. While employees usually have their taxes directly deducted from their salary, and thus hardly have an opportunity to cheat, the self-employed are required to file and pay their own income tax, value added tax, social insurance contributions, etc. There are various opportunities to render services for cash without an invoice, or to declare costs that were not business-related. These opportunities to secure some additional benefits could be tempting. Persons whose income generally goes directly into their own pockets and who at the end of the day sometimes have unexpectedly high taxes due are likely to see their contributions as a loss. As Kahneman and Tversky (1979) described in their prospect theory, individuals often react to losses by being more willing to take risks in the hope of restoring that loss. Empirically, one study (Kirchler, 1998) showed that primarily inexperienced self-employed people view taxes as a limitation of their freedom. This perceived limitation of freedom was correlated with reactance and the inclination towards tax evasion. People are motivated to enjoy once again the economic latitude they previously possessed. It could also be empirically demonstrated that reactance phenomena occur most often among entrepreneurs whose economic activities have only just begun (Kirchler, 1999; Muehlbacher & Kirchler, 2013). Flight into the shadow economy through tax evasion provides an avenue of escape, allowing the realm of economic action that has been narrowed to be regenerated.

Resistance to taxes is especially high when the payment of taxes is perceived as a loss. According to prospect theory, it is expected that people who have, for example, already paid taxes in advance in the form of monthly contributions, but then have an additional sum to pay at the end of the fiscal year, experience this balance as a loss and attempt to counteract it. In contrast, people with the same total amount of tax liability who have already paid their taxes in advance, resulting in a year-end refund, experience this balance as a gain and demonstrate a corresponding willingness to declare revenue and expenses in proper form. A study by Cox and Plumley (1988; as cited in Webley et al., 1991) showed that these speculations may actually be accurate. The authors investigated 50,000 tax declarations and found that willingness to pay taxes depended upon whether a taxpayer was expecting a refund from the tax authorities or owed them an additional payment. For wage earners, willingness to pay taxes reached 96% when a refund exceeding US$ 1,000 was expected; when, on the other hand, a balance due of more than US$ 1,000 was expected, willingness to pay dropped to 89%. People with business income acted even more clearly according to the dictates of prospect theory: willingness to pay varied from 96% to 70% depending on whether they expected to receive a refund or make an additional payment. Similar results were reported by other researchers (e.g., Elffers & Hessing, 1997; Kirchler et al., 2005; Schepanski & Kelsey, 1990; Schepanski & Shearer, 1995; Thomas, 2013).

The general view, however, that the self-employed are overall unwilling to pay their taxes is not correct. This might apply to self-employed people in their early years, but the tendency towards tax evasion lessens with increasing work experience. Why are older self-employed individuals more honest than younger ones? This could be attributed to a change in values across generations. However, a positive correlation between age and tax honesty has been reported for a long time. Another explanation could be that the self-employed at the start of their business careers consider their gross income as their own real income. Instead of setting aside value added tax and calculating a realistic tax debt as well as social insurance contributions and setting these 'contributions' aside, the young self-employed may see their total incoming revenue as being at their disposal. This leads to problems when taxes need to be paid. Increasing experience could lead to the keeping of separate accounts; at least virtually. This mental accounting (Muehlbacher & Kirchler, 2013) protects against surprises. In addition, there is no longer the impression that taxes represent unforeseen costs that probably leads to a sense of loss and increasing risk propensity.

Besides the factors described above, the 'distance' between taxpayers and tax authorities is relevant. On the one hand, this concerns geographical distance. For instance, Hartner, Rechberger, Kirchler and Wenzel (2011) and Hartner-Tiefenthaler, Kubicek, Kirchler, Rechberger and Wenzel (2012) showed that willingness to pay taxes to local or national authorities differs from willingness to comply with hypothetical taxes paid directly to the EU. Alongside other factors, social and national identity plays a crucial role. On the other hand, this concerns social distance – how close or distant taxpayers feel to tax authorities. Social distance transfers into different '**motivational postures**' as standpoints that taxpayers take in their interaction with the tax authorities. The work of Braithwaite (2003, 2009) shows that taxpayers differ strongly in terms of their motivation to comply with tax law. She attributes a positive basic attitude to the majority of taxpayers. Many feel morally committed to contribute to society. Braithwaite distinguishes between five motivational postures. The two positive motivational postures of 'commitment' and 'capitulation' combine views that express a feeling of responsibility to behave in the interest of society and to cooperate. The remaining three postures express negative tendencies in terms of motivation. 'Resistant taxpayers' doubt the good intentions of the financial authorities and the government and fight against paying taxes as a way of recapturing their rights. 'Disengaged taxpayers' are characterised by a similar attitude, but they have already abandoned the struggle for their rights and see no point in cooperating with the authorities. Finally, there are the 'game players', individuals who do not respect the law as such but rather see it as something that can be cleverly used to one's own advantage. Grey areas in legislation are used to lower individual tax burden without scruples.

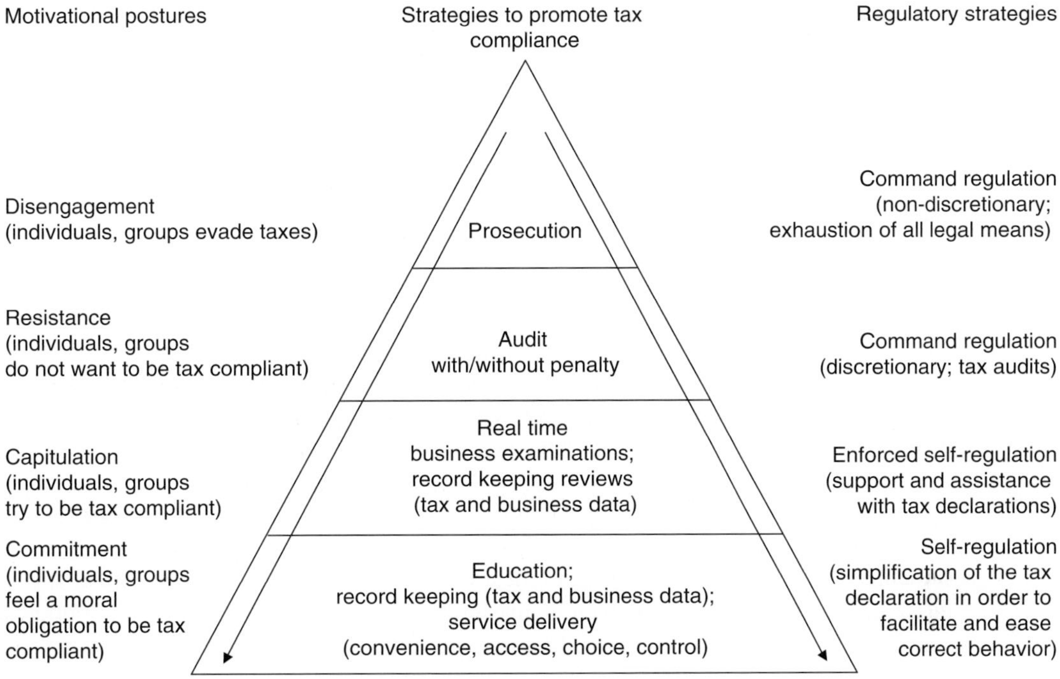

Figure 8.7 Australian Taxation Office compliance model (Braithwaite, 2003, p. 3)

Positive motivational postures dominate in society and should not be destroyed through mistrust, controls and harsh sanctions. Braithwaite thus argues for a differentiated approach to regulation on the part of the authorities (Figure 8.7). Taxpayers should be treated according to their motivation, and violations of the law should be sanctioned accordingly. Taxpayers should not be seen as supplicants before the financial authorities, but rather as clients. Generally, a service orientation and a sensitive approach on the part of tax authorities is needed, whereas 'an iron fist in a velvet glove' should await all those who repeatedly violate the law.

The differential approach primarily focuses on distinctions among taxpayers. Age, traditional gender roles, personal values, motivational tendencies, situative differences and the opportunity to cheat are significant in this approach. Taxpayers are not seen as an anonymous mass with one dominant motivation for behaviour, but are divided into various types. Depending on taxpayers' willingness to cooperate and the situative characteristics in which they find themselves, different approaches on the part of tax authorities are required. Referring to Figure 8.6, in this tradition of research, the authority of tax officials is not questioned. However, a service orientation is emphasised to facilitate and increase compliance (McKee, Siladke & Vossler, 2011) and differential approaches to taxpayers are imperative. There is no single dominant, successful strategy to ensure compliance; instead, regulatory measures are required that respond to taxpayers' individual characteristics and situational circumstances.

8.5.4 The 'Psychological Contract'

Taxpayers do react to aversive stimuli such as controls and sanctions. However, they also react to fairness and the violation of rules of fairness on the part of the authorities, as well as to social norms, and often have an intrinsic motivation to cooperate. Intrinsic motivation or tax morale is related to what Schmölders (1960) described as tax mentality: 'Tax morale is anchored in citizens' tax mentality and in their consciousness as citizens, which is the basis of their inner acceptance of their tax duties and of their acknowledgment of the sovereignty of the state' (p. 97 f). Other authors also highlighted intrinsic motivation: Braithwaite and Ahmed (2005) referred to an internalised obligation; Frey (1997a) as well as Alm and Torgler (2006) referred to an intrinsic motivation to pay taxes. Orviska and Hudson (2002) referred to the concept of civic duty. Civic duty proposes that people are motivated by a sense of responsibility and loyalty to society. Responsible citizens with high levels of civic duty are collaborative even if the system allows for non-compliance. Their behaviour is regulated not externally by audits and sanctions but by their concern for society and by an intrinsic motivation to cooperate.

Audits and sanctions can undermine an intrinsic willingness to cooperate and lead to effects the opposite of those intended. Frey (1992, 1997b) speaks of a 'crowding out' phenomenon when external stimuli such as punishments or inadequate rewards for cooperation destroy intrinsic motivation.

That punishment can have effects contrary to deterrence was impressively shown in a study by Gneezy and Rustichini (2000). Sanctions do not necessarily serve as an effective deterrent, but are sometimes seen as a price to be paid for desired liberties. When the management at day care centres in Israel observed that parents were consistently picking up their children late (albeit with a bad conscience), they introduced a fine. The amount of the fine depended on how late the parents were. This action did indeed have an effect; however, the effect was the exact opposite of increased punctuality. Now, parents picked up their children even later, but without any feelings of guilt or promises to be on time in the future: they were in fact happy to pay the price for extended childcare. Tax offences are also often impossible to counter with negative financial sanctions. A sentence of community service, feelings of shame and a loss of reputation are frequently much more effective (Braithwaite & Wenzel, 2008).

Feld and Frey (2007, 2010) plead for a cooperative relationship between authorities and taxpayers to promote the likelihood of tax honesty as well as to stabilise it. Taxpayers are not subjects but cooperation partners, and politicians and authorities are entrusted with the task of frugally managing the tax budget and responding to the needs of the population.

The construct of the '**psychological contract**' between employees and management in organisations (Rousseau, 1995) describes the implicit assumptions of rights and duties each side has. Applying this construct to the tax context, it can be assumed that expectations and commitments between tax authorities and taxpayers exist that go beyond legal regulations. In establishing a norm of reciprocity, commitment from one party requires an equivalent commitment from the other. By focusing on the 'reciprocity of commitments' between authorities and taxpayers, it becomes clear that taxpayers might respond to pressure with reactance. Those who presume a 'cops and robbers' situation actually turn to the other side and become robbers who will try various tricks to escape the authorities.

Authorities can presume that taxpayers understand that public goods need to be funded and that this funding has to be provided by the taxpayer. It is ultimately in their own interest to ensure the provision of public goods. The psychological contract implies that citizens entrust their money to a tax authority to invest it in sensible projects decided by the reigning politicians, providing long-term benefits. It is expected that authorities and politicians will not violate the trust placed in them. The psychological contract 'regulates' an approach of mutual respect and openness between partners. This relationship is characterised by mutual loyalty and emotional ties. The disappointment of expectations represents a violation of the contract, the rattling of mutual trust, and scepticism in terms of the willingness of the other party to cooperate, and might even lead to a termination of cooperation in some cases. When taxpayers trust the authorities, cooperation can be expected of them; however, if they do not trust the authorities, cooperation can at best be obtained by force.

With the postulation of a psychological contract between taxpayers and authorities, attention shifts from the taxpayer as a single entity to the relationship between tax authorities and taxpayers. Taxpayers are seen as cooperative partners who have a sense of community and recognise the value of cooperation. All the same, they also expect to be treated as partners, and they react to signals of mistrust – such as audits and fines – with mistrust. Instead of tax compliance (which suggests a hierarchical structure between authorities and taxpayers), we speak here of '**tax cooperation**': correct taxpaying from a perspective of equality. Referring to Figure 8.6, in this tradition of research, tax officials' position of authority is questioned; in its stead, the focus is on equal-status partners whose cooperation is not predominantly formally regulated, but rather regulated by a psychological contract.

8.5.5 Interaction Climate

Under the premise of rational decision-making it is assumed that all taxpayers seek to maximise their own selfish gains, and that the state and its authorities, who have the 'natural right' to obligate their subjects to the payment of taxes, need to use audits and fines to achieve that goal. Under the premise of a 'psychological contract', an egalitarian relationship between authorities and taxpayers is assumed. Cooperation works as long as neither party disappoints the other.

In what Kirchler (2007) and Kirchler et al. (2008) have called the '**slippery slope framework**', it is assumed that tax behaviour is a function of trust in tax authorities and power of tax authorities. Not only the relationship between authorities and citizens but also the climate of interaction is considered as significant in determining whether cooperation takes place voluntarily or needs to be obtained using coercion. Looking at Figure 8.6, this means that all actors and their relationships need to be taken into account and that the entire system of interaction needs to be structured in a way that promotes cooperation. Government and tax authorities are no longer seen as superior agencies that compel legal compliance in general and tax honesty in particular. Rather, they are thought to act in the service of citizens in order to increase the well-being of the community. Instead of intensifying the enforcement of compliance, a shaping of the interaction climate to promote fairness, mutual trust and cooperation gains importance. This corresponds to the 'trust paradigm' that Alm and Torgler (2011) identify as one of the three paradigms of tax administration. In the traditional '**enforcement paradigm**', taxpayers are treated as potential criminals, and tax honesty is to be achieved through audits and fines. In the '**service paradigm**', the need to ease tax honesty by offering services is acknowledged. Tax authorities are supposed to provide services to taxpayers that facilitate compliance with the law (see Olson, 2015). The '**trust paradigm**' emphasises the importance of building trust to promote tax honesty. Trust is built between interacting parties based on expectations on the part of both taxpayers and tax authorities, assuming that the other party will act beneficially rather than detrimentally (Gambetta, 1988).

In the slippery slope framework, a distinction is made between two kinds of tax honesty: voluntary cooperation and enforced compliance (Figure 8.8). Voluntary cooperation primarily depends on trust in the state and its authorities. If cooperation does not take place voluntarily, tax honesty can be secured by force to the extent that the state authorities have enough power to exert sufficient pressure on the offender. While voluntary compliance is assumed to be an intuitive, spontaneous cooperative reaction, enforced compliance originates from extended decisions on whether it pays to take the risk

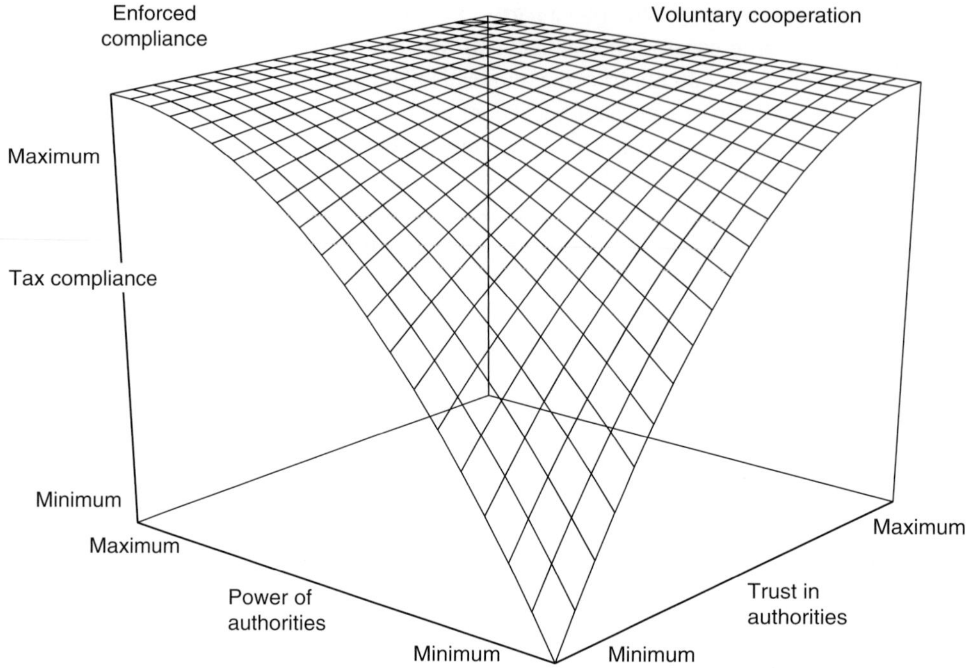

Figure 8.8 The slippery slope framework (Kirchler, Hoelzl & Wahl, 2008, p. 212)

of evasion or not (see Rand, Greene & Nowak, 2012, on spontaneous giving and calculated greed). State power is understood to include all measures that serve the purpose of deterrence. They include the (perceived) audit frequency and the severity of negative sanctions. On the other hand, voluntary tax honesty rises with increasing trust in the authorities – that is, when the tax system is felt to be just, taxpayers are treated fairly (see Tyler et al., 2015), and cooperation has become the social norm in the state.

The slippery slope framework assumes that tax payments are influenced by a combination of trust in authorities and power of authorities. If both trust and power are at a minimum level, tax payments are assumed to be low; taxpayers act selfishly by maximising their own gains through tax evasion. When trust in authorities increases, tax payments are also assumed to increase. Furthermore, if the power of authorities – defined as tax authorities' capacity to detect and punish tax crimes – increases, tax payments are expected to increase as well.

Wahl, Kastlunger and Kirchler (2010) empirically tested whether tax payments are high in cases of trustworthy authorities as well as in cases of draconian deterrence and fines. Moreover, they studied the quality of and motivations for compliance as a function of trust and power. When trust in state authorities is high and when taxpayers feel morally committed to contributing to the general welfare of society, it can be assumed that taxpayers will comply with laws and not think extensively about how to optimise their individual goals. Therefore, tax payments originating from trust have a voluntary character. If authorities exert power and act in an untrustworthy manner, taxpayers are likely to weigh up potential gains against the costs of evasion and pay their taxes. Taxpayers can feel forced by the authorities to contribute; this can lead to reactance and attempts to think strategically about how to avoid tax pressure. The probability of tax evasion increases with the reduction of efficient controls and punishment, as do attempts to use loopholes to one's best advantage. The difference between voluntary cooperation and enforced compliance is mirrored in taxpayers' behaviour and in its underlying motivations. Referring to Braithwaite's (2003) motivational postures, commitment and resistance motives should co-vary with variations in trust and voluntary cooperation and with power and enforced compliance.

A laboratory experiment provided support to these assumptions (Wahl et al., 2010). Participants imagined living in a fictitious country, named Varosia, and paying their taxes to authorities that were either trustworthy or not, and powerful or not. Participants were randomly assigned to one of the four experimental conditions and were informed about (a) their income in twenty tax-filing periods (3,500 experimental currency units, ECU), (b) their tax liability in each period (1,400 ECU = 40%), (c) the audit probability (10%), and (d) the fine in the event of detected evasion (equal to the evaded amount). In each period, participants decided how much tax to pay, from zero ECU to 1,400 ECU. After filing taxes, motivational postures were assessed. Table 8.5 shows the average tax payments by trust and power over twenty taxpaying periods. Participants contributed more if authorities were described as trustworthy rather than untrustworthy, and if authorities were described as powerful rather than weak. Tax payments were highest when trust and power were high and lowest when trust and power were low. The motivational posture commitment (a proxy for voluntary cooperation) and the motivational posture resistance (a proxy for enforced compliance) varied with trust and power. Voluntary compliance was highest when authorities were trustworthy and powerful, whereas enforced compliance was lowest in this case and increased when power increased and trust decreased. Similar results confirming the assumptions of the slippery slope framework were obtained in an online study that additionally revealed that, in cases of low trust and high power, strategic taxpaying behaviour – an indicator of deliberate decision-making – is likely to occur. Participants contributed the most when trust and power were high and the least when trust and power were low. Measures of the motives voluntary cooperation and enforced compliance varied with trust and power. Voluntary compliance was highest when authorities were trustworthy and powerful, whereas enforced compliance was lowest when authorities were trustworthy and weak; enforced compliance also increased when power increased and trust decreased.

The power-enhancing and trust-building measures proposed in the slippery slope framework are likely to affect each other, and therefore may have complex interactions and dynamics over time. However, the nature of this interplay is far from clear. On the one hand, it can be argued that the exertion of power may evoke suspicion and mistrust in the group upon which the measures are imposed, resulting in a vicious circle: mistrust in one party provokes mistrust in the other party, which justifies and deepens the mistrust in the first (e.g., Castelfranchi & Falcone, 2010; Farrell & Knight, 2003; Nooteboom, 2002). On the other hand, it can also be argued that power positively affects trust. Bachmann (2001) proposed that depersonalised forms of power (i.e., the power of a system) such as the law can be perceived as a necessary precondition for trust. Similarly, Mulder, Verboon and De Cremer (2009) argued that the law and its enforcement define the norms to be followed. Further, if sanctioning systems are perceived as a means of enforcing societal norms, trust would also increase due to authorities' power (Mulder, van Dijk, De Cremer & Wilke, 2006).

Power- and trust-building measures involve complex dynamics; hence, further research is needed to understand their interplay and their effects on citizens' compliance. What seems important, however, is to distinguish between different forms of power and different forms of trust. Regarding power, the most prominent taxonomy stems from French and Raven (1959), who differentiated five bases of power, especially 'legitimate power' and 'coercive power'. Transferred to the tax context, **legitimate power** is based on positive evaluations of authorities' power and positive attitudes towards authorities, whereas **coercive power** is based on tax

Table 8.5 Estimated means and standard errors of mean tax payments, enforced tax compliance and voluntary tax compliance by trust and power (from Wahl et al., 2010, p. 392)

	Low trust		High trust	
Dependent variables	Low power $n = 30$	High power $n = 31$	Low power $n = 30$	High power $n = 29$
Mean tax payments	655.83 (80.87)[a]	795.97 (78.22)[a]	718.74 (81.20)[a]	1042.58 (80.60)[b]
Voluntary tax compliance	2.81 (0.22)[a]	2.59 (0.22)[a]	4.49 (0.22)[b]	5.21 (0.22)[c]
Enforced tax compliance	3.78 (0.16)[a]	4.81 (0.16)[b]	2.93 (0.16)[c]	3.37 (0.16)[ac]

Note: Higher scores indicate higher tax payments and higher agreement with the two forms of compliance. Means are corrected for covariates gender, age, and income. Standard errors are given in parentheses. Estimated means with differing letters in the same row differ at $p < 0.05$.

authorities' ability to enforce a law regardless of its societal acceptance. It is likely that different types of power have different effects on trust. However, only a few of the discussions on the relationship between power and trust make these distinctions. For example, Korczynski (2000) argued that, whereas trust will be undermined if power is used to coerce cooperation, power exerted by an authority that is seen as legitimate can increase the quality of trust based on rational considerations. Similarly, Das and Teng (1998) argued that formal control mechanisms in organisations (e.g., a strict performance evaluation procedure) undermine trust, whereas social control mechanisms (e.g., stressing organisational values, norms and culture) enhance trust. Choudhury (2008) argued that power and control decrease trust when controls include out-dated rules, whereas the opposite is true when the exertion of power is rule-based and authorities monitor actions in a fair manner. As long as the power of authorities is perceived as legitimate, it probably has a positive effect on citizens' trust. On the other hand, coercive power probably has a negative effect on trust (Leonidou, Talias & Leonidou, 2008). Balliet and Van Lange (2013) investigated effects of trust on the effectiveness of measures of power. In their meta-analysis, they find that punishment promotes cooperation more effectively in societies with high trust. They argue that trust makes punishment work because society members count on each other and punish norm violations.

Different types of trust are also distinguished in the literature (Castelfranchi & Falcone, 2010; Lewis & Weigert, 1985; Tyler, 2003). Most conceptualisations separate a form of trust resulting from automatic and affective processes from another form based on a rational assessment of the predictability and competence of others and their trustworthiness. In the context of tax behaviour, the interplay between types of power and trust has been investigated by Hofmann, Gangl, Kirchler and Stark (2014).

Among financial authorities, recognition is growing that trust-building measures promote cooperation and are an important element of praxis. In the Netherlands, new forms of the interaction between authorities and taxpaying companies, known as '**horizontal monitoring**', are being tested (Gribnau, 2015b). Dutch, Austrian and other countries' tax authorities are switching from traditional vertical monitoring to horizontal monitoring. Vertical monitoring is based on checking tax files retroactively, whereas horizontal monitoring focuses on working in the present based on mutual trust, understanding and transparency between taxpayers and the authorities.

Horizontal monitoring is based on a good relationship between the taxpayer and the authorities, which is recorded in a compliance agreement.

8.6 Synergistic versus Antagonistic Climates: Recommended Practice

Even if most citizens accept the state as an authoritarian, paternalistic tax collector, and even if taxes seem legally justified and must be paid by all individuals with an income, there is the question of whether tax honesty is actually the norm rather than the exception. If taxpayers are assumed to be selfish, profit-maximising individuals, we unavoidably arrive at the conclusion that contributions are not made voluntarily, but are only paid when taxpayers are subject to legal coercion. This view is posited as the point of departure for all economic considerations of tax behaviour. According to these assumptions, strategies to secure tax honesty have been developed that are used by the authorities. However, the success these strategies promise in theory remains elusive in practice.

The slippery slope framework integrates economic and psychological perspectives on compliance. Successful interaction between citizens and authorities requires a synergistic climate in the state as a whole, rather than an antagonistic opposition. Elected officials and authorities have to orient themselves towards administering and shaping the country in line with the mandate of the people. Nevertheless, they also ought to be able to ensure that those willing to cooperate are not exploited by 'free-riders' acting selfishly. Non-cooperative citizens need to be led back to the values of the community by way of strict regulatory measures, or they must be denied the opportunity to abuse social values selfishly. It is thus necessary to apply strategies based on both economic and psychological arguments to promote mutual trust and cooperation. Alm and Torgler (2011) and James, Hasseldine, Hite and Toumi (2003) stipulated a series of measures that can be summed up as follows:

- Tax law must be simplified so that taxpayers understand it.
- Instead of a plethora of rules with exceptions, principles of behaviour need to be fixed in the law to minimise the room for interpretation and negotiation.
- Tax authorities and above all tax auditors need to be efficiently trained so that they are experts in tax law and are able to treat taxpayers according to their motivations and abilities in order to apply regulation strategies effectively.
- Tax authorities need to cooperate intensively with legislators, judges and international authorities.
- The use of tax money must be transparent; advertising campaigns should be used to inform the public of the services available so that the fair exchange of tax contributions for state services is clear.
- Social norms of correct behaviour need to be promoted and communicated, and measures need to be taken that strengthen citizens' and residents' identification with the community.
- Justice needs to be achieved on the distributive, procedural and retributive levels.
- Taxpayers need to be segmented according to their needs so that appropriate services can be offered to facilitate tax honesty, tailored to meet individual needs at the 'point of sale'.
- Audits are necessary to protect honest taxpayers from free-riders. Audits need to be directed at high-risk groups and to be effectively implemented.
- Negative sanctions are necessary at an adequate level and in the proper form, and should depend on the tax offender's ability to pay. Fines or prison sentences are two possible forms of retribution,

while the publication of offenders' names or the requirement of compulsory community service represent alternative sanctions.

The trend in tax behaviour research indicates a move from understanding taxpayers as selfish individuals trying to maximise their own gains to individuals with a sense of community who are ready to cooperate if all agents in the social system and the state contribute to a climate of mutual trust. The list of suggestions above combines considerations from economic and psychological research. In doing so, with regard to tax behaviour no ultimate preference is given to either of the two perspectives. Instead, we take account of the fact that all research paradigms and perspectives offer essential contributions to understanding tax behaviour and also note the great promise contained in integrating findings from the two disciplines. Indeed, Alm and Torgler (2011) argued that

> a full house of compliance strategies is needed to combat tax evasion, strategies that include the traditional 'enforcement' paradigm suggested by and consistent with neoclassical theory, a less traditional 'service' paradigm that recognizes the important role of a 'kinder and gentler' tax administration in encouraging compliance, and, importantly, a new 'trust' paradigm that is built on the foundation of ethics, in which the tax administration must recognize that it can erode the ethics of taxpayers by its own decisions. (Alm & Torgler, 2011, p. 635)

Conclusion

Tax income is essential for the maintenance of a society and its government. It is used to finance public services and civil servants and to correct injustices in the distribution of resources between a society's richer and poorer members. This should increase happiness, since income inequality and happiness have an inverse correlation. Consequently, revenue lost in the shadow economy is more than just a nuisance, as it is money that could be put to good use. Most people accept the necessity of paying taxes, yet they favour reduction of taxes while simultaneously desiring better public services. In addition, tax guidelines are perceived as too complicated. It is important to increase tax compliance, especially among the black sheep, to avoid a social contribution dilemma.

Nonetheless, just because some taxpayers try to evade taxes, not everyone should be treated as a potential criminal. Intrinsically motivated voluntary cooperation could suffer under a climate of coercive power. An environment with high trust in an authority that treats taxpayers justly and according to their behaviour, using a norm of reciprocity combined with high legitimate power to punish offenders adequately, is most promising. This conclusion marks a shift from an enforcement paradigm to a service paradigm for tax authorities; new strategies like horizontal monitoring are among the first practical applications of this new orientation.

Summary

- In the narrowest sense, the shadow economy comprises work and the exchange of goods on the black market with the aim of evading taxes and fees. In a broader sense, housework and helping one's neighbours also count – as do illegal activities like drug dealing, smuggling and dealing in stolen goods.
- Tax morale is an intrinsic motivation arising from the moral obligation to pay taxes correctly.
- The field of public finance justifies taxes with the equivalence or interest theory, insurance theory and sacrifice theory.
- The Lorenz curve relates the cumulative percentage of the population and the cumulative percentage of the population's total income. The Gini coefficient provides a summary measure of income inequality.
- Taxes and transfers can be appropriate regulatory tools aiding in the creation of a more just income distribution. However, the income gap has become significantly wider in the past few decades, with large income disparities even after taxes and transfers.
- Tax compliance describes taxpayers' willingness to pay their taxes. Non-compliance represents the most inclusive conceptualisation of the failure to meet tax obligations, regardless of whether that failure was intentional.
- Tax evasion behaviour is a deliberate act of non-compliance that results in the payment of less tax than actually owed. Tax avoidance, on the other hand, is within the legal framework of the tax law.
- Determinants of tax compliance can be organised into two groups: economic determinants on the one hand, such as frequency of audits, fines, marginal tax rate, income size and opportunity to avoid or to evade taxes, and psychological determinants on the other hand, such as complexity of tax law, attitudes, personal and social norms, procedural justice and retributive justice.
- Audits and fines seem to have a clear deterrent effect, albeit only a slight one. However, they do not have a long-lasting effect. In experiments, taxpayers' compliance showed a strong decrease immediately after an audit. Furthermore, audits and the threat of negative sanctions can be perceived as signalling a lack of trust, thus promoting deliberate decision-making.
- Not only negative sanctions affect taxpayer behaviour; social norms need to be accounted for as well. Likewise, socio-demographic, cultural and personality-specific variables are influential.
- The self-employed, in particular, are considered as a high-risk group for tax evasion. The general view, however, that the self-employed are overall unwilling to pay their taxes is also not correct. This may apply to self-employed people in their early years, but the tendency towards tax evasion lessens with increasing work experience.
- The slippery slope framework assumes that tax payments are influenced by trust and the power of authorities. High power and trust lead to high tax compliance. As long as the power of authorities is perceived as legitimate, it seems to have a positive effect on citizens' trust. On the other hand, coercive power seems to have a negative effect on trust.

- The psychological contract implies that citizens entrust their money to a tax authority to invest it in sensible projects. This relationship is characterised by mutual loyalty and emotional ties. The disappointment of expectations represents a violation of the contract.
- In the 'enforcement paradigm', taxpayers are treated as potential criminals, while the 'service paradigm' acknowledges the need to ease tax honesty by offering services.

Questions

1 What is the 'insurance theory' regarding the justification of taxes?
2 What does a Gini coefficient of 1 mean?
3 What is 'capitulative compliance'?
4 What is 'coercive power' in the context of the slippery slope model?
5 What is the 'bomb crater effect'?

FURTHER READING

Braithwaite, J. (2005). *Markets in vice, markets in virtue*. Leichhardt: The Federation Press.

Braithwaite, V. A. (ed.) (2001). *Taxing democracy: Understanding tax avoidance and evasion*. Aldershot: Ashgate.

Kirchler, E. (2007). *The economic psychology of tax behaviour*. Cambridge: Cambridge University Press.

Torgler, B. (2007). *Tax compliance and tax morale: A theoretical and empirical analysis*. Cheltenham: Edward Elgar.

9 Collective Production: Work and Unemployment

Overview

Modern societies are characterised by extreme specialisation and division of labour, and production is highly intertwined. In consequence, production is a topic of relevance on the society level. Societies develop specific views on the meaning of work. These views shape opinions about how work should be structured and about people who do not find work.

The meaning of paid work has undergone a number of changes in the course of history. Work was at one time considered a burden, and those who could afford not to work did not. Later, work came to be seen as a service to society. Presently, it is postulated that work must both be a service to society and satisfy workers' extrinsic and intrinsic needs. In particular, the focus on intrinsic motivation and its connection to job performance and well-being is relevant for questions of how to structure work. Changes have also occurred in working time over the decades, and consequently the focus is on the importance of leisure. The question is how work and leisure influence each other, and how work–life balance can contribute to both performance and well-being.

The labour market structure has changed as well. The trend towards greater flexibility in employment relationships means that people more often need to search for work. Consequences of job loss are not only of an economic nature, but also of a social and psychological nature. Unemployment has severe psychosocial effects and is connected with physical and psychological well-being. However, consequences of unemployment are not the same for everyone – they are moderated by a number of psychological variables, for example the subjective importance of work. Chances for re-employment also differ depending on psychological variables such as self-esteem and job search strategies.

Introduction

In most societies, work has a central role. People invest a lot of time and energy into paid work. Young people seek education and training, be it in the form of an apprenticeship, school or university, to secure a better chance of getting a job they desire. Work is important for identity, for an understanding of who we are. Additionally, many societies see the work of individuals as a way to evaluate their worth in the community. Consequently, the loss of a job is often stigmatised and connected with a decline in social standing, sometimes even accompanied by feelings of resignation and depression.

9.1 Work

The meaning of work has changed over the centuries, and today it has several psychological components that go beyond just securing one's living. It is currently acknowledged that work should also provide intrinsic motivation and that organisational outcomes are influenced by an interplay of job demands and job resources. In recent decades, the focus has also shifted to leisure as non-working time, and its relevance for job performance and well-being.

9.1.1 Historical Changes in the Meaning of Work

The bulk of adults' time – with the exception of time spent asleep – is occupied by paid and unpaid work. Paid employment and housework, as well as the rhythm of work, structure the daily lives of many people. Despite its importance, the time spent working is often perceived as burdensome. The time under one's direct control, in contrast, becomes precious leisure time. According to Lipset (1992, p. 45), 'the idea that human beings should work hard because it is virtuous, or contributes to the common good, or allows them to accumulate personal possessions and wealth is a relatively recent phenomenon'. In ancient times and in the Middle Ages, work was regarded as a dishonourable activity. The Greeks saw work as a curse. Aristotle despised working people and viewed work as unrighteous (Unrein, 1978). During the Middle Ages, meeting physical needs and avoiding idleness – which was regarded as a sin – became the central functions of work (Hill, 1992).

The Reformation, the renewal movement in Western Europe during the sixteenth century, brought a new perspective to work. Martin Luther and John Calvin were two key religious leaders during this period in history who were discontented with the Catholic Church. Luther disagreed with the medieval concept that one form of work was superior to another – as in monastic life versus physical labour – and regarded all kinds of work as being of equal dignity. Both Luther and Calvin saw work as a societal duty, yet they had different views on occupational selection and the accumulation of wealth. Luther claimed that people should carry out the occupation they were born into, and thereby serve God. He claimed that a person should earn only enough to meet basic needs, but not to aggregate monetary wealth, which he regarded as sinful. Calvin, on the other hand, viewed it as one's duty to choose an occupation that allowed one to earn the greatest profit. He encouraged people to pursue high profits, not for personal wealth, which he also regarded as sinful, but in order to reinvest it into further ventures. Calvin believed that the only way to find out if a person would get a place in heaven was through his success in a profession (Hill, 1992; Lipset, 1992). Max Weber (1968) emphasised that Calvinistic puritanism and Lutheran pietism led to an understanding of work as a service to God, leading to a work ethic of diligence, conscientiousness, punctuality and deferred gratification. He did not state – as is often claimed – that capitalism was derived directly from Protestant ethics, but believed rather that Protestant ethics laid the societal basis for capitalist ideas.

With the transition from the late Middle Ages to the early modern period, a restructuring of the medieval social order began to take place. The number of beggars and vagabonds grew. Problems of social integration cropped up for the first time to a greater extent. 'A new sensibility to poverty and to the duties of assistance, new forms of reaction to the economic problems of unemployment and idleness, a new ethic of work' arose (Foucault, 1965, p. 46). Work primarily served to fulfil economic goals and as a means of personal development. Böhrs (1969) particularly emphasised economic goals in his understanding of human work as the deployment of a person's physical, mental and spiritual talents for the satisfaction of his material and non-material needs. Presently, Protestant norms such as fulfilling one's obligations, a strong work ethic and obedience appear to be less worth striving for. Work and thrift have lost some of their value, while privacy and freedom have become more highly valued.

Several decades ago, Inglehart (1977, 2000) argued that materialist values would soon make way for postmaterialist values: when work is scarce, it is evaluated particularly positively. That which is scarce appears valuable and that which can be found in excess loses value. Many people in the industrialised world have come to take material prosperity for granted. This has come at the cost of discipline, conscientiousness, a sense of duty and the willingness to make sacrifices. As prosperity becomes a given, work is considered a nuisance and **postmaterialist values** emphasising autonomy and self-expression become more valuable. This includes a higher valuation of leisure time and hedonic experiences. However, Opaschowski (2001) argued that hedonism does not necessarily distract from performance: work and pleasure are both part of life. Those who cannot enjoy life will not be able to sustain high levels of performance over the long run. Rather, they will be burned out by their work.

Values in the world of work and the demands put on paid employment change over time. While some studies emphasise the increasing importance of income, others emphasise that work should provide opportunities for personal development. According to Maas and Schüller (1990), several changes can be identified: from short-term to long-term thinking, from centralised to decentralised ways of making decisions, from external determination to self-determination, and to a certain extent from economy to ecology.

There are different ways of studying developments over time. One way is a repeated cross-sectional approach, meaning that different samples are compared over time. Kalleberg and Marsden (2013) investigated the development of work-related values in the United States with this approach. A representative sample of members of the workforce was drawn at sixteen points in time between 1973 and 2006 and interviewed about values. It was then possible to investigate changes in work-related values by comparing the sixteen different samples with each other. Participants were given five job characteristics to rank. The characteristics were high income, job stability, working hours, opportunities for advancement and feelings of accomplishment. The first four can be regarded as extrinsic and the last as intrinsic. Their results showed that the intrinsic job characteristic was ranked highest throughout the study period. The importance of a high income and job stability grew over the years. The authors explain this by pointing to the vast changes in the labour market that occurred during this time, including growing job insecurity, wage inequality, and high demand for skilled workers due to technological changes. They also show that workers with low education emphasise income relative to other work values.

Another way to study developments over time is to interview the same sample over a longer period of time – a longitudinal approach. In the context of work-related values, this allows for an investigation of stability and changes in work-related values across the life span, as Jin and Rounds (2012) conducted in their meta-analysis. They studied the development of four value categories: intrinsic, extrinsic, social and status. Ryan and Deci (2000) postulated in their 'self-determination theory' that intrinsic motivation results from satisfied needs for competence, autonomy and psychological relatedness. In Jin and Rounds (2012), intrinsic values include creativity, learning, independence and opportunities to utilise one's abilities. Extrinsic values include financial success, security and a good work environment. Social values include helping other people, working with people and social relations. Status values include prestige, advancement, authority, and power and control. Jin and Rounds (2012) found that intrinsic values remained stable over time. Extrinsic values decreased during adolescence and one's college years, and then increased again when individuals started their first jobs. Social values decreased consistently with age. Status values showed a decreasing trend from adolescence to young adulthood, but increased again after the age of 26. The combination of these results indicates that intrinsic values have great importance to both older and younger generations and fluctuate very little over time.

The evaluation of work and attitudes towards work differ from person to person. People who are highly involved in their work appear to have high demands that many jobs cannot fully satisfy. People who are less work-oriented, on the other hand, devalue the importance of work as a dominant sphere of life, view paid work primarily as an opportunity to earn money, and seek fulfilment in the private sphere and in their leisure time in order to compensate (Opaschowski, 1982).

In addition to differences among individuals, cultural differences also exist in terms of the meaning of work and demands made on work. Repeated surveys about postmaterialist and materialist orientations, and the meaning of work, as well as satisfaction with one's work (Beretta, 1993) showed that postmaterialist value systems were most dominant in Austria, the Netherlands, Norway and Germany at the data collection points. Materialist values prevailed in Ireland, Northern Ireland, the USA and the UK. In Italy, Hungary and Israel, materialist and postmaterialist values were balanced. It can be surmised that work loses importance as postmaterialist value orientations gain ground, and work is no longer seen as the most important life activity. In most nations – independent of the dominant value orientation – very few people agree with the statement that work is the most important thing in life. Satisfaction with one's work is markedly dependent on one's value system: people who have developed postmaterialist values and perceive work as an opportunity to satisfy intrinsic needs are more likely to report that they are happy with their work than people with materialist values who view their work as an opportunity to fulfil extrinsic motivations. A more recent review of the effects of national culture on the meaning of work (Rosso, Dekas & Wrzesniewski, 2010) indicates that, regardless of national culture, work centrality, intrinsic factors and financial motivations tend to be relatively high. The authors' conclusion is that the variance within a culture is larger than that between different cultures with regard to the meaning of work. Similar results were found by Kuchinke et al. (2011), who reported that work centrality was high in eight different countries. Work was ranked second to family as the most important life domain. When confronted with the scenario of a high lottery win, most participants in all eight countries indicated that they would prefer to continue working even though it was no longer financially necessary.

On the one hand, work is considered an opportunity for personal development and is therefore seen as the point of intersection between strenuous effort and the joys of accomplishment. According to this view, work contains that which in everyday understanding is typically ascribed to leisure time. On the other hand, work can be a burden that stands in sharp contrast to the pleasures of free time. Not uncommonly is leisure viewed as the opposite of work. Before further elaborating on the balance of work and leisure, we will first define work as it is understood at present, and describe in more detail the importance of the design and structure of work for motivation and satisfaction.

9.1.2 The Structure of Work

The following definitions of work highlight both the goals of work and the input in the form of material and psychological resources:

> Work is a change in nature on the basis of a dialectical mediation process between man and nature (subject and object) which is consciously intended by man for the purpose of creating optimal living conditions through the deployment of psycho-physical powers and with the help of technological energies and resources. (Schmale, 1983, pp. 46–7)

> Work can be defined as systematic human activity directed toward an economic or organisational goal, which involves the deployment of physical and mental abilities. Work, therefore, consists of methodical actions directed toward the fulfilment of tasks that are part of economic or organisational processes under specific conditions and through the utilisation of various resources (particularly tools and technical resources, as well as human abilities and achievements). (Nerdinger, Blickle & Schaper, 2011, p. 6)

Work should be designed so that it contains a high degree of motivation potential for those doing the work. The theoretical basis for intrinsically motivating work was developed by Hackman and Oldham (1976) in their **job characteristics model**. According to this theory, work must be designed according to three fundamental conditions: (a) knowledge must be provided about the results of current tasks, especially about the quality of the steps one has taken; (b) one must assume responsibility for the outcomes resulting from one's work; and (c) the significance of one's work must be perceptible.

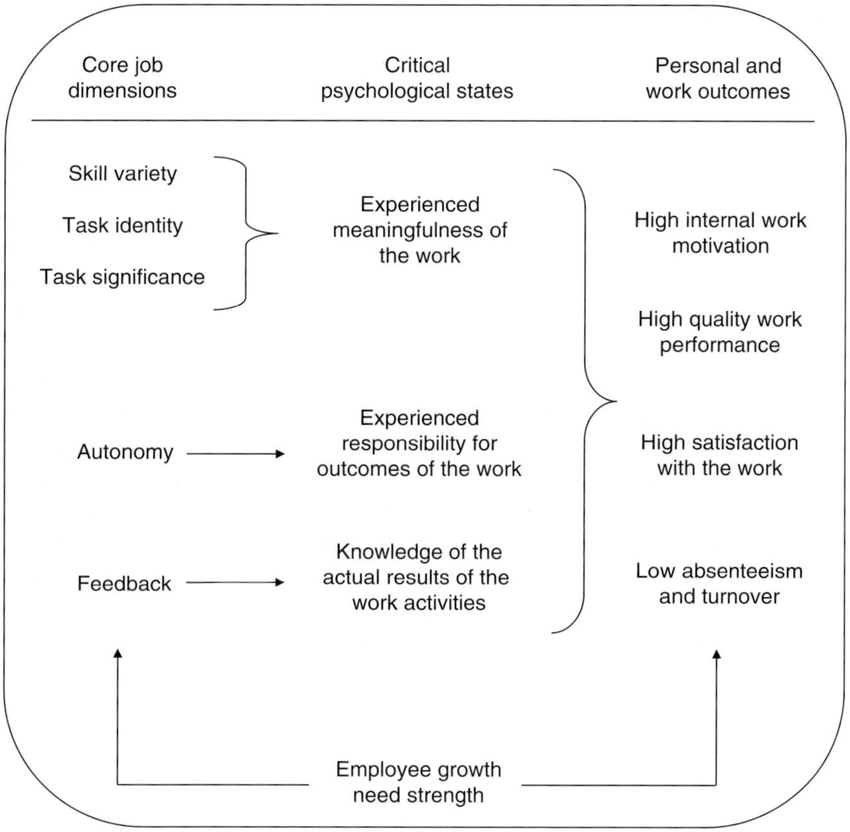

Figure 9.1 Job characteristics model of work motivation (Hackman & Oldham, 1976, p. 256)

These fundamental psychological dimensions are determined by five job dimensions or task characteristics (Figure 9.1): variety in the skills required, the comprehensiveness of the task (termed 'task identity'), the significance of the task, autonomy and feedback from the task. The theory further assumes that individual differences in the need for personal development ('employee growth need strength') moderate the link between task characteristics and outcomes.

The **motivating potential score** – that is, the degree to which a task can be intrinsically motivating – of a given task can be calculated from task characteristics using the following formula (Hackman & Oldham, 1976, p. 258):

$$\text{Motivating potential score} = \left[\frac{\text{Skill variety} + \text{Task identity} + \text{Task significance}}{3}\right] * \text{Autonomy} * \text{Feedback}$$

The additive operation represents that for experienced meaningfulness the sub-components skill variety, task identity and task significance can balance one another, with strength in one helping to compensate for weakness in another. The multiplicative operation represents that all three components – experienced meaningfulness, experienced responsibility and knowledge about the results – are indispensable conditions for work to be perceived as motivating.

Work should be structured so that it is comprehensive and not monotonous. It should have meaning both for those doing the work and for society as a whole. Moreover, carrying out one's work should offer opportunities for autonomy, and clear information should be given regarding progress achieved towards reaching objectives. Job motivation and job satisfaction are closely linked to one another and are conducive to better performance. Indeed, it can be empirically demonstrated that highly productive companies are usually the ones with a good work culture. Additionally, employee satisfaction and employee engagement co-vary with profitability and productivity (Harter, Schmidt & Hayes, 2002; McGuigan, McGuigan & Mallett, 2015; Sanchez & McCauley, 2006).

Today's work environment is changing. Globally competitive markets have forced organisations to shift from hierarchical and centralised structures to decentralised and flexible ones (Cascio, 2013). Rosa (2003) emphasised that Western societies are in a process of technological acceleration, acceleration of social change and a general acceleration of the pace of life. These changes have led to new ways of working. Voß and Pongratz (1998) describe an increase in employers' expectations regarding employee self-organisation as a consequence of this change, meaning that employees now need to plan and structure their workdays more autonomously. Knowledge workers are particularly independent of any specific workspace, a fact that has led to more frequent home office arrangements and target agreements instead of fixed working hours. Employers are seeking employees who are flexible, motivated, independent and responsible. According to Hackman and Oldham's (1976) model, increasing autonomy should always lead to higher levels of intrinsic work motivation. However, Korunka and Kubicek (2013) argue that high autonomy can lead to stress when paired with high flexibility, increased pressure to perform and little operational regulation, all three of which are common in today's work environment. Hence, factors influencing work-related response variables cannot be analysed in isolation from other relevant influences; they must be considered in light of the prevailing work context.

One model that considers both the work context and the characteristics of the working person is the **job demands-resources model** (JD-R; Bakker & Demerouti, 2007) (Figure 9.2). This model is based on the assumption that two general classes of factors exist for every type of occupation: job demands and job resources. Job demands resemble physiological and/or psychological costs. Included in this category are, for example, a high pressure to perform, an unhealthy physical environment and emotionally demanding interactions with clients. While job demands are not necessarily always negative, they have the potential to evolve into job strains and thus ultimately lead to stress. Job resources, on the other hand, fulfil three main functions. First, they act as a moderator between job demands and possible strains, thereby reducing the effects of job demands on strains. Second, job resources help employees achieve work goals by enhancing motivation, in line with the basic assumptions of Hackman and Oldham's (1976) job characteristics model. Third, on a personal level, job resources stimulate learning, growth and development. Furthermore, job demands have a moderating effect on the positive relationship between job resources and motivation. Job resources have particularly beneficial effects on workers' motivation when job demands are high. Thus, the combined effect of job demands and job resources is either strain or motivation. While strains are assumed to influence organisational outcomes negatively, motivation has a positive effect.

While Figure 9.2 shows autonomy as a job resource in the JD-R model, Bakker and Demerouti (2007) emphasise that the particular factors that are viewed as job demands or job resources can vary depending on the occupational setting, which is a key strength of the model. The unique characteristics of each working context can be taken into account and evaluated as either beneficial or challenging for employees. In this vein, in certain jobs autonomy could be classified

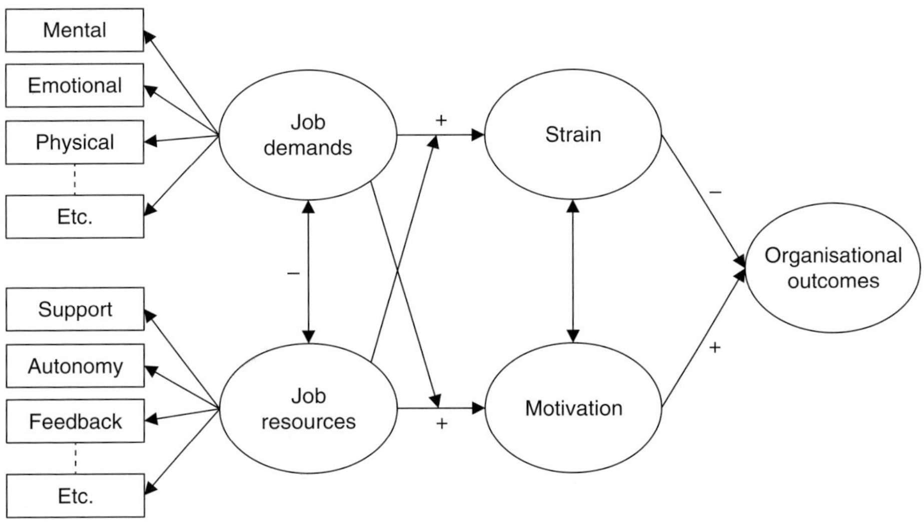

Figure 9.2 Job demands-resources model (Bakker & Demerouti, 2007, p. 313)

as a demand instead of a resource. This is particularly the case for knowledge workers who must come to terms with new working environments.

The relationship between job satisfaction and subjective well-being has occupied social scientists for a long time. On one hand, a generalised positive correlation between the two, a spillover effect, has been proposed. On the other hand, a compensation effect has also been postulated, according to which the relationship between job and life satisfaction must be negative. A segregation effect – no correlation – has also been proposed. In a study of 459 Canadian office workers, Gosselin (2000) and Dolan and Gosselin (1998) found a generalisation effect in 49% of participants, compensation effects in 44% of participants and segregation effects in 7%. Numerous studies have demonstrated the importance of satisfaction with one's work for general life happiness levels. In a meta-analysis, Bowling, Eschleman and Wang (2010) found an average correlation of $r = 0.40$ between global job satisfaction and life satisfaction, supporting a spillover effect. Similar correlations were found for happiness ($r = 0.36$), positive affect ($r = 0.38$) and the absence of negative affect ($r = 0.27$). However, the causal direction is unclear and may be reciprocal or due to third variables. For longitudinal studies, Bowling et al. (2010) found somewhat stronger effects from subjective well-being (at time 1) to job satisfaction (at time 2) than from job satisfaction (at time 1) to subjective well-being (at time 2). Personal dispositions, such as core self-evaluations, have been found to influence both job satisfaction and life satisfaction (Judge, Locke, Durham & Kluger, 1998).

9.1.3 Work and Leisure

Over 100 years ago, people spent more than 80 hours per week working, every day was a work day, and holiday time was unknown to working people. Accordingly, the question as to the importance of leisure time was not even on academics' radar, particularly not with regard to its effect on work. Time spent working reached its peak in the middle of the nineteenth century and has sunk since the Industrial Revolution, meaning that more leisure time is now available and can be used by each individual as seen fit.

The concept of a balance between work and free time is particularly important because it became difficult to set boundaries between the main areas of life. This is due to fundamental changes in the social, technical and operational frameworks in which professional work – and indeed, life in general – are embedded. The disintegration of the temporal boundaries between work, free time and the private sphere that are seen in new forms of work (e.g., telecommuting, working from home, etc.), and the difficulty of balancing responsibility for professional work and family work and dividing it up fairly between romantic partners have led to greater academic interest in the question of **work–life balance** (e.g., Klumb & Gemmiti, 2011; Moser, 2007; Prantl, 2005; Zaugg, 2006). This concept refers to the distribution of working and non-working time as well as to subjective feelings of balance and satisfaction with regard to this distribution. Research in this field focuses on the compatibility of family, private life and career success; the organisation of these spheres of life; and the balancing of employers' and employees' interests.

In their literature review, Kalliath and Brough (2008) determined that a clear definition of work–life balance does not yet exist. The literature references the multiple roles occupied by one person, the equal distribution of time for various roles and satisfaction with these roles, acceptance of the importance of various roles, conflict between roles and perceived feelings of control over various roles. The authors propose integrating these aspects, providing the definition that 'work–life balance is the individual perception that work and non-work activities are compatible and promote growth in accordance with an individual's current life priorities' (p. 326).

Ideally, work experiences, leisure time experiences and experiences in the private sphere are all satisfying and compatible with one another. However, work is often structured in such a way that people do not find fulfilment. Things that are not possible at one's job can sometimes be sought out in one's free time and thus compensated for. When needs that are left unsatisfied and abilities that are left to languish at work are developed in one's free time, work and free time complement one another. The views of the association between paid work and free time can be organised into four extreme positions (Büssing, 1992; Hoff, 1986, 1993; Stengel, 1988; Ulich & Ulich, 1977):

(a) According to the **neutrality hypothesis** (also called autonomy hypothesis or segmentation hypothesis), modes of behaviour and experiences at work and during leisure time have no connection to one another. The implicit assumption is that people are capable of making clear distinctions between various spheres of life and of reacting completely differently in different situations. Personality characteristics that, for example, lead to certain experiences and behaviours at work would have to be of little importance during one's free time. On the other hand, certain personality factors that are important for the activities in one's free time have little effect on work outcomes. Looking at this hypothesis, the objection can be made that people cannot be split into two parts – a 'work time person' and a 'leisure time person'. Critical holistic constructs such as personality cannot be reconciled with the segmentation hypothesis.

(b) In contrast to the neutrality hypothesis, the generalisation and compensation hypotheses propose that experiences and behaviours at work influence experiences and behaviours during leisure time (or vice versa). The distinction between the terms generalisation and compensation refers to whether reinforcing or balancing effects are assumed. According to the **generalisation hypothesis**, positive experiences at work are generalised to leisure time as well, resulting in leisure time that is actively structured and considered enjoyable. According to the **compensation hypothesis**, positive experiences during one's free time balance out negative experiences at work.

(c) While the generalisation and compensation hypotheses assume unidirectional effects from work on free time (or vice versa), the **interaction hypothesis** argues that experiences and behaviours at work and during free time both exert influence on one another. Work and free time have mutual effects on one another.

(d) The fact that the available data from various empirical studies are so confusing suggests that experiences at work are associated with free-time activities and experiences through third variables. The **congruence hypothesis** regarding the interaction between free time and work proposes that experiences and modes of behaviour at work and during free time are indeed associated with one another; however, the correlation is governed by third variables.

When empirical findings do not confirm the neutrality hypothesis, they often support the generalisation or interaction hypothesis and only rarely the compensation hypothesis. Argyris (1959) investigated the leisure time activities of blue-collar workers at various companies in the metalworking industry that differed from one another primarily in terms of their technological set-up. In one department, tasks had to be carried out that made relatively high demands on workers' skills. According to Argyris (1959), workers in this department were significantly more active and more creative in their free time than their colleagues in another department with partially automated work processes where lower demands were made on workers' skills. However, more recent studies have also found support for the congruence hypothesis. Sonnentag (2012) emphasises that detachment from work during leisure time is most relevant to well-being and job performance. **Job detachment** means refraining from job-related activities and thoughts during after-work hours. Sonnentag (2012) explains that the connection between stressful job-related situations and high levels of psychological strain is reduced if job detachment is high. People who successfully detach from work during their leisure time report higher levels of psychological well-being and feel more refreshed at the beginning of a working week. This shows that the association between work and leisure time is moderated by detachment from work.

The question of how and to what extent experiences at work and during free time mutually shape one another has not yet been conclusively settled. It is nevertheless clear that increases in time spent at work come at the cost of free time and vice versa. A person who decides to accept a job or to expand his working hours will consider the loss of free time as a cost factor in his deliberations. If work is perceived to be more burdensome than free time, the benefits gained from work must at least balance out the costs incurred from the loss of free time. Conversely, being freed from the burden of work could be experienced as positive. However, as research on unemployment shows, for most people a loss of work is a severely negative event.

9.2 Unemployment

Job loss is one of the greatest worries for people. Concerns about work, income and maintaining one's standard of living are especially high in times of economic crisis. In 2010, the risk of unemployment was the most frequently mentioned and negatively evaluated association with the financial and economic crises (Gangl, Kastlunger, Kirchler & Voracek, 2012).

Unemployment is not just a problem for the unemployed themselves and their families: it is also a political problem and a problem affecting society as a whole. For that reason, in most countries, periodic measurements are taken of the proportion of unemployed persons in the total population, and an increase in the number of unemployed people is discussed with great concern.

The International Labour Organisation (ILO) defines people as unemployed if they meet all of the following criteria: they are without work, currently available for work and actively seeking work (Hussmanns, 2007). Eurostat, the statistical office of the European Union, and the Bureau of Labour

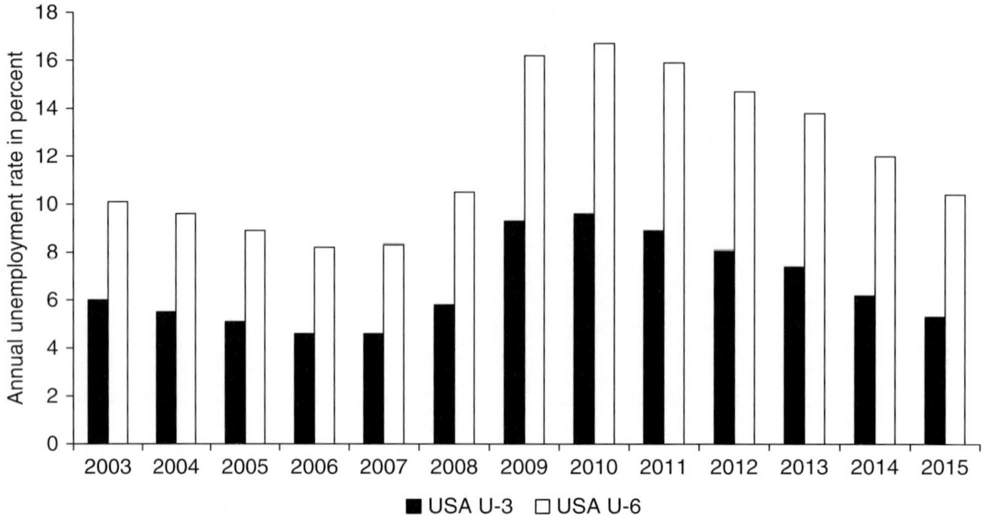

Figure 9.3 Annual unemployment rate in the USA 2003–15 as assessed by two different methods, U-3 and U-6 (data from www.bls.gov/lau/stalt_archived.htm, accessed 1 March 2017)

Statistics, a federal agency in the United States, measure the unemployment rate based on the ILO definition. Both define job seekers as people who have actively looked for a job in the previous four weeks, e.g., had a job interview, contacted an employment agency, sent out résumés, etc. Data are collected in a representative sample of the total population and then extrapolated to the population as a whole.

The ILO definition of unemployment fails to fully represent the job market situation. By definition, people are already regarded as being employed if they work for at least one hour within the reference period. In the United States, this reference period is defined as the week in which the current survey is conducted. Hence, part-time and temporary work is regarded as employment, regardless of a person's desire for a full-time job. Additionally, long-term unemployed people who may feel discouraged and have not made an active effort to find a job in the previous four weeks are not considered to be unemployed for the purposes of the official unemployment rate. Hence, the Bureau of Labour Statistics publishes – in addition to the official unemployment rate that follows the ILO definition (labelled as U-3) – other unemployment rates (from U-1 to U-6). The most extensive unemployment rate is U-6. It includes all people without work, who are discouraged, who have a part-time job due to economic reasons, or who indicate that they want and are available for a job but have not looked for one in the previous four weeks. When U-3 is compared to U-6, a large difference becomes evident (Figure 9.3). Different definitions of unemployment create different representations of the labour market. Considering that the unemployment rate is an important indicator of the state of the economy, the definition of unemployment can have political relevance. One advantage of the common use of the ILO definition is the easy comparability of unemployment rates amongst many countries.

9.2.1 Psychosocial Consequences of Unemployment

Unemployment represents a macroeconomic, a political and most importantly a psychosocial problem for those directly affected by it. Unemployment also has a beneficial potential by removing the stresses and burdens associated with work, increasing one's leisure time and therefore opportunities to be with one's partner, family members and friends, and offering the chance for a fresh start in one's working career. Nonetheless, Frese and Mohr (1978) identified a variety of losses associated with unemployment. Unemployment often entails the loss of (a) the structuring of daily life through work, (b) economic security, (c) career prospects, (d) social recognition, (e) social contacts with work colleagues, (f) one's feeling of importance to society, (g) stimuli from one's social environment, and – particularly for men in traditional relationships – (h) the role of the breadwinner in the family.

Unemployment is a shocking life event that represents a rupture in the social biographies of those affected by it (Wacker, 1983). Losing one's job means more than just being excluded from the production process. It is a threat to the entire fabric of one's life. In many countries today, unemployment does not endanger material reproduction any more, since the social safety net provided by unemployment insurance alleviates the most egregious financial problems. Nevertheless, economic distress still forces the unemployed to curtail their previous lifestyle (Waters & Moore, 2001).

The first studies on the psychosocial effects of unemployment date back to the time of the Great Depression in the 1930s. According to official data, the unemployment rate in industrialised countries in the 1930s rose to over 20% (Jahoda, 1983). Studies on the effects of unemployment on physical health came to often devastating conclusions. A medical examination of a school in a Welsh community with a 58% unemployment rate found that roughly 21% of children were undernourished (Save the Children International Union, 1933). The situation in Poland was even worse: 25% of the children surveyed did not get any breakfast at all, 5% received only dry bread, and 50% got dry bread and tea. Studies on the adult population's state of health, however, give the impression that overall health improved with unemployment when the former working conditions were unfavourable. Jahoda, Lazarsfeld and Zeisel (1971) reported that people from the Austrian village of Marienthal who had worked in the village factory's spinning and weaving departments became healthier after the factory shut down and they lost their jobs. They were no longer exposed to the noise and air pollution that had put them at risk of tuberculosis. Jahoda (1983, p. 40) argued that these contradictory findings in terms of health detriments can be brought into agreement. On the one hand, no longer being exposed to harmful working conditions can have a positive short-term effect on one's health. On the other hand, it takes some time for the effects of malnutrition on health to become apparent.

Symptoms of mental illness in particular seem to increase when the unemployment rate rises: Brenner (1979) found that economic crises and unemployment correlate with hospitalisation rates in psychiatric facilities and rates of heart disease in the long run. Economic crises also lead to an increase in rates of depression and suicide (Farmer, Preston & O'Brien, 1977; Walbran, MacMahon & Bailey, 1965). Vigderhous and Fishman (1978) considered the unemployment rate to be the strongest predictor of short- and long-term changes in suicide rates in the English-speaking world. Newman and Bland (2007) investigated suicide attempts in Canada and determined that unemployment leads to higher parasuicide rates. Boor (1980) confirmed the link between unemployment and suicide in Canada, France, Germany, Japan, Sweden and the United States, but did not find significant correlations for Italy and the United Kingdom. Schöny, Grausgruber and Sommereder (1988) analysed suicides in Austria for the period 1977–84, finding an average suicide rate of 25.0 suicides per 100,000 people. For unemployed men, the rate rose to 167.0, whereas the rate for unemployed women was relatively low, namely at 16.6. Moser, Fox, Jones and Goldblatt (1986) also reported high suicide rates for unemployed men, roughly 70% above the comparison level. Huikari and Korhonen (2016) explored suicide rates in Finland during 1991 and 2011 and found that unemployment expectations have a negative effect on well-being and that regional, working-age male suicide rates increase. Working-age males suffer especially from unemployment if regional unemployment rates are low relative to the average rate in Finland. Using time series analysis, Ceccherini-Nelli and Priebe (2011) studied the associations over time between death rates by suicide and three major economic factors – unemployment, real gross domestic product per capita (RGDP) and the consumer price index (CPI). Data sets from the UK (1901–2006), the USA (1900–97), France (1970–2004) and Italy (1970–2001) were included in the analyses. High rates of unemployment were associated with higher suicide rates in all four countries in the long run. The association between suicide rates and the remaining two economic factors (RGDP and CPI) applied to France and Italy only and was less consistent overall. Noh (2009) found higher suicide rates at higher income levels and in wealthier countries in particular. Alcohol consumption is a well-known risk factor for suicide and could be one possible mediator of increased suicide rates during unemployment (Sher, 2005). Khan, Murray and Barnes (2002) showed that short-term unemployment leads to a reduction in alcohol use, while longer periods of unemployment are tied to an increase in alcohol consumption.

Using meta-analytic techniques on 104 empirical studies with 146 independent samples, McKee-Ryan, Song, Wanberg and Kinicki (2005) examined the impact of unemployment on physical and psychological well-being. (a) Physical well-being was divided into subjective health (self-reports) and objective health (medical measurements). Unemployed workers displayed significantly lower subjective and objective physical health in cross-sectional comparisons between employed and unemployed workers. However, in longitudinal comparisons where workers were followed from employment into unemployment, job loss had no effect on subjective physical health (no data on objective physical health were available). This indicates that high-risk health behaviour occurs during a longer period of unemployment and not immediately after job loss. (b) Psychological well-being was defined as mental health and life satisfaction. Both were significantly lower in the group of unemployed workers in cross-sectional analyses. A significant reduction in mental health was also reported following job loss. However, it is important to consider that newly unemployed workers differ in their sensitivity and vulnerability to this type of life event (Lazarus & Folkman, 1984). One person might view unemployment as a threat, while another might see it as a challenge. The perspective one takes depends on one's cognitive appraisal, an evaluative framework determining whether an event will be viewed as stressful. Indeed, stress appraisals were negatively associated with mental health during unemployment (McKee-Ryan et al., 2005). Higher levels of mental health and life satisfaction were reported for unemployed persons with high re-employment expectations.

Already in the 1930s, studies delivered a comprehensive picture of psychological well-being during a period of unemployment. Among the most famous is the classic work on unemployment in the Austrian village of **Marienthal** (Jahoda et al., 1971). Starting at the end of 1931 and continuing into the following year, researchers at the University of Vienna provided a detailed picture of the situation in Marienthal. When the only factory – a flax mill operating since 1830 – was shut down, a large majority of residents became unemployed. Numbers and statistics captured life in the village on 120 workdays in various ways. A list of residents, crime statistics, accounting data from the consumer cooperative, library and election statistics and data on in- and out-migration were studied. The village's teachers, pastor and local businesspeople were asked to describe daily life. Schoolchildren were given purposefully selected composition topics in order to gain a sense of the situation from their perspective. Some people were interviewed about their life biographies; other people were asked to report on their meals and the ways they spent their time. Walking speed on the streets was measured and conversations in pubs were recorded. Finally, attempts were made to reconstruct the historical development of Marienthal on the basis of records and personal interviews with representatives of political parties, associations and societies, and other institutions. At the time of data collection, a total of 1,486 people were living in 478 households in Marienthal. In 358 households, at least one person had to collect unemployment benefits or welfare payments; nine households had to make ends meet without any public assistance at all; eighteen households received retirement benefits and in only ninety-three households was at least one person employed.

The financial losses bore down hard on village residents. The strains were so clearly traceable to residents' financial deficits that the research team was able to detect four types of unemployed people: the unbroken, the resigned, the despairing and the apathetic. Their circumstances ranged from bearable to hopeless depending on the per capita financial resources available. Jahoda (1983, pp. 43–4) wrote: 'If one assigns the financial resources of those with unbroken morale a value of 100, the resigned can be rated at 88, the despairing at 74 and the apathetic at 56.' The unbroken were able to keep their households above water, parents took care of their children, and, in general, people reported being in quite a good state, made plans for the future and continued their attempts to find work. Conversely, people labelled as apathetic were in a state of complete languishment. In the most severely afflicted group, children were neglected and the household fell apart. The dominant mood could be described as indifferent and inert, with residents passively watching life pass them by. Household economic management did not focus on meeting the family's most important needs; rather, it was markedly more irrational than in the other three groups. Family conflicts became more frequent, and alcoholism became an increasingly intransigent problem. The resigned, whose financial situation was somewhat worse than that of the unbroken, seemed to have made peace with their situation. They had few plans for the future and appeared to be without hope. Their needs and wants were reduced to a bare minimum. Nevertheless, in most families, the household remained well maintained, children were attentively cared for and well-being was generally good. The despairing also took care of their children and kept their households afloat; however, their emotional suffering was greater: despair, depression, hopelessness and the feeling that all efforts were futile dominated. Efforts to acquire work and improve one's circumstances proved unsuccessful, leading this group to focus on the ideal past rather than the dismal future. This classification scheme for the unemployed has a descriptive and static character. On the basis of these four types, however, Jahoda et al. (1971, p. 74) proposed a process-based model that begins with losing one's job and describes a slow but constant deterioration of one's psychological and material life situation.

This gradual process of breakdown also becomes manifest in changes in the experience and usage of time. This was especially true for the unemployed men in Marienthal, who, as many women complained, came late to lunch despite having unlimited time to spare (Table 9.1). Measurements of walking speed on the streets showed that the men moved more slowly and more often came to a stop than the women, who still had household duties. Time usage surveys made clear that the men's days had become empty and homogeneous. Only the regularity of meals formed significant temporal reference points. Otherwise, time was killed by sitting around, going for walks and standing around in the streets. Sundays and holidays lost their importance. Everything that could not be latched on to the fixed points represented by the men's daily undertakings no longer had any meaningful connection to their existence.

With regard to this, Jahoda et al. (1971) wrote:

> Anyone who knows how tenaciously the working class has fought for more leisure ever since it began to fight for its rights might think that even amid the misery of unemployment, men would still benefit from having unlimited free time. On examination this leisure proves to be a tragic gift. Cut off from their work and deprived of contact with the outside world, the workers of Marienthal have lost the material and moral

Table 9.1 Example of a time usage survey for an unemployed man and a woman in the Marienthal study (Jahoda et al., 1971, p. 68 and p. 75)

Time usage survey for a 33-year-old unemployed man		Typical time usage survey for a woman	
a.m.		a.m.	
6–7	Getting up.	6–7	Get dressed, light the fire, prepare breakfast.
7–8	Wake the boys because they have to go to school.	7–8	Wash and get ready, dress the children and take them to school.
8–9	When they have gone, I go down to the shed to get wood and water.	8–9	Wash up, go shopping.
9–10	When I get back up to the house my wife always asks me what she ought to cook; to avoid the question I go off into the field.	9–10	Tidy the rooms.
10–11	In the meantime, midday comes around.	10–11	Start preparing the meal.
11–12	[empty]	11–12	Finish cooking the meal and have lunch.
p.m		p.m	
12–1	We eat at one o'clock; the children don't come home from school until then.	12–1	Do the washing-up and clear up the kitchen.
1–2	After the meal I take a look at the newspaper.	1–2	Take the children to the kindergarten.
2–3	Go out.	2–3	Sewing and darning.
3–4	Go to Treer's (the shopkeeper's).	3–4	Sewing and darning.
4–5	Watch trees being cut down in the park; a pity about the park.	4–5	Sewing and darning.
5–6	Go home.	5–6	Fetch the children.
6–7	Then it's time for the evening meal – noodles and semolina pudding.	6–7	Have supper.
7–8	Go to bed.	7–8	Undress the children, wash and put them to bed.
		8–9	Sewing.
		9–10	Sewing.
		10–11	Go to bed.

> incentives to make use of their time. Now that they are no longer under any pressure, they undertake nothing new and drift gradually out of an ordered existence into one that is undisciplined and empty. (p. 66)

In addition to the breakdown in temporal structure came the depressing feeling that one was no longer needed. This is because it is primarily work that connects the individual to society and provides a sense of self-worth. Now, a different feeling, namely resignation, spread. As the length of unemployment increased, so did the subjective certainty that there was nothing that could be done to break out of the current hopeless situation. Irreversibility, despondency and resignation made their presence felt. It is obvious that such dismal circumstances also affect one's closest social relationships. Nevertheless, Jahoda et al. (1971) did not find a clear, unidirectional correlation between unemployment and family harmony. According to their study, unemployment seemed to bring the members of harmonious families closer together than they had been before. In other families, smouldering conflicts would rise to the surface and quarrels might even cause partners to separate.

Criticism of research on the unemployed during the time of the Great Depression can be found in Cole (2007). The conditions in those days cannot be extrapolated to the present time. More explicitly, Cole argues that unemployment benefits as they are known today did not exist back then, and that circumstances for the unemployed are therefore different today. However, psychological burdens on the unemployed today are comparable with those over eight decades ago, despite relatively better material conditions. Then as now, the loss of one's job and the shake-up in the familiar rhythm of life, in the oscillation between work and free time, creates problems in the organisation of one's daily life. It remains true today that exclusion from the social process of work is connected to a profound destabilisation in an individual's life perspective and thus creates experiences of social isolation, dependency and impotence. Although those who do not conduct themselves in accordance with economic dictates do not immediately meet their downfall today, the threat of decline looms (Adorno, 1972).

Most of the time, unemployment comes with the loss of social contacts, a slip into social isolation and a growing feeling of helplessness and powerlessness. It is a fundamental disruption in personal identity formation and self-development. In addition to the social safety net provided by society, a society's social orientation also plays an important role in the experience of unemployment. In a study by Martella and Maass (2000), unemployed people in collectivist societies, such as southern Italy, were less dissatisfied with their lives than unemployed people in individualist northern Italy. Unemployed people from collectivist societies have a stronger social network available to them and can count on support from their relatives and friends. Furthermore, it appears that they tend to attribute externally failures in general and their unemployment in particular. Martella and Maass also pointed out that life satisfaction among the unemployed is higher when daily structure is preserved. Time structure and collectivism do not eliminate but may reduce the adverse effects of unemployment. Comparing twenty-eight countries, Stavrova, Schlösser and Fetchenhauer (2011) found differences in the effects of unemployment on life satisfaction in different societies. They show that the amount of welfare state provision to the unemployed is not associated with life satisfaction. Instead, the injunctive norm to work, which specifies which behaviours are accepted within a society, has a significant effect on life satisfaction during unemployment. Exposure to external social sanctions leads to a reduction in life satisfaction. Hence, the life satisfaction of the unemployed in Germany is lower than in the United States, as the injunctive norm to work is higher in the former.

Unemployment does not only lead to the aforementioned consequences with respect to the unemployed and their families, but is also tied to changes in political beliefs and has an influence on the political and social activities of the unemployed. The Marienthal study was able to point out a decrease in the number of subscriptions to the Socialist Party newspaper, which fell by 60% between 1927 and 1930. Membership in societies, associations and political parties went down as well, and political conflicts lost some of their passion, explosiveness and bite. Beales and Lambert (1934) reported for England that trade union membership went down during the crisis and that interest in political happenings in general as well as in local politics sank. What remains intact for the unemployed, however, is an emotional rebellion against the existing social system. After analysing fifty-seven biographies of unemployed Poles in the 1930s, Zawadski and Lazarsfeld (1935) came to the following conclusion:

> The general impression which one gets in going through the biographies is that the experiences of unemployment are a preliminary step for the revolutionary mood, but that they do not lead by themselves to a readiness for mass action; metaphorically speaking, these experiences only fertilize the ground for revolution, but do not generate it. (p. 249)

Unemployment often becomes associated with extreme political opinions. Bay and Blekesaune (2002) investigated the impact of unemployment on political marginalisation among young people in eleven European countries using the Eurobarometer Survey of Young Europeans from 1990. Only 12% of employed and 9% of unemployed youth responded affirmatively to the question 'What sort of things interest you a lot? National Politics?' A larger proportion of unemployed than employed youth were dissatisfied with the way democracy works in their country, meaning that young unemployed people lack political confidence. Political extremism was measured by asking participants to consider 'three basic kinds of attitudes towards the society we live in'. The alternatives included revolutionary actions, reforms and strongly defending society against subversive forces. Unemployed young people expressed revolutionary opinions more frequently than young people with jobs; however, the number of revolutionaries within both the employed and unemployed populations was very low. Bay and Blekesaune conclude that raising political interest among young people in general is a greater challenge for Europe than the fact that there are small political differences between employed and unemployed youth.

Whether or not unemployment is correlated with higher crime rates has not been clearly determined. According to Cantor and Land (1985), criminal behaviour is influenced by the factors 'criminal motivation' and 'criminal opportunity'. Unemployment can be seen as an indicator of a poor economic climate, and the authors assume that a poor economic climate might lead to an increase in criminal motivation and thereby to higher crime rates. On the other hand, a poor economic climate could also lead to low criminal opportunity (for example, because unemployed people spend more time at home and therefore are better able to guard their property) and thereby to less crime. An analysis by Phillips and Land (2012) provides support for this model. They found that for US county-level data over the period 1978–2005, unemployment rates were only weakly related to overall crime rates. However, for property crimes such as burglary or theft, consistent patterns were found: criminal opportunity (as indicated by current unemployment rate) was negatively correlated with changes in crime rates, whereas criminal motivation (as indicated by changes in the unemployment rate in comparison to the year before) was positively correlated.

9.2.2 Differential Impact of Unemployment

Impacts of unemployment depend on personal characteristics, the social context and situational factors (e.g., Warr, 1983). In the following section, variables that influence individual reactions to unemployment will be discussed.

9.2.2.1 Length of Unemployment

Unemployment is not a single isolated event; the psychosocial consequences of unemployment depend primarily on its length. The importance of the length of unemployment was already recognised at the time of the Great Depression. Analysing reports from unemployed people in Warsaw, Zawadski and Lazarsfeld (1935) discovered a process by which the unemployed 'adapted' to their fate. Later, Eisenberg and Lazarsfeld (1938) developed a **four-phase model of unemployment** describing the course of this adaptation. According to this model, losing one's

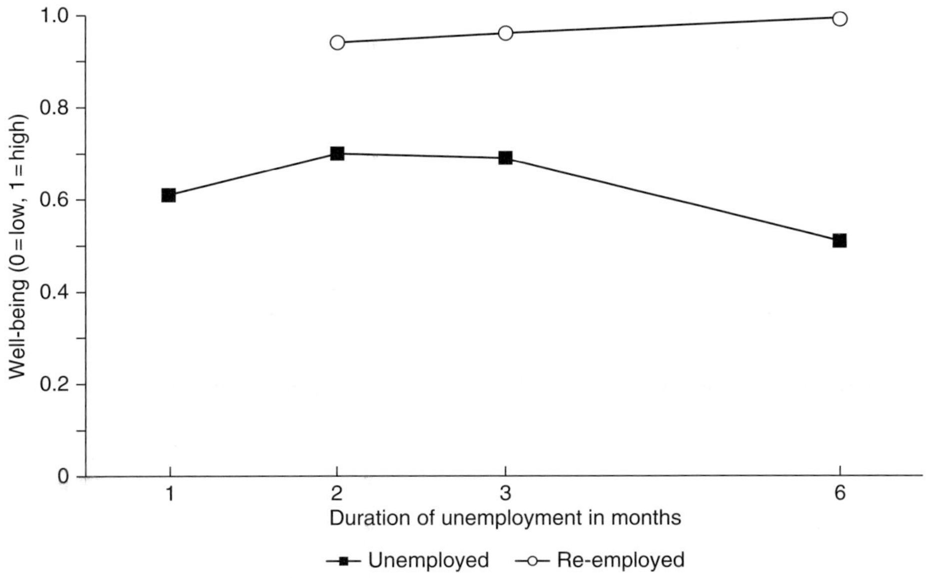

Figure 9.4 Psychological well-being as a function of employment status and the length of unemployment (Kirchler, 1984a, p. 70)

job is first experienced as (1) a shock. This is followed by a phase of (2) optimism accompanied by intensive efforts to find work again. After a series of unsuccessful job applications, they enter a phase of (3) pessimism, characterised by anxiety and fear, which finally gives way to a sustained state of (4) fatalism, in which unemployment is perceived as an unalterable fate. Briar (1977), Harrison (1976), Hill (1978), Hilpert (1981) and Hopson and Adams (1976) formulated similar phase models. They all speak of an initial trauma. After the period of optimism that follows, the unemployed drift into a phase of pessimism, which ends in apathy and fatalistic thinking.

The four-phase model of adaptation to unemployment was confirmed in a diary study by Kirchler (1984a). Figure 9.4 shows that psychological well-being for unemployed study participants was poor at the beginning. After a while, their state recovered and remained stable for some time. Following this phase of optimism, a drop in average well-being could be noted in the sixth month after the original job loss. In comparison, the well-being of those who found work again steadily increased up to a relatively high average level.

The process of 'adjusting' to unemployment can be explained on the basis of Seligman's (1975) **theory of learned helplessness**. According to this theory, people learn to become helpless when they have no influence or control over adverse conditions. Typical reactions to a lack of opportunities for control include passive, resigned and rigid modes of behaviour accompanied by failure-oriented attitudes. Frese (1977) developed the concept of **subjective control**, defined as the number of behavioural options that allow a person to deal with situational conditions in ways that serve his or her individual goals, needs, interests and desires. Subjective control factors are described as generalised expectations in the sense of Rotter, Chance and Phares (1972). Although generalised expectations are basically stable, they can be changed by environmental influences that run contrary to expectations. Frese (1979) analysed the phenomenon of unemployment on the basis of this theory, which seeks to capture the relationship between objective conditions and subjective interpretations. He was able to compare unemployed people and people who were later re-employed. He then focused on people who were employed for a short time and afterwards became unemployed again. His results confirmed the hypothesis that expectations of a lack of control are accompanied by depressiveness. In the beginning, hope for control remained intact despite a present lack of opportunities for control; however, it decreased over time with continuing unemployment. Among people whose hope for control was high at the beginning, long-term unemployment or repeated unemployment led to higher levels of depressiveness later, compared to people with 'realistic hopelessness' at the beginning. The longer the state of unemployment lasted, the more consequences like lower expectations of control and hopelessness became evident as well.

Lucas (2007) asked whether critical life events, such as the loss of a job, have long-term effects on subjective well-being from the perspective of **set-point models**. These models postulate that drops in life satisfaction triggered by life-altering events balance out over time due to adaptation processes, causing life satisfaction to again reach its original level. Thus, the long-term unemployed should become accustomed to their fate and therefore be just as content as before losing their jobs. This, however, does not appear to be the case, as Paul and Moser (2009a, 2009b) showed. Health and well-being worsen as the length of unemployment increases, and new declines in health can be detected even after a period of 29 months. The longer a person remains unemployed, the more severe the negative effects on health and well-being become, especially when unemployment benefits are not available and financial resources are scarce.

A particularly thorough piece of research on the effects of the length of unemployment was conducted by Wagner (1999). In a survey study with eight points of measurement in the time between 1995 and 1997, he followed 350 people from a manufacturing company in the metalworking industry through a massive restructuring process. At the first point of measurement, the workers had been notified about the company's rationalisation plans; however, it was not yet clear which departments would be shut down and who would be affected by layoffs. Two months later, the layoffs had been made public, but the severance period would last a few more months. At the third point of data collection, the laid-off workers had just left the company. These three measurement points can be seen as times of job uncertainty, anticipated dismissal and finally dismissal. Four further surveys were conducted at two-month intervals, and a final survey took place fifteen months after the layoffs.

After being laid off, some survey respondents found another job quickly, while others remained unemployed during the entire period of data collection. As the duration of unemployment increased, scores on all psychological measurements declined. Scores for depressiveness and health complaints were low at the first measurement point. They increased significantly in the anticipation phase and sank after workers were dismissed, at the beginning of unemployment. However, they rose sharply as the period of unemployment dragged on. Values for self-esteem were the mirror image of this. Workers who were not affected by unemployment exhibited lower scores of depressiveness and hardly suffered any health complaints. Those who found work again also reported low depressiveness scores and displayed hardly any physical symptoms after beginning their new jobs (Wagner, 1999).

9.2.2.2 Subjective Importance of Work

As the length of unemployment increases, it can be assumed that the probability of depressiveness will increase and the search for a position will languish. However, one might argue that this phenomenon is most pronounced among people who throw themselves into the job search with particular vigour and those for whom work is especially important. The repeated experience of failure in their attempts to find a new job may be the reason they are prone to fall into a depressive state. In this view, it is not languidness and depression that correlate with one another; rather, the active, unsuccessful job search is associated with the onset of depression. This hypothesis, which contradicts the theory of learned helplessness, was examined by Feather and Davenport (1981). They analysed the link between unemployment and depression on the assumption that depressive moods would be especially prevalent among unemployed people with high motivation to find work; conversely, when motivation is low, unemployment would have few negative psychological consequences. They surveyed 212 unemployed young people regarding their expectations and motivation to find work, the importance of work, the perceived causes of their unemployment, and depressiveness. In fact, people with higher motivation to find work did indeed have higher scores for depression. Unemployed people in depressive states placed a high value on work, tried hard to find work and had higher hopes of finding another job at the beginning of their period of unemployment. Those who made great efforts to find a new job tended to attribute the causes of their unemployment to external circumstances rather than to factors within themselves.

The duration of unemployment and the subjective importance of work are significant moderator variables with respect to the psychological effects of unemployment. Work- and career-oriented people experience unemployment significantly more negatively than people who attach little importance to work (Fröhlich, 1979). When a person views their job as a 'lifetime post', identifies with the substance of their work and considers their professional career to be important, losing their job becomes a tragic reversal of fortune.

Along these lines of reasoning, it might be assumed that those people who place an especially high importance on work experience job loss as especially shocking, but immediately begin actively searching for a new job. Over the course of time, when their repeated interviews with various companies are followed by rejections, hopelessness increases. Finally, all activity peters out and this leads to resignation. At the beginning of their unemployment, people with a high work orientation will be in a depressive state, but in accordance with reactance theory and expected value theory, they will also be especially active. During a prolonged period of unemployment, the job search will languish; depressiveness will either increase even further, or unemployment will not seem as distressing as before because the subjective importance of work will have decreased. People with a low work orientation are probably less negatively affected by the onset of unemployment, and react less intensively to a prolonged period of unemployment.

9.2.2.3 Subjective Causes of Unemployment

The social stigmatisation of the unemployed as 'dossers' and 'freeloaders' has had such a large effect that many unemployed people not only are unable to defend themselves against this image, they even internalise it and often start to believe themselves that unemployed people are lazy and don't want to work. Adopting these accusations of blame from society increases the strain one is under and subsequently leads to higher scores of depression, apathy and resignation, while resulting in a negative self-image and a lower willingness to acknowledge psychological problems and undergo appropriate treatment (Kieselbach & Schindler, 1984).

When asking about the causes of unemployment, one must differentiate between the causes of national unemployment and the reasons why one particular individual lost their job rather than a colleague. Kieselbach and Offe (1979; see also Schumacher, 1986) argued that the intermingling of these two levels of explanation serves as a strategy for shifting the blame for individual fates to the individuals themselves. For instance, unemployed people's lack of willingness to make concessions is seen as an individual-level explanation of why the unemployment rate might be increasing.

Wahl, Pollai and Kirchler (2013) conducted a study to investigate whether the unemployed differ from members of seven other occupational categories with regard to the perceived status of their category and their identification with it. The total of eight occupational categories can be divided into three main groups: the group of long-term employed containing entrepreneurs and business owners, white-collar workers, blue-collar workers and public servants; the group of short-term employed containing students, people undergoing compulsory military service, and conscientious objectors performing mandatory community service; and the group of unemployed. Participants had to answer questions regarding their identification with their own category (e.g., 'I identify closely with my occupational category') and the perceived status of their category (e.g., 'My occupational group has a lot of prestige'). Results showed that the unemployed both rated their category as having a significantly lower status than the other groups and displayed a significantly lower identification with their category. In addition to the questions on status and identification, participants were given all eight occupational categories as a stimulus. They were then first asked to think of a typical member of each of these categories and then to freely associate and to record what words came to mind. They were also asked to write down whether each association was positive, neutral or negative from their perspective. The associations for each stimulus were analysed separately for those who belonged to the occupational category given as a stimulus and for those who belonged to one of the seven other categories. Thus, for each stimulus (e.g., entrepreneurs), there are in-group associations created by the entrepreneurs in the sample, as well as out-group associations reported by all the other participants who belonged to different occupational categories. Staying with the stimulus example 'entrepreneurs', entrepreneurs mentioned positive words, such as 'determined', 'prepared to take risks', 'innovative', 'hardworking' and 'responsible' for their own category most frequently, whereas members of the other categories mentioned less positive words most often, such as 'suit', 'determined', 'stress', 'a lot of money' and 'arrogant'. In contrast, a typical unemployed person was described very negatively both by the unemployed themselves (in-group) and by the other occupational categories (out-group). The most frequent words were 'lazy', 'depressed', 'unwilling to work' and 'desperate'. In the next step, an index for the evaluative components of the associations ranging from +1 to –1 was computed; high positive values indicate a positive evaluation of the occupational category and high negative values indicate a negative evaluation. For all stimuli, these indices were calculated for the in-group perception (e.g., how entrepreneurs evaluated associations with the stimulus word 'entrepreneur'), for the perception by out-groups (e.g., how all other participants evaluated associations with the stimulus word 'entrepreneur'), and for the in-group perception of the out-groups (e.g., how entrepreneurs evaluated associations to all other stimulus words). Overall, the unemployed category was evaluated most negatively. The categories entrepreneurs, white-collar workers, public servants and military service members were evaluated significantly better by the respective in-group than by the out-groups. The self-evaluations produced by the unemployed did not significantly differ from the evaluations of unemployed provided by members of the other categories. Furthermore, only the unemployed evaluated their own category (i.e., their in-group) as significantly worse than the other categories. This means that the unemployed show not only no in-group favouritism, but also a significant degree of out-group favouritism.

These results show that unemployment is evaluated as undesirable not only by employed people but also by the unemployed themselves. This can be seen as a handicap when it comes to forming a lobby to represent the political interests of unemployed people. On the other hand, out-group favouritism and in-group rejection might encourage job-seeking activities.

The most radical form of blaming the victim consists of the belief that unemployment is caused by the unemployed themselves. If laziness, psychological lability and insufficient education are seen as causes of unemployment, not only are the unemployed themselves to blame for their fate, they also have hardly any chance of becoming reintegrated into economic processes, which are only willing to make room for the industrious. Godofsky, van Horn and Zukin (2010) interviewed 818 US residents on the causes of high unemployment. About a quarter (26%) of the working sample and 17% of the unemployed sample thought that high levels of unemployment are due to the fact that the unemployed do not want to work; 79% placed blame on the limited supply of available jobs not meeting the demand for work. Nearly three-quarters blamed global competition and cheap labour from other countries, and 47% claimed that high unemployment rates are caused by illegal immigrants taking jobs away from Americans. Furnham (1982) made a distinction between individualistic, societal and fatalistic causal attributions. He argued that employed people tend to look for explanations within the unemployed themselves, while unemployed people suspect that the causes lie in economic changes, societal developments and political actions. Grau and Thomsen (1985) spoke with unemployed men about the accusation that the unemployed are unwilling to work and asked them for explanations. Nearly a quarter (23.1%) of respondents were of the opinion that the roots of this accusation can be found in the unemployed person him- or herself, in misconduct on the job, excessive alcohol consumption, the voluntary decision to quit and so on. One-fifth (19.2%) pointed to social stigmatisation; 30.7% believed that such sweeping accusations were too general; 15.4% viewed this insult as a way to upset and attack groups of people in a weakened social position; and 11.5% named envy and frustration as reasons. The authors, subsequently, asked about the causes of other unemployed people's unwillingness to work and found confirmation for a strong self-exculpatory tendency.

In a diary study conducted by Kirchler (1984a), unemployed people blamed themselves for being in a negative mood in 40% of cases and blamed other people in 23% of cases. Re-employed people, on the other hand, blamed themselves for their negative mood in only 30% of cases and blamed other people in 34% of cases. General economic conditions were cited by both groups equally, often as the source of their negative mood (16% versus 17%, respectively).

9.2.2.4 Personality Characteristics

Is it possible to identify personality factors that determine unemployment? It cannot be simply presumed that people with certain personality characteristics are, in general, more likely to become unemployed than other people. Yet, it can be expected that confident, adaptable, flexible, robust, enthusiastic people with high self-esteem are better able to cope with difficulties during unemployment than people who are anxious, emotionally unstable or reserved. Resilient, stress-resistant, extraverted people whose behaviour falls within the normal range seem to find work again more quickly than others (Warr, 1983).

Uysal and Pohlmeier (2011) used the Big Five personality traits to investigate whether both unemployed people's probability of getting a new job and their job search intensity are driven by personality traits. Conscientiousness had a positive association with the probability of finding a job, while a contrasting effect was found for neuroticism. The subsequent duration of employment was associated negatively with conscientiousness, but positively with neuroticism. For women and workers with immigrant backgrounds, openness made the job search easier. Yap, Anusic and Lucas (2012) found an association between agreeableness and life satisfaction after a job loss. People high in agreeableness reacted less negatively to unemployment; however, there were no differences in the long run between people with high and low values in this personality dimension. Neither study found significant effects for extraversion.

9.2.2.5 Socio-demographic Characteristics

Even though a curvilinear relationship between age and reactions to unemployment has been seemingly confirmed (Daniel, 1974; Hepworth, 1980), caution is in order. In reality, the age of the unemployed person probably should not be assigned an important role as a moderator variable. Age is correlated with financial obligations, social and familial expectations, career hopes, chances of re-employment, difficulties mastering a new job, retaining previously acquired skills and knowledge, and other factors. Thus, it is likely that these variables associated with age determine reactions to unemployment rather than age itself. Finally, it should be considered that different age groups need to deal with particular challenges at different times and in changing environments.

Depending on societal stereotypes of gender roles and local ideologies, men or women might be 'required' to perform paid work. In Western industrial societies, the image of a woman who does not work for pay but instead runs the household still exists. A man without a job does not fulfil the societal stereotype, and therefore would experience unemployment more negatively than a comparable woman. Paul and Moser (2009a, 2009b) also proceed from the assumption that job loss has stronger negative effects on health for men than for women. In a meta-analysis taking 237 cross-sectional studies into consideration, they were able to detect differences between unemployed men's and women's mental health states. Gender proved to be a significant and stable variable in terms of mental health. Unemployed men were more susceptible to health problems than unemployed women. For women, the family represents an alternative sphere of work that lessens the burden of unemployment (Cohn, 1978). Brandes (1977) noted that, most of the time, women perceive their unemployment

> as less of a burden than the unemployment of a man, due to the possibility they have of withdrawing to the domestic sphere at any time and making that their principal duty – and for the family, this is true in financial terms. When they become unemployed, women's gendered self-image is often less affected than is the case with men, whose understanding of their gender role traditionally consists of serving as the family breadwinner. (Brandes, 1977, p. 220)

On the contrary, Warr (1983) reported that unemployment affects women just as negatively as men when their work had previously served to finance their livelihood. The results of a study by Kirchler and Nowy (1988) completely contradict the seemingly plausible hypothesis that effects of unemployment differ by gender. Their study proceeded from the assumption that men and women would experience their unemployment differently depending upon their understanding of gender roles. According to this, traditionally minded women would find their personal fulfilment within the family, and even if they do not view paid employment as a burden, they do see it as an obstacle keeping them from devoting themselves fully to the family. An end to employment would, in this view, be a relief, or at least not a burden. Traditionally minded men see paid work as their primary function in society, and their usefulness and self-worth should evaporate with the loss of a job. Progressive women extract themselves from the family by taking a job, which has an important place in their lives alongside their partner, their children, etc. They ought to experience unemployment as a negative major life event. Progressive men, conversely, should have an array of areas in addition to work in which they achieve self-actualisation and, therefore, assign a lower importance to work than their traditionally minded male colleagues. They should experience job loss as a less dramatic occurrence than traditional men. This interplay between gender and ideas about gender roles was not confirmed in Kirchler and Nowy's (1988) study. Nevertheless, a main effect of gender on general satisfaction and well-being scores was found, but not, however, in the expected direction. Rather, men seemed to be less affected by their unemployment than women. Women indicated that they were more depressed, more anxious, more tired and more often upset than men. They tended to be less often in a good mood, were more often nervous, and above all were less satisfied with their education and their health than men. However, one might argue that men are less willing and able to talk about feelings, fears, weaknesses and sadness than women and therefore tend to downplay negative experiences.

In addition to age and gender, the social class and financial status of the unemployed person also act as moderator variables. Social status is often defined on the basis of a person's income, available material resources, education, job and position of social influence. Even though unemployment today can no longer be equated with destitution, financial troubles among the unemployed have in no way been eliminated. Even today, prolonged unemployment intensifies financial distress, particularly in lower-class families. Financial distress is often an indirect burden as well. For example, as a cost-cutting measure, leisure activities often have to be cut down on, which can lead to frustration and irritability (Schultz-Gambard & Balz, 1988). Unemployed people belonging to higher social classes are knocked off a 'higher perch', meaning that their prestige and social recognition tends to be more at risk than members of lower social classes. However, they are better able to solve the problems presented by unemployment than financially disadvantaged persons due to their social contacts and more flexible material position. Hepworth (1980) was able to show that workers with qualitatively worse jobs exhibited lower self-esteem and higher psychological morbidity than workers who had lost a higher position. Thomas and Madigan (1974) reported similar findings: higher-skilled workers felt like they were under less stress at the onset of unemployment than did low-skilled workers. Hartley's (1980) findings are also in line with this. She found no difference in self-esteem between employed and unemployed executives. In contrast, the employed and the unemployed among members of lower classes showed a corresponding difference in their self-esteem.

9.2.2.6 Personal Activities

Losing one's job is accompanied by a massive increase in free time. The more meaningfully this free time can be structured and used, the lower the psychological burdens of unemployment should be (Warr & Payne, 1983). Schultz-Gambard and Balz (1988) emphasise the importance of meaningful activities during unemployment. Frese and Mohr (1978; see also Leggett, 1968) report, for example, that unemployed people who are organised and active in a trade union exhibit lower scores for depression than others. McKee-Ryan et al. (2005) also report a positive relationship between mental health and the ways unemployed individuals structure their time. However, a lack of financial opportunities, insufficient personal skills, a lack of publicly sponsored measures or a lack of social relationships can prevent the unemployed from taking part in meaningful activities. In this case, the effects of unemployment are especially negative (Fryer & Payne, 1984; Hepworth, 1980).

9.2.2.7 Experience with Unemployment

In addition to the moderator variables already mentioned, previous experiences with unemployment and the knowledge that other people share one's fate can also lead to differences in reactions to unemployment. The assumption that repeated experiences of unemployment have increasingly negative effects on the unemployed person's psychological well-being stands in opposition to the hypothesis that unemployed people begin to develop coping strategies as the length of their experience with unemployment grows and are therefore better able to put up with their situation. Hepworth (1980) proposed that frequent exits from the labour market and the loss of career continuity associated with it carry negative consequences for the people involved. Erwin Kirchler (1988) was able to find evidence supporting Hepworth's hypothesis, namely that people who have been unemployed before have a more difficult time finding work again than people who have lost a job for the first time.

It can be assumed that unemployed people are better able to come to terms with their fate when they live in a region where unemployment is not an isolated phenomenon, but one that directly affects many people. In these regions, unemployment is not an individualised problem, but rather a form of shared suffering. The social stigma of unemployment, since it applies to many people, is probably a smaller burden for each individual. Cohn (1978) reported that in regions with a high unemployment rate, the unemployed are more content than in regions with lower rates. High rates of unemployment seem to counteract the feeling of belonging to a group on the margins of society while reducing accusations of blame and thus negative well-being. On the other hand, it can be assumed that those unemployed people who live in structurally unfavourable regions are in an especially bad situation. High unemployment rates imply that each individual unemployed person has a smaller chance of finding another job due to increased competition. The higher the local unemployment rate, the stronger the feelings of powerlessness and helplessness could become and, subsequently, unemployed people might evaluate their situation as more unfavourable (Daniel, 1974).

9.2.2.8 Social, Emotional and Informational Support

By actively participating in associations, societies and clubs, but also by working on the black market, unemployed people increase their access to information about job openings. Unemployed people who have access to relevant public and private institutions and who draw on them in dealing with their situation and finding work again perceive their circumstances to be less negative than other people. Winter-Ebmer and Zweimüller (1991) also found that unemployed people who participate in training programmes offered by the government unemployment office have better chances of re-employment. In addition, people who have hopes of becoming re-employed are likely to be better able to cope with their situation while unemployed.

Just as associations, societies, clubs and institutions can provide unemployed people with social and informational support, informal advisors, acquaintances and relatives can also help unemployed people find work again and make the period of unemployment easier to put up with. Family members and friends, in particular, can provide emotional support. They provide a 'buffer function' which can minimise the severe shock when unemployment occurs (Gore, 1978). Silver and Wortman (1980) considered the following to be individual effect components of social support: (a) the esteem in which one is held by others, (b) confirmation of one's own beliefs, interpretations and feelings by others, (c) the opportunity to confide one's feelings and thoughts, (d) the opportunity to receive material and informational help, and (e) having other people strengthen one's self-confidence and the security that comes from being part of a social network. People who receive social and emotional support are able to maintain their sense of self-worth even after losing their jobs, because they do not define their worth solely in terms of their work performance.

9.2.3 Determinants of Re-employment

What determines whether an unemployed person finds work again? Zikic and Klehe (2006) emphasised the importance of drawing unemployed people's attention to their strengths and resources and away from the negative aspects of unemployment. In their attempts to come to terms with their jobless situation, unemployed people become independent and autonomous actors whose perceived self-efficacy can be positively influenced by the exploration of career options (Kanfer & Hulin, 1985; Wanberg, Kanfer & Rotundo, 1999). Wanberg, Glomb, Song and Sorenson (2005) discovered that unemployed people with a positive self-concept were able to find work again more quickly. A positive self-concept consists of high self-esteem, generalised self-efficacy, perceived control and emotional stability.

The intensity of job search increases the chance of re-employment (Wanberg, Watt & Rumsey, 1996). Chances for re-employment were higher for younger individuals with the same job-seeking intensity as older individuals in the sample. However, job-search intensity only has a small effect on re-employment quality (Wanberg, Song & Hough, 2002).

Finally, job search strategies matter (Koen, Klehe, Van Vianen, Zikic & Nauta, 2010). Among other variables, they studied three different types of job search strategies as predictors of re-employment quality: an exploratory strategy, a focused strategy and a haphazard strategy. An exploratory strategy involves a full exploration of options and openness to new opportunities in various fields. A focused strategy is characterised by a goal-directed and selective job search. Job offers are scanned for requirements, qualifications and interests. A haphazard strategy involves the application of trial-and-error during the job search and switching between different tactics without first conducting thorough research. An exploratory strategy leads to a higher number of job offers. Yet, contradicting the authors' predictions, this strategy leads to a decrease in re-employment quality a few months later. A possible explanation is that an exploratory job search strategy might lead to a variety of different jobs, sometimes in unfamiliar fields, which could lead to a dissatisfying experience. Another reason might be the re-employment situation itself, in which people may feel pressured to accept any job offer they receive. A focused strategy leads to an increase in job offers, but no association with re-employment quality was found. A haphazard strategy has a negative effect on re-employment quality. Koen et al. (2010) showed that this strategy is mainly applied when people are undecided about their future. Successful job search involves following a deliberate job search strategy, considering career planning and decision-making, and being confident about the job search.

Conclusion

As the meaning of work has changed, both the structure of work and its interplay with leisure have become more important. In both theoretical and applied discourses, intrinsic motivation to work and work–life balance have gained prominence. At the same time, unemployment still imposes a serious burden on a person. Both objective factors such as the length of unemployment and experience with unemployment and psychological factors have a significant influence on the impact of unemployment on well-being. Social and emotional support can mitigate the effects of unemployment on well-being.

Summary

- The meaning of work has changed over time, and currently is seen both as a service to society and as a way to satisfy workers' extrinsic and intrinsic needs.
- Work should be designed so that it has a high degree of motivating potential, that is, it can be intrinsically motivating. Job demands and job resources interact and influence organisational outcomes.
- The satisfaction with one's work is closely related to general life happiness. Furthermore, the balance between work and leisure is particularly important.
- Unemployment goes along with the loss of structure of daily life through work, economic security, career prospects, social recognition, social contacts with work colleagues, one's feeling of importance to society, stimuli from one's social environment and role of the breadwinner.
- Unemployment has severe consequences for physical and psychological well-being.
- Psychological well-being varies with the length of unemployment: after the initial trauma and a period of optimism that follows, the unemployed drift into a phase of pessimism, which ends in apathy, fatalistic thinking and learned helplessness. The longer people remain unemployed and the less they can partake in meaningful activities, the more severe the negative effects on health and well-being become.
- Social and emotional support can mitigate the effects of unemployment and enables people to maintain their sense of self-worth even after losing their jobs.

Questions

1. What are the core assumptions of the job characteristics model (Hackman & Oldham, 1976)?
2. What is work–life balance?
3. Which four positions about the relation between work and leisure can be distinguished?
4. How do subjective causes of unemployment moderate the impact of unemployment on well-being?
5. What is the four-phase model of unemployment (Eisenberg & Lazarsfeld, 1938)?

FURTHER READING

Feather, N. T. (1990). *The psychological impact of unemployment*. New York: Springer.

Jahoda, M., Lazarsfeld, P., & Zeisel, H. (1971). *Marienthal: The sociography of an unemployed community*. Chicago, IL: Aldine-Atherton.

Layard, R. (1999). *Tackling unemployment*. London: Palgrave Macmillan.

Rosa, H. (2013). *Social acceleration: A new theory of modernity*. New York: Columbia University Press.

Williams, C. C. (2007). *Rethinking the future of work: Directions and visions*. Basingstoke: Palgrave Macmillan.

10 Collective Prosperity: Wealth and Happiness

Overview

This chapter introduces well-being and happiness in general and particularly discusses the relationship between happiness and wealth. People strive for well-being, happiness, contentment and high quality of life. These factors are important socio-political measures at the country level as well. Empirical research on happiness and satisfaction has intensified in recent years and 'positive psychology' has become an important research trend. Periodic surveys of life satisfaction and satisfaction with specific areas of life are conducted, and determinants and consequences of satisfaction are investigated.

The terms well-being, happiness, satisfaction and quality of life are often used synonymously. What is meant is a good, pleasant, either short-lived or long-lasting and more or less intensely perceived emotional state. However, sometimes these terms are defined and operationalised differently, making it difficult to compare the results of empirical studies. Sometimes one term encompasses the other, sometimes it does not. Sometimes the terms refer to processes, sometimes to outcomes. Attempts have been made to make a clear definitional distinction between various aspects of life satisfaction by differentiating between life chances versus life outcomes on the one hand, and between inner versus outer qualities on the other. Numerous proposals for measuring one or more dimensions of quality of life, satisfaction and well-being can be found in the social scientific literature. In addition to uni- and multidimensional instruments that collect data on respondents' subjective views, external assessment instruments are often applied in health research. However, external assessments are controversial, given that well-being, satisfaction and quality of life represent subjective experiences. Therefore, surveys and time-sample diaries are frequently used to assess subjective evaluations of well-being and satisfaction. Nevertheless, none of the applied methods is free of biases and critique.

National happiness indices vary considerably across countries. Since the highest values are measured in the Western industrialised world and the lowest in the third and fourth worlds, it can be assumed that satisfaction is correlated with economic prosperity. People in rich countries do tend to be more satisfied than people in poor countries, and rich people in industrialised countries are happier than poor people. However, the most important determinants of individual satisfaction correspond not to material aspects but rather to a well-functioning partnership, a close circle of friends, participation in clubs and organisations, volunteer work, having a job as opposed to being unemployed, religious faith and, last but not least, a personal disposition favouring optimism and satisfaction. In addition, psychological processes are also relevant to understanding well-being and satisfaction, including adaptation processes, aspiration levels and social comparisons.

Numerous studies indicate that the satisfaction originating from material prosperity is only temporary. People quickly get used to their improved living situation. People who become materially prosperous are more satisfied for a short period of time, but they soon take their improved position for granted and use it as the neutral reference point for evaluating their position in life. Wealth alone does not guarantee satisfaction. National happiness seems to depend on material wealth up to a certain point, after which other factors gain weight in determining happiness.

Introduction

Almost all modern nations emphasise the importance of economic growth to smooth the way for increasing wealth and standard of living. Relentlessly we strive to achieve goals that are ever more ambitious, and even a slow growing economy is often perceived as already worrisome. This comes at great costs. So is it worth the trouble? Does more wealth lead to happiness and satisfaction with life? One could argue that being happy and satisfied with one's own life is the ultimate goal humans seek. This raises the question of whether it is the best choice to invest our time and effort in the pursuit of wealth. The goal is to understand what determines happiness and to evaluate the role of income. First, this chapter provides a definition for happiness and subsequently discusses how it can be measured accurately. Lastly, the complex interaction between income and subjective well-being is examined.

10.1 Life Satisfaction

People strive for well-being, happiness and contentment. In ancient Greece, philosophers such as Aristippus of Cyrene, Democritus, Plato, Aristotle and Epicurus devoted significant studies to the highest good attainable by humankind: happiness or *eudemonia*. Aristotle characterised happiness as the goal of all human action. The American Declaration of Independence of 4 July 1776 viewed the pursuit of happiness as an inalienable right of humankind, on equal footing with the rights to life and liberty. Frey (2008) described the pursuit of happiness as the ultimate human goal.

Happiness, satisfaction and a high quality of life in a country are important socio-political measures. As part of reporting on social life in various countries around the world, prosperity indices and social indicators are periodically generated. The origin of quality of life research lies in the social scientific study of prosperity. At first, primarily social and economic indicators of quality of life were collected, such as income level, material security, healthcare availability, political freedom, social justice and rule of law. The concept of quality of life was developed within the context of the social sciences and medicine, while well-being and satisfaction primarily have been investigated from a psychological perspective. Today, data on subjective factors, such as well-being and life satisfaction, are included in surveys, and quality of life is increasingly understood as an individual-specific concept. In that regard, quality of life is conceived as the subjective evaluation of life conditions. The level of well-being and satisfaction among the citizens of a country determines its quality of life (Schumacher, Klaiberg & Brähler, 2003; Zapf, 2000; Zapf, Schupp & Habich, 1996).

For a long time, research on satisfaction was under the purview of psychology and sociology (e.g., Kahneman, Diener & Schwarz, 1999; Mayring, 1991; Veenhoven, 1984). However, a common point of criticism was that psychology places too much emphasis on negative experiences and deficiencies rather than focusing on those aspects that make people happy. As a counterpoint, '**positive psychology**' studies positive experiences such as happiness and satisfaction. It has become an important research trend. In particular, the psychologist Martin Seligman mapped out a theoretical framework for positive psychology (Peterson & Seligman, 2004). Since 2000, a scholarly journal exclusively dedicated to the topic of satisfaction has been in existence (*Journal of Happiness Studies*). Periodic surveys of life satisfaction and satisfaction with specific areas of life are conducted, and Ruut Veenhoven has built a World Database of Happiness (http://worlddatabaseofhappiness.eur.nl) that summarises average national life satisfaction scores and records determinants and consequences of satisfaction. Within this database, the results of thousands of studies on life satisfaction are stored.

Similarly, economics has now moved away from the exclusive consideration of traditional utility theory and prosperity to a more explicit consideration of subjective satisfaction and the satisfaction of nations, as well as the socio-economic determinants of these (e.g., Easterlin, 1974; Frey, 2008; Frey & Stutzer, 2002; Scitovsky, 1976; Stutzer, 2003). Theology has also entered the fray of happiness research (Bucher, 2009), as have other disciplines. According to van Raaij's model (1981) of research questions in economic psychology (Figure 1.7 in Chapter 1), consumer behaviour brings about economic changes, which in turn have an effect on subjective well-being and national satisfaction. Subjective well-being is associated with satisfaction after purchasing a good; with experiences with products, services and claims; with work opportunities and job security; and with general conditions related to economic policy. When economics was just getting started as a discipline, happiness and satisfaction were understood as being closely related to the economy. Because it did not seem possible to measure satisfaction with sufficient precision, satisfaction was defined as utility. People were expected to focus their behaviour towards the maximisation of utility, with the assumption that their behaviour reveals what offers them the greatest utility. Rather than measuring utility directly, it was assumed that the alternative selected by a decision-maker out of a set of possible alternatives represents the best alternative for them. Similarly, it was assumed that the actions a person takes constitute the optimal ones for them. However, if people are actually only capable of rational action to a limited extent, the alternatives they choose may not necessarily reflect their actual preferences, and the conclusion that the chosen alternative is the one a person liked best might not be correct (Kahneman & Krueger, 2006).

High productivity and opportunities for consumption due to high income are equated with happiness and satisfaction. The presumed high correlation between income and satisfaction was first called into question in the 1970s, when Easterlin (1974) compared changes in US national satisfaction with economic data over the years. Results indicated that, despite economic improvements, satisfaction remained the same. Layard (2005) criticised the long-standing approach of economists to equate people's life satisfaction with their buying power; however, money alone does not make a person happy and a nation's happiness level does not depend solely on its gross domestic product.

10.2 Definitions of Well-being, Happiness, Satisfaction and Quality of Life

The terms well-being, happiness, satisfaction and quality of life are often used synonymously. All of these terms refer to a good, pleasant, either short-lived or long-lasting and more or less intensely emotional state. However, sometimes these constructs are defined and operationalised differently, making it difficult to compare the results of empirical studies. Sometimes one term encompasses the other, sometimes it does not. Sometimes the terms refer to processes, sometimes to outcomes.

Veenhoven (2000) attempted to make a clear definitional distinction between various aspects of life satisfaction by suggesting four **qualities of life**, differentiating between life chances versus life

Table 10.1 Four qualities of life (adapted from Veenhoven, 2000, p. 11)

	Outer qualities	Inner qualities
Life chances	Liveability of the environment	Life-ability of the person
	Ecological (e.g., moderate climate, clean air, spacious housing) Social (e.g., freedom, equality, brotherhood) Economic (e.g., wealthy nation, generous social benefits, smooth economic development) Cultural (e.g., flourishing of arts and sciences, mass education) A comparable concept in economics is the market.	Physical health (negative: free of disease; positive: energetic, resilient) Mental health (negative: free of mental defects; positive: autonomous, creative) Knowledge (e.g., literacy, schooling) Skills (e.g., intelligence, manners) Art of living (e.g., varied lifestyle, differentiated taste) A comparable concept in economics is capital.
Life outcomes	Objective utility of life	Subjective appreciation of life
	External utility (e.g., in intimate relationships: rearing children, caring for friends; e.g., for society: being a good citizen; e.g., for mankind: leaving behind an invention) Moral perfection (e.g., authenticity, compassion, originality) A comparable concept in economics would be public goods.	Appraisal of life aspects (e.g., satisfaction with job, satisfaction with variety) Prevailing moods (e.g., depression, ennui; enthusiasm) Overall appraisals (affective: general mood level; cognitive: contentment with life) A comparable concept in economics is private profit.

outcomes on the one hand, and between inner qualities versus outer qualities on the other. Life chances are opportunities that could be used – but not always are – actually to lead a good life. Life outcomes represent the way a person actually uses these opportunities. Inner qualities refer to characteristics of people themselves, while outer qualities represent life circumstances and situational conditions. The combination of these differentiation criteria results in a 2 × 2 diagram with different qualities of life (Table 10.1).

Satisfaction can refer to specific areas of life or to life as a whole, and can be either fleeting or long-lasting. For example, pleasure represents a temporary feeling that relates to only one aspect of life, while temporary religious experiences can have a profound impact on a person's life as a whole. Job satisfaction is a long-lasting emotional state related to one area of life, while life satisfaction is durable as well but related to a person's life as a whole.

Mayring (1991) differentiated between momentary experiences of happiness and biographically situated life happiness. While momentary feelings of happiness are situationally determined, are temporally fleeting and therefore last only a short amount of time, life happiness lasts longer, has its roots in the person and is little affected by situational conditions. Momentary experiences of happiness arise from positive emotions like joy and enthusiasm. They are experienced intensely, lead to increased feelings of self-worth and a positive self-concept, and promote social interests as well as the ease with which a person makes social connections. Life happiness, on the other hand, builds upon concrete experiences of happiness and results from a cognitive evaluation of one's own goals, opportunities and achievements.

Schumacher et al. (2003) summarised various approaches to differentiate well-being into emotional and evaluative components. In their theory of subjective well-being, Diener and colleagues (Diener, 1984, 2000; Diener, Suh, Lucas & Smith, 1999; Diener, Suh & Oishi, 1997) assume that subjective well-being comprises an emotional or affective component on the one hand and a cognitive-evaluative component on the other. Positive and negative affect as well as happiness as a long-lasting positive emotional state form the emotional component and determine subjective **emotional well-being** (Diener & Lucas, 2000). The cognitive-evaluative component, on the other hand, comprises general and specific **life satisfaction** (e.g., Fahrenberg, Myrtek, Schumacher & Brähler, 2000). While well-being as a positively or negatively tinged emotional state is situationally determined, it is assumed that life satisfaction or domain-specific satisfaction, such as job or relationship satisfaction, is longer lasting. Becker (1994) formulated his concepts of momentary and habitual well-being in a similar manner, with the former referring to a person's current state and the latter to the aggregate of their emotional experiences. Adding a distinction between mental and physical well-being, Schumacher et al. (2003) differentiated between four **forms of well-being**: (a) momentary mental well-being (e.g., joy, feelings of happiness); (b) habitual mental well-being, characterised by persistent optimism; (c) momentary physical well-being, characterised by feelings of strength and vitality; and (d) habitual physical well-being, based on a persistent freedom from physical ailments. In the end, people's subjective evaluation of their habitual mental and physical well-being represents their general life satisfaction. Daniel Kahneman also made a distinction between two terms for well-being. 'Subjective well-being' is measured when people indicate how happy they feel. 'Objective well-being' represents the sum of momentary utility across a certain period of time (Kahneman, 1999). Frey (2008) – building on Nettle (2005) – made a distinction between three concepts of happiness:

(a) Current mood or positive and negative affect, which can arise from joy, gratitude or enjoyment, but also anger, fear or reluctance. Positive affect is frequently described as happiness.
(b) Satisfaction with life in general, or life satisfaction.
(c) Quality of life, which arises from taking full advantage of one's opportunities.

According to Frey and Stutzer (2000), well-being, happiness and life satisfaction are highly correlated with one another. The terms can be used synonymously in research on national satisfaction and quality of life. However, a distinction still needs to be made between momentary affect on the one hand and long-lasting well-being or satisfaction on the other hand. For example, studies investigating momentary states show that divorced women are less likely to conduct activities they consider unpleasant and are more frequently in a good mood than married women. If satisfaction were viewed solely as the aggregate of momentary moods, life satisfaction of divorced women would be higher than that of married women. However, women in stable romantic partnerships are actually happier than divorced women (Kahneman et al., 1999; see also Diener & Eunkook, 2003; Gilbert, 2006).

In his **PERMA model**, Seligman (2011) isolates five factors considered as essential for well-being: Positive emotions (P), Engagement (E), Close Relations (R), Meaning (M) and Accomplishment (A). The model attempts to make the theory of well-being applicable to support programmes for institutions and individuals. By evaluating the five factors that according to Seligman influence well-being, specific deficits can be revealed and subsequently may become targets for improvement. A study of Australian school students (Adler, Kern, Waters & White 2015) was able to confirm the factors of the PERMA model empirically, concluding that well-being needs to be understood as a multidimensional construct. Rath and Harter (2010) also support a differentiated view of well-being.

Based on data from the Gallup Organisation, they differentiate between five critical areas: career well-being, social well-being, financial well-being, physical well-being and community well-being.

From these distinctions, it becomes clear why well-being is gaining more and more acceptance among researchers as opposed to terms such as happiness. With so many variables determining our emotional state, a precise but complex construct is required. In everyday life and in many people's minds, the definition of happiness is too diffuse, posing problems for research and practice.

10.3 Measuring Satisfaction

In the social scientific literature, numerous proposals for measuring one or more dimensions of quality of life, satisfaction and well-being can be found (e.g., Schumacher et al. 2003). In health research, in addition to uni- and multidimensional instruments that collect data on respondents' subjective views, external assessment instruments are often applied. These are based on the assumption that people's quality of life – at least in terms of their state of health – can be specified by outside observers (e.g., doctors, nursing staff). However, external assessments are controversial, given that well-being, satisfaction and quality of life represent subjective experiences and subjective assessments. For example, investigations of financial decision-making in intimate partnerships have shown that married couples are not able to make precise evaluations of each other's emotional states and their causes. Kirchler (1989) had twenty-one couples record their current state, subjective speculations regarding the cause of this state, and their current needs in a time-sample diary up to six times a day over the course of a month. At the same time, and in their partner's presence, they assessed the partner's emotional state, the causes of that state, and his or her needs. On average, participants correctly assessed their partner's current emotional state two-thirds of the time; the causes of that state were also similarly assessed by both partners (the affected person and the observer) around two-thirds of the time. Speculation on one's partner's current needs matched that person's actually reported needs only a bit more than half of the time. Thus, it is not surprising that current research typically assesses people's well-being directly, conducting either interviews or surveys.

Socio-economic surveys of happiness or a group or nation's life satisfaction do not typically make distinctions between happiness, mood, state, satisfaction and quality of life. People are asked how satisfied they are in general, using simple questions with only a few possible answers. By calculating the mean within a representative sample, an estimate of the level of life satisfaction in a given country can be obtained. A summary of typical questions in surveys conducted across the globe can be found in Grimm (2006, p. 5). The General Social Survey, USA, asks: 'Taken all together, how would you say things are these days – would you say that you are very happy, pretty happy or not too happy?' In the Eurobarometer Survey, four answers are possible: 'On the whole, are you very satisfied, fairly satisfied, not very satisfied, or not at all satisfied with the life you lead?' In a similar question, the World Value Survey allows ten possible answers: 'All things considered, how satisfied are you with your life as a whole?' (1 = dissatisfied; 10 = satisfied).

It is important to bear in mind that the measurement of well-being, satisfaction or quality of life using traditional survey instruments is not straightforward. There are a number of potential problems inherent to the method, and numerous psychological findings point to systematic errors (e.g., Bless, 1997; Diener & Tov, 2012; Nisbett & Ross, 1980; Ross, 1977; Ross & Nisbett, 1991; Schwarz, 1996, 1998, 1999). The remainder of this section reports on a few typical sources of error and part of it has been taken directly from Kirchler, Rodler, Hoelzl and Meier (2001).

One potential problem comes from social desirability and stereotype use. Possible distortions due to the tendency to provide socially desirable answers need to be taken into account. For example, in surveys about relationship quality, people often massively overestimate their own satisfaction. On a 7-point scale, it is not uncommon for satisfaction ratings to average around 6, indicating a very high level of satisfaction. This is in sharp contrast to the expected average value of a hypothetical characteristic with a normal distribution on a 7-point scale. In representative Dutch samples, Buunk and van der Eijnden (1997) found that more than 53% of respondents rate their relationship satisfaction as higher than the average level of relationship satisfaction in the population. Roughly 45% believed that their relationship was just as happy as other people's relationships, while only 10% of respondents indicated that their relationship was less happy. When complex pieces of information need to be processed (such as past experiences in one or more areas of life) which further are supposed to be aggregated into a total satisfaction index, survey respondents typically fall back on and report stereotypes and prejudices. This is even more likely when little time is available, and as well as when events were not perceived and processed with one's full attention and therefore are remembered poorly. Easily available experiences, and experiences that stand out in one's memory, often receive significantly more weight in judgments about satisfaction than more common but less salient experiences. Research on judgment heuristics (Tversky & Kahneman, 1974) provides an explanation for this.

A second potential problem comes from correctly distinguishing between experience and memory in studies of well-being. Mixing up experiences and memories is a possible source of error among both researchers and research participants. Everyday experiences are complex. People cognitively structure everyday life in subjective ways. In surveys, opportunities to subjectively structure one's experienced reality (e.g., in terms of determinants of satisfaction) are severely restricted. The type of questions, their level of differentiation and the prescribed answer alternatives are rooted in the researchers' view of reality and leave little room for a subjective reconstruction of respondents' reality. Advocates of survey techniques can only counter with the argument that it would probably be quite difficult to answer questions that do not correspond to one's own view of reality, as such questions would be incomprehensible. However, the fact that a questionnaire is completed does not necessarily mean that a survey is comprehensible for respondents. It is quite easy to tick off an arbitrary answer choice in order to satisfy the researcher, which facilitates a quick escape from the survey situation. Glick and Gross (1975) urged that social scientific research should operate with fewer restrictions in the future. Study participants should be given more latitude, with less intervention from researchers. Research designs and methods need to allow participants to report their subjective reality.

A third potential problem comes from mood. Memories and reports on past events – such as those called upon when completing a satisfaction survey – can be distorted by mood (Bower, 1981; Fiedler, 1991; Forgas, 1991; Schwarz, Strack, Kommer & Wagner, 1987). Bower (1981) argued that experiences congruent with one's current mood are remembered better than those that are incongruent with one's current mood. If respondents are in a good mood at the time they take a survey, they tend to remember pleasant events rather than unpleasant ones and provide correspondingly biased estimates of probabilities of occurrence and evaluations of experiences. According to Schwarz (1987), a person's current mood not only is responsible for errors in memory but is also itself used as a source of information for evaluating experiences. For example, when workers are in a good mood during a survey on job satisfaction, they tend to evaluate their work positively as a whole. However, this is not the case only because they remember more positive experiences than negative ones, overestimate the probability of occurrence of positive experiences at work and give those experiences too much weight in their assessment. On the basis of their current good mood they also conclude that they are satisfied with their work. In other situations, atmosphere and well-being serve as an anchor for judgments that are made in contrast to them. Finally, Bohner, Bless, Schwarz and Strack (1988) determined that people tend to look more intensely for the causes of negative events than for the causes of positive events or events to which they are emotionally indifferent. When an intensive search for causes is conducted, it can be assumed that more attention is paid and information is more thoroughly processed. Consequently, negative events are remembered more accurately than neutral or positive events. The influence of mood on satisfaction judgments has been demonstrated in a number of influential studies. For example, on the campus of University of Illinois at Urbana-Champaign, Schwarz (1987) arranged that one group of students 'found' 20 cents on top of a copy machine, while another group did not. Afterwards, the students were surveyed on their current state and their life satisfaction. Not just the students' current moods but also their life satisfaction was higher after 'finding' the 20 cents. Similar differences in life satisfaction were found between groups of people surveyed on sunny versus rainy days (Schwarz & Clore, 1983), between groups of sports fans surveyed before and after a football game in which their favourite team has won, or between groups surveyed in an aesthetically pleasing room versus an unpleasant room (Schwarz et al. 1987). Brief, Butcher and Roberson (1995) confirmed these findings but also pointed to a differential effect according to respondents' dispositional temperament. They invited hospital employees to participate in a study and greeted half of the participants with cookies and beverages, while the other half received no refreshments. Employees were then surveyed on their job satisfaction and given a test measuring their affective dispositions. Even people with dispositions towards negative affectivity tended to give higher satisfaction ratings when they were treated to refreshments beforehand; however, their evaluations were generally less contextually dependent than those of the people with positive affectivity. But recent research suggests that effects of mood on the measurement of life satisfaction are small or nonsignificant. Yap et al. (2016) report on nine studies closely modelled on previous work (Schwarz, 1987; Schwarz & Clore, 1983; Schwarz et al., 1987) and conclude that the current mood does not have a profound impact on judgments of life satisfaction.

A fourth potential problem comes from question wording. Answers to satisfaction questions may depend on how specific or general the question is. Strack, Martin and Schwarz (1988) assumed that people generate different answers to specific questions about their satisfaction with various areas of life compared to more general questions. Specific questions encourage people to remember and evaluate specific events, while general questions encourage a more global, less differentiated remembering. The order in which specific and global questions are asked can also lead to different answers, since the memories and answers given in response to one question can influence the assessment process for the next. Strack and colleagues (1988) investigated answers to questions on life satisfaction in general and satisfaction with one's current romantic relationship. In the first experimental condition, the question regarding relationship satisfaction was posed after the global satisfaction question. In the second condition, the specific question was posed immediately before the global satisfaction question, with the assumption that more specific content would be taken into consideration when evaluating global satisfaction compared to the first condition. In the third condition, the order of the questions from specific to global remained the same; however, respondents were explicitly told beforehand that they would be asked about their satisfaction with two completely different areas of life. In each case, answers were given on an 11-point scale. Table 10.2 summarises the correlations between answers to the two questions under each experimental condition. The size of the correlation depended on whether participants thought about content related to a specific subject before answering the global question. However, a possible objection to this is that the correlations may have been distorted by the fact that both questions were

Table 10.2 Correlation between specific relationship satisfaction or frequency of meeting up with one's partner and global life satisfaction under three experimental conditions (Strack et al., 1988, pp. 435 and 437)

	Experimental conditions		
	Global question before specific question	Specific question before global question	Specific question before global question; different areas pointed out
Experiment 1	$r = 0.16$ ($n = 60$)	$r = 0.55$ ($n = 60$)	$r = 0.26$ ($n = 60$)
Experiment 2	$r = -0.12$ ($n = 60$)	$r = 0.66$ ($n = 60$)	$r = 0.15$ ($n = 60$)

Table 10.3 High- and low-frequency answer choices (Schwarz & Scheuring, 1988, p. 489)

Questions: How often do you have intercourse with your partner? How often do you masturbate?	
High-frequency answer choices	Low-frequency answer choices
( ) Several times a day	( ) Several times a week
( ) Once a day	( ) Once a week
( ) 3 to 4 times a week	( ) Once every two weeks
( ) 2 times a week	( ) Once a month
( ) Once a week	( ) Less than once a month
( ) Less than once a week	( ) Never

answered on the same scale. Thus, Strack et al. (1988) conducted a further experiment that was nearly identical to the first, but with the following exception: instead of asking about relationship quality, participants were asked an open-ended question about how often they met up with their partner. The correlations were in line with those in the first experiment (Table 10.2). However, the size of these effects has recently been questioned. Schimmack and Oishi (2005) conducted a meta-analysis and found the overall effect to be small, and conceptual replications confirmed that item order has rather small effects.

Finally, problems may arise because answers in a survey also depend on the answer choices available. This does not only mean that researchers lay out their view of reality by defining possible answer choices, forcing respondents to provide an answer within a predetermined framework. It also means that the way in which the answer scale is differentiated can influence survey results, as Schwarz and Scheuring (1988) convincingly showed. They asked participants to indicate on a 6-point scale how frequently they had sex with their partner and how frequently they masturbated. In one experimental condition, answers were differentiated at the high-frequency end of the scale; in the other condition, answers were differentiated on the low-frequency end (Table 10.3). Afterwards, participants were asked to rate their relationship satisfaction on an 11-point scale. When high-frequency answer choices were given, the results indicated that roughly 77% of respondents had intercourse with their partner at least once a week, while roughly 69% reported masturbating at least once a week. In the condition with the low-frequency answer choices, the percentage sank to roughly 39% for intercourse and roughly 42% for masturbation. Relationship satisfaction was equally high in each condition. Similar results were reported in a survey on the frequency of watching television (Schwarz & Hippler, 1987).

In light of the considerations just discussed, neither observational procedures nor survey designs asking about past events seem suitable for collecting data about people's experiences. The conspicuous lack of ecological validity and problems with the mood-dependent remembering of banal events, as well as judgment errors as a result of current mood and survey construction, can be reduced by using a diary method. Diaries, which require experiences to be recorded as they are being experienced, also provide an opportunity to study processes rather than just collecting data on compressed experiences. It can be further assumed that the repeated recording of experiences in everyday life leads participants gradually to pay more attention to them, increasing the reliability of the reports (Rehn, 1981). Epstein (1986) reported that the precision of prognoses also increases when aggregate data recorded at several time points are available. Overall, diaries seem to be particularly well suited to measure well-being, reducing the problems of traditional survey methods described above. However, it should not be forgotten that reliable and valid measurements are also possible with surveys, as long as efforts are made to avoid systematic errors. Measures of a person's happiness obtained by appropriate surveys correlate with statements about that person's satisfaction given by family members and friends. People who indicate greater levels of happiness in surveys smile more frequently, have a greater tendency to initiate social contacts, and are more helpful and less likely to miss work. They also get less frequently involved in conflicts with co-workers, seem more energetic, flexible and proactive, and have a greater tolerance for frustration. They express greater optimism about the future, remember more positive emotional states in the past than negative ones, and are at a lower risk of suicide as well as healthier overall (Stutzer, 2003).

Diaries have long been applied in well-being studies. Larson and Bradney (1988) recorded individuals' current well-being in the presence of friends or relatives using a diary. Almeida and Kessler (1998), Almeida, Wethington and Chandler (1999), Bolger, DeLongis, Kessler and Schilling (1989) and Bolger, DeLongis, Kessler and Wethington (1989) investigated experiences of stress in everyday life and the spill-over effects of work on intimate relationships. Laireiter, Baumann, Reisenzein and Untner (1997) conducted research on social networks using diaries. Data on interaction processes between partners have also been successfully collected using diaries (Auhagen, 1987, 1991; Brandstätter & Wagner, 1994; Duck, 1991; Feger & Auhagen, 1987; Kirchler, 1988a, 1988b).

On the basis of Lersch's (1962) phenomenology of experience and Vetter's (1966) philosophical-anthropological reflections on feelings, Brandstätter (1977) constructed a **time-sample diary** that allows an analysis of well-being in everyday life and, in a modified form, also appears to be well suited to investigate everyday life in the family. On an ongoing basis, study participants report their current mood, provide causes for their current state, and briefly describe objective characteristics of the situation (e.g., where they are at the moment, what they are doing and who else is present). Thus, the diary consists of question sheets that rather represent an aid in composing a memory fragment than an attempt to force a predetermined structure onto an individual area of life. The diary entries are scheduled to be made at random predetermined times – several times a day and over a longer period of time. In order to maintain the complete confidentiality of the entries, study participants themselves are trained to conduct classificatory content analyses of their diaries. On a data sheet, each participant reports (a) the date and the scheduled and actual times at which the entry is completed, (b) their current state, (c) the quality of their current mood, (d) the sources of this state, (e) current needs, (f) current location, (g) the activity currently performed and (h) everyone who is present. In addition to the diary, participants are asked to complete diagnostic instruments related to personality traits. This allows a differential social-psychological analysis of their emotional states and how they are influenced by specific events.

A series of studies have confirmed that a diary of emotional states is a useful research method and that the significant expenses associated with it are justified from an economic perspective. These studies asked groups of 20–35 people – university students (Brandstätter, 1981), female homemakers (Brandstätter, 1983; Rodler & Kirchler, 1998), military recruits (Kirchler, 1984b), the unemployed (Kirchler, 1984a) and private-sector employees (Auinger, 1987; Kirchler & Schmidl, 2000) – to keep diaries over a period of one to six months. Kahneman and Krueger (2006) and Kahneman, Krueger, Schkade, Schwarz and Stone (2004) similarly stressed the advantages of diary studies. In order to reduce the significant amount of effort required by participants – who need to record their emotional state several times a day – they developed a somewhat more efficient method: the **day reconstruction method**. In this method, participants review each day by noting their experiences and feelings in the diary in a timely manner.

10.4 National and Subjective Life Satisfaction

Veenhoven's (2016a) World Database of Happiness (http://worlddatabaseofhappiness.eur.nl) contains average life satisfaction values for many countries, a selection of which are presented in Table 10.4. A value of 0 represents dissatisfaction, while 10 represents the highest possible satisfaction. According to the data, people from Costa Rica and Denmark are the happiest on earth. The lowest levels of satisfaction were recorded in Togo and Tanzania. The USA is in 22nd place with a score of 7.3, Germany and Austria come in 25th and 26th places with scores of 7.2, and the UK is in 30th place with a score of 7.1.

At this point, the question arises regarding the determinants of satisfaction. Since the highest values are seen in the Western industrialised world, while the lowest are recorded in the third and fourth world, it could be assumed that satisfaction is correlated with economic prosperity. However, most analyses show a weak correlation between economic data and satisfaction. People in rich countries do tend to be more satisfied than people in poor countries, and rich people in industrialised countries are happier than poor people. However, the most important determinants of (individual) satisfaction are not material factors but rather a well-functioning partnership, a close circle of friends, participation in clubs and organisations, volunteer work, having a job as opposed to being unemployed, religious faith, and last but not least a personal disposition favouring optimism and satisfaction (e.g., Frey, 2008; Stutzer, 2003).

Frey (2008) and Stutzer (2003) make a distinction between five determinants of well-being and satisfaction: (a) personality factors, (b) socio-demographic factors, (c) economic factors, (d) situational factors and (e) institutional factors:

(a) Personality factors such as self-esteem, perceived control, optimism, extraversion and a stable emotional foundation are correlated with well-being. In addition, a portion of people's 'capability' for well-being appears to be inheritable. According to a twin study by Tellegen, Lykken, Bouchard, Wilcox, Segal and Rich (1988), genetic differences could be responsible for as much as 40% of subjective well-being. High sociability is an especially important personality factor in terms of well-being, while anxiety, hostility and impulsiveness are negatively associated with satisfaction. High levels of neuroticism and mental illness are also negatively correlated with satisfaction, while physical health, particularly health status as determined by doctors, is weakly correlated with satisfaction. Sociability is positively correlated with social connections, and a tight social network provides opportunities for positive emotional experiences and social support. People who believe that their life has 'meaning' are

Table 10.4 Average happiness in selected countries, 2005–14 (Veenhoven, 2016a)

	Code	Nation	Satisfaction with life (scale 0–10)	Number of surveys
1	CR	Costa Rica	8.5	1
2	DK	Denmark	8.4	7
3	MX	Mexico	8.3	4
4	IS	Iceland	8.1	3
5	CA	Canada	8.0	1
6	CH	Switzerland	8.0	8
7	NO	Norway	8.0	6
8	FI	Finland	7.9	7
9	CO	Colombia	7.9	3
10	VE	Venezuela	7.8	1
[...]				
150	MZ	Mozambique	3.8	1
151	NE	Niger	3.8	1
152	MG	Madagascar	3.7	1
153	KE	Kenya	3.7	1
154	CG	Congo (Brazzaville)	3.7	1
155	SL	Sierra Leone	3.5	1
156	BJ	Benin	3.0	1
157	BI	Burundi	2.9	1
158	TG	Togo	2.6	1
159	TZ	Tanzania	2.5	1

Note: Life satisfaction was measured asking how much people enjoy their life as a whole on a scale ranging from 0 to 10.

as a whole more content with themselves and the world than people who do not perceive such meaning. Whether this meaning arises from religious values or volunteer work or is expressed via what appears to others as a quirky hobby is not important. One example of this is a study by Vázquez (2013), who interviewed garbage collectors at a landfill in Nicaragua. Despite their low income, many garbage collectors stated that they were happy and were optimistic about the future. Most of them pointed to social activities and leisure time as the source of their happiness.

(b) Socio-demographic factors such as age, gender, marital status and education have also been investigated in correlation with satisfaction. Summarising studies on age, gender and educational differences, Stutzer (2003) argues that differences in satisfaction are small overall; however, older people and women tend to have higher scores than younger people and men. According to Dolan, Peasgood and White (2008), age and well-being show a U-shaped relation. Younger and older people are the happiest, while people between 32 and 50 are the least satisfied. Stone, Schwartz, Broderick and Deaton (2010) observed similar results in the USA. Various studies have found high satisfaction rates among married couples whose children are already grown up and have left home. Among both men and women, married people are happier than divorced, widowed and single people. Another important factor influencing well-being involves what is known as '**daily hassles**': events that occur on a day-to-day basis and by themselves only produce minor stress, but cumulatively impact well-being (e.g., Kanner, Coyne, Schaefer & Lazarus, 1981). Thus, it is not surprising that couples have lower satisfaction scores when their children are still at home and strongly dependent on their parents. During that time, parents tend to have more concerns, and are required to put in more work in the household and in raising their children, as well as reporting more frequent conflicts and fights (Kirchler et al., 2001). The high value accorded to romantic partnerships begs the question of the role of intimacy and sex as determinants of happiness. To answer this, Blanchflower and Oswald (2004) analysed data from 16,000 Americans on questions related to happiness, money and sex. For the most part, it was determined that frequency of sex was significantly positively correlated with happiness regardless of respondents' gender or age. Married couples indicated that they had sex more frequently than unmarried couples – with the same partner – and more highly educated people reported lower frequencies than respondents with lower education. Sexual orientation and income had no statistically significant effects on the frequency of sex or life satisfaction.

(c) Economic factors such as income and material possessions, unemployment and the level of inflation are also correlated with satisfaction. Income, in particular, ought to be highly correlated with satisfaction, since a high income provides many opportunities for consumption and thus for satisfying one's material needs, at least. However, a certain income level, lottery winnings, or material possessions are often not seen as guarantees of happiness. Money can be comforting, but it does not really make people happy in the long run. People tend to overestimate the happiness that a higher salary or winning the lottery will bring. After a period of exhilaration, people become habituated to their new living standards. In the same way, they get used to having luxury cars, dream apartments and other material possessions. Veenhoven (1991) points to two guiding messages here: the postulate that 'standards of comparison adjust', which states that people's aspiration level adjusts to their perceived surroundings and thus increases in response to a perceived improvement in circumstances. He also cites the inference that 'happiness is insensitive to actual quality of life', which states that assessed aspiration levels are arbitrary, with the implication that even people in objectively bad circumstances can be happy. However, Veenhoven also argues that satisfaction is not only based on comparative processes and that people's aspiration levels do not adjust to their circumstances without exception. Rather, feelings of happiness are based on fulfilling bio-psychological needs that do not recalibrate themselves to fit the situation at hand, thus revealing the limits of human adaptability: people who experience chronic hunger, physical danger and social isolation cannot be happy. In these cases, happiness is not relative since it is based on fulfilling these aforementioned bio-psychological needs.

However, why do so many people strive to increase their income, when, according to this line of argumentation, it will not bring them any lasting benefits? Ahuvia (2008) described two factors that cause people to continue to strive for income increases despite multiple past experiences that a rise only leads to a temporary increase in satisfaction rather than a lasting effect (at least at levels above that of mere subsistence). First, he suggested that people do not learn from past experiences of these adaptive processes – for evolutionary reasons, people suffer under a continuously recurring amnesia. This amnesia causes people to continue believing that they will be able to achieve lasting satisfaction by putting in the effort necessary to achieve their goals; this, in turn, increases their motivation. Since a hypothetical person who is currently very happy will not expend much effort to improve his or her situation further, achieving satisfaction for several years after reaching one's goals would decrease motivation and thus be maladaptive. Second, Ahuvia (2008) postulated that the social recognition people hope to achieve via a high income serves as a motivational system that can act independently of or even contrary to the desire to be happy. Up to a certain point, income growth has a strong positive effect on people's satisfaction level – for example, if their basic need for food could not be satisfied before because of a lack of money. However, the motivational system described above does not automatically shut down after this point has been reached. Beyond this point, striving for greater social recognition via a higher income might develop into an independent motivational system that comes into competition with the desire for satisfaction.

Nevertheless, the influence of consumption and satisfaction with one's own economic opportunities on life satisfaction should not be completely disregarded. Money can make people happy – but only up to a certain point. According to Kahneman and Deaton (2010), US Americans appear to become happier as their income rises up to a salary level of US$ 75,000. Above this amount, happiness depends on other factors. According to Caporale, Georgellis, Tsitsianis and Ping Yin (2009), a clear correlation between income and happiness can be demonstrated by comparing income groups. Regression coefficients increased steadily from the lowest category (weekly income of below €120) to the highest (above €2,310) and were all statistically significant. Their results indicate that moving from the lowest to the highest income group is associated with a 1.08-point increase in satisfaction scores on an 11-point scale (0 = extremely unsatisfied, 10 = extremely satisfied).

Easterlin (2001) likewise confirmed a relatively clear correlation between US household income in 1994 and happiness. Figure 10.1 depicts the population distribution of various happiness categories for seven income groups in the USA in 1994. While only 16% of respondents in the bottom category claimed to be 'very happy', this number rose to 44% in the highest income category. The proportion of 'not too happy' people decreased from 23% in the bottom category to 6% in the highest category. According to Stutzer (2003), the Eurobarometer Surveys from 1975 to 1991 paint a similar picture. Nearly 90% of people in the highest income quartile indicate that they are 'fairly happy' or 'very happy'. Meanwhile, only two-thirds of people in the bottom income quartile indicate that they are 'fairly happy' or 'very happy' with their life.

Unemployment is experienced particularly negatively, even when financial safeguards are provided. Noh (2009) analysed suicide data for twenty-four OECD countries in the period 1980–2002, reporting that unemployment is highly correlated with suicide rates in high-income countries. Being unemployed does not just mean losing one's social contacts, a significant source of self-esteem, time structure and a sense of making an important contribution to society – it also makes a person feel useless (Kirchler, 1993a). Lower satisfaction scores have been found among unemployed people looking for work, but not among other groups of people who do not receive a regular wage: pensioners, university students and people who are highly involved in housework and family work have satisfaction scores that are just as high as people who work for pay (Leu, Burri & Priester, 1997). Notably, people do not seem to get used to unemployment; at least, this can be concluded from data on their long-term well-being. However, according to Caporale et al. (2009), the influence of unemployment on subjective satisfaction should not be exclusively seen as a negative one. Re-entering working life after a period of unemployment has a positive influence on satisfaction. This satisfaction bonus is highest when the period of unemployment was within the last 12 months. Over a longer period, the positive effect on well-being weakens. The authors explain this correlation by the fact that the additional income generated by taking a job is perceived especially strongly when the period of unemployment lies within the last 12 months and exerts a sustainable influence on satisfaction.

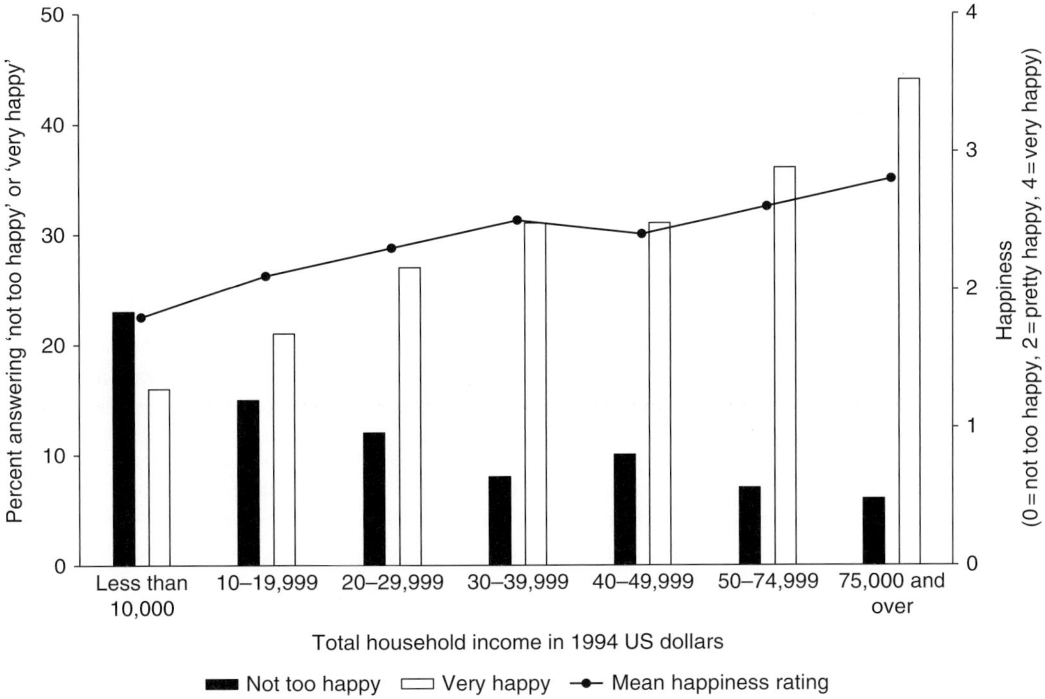

Figure 10.1 Population distribution of happiness categories for seven income groups in the USA in 1994 (data from Easterlin, 2001, p. 468)

With regard to inflation, Stutzer (2003) determined that people do not adjust their behaviour to (expected) inflation, as classical economic theory would suggest, but they react emotionally to price increases. Inflation is linked to dissatisfaction. Di Tella, MacCulloch and Oswald (2001) confirmed that inflation has a systematic influence on subjective well-being, with a 5% increase in the inflation rate resulting in a decline of 0.05 units on a 4-point scale of subjective well-being. This translates into 5% of the population slipping from the 'very happy' category into the 'fairly happy' category.

(d) Situational factors such as work and living conditions and social relationships with one's co-workers, relatives and friends are also relevant for satisfaction. Working a lot and having only limited free time tends to make people unhappy, unless their work is demanding and fully absorbing: something that they can concentrate on, experience success in, and become so engrossed in that they forget the world around them. Job satisfaction is a vibrant research area in applied psychology. Although Büssing, Bissels, Fuchs and Perrar (1999) argued that the deluge of studies on job satisfaction has dropped off somewhat from the more than 3,000 investigations counted by Locke (1976) in the middle of the 1970s, the topic still remains quite attractive. This is due to the assumption – which has also been at least partially empirically confirmed – that satisfaction is positively correlated with performance and negatively correlated with absenteeism and employee turnover, as well as that satisfied employees develop stronger allegiance to the company (Weinert, 1998). Satisfaction can also be understood from a humanistic perspective, defining it as an opportunity for self-development and self-expression, which is of critical importance for maintaining and promoting health. 'Maintaining workers' health and physical, mental and social well-being is a central concern from the perspective of occupational and health protection, the perspective of work design for personal development, and from a socio-political and business perspective' (Frieling & Sonntag, 1999, p. 193). People's careers often mean a lot to them, as they are a source of meaning and personal value in society. Krieger and Sheldon (2014) compared lawyers who were either intrinsically or extrinsically motivated. Intrinsically motivated lawyers indicated higher levels of well-being despite lower salaries, which the authors explain by their conviction of doing meaningful and well-respected work. The majority of workers look for responsibility and self-determination at work and want to be given opportunities to apply and improve their talents and skills. A high value is frequently placed on acquiring new skills. Varied, creative and even difficult assignments are typically preferred over simple, routine tasks. The experience of making a meaningful contribution to the organisation or to society matters, despite the fact that the significance of work varies from person to person. On the basis of empirical evidence, Weinert (1998) wrote that, in general, a high level of job satisfaction requires working conditions that are

> mentally stimulating, well-suited to the worker's physical and mental needs, convey a feeling of success, and provide opportunities for workers to apply and expand their interests and talents. Employees should experience respect and self-esteem as a result of their accomplishments, while the compensation system should be viewed by employees as appropriate and should be linked to individual performance. The prevailing leadership style should promote personal responsibility and proactiveness and should be conducive to workers' personal development. (p. 215 f)

During work, '**flow**' – as the feeling of being completely absorbed in an activity – is sometimes possible when workers' capabilities and the difficulty of their assignments are equally high (Csikszentmihalyi, 1990). Helliwell and Huang (2008) determined that working conditions that have nothing to do with income level have an enormous influence on life satisfaction. People who have more trusting relationships with their bosses and co-workers gain as much satisfaction on average as they would receive from a massive salary rise.

Frey (2008) and Stutzer (2003) determined that long commutes to work can reduce satisfaction. The more time respondents spent commuting each day, the less satisfied they were with their lives. People who need less than 10 minutes to get to work each day describe themselves as more satisfied than people who need more than 30 minutes a day. Kaun (2005) also confirms this. He describes long working hours and stressful commutes as negative effects of work. People also spend too much time on tasks that bring them little satisfaction. Rather than spending time with family or friends, they sit in front of the TV and compare themselves to the 'rich and famous' (Kaun, 2005). Frey (2008) noted that many people do not have their TV consumption under control, and spend more time in front of the TV than is good for them. His study was based on a survey on TV habits and life satisfaction among more than 42,000 people in twenty-two European countries. He found that people who watch TV for less than half an hour a day are more satisfied with their lives than people who spend more time watching TV, with an especially large decline in satisfaction observed when people spend more than 2.5 hours a day in front of the TV. Frey (2008) concedes that it is not clear whether people who are less satisfied with their opportunities and circumstances in life watch more TV or whether watching TV leads to dissatisfaction. One explanation of the inclination towards excessive TV consumption that sounds plausible to him is the utility arising from relaxation and entertainment. This stands in opposition to the costs associated with excessive TV consumption, such as neglecting social connections.

Good social connections are particularly relevant to satisfaction. Work-related requirements for mobility and flexibility, or excessive TV consumption etc., make it more difficult to build social connections. Social connections are a constant source of novelty, which promotes attentiveness, curiosity and engagement. In contrast, the novelty of material things with which consumers can surround themselves quickly wears off, making them poor sources of happiness. Therefore, it does not make sense to strive for material possessions – instead, people should focus on forming social connections. Kahneman (2006) suggested in a newspaper interview that people should go on holiday, give each other gifts or throw parties rather than buy a mansion or a great car. They should give their full attention to current activities, as it is better to do less but have fewer distractions. They also need to manage their attention more efficiently and allow themselves to be less impressed by what other people have or are doing.

(e) Institutional factors such as political participation and political decentralisation have been primarily investigated as determinants of satisfaction by Frey (2008) and Stutzer (2003). In general, life satisfaction is higher in countries with civil liberties and political freedom of expression, with economic freedom in the form of free exchange of goods and labour as well as personal liberties in the form of religious freedom, freedom of travel, etc., than in countries in which freedoms are restricted. Within this framework, political freedom is more important in more prosperous countries, while economic freedom is more important in poorer countries. Types of governance that preserve freedoms, function efficiently and grant their citizens the right to political participation have a positive effect on life satisfaction. According to Helliwell and Huang (2008), good governance is especially relevant in explaining national differences in quality of life. Stability and security, especially distributive and procedural justice on the part of state authorities, are positively correlated with satisfaction. In contrast, political and economic deregulation and liberalisation are unsettling and undermine trust in the authorities and one's fellow human beings.

In addition to these determining factors, three psychological processes are also relevant to understanding well-being and satisfaction (Frey, 2008; Stutzer, 2003):

(a) Adaptation processes are important because people become habituated to changed circumstances. After a while, their well-being adjusts to changes, in line with the theory of hedonic adaptation.
(b) Aspiration levels are also important. Assessments of one's own situation are made with reference to standards and expectations. Satisfaction increases when aspirations are fulfilled. However, aspirations do not always remain the same. On the one hand, aspirations can rise after having been fulfilled, creating a renewed discrepancy between the current situation and one's expectations. On the other hand, aspirations can be reduced so that the current situation seems increasingly satisfactory. The importance of aspirations for well-being is primarily reflected in Bruggemann, Groskurth and Ulich's (1975) satisfaction model. They postulate that dynamics in aspiration levels can result in various forms of job satisfaction: stabilised satisfaction, progressive satisfaction, resigned satisfaction, pseudo-satisfaction, fixated dissatisfaction and constructive dissatisfaction. Comparing existing advantages and disadvantages (current state) with expectations (target state) may result in only minor divergences, leading to stabilised satisfaction. When aspirations rise and are met, progressive satisfaction is the result. A wide gap between current and target states can lead to diffuse dissatisfaction, which triggers a reduction in aspirations, resulting in **resigned satisfaction**. If aspirations remain constant, people can 'correct' their perceptions and convince themselves that they are content with their current situation. This results in a form of satisfaction despite a discrepancy between current and target states; however, it is only pseudo-satisfaction. When current and target states diverge, dissatisfaction only arises when aspirations remain constant and no distortions of perception take place. In these cases either no attempts are made to resolve

the issue (fixated dissatisfaction) or the person actively searches for constructive improvements (constructive dissatisfaction).

(c) Finally, social comparisons are also important. Since there are no absolute measures of happiness, people compare their situation with those of other people. Whether one's own income is viewed as high or low depends on how much money other people make.

A survey on personal happiness in Austria was conducted just after the outbreak of the global financial crisis, which gained widespread media attention with the bankruptcy of the US investment bank Lehman Brothers in the middle of September 2008. The data seemed to confirm that personal happiness defied the economic crisis: reported reasons for happiness included health, fulfilling work and a strong long-term relationship. Winning the lottery, wealth or stable economic conditions were not considered relevant reasons for happiness, even during a period of crisis (Market Institut, 2009).

Not only has satisfaction research in various disciplines generated an abundance of empirical results, it has also found its way into popular science literature, leading to both guidebooks on individual happiness and socio-political recommendations for governments (e.g., Bucher, 2009; Frey, 2008; Mayrhofer, Meyer & Steyrer, 2005).

10.5 Life Satisfaction and Gross Domestic Product

Numerous studies indicate that the satisfaction stemming from material prosperity is only temporary. People quickly get used to their improved living situation. People who become materially prosperous are more satisfied for a short period of time, but they soon take their improved position for granted and use it as the neutral reference point for evaluating their position in life. Striving for material happiness doesn't seem to be worth it: we risk winding up in a treadmill of happiness expectations. But is there a world imaginable in which the poorest sick beggar with no family or friends can be just as happy as the richest person in the country, who has a caring network of family and friends and enjoys all conceivable forms of financial, social and emotional support? Diener, Lucas and Scollon (2006) invite us to imagine further whether it is possible that the citizens of a country ruled by a horrific dictator, in which criminality, slavery and inequality reign, are not any less happy with their lives than citizens of a country with a stable democracy, social prosperity and security. Does it matter at all in the long run whether or not we make an effort to improve living conditions? Is there really no demonstrable long-term effect of economic growth on subjective life satisfaction? That seems highly implausible. However, the situations described above are actually not completely absurd. They are based on a widely accepted model of subjective well-being. This model was termed the '**hedonic treadmill**' by Brickman and Campbell (1971). The assumption is that emotional reactions are comparable to the phenomenon of sensory adaptation: just as we no longer notice fragrances and odours after a while, neither do we perceive positive or negative changes after a certain period of time. We get used to our changed circumstances and are just as happy as we used to be. Every yearned-for change, love, power, success or possession makes us temporarily happier (Myers, 1992), but well-being, happiness and satisfaction are short-lived. Diener et al. (2006) similarly argue that adaptation and habituation effects are strong. However, they do not fully support the assertions of the hedonic treadmill model: in actuality, intervention programmes at the individual, organisational and societal level are effective in the long term. Specifically, they cite studies in which targeted changes in people's activities, friendliness and assistance do result in long-term increases in satisfaction. From the field of organisational psychology, it is known that the way in which work is structured can generate sustainable changes in satisfaction, while on the societal level, studies exist that demonstrate not only that satisfaction differs between demographic groups and across countries, but also that certain political, economic and social contextual conditions have a lasting influence on satisfaction.

Economic growth means more money and more opportunities for the citizens of a country to fulfil their desires. Wealth alone does not guarantee satisfaction, but neither does it seem credible that citizens' income and a country's economic performance are completely irrelevant. Even if people become quickly habituated to material prosperity, hence only experiencing temporary delights in a salary rise, it is implausible that a country's economic performance has no influence on life satisfaction. In traditional economic thought, money is seen as an indicator of happiness. More money means that more desires can be fulfilled and a higher level of satisfaction can be reached. Gross domestic product (GDP) measures the economic performance of a country in terms of the market value of all products and services generated over a certain period of time. A higher GDP ought to be correlated with higher satisfaction in a country.

In their **self-determination theory**, Ryan and Deci (2000) define the needs for autonomy, competence and relatedness (i.e., social relationships) as fundamental psychological needs, which should lead to greater well-being and mental health if fulfilled. Technological advancement and economic development allow increasingly more people to reduce their working hours and use the additional time as they please. In the past, not only did the proportion of free time increase steadily (although Kaun, 2005, has a different opinion on this), income and buying power also rose, resulting in greater opportunities to acquire goods and make use of services. When goods serve to satisfy desires, as assumed in economic science, people today, overall, ought to be happier than in previous decades. The fundamental assumption is that a higher income makes people happier. Conversely, a reduction in income should lead to dissatisfaction and discontent. Brenner (1979) demonstrated that economic crises and the financial losses associated with them led not only to subjective dissatisfaction, but also to health problems among those affected, including their family members. Over the past century, hospitalisation rates in US psychiatric facilities have fallen during times of economic prosperity, whereas significant increases in hospitalisation rates have been reported in times of economic crisis.

Are satisfaction, well-being and happiness actually correlated with a person's or a nation's economic opportunities (or not)? Traditional economic theory dictates that the correlation ought to be high. However, already Easterlin (1974) compared survey reports of people's life satisfaction over the years with economic data, finding that happiness in industrialised countries had stagnated despite continued increases in prosperity. This pattern has remained the same since. Figure 10.2 shows the developments of wealth and happiness in the USA. One line indicates the real gross domestic product per capita from 1947 to 2016 and shows a steady increase in wealth. The other line shows happiness ratings over time. The data used are from 3-step verbal happiness measures (Veenhoven, 2017), available from 1946 to 2010 (missing years are indicated by the dashed lines). The happiness line shows no change over time, indicating that happiness ratings on average remained the same.

Scitovsky (1976) evaluated the correlation between economic changes and satisfaction by analysing the percentage of people who describe themselves as satisfied or dissatisfied over a period of nearly 25 years, and comparing these satisfaction statements with income. From 1946 to 1970, while per capita income in the USA rose by 62%, the percentage of very satisfied people remained constant at roughly 47% (with variation from 39% to 62%). Using Scitovsky's (1976, p. 134 f) data to calculate the distribution of the US population according to satisfaction (on a scale from 1 = not satisfied or not very satisfied, 2 = fairly satisfied, 3 = very satisfied) and income yielded a pattern like the one depicted in Figure 10.3.

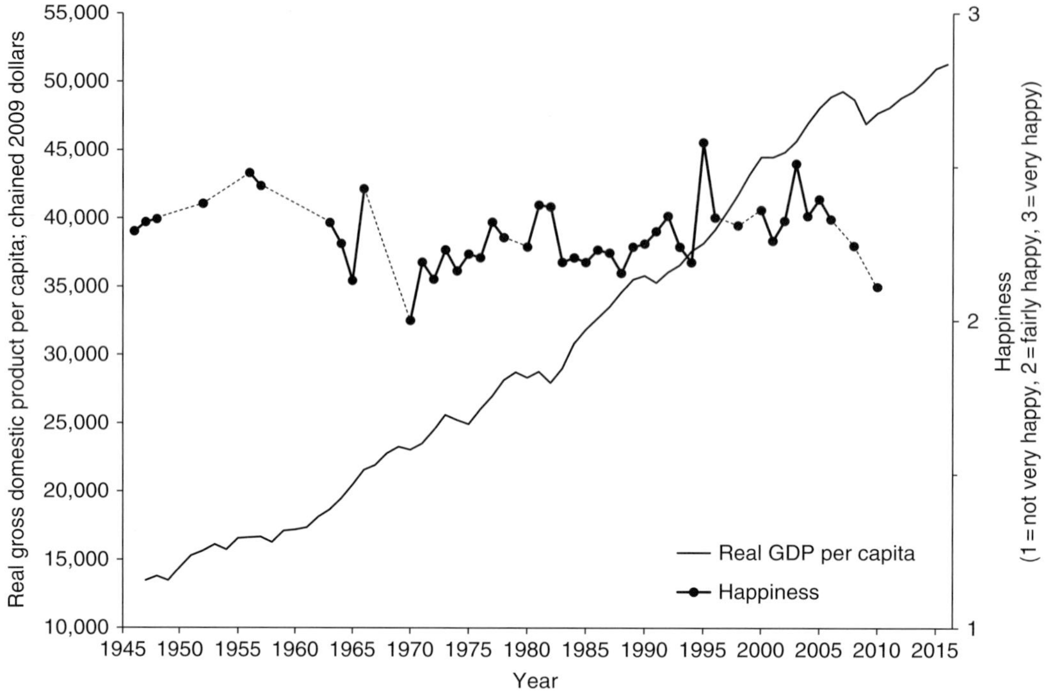

Figure 10.2 Happiness and real gross domestic product per capita, USA 1946–2016 (data from Veenhoven, 2017 and US Bureau of Economic Analysis, 2017)

The data show that US citizens did not become any happier from 1946 to 1970: there is little variation in the average satisfaction curve calculated across each period of data collection; it remains constant at a value of around 2.30 to 2.40. On the other hand, a person's income does seem to be correlated with higher satisfaction scores: the average satisfaction curve calculated across income groups shows significant variation, rising from 1.93 in the lowest groups (with income under US$ 1,000) to 2.45 in the highest income group. Scitovsky (1976) summarised:

> The puzzle is that rising in rank on the income scale seems to improve one's chances of happiness, but a rise in one's income when everybody's income is rising does not. The obvious explanation would be that one's happiness depends on where one stands in relation to the Joneses and not at all on one's absolute standard of living. (p. 135)

Differences in income and the opportunity to generate wealth lead to questions about fair wages, the fair distribution of wealth and general human satisfaction. Similarly to Scitovsky, Marx (1847/1973) made an observation to this effect that is of relevance to social psychology. He explains why satisfaction can vary as income rises but does not necessary need to do so. A house might be either large or small. As long as the houses around it are also small, the small house satisfies all social requirements in terms of living space. However, if there is a palace next door that towers above the small house, it shrinks to the size of a hut. This observation makes two points: first, that all evaluations are relative and are based on comparisons; second, that people learn about themselves by comparing themselves to others and come to a positive, neutral or negative self-assessment based on this comparative social evaluation process. Diener (1984) came to the same conclusion, summarising various empirical studies on subjective well-being. He argued that a positive

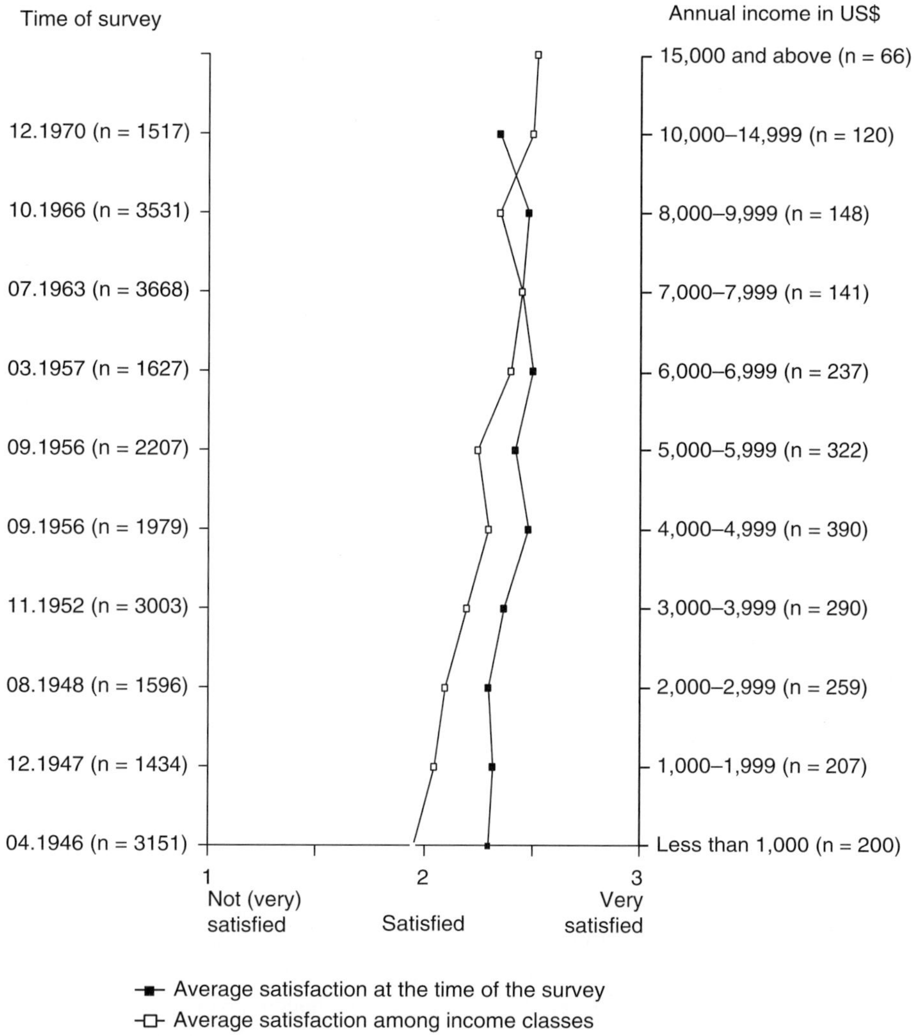

Figure 10.3 Variation in satisfaction depending on the time of survey and respondents' annual income in US$ (Scitovsky, 1976, p. 134 f)

relationship exists between the satisfaction levels of a country's citizens, their satisfaction with their own income and with their level of income relative to that of others. Scitovsky's (1976) data suggest that income is positively correlated with satisfaction. Similarly, Cheung's (1998) investigations of well-being among citizens of Hong Kong and their class affiliation suggest that income and satisfaction are positively correlated with one another. However, satisfaction was correlated not with absolute income level, but rather with better financial opportunities compared to other people. When one's income is just as high as or lower than others' income, satisfaction should remain the same or could even decline amid a general increase in buying power. Technological advancement, economic growth and shifts in values should lead to an inflation of living standards (Wiswede, 1991), meaning that a dynamic of multiplying demands can arise as opportunities to fulfil needs and wants increase. 'Thus, improving opportunities cannot keep pace with inflationary desires', summarised Wiswede (p. 143). For this reason, a nation's satisfaction does not increase over time

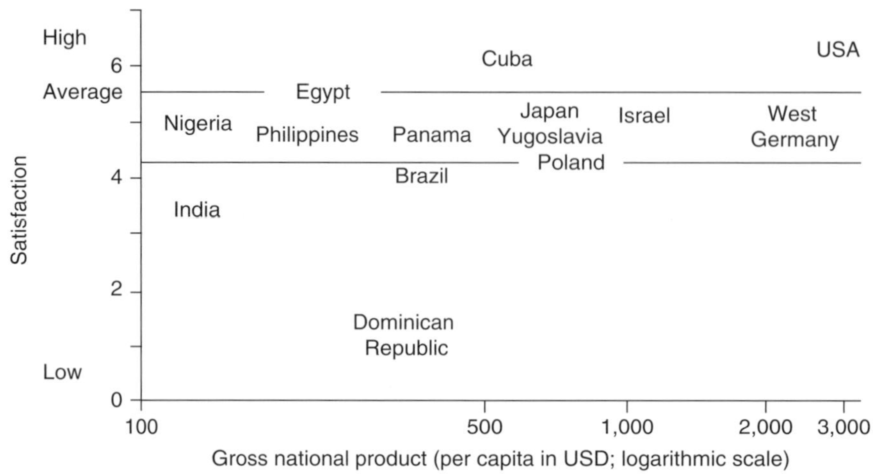

Figure 10.4 Correlation between gross national product and satisfaction (Easterlin, 1974, p. 106)

even when per capita income increases. Similarly, no significant positive correlation between gross domestic product and residents' well-being can be discerned in cross-country comparisons. This proposition is supported by a famous study by Easterlin.

Easterlin (1974) conducted a cross-cultural investigation of the relationship between gross domestic product and personal well-being. Well-being was measured in fourteen countries according to the Cantril scale (Cantril, 1965). Respondents were instructed to set the endpoints of the scale subjectively, in such a way that one endpoint symbolised the well-being that would result from fulfilling all of their desires and goals, while the other end of the scale represented the discontent that would be experienced if all their worries and fears were to be realised. They were then asked to mark their current personal well-being on this scale. As Figure 10.4 shows, average national well-being and the gross national product of various countries do not seem to co-vary with one another in Easterlin's data. Only the average well-being scores for the USA, India and the Dominican Republic point to a slight positive correlation with the macroeconomic indicators.

According to Easterlin (1974), economic changes do not lead to changes in well-being. Although on average richer people in a country are happier than poorer people, happiness in a country remains the same despite growth in material prosperity. This phenomenon is known as the **Easterlin paradox**. One explanation is that people compare their material opportunities with one another, hence a person's well-being should increase when their opportunities improve in comparison to those of a reference group. An absolute improvement in everyone's economic conditions appears to have little bearing on subjective life happiness. Similarly, a general increase in wages in a country does not significantly affect life satisfaction. People who earn more money are happier than workers who earn less, but an increase in everyone's wages does not lead to a change in satisfaction.

A study conducted by Solnick and Hemenway (1998) confirmed the assumption that the impact of absolute income pales in comparison to that of relative income. Students were asked to indicate in which world they would rather live: one in which they earn 50,000 dollars and everyone else earns half as much, or one in which they earn 100,000 dollars with the same purchasing power (i.e., prices remain the same) but everyone else earns twice as much. Most participants selected the first option, even though their consumption opportunities would have been significantly greater in the second scenario. A study by Lembregts and Pandelaere (2014) deserves mention in this context. They investigated the impact of relative wage increases on perceived inequality. Even though the wages of all participants increased by the same percentage, perceived inequality rose. This observation is also of interest in terms of the correlation between happiness and income. What happens when a country's income rises, and everyone earns 20% more? Are people just as happy as before, because they are just as rich or poor as they used to be in comparison to everyone else? Or do small initial absolute income differences eventually lead to a large gap, generating feelings of unfairness and jealousy? If so, what is the threshold for this? Even though relative income is the heavyweight in the ring, absolute income can tip the scale in certain circumstances.

Inspired by Easterlin's work, Rojas (2007) took up the question of whether or not money makes people happy. The point of departure for his study, conducted in Mexico in 2001, was the '**conceptual-referent theory of happiness**', according to which every person has a different definition of subjective well-being. People evaluate their lives according to their own understanding of subjective well-being in order to determine whether they are happy. Rojas found two opposing attitudes in his study: people place value on either inner factors or outer factors. For people with an internal orientation, money has little to do with happiness. They believe that happiness arises from within a person and does not depend on outside factors. Self-acceptance, a feeling of belonging, and emotional security play a central role for them. People with an external orientation think that happiness is affected by external factors. They place greater value on material things, wealth, possessions and fame. For them, income plays a significant role in whether or not they are happy. Rojas' study in Mexico found that 61.4% of respondents viewed happiness as influenced by external factors.

Stanovnik's (1992) findings speak against the assumption that a person's absolute level of financial opportunities has no effect on subjective satisfaction. He investigated Slovenian households' income levels, finding that satisfaction with one's income declines as income falls. Veenhoven (1984) launched a particularly vehement criticism of Easterlin's (1974) study, arguing that, according to the latter's hypothesis, even people in poor regions, battling famine and forced to fight for even their most basic needs, should feel happy as long as everyone else in their comparison group is in the same position. Not only does this argument lead to disastrous ignorance of third world poverty, it also does not hold up empirically. Easterlin's investigation focused on relatively prosperous nations, neglecting any really poor countries. This may be the reason why the correlation between subjective happiness and economic indicators did not turn out to be significant in his study. It could be the case that, in actual fact, satisfaction depends not just on interpersonal comparative processes but also on absolute economic conditions. In order to test these assumptions, more diverse countries need to be compared with one another. Figure 10.5 illustrates the correlation between average national well-being and gross national product in various rich and poor countries according to Veenhoven (1984). It is apparent that well-being is lower on relatively poor continents such as Asia and Africa than on richer continents such as North America, Australia and Europe.

To present more recent data, we assessed the relationship between GDP 2014 published by the World Bank Group (2016) and satisfaction with life and 'happy life years' published by Veenhoven (2016b). Happy life years is a variable that weights life satisfaction with life expectancy. The two happiness indicators have a non-linear relation with GDP, as Figures 10.6a and 10.6b show: countries with low GDP seem to vary considerably with regard to happiness indicators. With increasing GDP, happiness increases but the increase slows down if GDP reaches highest levels.

In 1994, Veenhoven compared subjective happiness in thirty-one countries once again. Against Easterlin's expectations, he found severe differences between nations. Average subjective well-being was higher in Iceland, Ireland, Canada, Australia, Great Britain and Scandinavian countries than in countries like India, Greece, White Russia, Portugal, South Korea or Mexico. While Easterlin

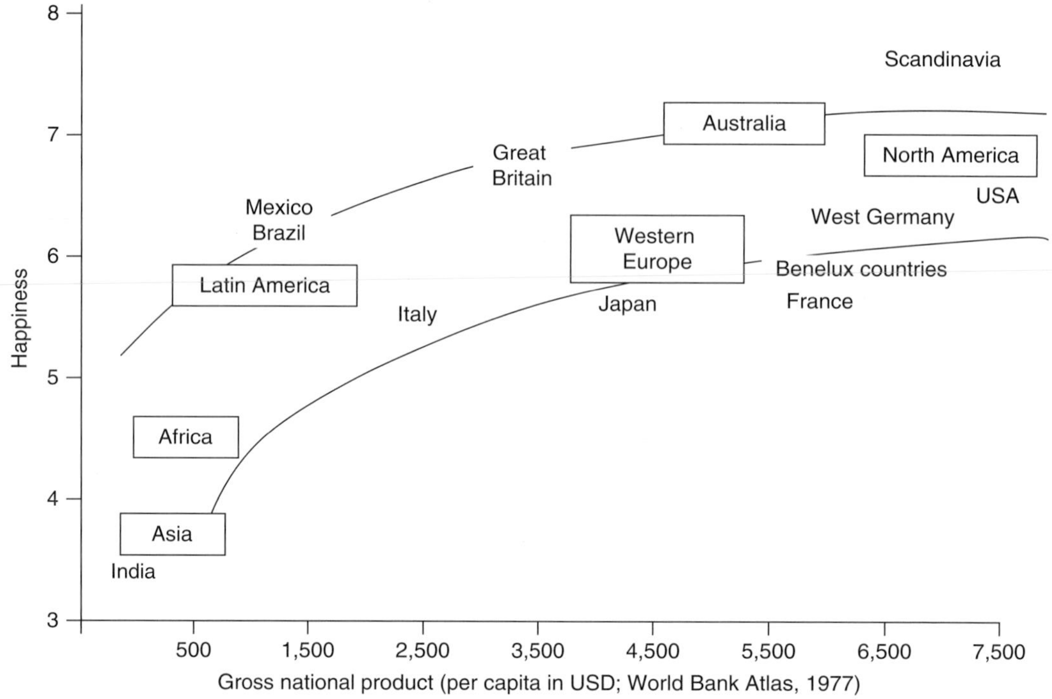

Figure 10.5 Correlation between gross national product and happiness in different parts of the world (Veenhoven, 1984, p. 149)

(1974) found no differences in satisfaction across nations in the 1970s, Veenhoven (1994) demonstrated significant differences two decades later up to the present day. Veenhoven concluded that absolute life conditions rather than relative ones are of significance for life satisfaction, which constitutes the reason why differences between nations could be confirmed.

At this point, one could speculate that the difference in findings can be explained by a worldwide intensification of mass communication rather than different economic conditions per se. Deaton (2008) argued that health is important and so is income to afford a good life. But there are other factors which are irrelevant as long as people are not aware that they are lacking something which others possess or which is taken for granted in other countries:

> People may adapt to misery and hardship, and cease to see it for what it is. People do not necessarily perceive the constraints caused by their lack of freedom; the child who is potentially a great musician but never has a chance to find out will not express a lack of life satisfaction. Whole groups can be taught that their poor health or their lack of political participation are natural or even desirable aspects of a good world. (p. 69)

Nowadays, even people in less developed countries have some idea of the living standards in economically developed countries and are able to draw comparisons. In the past, such comparative processes were nearly impossible due to limited mass communication. However, this interpretation remains speculation. Other arguments for differences between past and recent analyses of wealth and happiness stress the fact that recent analyses also include the poorest countries, the data structure has changed (e g., the inclusion of countries from the former Soviet Union), and samples are more representative than they were in former analyses (Deaton, 2008).

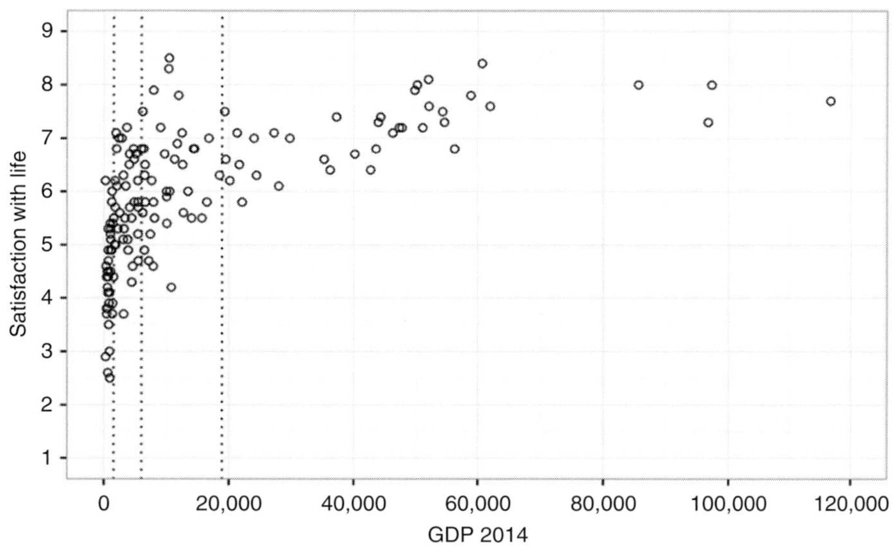

Figure 10.6a Relationship between GDP 2014 and satisfaction with life (dotted lines indicate 1st, 2nd (= median) and 3rd quartile of GDP in 149 countries). Data from Veenhoven (2016b) and World Bank Group (2016).

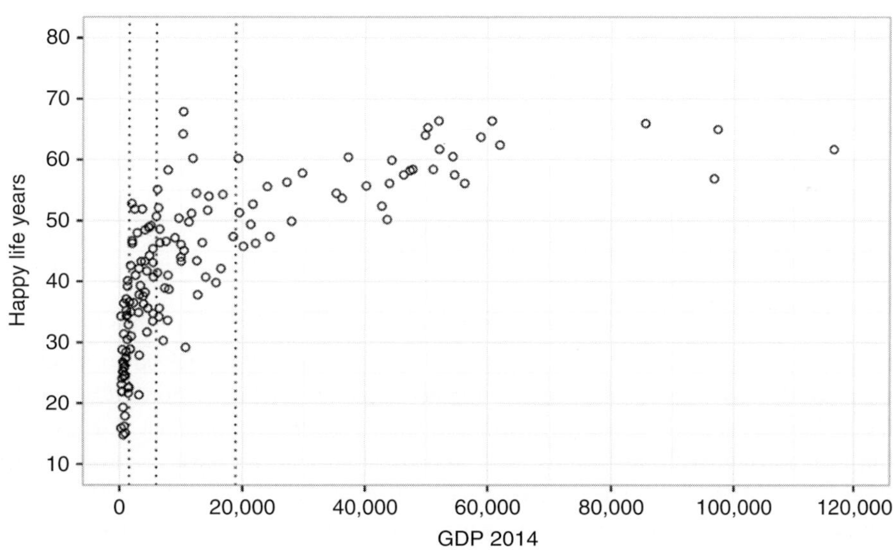

Figure 10.6b Relationship between GDP 2014 and happy life years (dotted lines indicate 1st, 2nd (= median) and 3rd quartile of GDP in 149 countries). Data from Veenhoven (2016b) and World Bank Group (2016).

According to another line of thought, national differences in satisfaction could be rooted in cultural differences rather than differences in income. It could be the case that some nations are more prone to melancholy, while others are more prone to levity and confidence. However, it is troubling that, for instance, Finland places much higher than Italy. Veenhoven (1994) argued that comparing the well-being of East and West Germans after reunification allows for a test of economic versus cultural aspects: Germany was divided for a period of around five decades. This amount of time is nowhere near sufficient to cause shifts in cultural traits; moreover, opportunities for contact between East and West Germans persisted even during the time of the Iron Curtain despite a number of challenges. If differences in well-being are rooted in cultural aspects, equal satisfaction scores would be found among East and West Germans, however, this should not be the case if well-being was correlated with financial means. It turns out that the two newly reunified sections of the country exhibited significant differences (Landua, 1992; Veenhoven, 1994).

In the end, the view can be confirmed that a high quality of life, material prosperity, security, and opportunities to satisfy one's needs and wants lead to greater well-being in a country. However, it might still be the case that different determinants of satisfaction are relevant in different countries. This hypothesis seems plausible: the wealth and poverty of various countries as well as differences among demographic groups within a country are associated with different subjective well-being scores. It can also be argued that the correlation between life satisfaction and economic prosperity may be higher than shown in the data, given that the typical measure used to define economic prosperity, gross domestic product (GDP), is prone to error. GDP rises when people work a lot. However, work is only strongly correlated with satisfaction when it is meaningful and fosters personal development. Some factors linked to satisfaction and a high quality of life, such as ecological values, job security and the value of free time, are not taken into account in GDP. On the other hand, many factors that definitely do not make people happy, such as destruction and crime, are reflected in GDP. GDP increases after natural disasters and armed conflicts because destruction and rebuilding promote greater production. Similarly, when crime rises in a country, expenditures on security and crime-fighting are increased; these are also reflected in GDP.

Finally, it should be pointed out that arguments about the correlation between economic development and satisfaction have significant socio-political effects. If, on the one hand, a country's well-being remains unaffected by material conditions due to continuous adjustments to aspirations, striving for growth and economic prosperity no longer has any meaning, nor do efforts to redistribute resources between the first and the third world. If, on the other hand, material possessions are recognised as significant to human happiness, both individuals and national economies may be forced onto a treadmill of production and consumption focused on generating wealth even at the expense of other people.

With regard to this dilemma, the British 'happiness economist' Layard (2005) argued that a high marginal tax rate or union rules limiting working hours should indeed be viewed positively, as they help rein in the desire continually to improve performance, which is detrimental to well-being. According to Häring and Storbeck (2007), a statement by Benjamin Friedman, economist at Harvard University, stands in contradiction with this. In his view, economic growth can have positive consequences for society, such as accelerating the development of democratic values, tolerance and fairness.

What can economists and politicians learn from happiness research? Happiness economists advise politicians to focus on what people say makes them happy rather than what economic theories would expect to make them happy. Frey (2008), Frey and Stutzer (2002) and Stutzer (2003) summarise economic and political factors which influence life satisfaction levels in a country (see also Diener & Tov, 2012). They emphasise the importance of income up to a certain point, taxation policies that reduce inequality and fight poverty, social policies that propagate full employment rather than joblessness, democratic values and government's responsiveness to its citizens as important socio-political goals. Finally, research on subjective well-being in society should be used to evaluate the effects of state spending on public goods, as happiness in a country cannot be solely derived on the basis of the level of state expenditure.

Conclusion

So does money make you happy? This may be a simple question, yet the answer to it is not. Economic changes have an effect on well-being and satisfaction. People in rich countries and with high income report higher subjective well-being, but it is puzzling why increases in income do not necessarily lead to increases in happiness. Not only the absolute income but also the relative income seems to matter to people. In addition, expectations and aspirations or the adaptation to a raised income as a new reference point have to be considered. The experienced happiness of a higher standard of living may fade away when a person gets used to it, and a promotion may not even have a positive effect when one's hope for the included salary rise is disappointed. Mediating processes, such as self-determination or the perception of fairness, are another possible explanation. Lastly, there are far more important variables that determine happiness than income and money, most notably friendship, intimate partnership and meaning in life.

Summary

- The terms well-being, happiness, satisfaction and quality of life are often used as synonyms. However, sometimes these terms are defined and operationalised differently, making it difficult to compare the results of empirical studies. The definition of happiness is too diffuse, making it problematic for research and practice.
- Subjective well-being comprises an emotional or affective component, in particular positive and negative affect on the one hand and a cognitive-evaluative component, namely general and specific life satisfaction, on the other. However, a distinction needs to be made between momentary affect on the one hand and long-lasting well-being or satisfaction on the other.
- The most used method to operationalise well-being is self-assessment. Yet it has many drawbacks: socially desirable answers, falling back on stereotypes and prejudices, distortion of memories and reports, and mood-dependent remembering.
- Neither observational procedures nor survey designs asking about past events seem suitable for collecting data about people's experiences. New methods like the daily reconstruction method are promising.
- Subjective life satisfaction is determined by personality factors (e.g., self-esteem), socio-demographic factors (e.g., age or gender), economic factors (e.g., income or unemployment), situational factors (e.g., work and living conditions) and institutional factors (e.g., political freedom).
- People's aspiration levels adjust to their perceived surroundings. Adaptation and habituation effects are strong, leading to the so-called 'hedonic treadmill'. People work even beyond the point where money makes them happy, partly because they do not learn from past experiences of adaptive processes, but also because social recognition serves as a motivational system.
- Self-determination theory postulates that needs for autonomy, competence and relatedness are fundamental psychological needs that lead to greater well-being and mental health if fulfilled.
- Economic changes do not necessarily lead to changes in well-being. Life happiness in a country remains the same despite growth in material prosperity.

Questions

1. What are 'inner qualities' according to Veenhoven (2000) in the context of life satisfaction?
2. What is the 'hedonic treadmill' model with regards to income?
3. What does 'standards of comparison adjust' mean in the context of income and satisfaction?
4. Why is the use of GDP problematic in studies of wealth and happiness?
5. What is the 'Easterlin paradox'?

FURTHER READING

Anand, P. (2016). *Happiness explained: What human flourishing is and what we can do to promote it*. Oxford: Oxford University Press.

Diener, E., & Biswas-Diener, R. (2008). *Happiness: Unlocking the mysteries of psychological wealth*. Malden, MA: Blackwell.

Frey, B. S. (2008). *Happiness: A revolution in economics*. Cambridge, MA: MIT Press.

Kahneman, D., Diener, E., & Schwarz, N. (eds.) (1999). *Well-being: The foundations of hedonic psychology.* New York: Sage.

KEY TERMS

1/n heuristic The 1/n heuristic is a **heuristic** based on naive diversification. Investors tend to spread their assets equally among several options without taking into account the risks of each option and the correlations between risks.

9-ending prices 9-ending prices are **psychological prices** that have the digit 9 at a significant ending place (e.g., 15.90). They can influence consumers through **image effects** and **level effects**.

accommodation In the **cognitive-developmental theory**, accommodation is a process of adaptation of the individual to the environment.

action orientation Action orientation refers to people's tendency to convert their intentions into actions. (Compare **state orientation**.)

affect heuristic The affect heuristic is a **heuristic** where judgments are based on cues from positive and negative affect.

affective forecasting Affective forecasting is the prediction of emotional reactions to future events.

AIDA model The AIDA model assumes that advertising works through the stages of attention (A), interest (I), desire (D) and action (A). It is a **hierarchy-of-effects model**.

altruistic punishment Altruistic punishment is punishment dealt out by people although they do not profit from this punishment and even when they incur costs by doing so.

ambiguity effect The ambiguity effect assumes that decision-makers prefer **risky decisions** to **ambiguous decisions**.

ambiguous decisions Ambiguous decisions are a subset of **decisions under uncertainty** where the probabilities of consequences of alternatives are only vaguely known.

anchoring In the **theory of social representations**, anchoring is a process where the social representation is linked to existing categories.

anchoring and adjustment heuristic The anchoring and adjustment heuristic is a **heuristic** where judgments are based on a starting value and (inadequately) adjusted from that value.

anticipated emotions Anticipated emotions are emotions concerning the consequences of a decision. They are part of **integral affect**.

anticipatory emotions Anticipatory emotions are emotions concerning the immediate visceral reactions to risk in a decision. They are part of **integral affect**.

Asian disease problem The Asian disease problem is a decision problem where decision-makers need to choose between two intervention programmes with certain or risky consequences. It demonstrates that risk preferences are influenced by **framing effects**.

assimilation In the **cognitive-developmental theory**, assimilation is a process of adaptation of the environment to the individual.

assimilation effects Within **social categorisation theory**, assimilation effects describe how similarities within a category are perceived as more pronounced than they actually are. (Compare **contrast effects**.)

attitudes Attitudes are summary evaluations of objects. Attitudes can refer to all kinds of objects (e.g., ideas, topics, physical items, people, etc.) and evaluate such objects from negative to positive.

autonomous decisions In the **model of purchase decisions in private households**, autonomous decisions are decisions made by one partner while taking into account the other partner's preferences.

availability heuristic The availability heuristic is a **heuristic** where judgments are based on the ease with which pieces of information can be generated or retrieved from memory.

axioms In decision theory, axioms are basic assumptions about preferences that form the core of the rationality assumption. The most important axioms are **completeness**, **transitivity**, **reflexivity**, **non-satiation**, **continuity** and **convexity**.

backward induction Backward induction is an analysis of repeated decision problems (e.g., a limited number of rounds of a **prisoner's dilemma**) that starts from considering the rational solution in the last round. From that solution, the rational solution in the previous round can be derived, and so on.

beauty contest The beauty contest is a decision problem where decision-makers have to give an estimate that requires them to put themselves in the position of the other players, take their limited rationality into account in their own estimate, and anticipate the others' estimates (e.g., writing down the number corresponding to two-thirds of the mean of all numbers written down by all participants).

belief in a just world The theory of belief in a just world assumes that people have the need to assume they live in a world that is just, and where outcomes are not determined by random events.

better-than-average effect The better-than-average effect assumes that people believe that they are better than others, in the sense that their positive traits are more developed and their negative traits are less developed than those of other people.

bomb crater effect The bomb crater effect describes the finding that, in tax experiments with several rounds, compliance often strongly drops after an audit.

bounded rationality Bounded rationality assumes that the human ability to behave rationally is limited.

centipede game The centipede game is a decision problem where decision-makers repeatedly can either keep a money amount or pass it on to another person. If they pass it on, the amount is multiplied by some factor and then the other person can decide to keep the resulting amount or give it back.

choice bracketing Choice bracketing describes whether several decisions are considered jointly or in isolation.

coercive power In tax research, coercive power is based on tax authorities' ability to enforce a law regardless of its societal acceptance. (Compare **legitimate power**.)

cognitive-developmental theory The cognitive-developmental theory assumes that intelligence develops through adaptation processes of **assimilation** and **accommodation**. It assumes four stages: **sensorimotor intelligence**, **preoperational thought**, **concrete operational thought** and **formal operations**.

common sense Related to the theory of social representations, common sense refers to the sum of knowledge within a community that forms the basis for actions.

compensation hypothesis The compensation hypothesis assumes that positive experiences and behaviour during leisure time balance out negative experiences at work. (Compare **neutrality hypothesis**, **generalisation hypothesis**, **interaction hypothesis**, **congruence hypothesis**.)

completeness Completeness is an **axiom** in decision theory stating that actors can rank alternatives into a preference order.

compulsive buying Compulsive buying describes **pathological buying** behaviour as driven by a reduction in tension and anxiety provided by shopping.

conceptual-referent theory of happiness The conceptual-referent theory of happiness assumes that people have different definitions of subjective well-being, and evaluate their lives according to their own understanding of subjective well-being.

concrete operational thought Concrete operational thought is the third stage in the **cognitive-developmental theory**, ranging from 7 to 11 years of age. It is characterised by loss of egocentrism and the ability for coordinated and reversible transformations.

conflict A conflict is a difference of opinion among the people concerned. Conflicts are differentiated into **probability conflicts**, **value conflicts** and **distribution conflicts**.

congruence hypothesis The congruence hypothesis assumes that experiences and behaviour at work and during leisure time are associated with one another through third variables. (Compare **neutrality hypothesis**, **generalisation hypothesis**, **compensation hypothesis**, **interaction hypothesis**.)

conjunction fallacy The conjunction fallacy assumes that people do not take into account that combined events cannot be more likely than the constituting single events.

Consumer Sentiment Index The Consumer Sentiment Index measures consumers' subjective feelings about their individual financial situation and overall economic conditions at present and in the future.

continuity Continuity is an **axiom** in decision theory stating that the loss of a specific quantity of a Good A can be compensated with receiving a specific quantity of another Good B.

contrast effects Within **social categorisation theory**, contrast effects describe how differences between categories are perceived as more pronounced than they actually are. (Compare **assimilation effects**.)

convexity Convexity is an **axiom** in decision theory stating that actors possessing a small amount of Good A and a large amount of Good B will only be indifferent to the loss of part of A if they receive a proportionally larger quantity of B in return.

core elements In the **theory of social representations**, core elements are those central parts of a social representation that define its meaning and organise it.

cost minimisation principle The cost minimisation principle states that a given result should be achieved with the minimum of resources.

creeping determinism Related to **hindsight bias**, creeping determinism describes the belief that something 'had to turn out this way' after knowing the outcome.

daily hassles Daily hassles are events that occur on a day-to-day basis and by themselves only produce minor stress, but cumulatively impact well-being.

day reconstruction method The day reconstruction method asks respondents to review their day and report their experiences (e.g., well-being) during parts of the day.

decision anomalies Decision anomalies are deviations from the rational model.

decision diary The decision diary is a specific form of **diary methods** to study decision-making in close relationships.

decisions under certainty Decisions under certainty are decisions where no probabilities are involved regarding the consequences of alternatives. (Compare **decisions under uncertainty**.)

decisions under uncertainty Decisions under uncertainty are decisions where the consequences of alternatives only occur with some probability. They are differentiated into **risky decisions** and **ambiguous decisions**. (Compare **decisions under certainty**.)

descriptive decision models Descriptive decision models describe how individuals actually make decisions. (Compare **normative decision models**, **prescriptive decision models**.)

diary methods Diary methods are measures (usually short questionnaires) that are repeatedly completed in a real-life situation, at either a specific time or a specific event.

dictator game The dictator game is a decision problem where decision-makers have to divide a good (e.g., a sum of money) between themselves and another person. The other person has to accept the proposed division. (Compare **ultimatum game**.)

disposition effect The disposition effect assumes that investors hold on to losing stocks for too long, and sell winning stocks too quickly.

distribution conflicts Distribution conflicts are one form of **conflict** where people disagree about the distribution of resources.

doing gender Doing gender refers to attempts to neutralise violations of societal gender norms (e.g., the 'male breadwinner').

double-entry mental accounting model The double-entry mental accounting model assumes that transactions are booked in mental accounts as streams of future pleasure of consumption and pain of payment. These streams can be linked in the mental account to varying degrees (coupling).

EAST EAST is a framework for **nudges** and highlights that, for a specific behaviour to be encouraged, it should be made Easy, Attractive and Social, and that nudges should occur Timely.

Easterlin paradox The Easterlin paradox assumes that although on average richer people in a country are happier than poorer people, happiness in a country remains the same despite growth in material prosperity.

economic expectations Economic expectations are conjectures about future economic events, based on past experiences, learning processes, and knowledge and opinions about new circumstances.

economic psychology Economic psychology is the branch of psychology that studies the psychological mechanisms and processes that underlie consumption and other economic behaviour.

economic theory of criminal behaviour The economic theory of criminal behaviour assumes that criminal behaviour can be understood as consideration of costs and benefits, and therefore the threat of punishment has a deterrent effect if crimes are discovered and punished.

editing phase In **prospect theory**, the editing phase is the first stage of the decision-making process where options are subjectively restructured and simplified. In particular, a reference point is chosen that defines outcomes as gains or losses.

efficient markets hypothesis The efficient markets hypothesis assumes that all of the information available at a given time should be reflected in the price of the traded securities.

elaboration likelihood model The elaboration likelihood model (ELM) assumes that persuasion can occur through a central or a peripheral route. It is an **information processing model**.

elimination heuristic The elimination heuristic is a **heuristic** where decisions are based on sequential elimination of alternatives.

Ellsberg paradox The Ellsberg paradox is an illustration that decision-makers behave inconsistently between two formulations of the decision situation that have mathematically identical possible gains but differ in ambiguity. It demonstrates the **ambiguity effect**.

emotional well-being Emotional well-being is the affective component of subjective well-being. (Compare **life satisfaction**.)

endowment effect The endowment effect states that a good immediately becomes more valuable after a person has taken possession of it.

enforcement paradigm In tax research, the enforcement paradigm refers to a view of taxpayers as potential criminals, so that tax honesty is to be achieved through audits and fines. (Compare **service paradigm**, **trust paradigm**.)

entrepreneur An entrepreneur is a person who detects or creates business opportunities and exploits these opportunities through small and medium-sized firms.

entrepreneurial alertness Entrepreneurial alertness refers to the ability to discern business opportunities precisely and quickly and to have a 'feel' for them.

equilibrium wage In economic analyses of labour markets, the equilibrium wage (or market-clearing wage) is the wage where supply and demand for labour correspond to each other.

equity theory Equity theory assumes that perceptions of fairness are a function of comparing one's own ratio of outcomes to inputs with the ratio of outcomes to inputs of other people.

euro illusion Euro illusion is a specific form of **money illusion** and describes that the perception of prices in euros is influenced by the respective original currency and the exchange rates.

evaluation phase In **prospect theory**, the evaluation phase is the second stage of the decision-making process where options are evaluated according to the **value function** and the **weighting function**.

expensive = good heuristic See **price–quality heuristic**.

extensive decisions Extensive decisions are decisions that involve complex information processing.

fair wage–fair effort hypothesis The fair wage–fair effort hypothesis assumes that workers' behaviour in the labour market is governed by fairness: they respond to higher wages with higher effort and to lower wages with lower effort.

fast and frugal heuristics Fast and frugal heuristics (**heuristic**) are decision-making aids that allow a complex problem to be solved in a short period of time, using only a few pieces of information.

financial capability Financial capability includes **financial literacy**, but also skills as well as confidence and attitudes regarding financial concepts.

financial literacy Financial literacy is the ability to understand and use financial concepts.

financial psychology Financial psychology (as a subsection of **economic psychology**) studies experience and behaviour when dealing with money or highly liquid investments.

flow Flow describes the feeling of being completely absorbed in an activity.

formal operations Formal operations is the fourth stage in the **cognitive-developmental theory**, ranging from 11 years of age to adulthood. It is characterised by the independence of mental operations of the concrete object and the ability to reason formally.

forms of well-being Four different forms of well-being are distinguished: momentary mental well-being, habitual mental well-being, momentary physical well-being and habitual physical well-being.

four-phase model of unemployment The four-phase model of unemployment assumes that unemployed persons go through phases of shock, optimism, pessimism and fatalism.

framing effects Framing effects assume that decision-makers' preferences depend on the problem presentation.

full employment In economic analyses of labour markets, full employment refers to the employment situation at the **equilibrium wage**. (Compare **voluntary unemployment**.)

fundamental law of effect The fundamental law of effect states an increase in the probability of occurrence of the behaviour that receives the most reinforcement. (Compare **law of relative effect**.)

gambler's fallacy The gambler's fallacy describes the mistaken belief that, after a sequence of one outcome, the other outcome becomes more likely (e.g., black and red in roulette). (Compare **hot hand fallacy**.)

garbage can model The garbage can model assumes that decisions occur as a coincidental combination of problems, solutions and decision-makers. It is a **descriptive decision model**.

generalisation hypothesis The generalisation hypothesis assumes that positive experiences and behaviour at work are generalised to leisure time as well. (Compare **neutrality hypothesis**, **compensation hypothesis**, **interaction hypothesis**, **congruence hypothesis**.)

Gini coefficient The Gini coefficient measures the degree of concentration in a country's income distribution. It measures the area between the **Lorenz curve** and an equal distribution line, relative to the total area under the equal distribution line.

groupthink Groupthink describes the phenomenon that groups make suboptimal decisions. It occurs in highly cohesive groups and leads to suboptimal solutions through failure to define goals, selective information processing, insufficient evaluation of consequences and poor implementation plans.

hedonic editing See **hedonic framing**.

hedonic framing Hedonic framing (or hedonic editing) states that, in **mental accounting**, gains and losses can be viewed in specific ways (integrated or separated) to increase satisfaction.

hedonic treadmill The hedonic treadmill is a model of subjective well-being that assumes that people quickly adapt to changed circumstances and after a short while are just as happy as before.

hedonism Hedonism describes the search for pleasure and for increased gratification.

herd behaviour Herd behaviour is a tendency among investors to follow the behaviour of other investors blindly. (Compare **information cascades**.)

heuristics Heuristics are rules of thumb that allow reaching a judgment or a decision quickly in a complex situation. Examples for heuristics are the **availability heuristic**, **representativeness heuristic**, **anchoring and adjustment heuristic**, **mood-as-information heuristic**, **affect heuristic**, **price–quality heuristic** and **1/n heuristic**. So-called **fast and frugal heuristics** include the **recognition heuristic**, **take-the-best heuristic** and **elimination heuristic**.

hierarchy-of-effects models In consumer behaviour, hierarchy-of-effects models describe the effects of advertising as mediated by cognitive, affective and conative (behavioural) processes. (Compare **information processing models**.)

hindsight bias The hindsight bias (or knew-it-all-along bias) states that, after learning an outcome, people tend to claim to have known that the event would turn out that way. (Compare **creeping determinism**.)

home bias The home bias states that investors tend to select stocks from their own country, and therefore ignore that the values of these stocks correlate more closely with one another than do the values of stocks from different countries.

homo economicus In decision theory, *homo economicus* is the paradigm of a utility-maximising and rationally behaving actor.

horizontal monitoring Horizontal monitoring is an approach to taxation based on a good relationship between the taxpayer and the authorities, which is recorded in a compliance agreement.

hot hand fallacy The hot hand fallacy describes the mistaken belief that, after a sequence of successes, another success becomes more likely (e.g., scoring in basketball). (Compare **gambler's fallacy**.)

house money effect The house money effect describes how previous gains can lead to greater risk seeking.

image effects Image effects state that **9-ending prices** influence the perception of the good or the perception of the relation between the good and the price.

impact bias In **affective forecasting**, the impact bias describes how the duration and intensity of emotional reactions to future events are often overestimated.

implicit favourite model The implicit favourite model assumes that decision-makers spontaneously choose one option, and then search for confirmation that this was the correct choice. It is a **descriptive decision model**.

incidental affect Incidental affect describes emotions and moods that are experienced at the time of decision-making but have no connection to the task at hand. (Compare **integral affect**.)

influence debts In the **model of purchase decisions in private households**, it is assumed that one partner may have more influence in a specific purchase decision and therefore incurs influence debts that need to be balanced out in future decisions.

influence tactics Influence tactics are ways in which partners in close relationships try to convince the other person of the accuracy of their own perspective and the advantages of their own preferences.

information cascades Information cascades describe situations where investors ignore their private information and imitate others. (Compare **herd behaviour**.)

information processing models In consumer behaviour, information processing models describe the effects of advertising by examining different routes through which information is processed by consumers. (Compare **hierarchy-of-effects models**.)

integral affect Integral affect describes emotions and moods that are directly linked to the decision itself. It comprises **anticipated emotions** and **anticipatory emotions**. (Compare **incidental affect**.)

integrative process model of consumer credit The integrative process model of consumer credit assumes that credit use can be described in three phases before, during and after credit take up.

interaction hypothesis The interaction hypothesis assumes that experiences and behaviour at work and during leisure time have mutual effects on one another. (Compare **neutrality hypothesis**, **generalisation hypothesis**, **compensation hypothesis**, **congruence hypothesis**.)

interaction principles In the **model of purchase decisions in private households**, it is assumed that close relationships differ in terms of power structure and harmony, and can be described by four interaction principles: love principle, credit principle, equity principle and egoism principle. These principles also govern the regulation of **utility debts**.

intrapreneurs Intrapreneurs are entrepreneurially oriented employees (e.g., considering founding their own business).

job characteristics model The job characteristics model assumes that intrinsically motivating work requires knowledge about results, experienced responsibility and experienced meaningfulness.

job demands–resources model The job demands–resources model assumes that organisational outcomes result from the interplay between job demands and job resources.

job detachment Job detachment means refraining from job-related activities and thoughts during after-work hours.

knew-it-all-along bias See **hindsight bias**.

law of relative effect The law of relative effect (or matching law) states that the selection ratio of various behavioural alternatives is proportional to the subjective value of the reinforcements attached to these alternatives and inversely proportional to the time that passes between the behaviour and its reinforcement. (Compare **fundamental law of effect**.)

legitimate power In tax research, legitimate power is based on positive evaluations of authorities' power and positive attitudes towards authorities. (Compare **coercive power**.)

less-is-more effect The less-is-more effect states that, in some cases, less knowledge can lead to better decisions because it allows using the **recognition heuristic**.

level effects Level effects state that **9-ending prices** influence the perception of the price as such.

life satisfaction Life satisfaction is the cognitive-evaluative component of subjective well-being. (Compare **emotional well-being**.)

logic of success The logic of success is an approach to decisions that focuses on delineating concrete goals in complex decision situations, and on taking into consideration interactions between goals.

Lorenz curve The Lorenz curve shows the distribution of income within a country. (Compare **Gini coefficient**.)

Marienthal Marienthal is the name of an Austrian village where a very influential study on the consequences of unemployment was conducted in the 1930s.

market-clearing wage See **equilibrium wage**.

matching law See **law of relative effect**.

melioration Melioration states that people often choose the alternative that puts them in a better position for the time being. In the long run, melioration can counteract maximisation.

mental accounting The theory of mental accounting assumes that people record the costs and benefits of various operations, and remember and settle them in event-specific ways. For example, people set aside specific sums of money in their budget for specific decision categories.

MINDSPACE MINDSPACE is a framework for **nudges** and summarises nine robust effects on behaviour: Messenger, Incentives, Norms, Defaults, Salience, Priming, Affect, Commitments and Ego.

model of purchase decisions in private households The model of purchase decisions in private households assumes that decisions are influenced by product type, power and harmony in the relationship and the resulting **interaction principles**, and **conflict** type, as well as regulation of benefits such as **utility debts** or **influence debts**.

money illusion Money illusion states that a perceived economic value of money amounts is influenced by the units in which they are represented.

Monty Hall dilemma The Monty Hall dilemma is a decision problem where decision-makers have to decide whether to revise a previous decision when presented with additional information. It demonstrates that people have difficulties understanding probabilities.

mood-as-information heuristic The mood-as-information heuristic is a **heuristic** where judgments are based on the current mood.

motivating potential score Within the **job characteristics model**, the motivating potential score describes the degree to which a task can be intrinsically motivating.

motivational postures In tax research, motivational postures are different standpoints that taxpayers take in their interaction with the tax authorities.

muddling through Muddling through assumes that decisions are taken in a step-by-step, incremental process. It is a **descriptive decision model**.

neutrality hypothesis The neutrality hypothesis assumes that experiences and behaviour at work and during leisure time have no connection to one another. (Compare **generalisation hypothesis**, **compensation hypothesis**, **interaction hypothesis**, **congruence hypothesis**.)

noise traders Noise traders are participants in financial markets who do not behave rationally, but instead do not take some information into account, place too much value on rumours, and make many more trades than would be the case among rational traders. (Compare **passive investors**.)

non-satiation Non-satiation is an **axiom** in decision theory stating that actors prefer to possess more of a good and not less.

norm of reciprocity The norm of reciprocity states that behaviours of others should be returned in kind (e.g., putting in more effort for higher wages).

normative decision models Normative decision models specify how an (idealised) individual should make optimal decisions. (Compare **descriptive decision models**, **prescriptive decision models**.)

nudges Nudges are attempts to structure decisions in a way that induces rational behaviour without curtailing individual freedom. A nudge is a means to encourage or steer behaviour, but without mandating or instructing, and ideally without the need for financial incentives or sanctions. Two frameworks are **MINDSPACE** and **EAST**.

objectification In the **theory of social representations**, objectification is a process where the social representation is made vivid through quasi-physical objects.

operant conditioning theory Operant conditioning theory assumes that the probability of a behaviour is increased by rewarding stimuli (reinforcers) following that behaviour. Primary reinforcers are rewarding in themselves; secondary reinforcers have acquired a reward quality through learning processes.

opportunity costs In decisions, opportunity costs are the costs that arise from selecting one alternative and therefore renouncing all other alternatives and their corresponding benefits.

passive investors Passive investors are participants in financial markets who do not behave rationally, but instead make purchases and then do not trade again for a long time, and make much fewer trades than would be the case among rational traders. (Compare **noise traders**.)

pathological buying Pathological buying is a more general term than **compulsive buying** or **shopping addiction**. It describes a preoccupation with shopping, strong urges to shop, and guilt after the frequent shopping episodes. Pathological buying is often accompanied by distress, marital conflicts and financial problems.

peak and end rule The peak and end rule states that, in retrospect, an experience is often not judged by its duration and the sum of all its elements, but is strongly influenced by outstanding elements and by the elements at the end.

peripheral elements In the **theory of social representations**, peripheral elements are those parts of a social representation that protect the stable core.

PERMA model The PERMA model assumes that five factors are essential for well-being: positive emotions (P), engagement (E), close relations (R), meaning (M) and accomplishment (A).

positive psychology Positive psychology is a branch in psychology that studies positive experiences such as happiness and satisfaction.

postmaterialist values Postmaterialist values are values emphasising autonomy and self-expression.

preoperational thought Preoperational thought is the second stage in the **cognitive-developmental theory**, ranging from 2 to 7 years of age. It is characterised by the development of internalisation. Thinking is limited by egocentrism, focusing, rigidity, realism and irreversibility.

prescriptive decision models Prescriptive decision models use decision theory to offer step-by-step suggestions on how to proceed in a decision situation in order to make an optimal decision. (Compare **normative decision models**, **descriptive decision models**.)

prevention focus Prevention focus is a motivational state in which people concentrate on protection and security, as well as on avoiding losses. (Compare **promotion focus**.)

price–quality heuristic The price–quality heuristic (or expensive = good heuristic) is a **heuristic** based on the belief that there is a positive correlation between price and quality.

prisoner's dilemma The prisoner's dilemma is a decision problem where two decision-makers independently have to decide between cooperation and defection. While from an individual perspective defection is the rational solution, the overall outcome is better if both cooperate.

probability conflicts Probability conflicts are a form of **conflict** where people agree about the goal, but disagree about the best way to reach the goal.

production possibilities curve The production possibilities curve (or production transformation curve) describes the maximum producible combinations of goods, given a specific level of resources that are used at full capacity.

production transformation curve See **production possibilities curve**.

profit maximisation principle The profit maximisation principle states that the maximum result possible should be achieved with a given quantity of resources.

projection bias The projection bias describes the tendency to assume that one's future feelings and preferences will be similar to the current feelings and preferences.

promotion focus Promotion focus is a motivational state in which people concentrate on growth and accomplishment, as well as on potential gains. (Compare **prevention focus**.)

prospect theory Prospect theory assumes that decision-making processes consist of an **editing phase** and an **evaluation phase**. The major elements in the evaluation phase are the **value function** and the **weighting function**.

psychological contract The psychological contract refers to implicit assumptions of rights and duties of management and employees. In tax research, it means the expectations and commitments between tax authorities and taxpayers that go beyond legal regulations.

psychological prices Psychological prices are prices that try to evoke the impression that they are considerably below a round number. One form is **9-ending prices**.

public goods game The public goods game is a decision problem where decision-makers can either keep a money amount or give part of it into a common pool. The sum of contributions in the common pool is usually multiplied by some factor and distributed equally to all decision-makers.

qualities of life Qualities of life are different aspects of life satisfaction that arise from a combination of life chances versus life outcomes and outer qualities versus inner qualities.

random walk hypothesis The random walk hypothesis assumes that, at the aggregate level, the prices of securities represent their fundamental values and vary only unsystematically.

RAWFS model The RAWFS model describes decision-making processes in uncertain decision situations as application of the tactics Reduction, Assumption-based reasoning, Weighing pros and cons, Forestalling and Suppression. It is a **descriptive decision model**.

recognition heuristic The recognition heuristic is a **heuristic** where decisions are based on familiarity with objects. When only one of two objects is recognised, that object is seen as more important.

reflective-impulsive model The reflective-impulsive model (RIM) assumes that a specific behaviour is not either impulsive or reflective, but often comprises components of both processes in different strength.

reflexivity Reflexivity is an **axiom** in decision theory stating that every bundle of alternatives is just as good as itself.

regret Regret is a negative emotion based on comparing alternatives and the consequences of alternatives. It can refer to decisions in the past or the future.

relative resources theory Relative resources theory assumes that influence in decisions in close relationships is determined by prevailing social norms and the partners' relative contributions of material and immaterial resources.

representativeness heuristic The representativeness heuristic is a **heuristic** where judgments are based on the similarity between an outcome and a model (e.g., a sample and a population).

resigned satisfaction Resigned satisfaction is satisfaction that results from lowering one's aspirations after initial dissatisfaction.

resource theory Resource theory assumes that social interactions are based on the exchange of different resources, including money, information, goods, services, status and love.

risk defusing operators Risk defusing operators are actions aimed at reducing the risk that negative consequences of a decision will occur.

risky decisions Risky decisions are a subset of **decisions under uncertainty** where the probabilities of consequences of alternatives are known.

role triangle The role triangle is a method to illustrate product-specific influence in purchase decisions and how influence is distributed between men and women in close relationships.

satisficing principle The satisficing principle states that in complex decision situations, decision-makers act within the limits of **bounded rationality** and are content with a satisfactory alternative instead of the optimal alternative. It is a **descriptive decision model**.

selective outcome correction process In the context of the euro introduction, a selective outcome correction process shows that errors that occur in price comparison are more likely to be detected and corrected when they are inconsistent with expectations.

self-determination theory Self-determination theory assumes that autonomy, competence and relatedness (i.e., social relationships) are fundamental psychological needs, and that their fulfilment leads to greater well-being.

sensorimotor intelligence Sensorimotor intelligence is the first stage in the **cognitive-developmental theory**, ranging from birth to approximately 2 years of age. It is characterised by first reflexive reactions, first motoric habits, the linking of means and ends, and active experimenting.

service paradigm In tax research, the service paradigm refers to a view that tax honesty can be achieved by easing the way through service offerings. (Compare **enforcement paradigm**, **trust paradigm**.)

set-point models Set-point models assume that drops in life satisfaction triggered by life-altering events balance out over time due to adaptation processes.

shadow economy In a broad sense, the shadow economy comprises those economic activities and the income derived from them that circumvent or avoid government regulation, taxation or observation. In a narrow sense, the shadow economy is the market-based legal production of goods and services that is deliberately concealed from public authorities.

shopping addiction Shopping addiction describes **pathological buying behaviour** as driven by intense positive feelings experienced during shopping.

slippery slope framework The slippery slope framework assumes that tax behaviour is a function of trust in tax authorities and power of tax authorities.

social categorisation theory Social categorisation theory assumes that information about persons and objects is cognitively represented in schemata that are formed through categorisation. Processes of social categorisation help to structure social events and therefore offer a basis for actions.

social dilemma A social dilemma is a decision problem where individual interests are opposed to the goals of the community. Individuals can gain by acting selfishly, but the community (and ultimately the individual) are harmed if too many individuals act selfishly.

social identity theory Social identity theory assumes that people strive for a satisfactory self-concept. Part of the self-concept is determined by membership in groups. Social identity arises from categorisation processes in which the social environment is divided into 'own' and 'other' environment.

speculative bubble A speculative bubble is a situation where a large difference between the market price of an investment and its fundamental value occurs.

St Petersburg paradox The St Petersburg paradox is an illustration that decision-makers do not base decisions on expected value.

starting low but ending high effect The starting low but ending high effect describes that, in auctions, low starting prices can lead to high final prices.

state orientation State orientation refers to a person's tendency to be bound up in thoughts that relate to current, past or future states and that impede the systematic implementation of an action. (Compare **action orientation**.)

subjective control Subjective control is defined as the number of behavioural options that allow a person to deal with situational conditions in ways that serve his or her individual goals, needs, interests and desires.

subjective expected utility theory (SEU) Subjective expected utility theory assumes that decision-makers choose the option with the highest subjective expected utility. Subjective expected utility is the sum of the products of the subjective probabilities and the subjective utility of the consequences.

sunk cost effect The sunk cost effect states that it is more likely that an endeavour is continued when resources have already been invested, even when these resources are irretrievable.

syncratic decisions Syncratic decisions are decisions made jointly by two or more persons in a household.

synthetic families Synthetic families are groups of strangers that mimic a traditional family structure by consisting of a male and a female participant of about equal age plus another younger person.

take-the-best heuristic The take-the-best heuristic is a **heuristic** where decisions are based on the one characteristic of options that seems especially relevant.

tax avoidance Tax avoidance refers to legal attempts to reduce tax liability by taking advantage of loopholes in the law. (Compare **tax evasion**, **tax circumvention**.)

tax circumvention Tax circumvention refers to attempts to reduce tax liability that are against the spirit and purpose of the law. (Compare **tax evasion**, **tax avoidance**.)

tax compliance Tax compliance describes taxpayers' willingness to pay their taxes.

tax cooperation Tax cooperation refers to correct taxpaying out of a perspective of equality.

tax evasion Tax evasion refers to illegal attempts to reduce tax liability by breaking the law. (Compare **tax avoidance**, **tax circumvention**.)

tax morale Tax morale is an intrinsic motivation arising from the moral obligation to pay taxes correctly.

tax swap A tax swap means selling losing stocks, using the money to buy stocks with similar risk and return prospects, and deducting the realised losses from the investor's taxes.

theory of learned helplessness The theory of learned helplessness assumes that people learn to become helpless when they have no influence or control over adverse conditions.

theory of social representations The theory of social representations assumes that people's opinions are a complex result of experiences, emotionally loaded judgments, and information that is subjectively experienced, transformed and cognitively available. Social representations consist of **core elements** and **peripheral elements**, and are formed through processes of **anchoring** and **objectification**.

time and outcome valuation model The time and outcome valuation model assumes that the value function in prospect theory becomes more flat for outcomes occurring in the future as compared to outcomes in the present.

time discounting Time discounting describes the preference for immediate utility vis-à-vis delayed utility in decisions where consequences occur at different points in time.

time-sample diary A time-sample diary is a **diary method** where respondents report at specific times on their current experience (e.g., well-being).

total models In consumer behaviour, total models are models that attempt to depict all purchasing and decision-making behaviour.

transitivity Transitivity is an **axiom** in decision theory stating that actors have a consistent preference order over alternatives.

trust Trust is the acceptance of vulnerability to the actions of another party. It is either reason-based, originating from experience of benevolence of the other party in the past, or implicit.

trust game The trust game is a decision problem where decision-makers can either keep a money amount or hand part of it to another person. That part is then usually multiplied by some factor. The other person can then decide whether to keep the resulting money amount or return part of it.

trust paradigm In tax research, the trust paradigm refers to a view that tax honesty can be achieved by building trust between tax authorities and taxpayers. (Compare **enforcement paradigm**, **service paradigm**.)

ultimatum game The ultimatum game is a decision problem where decision-makers have to divide a good (e.g., a sum of money) between themselves and another person. If the other person rejects the proposed division, both leave empty-handed. (Compare **dictator game**.)

utility debts In the **model of purchase decisions in private households**, it is assumed that one partner may have more utility from a specific purchase decision and therefore incurs utility debts that need to be balanced out in future decisions.

valence-instrumentality-expectancy theory The valence-instrumentality-expectancy theory (V-I-E theory) assumes that motivation is a function of the valuation of outcomes, the subjective connection between an action and outcomes, and the subjective belief about the feasibility of an action.

value conflicts Value conflicts are one form of **conflict** where people disagree about the goal to be pursued.

value congruence Value congruence refers to a fit between the values held by financial institutions and their clients. It is considered a basis of trust in institutions.

value function In **prospect theory**, the value function describes the relationship between objective outcomes (gain or loss relative to a reference point) and their subjective values. It is concave in the gains region and convex in the loss region ('S-shaped'). It is also steeper in the loss region.

Vienna Diary Study The Vienna Diary Study was an extensive study on household decision-making using the **decision diary**, conducted at the University of Vienna.

voluntary unemployment In economic analyses of labour markets, voluntary unemployment refers to the unemployment situation at the **equilibrium wage**. (Compare **full employment**.)

weighting function In **prospect theory**, the weighting function describes the relationship between objective probabilities and subjective decision weights.

windfall gains Windfall gains are unexpected gains. They are often treated differently than expected gains.

wisdom of the crowd Wisdom of the crowd refers to a statistical effect where an aggregate collective judgment is more accurate than individual judgments.

work–life balance Work–life balance refers to the distribution of working and non-working time as well as to subjective feelings of balance and satisfaction with regard to this distribution.

REFERENCES

Abouchedid, K., & Nasser, R. (2001). Poverty attitudes and their determinants in Lebanon's plural society. *Journal of Economic Psychology*, *22*, 271–82.

Abric, J. C. (1994). Méthodologie de recueil des représentations sociales [Methods for the collection of social representations]. In J. C. Abric (ed.), *Pratiques sociales et représentations* (pp. 59–82). Paris: Presses Universitaires de France.

Adams, J. S. (1963). Toward an understanding of inequity. *Journal of Abnormal and Social Psychology*, *67*, 422–36.

(1965). Inequity in social exchange. In L. Berkowitz (ed.), *Advances in experimental social psychology* (vol. 2, pp. 267–99). New York: Academic Press.

Addabbo, T., Emilia, R., Arrizabalaga, M.-P., Borderias, C., & Owens, A. (eds.). (2010). *Gender inequalities, households and the production of well-being in modern Europe*. Farnham: Ashgate.

Adler, A., Kern, M., Waters, L., & White, M. (2015). A multi-dimensional approach to measuring well-being in students: Application of the PERMA framework. *Journal of Positive Psychology*, *10*, 262–71.

Adorno, T. W. (1972). *Zum Verhältnis von Soziologie und Psychologie* [On the relationship between sociology and psychology]. Gesammelte Schriften 8. Frankfurt am Main: Suhrkamp.

Agnell, J., & Persson, M. (2000). Tax arbitrage and labor supply. *Journal of Public Economics*, *78*, 3–24.

Ahuja, R. D., & Stinson, K. M. (1993). Female-headed single parent families: An explanatory study of children's influence in family decision making. *Advances in Consumer Research*, *20*, 469–74.

Ahuvia, A. (2008). If money doesn't make us happy, why do we act as if it does? *Journal of Economic Psychology*, *29*, 491–507.

Ainslie, G., & Haslam, N. (1992). Hyperbolic discounting. In G. Loewenstein & J. Elster (eds.), *Choice over time* (pp. 57–92). New York: Sage.

Ajzen, I. (1985). From intentions to actions: A theory of planned behavior. In J. Kuhl & J. Beckman (eds.), *Action-control: From cognition to behavior* (pp. 11–39). Heidelberg: Springer.

(1987). Attitudes, traits and actions: Dispositional predictions of behavior in personality and social psychology. In L. Berkowitz (ed.), *Advances in experimental social psychology* (vol. 20, pp. 1–64). San Diego, CA: Academic Press.

Akerlof, G. A., & Shiller, R. J. (2009). *Animal spirits: How human psychology drives the economy, and why it matters for global capitalism*. Princeton, NJ: Princeton University Press.

(2015). *Phishing for phools: The economics of manipulation & deception*. Princeton, NJ: Princeton University Press.

Akerlof, G. A., & Yellen, J. L. (1988). Fairness and unemployment. *American Economic Review*, *78*, 44–9.

Ali, M. M., Cecil, H. W., & Knoblett, J. A. (2001). The effects of tax rates and enforcement policies on taxpayer compliance: A study of self-employed taxpayers. *Atlantic Economic Journal*, *29*, 186–202.

Alicke, M. D., & Govorun, O. (2005). The better-than-average effect. In M. D. Alicke, D. A., Dunning & J. I. Krueger (eds.), *The self in social judgement* (pp. 85–106). New York: Psychology Press.

Allen, M. W., Ng, S. H., & Leiser, D. (2005). Adult economic model and values survey: Cross-national differences in economic beliefs. *Journal of Economic Psychology*, *26*, 159–85.

Allingham, M., & Sandmo, A. (1972). Income tax evasion: A theoretical analysis. *Journal of Public Economics*, *1*, 323–38.

Alm, J. (1991). A perspective on the experimental analysis of taxpayer reporting. *Accounting Review*, *55*, 577–93.

Alm, J., Bloomquist, K. M., & McKee, M. (2015). On the external validity of laboratory tax compliance experiments. *Economic Inquiry*, *53*, 1170–86.

Alm, J., Jackson, B., & McKee, M. (1992). Estimating the determinants of taxpayer compliance with experimental data. *National Tax Journal*, *45*, 107–14.

Alm, J., Kirchler, E., & Muehlbacher, S. (2012). Combining psychology and economics in the analysis of compliance: From enforcement to cooperation. *Economic Analysis and Policy*, *42*, 133–51.

Alm, J., McClelland, G. H., & Schulze, W. D. (1992). Why do people pay taxes? *Journal of Public Economics*, *48*, 21–38.

Alm, J., Sanchez, I., & de Juan, A. (1995). Economic and noneconomic factors in tax compliance. *Kyklos*, *48*, 3–18.

Alm, J., & Torgler, B. (2006). Culture differences and tax morale in the United States and in Europe. *Journal of Economic Psychology*, *27*, 224–46.

(2011). Do ethics matter? Tax compliance and morality. *Journal of Business Ethics*, *101*, 635–51.

Almeida, D., & Kessler, R. (1998). Everyday stressors and gender differences in daily distress. *Journal of Personality and Social Psychology*, *75*, 670–80.

Almeida, D., Wethington, E., & Chandler, A. (1999). Daily transmission of tensions between marital dyads and parent–child dyads. *Journal of Marriage and Family*, *61*, 49–61.

Amar, M., Ariely, D., Ayal, S., Cryder, C. E., & Rick, S. I. (2011). Winning the battle but losing the war: The psychology of debt management. *Journal of Marketing Research*, *48*, 38–50.

Anand, P. (2016). *Happiness explained: What human flourishing is and what we can do to promote it*. Oxford: Oxford University Press.

Anderhub, V., Giese, S., Güth, W., Hoffmann, A., & Otto, T. (2001). Tax evasion with earned income: An experimental study. *Finanz Archiv*, *58*, 188–206.

Anderson, E. T., & Simester, D. I. (2003). Effects of $9 price endings on retail sales: Evidence from field experiments. *Quantitative Marketing and Economics*, *1*, 93–110.

Anderson, L. R., & Holt, C. A. (1997). Information cascades in the laboratory. *American Economic Review*, *87*, 847–62.

Andersson, M., Hedesström, M., & Gärling, T. (2014). A social-psychological perspective on herding in stock markets. *Journal of Behavioral Finance*, *15*, 226–34.

Andreassen, P. A. (1990). Judgmental extrapolation and market overreaction: On the use and disuse of news. *Journal of Behavioral Decision Making*, *3*, 153–74.

Andreoni, J., Erard, B., & Feinstein, J. S. (1998). Tax compliance. *Journal of Economic Literature*, *36*, 818–60.

Andreoni, J., & Petrie, R. (2008). Beauty, gender and stereotypes: Evidence from laboratory experiments. *Journal of Economic Psychology*, *29*, 73–93.

Angner, E., & Loewenstein, G. (2012). Behavioral economics. In U. Mäki (ed.), *Handbook of the philosophy of science: Philosophy of economics* (vol. 13, pp. 641–90). Amsterdam: Elsevier.

Antonides, G. (1991). *Psychology in economics and business*. Dordrecht: Kluwer.

(2011). The division of household tasks and household financial management. *Journal of Psychology*, *219*, 198–208.

Antonides, G., de Groot, I. M., & van Raaij, W. F. (2011). Mental budgeting and the management of household finance. *Journal of Economic Psychology*, *32*, 546–55.

Antonides, G., Farago, K., Ranyard, R., & Tyszka, T. (1997). Perceptions of economic activities: A cross-country comparison. In G. Antonides, W. F. van Raaij, & S. Maital (eds.), *Advances in economic psychology* (pp. 39–60). Chichester: Wiley.

Antonides, G., & Robben, H. S. J. (1995). True positives and false alarms in the detection of tax evasion. *Journal of Economic Psychology*, *16*, 617–40.

Argyris, C. (1959). The individual and organization: An empirical test. *Administrative Science Quarterly*, *4*, 145–67.

Ariely, D. (2008). *Predictably irrational: The hidden forces that shape our decisions*. New York: HarperCollins.

Ariely, D., & Norton, M. I. (2007). Psychology and experimental economics. *Current Directions in Psychological Science*, *16*, 336–9.

Arkes, H. R., & Blumer, C. (1985). The psychology of sunk cost. *Organizational Behavior and Human Decision Processes*, *35*, 124–40.

Arkes, H. R., Joyner, C. A., Pezzo, M. V., Nash, J. G., Siegel-Jacobs, K., & Stone, E. (1994). The psychology of windfall gains. *Organizational Behavior and Human Decision Processes*, *59*, 331–47.

Asch, S. E. (1946). Forming impressions of personality. *Journal of Abnormal and Social Psychology*, *41*, 258–90.

Aschenfelter, P., & Heckman, J. (1974). The estimation of income and substitution effects in a model of family labour supply. *Econometrica*, *42*, 73–85.

Ashby, K. J., & Burgoyne, C. B. (2008). Separate financial entities? Beyond categories of money management. *Journal of Socio-Economics*, *37*, 458–80.

Athayde, R. (2009). Measuring enterprise potential in young people. *Entrepreneurship Theory and Practice*, *3*, 481–500.

Atkin, C. K. (1978). Observation of parent–child interaction in supermarket decisionmaking. *Journal of Marketing*, *42*, 41–5.

Atkinson, A., McKay, S., Kempson, E., & Collard, S. (2006). *Levels of financial capability in the UK: Results of a baseline survey (Consumer Research Report 47, March 2006)*. London: Financial Services Authority.

Attridge, M., & Berscheid, E. (1994). Entitlement in romantic relationships in the United States: A social-exchange perspective. In M. J. Lerner & G. Mikula (eds.), *Entitlement and the affectional bond* (pp. 117–48). New York: Plenum Press.

Au, K., Chan, F., Wang, D., & Vertinsky, I. (2003). Mood in foreign exchange trading: Cognitive processes and performance. *Organizational Behavior and Human Decision Processes*, *9*, 322–38.

Auhagen, A. E. (1987). A new approach for the study of personal relationships: The double diary approach. *German Journal of Psychology*, *11*, 3–7.

(1991). *Freundschaft im Alltag: Eine Studie mit dem Doppeltagebuch* [Friendship in everyday life: A double diary study]. Berne: Huber.

Auinger, F. (1987). *Subjektives Wohlbefinden als Klimabarometer in Organisationen. Eine Studie mit dem Zeitstichprobentagebuch* [Subjective well-being as a climate barometer in organisations. A time-sample diary study] (unpublished thesis). University of Linz, Austria.

Autio, M., Wilska, T.-A., Kaartinen, R., & Lähteenmaa, J. (2009). The use of small instant loans among young adults: A gateway to a consumer insolvency? *International Journal of Consumer Studies*, *33*, 407–15.

Averbeck, D. (2010). *Die Rolle der Behavioral Finance bei der Preisbildung an Aktienmärkten: Implikationen für die Entstehung von Spekulationsblasen* [The role of behavioural finance in price formation on stock markets: Implications for the formation of speculative bubbles]. Saarbrücken: VDM.

Axelrod, R. (1984). *The evolution of cooperation*. New York: Basic Books.

Ayres, I., Raseman, S., & Shih, A. (2013). Evidence from two large field experiments that peer comparison feedback can reduce residential energy usage. *Journal of Law Economics and Organization*, *29*, 992–1022.

Babin, B. J., Darden, W. R., & Griffin, M. (1994). Work and/or fun: Measuring hedonic and utilitarian shopping value. *Journal of Consumer Research*, *20*, 644–56.

Bachmann, R. (2001). Trust, power and control in trans-organizational relations. *Organization Studies*, *22*, 337–65.

Baker, H. K., & Nofsinger, J. R. (2002). Psychological biases of investors. *Financial Services Review*, *11*, 97–116.

Bakker, A. B., & Demerouti, E. (2007). The job demands–resources model: State of the art. *Journal of Managerial Psychology*, *22*, 309–28.

Baldry, J. C. (1987). Income tax evasion and the tax schedule: Some experimental results. *Public Finance*, *42*, 357–83.

Balliet, D., & Van Lange, P. A. (2013). Trust, punishment, and cooperation across 18 societies: A meta-analysis. *Perspectives on Psychological Science*, *8*, 363–79.

Banducci, S. A., Karp, J. A., & Loedel, P. H. (2003). The Euro, economic interests and multi-level governance. Examining support for the common currency. *European Journal of Political Research*, *42*, 685–703.

Banerjee, A. V. (1992). A simple model of herd behavior. *Quarterly Journal of Economics*, *107*, 797–817.

Barber, B. M., Odean, T., & Zheng, L. (2005). Out of sight, out of mind: The effects of expenses on mutual fund flows. *Journal of Business*, *78*, 2095–120.

Barlés-Arizón, M.-J., Fraj-Andrés, E., & Martínez-Salinas, E. (2008). What is the partner's role in the family decision-making? The use of different dissuasive tactics. Paper presented at the IAREP/SABE World Meeting, September, Rome.

Bastounis, M., Leiser, D., & Roland-Lévy, C. (2004). Psychosocial variables involved in the construction of lay thinking about the economy: Results of a cross-national survey. *Journal of Economic Psychology*, *25*, 263–78.

Bates, J. M., & Gabor, A. (1986). Price perception in creeping inflation: Report on an enquiry. *Journal of Economic Psychology*, *7*, 291–314.

Bay, A.-H., & Blekesaune, M. (2002). Youth, unemployment and political marginalization. *International Journal of Social Welfare*, *11*, 132–9.

Bazerman, M. H. (1990). *Managerial decision making*. New York: Wiley.

(1994). *Judgment in managerial decision making*. New York: Wiley.

Beales, A. L., & Lambert, R. S. (1934). *Memoires of the unemployed*. London: Gollancz.

Beatty, S. E., & Talpade, S. (1994). Adolescent influence in family decision making: A replication with extension. *Journal of Consumer Research*, *21*, 332–41.

Becker, G. S. (1968). Crime and punishment: An economic approach. *Journal of Political Economy*, *76*, 169–217.

(1976). *The economic approach to human behavior*. Chicago, IL: University of Chicago Press.

Becker, P. (1994). Theoretische Grundlagen [Theoretical foundations]. In A. Abele & P. Becker (eds.), *Wohlbefinden: Theorie – Empirie – Diagnostik* (pp. 13–49). Weinheim: Juventa.

Belch, M. A., & Willis, L. A. (2002). Family decision at the turn of the century: Has the changing structure of households impacted the family decision-making process? *Journal of Consumer Behaviour*, *2*, 111–24.

Belk, R. W. (1988). Possessions and the extended self. *Journal of Consumer Research*, *15*, 139–62.

Belk, R. W., & Wallendorf, M. (1990). The sacred meanings of money. *Journal of Economic Psychology*, *11*, 35–67.

Bell, D. (1976). *The cultural contradictions of capitalism*. London: Heineman.

Bell, D. E. (1982). Regret in decision making under uncertainty. *Operations Research*, *30*, 961–81.

Bénabou, R., & Tirole, J. (2006). Belief in a just world and redistributive politics. *Quarterly Journal of Economics*, *121*, 699–746.

Benartzi, S., & Thaler, R. (1995). Myopic loss aversion and the equity premium puzzle. *Quarterly Journal of Economics*, *110*, 73–92.

(2001). Naive diversification strategies in defined contribution saving plans. *American Economic Review*, *91*, 79–98.

Bennett, F. (2013). Researching within-household distribution: Overview, developments, debates, and methodological challenges. *Journal of Marriage and Family*, *75*, 582–97.

Ben-Yoav, O., & Pruitt, D. G. (1984). Accountability to constituents: A two-edged sword. *Organizational Behavior and Human Performance*, *34*, 283–94.

Beretta, C. (1993). Gli atteggiamenti verso il lavoro [Attitudes toward work]. *Social Trends: Informazioni sul Cambiamento Socioculturale*, *59*, 1–15.

Berggren, N., Jordahl, H., & Poutvaara, P. (2013). The looks of a winner: Beauty and electoral success. *Journal of Public Economics*, *94*, 8–15.

Bernthal, M. J., Crockett, D., & Rose, R. L. (2005). Credit cards as lifestyle facilitators. *Journal of Consumer Research*, *32*, 130–45.

Bertaut, C. C., Haliassos, M., & Reiter, M. (2009). Credit card debt puzzles and debt revolvers for self control. *Review of Finance*, *13*, 657–92.

Berthoud, R., & Kempson, E. (1992). *Credit and debt: The PSI report*. London: Policy Studies Institute.

Berti, A. E., & Bombi, A. S. (1981). *Il mondo economico nel bambino* [The economic world of the child]. Florence: La Nuova Italia.

Berti, A. E., Bombi, A. S., & De Beni, R. (1986). Acquiring economic notions: Profit. *International Journal of Behavioral Development*, *9*, 15–29.

Besharat, A., Carrillat, F. A., & Ladik, D. M. (2014). When motivation is against debtors' best interest: The illusion of goal progress in credit card debt repayment. *Journal of Public Policy & Marketing*, *33*, 143–58.

Betti, G., Dourmashkin, N., Rossi, M., & Yin, Y. P. (2007). Consumer over-indebtedness in the EU: Measurement and characteristics. *Journal of Economic Studies*, *34*, 136–56.

Biais, B., & Weber, M. (2009). Hindsight bias and investment performance. *Management Science*, *55*, 1018–29.

Bisdee, D., Daly, T., & Price, D. (2013). Behind closed doors: Older couples and the gendered management of household money. *Social Policy and Society*, *12*, 163–74.

Blackwell, C. (2007). *A meta-analysis of tax compliance experiments* (International Studies Program Working Paper 07–24). Atlanta, GA: Andrew Young School of Policy Studies, Georgia State University.

Blanchflower, D. G., & Oswald, A. J. (2004). Money, sex and happiness: An empirical study. *Scandinavian Journal of Economics*, *106*, 393–415.

Blank, H., & Fischer, V. (2000). 'Es musste eigentlich so kommen': Rückschaufehler bei der Bundestagswahl 1998 ['It had to turn out that way': Hindsight bias in the German parliamentary elections in 1998]. *Zeitschrift für Sozialpsychologie*, *31*, 128–42.

Blau, P. M. (1964). *Exchange and power in social life*. New York: Wiley.

Bless, H. (1997). *Stimmung and Denken: Ein Modell zum Einfluß von Stimmungen auf Denkprozesse* [Mood and thought: A model of the influence of moods on thought processes]. Berne: Huber.

Bloch, P. H., Sherrell, D. L., & Ridgway, N. M. (1986). Consumer search: An extended framework. *Journal of Consumer Research*, *13*, 119–26.

Blood, R. O., & Wolfe, D. W. (1960). *Husbands and wives: The dynamics of married living*. Glencoe, IL: Free Press.

Bodell, R. W., Kerton, R. R., & Schuster, R. W. (1986). Price as a signal of quality – Canada in the international context. *Journal of Consumer Policy*, *9*, 431–44.

Bodi, O., Mikula, G., & Riederer, B. (2010). Long-term effects between perceived justice in the division of domestic work and women's relationship satisfaction. Testing for moderation effects. *Social Psychology*, *41*, 57–65.

Bohner, G., Bless, H., Schwarz, N., & Strack, F. (1988). What triggers causal attributions? The impact of valence and subjective probability. *European Journal of Social Psychology*, *18*, 335–45.

Böhrs, H. (1969). Arbeit [Work]. In E. Grochla (ed.), *Handwörterbuch der Organisation* (pp. 85–8). Stuttgart: Poeschel.

Boissevain, J. (1974). *Friends of friends: Networks, manipulators and coalitions*. Oxford: Blackwell.

Bolger, N., DeLongis, A., Kessler, R. C., & Schilling, E. A. (1989). Effects of daily stress on negative mood. *Journal of Personality and Social Psychology*, *57*, 808–18.

Bolger, N., DeLongis, A., Kessler, R. C., & Wethington, E. (1989). The contagion of stress across multiple roles. *Journal of Marriage and Family*, *51*, 175–83.

Boor, M. (1980). Relationships between unemployment rates and suicide rates in eight countries, 1962–1976. *Psychological Reports*, *47*, 1095–1101.

Borges, B., Goldstein, D. G., Ortmann, A., & Gigerenzer, G. (1999). Can ignorance beat the stock market? In G. Gigerenzer, P. M. Todd, & ABC Research Group (eds.), *Simple heuristics that make us smart* (pp. 59–72). Oxford: Oxford University Press.

Bornstein, G., Kugler, T., & Ziegelmeyer, A. (2004). Individual and group decisions in the centipede game: Are groups more 'rational' players? *Journal of Experimental Social Psychology*, *40*, 599–605.

Bourdieu, P. (1983). Ökonomisches Kapital – kulturelles Kapital – soziales Kapital [Economic capital – cultural capital – social capital]. In R. Kreckel (ed.), *Soziale Ungleichheiten* (pp. 183–98). Göttingen: Otto Schwartz.

(1984). *Distinction: A social critique of the judgment of taste*. London: Routledge.

Bower, G. H. (1981). Mood and memory. *American Psychologist*, *36*, 129–48.

Bowling, N. A., Eschleman, K. J., & Wang, Q. (2010). A meta-analytic examination of the relationship between job satisfaction and subjective well-being. *Journal of Occupational and Organizational Psychology*, *83*, 915–34.

Boyle, P.-J., & Lathrop, E.-S. (2009). Are consumers' perceptions of price–quality relationships well calibrated? *International Journal of Consumer Studies*, *33*, 58–63.

Brachinger, H. W. (2005). Der Euro als Teuro? Die wahrgenommene Inflation in Deutschland [Euro as Teuro? Perceived inflation in Germany]. *Wirtschaft und Statistik*, *9*, 999–1013.

Braithwaite, J. (2005). *Markets in vice, markets in virtue*. Leichhardt: The Federation Press.

(2008). *Regulatory capitalism: How it works, ideas for making it work better*. Cheltenham: Elsevier.

Braithwaite, V. (ed.) (2001). *Taxing democracy: Understanding tax avoidance and evasion*. Aldershot: Ashgate.

(2003). Dancing with tax authorities: Motivational postures and non-compliant actions. In V. Braithwaite (ed.), *Taxing democracy* (pp. 1–11). Aldershot: Ashgate.

(2009). *Defiance in taxation and governance: Resisting and dismissing authority in a democracy*. Cheltenham: Edward Elgar.

Braithwaite, V., & Ahmed, E. (2005). A threat to tax morale: The case of Australian higher eduction policy. *Journal of Economic Psychology*, *26*, 523–40.

Braithwaite, V., & Wenzel, M. (2008). Integrating explanations of tax evasion and avoidance. In A. Lewis (ed.), *The Cambridge handbook of psychology and economic behaviour* (pp. 304–31). Cambridge: Cambridge University Press.

Brandes, V. (1977). Arbeitslosigkeit in der Bundesrepublik: Erscheinungsformen, Auswirkungen, Verarbeitungsformen und Abwehrperspektiven [Unemployment in the Federal Republic of Germany]. In H.-G. Backhaus et al. (eds.), *Gesellschaft: Beiträge zur Marxschen Theorie 10* (pp. 187–245). Frankfurt am Main: Suhrkamp.

Brandstätter, H. (1977). Wohlbefinden and Unbehagen [Well-being and discontent]. In W. H. Tack (ed.), *Bericht über den 30. Kongreß der Deutschen Gesellschaft für Psychologie in Regensburg* (vol. 2, pp. 60–2). Göttingen: Hogrefe.

(1981). Time sampling of subjective well-being. In H. Hartmann, W. Molt & P. Stringer (eds.), *Advances in economic psychology* (pp. 63–76). Heidelberg: Meyn.

(1983). Emotional responses to other persons in everyday life situations. *Journal of Personality and Social Psychology*, *45*, 871–83.

(1987). Gruppenleistung und Gruppenentscheidung [Group performance and group decision-making]. In D. Frey & S. Greif (eds.), *Sozialpsychologie: Ein Handbuch in Schlüsselbegriffen* (pp. 182–6). Munich: Urban & Schwarzenberg.

(1988a). Becoming an entrepreneur – a question of personality structure? Paper presented at the 13th Annual Colloquium of IAREP, Leuven, Belgium.

(1988b). Sechzehn Persönlichkeits-Adjektivskalen (16 PA) als Forschungsinstrument anstelle des 16 PF [16 personality adjectives (16 PA) scales as a research instrument instead of the 16 PF]. *Zeitschrift für Experimentelle und Angewandte Psychologie*, *35*, 370–91.

(1997). Becoming an entrepreneur – a question of personality structure? *Journal of Economic Psychology*, *18*, 157–77.

(2011). Personality aspects of entrepreneurship: A look at five meta-analyses. *Personality and Individual Differences*, *51*, 222–30.

Brandstätter, H., Güth, W., & Kliemt, H. (2009). *Psychology and economics rather than psychology versus economics: Cultural differences but no barriers! (Jena Economic Research Papers 17)*. Jena: Max Planck Institute of Economics.

Brandstätter, H., & Wagner, W. (1994). Erwerbsarbeit der Frau and Alltagsbefinden von Ehepartnern im Zeitverlauf [Women's paid work and married couples' everyday well-being over the course of time]. *Zeitschrift für Sozialpsychologie*, *25*, 126–46.

Braunstein, S., & Welch, C. (2002). Financial literacy: An overview of practice, research, and policy. *Federal Reserve Bulletin*, *88*, 445–57.

Braybrooke, D., & Lindblom, C. E. (1963). *A strategy of decisions*. Glencoe, IL: Free Press.

Breakwell, G. M. (2007). *The psychology of risk*. Cambridge: Cambridge University Press.

Brenner, H. H. (1979). *Wirtschaftskrisen, Arbeitslosigkeit und psychische Erkrankung* [Economic crises, unemployment and mental illness]. Munich: Urban & Schwarzenberg.

Breuer, W., Hens, T., Salzmann, A. J., & Wang, M. (2015). On the determinants of household debt maturity choice. *Applied Economics*, *47*, 449–65.

Briar, R. (1977). The effect of long-term unemployment on workers and their families. *Dissertation Abstracts International*, *37*, 6062.

Brickman, P., & Campbell, D. T. (1971). Hedonic relativism and planning the good society. In M. H. Appley (ed.), *Adaptation level theory: A symposium* (pp. 287–302). New York: Academic Press.

Bridges, S., & Disney, R. (2010). Debt and depression. *Journal of Health Economics*, *29*, 388–403.

Brief, A. P., Butcher, A. H., & Roberson, L. (1995). Cookies, disposition, and job attitudes: The effects of positive mood-inducing events and negative affectivity on job satisfaction in a field experiment. *Organizational Behavior and Human Decision Processes*, *62*, 55–62.

Briesch, R. A., Krishnamurthi, L., Mazumdar, T., & Raj, S. P. (1997). A comparative analysis of reference price models. *Journal of Consumer Research*, *24*, 202–14.

Brockhaus, R. H. (1982). The psychology of the entrepreneur. In C. A. Kent, D. Sexton, & K. Vesper (eds.), *Encyclopedia of entrepreneurship* (pp. 39–57). Englewood Cliffs, NJ: Prentice Hall.

Brooks, P., & Zank, H. (2005). Loss averse behaviour. *Journal of Risk and Uncertainty*, *31*, 301–25.

Brown, R. (1988). *Group processes: Dynamics within and between groups*. Worcester, MA: Billing and Sons.

Brown, S., Garino, G., & Taylor, K. (2012). Household debt and attitudes toward risk. *Review of Income and Wealth*, *59*, 283–304.

Brown, S., Taylor, K., & Wheatley Price, S. (2005). Debt and distress: Evaluating the psychological cost of credit. *Journal of Economic Psychology*, *26*, 642–63.

Brown, Z., Johnstone, N., Hascic, I., Vong, L., & Barascud, F. (2013). Testing the effects of defaults on the thermostat settings of OECD employees. *Energy Economics*, *39*, 128–34.

Bruggemann, A., Groskurth, P., & Ulich, E. (1975). *Arbeitszufriedenheit* [Job satisfaction]. Berne: Huber.

Bruner, G. C., & Pomazal, R. J. (1988). Problem recognition: The crucial first stage of the consumer decision process. *Journal of Services Marketing*, *2*, 43–53.

Bruner, J., & Goodman, C. (1947). Value and need as organising factors in perception. *Journal of Abnormal and Social Psychology*, *42*, 33–44.

Brunswick, E. (1949). *Systematic and representative design of psychological experiments*. Berkeley: University of California Press.

Bucher, A. A. (2009). *Psychologie des Glücks: Ein Handbuch* [Psychology of happiness: A handbook]. Weinheim: Beltz.

Buijzen, M., & Valkenburg, P. M. (2008). Observing purchase-related parent–child communication in retail environments: A developmental and socialization perspective. *Human Communication Research*, *34*, 50–69.

Burgoyne, C. B. (1995). Financial organisation and decision-making within western 'households'. *Journal of Economic Psychology*, *16*, 421–30.

(2008). Introduction: Special issue on the household economy. *Journal of Socio-Economics*, *37*, 455–7.

Burgoyne, C. B., Clarke, V., & Burns, M. (2011). Money management and views of civil partnership in same-sex couples: Results from a UK survey of non-heterosexuals. *Sociological Review*, *59*, 685–706.

Burgoyne, C. B., & Kirchler, E. (2008). Financial decisions in the household. In A. Lewis (ed.), *The Cambridge handbook of psychology and economic behaviour* (pp. 132–54). Cambridge: Cambridge University Press.

Burgoyne, C. B., Routh, D., & Ellis, A. (1999). The transition to the Euro: Some perspectives from economic psychology. *Journal of Consumer Policy*, *22*, 91–116.

Burns, A. C., & Gentry, J. W. (1990). Toward improving household consumption behavior research: Avoidance of pitfalls in using alternative household data collection procedures. *Advances in Consumer Research*, *17*, 518–20.

Burns, M. L., Burgoyne, C. B., & Clarke, V. (2008). Financial affairs? Money management in same-sex relationships. *Journal of Socio-Economics*, *37*, 481–501.

Burns, T. (1976). Spousal involvement and empathy in jointly-resolved and authoritatively-resolved purchase sub-decisions. *Advances in Consumer Research*, *3*, 199–207.

Burns, T., & Granbois, D. H. (1977). Factors moderating the resolution of preference conflict in family automobile purchasing. *Journal of Marketing Research*, *14*, 77–86.

Burris, V. (1983). Stages in the development of economic concepts. *Human Relations*, 9, 791–812.

Büssing, A. (1992). Subjektive Vorstellungen und Vorstellungsmuster zum Verhältnis von Arbeit und Freizeit: Konzept und Methode [Subjective notions and perception patterns on the relationship between work and leisure time: Concept and method]. *Zeitschrift für Arbeits- und Organisationspsychologie*, *36*, 63–76.

Büssing, A., Bissels, T., Fuchs, V., & Perrar, K.-M. (1999). A dynamic model of work satisfaction: Qualitative approaches. *Human Relations*, *52*, 999–1028.

Buunk, B. P. (2001). Perceived superiority of one's own relationship and perceived prevalence of happy and unhappy relationships. *British Journal of Social Psychology*, *40*, 565–74.

Buunk, B. P., & Van der Eijnden, R. J. J. M. (1997). Perceived prevalence, perceived superiority, and relationship satisfaction: Most relationships are good, but ours is the best. *Personality and Social Psychology Bulletin*, *23*, 219–28.

Caginalp, G., Porter, D., & Smith, V. (2000). Overreactions, momentum, liquidity, and price bubbles in laboratory and field asset markets. *Journal of Psychology and Financial Markets*, *11*, 24–48.

Calderwood, G., & Webley, P. (1992). Who responds to changes in taxation? The relationship between taxation and incentive to work. *Journal of Economic Psychology*, *13*, 735–48.

Camerer, C. (1995). Individual decision making. In J. H. Kagel & A. E. Roth (eds.), *The handbook of experimental economics* (pp. 587–703). Princeton, NJ: Princeton University Press.

Camerer, C., Babcock, L., Loewenstein, G., & Thaler, R. (1997). Labor supply of New York City cabdrivers: One day at a time. *Quarterly Journal of Economics*, *112*, 407–41.

Camerer, C. F., Cohen, J. D., Fehr, E., Glimcher, P. W., & Laibson, D. (2015). Neuroeconomics. In J. H. Kagel & A. Roth (eds.), *The handbook of experimental economics* (pp. 153–216). Princeton, NJ: Princeton University Press.

Camerer, C., Loewenstein, G., & Prelec, D. (2005). Neuroeconomics: How neuroscience can inform economics. *Journal of Economic Literature*, *43*, 9–64.

Campbell, C. (1987). *The romantic ethic and the spirit of modern consumerism*. Oxford: Blackwell.

Canner, G. B., & Luckett, C. A. (1991). Payment of household debts. *Federal Reserve Bulletin*, *77*, 218–29.

Cantillon, S. (2013). Measuring differences in living standards within households. *Journal of Marriage and Family*, *75*, 598–610.

Cantor, D., & Land, K. C. (1985). Unemployment and crime rates in the post-world war II United States: A theoretical and empirical analysis. *American Sociological Review*, *50*, 317–32.

Cantril, H. (1965). *The pattern of human concerns*. New Brunswick, NJ: Rutgers University Press.

Caporale, G., Georgellis, Y., Tsitsianis, N., & Ping Yin, Y. (2009). Income and happiness across Europe. Do reference values matter? *Journal of Economic Psychology*, *30*, 42–51.

Cascio, W. F. (2013). *Managing human resources: Productivity, quality of work life, profits* (9th edn). New York: McGraw-Hill.

Castelfranchi, C., & Falcone, R. (2010). *Trust theory: A socio-cognitive and computional model*. Chichester: John Wiley & Sons.

Ceccherini-Nelli, A., & Priebe, S. (2011). Economic factors and suicide rates: Associations over time in four countries. *Social Psychiatry and Psychiatric Epidemiology*, *46*, 975–82.

Chaiken, S. (1980). Heuristic versus systematic information processing and the use of source versus message cues in persuasion. *Journal of Personality and Social Psychology*, *39*, 752–66.

Chen, G., Kim, K., Nofsinger, J., & Rui, O. (2007). Trading performance, disposition effect, overconfidence, representativeness bias and experience of emerging market investors. *Journal of Behavioral Decision Making*, *20*, 425–51.

Chen, S., & Chaiken, S. (1999). The heuristic-systematic model in its broader context. In S. Chaiken & Y. Trope (eds.), *Dual-process theories in social psychology* (pp. 73–96). New York: Guilford.

Cheung, C. (1998). Impacts of class on Hong Kong people's well-being. *Human Relations*, *51*, 89–119.

Cheung, F. M., & Halpern, D. F. (2010). Women at the top: Powerful leaders define success as work + family in a culture of gender. *American Psychologist*, *65*, 182–93.

Chin, J. L. (2010). Introduction to the special issue on diversity and leadership. *American Psychologist*, *65*, 150–6.

Choudhury, E. (2008). Trust in administration: An integrative approach to optimal trust. *Administration & Society*, *40*, 586–620.

Christen, M., & Morgan, R. M. (2005). Keeping up with the Joneses: Analyzing the effect of income inequality on consumer borrowing. *Quantitative Marketing and Economics*, *3*, 145–73.

Christian, C. W. (1994). *Voluntary compliance with the individual income tax: Results from the 1988 TCMP study* (The IRS Research Bulletin, Publication 1500 Rev 9 94). Washington, DC: Department of the Treasury, Internal Revenue Service.

Cialdini, R. B. (2001). *Influence: Science and practice* (4th edn). Boston, MA: Allyn & Bacon.

Ciavarella, M., Buchholtz, A., Riordan C., Gatewood, R., & Stokes, G. (2004). The big five and venture survival: Is there a linkage? *Journal of Business Venturing*, *19*, 265–483.

Clark, M. S., & Chrisman, K. (1994). Resource allocation in intimate relationships: Trying to make sense of a confusing literature. In M. J. Lerner & G. Mikula (eds.), *Entitlement and the affectional bond* (pp. 65–88). New York: Plenum Press.

Clark, M. S., & Mills, J. (1979). Interpersonal attraction in exchange and communal relationships. *Journal of Personality and Social Psychology*, *37*, 12–24.

Clark, M. S., Mills, J., & Powell, M. C. (1986). Keeping track of needs in communal and exchange relationships. *Journal of Personality and Social Psychology*, *51*, 333–8.

Clark, M. S., & Reis, H. T. (1988). Interpersonal processes in close relationships. *Annual Review of Psychology*, *39*, 609–72.

Clotfelter, C. (1983). Tax evasion and tax rates: An analysis of individual returns. *Review of Economics and Statistics*, *65*, 363–73.

Cochard, F., Nguyen Van, P., & Willinger, M. (2004). Trusting behavior in repeated investment game. *Journal of Economic Behavior and Organization*, *55*, 31–44.

Codol, J. P. (1986). Evaluation and expression of similarities and differences between peers. *Année Psychologique*, *86*, 527–50.

Cohen, M. D., March, J. G., & Olsen, J. P. (1972). A garbage can model of organizational choice. *Administrative Science Quarterly*, *17*, 1–15.

Cohn, R. M. (1978). The effect of employment status change on self-attitudes. *Social Psychology*, *41*, 81–93.

Cole, M. (2007). Re-thinking unemployment: A challenge to the legacy of Jahoda et al. *Sociology*, *41*, 1133–49.

Coleman, J. S. (1988). Social capital in creation of human capital. *American Journal of Sociology*, *94*, 95–120.

Collins, J. H., & Plumlee, R. D. (1991). The taxpayer's labor and reporting decision: The effect of audit schemes. *Accounting Review*, *66*, 559–76.

Connolly, T., & Butler, D. (2006). Regret in economic and psychological theories of choice. *Journal of Behavioral Decision Making*, *19*, 139–54.

Corfman, K. P. (1987). Group decison-making and relative influence when preferences differ: A conceptual framework. In E. C. Hirschman & J. Sheth (eds.), *Research in consumer behavior* (vol. 2, pp. 223–57). Greenwich, CT: JAI.

Corfman, K. P., & Lehmann, D. R. (1987). Models of cooperative group decision-making and relative influence: An experimental investigation of family purchase decisions. *Journal of Consumer Research*, *14*, 1–13.

Cornicello, G. (2003). Behavioural finance and speculative bubble (unpublished thesis). Università Commerciale Luigi Bocconi, Milan.

Cosma, S., & Pattarin, F. (2011). Attitudes, personality factors and household debt decisions: A study of consumer credit. In P. Molyneux (ed.), *Bank strategy, governance and ratings* (pp. 194–216). Basingstoke: Palgrave Macmillan.

Couprie, H. (2007). Time allocation within the family: Welfare implications of life in a couple. *Economic Journal*, *117*, 287–305.

Cox, D., & Plumley, A. (1988). Analysis of voluntary compliance rates for different income source classes (unpublished report). Washington, DC: International Revenue Service, Research Division.

Cram, F., & Ng, S. H. (1994). Children's understanding of public ownership. *European Journal of Social Psychology*, *24*, 469–80.

Croden, N. (2000). Credit use among low income groups. In A. Fleiss (ed.), *Research yearbook 1999/2000, Department of Social Security* (pp. 7–16). Leeds: Corporate Document Services.

Cross, P. (1977). Not can but will college teachers be improved? *New Directions for Higher Education*, *17*, 1–15.

Csikszentmihalyi, M. (1990). *Flow: The psychology of optimal experience*. New York: Harper & Row.

Cuervo, A., Ribeiro, D., & Roig, S. (eds.) (2007). *Entrepreneurship: Concepts, theory and perspective*. Berlin: Springer.

Curtin, R. (1979). Consumer pessimism nears record level. *Economic Outlook USA*, *6*, 80–2.

Daly, M., & Rake, K. (2003). *Gender and the welfare state: Care, work and welfare in Europe and the USA*. Cambridge: Polity Press/Blackwell.

Daniel, W. W. (1974). *A national survey of the unemployed*. London: Political and Economic Planning Institute.

Das, T. K., & Teng, B.-S. (1998). Between trust and control: Developing confidence in partner cooperation in alliances. *Academy of Management Review*, *23*, 491–512.

Davidsson, P. (1987). Need for achievement & entrepreneural activity in small firms. Paper presented at the 12th Annual Colloquium of IAREP, Ebeltoft, Denmark.

Davies, E., & Lea, S. E. G. (1995). Student attitudes to student debt. *Journal of Economic Psychology*, *16*, 663–79.

Davis, D. D., & Holt, C. A. (1993). *Experimental economics*. Princeton, NJ: Princeton University Press.

Davis, H. L. (1972). *Determinants of marital roles in a consumer purchase decision* (Working Paper 72–14). Brussels: European Institute for Advanced Studies in Management.

(1976). Decision making within the household. *Journal of Consumer Research*, *2*, 241–60.

Davis, H. L., & Rigaux, B. P. (1974). Perception of marital roles in decision processes. *Journal of Consumer Research*, *1*, 51–62.

Dawes, R. M. (1980). Social dilemmas. *Annual Review of Psychology*, *31*, 169–93.

De, D. A. (2005). *Entrepreneurship: Gründung und Wachstum von kleinen und mittleren Unternehmen* [Entrepreneurship: Foundation and growth of small and medium enterprises]. Munich: Pearson Studium.

De Dreu, C. K. W., Lualhati, C., & McCusker, C. (1994). Effects of gain–loss frames on satisfaction with self–other outcome–differences. *European Journal of Social Psychology*, *24*, 497–510.

de Henau, J., & Himmelweit, S. (2013). Unpacking within-household gender differences in partners' subjective benefits from household income. *Journal of Marriage and Family*, *75*, 611–24.

de Kam, F. (1992). Tax reform: Dreaming about tough realities. *Journal of Economic Psychology*, *13*, 679–86.

De Meza, D., Irlenbusch, B., & Reyniers, D. (2008). *Financial capability: A behavioural economics perspective* (Consumer Research Report 69, July 2008). London: Financial Services Authority.

de Quervain, D. J.-F., Fischbacher, U., Treyer, V., Schellhammer, M., Schnyder, U., Buck, A., & Fehr, E. (2004). The neural basis of altruistic punishment. *Science*, *305*, 1254–8.

De Rosa, A. (1995). Le 'réseau d'associations' comme méthode d'étude dans la recherche sur les representationes sociales: Structure, contenus et polarité du champ sémantique [The 'associative network' as a research method for social representations: Structure, contents and polarity of semantic fields]. *Cahiers Internationaux de Psychologie Sociale*, *28*, 96–112.

Deaton, A. (2008). Income, health, and well-being around the world: Evidence from the Gallup World Poll. *Journal of Economic Perspective*, *22*, 53–72.

DeBondt, W. F. M. (2008). Stock prices: Insights from behavioral finance. In A. Lewis (ed.), *The Cambridge handbook of psychology and economic behaviour* (pp. 64–104). Cambridge: Cambridge University Press.

DeBondt, W. F. M., & Thaler, R. (1985). Does the stock market overreact? *Journal of Finance*, *40*, 793–808.

(1987). Further evidence on investor overreaction and stock market seasonality. *Journal of Finance*, *42*, 557–81.

Dehm, H., & Müller-Peters, A. (2001). The impact of economic representations and national identity on the attitude towards the Euro. In C. Roland-Lévy, E. Kirchler, E. Penz, & C. Gray (eds.), *Everyday representations of the economy* (pp. 205–31). Vienna: WUV.

Delgado, M. R., Locke, H. M., Stenger, V. A., & Fiez, J. A. (2003). Dorsal striatum responses to reward and punishment: Effects of valence and magnitude manipulations. *Cognitive, Affective & Behavioral Neuroscience*, *3*, 27–38.

DellaVigna, S. (2009). Psychology and economics. Evidence from the field. *Journal of Economic Literature*, *47*, 315–72.

Desmarais, S., & Lerner, M. J. (1994). Entitlements in close relationships: A justice-motive analysis. In M. J. Lerner & G.

Mikula (eds.), *Entitlement and the affectional bond* (pp. 43–64). New York: Plenum Press.

Deutsch, M. (1975). Equity, equality and need: What determines which value will be used as the basis of distributive justice? *Journal of Social Issues*, *31*, 137–48.

(1985). *Distributive justice: A socio-psychological perspective*. New Haven, CT: Yale University Press.

Deutsche Bundesbank (2004). *Der Euro und die Preise: Zwei Jahre später* (Deutsche Bundesbank Monatsbericht Januar 2004, pp. 15–28). Frankfurt am Main: Deutsche Bundesbank.

Dewey, J. (1910). *How we think*. Boston, MA: D. C. Heath.

Dhar, R., & Zhu, N. (2006). Up close and personal: Investor sophistication and the disposition effect. *Management Science*, *52*, 726–40.

Di Tella, R., MacCulloch, R. J., & Oswald, A. J. (2001). Preferences over inflation and unemployment: Evidence from surveys of happiness. *American Economic Review*, *91*, 335–41.

Diacon, S., & Hasseldine, J. (2007). Framing effects and risk perception: The effect of prior performance presentation format on investment fund choice. *Journal of Economic Psychology*, *28*, 31–52.

Díaz-Martínez, C., Dema, S., & Ibánez, M. (2007). The intertwining of money and love in couple relationships. In J. Stocks, C. Díaz-Martínez, & B. Halleröd (eds.), *Modern couples sharing money, sharing life* (pp. 100–42). Basingstoke: Palgrave Macmillan.

Dickson, P. R., & Sawyer, A. G. (1990). The price knowledge and search of supermarket shoppers. *Journal of Marketing*, *54*, 42–53.

Diekmann, A. (2009). *Spieltheorie: Einführung, Beispiele, Experimente* [Game theory: Introduction, examples, experiments]. Reinbek: Rowohlt.

Diener, E. (1984). Subjective well-being. *Psychological Bulletin*, *95*, 542–75.

(2000). Subjective well-being: The science of happiness and a proposal for a national index. *American Psychologist*, *55*, 34–43.

Diener, E., & Biswas-Diener, R. (2008). *Happiness: Unlocking the mysteries of psychological wealth*. Malden, MA: Blackwell.

Diener, E., & Eunkook, M. S. (eds.) (2003). *Culture and subjective well-being*. Cambridge, MA: MIT Press.

Diener, E., & Lucas, R. E. (2000). Subjective emotional well-being. In M. Lewis & J. M. Haviland-Jones (eds.), *Handbook of emotions* (2nd edn, pp. 325–37). New York: Guilford.

Diener, E., Lucas, R. E., & Scollon, C. N. (2006). Beyond the hedonic treadmill: Revising the adaptation theory of well-being. *American Psychologist*, *61*, 305–14.

Diener, E., Suh, E., & Oishi, S. (1997). Recent findings on subjective well-being. *Indian Journal of Clinical Psychology*, *24*, 25–41.

Diener, E., Suh, E., Lucas, R. E., & Smith, H. L. (1999). Subjective well-being: Three decades of progress. *Psychological Bulletin*, *125*, 276–302.

Diener, E., & Tov, W. (2012). National accounts of well-being. In K. C. Land, A. C. Michalos & M. J. Sirgy (eds.), *Handbook of social indicators and quality of life research* (pp. 137–57). New York: Springer.

DiFonzo, N., & Bordia, P. (1997). Rumor and prediction: Making sense (but losing dollars) in the stock market. *Organizational Behavior and Human Decision Processes*, *71*, 329–53.

Dittmar, H. (1992). *The social psychology of material possessions: To have is to be*. Hemel Hempstead: Harvester Wheatsheaf.

Dittmar, H., Beattie, J., & Friese, S. (1996). The role of self-discrepancies in shopping addiction. Paper presented at the 21th Annual Colloquium of IAREP, Paris.

Dohmen, T., Falk, A., Huffman, D., & Sunde, U. (2009). Homo reciprocans: Survey evidence on behavioural outcomes. *Economic Journal*, *119*, 592–612.

Doise, W. (1978). *Groups and individuals: Explanations in social psychology*. Cambridge: Cambridge University Press.

Dolan, P., Peasgood, T., & White, M. (2008). Do we really know what makes us happy? A review of the economic literature on the factors associated with subjective well-being. *Journal of Economic Psychology*, *29*, 94–122.

Dolan, S. L., & Gosselin, E. (1998). *Job satisfaction and life satisfaction: Analysis of a reciprocal model with social demographic moderators* (Papers 98–02). University of Montreal, School of Industrial Relations.

Doms, M., & Morin, N. (2004). Consumer sentiment, the economy, and the news media. *Finance and Economics Discussion Series*, *51*, 1–70.

Donkers, B., & van Soest, A. (1999). Subjective measures of household preferences and financial decisions. *Journal of Economic Psychology*, *20*, 613–42.

Dörner, D. (1996). *The logic of failure: Recognizing and avoiding error in complex situations*, trans. R. & R. Kimber. New York: Metropolitan Books.

(2010, October). *Die Logik des Gelingens?* [The logic of success?] Lecture at the Vienna University of Economics and Business Administration, Vienna.

Dornstein, M. (1987). Taxes: Attitudes and perceptions and their social bases. *Journal of Economic Psychology*, *8*, 55–76.

Douglas, J., & Isherwood, B. (1979). *The world of goods*. Harmondsworth: Penguin.

Dowling, M., & Lucey, B. M. (2005). The role of feelings in investor decision-making. *Journal of Economic Surveys*, *19*, 211–37.

Dubin, J. A., Graetz, M. J., & Wilde, L. L. (1990). The effect of audit rates on the federal individual income tax, 1977–1986. *National Tax Journal*, *43*, 395–409.

Duck, S. (1991). Diaries and logs. In B. M. Montgomery & S. W. Duck (eds.), *Studying social interaction* (pp. 141–61). New York: Guilford.

Duesenberry, J. S. (1949). *Income, saving and the theory of consumer behavior*. Cambridge, MA: Harvard University Press.

Duggan, M. (1999). Share markets and psychology. In P. E. Earl & S. Kemp (eds.), *The Elgar companion to consumer research and economic psychology* (pp. 531–7). Cheltenham: Edward Elgar.

Dunning, D., Anderson, J. E., Schlösser, T., Ehlebracht, D., & Fetchenhauer, D. (2014). Trust at zero acquaintance: More a matter of respect than expectation of reward. *Journal of Personality and Social Psychology*, *107*, 122–41.

Dunning, D., Fetchenhauer, D., & Schlösser, T. M. (2012). Trust as a social and emotional act: Noneconomic considerations in trust behavior. *Journal of Economic Psychology*, *33*, 686–94.

Durkheim, É. (1898). Représentations individuelles et représentations collectives [Individual and collective representations]. *Revue de Métaphysique et de Morale*, *6*, 273–302.

Eagly, A. H., & Chin, J. L. (2010). Diversity and leadership in a changing world. *American Psychologist*, *65*, 216–24.

Eagly, A. H., Johannesen-Schmidt, M. C., & van Engen, M. I. (2003). Transformational, transactional, and laissez-faire leadership styles: A meta-analysis comparing women and men. *Psychological Bulletin*, *129*, 569–91.

Earl, P. E., & Kemp, S. (eds.) (1999). *The Elgar companion to consumer research and economic psychology*. Cheltenham: Edward Elgar.

Easterlin, R. A. (1974). Does economic growth improve the human lot? Some empirical evidence. In P. A. David & M. W. Reder (eds.), *Nations and household in economic growth* (pp. 89–125). New York: Academic Press.

(1995). Will raising the incomes of all increase the happiness of all? *Journal of Economic Behavior and Organization*, *27*, 35–48.

(2001). Income and happiness: Toward a unified theory. *Economic Journal*, *111*, 465–84.

Ebner, M. L., Korunka, C., Frank, H., & Lueger, M. (2008). Intrapreneurship in der beruflichen Erstausbildung: Versuch einer begrifflichen Klärung und Operationalisierung [Intrapreneurship in primary career training: An attempt at conceptual clarification and operationalisation]. *Zeitschrift für Personalforschung*, *22*, 291–311.

Ebster, C., Wagner, U., & Neumüller, D. (2009). Children's influences on in-store purchase. *Journal of Retailing and Consumer Services*, *16*, 145–54.

Eckel, C. C., & Grossman, P. (1997). Equity and fairness in economic decisions: Evidence from bargaining experiments. In G. Antonides, W. F. van Raaij, & S. Maital (eds.), *Advances in economic psychology* (pp. 281–302). Chichester: John Wiley & Sons.

Eckel, C. C., & Wilson, R. K. (2004). Is trust a risky decision? *Journal of Economic Behavior & Organization*, *55*, 447–65.

Edgeworth, F. Y. (1881). *Mathematical physics: An essay on the application of mathematics to the moral sciences*. London: C. Kegan Paul & Co.

Edlund, J. (2003). Attitudes towards taxation: Ignorant and incoherent? *Scandinavian Political Studies*, *26*, 145–67.

Edwards, W. (1954). The theory of decision making. *Psychological Bulletin*, *51*, 380–417.

Eisenberg, G. P., & Lazarsfeld, P. (1938). The psychological effects of unemployment. *Psychological Bulletin*, *35*, 358–90.

el Sehity, T., Hoelzl, E., & Kirchler, E. (2005). Price developments after a nominal shock: Benford's Law and psychological pricing after the euro introduction. *International Journal of Research in Marketing*, *22*, 471–80.

el Sehity, T., & Kirchler, E. (2006). Soziale Repräsentationen (Vorstellungen) [Social representations]. In H.-W. Bierhoff & D. Frey (eds.), *Handbuch der Sozialpsychologie und Kommunikationspsychologie* (pp. 486–93). Göttingen: Hogrefe.

el Sehity, T., Kirchler, E., & Brandstätter, E. (2005). Preiswahrnehmung [Price perception]. In D. Frey, L. von Rosenstiel, & C. Graf Hoyos (eds.), *Wirtschaftspsychologie* (pp. 291–4). Basel: Beltz.

el Sehity, T., Kirchler, E., & Muehlbacher, S. (2003). Rise and decline of social objects: Ten case studies on the social development of meaning structures. Paper presented at the IAREP (International Association for Research in Economic Psychology) Euro-Workshop, Vienna, July.

Elffers, H., & Hessing, D. J. (1997). Influencing the prospects of tax evasion. *Journal of Economic Psychology*, *18*, 289–304.

Elffers, H., Robben, H. S. J., & Hessing, D. J. (1991). Underreporting income: Who is the best judge – taxpayer or tax inspector? *Journal of Royal Statistical Society*, *154*, 125–7.

(1992). On measuring tax evasion. *Journal of Economic Psychology*, *13*, 545–67.

Elffers, H., Weigel, R. H., & Hessing, D. J. (1987). The consequences of different strategies for measuring tax evasion behavior. *Journal of Economic Psychology*, *8*, 311–37.

Elizabeth, V. (2001). Managing money, managing coupledom: A critical examination of cohabitants' money management practices. *Sociological Review*, *49*, 389–411.

Ellsberg, D. (1961). Risk, ambiguity, and the savage axioms. *Quarterly Journal of Economics*, *75*, 643–69.

Engel, C. (2011). Dictator games: A meta study. *Experimental Economics*, *14*, 583–610.

Engel, J. F., Blackwell, R. D., & Miniard, P. W. (2007). *Consumer behavior* (10th edn). Fort Worth, TX: Dryden Press.

Englich, B., Mussweiler, T., & Strack, M. (2006). Playing dice with criminal sentences: The influence of irrelevant anchors on experts' judicial decision making. *Personality and Social Psychology Bulletin*, *32*, 188–200.

Engström, P., Nordblom, K., Ohlsson, H., & Persson, A. (2011). *Loss evasion and tax aversion* (Working Paper Series 2011:17). Uppsala: Uppsala University, Department of Economics.

Epstein, S. (1986). Does aggregation produce spuriously high estimates of behavior stability? *Journal of Personality and Social Psychology*, *50*, 1199–1210.

(1994). Integration of the cognitive and the psychodynamic unconscious. *American Psychologist*, *49*, 709–24.

Epstein, S., & Pacini, R. (1999). Some basic issues regarding dual-process theories from the perspective of cognitive-experiential theory. In S. Chaiken & Y. Trope (eds.), *Dual-process theories in social psychology* (pp. 462–82). New York: Guilford.

Etzioni, A. (1988). *The moral dimension: Toward a new economics*. New York: Free Press.

European Central Bank (2014). *The euro area bank lending survey, 3rd quarter of 2014*. Retrieved from www.ecb.europa.eu/stats/money/surveys/lend/html/index.en.html (accessed 13 July 2016).

European Opinion Research Group (2001). *Eurobarometer 55*. Brussels: European Commission.

(2002). *Perception of the euro – first elements*. Brussels: European Commission.

Evans, J. St. B. T. (1989). *Bias in human reasoning: Causes and consequences*. Brighton: Erlbaum.

(2006). The heuristic-analytic theory of reasoning: Extension and evaluation. *Psychonomic Bulletin and Review*, *13*, 378–95.

(2008). Dual-processing accounts of reasoning, judgment and social cognition. *Annual Review of Psychology*, *59*, 255–78.

(2012). Questions and challenges for the new psychology of reasoning. *Thinking & Reasoning*, *18*, 5–31.

Evans, J. St. B. T., & Over, D. E. (1996). *Rationality and reasoning*. Hove: Psychology Press.

Evans, J. St. B. T., & Stanovich, K. E. (2013a). Dual-process theories of higher cognition: Advancing the debate. *Perspectives on Psychological Science*, *8*, 223–41.

(2013b). Theory and metatheory in the study of dual processes: Reply to comments. *Perspectives on Psychological Science*, *8*, 263–71.

Evertsson, L., & Nyman, C. (2012). Perceptions and practices in independent management: Blurring the boundaries between 'mine', 'yours' and 'ours'. *Journal of Family Economic Issues*, *33*, 389–506.

Faber, R. J., & O'Guinn, T. C. (1992). A clinical screener for compulsive buying. *Journal of Consumer Research*, *19*, 459–69.

Fahrenberg, J., Myrtek, M., Schumacher, J., & Brähler, E. (2000). *Fragebogen zur Lebenszufriedenheit (FLZ): Handanweisung* [Questionnaire on life satisfaction: Manual]. Göttingen: Hogrefe.

Falk, A., Fehr, E., & Zehnder, C. (2006). Fairness perception and reservation wages – the behavioral effects of minimum wage laws. *Quarterly Journal of Economics*, *121*, 1347–81.

Falk, A., & Heckman, J. J. (2009). Lab experiments are a major source of knowledge in the social sciences. *Science*, *326*, 535–8.

Fama, E. F. (1965). The behavior of stock market prices. *Journal of Business*, *38*, 34–105.

(1970). Efficient capital markets: A review of theory and empirical work. *Journal of Finance*, *25*, 383–417.

Farmer, R. D. T., Preston, D. T., & O'Brian, S. E. M. (1977). Suicide mortality in greater London: Changes during the past 25 years. *British Journal of Preventive Social Medicine*, *31*, 171–7.

Farrell, H., & Knight, J. (2003). Trust, institutions, and institutional change: Industrial districts and the social capital hypothesis. *Politics and Society*, *31*, 537–66.

Fassinger, R. E., Shullman, S. L., & Stevenson, M. R. (2010). Toward an affirmative lesbian, gay, bisexual, and transgender leadership paradigm. *American Psychologist*, 65, 201–15.

Feagin, J. R. (1975). *Subordinating the poor*. Englewood Cliffs, NJ: Prentice Hall.

Feather, N. T. (1990). *The psychological impact of unemployment*. New York: Springer.

Feather, N., & Davenport, P. (1981). Unemployment and depressive affect: A motivational and attributional analysis. *Journal of Personality and Social Psychology*, *41*, 422–36.

Feger, H., & Auhagen, A. E. (1987). Unterstützende soziale Netzwerke: sozialpsychologische Perspektiven [Supportive social networks: Social psychological perspectives]. *Zeitschrift für Klinische Psychologie*, *86*, 353–67.

Fehr, E. (2001). Unvollständige Arbeitsverträge schaffen Arbeitslosigkeit: Die Folgen von fairem Verhalten auf dem Arbeitsmarkt. [Incomplete work contracts create unemployment: The consequences of fair behaviour on the labor market]. *Neue Zürcher Zeitung*, 13/14 January, p. 27.

(2002). The economics of impatience. *Nature*, *415*, 269–72.

Fehr, E., Bernhard, H., & Rockenbach, B. (2008). Egalitarianism in young children. *Nature*, *454*, 1079–84.

Fehr, E., & Fishbacher, U. (2003). The nature of human altruism. *Nature*, *425*, 785–91.

Fehr, E., & Gächter, S. (2002). Altruistic punishment in humans. *Nature*, *415*, 137–40.

Fehr, E., Goette, L., & Zehnder, C. (2009). A behavioral account of the labor market: The role of fairness concerns. *Annual Review of Economics*, *1*, 355–84.

Fehr, E., Kirchler, E., Weichbold, A., & Gächter, S. (1998). When social norms overpower competition: Gift exchange in experimental markets. *Journal of Labor Economics*, *16*, 321–54.

Fehr, E., & Schmidt, K. M. (1999). A theory of fairness, competition, and cooperation. *Quarterly Journal of Economics*, *114*, 817–68.

Feige, E. (2016). Reflections on the meaning and measurement of unobserved economies: What do we really know about the 'shadow economy'? *Journal of Tax Administration, 2*, [no pagination].

Feinstein, J. (1991). An econometric analysis of income tax evasion and its detection. *Rand*, *22*, 14–35.

Feld, L. P., & Frey, B. S. (2007). Tax compliance as the result of a psychological tax contract: The role of incentives and responsive regulation. *Law & Policy*, *29*, 102–20.

(2010). Tax evasion and the psychological tax contract. In J. Alm, J. Martinez-Vazquez, & B. Torgler (eds.), *Developing alternative frameworks for explaining tax compliance* (pp. 74–94). London: Routledge.

Fennis, B. M., & Stroebe, W. (2016). *The psychology of advertising* (2nd edn). London: Routledge.

Fenzl, T. (2009). *Die Massenpsychologie der Finanzmarktkrise: US-Immobilienblase, Subprime desaster, Schulden-bubble und ihre Auswirkungen* [Mass psychology of the financial market crisis: The US real estate bubble, subprime disaster, debt bubble and their effects]. Vienna: Springer.

Fenzl, T., & Brudermann, T. (2008). Die Vortester-Strategie – Umgang mit unbekannten Risiken [The pretester strategie]. *Wirtschaftspsychologie Aktuell*, *4*, 39–41.

Fernandes, D., Lynch Jr, J. G., & Netemeyer, R. G. (2014). Financial literacy, financial education, and downstream financial behaviors. *Management Science*, *60*, 1861–83.

Ferrari, L., & Romano, D. F. (1999). *Mente e denaro: introduzione alla psicologia economica* [Money and the mind: Introduction to economic psychology]. Milan: Raffaello Cortina.

Festinger, L. (1957). *A theory of cognitive dissonance*. Stanford, CA: Stanford University Press.

Fetchenhauer, D., & Dunning, D. (2010). Why so cynical? Asymmetric feedback underlies misguided skepticism regarding the trustworthiness of others. *Psychological Science*, *21*, 189–93.

(2012). Betrayal aversion versus principled trustfulness – how to explain risk avoidance and risky choices in trust games. *Journal of Economic Behavior & Organization*, *81*, 534–41.

Fiedler, K. (1991). On the task, the measures and the mood in research on affect and social cognition. In J. P. Forgas (ed.),

Emotion and social judgments (pp. 83–104). Oxford: Pergamon Press.

Filiatrault, P., & Ritchie, J. R. B. (1980). Joint purchasing decisions: A comparison of influence structure in family and couple decision-making units. *Journal of Consumer Research*, *7*, 131–40.

Filley, A. C. (1975). *Interpersonal conflict resolution*. Glenview, IL: Scott, Foresman.

Finucane, M. L., Alhakami, A., Slovic, P., & Johnson, S. M. (2000). The affect heuristic in judgments of risks and benefits. *Journal of Behavioral Decision Making*, *13*, 1–17.

Fischer, C. M., Wartick, M., & Mark, M. M. (1992). Detection probability and taxpayer compliance: A review of the literature. *Journal of Accounting Literature*, *11*, 1–46.

Fischer, K., & Fischer, I. (1988). Konsumklimaforschung: Zur Analyse der privaten Nachfrage [Consumer confidence research: On the analysis of private demand]. *Jahrbuch der Absatz- und Verbrauchsforschung*, *4*, 334–51.

Fischer, L., & Fischer, O. (2010). Übertarifliche Bezahlung als Determinante von Gerechtigkeitsperzeption und Motivation von Arbeitnehmern in Deutschland [Payment above collective contracts as a determinant of German employees' motivation and perceptions of fairness]. In E. H. Witte & T. Gollan (eds.), *Sozialpsychologie und Ökonomie* (pp. 126–43). Lengerich: Pabst.

Fischer, L., Katzer, C., & Kiell, G. (2002). Der TEURO und die Geldillusion [The TEURO and money illusion]. *Wirtschaftspsychologie*, *4*, 43–60.

Fischer, L., & Mörsch, C. (1999). Themen und Konzepte einer allgemeinen Finanzpsychologie – sozialpsychologische Grundlagen und wirtschaftliche Anwendungsbereiche [Themes and concepts of general financial psychology: Social psychological foundations and economic areas of application]. In L. Fischer, T. Kutsch & E. Stephan (eds.), *Finanzpsychologie* (pp. 11–46). Munich: Oldenburg.

Fischer, P., Jonas, E., Frey, D., & Kastenmüller, A. (2008). Selective exposure and decision framing: The impact of gain and loss framing on confirmatory information search after decisions. *Journal of Experimental Social Psychology*, *44*, 312–20.

Fischhoff, B. (1975). Hindsight ≠ foresight: Effect of outcome knowledge on judgment under uncertainty. *Journal of Experimental Psychology: Human Perception and Performance*, *1*, 288–99.

Fischhoff, B., & Beyth, R. (1975). 'I knew it would happen': Remembered probabilities of once-future things. *Organizational Behavior & Human Performance*, *13*, 1–16.

Fishbein, M., & Ajzen, I. (1975). *Belief, attitude, intention and behavior*. Reading, MA: Addison Wesley.

Fisher, I. (1928). *The money illusion*. New York: Adelphi.

Fishlow, A., & Friedman, J. (1994). Tax evasion, inflation and stabilization. *Journal of Development Economics*, *43*, 105–23.

Fiske, A. P., & Tetlock, P. E. (1997). Taboo trade-offs: Reactions to transactions that transgress the spheres of justice. *Political Psychology*, *18*, 255–97.

Fleming, R. (1997). *The common purse: Income sharing in New Zealand families*. Auckland: Auckland University Press/ Bridget Williams Books.

Foa, U. G., & Foa, E. B. (1974). *Societal structures of the mind*. Springfield, IL: Thomas.

Fodor, J. (1983). *The modularity of mind*. Scranton, PA: Crowell.

(2001). *The mind doesn't work that way*. Cambridge, MA: MIT Press.

Foreman, P., & Murnighan, J. K. (1996). Learning to avoid the winner's curse. *Organizational Behavior and Human Decision Processes*, *67*, 170–80.

Forester, J. (1984). Bounded rationality and the politics of muddling through. *Public Administration Review*, *44*, 23–31.

Forgas, J. P. (ed.) (1991). *Emotion and social judgments*. Oxford: Pergamon Press.

Foucault, M. (1965). *Madness and civilisation: A history of insanity in the age of reason*, trans. R. Howard. New York: Vintage.

Fox, S., & Dayan, K. (2004). Framing and risky choice as influenced by comparison of one's achievements with others: The case of investment in the stock exchange. *Journal of Business and Psychology*, *18*, 301–20.

Foxall, G. R., & Goldsmith, R. E. (1994). *Consumer psychology for marketing*. London: Routledge.

Foxman, E. R., Tansuhaj, P. S., & Ekstrom, K. M. (1989a). Family members' perceptions of adolescents' influence in family decision making. *Journal of Consumer Research*, *15*, 482–91.

(1989b). Adolescents influence in family purchase decisions: A socialization perspective. *Journal of Business Research*, *18*, 159–72.

Frank, H., & Korunka, C. (1996). Zum Informations- und Entscheidungsverhalten von Unternehmensgründern. Der Zusammenhang von 'Handlungskontrolle' und Gründungserfolg [On the information and decision behaviour of entrepreneurs. The connection between action control and founding success]. *Zeitschrift für Betriebswirtschaft*, *66*, 947–63.

Frank, H., Korunka, C., & Lueger, M. (2002). *Entrepreneural spirit: Unternehmerische Orientierung und Gründungsneigung von Studierenden* [Entrepreneurial spirit: Entrepreneurial orientation and founding intentions of students]. Vienna: WUV.

Frank, H., Lueger M., & Korunka, C. (2007). The significance of personality in business start-up intentions, start-up realization and business success. *Entrepreneurship & Regional Development*, *19*, 227–51.

Franke, N., & Lüthje, C. (2002). Studentische Unternehmensgründungen – dank oder trotz Förderung? [Students' founding of companies – thanks to or despite sponsoring?]. *Schmalenbachs Zeitschrift für Betriebswirtschaftliche Forschung*, *54*, 96–112.

Frederick, S. (2005). Cognitive reflection and decision making. *Journal of Economic Perspectives*, *19*, 25–42.

Frederick, S., Loewenstein, G., & O'Donoghue, T. (2002). Time discounting and time preference: A critical review. *Journal of Economic Literature*, *40*, 351–401.

Freiberg, A. (2010). *The tools of regulation*. Leichhardt: The Federation Press.

French, J., & Raven, B. (1959). The bases of social power. In D. Cartwright (ed.), *Studies in social power* (pp. 150–67). Ann Arbor: University of Michigan.

French, K., & Poterba, J. (1991). Investor diversification and international equity markets. *American Economic Review*, *81*, 222–6.

Frese, M. (1977). *Psychische Störungen bei Arbeitern* [Mental disorders in workers]. Salzburg: Otto Müller.

(1979). Arbeitslosigkeit, Depressivität und Kontrolle. Eine Studie mit Wiederholungsmessung [Unemployment, depressiveness and control. A study with repeated measures]. In T. Kieselbach & H. Offe (eds.), *Arbeitslosigkeit: individuelle Verarbeitung, gesellschaftlicher Hintergrund* (pp. 222–57). Darmstadt: Steinkopff.

(ed.) (1998). *Erfolgreiche Unternehmensgründer* [Successful entrepreneurs]. Göttingen: Hogrefe.

Frese, M., & Gielnik, M. M. (2014). The psychology of entrepreneurship. *Annual Review of Organizational Psychology & Organizational Behavior*, *1*, 413–38.

Frese, M., & Mohr, G. (1978). Die psychopathologischen Folgen des Entzugs von Arbeit: Der Fall Arbeitslosigkeit [The psychopathological effects of withdrawal from work: The case of unemployment]. In M. Frese, S. Greif & N. Semmer (eds.), *Industrielle Psychopathologie* (Schriftenreihe zur Arbeitspsychologie 23) (pp. 282–320). Berne: Huber.

Frey, B. S. (1990). Entscheidungsanomalien: Die Sicht der Ökonomie [Decision-making anomalies: The perspective of economics]. *Psychologische Rundschau*, *41*, 67–83.

(1992). Tertium datum: Pricing, regulating, and intrinsic motivation. *Kyklos*, *45*, 161–84.

(1997a). *Not just for the money: An economic theory of personal motivation*. Cheltenham: Edward Elgar.

(1997b). A constitution for knaves crowds out civic virtues. *Economic Journal*, *107*, 1043–53.

(2008). *Happiness: A revolution in economics*. Cambridge, MA: MIT Press.

Frey, B. S., & Benz, M. (2007). Die psychologischen Grundlagen des Marktmodells (Homo oeconomicus) [The psychological foundations of the market model (Homo economicus)]. In L. von Rosenstiel & D. Frey (eds.), *Enzyklopädie der Psychologie, Marktpsychologie* (vol. 5, pp. 1–26). Göttingen: Hogrefe.

Frey, B. S., & Stutzer, A. (2000). Happiness, economy and institutions. *Economic Journal*, *110*, 918–38.

(2002). *Happiness and economics: How the economy and institutions affect well-being*. Princeton, NJ: Princeton University Press.

Frey, B. S., & Torgler, B. (2007). Tax morale and conditional cooperation. *Journal of Comparative Economics*, *35*, 136–59.

Frey, D., & Stahlberg, D. (1990). Erwartungsbildung und Erwartungsveränderung bei Börsenakteuren [Expectation formation and changes in expectations among actors on the stock market]. In P. Maas & J. Weibler (eds.), *Börse und Psychologie* (pp. 102–39). Cologne: Deutscher Instituts-Verlag.

Frideres, J. S. (1973). Advertising, buying patterns, and children. *Journal of Advertising Research*, *13*, 34–6.

Friedland, N. (1982). A note on tax evasion as a function of the quality of information about the magnitude and credibility of threatened fines: Some preliminary research. *Journal of Applied Social Psychology*, *12*, 54–9.

Friedland, N., Maital, S., & Rutenberg, A. (1978). A simulation study of income tax evasion. *Journal of Political Economics*, *10*, 107–16.

Friedrichs, J. (1982). *Methoden empirischer Sozialforschung* [Methods of empirical social research]. Opladen: Westdeutscher Verlag.

Frieling, E., & Sonntag, K.-H. (1999). *Lehrbuch Arbeitspsychologie* [Textbook work psychology] (2nd edn). Berne: Huber.

Fröhlich, D. (1979). *Psychosoziale Folgen der Arbeitslosigkeit: Eine empirische Untersuchung in Nordrhein-Westfalen* [Psychosocial effects of unemployment: An empirical study in North Rhine-Westphalia]. Cologne: Institut zur Erforschung sozialer Chancen.

Fryer, D., & Payne, R. L. (1984). Proactive behavior in unemployment: Findings and implications. *Leisure Studies*, *3*, 273–95.

Furnham, A. F. (1982). The Protestant work ethic and attitudes towards unemployment. *Journal of Occupational Psychology*, *55*, 277–85.

(1984). Many sides of the coin: The psychology of money usage. *Personality and Individual Differences*, *5*, 95–103.

(1988). Unemployment. In W. F. van Raaij, G. M. Van Veldhoven, & K.-E. Wärneryd (eds.), *Handbook of economic psychology* (pp. 594–673). Dordrecht: Kluwer.

(2001). Parental attitudes of pocket money/allowances for children. *Journal of Economic Psychology*, *22*, 397–422.

(2005). Understanding the meaning of tax: Young people's knowledge of the principles of taxation. *Journal of Socio-Economics*, *34*, 703–13.

(2014). *The new psychology of money*. London: Routledge.

Furnham, A. F., & Kirkcaldy, B. (2000). Economic socialization: German parents' perceptions and implementations of allowances to educate children. *European Psychologist*, *5*, 202–15.

Furnham, A. F., & Lewis, A. (1986). *The economic mind: The social psychology of economic behaviour*. Brighton: Wheatsheaf.

Fürst, R. A., Heil, O. P., & Daniel, J. F. (2004). Die Preis–Qualitäts-Relation von deutschen Konsumgütern im Vergleich eines Vierteljahrhunderts [The price–quality-relation of consumer goods in Germany over a quarter of a century]. *Die Betriebswirtschaft*, *64*, 538–49.

Gabor, A., & Granger, C. (1961). On the price consciousness of consumers. *Applied Statistics*, *10*, 170–80.

Gabriel, Y., & Lang, T. (1995). *The unmanageable consumer*. London: Sage.

Gal, D., & McShane, B. B. (2012). Can small victories help win the war? Evidence from consumer debt management. *Journal of Marketing Research*, *49*, 487–501.

Galinsky, A. D., & Mussweiler, T. (2001). First offers as anchors: The role of perspective-taking and negotiator focus. *Journal of Personality and Social Psychology*, *81*, 657–69.

Gambetta, D. (ed.) (1988). *Trust: Making and breaking co-operative relations*. Oxford: Basil Blackwell.

Gamble, A., Gärling, R., Charlton, J., & Ranyard, R. (2002). Euro illusion: Psychological insights into price evaluations with a unitary currency. *European Psychologist*, *7*, 302–11.

Gamble, A., Gärling, R., Västfjäll, D., & Marell, A. (2003). Consumer choice biased by nominal representation of price.

Paper presented at the IAREP (International Association for Research in Economic Psychology) Euro-Workshop, Vienna, July.

Ganesh, G. (1997). Spousal influence in consumer decisions: A study of cultural assimilation. *Journal of Consumer Marketing*, *14*, 132–55.

Gangl, K., Kastlunger, B., Kirchler, E., & Voracek, M. (2012). Confidence in the economy in times of crisis: Social representations of experts and laypeople. *Journal of Socio-Economics*, *41*, 603–14.

Garboua, L., Masclet, D., & Montmarquette, C. (2009). A behavioral Laffer curve: Emergence of a social norm of fairness in a real effort experiment. *Journal of Economic Psychology*, *30*, 147–61.

Gärling, T., Kirchler, E., Lewis, A., & van Raaij, W. F. (2009). Psychology, financial decision making, and financial crises. *Psychological Science in the Public Interest*, *10*, 1–47.

Gasana, P. U. (2009). Relative status and interdependent effects in consumer behaviour. *Journal of Socio-Economics*, *38*, 52–9.

Gassner, W. (1983). Steuervermeidung, Steuerumgehung, Steuerhinterziehung [Tax avoidance, tax circumvention, tax evasion] (unpublished manuscript). Vienna University of Economics and Business Administration.

Gathergood, J. (2012). Self-control, financial literacy and consumer over-indebtedness. *Journal of Economic Psychology*, *33*, 590–602.

Gathergood, J., & Weber, J. (2014). Self-control, financial literacy & the co-holding puzzle. *Empirical Behavioral Finance*, *107*, 455–69.

Gedenk, K., & Sattler, H. (1999). The impact of price thresholds on profit contribution – should retailers set 9-ending prices? *Journal of Retailing*, *75*, 33–57.

Gehring, W. J., & Willoughby, A. R. (2002). The medial frontal cortex and the rapid processing of monetary gains and losses. *Science*, *295*, 2279–82.

Genze, F. (2006). Immobilienpreisblase als wirtschaftspolitisches Problem – der Fall Spanien. [Real estate price bubbles as problem of economic policy – the case of Spain] (unpublished thesis). Norderstedt: GRIN.

Gershuny, J. I., & Pahl, R. E. (1981). Work outside employment: some preliminary speculations. In S. Henry (ed.), *Informal institutions* (pp. 73–88). New York: St. Martin's.

Gërxhani, K., & Schram A. (2006). Tax evasion and income source: A comparative experimental study. *Journal of Economic Psychology*, *27*, 202–22.

Gigerenzer, G. (2004a). *Das Einmaleins der Skepsis: über den richtigen Umgang mit Zahlen und Risiken* [Skepticism 101: On the correct handling of numbers and risks]. Berlin: Berliner Taschenbuch Verlag.

(2004b). Fast and frugal heuristics: The tools of bounded rationality. In D. Koehler & N. Harvey (eds.), *Blackwell handbook of judgment and decision making* (pp. 62–88). Oxford: Blackwell.

(2015). *Simply rational: Decision making in the real world.* Oxford: Oxford University Press.

Gigerenzer, G., & Hoffrage, U. (1995). How to improve Bayesian reasoning without instruction: Frequency formats. *Psychological Review*, *102*, 684–704.

Gigerenzer, G., & Hug, K. (1992). Domain-specific reasoning: Social contracts, cheating, and perspective change. *Cognition*, *43*, 127–71.

Gigerenzer, G., Todd, P. M., & ABC Research Group (1999). *Simple heuristics that make us smart.* Oxford: Oxford University Press.

Gilbert, D. (2006). *Stumbling on happiness.* New York: Knopf Doubleday.

Gilbert, D. T., Pinel, E. C., Wilson, T. D., Blumberg, S. J., & Wheatley, T. P. (1998). Immune neglect: A source of a durability bias in affective forecasting. *Journal of Personality and Social Psychology*, *75*, 617–38.

Gillibrand, R., Lam, V., & O'Donnell, V. (2011). *Developmental psychology.* Upper Saddle River, NJ: Prentice Hall.

Gilovich, T., & Medvec, V. H. (1995). The experience of regret: What, why, and when. *Psychological Review*, *102*, 379–95.

Gintis, H. (2000). *Game theory evolving: A problem centered introduction to modeling strategic interaction.* Princeton, NJ: Princeton University Press.

Glick, B., & Gross, S. (1975). Marital interaction and marital conflict: A critical evaluation of current research strategies. *Journal of Marriage and Family*, *37*, 505–12.

Glimcher, P. W., Camerer, C. F., Fehr, E., & Poldrack, R. A. (eds.) (2009). *Neuroeconomics: Decision making and the brain.* Amsterdam: Elsevier.

Gneezy, A., Gneezy, U., & Lauga, D. O. (2014). A reference-dependent model of the price–quality heuristic. *Journal of Marketing Research*, *51*, 153–64.

Gneezy, U., & Rustichini, A. (2000). A fine is a price. *Journal of Legal Studies*, *29*, 1–18.

Godofsky, J., van Horn, C., & Zukin, C. (2010). *American workers assess an economic disaster.* New Brunswick, NJ: John J. Heldrich Center for Workforce Development, Rutgers University. Retrieved from www.heldrich.rutgers.edu/sites/default/files/products/uploads/Work_Trends_September_2010.pdf.

Goldoni, C. (1928). *The servant of two masters* (trans. E. J. Dent). Cambridge: Cambridge University Press.

Goldstein, D. G., & Gigerenzer, G. (1999). The recognition heuristic. How ignorance makes us smart. In G. Gigerenzer, P. M. Todd & ABC Research Group (eds.), *Simple heuristics that make us smart* (pp. 37–58). Oxford: Oxford University Press.

(2002). Models of ecological rationality: The recognition heuristic. *Psychological Review*, *109*, 75–90.

Goldstein, N. J., Cialdini, R. B., & Griskevicius, V. (2008). A room with a viewpoint: Using social norms to motivate environmental conservation in hotels. *Journal of Consumer Research*, *35*, 472–82.

Goode, J. (2010). The role of gender dynamics in decisions on credit and debt in low income families. *Critical Social Policy*, *30*, 99–119.

Goode, J., Callender, C., & Lister, R. (1998). *Purse or wallet? Gender inequalities and income distribution within families on benefits.* London: Policy Studies Institute.

Goodman, P. S., & Friedman, A. (1971). An examination of Adams' theory of inequity. *Administrative Science Quarterly*, *16*, 271–88.

Gore, S. (1978). The effect of social support in moderating the health consequences of unemployment. *Journal of Health and Social Behavior*, *19*, 157–65.

Gosselin, E. (2000). La nature, la direction et l'intensité de la relation unissant la satisfaction au travail et la satisfaction hors travail: une analyse psycho-temporelle [The nature, direction and intensity of the relationship between job satisfaction and satisfaction outside work: A psycho-temporal analysis] (unpublished thesis). University of Montreal, School of Industrial Relations, Canada.

Gourville, J. T., & Soman, D. (1998). Payment depreciation: The behavioral effects of temporally separating payments from consumption. *Journal of Consumer Research*, *25*, 160–74.

Graffeo, M., Ritov, I., Bonini, N., & Hadjichristidis, C. (2015). To make people save energy tell them what others do but also who they are: A preliminary study. *Frontiers in Psychology*, *6*, 1287.

Granberg, D., & Brown, T. A. (1995). The Monty Hall dilemma. *Personality and Social Psychology Bulletin*, *21*, 711–23.

Granbois, D. H., & Summers, J. O. (1975). Primary and secondary validity of consumer purchase probabilities. *Journal of Consumer Research*, *1*, 31–8.

Grau, U., & Thomsen, K. (1985). Die Attribuierung des Vorwurfs der Arbeitsunwilligkeit. Zur Rolle der Arbeitslosen [The attribution of the charge of unwillingness to work. On the role of the unemployed]. In T. Kieselbach & A. Wacker (eds.), *Individuelle und gesellschaftliche Kosten der Massenarbeitslosigkeit* (pp. 107–19). Weinheim: Beltz.

Gravelle, H., & Rees, R. (1981). *Microeconomics*. London: Longman.

Gray-Little, B., & Burks, N. (1983). Power and satisfaction in marriage: A review and critique. *Psychological Bulletin*, *93*, 513–38.

Green, D. P., Kahneman, D., & Kunreuther, H. (1994). How the scope and method of public funding affect willingness to pay for public goods. *Public Opinion Quarterly*, *58*, 49–67.

Greenberg, J. (1982). Approaching equity and avoiding inequity in groups and organizations. In J. Greenberg & R. J. Cohen (eds.), *Equity and justice in social behavior* (pp. 389–435). New York: Academic Press.

(1983). Equity and equality as clues to the relationship between exchange participants. *European Journal of Social Psychology*, *13*, 195–6.

(1988). Equity and workplace status: A field experiment. *Journal of Applied Psychology*, *73*, 606–13.

(1990). Employee theft as a reaction to underpayment inequity: The hidden costs of pay cuts. *Journal of Applied Psychology*, *75*, 561–8.

Greenwald, A. G. (1968). Cognitive learning, cognitive response to persuasion, and attitude change. In A. G. Greenwald, T. C. Brock, & T. M. Ostrom (eds.), *Psychological foundations of attitudes* (pp. 147–70). San Diego, CA: Academic Press.

Greitemeyer, T., Schulz-Hardt, S., Popien, G., & Frey, D. (2005). Der Einfluss versunkener monetärer und zeitlicher Kosten auf Ressourcenallokationen [The influence of sunk monetary and time costs on resource allocation]. *Zeitschrift für Arbeits- und Organisationspsychologie*, *49*, 35–43.

Greitemeyer, T., Schulz-Hardt, S., Traut-Mattausch, E., & Frey, D. (2002). Erwartungsgeleitete Wahrnehmung bei der Einführung des Euro: Der Euro ist nicht immer ein Teuro [Expectation-guided perception during the introduction of the euro: The euro is not always a Teuro]. *Wirtschaftspsychologie*, *4*, 22–8.

(2005). The influence of price trend expectations on price trend estimates: Why the euro seems to make life more expensive. *Journal of Economic Psychology*, *26*, 541–8.

Greitemeyer, T., Traut-Mattausch, E., & Frey, D. (2008). *Psychologische Konsequenzen der Euro-Einführung* [Psychological consequences of the introduction of the euro] (Information 7). Munich: Roman Herzog Institut.

Gribnau, H. (2015a). Corporate social responsibility and tax planning: Not by rules alone. *Social & Legal Studies*, *24*, 225–50.

(2015b). Corporate compliance: Some procedural tax law issues. In R. Russo (ed.), *Tax assurance* (pp. 183–216). Deventer: Kluwer.

Grimm, J. (2006). *Ergebnisse der Glücksforschung als Leitfaden für politisches Handeln?* [Results of happiness research as a guide for political action?] (Discussion Paper 14). Flensburg: University of Flensburg, International Institute of Management.

Grinblatt, M., Keloharju, M., & Linnainmaa, J. T. (2012). IQ, trading behavior, and performance. *Journal of Financial Economics*, *104*, 339–62.

Groenland, E. A. G. (1992). Developing a dynamic research strategy for the economic psychological study of taxation. *Journal of Economic Psychology*, *13*, 589–96.

Groenland, E. A. G., Bloem, J. G., & Kuylen, A. A. A. (1996). Prototypicality and structure of the saving concept for consumers. *Journal of Economic Psychology*, *17*, 691–708.

Groenland, E. A. G., & Van Veldhoven, G. M. (1983). Tax evasion and mechanisms of social control: A comparison with grand and petty theft. *Journal of Economic Psychology*, *2*, 213–30.

Groenland, E. A. G., & Wahlund, R. (1996). Household saving behaviour and financial management. *Journal of Economic Psychology*, *17*, 669–75.

Guala, F., & Mittone, L. (2005). Experiments in economics: External validity and the robustness of phenomena. *Journal of Economic Methodology*, *12*, 495–515.

Gummerum, M., Hanoch, Y., Keller, M., Parsons, K., & Hummel, A. (2010). Preschoolers' allocations in the dictator game: The role of moral emotions. *Journal of Economic Psychology*, *31*, 25–34.

Gunnarsson, J., & Wahlund, R. (1997). Household financial strategies in Sweden: An explanatory study. *Journal of Economic Psychology*, *18*, 201–33.

Guo, Z. (2002). Behavioral Finance: Die empirische Überprüfbarkeit behavioraler Modelle [Behavioral finance: The empirical testability of behavioural models] (unpublished thesis 2625). University of St Gallen.

Gupta, V. K., Turban, D. B., Wasti, S. A., & Sikdar, A. (2009). The role of gender: Stereotypes in perceptions of entrepreneurs and intention to become an entrepreneur. *Entrepreneurship Theory and Practice*, *33*, 397–417.

Gurtner, A., Tschan, F., Semmer, N., & Nägele, C. (2007). Getting groups to develop good strategies: Effects of reflexivity interventions on team process, team performance, and shared mental models. *Organizational Behavior and Human Decision Processes*, *102*, 127–42.

Güth, W. (1994). Distributive justice. A behavioral theory and empirical evidence. In H. Brandstätter & W. Güth (eds.), *Essays on economic psychology* (pp. 153–76). Berlin: Springer.

(1999). *Spieltheorie und ökonomische (Bei)Spiele* [Game theory and economic games and examples] (2nd edn). Berlin: Springer.

Güth, W., & Kocher, M. (2014). More than thirty years of ultimatum bargaining experiments: Motives, variations, and a survey of the recent literature. *Journal of Economic Behavior & Organization*, *108*, 396–409.

Güth, W., & Tietz, R. (1990). Ultimatum bargain behavior – a survey and comparison of experimental results. *Journal of Economic Psychology*, *11*, 417–49.

Hackman, J. R., & Oldham, G. R. (1976). Motivation through the design of work: Test of a theory. *Organizational Behavior and Human Performance*, *16*, 250–79.

Haferkamp, A., Fetchenhauer, D., Belschak, F., & Enste, D. (2009). Efficiency versus fairness: The evaluation of labor market policies by economists and laypeople. *Journal of Economic Psychology*, *30*, 527–39.

Hahn, L., Hoelzl, E., & Pollai, M. (2013). The effect of payment type on product-related emotions: Evidence from an experimental study. *International Journal of Consumer Studies*, *37*, 21–8.

Halleröd, B., Díaz-Martínez, C., & Stocks, J. (2007). Doing gender while doing couple: Concluding remarks. In J. Stocks, C. Díaz-Martínez, & B. Halleröd (eds.), *Modern couples sharing money, sharing life* (pp. 143–55). Basingstoke: Palgrave Macmillan.

Hallsworth, M. (2014). The use of field experiments to increase tax compliance. *Oxford Review of Economic Policy*, *30*, 658–79.

Hallsworth, M., List, J. A., Metcalfe, R. D., & Vlaev, I. (2014). *The behavioralist as tax collector: Using natural field experiments to enhance tax compliance* (NBER Working Paper 20007). Cambridge, MA: National Bureau of Economic Research.

Halpern, D. (2015). *Inside the nudge unit: How small changes can make a big difference*. London: H. W. Allen.

Hamermesh, D. S. (2011). *Beauty pays: Why attractive people are more successful*. Princeton, NJ: Princeton University Press.

Hamermesh, D. S., & Biddle, J. E. (1994). Beauty and the labor market. *American Economic Review*, *84*, 1174–94.

Hammond, J. S., Keeney, R. L., & Raiffa, H. (1998). The hidden traps in decision making. *Harvard Business Review*, *76*, 47–58.

Hammond, K. R. (1996). *Human judgment and social policy*. Oxford: Oxford University Press.

Hanf, C.-H., & von Wersebe, B. (1994). Price, quality, and consumers' behaviour. *Journal of Consumer Policy*, *17*, 335–48.

Hansen, P. G., Jespersen, A. M., & Skov, L. R. (2015). Size matters! A choice architectural field experiment in reducing food waste. *Menu: Journal of Food and Hospitality Research*, *4*, 11–15.

Hansmeyer, K.-H., & Mackscheidt, K. (1977). Finanzpsychologie [Financial psychology]. In F. Neumark, N. Andel, & H. Haller (eds.), *Handbuch der Finanzwissenschaft* (3rd edn, vol. 1, pp. 553–83). Tübingen: J. C. B. Mohr (Paul Siebeck).

Hantrais, L. (1999). Socio-demographic change, policy impacts and outcomes in social Europe. *Journal of European Social Policy*, *9*, 291–309.

Harcar, T., & Spillan, J. E. (2006). Exploring Latin American family decision-making using correspondence analysis. *Journal of World Business*, *41*, 221–32.

Häring, N., & Storbeck, O. (2007). *Ökonomie 2.0: 99 überraschende Erkenntnisse* [Economics 2.0: 99 surprising findings]. Stuttgart: Schäffer-Poeschel.

Harrison, R. (1976). The demoralizing experience of prolonged unemployment. *Department of Employment Gazette*, *4*, 339–48.

Harter, J. K., Schmidt, F. L., & Hayes, T. L. (2002). Business-unit-level relationship between employee satisfaction, employee engagement, and business outcomes: A meta-analysis. *Journal of Applied Psychology*, *87*, 268–79.

Hartl, B., Kirchler, E., & Muehlbacher, S. (2013). Geschlechtsstereotype auf Führungsebene zwischen 1974 und 2010. Eine Analyse verstorbener weiblicher und männlicher Führungskräfte [Gender stereotypes on leadership level between 1974 and 2010. An analysis of deceased female and male leaders]. *Zeitschrift für Arbeits- und Organisationspsychologie*, *57*, 121–31.

Hartley, J. (1980). Psychological approaches to unemployment. *Bulletin of the British Psychological Society*, *33*, 412–14.

Hartner, M., Rechberger, S., Kirchler, E., & Wenzel, M. (2011). Perceived distributive fairness of EU transfer payments, outcome favorability, identity, and EU-tax compliance. *Law & Policy*, *33*, 59–81.

Hartner-Tiefenthaler, M., Kubicek, B., Kirchler, E., Rechberger, S., & Wenzel, M. (2012). Perceived distributive fairness of European transfer payments and EU-taxes in Austria, the Czech Republic, and the United Kingdom. *Applied Psychology: An International Review*, *61*, 454–78.

Hastie, R. (1982). Comment: consumers' memory for product knowledge. In A. Mitchell (ed.), *Advances in consumer research* (vol. 9, pp. 72–3). Ann Arbor, MI: Association for Consumer Research.

Hatfield, E., & Traupmann, J. (1981). Intimate relationships: A perspective from equity theory. In S. W. Duck & R. Gilmour (eds.), *Personal relationships, vol. 1, Studying personal relationships* (pp. 165–78). London: Academic Press.

Hatfield, E., Traupmann, J., Sprecher, S., Utne, M., & Hay, J. (1985). Equity and intimate relations: Recent research. In W. Ickes (ed.), *Compatible and incompatible relationships* (pp. 91–117). New York: Springer.

Hatfield, E., Utne, M. K., & Traupman, J. (1979). Equity theory and intimate relationships. In R. L. Burgess & T. L. Huston (eds.), *Social exchange in developing relationships* (pp. 99–133). New York: Academic Press.

Hawkins, S. A., & Hastie, R. (1990). Hindsight: Biased judgments of past events after the outcomes are known. *Psychological Bulletin*, *107*, 311–27.

Haws, K. L., Bearden, W. O., & Nenkov, G. Y. (2012). Consumer spending self-control effectiveness and outcome elaboration prompts. *Journal of the Academy of Marketing Science*, *40*, 695–710.

Hayati, D., & Karami, E. (2005). Typology of causes of poverty: The perception of Iranian farmers. *Journal of Economic Psychology*, *26*, 884–901.

Heath, C., Huddart, S., & Lang, M. (1999). Psychological factors and stock option exercise. *Quarterly Journal of Economics*, *114*, 601–27.

Heath, C., & Soll, J. B. (1996). Mental budgeting and consumer decisions. *Journal of Consumer Research*, *23*, 40–52.

Heckhausen, H. (1989). *Motivation und Handeln* [Motivation and behaviour] (2nd edn). Berlin: Springer.

Hedesström, T., Svedsäter, H., & Gärling, T. (2007). Determinants of the use of heuristic choice rules in the Swedish premium pension scheme: An internet-based survey. *Journal of Economic Psychology*, *28*, 113–26.

Hegtvedt, K. A. (1989). Fairness conceptualizations and comparable worth. *Journal of Social Issues*, *45*, 81–97.

Heidhues, P., & Kőszegi, B. (2010). Exploiting naïvete about self-control in the credit market. *American Economic Review*, *100*, 2279–303.

Heifetz, A., & Pauzner, A. (2005). Backward induction with players who doubt others' faultlessness. *Mathematical Social Sciences*, *50*, 252–67.

Hektner, J. M., Schmidt, J. A., & Csikszentmihalyi, M. (2007). *Experience sampling method: Measuring the quality of everyday life*. London: Sage.

Helliwell, J., & Huang, H. (2008). How's your government? International evidence linking good government and well-being. *British Journal of Political Science*, *38*, 595–619.

Helson, H. (1964). *Adaptation-level theory*. Oxford: Harper & Row.

Henrich, J., Boyd, R., Bowles, S., Camerer, C., Fehr, E., Gintis, H., & McElreath, R. (2001). In search of Homo economicus: Behavioral experiments in 15 small-scale societies. *American Economic Review*, *91*, 73–8.

Henrichsmeyer, W., Gans, O., & Evers, I. (1982). *Einführung in die Volkswirtschaftslehre* [Introduction to economics]. Stuttgart: UTB-Ulmer.

Henry, S. (1978). *The hidden economy*. London: Martin Robertson.

Hepworth, S. J. (1980). Moderating factors of the psychological impacts of unemployment. *Journal of Occupational Psychology*, *53*, 139–45.

Herkner, W. (1993). *Lehrbuch Sozialpsychologie* [Textbook social psychology] (5th edn). Berne: Huber.

Herrnstein, R. J. (1961). Relative and absolute strength of responses as a function of frequency of reinforcement. *Journal of the Experimental Analysis of Behaviour*, *4*, 267–72.

(1990). Rational choice theory: Necessary but not sufficient. *American Psychologist*, *45*, 356–67.

(1991). Experiments on stable suboptimality in individual behavior. *American Economic Review*, *81*, 360–4.

Herrnstein, R. J., Loewenstein, G., Prelec, D., & Vaughan, W. Jr. (1993). Utility maximization and melioration: Internalities in individual choice. *Journal of Behavioral Decision Making*, *6*, 149–85.

Herrnstein, R. J., & Prelec, D. (1991). Melioration: A theory of distributed choice. *Journal of Economic Perspectives*, *5*, 137–56.

Hertwig, R., & Herzog, S. M. (2009). Fast and frugal heuristics: Tolls of social rationality. *Social Cognition*, *27*, 661–98.

Hertwig, R., & Ortmann, A. (2001). Experimental practices in economics: A methodological challenge for psychologists? *Behavioral and Brain Sciences*, *24*, 383–403.

Hessing, D. J., Elffers, H., & Weigel, R. (1988). Exploring the limits of self-reports and reasoned action: An investigation of the psychology of tax evasion behavior. *Journal of Personality and Social Psychology*, *54*, 405–13.

Hessing, D. J., Kinsey, K. A., Elffers, H., & Weigel, R. H. (1988). Tax evasion behavior: Measurement strategies and theoretical models. In W. F. van Raaij, G. M. Van Veldhoven, & K.-E. Wärneryd (eds.), *Handbook of economic psychology* (pp. 517–37). Dordrecht: Kluwer.

Hewstone, M., Jaspars, J., & Lalljee, M. (1982). Social representations, social attribution and social identity: The intergroup attribution images of 'public' and 'comprehensive' schoolboys. *European Journal of Social Psychology*, *12*, 241–69.

Hey, J. D. (1991). *Experiments in economics*. Oxford: Blackwell.

Heyman, J., & Ariely, D. (2004). Effort for payment: A tale of two markets. *Psychological Science*, *15*, 787–93.

Higgins, E. T. (1997). Beyond pleasure and pain. *American Psychologist*, *52*, 1280–1300.

(1998). Promotion and prevention: Regulatory focus as a motivational principle. In M. P. Zanna (ed.), *Advances in experimental social psychology* (vol. 30, pp. 1–46). San Diego, CA: Academic Press.

Hilgert, M. A., Hogarth, J. M., and Beverly, S. G. (2003). Household financial management: The connection between knowledge and behavior. *Federal Reserve Bulletin*, *89*, 309–22.

Hill, J. (1978). The psychological impact of unemployment. *New Society*, *43*, 118–20.

Hill, R. (1972). Modern systems theory and the family: A confrontation. *Social Science Information*, *10*, 7–26.

Hill, R. B. (1992). The work ethic as determined by occupation, education, age, gender, work experience and empowerment. *Dissertation Abstracts International*, 53-07A, 2343.

Hilpert, H. R. (1981). Psychische und psychosomatische Beschwerdebilder bei Arbeitslosen [Psychic and psychosomatic symptoms among the unemployed]. *Zeitschrift für Arbeits- und Organisationspsychologie*, *3*, 151–9.

Himmelweit, S., Santos, C., Sevilla, A., & Sofer, C. (2013). Sharing of resources within the family and the economics of household decision making. *Journal of Marriage and Family*, *75*, 625–39.

Hirschman, E. C., & Holbrook, M. B. (1982). Hedonic consumption: Emerging concepts, methods, and propositions. *Journal of Marketing*, *46*, 92–101.

Hirshleifer, H., & Shumway, T. (2003). Good day sunshine: Stock returns and the weather. *Journal of Finance*, *58*, 1009–32.

Hirst, D. E., Joyce, E. J., & Schadewald, M. S. (1994). Mental accounting and outcome contiguity in consumer-borrowing decisions. *Organizational Behavior and Human Decision Processes*, *58*, 136–52.

Hirst, W., Phelps, E. A., Meksin, R., Vaidya, C. J., Johnson, M. K., Mitchell, K. J., . . . & Olsson, A. (2015). A ten-year follow-up of a study of memory for the attack of September 11, 2001: Flashbulb memories and memories for flashbulb events. *Journal of Experimental Psychology: General*, *144*, 604–23.

Hite, P. A. (1987). An application of attribution theory in taxpayer noncompliance research. *Public Finance*, *42*, 105–18.

(1988). An examination of the impact of subject selection on hypothetical and self-reported taxpayer noncompliance. *Journal of Economic Psychology*, *9*, 445–66.

Hjorth-Andersen, C. (1992). Alternative interpretations of price–quality-relations. *Journal of Consumer Policy*, *15*, 71–82.

Hmieleski, K. M., & Baron, R. A. (2008). When does entrepreneurial self-efficacy enhance versus reduce firm performance? *Strategic Entrepreneurship Journal*, *2*, 57–72.

Hoelzl, E. (2015). *Consumer credit decisions in a dual-process perspective. DFG-Grant HO 4767/2–1 proposal within the research unit FOR 1882: Psychoeconomics*. University of Cologne.

Hoelzl, E., Kamleitner, B., & Kirchler, E. (2011). Loan repayment plans as sequences of instalments. *Journal of Economic Psychology*, *32*, 621–31.

Hoelzl, E., & Kirchler, E. (2005). Attribution and hindsight bias for economic developments. *Applied Psychology*, *90*, 167–74.

Hoelzl, E., Kirchler, E., & Rodler, C. (2002). Hindsight bias in economic expectations: I knew all along what I want to hear. *Applied Psychology*, *87*, 437–43.

Hoelzl, E., Pollai, M., & Kamleitner, B. (2009). Experience, prediction and recollection of loan burden. *Journal of Economic Psychology*, *30*, 446–54.

Hoeve, M., Stams, G. J. J., van der Zouwen, M., Vergeer, M., Jurrius, K., & Asscher, J. J. (2014). A systematic review of financial debt in adolescents and young adults: Prevalence, correlates and associations with crime. *PloS ONE*, *9*, e104909.

Hoff, E.-H. (1986). *Arbeit, Freizeit und Persönlichkeit: wissenschaftliche und alltägliche Vorstellungsmuster* [Work, leisure and personality: Scientific and everyday patterns of representation]. Berne: Huber.

(1993). Freizeit [Leisure]. In A. Schorr (ed.), *Handwörterbuch der Angewandten Psychologie* (pp. 249–55). Bonn: Deutscher Psychologen Verlag.

Hoffrage, U., & Reimer, T. (2004). Models of bounded rationality: The approach of fast and frugal heuristics. *Management Revue*, *15*, 437–57.

Hofmann, E., Gangl, K., Kirchler, E., & Stark, J. (2014). Enhancing tax compliance through coercive and legitimate power of tax authorities by concurrently diminishing or facilitating trust in tax authorities. *Law & Policy*, *36*, 290–313.

Hofmann, E., Kamleitner, B., Kirchler, E., & Schulz-Hardt, S. (2006). Kaufkraftschwund nach der Währungsumstellung. Zur erwartungsgeleiteten Wahrnehmung des (T)Euro [Purchase power loss after the currency changeover: on the expectation-based perception of the (T)euro]. *Wirtschaftspsychologie*, *8*, 98–108.

Holbrook, M. B., & Hirschman, E. C. (1982). The experiential aspects of consumption: Consumer fantasies, feelings, and fun. *Journal of Consumer Research*, *9*, 132–40.

Holt, D. B. (1995). How consumers consume: A typology of consumption practices. *Journal of Consumer Research*, *22*, 1–16.

Homans, G. C. (1961). *Social behavior: Its elementary forms*. New York: Harcourt, Brace & World.

(1974). *Social behaviour: Its elementary forms* (2nd edn). New York: Harcourt, Brace Javanovich.

Hopson, B., & Adams, J. (1976). Towards an understanding: Defining some boundaries of transition dynamics. In J. Adams, J. Hayes, & B. Hopson (eds.), *Transition: Understanding and managing personal change* (pp. 3–25). London: Martin Robertson.

Hornik, J. (1982). Situational effects on the consumption of time. *Journal of Marketing*, *46*, 44–55.

Howard, J., & Sheth, J. N. (1969). *The theory of buyer behavior*. New York: Wiley.

Hsee, C. K., & Rottenstreich, Y. (2004). Music, pandas, and muggers: On the affective psychology of value. *Journal of Experimental Psychology: General*, *133*, 23–30.

Hubel, W. (1986). *Der Einfluß der Familienmitglieder auf gemeinsame Kaufentscheidungen* [The influence of family members on joint purchasing decisions]. Berlin: Duncker und Humblot.

Huber, O. (2007). Behavior in risky decisions: Focus on risk defusing. In M. Abdellaoui, R. D. Luce, M. Machina & B. Munier (eds.), *Uncertainty and risk: Mental, formal, experimental representations* (pp. 291–306). Berlin: Springer.

(2012). Risky decisions: Active risk management. *Current Directions in Psychological Science*, *21*, 26–30.

Huber, O., & Huber, O. W. (2003). Detectability of the negative event: Effect on the acceptance of pre- or post-event risk-defusing actions. *Acta Psychologica*, *113*, 1–21.

(2008). Gambles vs. quasi-realistic scenarios: Expectations to find probability and risk-defusing information. *Acta Psychologica*, *127*, 222–36.

Huber, O., & Macho, S. (2001). Probabilistic set-up and the search for probability information in quasi-naturalistic decision tasks. *Risk, Decision and Policy*, *6*, 1–16.

Huikari, S. & Korhonen, M. (2016). The impact of unemployment on well-being: Evidence from the regional level suicide data in Finland. *Social Indicators Research*, *128*, 1103–19.

Hunt, M. O. (2004). Race/ethnicity and beliefs about wealth and poverty. *Social Science Quarterly*, *85*, 827–53.

Hurtig, M.-C., & Pichevin, M.-F. (1990). Salience of the sex category system in person perception: Contextual variations. *Sex Roles*, *22*, 369–95.

Hussmanns, R. (2007). *Measurement of employment, unemployment and underemployment – current international standards and issues in their application*. Geneva: International Labour Organisation. Retrieved from www.ilo.org/wcmsp5/groups/public/–dgreports/–stat/documents/publication/wcms_088394.pdf.

Huston, S. J. (2010). Measuring financial literacy. *Journal of Consumer Affairs*, *44*, 296–316.

(2012). Financial literacy and the cost of borrowing. *International Journal of Consumer Studies*, *36*, 566–72.

Ichheiser, G. (1949). Misunderstanding in human relations: A study in false social perception. *American Journal of Sociology*, *55*, 1–70.

Ikenberry, D. L., Rankine, G., & Stice, E. K. (1996). What do stock splits really signal? *Journal of Financial and Quantitative Analysis*, *31*, 299–317.

Imkamp, H. (2004). Mangelnde Funktionsfähigkeit von Konsumgütermärkten? [Deficient functioning of consumer goods markets?]. *Jahrbuch für Wirtschaftswissenschaften*, *55*, 106–25.

(2008). A new look at old coefficients. The price–quality relationship re-evaluated. *Journal of Consumer Policy*, *31*, 139–45.

Inglehart, R. (1977). *The silent revolution: Changing values and political styles among western publics*. Princeton, NJ: Princeton University Press.

(2000). Globalization and postmodern values. *Washington Quarterly*, *23*, 215–18.

Institute for Government & Cabinet Office (2010). *MINDSPACE: Influencing behaviour through public policy*. London: Institute for Government & Cabinet Office. Retrieved from www.instituteforgovernment.org.uk/our-work/better-policy-making/mindspace-behavioural-economics (accessed 27 November 2016).

Isen, A. M. (2000). Positive affect and decision making. In M. Lewis & J. M. Haviland-Jones (eds.), *Handbook of emotions* (2nd edn, pp. 417–35). London: Guilford.

Isler, L., Popper, E. T., & Ward, A. (1987). Consumer socialisation and frequency of shopping with children. *Journal of the Academy of Marketing Science*, *19*, 155–63.

Jacob, K., & Richter, G. P. (2005). Absichten zur Gründung eines Unternehmens bei Studierenden [Students' intentions related to founding a company]. *Wirtschaftspsychologie*, *2*, 51–70.

Jahoda, M. (1982). *Employment and unemployment: A social-psychological analysis*. Cambridge: Cambridge University Press.

(1983). *Wieviel Arbeit braucht der Mensch?* [How much work does a person need?]. Weinheim: Beltz.

Jahoda, M., Lazarsfeld, P., & Zeisel, H. (1971). *Marienthal: The sociography of an unemployed community*. Chicago, IL: Aldine-Atherton.

James, S. (1992). Taxation and female participation in the labour market. *Journal of Economic Psychology*, *13*, 715–34.

James, S., & Alley, C. (2002). Tax compliance, self-assessment and tax administration. *Journal of Finance and Management in Public Services*, *2*, 27–42.

James, S., Hasseldine, J. D., Hite, P. A., & Toumi, M. (2003). Tax compliance policy: An international comparison and new evidence on normative appeals and auditing. Paper presented at the ESRC Future Governance Workshop, Institute for Advanced Studies, Vienna, December.

Janis, I. L. (1972). *Victims of groupthink*. Boston, MA: Houghton Mifflin.

Janiszewski, C., & Lichtenstein, D. R. (1999). A range theory account of price perception. *Journal of Consumer Research*, *25*, 353–68.

Jann, B. (2008). *Erwerbsarbeit, Einkommen und Geschlecht: Studien zum Schweizer Arbeitsmarkt* [Paid employment, income and gender: Studies on the labor market in Switzerland]. Wiesbaden: VS Verlag für Sozialwissenschaften.

Jebabli, I., Arouri, M., & Teulon, F. (2014). On the effects of world stock market and oil price shocks on food prices: An empirical investigation based on TVP-VAR models with stochastic volatility. *Energy Economics*, *45*, 66–98.

Jin, J., & Rounds, J. (2012). Stability and change in work values: A meta-analysis of longitudinal studies. *Journal of Vocational Behavior*, *80*, 326–39.

Johnson, E., Camerer, C., Sen, S., & Rymon, T. (2002). Detecting failures of backward induction: Monitoring information search in sequential bargaining. *Journal of Economic Theory*, *104*, 16–47.

Johnson, E., Häubl, G., & Keinan, A. (2007). Aspects of endowment. A query theory of value construction. *Journal of Experimental Psychology: Learning, Memory, and Cognition*, *33*, 461–74.

Johnson, E., & Sherraden, M. S. (2007). From financial literacy to financial capability among youth. *Journal of Sociology and Social Welfare*, *34*, 119–46.

Johnson, H. B., & Hagerman, M. A. (2006). Kids' talk about class divides: Privileged children's perspectives on social class inequality. Paper presented at the Conference of the American Sociological Association, Montreal, August.

Johnson, N. D., & Mislin, A. A. (2011). Trust games: A meta-analysis. *Journal of Economic Psychology*, *32*, 865–89.

Jonas, E., & Frey, D. (2003). Searching for information about financial decisions in euro versus DM. *European Psychologist*, *8*, 92–6.

Jonas, E., Fritsche, I., & Greenberg, J. (2005). Currencies as cultural symbols – an existential psychological perspective on reactions of Germans toward the Euro. *Journal of Economic Psychology*, *26*, 129–46.

Jonas, E., Greitemeyer, T., Frey, D., & Schulz-Hardt, S. (2002). Psychological effects of the euro – experimental research on the perception of salaries and price estimations. *European Journal of Social Psychology*, *32*, 147–69.

Jonas, E., Greitemeyer, T., Graupmann, V., & Frey, D. (2002). Gewöhnung an den Euro – experimentelle Untersuchungen zur Schätzung von Preisen in DM vs. Euro vor und nach der Einführung des Euro [Adaption to the euro – experimental studies on price estimation in German marks vs. euro before and after the introduction of the euro]. *Wirtschaftspsychologie*, *4*, 29–35.

Judge, T. A., Locke, E. A., Durham, C. C., & Kluger, A. N. (1998). Dispositional effects on job and life satisfaction: The role of core evaluations. *Journal of Applied Psychology*, *83*, 17–34.

Jünemann, B., & Schellenberger, D. (eds.) (1997). *Psychologie für Börsenprofis: Die Macht der Gefühle bei der Geldanlage* [Psychology for stock market professionals: The power of feelings in investing]. Stuttgart: Schäffer-Poeschel.

Jung, J. Y., & Mellers, B. A. (2016). American attitudes towards nudges. *Judgment and Decision Making*, *11*, 62–74.

Jungermann, H., Brachinger, H. W., Belting, J., Grinberg, K., & Zacharias, E. (2007). The euro changeover and the factors influencing perceived inflation. *Journal of Consumer Policy*, *30*, 405–19.

Jungermann, H., Pfister, H.-R., & Fischer, K. (2010). *Die Psychologie der Entscheidung* [Psychology of decision-making]. Heidelberg: Spektrum.

Kahneman, D. (1994). New challenges to the rationality assumption. *Journal of Institutional and Theoretical Economics / Zeitschrift für die gesamte Staatswissenschaft*, *150*, 18–36.

(1999). Objective happiness. In D. Kahneman, E. Diener & N. Schwarz (eds.), *Well-being: The foundations of hedonic psychology* (pp. 3–25). New York: Sage.

(2003). A perspective of judgment and choice. *American Psychologist*, *58*, 697–720.

(2006). Glück durch Geld ist eine Illusion [Happiness through money is an illusion]. Interview with Philip Wolff for the *Süddeutsche Zeitung*, 31 October. Retrieved from www.sued

deutsche.de/wissen/643/301640/text/ (accessed 13 July 2016).

(2011). *Thinking, fast and slow.* New York: Farrar, Straus and Giroux.

Kahneman, D., & Deaton, A. (2010). High income improves evaluation of life but not emotional well-being. *Proceedings of the National Academy of Sciences*, *107*, 16489–93.

Kahneman, D., Diener, E., & Schwarz, N. (eds.) (1999). *Well-being: The foundations of hedonic psychology.* New York: Sage.

Kahneman, D., & Frederick, S. (2002). Representativeness revisited: Attribute substitution in intuitive judgment. In T. Gilovich, D. Griffin, & D. Kahneman (eds.), *Heuristics and biases: The psychology of intuitive judgment* (pp. 49–81). Cambridge: Cambridge University Press.

Kahneman, D., Fredrickson, B. L., Schreiber, C. A., & Redelmeier, D. A. (1993). When more pain is preferred to less: Adding a better end. *Psychological Science*, *4*, 401–5.

Kahneman, D., Higgins, D., Hall, R., & Riepe, M. W. (1998). Aspects of investor psychology. Beliefs, preferences, and biases investment advisors should know about. *Journal of Portfolio Management*, *24*, 1–21.

Kahneman, D., & Klein, G. (2009). Conditions for intuitive expertise. *American Psychologist*, *64*, 515–26.

Kahneman, D., Knetsch, J. L., & Thaler, R. (1990). Experimental tests of the endowment effect and the Coase theorem. *Journal of Political Economy*, *98*, 1325–48.

Kahneman, D., & Krueger, A. B. (2006). Developments in the measurement of subjective well-being. *Journal of Economic Perspectives*, *20*, 3–24.

Kahneman, D, Krueger, A. B., Schkade, D. A., Schwarz, N., & Stone, A. A. (2004). A survey method for characterizing daily life experience: The day reconstruction method. *Science*, *306*, 1776–80.

Kahneman, D., Slovic, P., & Tversky, A. (1982). *Judgment under uncertainty: Heuristics and biases*. Cambridge: Cambridge University Press.

Kahneman, D., & Tversky, A. (1973). On the psychology of prediction. *Psychological Review*, *80*, 237–51.

(1979). Prospect theory: an analysis of decision under risk. *Econometrica*, *47*, 263–91.

(1984). Choices, values, and frames. *American Psychologist*, *39*, 341–50.

Kalleberg, A. L., & Marsden, P. V. (2013). Changing work values in the United States, 1973–2006. *Social Science Research*, *42*, 225–70.

Kalliath, T., & Brough, P. (2008). Work–life balance: A review of the meaning of the balance construct. *Journal of Management and Organization*, *14*, 323–7.

Kaltenthaler, K., & Anderson, C. (2001). Europeans and their money. Explaining public support for the common European currency. *European Journal of Political Research*, *40*, 139–70.

Kalugina, E., Radtchenko, N., & Sofer, C. (2009). How do spouses share their full income? Identification of the sharing rule using self-reported income. *Review of Income and Wealth*, *55*, 360–91.

Kamleitner, B., Hoelzl, E., & Kirchler, E. (2012). Credit use: Psychological perspectives on a multifaceted phenomenon. *International Journal of Psychology*, *47*, 1–27.

Kamleitner, B., & Kirchler, E. (2007). Consumer credit use: A process model and literature review. *Revue Européenne de Psychologie Appliquée / European Review of Applied Psychology*, *57*, 267–83.

Kan, M. Y., & Laurie, H. (2011). *Savings, investments, debts and psychological well-being in married and cohabiting couples* (ISER Working Paper 2010–42). Colchester: Institute for Social and Economic Research, University of Essex.

Kanfer, R., & Hulin, C. (1985). Individual differences in successful job searches following lay-off. *Personnel Psychology*, *38*, 835–48.

Kanner, A. D., Coyne, J. C., Schaefer, C., & Lazarus, R. S. (1981). Comparison of two modes of stress measurement: Daily hassles and uplifts versus major life events. *Journal of Behavioral Medicine*, *4*, 1–39.

Kaplanski, G., & Levy, H. (2010). Sentiment and stock prices: The case of aviation disasters. *Journal of Financial Economics*, *95*, 174–201.

Kastlunger, B., Dressler, S., Kirchler, E., Mittone, L., & Voracek, M. (2010). Sex differences in tax compliance: Differentiating between demographic sex, gender-role orientation, and prenatal masculinization (2D:4D). *Journal of Economic Psychology*, *31*, 542–52.

Kastlunger, B., Kirchler, E., Mittone, L., & Pitters, J. (2009). Sequences of audits, tax compliance, and taxpaying strategies. *Journal of Economic Psychology*, *30*, 405–18.

Katona, G. (1951). *Psychological analysis of economic behavior.* New York: Elsevier.

(1975). *Psychological economics*. Amsterdam: Elsevier.

Katona, G., Strümpel, B., & Zahn, E. (1971). *Zwei Wege zur Prosperität* [Two ways to prosperity]. Düsseldorf: Econ.

Kaun, D. E. (2005). Income and happiness: Earning and spending as sources of discontent. *Journal of Socio-Economics*, *34*, 135–50.

Kaynak, E., & Harcar, T. (2001). Consumers' attitudes and intentions towards credit card usage in an advanced developing country. *Journal of Financial Services Marketing*, *6*, 24–39.

Ke, D., Ng, L., & Wang, Q. (2009). Home bias in foreign investment decisions. *Journal of International Business Studies*, *41*, 960–79.

Keller, G. (2010). *Green Henry* (trans. A. M. Holt). Richmond: Calder.

Kelly, M. (1997). Do noise traders influence stock prices? *Journal of Money, Credit, and Banking*, *29*, 351–63.

Kemp, S. (1987). Estimation of past prices. *Journal of Economic Psychology*, *8*, 181–9.

(2004). Preferences for funding particular government services from flat or progressive tax. Paper presented at the Joint SABE/IAREP Annual Colloquium, Philadelphia, PA.

Kempson, E., Collard S., & Moore, N. (2005). *Measuring financial capability: an exploratory study* (Consumer Research Report 37, June). London: Financial Services Authority.

Keynes, J. M. (1936/1997). *The general theory of employment, interest and money.* New York: Harcourt, Brace & World.

Khan, S., Murray, R. P., & Barnes, G. E. (2002). A structural equation model of the effect of poverty and unemployment on alcohol abuse. *Addictive Behaviors*, *27*, 405–23.

Kiell, G., Müller-Peters, A., & Fischer, L. (2002). Steigende Europäische Identität bei den Deutschen – Ergebnisse einer Längsschnittstudie [Increasing European identity among Germans – results of a longitudinal study]. *Wirtschaftspsychologie*, *4*, 61–70.

Kieselbach, T., & Offe, H. (1979). Psychologische, gesundheitliche, soziale und politische Probleme als Folge von Arbeitslosigkeit: Ein kritischer Überblick [Psychological, health-related, social and political problems as a consequence of unemployment: A critical overview]. In T. Kieselbach & H. Offe (eds.), *Arbeitslosigkeit: individuelle Verarbeitung, gesellschaftlicher Hintergrund* (pp. 7–140). Darmstadt: Steinkopff.

Kieselbach, T., & Schindler, H. (1984). *Psychosoziale Auswirkungen von Arbeitslosigkeit und Hindernisse für eine Aktivierung Arbeitsloser* [Psychosocial effects of unemployment and obstacles to activating the unemployed]. (Bremer Beiträge zur Psychologie, Reihe C: Berichte aus der Wissenschaftlichen Einheit 'Arbeit, Arbeitslosigkeit und Persönlichkeitsentwicklung', 32). Bremen: University Bremen.

King, S., & Sheffrin, S. M. (2002). Tax evasion and equity theory: An investigative approach. *International Tax and Public Finance*, *9*, 505–21.

Kirchler, E. (1984a). *Alltagsbefinden und Arbeitslosigkeit* [Everyday well-being and unemployment]. Linz: Trauner.

(1984b). Befinden von Wehrpflichtigen in Abhängigkeit von personellen und situativen Gegebenheiten [The condition of military recruits dependent on personal and situational factors]. *Psychologie und Praxis*, *28*, 16–25.

(1988a). Diary reports on daily economic decisions of happy versus unhappy couples. *Journal of Economic Psychology*, *9*, 327–57.

(1988b). Marital happiness and interaction in everyday surroundings: A time sample diary approach for couples. *Journal of Social and Personal Relationships, 5*, 375–82.

(1989). *Kaufentscheidungen im privaten Haushalt* [Purchasing decisions in private households]. Göttingen: Hogrefe.

(1990). Spouses' influence strategies in purchase decisions as dependent on conflict type and relationship characteristics. *Journal of Economic Psychology*, *11*, 101–18.

(1992). Adorable woman, expert man – changing gender images of women and men in management. *European Journal of Social Psychology*, *22*, 363–73.

(1993a). *Arbeitslosigkeit: Psychologische Skizzen über ein anhaltendes Problem* [Unemployment: Psychological sketches of a persistent problem]. Göttingen: Hogrefe.

(1993b). Beeinflussungstaktiken von Eheleuten: Entwicklung und Erprobung eines Instrumentes zur Erfassung der Anwendungshäufigkeit verschiedener Beeinflussungstaktiken in familiären Kaufentscheidungen [Influence tactics of spouses: Development and testing of an instrument to measure the frequency of applicaton of various influence tactics in familial purchase decisions]. *Zeitschrift für Experimentelle und Angewandte Psychologie*, *40*, 102–31.

(1993c). Spouses' joint purchase decisions: Determinants of influence strategies to muddle through the process. *Journal of Economic Psychology*, *14*, 405–38.

(1996). *Zur Erfassung der Komplexität von ökonomischen Entscheidungen im privaten Haushalt und der Entscheidungsgeschichte* [On the measurement of the complexity of economic decisions in private households and their decision-making history]. Research presentation to the 40th Congress of the Deutsche Gesellschaft für Psychologie, September (German Psychological Society), Munich.

(1997a). The burden of new taxes: Acceptance of taxes as a function of affectedness and egoistic versus altruistic orientation. *Journal of Socio-Economics*, *26*, 421–37.

(1997b). Balance between giving and receiving: Tax morality and satisfaction with fiscal policy as they relate to the perceived just distribution of public resources. *Reitaku International Journal of Economic Studies*, *5*, 59–70.

(1997c). The unequal equality: Social stereotypes about female and male entrepreneurs. *Revue Internationale de Psychologie Sociale*, *10*, 63–77.

(1998). Differential representations of taxes: Analysis of free associations and judgments of five employment groups. *Journal of Socio-Economics*, *27*, 117–31.

(1999). Reactance to taxation: Employers' attitudes towards taxes. *Journal of Socio-Economics*, *28*, 131–8.

(2007). *The economic psychology of tax behaviour.* Cambridge: Cambridge University Press.

Kirchler, E., & Berger, M. M. (1998). Macht die Gelegenheit den Dieb? Einstellungen zu Steuern und Tendenzen zur Steuerhinterziehung [Does opportunity make the thief? Attitudes towards taxation and tendencies toward tax evasion]. *Jahrbuch für Absatz- und Konsumentenforschung*, *44*, 439–62.

Kirchler, E., el Sehity, T., & Kulich, C. (2004). *Preiswahrnehmung und Preisentwicklung im Eurokontext: Zur Rekonstruktion einer neuen Währung* [Price perception and price development in the context of the euro: On the reconstruction of a new currency] (project report to the Jubiläumsfonds der Oesterreichischen Nationalbank, project no. 9545). University of Vienna, Faculty of Psychology.

Kirchler, E., Fehr, E., & Evans, R. (1996). Social exchange in the labor market: Reciprocity and trust versus egoistic money maximation. *Journal of Economic Psychology*, *17*, 313–41.

Kirchler, E., Fischer, F., & Hoelzl, E. (2010). Price and its relation to objective and subjective product quality: Evidence from the Austrian market. *Journal of Consumer Policy*, *33*, 275–86.

Kirchler, E., & Gangl. K. (2015). Trust. In M. Altmann (ed.), *Real-world decision making: An encyclopedia of behavioral economics* (pp. 442–3). Santa Barbara, CA: Greenwood.

Kirchler, E., & Hoelzl, E. (2003). Economic psychology. *International Review of Industrial and Organizational Psychology*, *18*, 29–80.

(2006). Twenty-five years of the *Journal of Economic Psychology* (1981–2005): A report on the development of an interdisciplinary field of research. *Journal of Economic Psychology*, *27*, 793–804.

Kirchler, E., Hoelzl, E., & Kamleitner, B. (2008). Spending and credit use in the private household. *Journal of Socio-Economics*, *37*, 519–32.

Kirchler, E., Hoelzl, E., & Wahl, I. (2008). Enforced versus voluntary tax compliance: The 'slippery slope' framework. *Journal of Economic Psychology*, *29*, 210–25.

Kirchler, E., Maciejovsky, B., & Weber, M. (2005). Framing effects, selective information and market behavior: An experimental analysis. *Journal of Behavioral Finance*, *6*, 90–100.

Kirchler, E., & Meier, K. (1998). Vom Schilling zum Euro: Projekt Eurologistik [From the schilling to the euro: Project Eurologistik] (unpublished project report). University of Vienna, Faculty of Psychology.

Kirchler, E., Muehlbacher, S., Hoelzl, E., & Webley, P. (2009). Effort and aspirations in tax evasion: Experimental evidence. *Applied Psychology: An International Review*, *58*, 488–507.

Kirchler, E., Muehlbacher, S., Kastlunger, B., & Wahl, I. (2010). Why pay taxes? A review of tax compliance decisions. In J. Alm, J. Martinez-Vazques, & B. Torgler (eds.), *Developing alternative frameworks for explaining tax compliance* (pp. 15–31). London: Routledge

Kirchler, E., & Nowy, C. (1988). Wo bleibt das Glück am Herd? Geschlechtsspezifische Reaktionen auf Arbeitslosigkeit [What happened to home sweet home? Gender-specific reactions to unemployment]. *Wirtschafts- und sozialpolitische Zeitschrift des ISW*, *11*, 69–87.

Kirchler, E., & Pießlinger, C. (1992). Vestis virum reddit: Modische Kleider und deren Träger aus der Sicht der Designer, Händler, Verkäufer und Konsumenten [The clothes make the man: Fashionable clothes and their wearers from the perspective of designers, merchandisers, salespeople, and consumers]. *Jahrbuch der Absatz- und Verbrauchsforschung*, *1*, 21–53.

Kirchler, E., & Pitters, J. (2007). Kontraproduktives Verhalten durch Schädigung öffentlicher Güter [Counterproductive behaviour through damage to public goods]. In K. Moser (ed.), *Wirtschaftspsychologie* (pp. 357–78). Heidelberg: Springer.

Kirchler, E., Rodler, C., Hoelzl, E., & Meier, K. (2001). *Conflict and decision making in close relationships: Love, money and daily routine*. Hove: Psychology Press.

Kirchler, E., & Schmidl, D. (2000). Schichtarbeit im Vergleich: Befindensunterschiede and Aufmerksamkeitsvariation während der 8-Stunden- versus 12-Stunden-Schichtarbeit [Shift work in comparison: Differences in well-being and attentiveness during 8-hour and 12-hour shifts]. *Zeitschrift für Arbeits- and Organisationspsychologie*, *44*, 2–18.

Kirchler, E., Wagner, J., & Buchleitner, S. (1996). Der langsame Wechsel in Führungsetagen. Meinungen über Frauen und Männer als Führungspersonen [The slow shift in top management. Opinions of women and men as leaders]. *Zeitschrift für Sozialpsychologie*, *27*, 148–66.

Kirchler, E., & Wahl, I. (2010). Tax compliance inventory TAX-I: designing an inventory for surveys of tax compliance. *Journal of Economic Psychology*, *31*, 331–46.

Kirchler, E [Erwin]. (1988). *Individuelle Folgen des Arbeitsplatzverlustes: Ein psychologisches Modell zur Verarbeitung von Arbeitslosigkeit* [Individual consequences of losing one's job: A psychological model on processing unemployment] (unpublished thesis). University of Vienna.

Kirzner, I. M. (1979). *Perception, opportunity, and profit*. Chicago, IL: University of Chicago Press.

Klein, D. M., & Hill, R. (1979). Determinants of family problem-solving effectiveness. In W. R. Burr, R. Hill, F. I. Nye, & I. L. Reiss (eds.), *Contemporary theories about the family: Research bases theories* (vol. 1, pp. 493–548). New York: Free Press.

Klein, G. (1998). *Sources of power: How people make decisions*. Cambridge, MA: MIT Press.

Klumb, P. L., & Gemmiti, M. (2011). Harmonisierung von Berufs- und Privatleben: Vorsicht vor schnellen Lösungen [Harmonisation of work and private life: Caution with quick solutions]. In E. Bamberg, A. Ducki, & A.-M. Metz (eds.), *Handbuch Gesundheitsförderung und Gesundheitsmanagement in der Arbeitswelt* (pp. 259–78). Göttingen: Hogrefe.

Kluwer, E., & Mikula, G. (2002). Gender-related inequalities in the division of family work in close relationships: A social psychological perspective. *European Review of Social Psychology*, *13*, 185–216.

Knauth, O. (1949). Considerations in setting retail prices. *Journal of Marketing*, *14*, 1–12.

Knutson, B., Taylor, J., Kaufman, M., Peterson, R., & Glover, G. (2005). Distributed neural representation of expected value. *Journal of Neuroscience*, *25*, 4806–12.

Koen, J., Klehe, U.-C., van Vianen, A. E. M., Zikic, J., & Nauta, A. (2010). Job-search strategies and reemployment quality: The impact of career adaptability. *Journal of Vocational Behavior*, *77*, 126–39.

Kollmann, K., Simperl, K., & Huber, R. (2003). *Endbericht zur Euro-Begleitforschung* [Final report on the euro evaluation research]. Vienna: Kammer für Arbeiter und Angestellte.

Korczynski, M. (2000). The political economy of trust. *Journal of Management Studies*, *37*, 1–21.

Korunka, C., & Frank, H. (2005). Ökonomische Bildung von Schülern höherer Schulen [Economic education among high school students]. *Wirtschaftspsychologie*, *7*, 24–41.

Korunka, C., Frank, H., & Becker, P. (1993). Persönlichkeitseigenschaften von Unternehmensgründern: Erfolgsfaktor oder vernachlässigbare Restgröße in der Theorie der Unternehmensgründung [Personality characteristics of entrepreneurs: Success factor or negligible residual in the theory of founding a company]. *Internationales Gewerbearchiv*, *41*,169–88.

Korunka, C., Frank, H., & Lueger M. (2004). Die Bedeutung der Persönlichkeit für die Gründungsintention, die Gründungsrealisation und den Unternehmenserfolg [The importance of personality for entrepreneurial intentions, founding a company, and corporate success]. *Zeitschrift für Psychologie*, *212*, 25–39.

Korunka, C., Frank, H., Lueger, M., & Mugler, J. (2003). The entrepreneurial personality in the context of resources, environment, and the startup process – a configurational approach. *Entrepreneurship Theory and Practice*, *28*, 23–42.

Korunka, C., & Kubicek, B. (2013). Beschleunigung im Arbeitsleben: Neue Anforderungen und deren Folgen [Acceleration at work: New demands and their consequences]. In G. Junghanns & M. Morschhäuser (eds.), *Immer schneller, immer mehr: Psychische Belastung bei Wissens- und Dienstleistungsarbeit* (pp. 17–39). Wiesbaden: Springer.

Kostolany, A. (1997). '2 × 2 = 5 – 1': Börse ist Psychologie [The stock market is psychology]. In B. Jünemann & D. Schellenberger (eds.), *Psychologie für Börsenprofis: Die Macht der Gefühle bei der Geldanlage* (pp. xiv–xvi). Stuttgart: Schäffer-Poeschel.

Kotler, P. (1982). *Marketing-Management: Analyse, Planung und Kontrolle* [Marketing management: Analysis, planning and monitoring]. Stuttgart: Poeschel.

Kourilsky, M., & Murray, I. (1981). The use of economic reasoning to increase satisfaction with family decision making. *Journal of Consumer Research*, *8*, 183–8.

Krauss, S., & Wang, X. T. (2003). The psychology of the Monty Hall problem: Discovering psychological mechanisms for solving a tenacious brain teaser. *Journal of Experimental Psychology*, *132*, 3–22.

Krieger, L. S., & Sheldon, K. M. (2014). Service job lawyers are happier than money job lawyers, despite their lower income. *Journal of Positive Psychology*, *9*, 219–26.

Kroeber-Riel, W. (1991). In der Informationsflut überleben [Surviving in the information glut]. *Technologie & Management*, *2*, 14–19.

(1992). *Konsumentenverhalten* [Consumer behaviour] (5th edn). Munich: Vahlen.

Kroll, Y., Levy, H., & Rapoport, A. (1988). Experimental tests of the mean-variance model for portfolio selection. *Organizational Behavior and Human Decision Processes*, *42*, 388–410.

Kruger, J., & Dunning, D. (1999). Unskilled and unaware of it: How difficulties in recognizing one's own incompetence lead to inflated self-assessment. *Journal of Personality and Social Psychology*, *77*, 1121–34.

Ku, G., Galinsky, A. D., & Murnighan, J. K. (2006). Starting low but ending high: A reversal of the anchoring effect in auctions. *Journal of Personality and Social Psychology*, *90*, 975–86.

Kuchinke, K. P., Ardichvili, A., Borchert, M., Cornachione, E., Cseh, M., Kang, H., . . . & Zav'jalova, E. (2011). Work meaning among mid-level professional employees: A study of the importance of work centrality and extrinsic and intrinsic work goals in eight countries. *Asian Pacific Journal of Human Resources*, *49*, 264–84.

Kühberger, A. (1994). Risiko und Unsicherheit: Zum Nutzen des Subjective-Expected-Utility-Models [Risk and uncertainty: On the utility of the subjective expected utility model]. *Psychologische Rundschau*, *45*, 3–23.

(1995). The framing of decisions: A new look at old problems. *Organizational Behavior and Human Decision Processes*, *62*, 230–40.

Kuhl, J., & Goschke, T. (1994). A theory of action control: Mental subsystems, modes of control, and volitional conflict-resolution strategies. In J. Kuhl & J. Beckman (eds.), *Volition and personality: Action versus state orientation* (pp. 93–124). Seattle, WA: Hogrefe.

Kuß, A. (1980). Konsumklima als Einstellung zur Wirtschaftslage [Consumer confidence as attitude towards economic conditions]. In C. Graf Hoyos, W. Kroeber-Riel, L. von Rosenstiel, & B. Strümpel (eds.), *Grundbegriffe der Wirtschaftspsychologie: Gesamtwirtschaft – Markt – Organisation – Arbeit* (2nd edn, pp. 101–11). Munich: Psychologie Verlags Union.

Laibson, D. (1997). Golden eggs and hyperbolic discounting. *Quarterly Journal of Economics*, *112*, 443–77.

Laireiter, A.-R., Baumann, U., Reisenzein, E., & Untner, A. (1997). A diary method for the assessment of interactive social networks: The interval-contingent diary SONET-T. *Swiss Journal of Psychology*, *56*, 217–38.

Lamm, H., & Schwinger, T. (1983). Need consideration in allocation decisions: Is it just? *Journal of Social Psychology*, *119*, 205–9.

Landua, D. (1992). Satisfaction changes. *Social Indicators Research*, *26*, 221–41.

Lang, O., Nöhrbaß, K.-H., & Stahl, K. (1997). On income tax avoidance: The case of Germany. *Journal of Public Economics*, *66*, 327–47.

Langan-Fox, J., & Roth, S. (1995). Achievement motivation and female entrepreneurs. *Journal of Occupational and Organizational Psychology*, *68*, 209–19.

Langer, E., Blank, A., & Chanowitz, B. (1978). The mindlessness of ostensibly thoughtful action: The role of 'placebic' information in interpersonal interaction. *Journal of Personality and Social Psychology*, *36*, 635–42.

Larsen, J. T., McGraw, W., & Cacioppo, J. T. (2001). Can people feel happy and sad at the same time? *Journal of Personality and Social Psychology*, *81*, 684–98.

Larson, R. W., & Bradney, N. (1988). Precious moments with family members and friends. In R. M. Milardo (ed.), *Families and social networks* (pp. 107–26). Beverly Hills, CA: Sage.

Lassarre, D. (1995). *Psychologie sociale et économique* [Social and economic psychology]. Paris: Armand Colin.

Lauer, S. R., & Yodanis, C. (2011). Individualized marriage and the integration of resources. *Journal of Marriage and Family*, *73*, 669–83.

Laurie, H., & Gershuny, J. (2000). Couples, work and money. In R. Berthoud & J. Gershuny (eds.), *Seven years in the lives of British families: Evidence on the dynamics of change from the British Household Panel Survey* (pp. 45–72). Bristol: Policy Press.

Lavidge, R. J., & Steiner, G. A. (1961). A model for predictive measurements of advertising effectiveness. *Journal of Marketing*, *25*, 59–62.

Lawrence, E. C., & Elliehausen, G. (2008). A comparative analysis of payday loan customers. *Contemporary Economic Policy*, *26*, 299–316.

Layard, R. (1999). *Tackling unemployment*. London: Palgrave Macmillan.

(2005). *Happiness: Lessons from a new science*. London: Penguin.

Lazarus, R. S., & Folkman, S. (1984). *Stress, appraisal, and coping*. New York: Springer.

Lea, S. E. G. (1981). Inflation, decimalization and the estimated sizes of coins. *Journal of Economic Psychology*, *1*, 79–81.

Lea, S. E. G., Tarpy, R. M., & Webley, P. (1987). *The individual in the economy: A survey of economic psychology*. Cambridge: Cambridge University Press.

Lea, S. E. G., & Webley, P. (2006). Money as tool, money as drug: The biological psychology of a strong incentive. *Behavioral and Brain Sciences*, *29*, 161–209.

Lea, S. E. G., Webley, P., & Levine, R. M. (1993). The economic psychology of consumer debt. *Journal of Economic Psychology*, *14*, 85–119.

Lea, S. E. G., Webley, P., & Walker, C. M. (1995). Psychological factors in consumer debt: Money management, economic socialization, and credit use. *Journal of Economic Psychology*, *16*, 681–701.

Leavitt, H. J. (1954). A note on some experimental findings about the meanings of price. *Journal of Business*, *27*, 205–10.

Lee, H., Park J., Lee J., & Wyer R. S. (2008). Disposition effects and underlying mechanisms in e-trading of stocks. *Journal of Marketing Research*, *65*, 362–78.

Leggett, J. C. (1968). *Class, race, and labor*. London: Wiley.

Leiser, D. (1983). Children's conceptions of economics – the constitution of a cognitive domain. *Journal of Economic Psychology*, *4*, 297–317.

Leiser, D., & Drori, S. (2005). Naive understanding of inflation. *Journal of Socio-Economics*, *34*, 179–98.

Leiser, D., & Halachmi, R. B. (2006). Children's understanding of market force. *Journal of Economic Psychology*, *27*, 6–19.

Leiser, D., & Izak, G. (1987). The money size illusion as a barometer of confidence? The case of high inflation in Israel. *Journal of Economic Psychology*, *8*, 347–56.

Leiser, D., & Rötheli, T. F. (2010). The financial crisis – economic and psychological perspectives: Introduction to the special issue of the *Journal of Socio-Economics* on 'The Financial Crisis'. *Journal of Socio-Economics*, *39*, 117–18.

Lembregts, C., & Pandelaere, M. (2014). 'A 20% income increase for everyone?': The effect of relative increases in income on perceived income inequality. *Journal of Economic Psychology*, *43*, 37–47.

Lenartova, G. (2003). Prepared tax reform in the Slovak Republic according to the criteria of tax theory and practice. *Ekonomicky Casopis*, *51*, 664–87.

Leonidou, L. C., Talias, M. A., & Leonidou, C. N. (2008). Exercised power as a driver of trust and commitment in cross-border industrial buyer–seller relationship. *Industrial Marketing Management*, *37*, 92–103.

Lerner, M. J. (1980). *The belief in a just world: A fundamental delusion*. New York: Springer.

Lersch, P. (1962). *Aufbau der Person* [Structure of the person]. Munich: Barth.

Leu, R., Burri, S., & Priester, T. (1997). *Lebensqualität and Armut in der Schweiz* [Quality of life and poverty in Switzerland]. Berne: Haupt.

Leuthold, J. H. (1983). Home production and the tax system. *Journal of Economic Psychology*, *3*, 145–57.

Lewis, A. (1978). Perceptions of tax rates. *British Tax Review*, *6*, 358–66.

(1982). *The psychology of taxation*. Oxford: Martin Robertson.

(2008). *The Cambridge handbook of psychology and economic behaviour*. Cambridge: Cambridge University Press.

(2010). The credit crunch: Ideological, psychological and epistemological perspective. *Journal of Socio-Economics*, *39*, 127–31.

Lewis, A., Webley, P., & Furnham, A. (1995). *The new economic mind*. Hemel Hempstead: Harvester Wheatsheaf.

Lewis, J. D., & Weigert, A. J. (1985). Trust as a social reality. *Social Forces*, *63*, 967–85.

Lichtenstein, D. R., & Burton, S. (1989). The relationship between perceived and objective price-quality. *Journal of Marketing Research*, *26*, 429–43.

Lichtenstein, S., & Slovic, P. (1971). Reversals of preferences between bids and choices in gambling decisions. *Journal of Experimental Psychology*, *89*, 46–55.

Lichtenstein, S., Slovic, P., Fischhoff, B., Layman, B., & Combs, B. (1978). Judged frequency of lethal events. *Journal of Experimental Psychology*, *4*, 551–78.

Lieberman, M. D. (2003). Reflective and reflexive judgment processes: A social cognitive neuroscience approach. In J. P. Forgas, K. R. Williams, & W. von Hippel (eds.), *Social judgments: Implicit and explicit processes* (pp. 44–67). Cambridge: Cambridge University Press.

Liersch, A. (2013). Überschuldungsstatistik 2012: Die amtliche Statistik zur Situation überschuldeter Personen in Deutschland [Statistics on overindebtedness 2012: The official statistics on the situation of overindebted persons in Germany]. *Wirtschaft & Statistik, November*, 795–804.

Lindblom, C. E. (1959). The science of 'muddling through'. *Public Administration Review*, *19*, 79–88.

(1979). Still muddling, not yet through. *Public Administration Review*, *39*, 517–26.

Linnainmaa, J. (2005). *The individual day trader* (Working Paper). The Anderson Law School at UCLA, Los Angeles.

Lipset, S. M. (1992). The work ethic, then and now. *Journal of Labor Research*, *13*, 45–54.

Lipshitz, R., & Strauss, O. (1997). Coping with uncertainty: A naturalistic decision-making analysis. *Organizational Behavior and Human Decision Processes*, *69*, 149–63.

Livingstone, S. M., & Lunt, P. K. (1992). Predicting personal debt and debt repayment: Psychological, social and economic determinants. *Journal of Economic Psychology*, *13*, 111–34.

Locke, E. A. (1976). The nature and causes of job satisfaction. In M. D. Dunnette (ed.), *Handbook of industrial and organizational psychology* (pp. 1297–1351). New York: Wiley.

Loewenstein, G. (2007). Affect regulation and affective forecasting. In J. J. Gross (ed.), *Handbook of emotion regulation* (pp. 180–203). New York: Guilford.

Loewenstein, G., & Issacharoff, S. (1994). Source dependence in the valuation of objects. *Journal of Behavioral Decision Making*, *7*, 157–68.

Loewenstein, G., O'Donoghue, T., & Rabin, M. (2003). Projection bias in predicting future utility. *Quarterly Journal of Economics*, *118*, 1209–48.

Loewenstein, G., & Prelec, D. (1991). Negative time preference. *American Economic Review*, *81*, 347–52.

Loewenstein, G., & Thaler, R. H. (1989). Anomalies: Intertemporal choice. *Journal of Economic Perspectives*, *3*, 181–93.

Loewenstein, G., Weber, E. U., Hsee, C. K., & Welch, N. (2001). Risk as feelings. *Psychological Bulletin*, *127*, 267–86.

Loomes, G., & Sugden, R. (1982). Regret theory: An alternative theory of rational choice under certainty. *Economic Journal*, *92*, 805–24.

Lopes, L. L. (1994). Psychology and economics: Perspectives on risk, cooperation, and the marketplace. *Annual Review of Psychology*, *45*, 197–227.

Lotto, L., Rubaltelli, E., Rumiati, R., & Savadori, L. (2006). Mental representation of money in experts and nonexperts after the introduction of the euro. *European Psychologist*, *11*, 277–88.

Lucas, R. E. (2007). Adaptation and the set-point model of subjective well-being. *Current Directions in Psychological Science*, *16*, 75–9.

Lujansky, H., & Mikula, G. (1983). Can equity theory explain the quality and the stability of romantic relationships? *British Journal of Social Psychology*, *22*, 101–12.

Lunt, P. (1996). Discourses of savings. *Journal of Economic Psychology*, *17*, 677–90.

Lunt, P., & Livingstone, S. M. (1992). *Mass consumption and personal identity*. Buckingham: Open University Press.

Lusardi, A., & Mitchell, O. S. (2007a). Financial literacy and retirement preparedness: Evidence and implications for financial education. *Business Economics*, January, 35–44.

(2007b). Baby boomer retirement security: The roles of planning, financial literacy, and housing wealth. *Journal of Monetary Economics*, *54*, 205–24.

Lynch Jr, J. G., & Wood, W. (2006). Special issue editors' statement: Helping consumers help themselves. *Journal of Public Policy & Marketing*, *25*, 1–7.

Maas, P., & Schüller, A. (1990). Arbeit und Konsum – Wertewandel in zwei zentralen Bereichen des Lebens [Work and consumption – a shift in values in two central areas of life]. In I. Szallies & G. Wiswede (eds.), *Wertewandel und Konsum* (pp. 87–108). Landsberg am Lech: Moderne Industrie.

Maas, P., & Weibler, J. (eds.) (1990). *Börse und Psychologie: Plädoyer für eine neue Perspektive* [The stock market and psychology: Plea for a new perspective]. Cologne: Deutscher Institutsverlag.

MacGregor, D. G., Slovic, P., Dreman, D., & Berry, M. (2000). Imagery, affect, and financial judgment. *Journal of Psychology and Financial Markets*, *1*, 104–10.

Maciejovsky, B., Kirchler, E., & Schwarzenberger, H. (2007). Misperception of chance and loss repair: On the dynamics of tax compliance. *Journal of Economic Psychology*, *28*, 678–91.

MacIver, R. (1949). *The elements of social science*. London: Methuen.

Madden, C. S. (1982). The effect of conflict awareness on interspousal decision making in highly involving purchases (Unpublished thesis). University of Nebraska (Lincoln).

Manhire, J. T. (2016). Tax compliance as a wicked system. *Florida Tax Review*, *18*, 235–74.

Mannix, E. A., Tinsley, C. H., & Bazerman, M. (1995). Negotiations over time: Impediments to integrative solutions. *Organizational Behavior and Human Decision Processes*, *62*, 241–51.

March, J. G., & Romelaer, P. (1976). Position and presence in the drift of decisions. In J. G. March & P. Olsen (eds.), *Ambiguity and choice in organizations* (pp. 251–76). Bergen: Universitetsforlaget.

March, J. G., & Shapira, Z. (1992). Behavioral decision theory and organizational decision theory. In M. Zey (ed.), *Decision making: Alternatives to rational choice models* (pp. 273–303). Newbury Park, CA: Sage.

March, J. G., & Simon, H. A. (1958). *Organizations*. New York: Wiley.

Market Institut (2009). *Persönliches Glück trotzt der Wirtschaftskrise* [Personal happiness defies the economic crisis]. (Market Institut News, May 09/16). Linz.

Markowitz, H. (1959). *Portfolio selection: Efficient diversification of investments*. New York: Wiley.

Marques, F. J., & Dehaene, S. (2004). Developing intuition for prices in euros: Rescaling or relearning prices? *Journal of Experimental Psychology: Applied*, *10*, 148–55.

Martella, D., & Maass, A. (2000). Unemployment and life satisfaction: The moderating role of time structure and collectivism. *Journal of Applied Social Psychology*, *30*, 1095–1108.

Martinelli, A. (2001). Entrepreneurship. In N. J. Smelser & P. B. Baltes (eds.), *International encyclopedia of the social and behavioural sciences* (pp. 4545–52). Oxford: Pergamon.

Marx, K. (1847/1973). Lohnarbeit and Kapital [Wage-Labour and Capital]. In *Marx-Engels-Werke, herausgegeben vom Institut für Marxismus-Leninismus beim ZK der SED* (vol. 6, pp. 397–423). Berlin: Dietz.

Masclet, D., Noussair, C., & Tucker, S. (2003). Monetary and nonmonetary punishment in the voluntary contributions mechanism. *American Economic Review*, *93*, 366–80.

Mason, R., & Calvin, L. D. (1978). A study of admitted income tax evasion. *Law and Society Review*, *13*, 73–89.

Mayall, M. (2010). A feeling for finance: Motivations for trading on the stock exchange. *Emotion, Space and Society*, *3*, 103–10.

Mayer, R. C., Davis, J. H., & Schoorman, F. D. (1995). An integrative model of organizational trust. *Academy of Management Review*, *20*, 709–34.

Mayrhofer, W., Meyer, M., & Steyrer, J. (eds.) (2005). *Macht? Erfolg? Reich? Glücklich?* [Power? Success? Rich? Happy?]. Vienna: Linde.

Mayring, P. (1991). *Psychologie des Glücks* [Psychology of happiness]. Stuttgart: Kohlhammer.

McBarnet, D. (2001). When compliance is not the solution but the problem: From changes in law to changes in attitude. In V. A. Braithwaite (ed.), *Taxing democracy: Understanding tax avoidance and evasion* (pp. 229–44). Aldershot: Ashgate.

McCaffery, E. J., & Baron, J. (2003). Heuristics and biases in thinking about tax. *Annual Conference on Taxation and Minutes of the Annual Meeting of the National Tax Association*, *96*, 434–43.

(2004). Framing and taxation: Evaluation of tax policies involving household composition. *Journal of Economic Psychology*, *25*, 679–705.

McClelland, D. C. (1975). *Power: The inner experience*. New York: Irvington.

McClelland, D. C., & Boyatzis, R. E. (1982). Leadership motive pattern and long-term success in management. *Journal of Applied Psychology*, *67*, 737–43.

McGuigan, C. J., McGuigan, K., & Mallett, J. (2015). Re-examining the job satisfaction–job performance link: A study among Irish retail employees. *Irish Journal of Psychology*, *36*, 12–22.

McKee, M., Siladke, C., & Vossler, C. A. (2011). *Behavioral dynamics of tax compliance under an information services initiative (*MPRA Paper 38865). Munich: University Library of Munich.

McKee-Ryan, F., Song, Z., Wanberg, C. R., & Kinicki, A. (2005). Psychological and physical well-being during unemployment: A meta-analytic study. *Journal of Applied Psychology*, *90*, 53–76.

McKerchar, M. (1995). Understanding small business taxpayers: Their sources of information and level of knowledge of taxation. *Australian Tax Forum*, *12*, 25–41.

(2001). The study of income tax complexity and unintentional noncompliance: Research method and preliminary findings (ATAX Discussion Paper). University of Sydney, Orange.

McNeal, J. U. (1992). *Kids as customers: A handbook of marketing to children*. Lexington, KY: D. C. Heath.

Meier, K., & Kirchler, E. (1998). Social representations of the euro in Austria. *Journal of Economic Psychology*, *19*, 755–74.

Meier, S., & Sprenger, C. (2010). Present-biased preferences and credit card borrowing. *American Economic Journal: Applied Economics*, *2*, 193–210.

(2012). Time discounting predicts creditworthiness. *Psychological Science*, *23*, 56–8.

Meier-Pesti, K., & Kirchler, E. (2001). Price perceptions of an unfamiliar currency scale: Hypotheses about the adaptation to the Euro. Paper presented at the 26th annual congress of the IAREP, September (International Association for Research in Economic Psychology), Bath.

(2003a). Nationalism and patriotism as determinants of European identity and attitudes towards the euro. *Journal of Socio-Economics*, *32*, 685–700.

(2003b). Attitudes towards the euro by national identity and relative national status. *Journal of Economic Psychology*, *24*, 293–9.

(2003c). Economic psychological investigations. Paper presented at the Center for Consumer Research, September, Universität Göteborg.

Meilers, B. A., Schwartz, A., & Cooke, A. D. J. (1998). Judgment and decision making. *Annual Review of Psychology*, *49*, 447–77.

Metcalfe, J., & Mischel, W. (1999). A hot/cool-system analysis of delay of gratification: Dynamics of willpower. *Psychological Review*, *106*, 3–19.

Miceli, M. P. (1993). Justice and pay system satisfaction. In R. Cropanzano (ed.), *Justice in the workplace: Approaching fairness in human resource management* (pp. 257–83). Hillsdale, NJ: Erlbaum.

Michaels, J. W., Acock, A. C., & Edwards, J. N. (1986). Social exchange and equity determinants of relationship commitment. *Journal of Social and Personal Relationships*, *3*, 161–75.

Michaels, J. W., Edwards, J. N., & Acock, A. C. (1984). Satisfaction in intimate relationships as a function of inequality, inequity, and outcomes. *Social Psychology Quarterly*, *47*, 347–57.

Mikula, G. (1991). Wage-effort Hypothese aus der Sicht der Sozialpsychologie [Wage-effort hypothesis from the perspective of social psychology]. Lecture at the Department of Economics, Vienna University of Technology.

(2006). Social psychology of justice, just division of household labor, and the reconciliation of family and work demands. In P. A. M. Van Lange (ed.), *Bridging social psychology: The benefits of transdisciplinary approaches* (pp. 301–6). Mahwah, NJ: Erlbaum.

Mikula, G., Schoebi, D., Jagoditsch, S., & Macher, S. (2009). Roots and correlates of perceived injustice in the division of family work. *Personal Relationships*, *16*, 553–74.

Miller, G. R., & Boster, F. (1988). Persuasion in personal relationships. In S. W. Duck (ed.), *Handbook of personal relationships*. New York: Wiley.

Mills, J., & Clark, M. S. (1982). Exchange and communal relationships. In L. Wheeler (ed.), *Review of personality and social psychology* (vol. 3, pp. 121–44). Beverly Hills, CA: Sage.

Mischel, W. (1974). Processes in delay of gratification. In L. Berkowitz (ed.), *Advances in experimental social psychology* (vol. 7, pp. 249–92). New York: Academic Press.

Mitchell, O. S., & Lusardi, A. (2012). *Financial literacy: Implications for retirement security and the financial marketplace*. Oxford: Oxford University Press.

Mitchell, W. C. (1914). Human behaviour and economics: A survey of recent literature. *Quarterly Journal of Economics*, *29*, 1–47.

Mobius, M. M., & Rosenblat, T. S. (2006). Why beauty matters. *American Economic Review*, *96*, 222–35.

Modigliani, F. (1988). The role of intergenerational transfers and life cycle saving in the accumulation of wealth. *Journal of Economic Perspectives*, *2*, 15–40.

Montada, L. (1995). Die geistige Entwicklung aus der Sicht Jean Piagets [Mental development as viewed by Jean Piaget]. In R. Oerter & L. Montada (eds.), *Entwicklungspsychologie* (3rd edn, pp. 518–60). Weinheim: Psychologische Verlags Union.

Montada, L., & Lerner, M. J. (1998). *Responses to victimizations and belief in a just world*. New York: Plenum Press.

Montier, J. (2003). *Behavioral finance: Insights into irrational minds and markets*. New York: Wiley.

(2005). Seven sins of fund management: A behavioural critic. *Dresdner Kleinwort Wasserstein*, November. Retrieved from www.trendfollowing.com/whitepaper/Seven_Sins_o-DrKW-100436-N.pdf (accessed 13 July 2016).

(2007). *Behavioural investing: A practitioner's guide to applying behavioural finance*. Chichester: John Wiley & Sons.

(2010). *Die Psychologie der Börse: Der Praxisleitfaden für Behavioral Finance* [The psychology of the stock market: A praxis-oriented manual for behavioural finance]. Munich: FinanzBuch Verlag.

Moore, D. A., Kurtzberg, T. R., Fox, C. R., & Bazerman, M. H. (1999). Positive illusions and forecasting errors in mutual fund investment decisions. *Organizational Behavior and Human Decision Processes*, *79*, 95–114.

Morewedge, C. K., & Kahneman, D. (2010). Associative processes in intuitive judgment. *Trends in Cognitive Sciences*, *14*, 435–40.

Moscovici, S. (1961). *La psychanalyse, son image et son public* [Psychoanalysis: Its image and its public]. Paris: Presses Universitaires de France.

(1981). On social representations. In J. Forgas (ed.), *Social cognition: Perspectives on everyday understanding*. London: Academic Press.

(2000). *Social representations: Explorations in social psychology*. Cambridge: Polity Press.

Moscovici, S., & Hewstone, M. (1983). Social representations and social explanations: From the 'naive' to the 'amateur' scientist. In M. Hewstone (ed.), *Attribution theory, social and functional extension*. Oxford: Blackwell.

Moser, D. V., Evans III., J. H., & Kim, C. K. (1995). The effects of horizontal and exchange inequity on tax reporting decisions. *Accounting Review*, *70*, 619–34.

Moser, H. (1994). Zur Kritik der Sprache von Gesetzen. Anmerkungen eines Sprachwissenschaftlers [Towards a critique of the language of laws. Remarks from a linguist]. In C. Smekal & E. Theurl (eds.), *Stand und Entwicklung der Finanzpsychologie* (pp. 171–84). Baden-Baden: Nomos.

Moser, K. (2007). *Wirtschaftspsychologie* [Economic psychology]. Heidelberg: Springer.

Moser, K. A., Fox, A. J., Jones, D. R., & Goldblatt, P. O. (1986). Unemployment and mortality: Further evidence from the OPCS longitudinal study 1971–1981. *The Lancet*, *327*, 365–7.

Mowen, J. C., & Mowen, M. M. (1991). Time and outcome valuation: Implications for marketing decision making. *Journal of Marketing*, *55*, 54–62.

Muehlbacher, S., Hoelzl, E., & Kirchler, E. (2007). Steuerhinterziehung und die Berücksichtigung des Einkommens in der Strafbemessung [Tax evasion and the consideration of income in calculating penalties]. *Wirtschaftspsychologie*, *9*, 116–21.

Muehlbacher, S., Hofmann, E., Kirchler, E., & Roland-Lévy, C. (2009). Household decision making: Changes of female and male partners' roles? *Psychology and Economics*, *2*, 17–37.

Muehlbacher, S., & Kirchler, E. (2009). Origin of endowments in public good games: The impact of effort on contributions. *Journal of Neuroscience, Psychology, and Economics*, *2*, 59–67.

(2013). Mental accounting of self-employed taxpayers: On the mental segregation of the net income and the tax due. *FinanzArchiv*, *69*, 412–38.

Muehlbacher, S., Kirchler, E., Hoelzl, E., Ashby, J., Berti, C., Job, J., Kemp, S., Peterlik, U., Roland-Lévy, C., & Waldherr, K. (2008). Hard-earned income and tax compliance: A survey in eight nations. *European Psychologist*, *13*, 298–304.

Mueller, S. L., & Conway Dato-On, M. (2008). Gender-role orientation as a determinant of entrepreneurial self-efficacy. *Journal of Developmental Entrepreneurship*, *13*, 3–20.

Mukherjee, K. (2010). A dual system model of preferences under risk. *Psychological Review*, *177*, 243–55.

Mulder, L. B., van Dijk, E., De Cremer, D., & Wilke, H. A. M. (2006). Undermining trust and cooperation: The paradox of sanctioning systems in social dilemmas. *Journal of Experimental Social Psychology*, *42*, 147–62.

Mulder, L. B., Verboon, P., & De Cremer, D. (2009). Sanctions and moral judgments: The moderating effect of sanction severity and trust in authorities. *European Journal of Social Psychology*, *39*, 255–69.

Müller, A., Mitchell, J. E., & de Zwaan, M. (2015). Compulsive buying. *American Journal on Addictions*, *24*, 132–7.

Müller-Peters, A., Pepermans, R., & Kiell, G. (1998). *The psychology of the European Monetary Union: A cross-national study of attitudes towards the euro* (Report for the European Commission). University of Cologne and Vrije Universiteit Brussels.

Müller-Peters, A., Pepermans, R., Kiell, G., & Farhangmehr, M. (eds.) (2001). *The psychology of European Monetary Union: A cross-national study of public opinion towards the euro.* Santiago de Compostela: Grafinova.

Münsterberg, H. (1912). *Psychologie und Wirtschaftsleben: Ein Beitrag zur angewandten Experimentalpsychologie* [Psychology and economic life: A contribution to applied experimental psychology]. Leipzig: Barth.

Mussweiler, T., & Englich, B. (2003). Adapting to the euro: Evidence from bias reduction. *Journal of Economic Psychology*, *24*, 285–92.

(2004). Sicherheit im Umgang mit dem Euro – Evidenz für eine schnelle Gewöhnung an die neue Währung [Confidence in managing the euro – evidence for a swift adaptation to the new currency]. *Wirtschaftspsychologie*, *6*, 66–70.

Mussweiler, T., & Schneller, K. (2003). What goes up must come down: How charts influence decisions to buy and sell stocks. *Journal of Behavioral Finance*, *4*, 121–30.

Myers, D. (1992). *The pursuit of happiness*. New York: William Morrow.

Na, W., Son, Y., & Marshall, R. (1998). An empirical study of the purchase role structure in Korean families. *Psychology & Marketing*, *15*, 563–76.

(2003). Purchase-role structure in Korean families: Revisited. *Psychology & Marketing*, *20*, 47–57.

Nagel, R. (1995). Unraveling in guessing games: An experimental study. *American Economic Review*, *85*, 1313–26.

Navarro-Martinez, D., Salisbury, L. C., Lemon, K. N., Stewart, N., Matthews, W. J., & Harris, A. J. L. (2011). Minimum required payment and supplemental information disclosure effects on consumer debt repayment decisions. *Journal of Marketing Research*, *48*, 60–77.

Nenkov, G. Y., Inman, J. J., & Hulland, J. (2008). Considering the future: The conceptualization and measurement of elaboration on potential outcomes. *Journal of Consumer Research*, *35*, 126–41.

Nerdinger, F. W. (1995). *Motivation und Handeln in Organisationen* [Motivation and behaviour in organisations]. Stuttgart: Kohlhammer.

Nerdinger, F. W., Blickle, G., & Schaper, N. (2011). *Arbeits- und Organisationspsychologie* [Work and organisational psychology] (2nd edn). Berlin: Springer.

Nestler, S., Blank, H., & von Collani, G. (2008). Hindsight bias doesn't always come easy: Causal models, cognitive effort, and creeping determinism. *Journal of Experimental Psychology: Learning, Memory, and Cognition*, *34*, 1043–54.

Nettle, D. (2005). *Happiness: The science behind your smile.* Oxford: Oxford University Press.

Newman, S. C., & Bland, R. C. (2007). Case-control study of unemployment and parasuicide. *Comprehensive Psychiatry*, *48*, 511–15.

Nicosia, F. M. (1966). *Consumer decision processes*. Englewood Cliffs, NJ: Prentice Hall.

Niederle, M., & Vesterlund, L. (2007). Do women shy away from competition? Do men compete too much? *Quarterly Journal of Economics*, *122*, 1067–1101.

Nisbett, R., Peng, K., Choi, I., & Norenzayan, A. (2001). Culture and systems of thought: Holistic vs. analytic cognition. *Psychological Review*, *108*, 291–310.

Nisbett, R., & Ross, L. (1980). *Human inferences: Strategies and shortcomings of social judgment.* Englewood Cliffs, NJ: Prentice Hall.

Nivoix, S., & Roland-Lévy, C. (2002). Attitudes et représentations liées au changement de monnaie et conversions des unités monétaires [Attitudes and representations related to currency change and conversion of monetary units]. *Economies et Sociétés*, *36*, 175–92.

Nofsinger, J. R. (2005). Social mood and financial economics. *Journal of Behavioral Finance*, *6*, 144–60.

Noh, Y.-H. (2009). Does unemployment increase suicide rates? The OECD panel evidence. *Journal of Economic Psychology*, *30*, 575–82.

Nooteboom, B. (2002). *Trust: Forms, foundations, functions, failures and figures*. Cheltenham: Edward Elgar.

Northcraft, G. B., & Neale, M. (1987). Experts, amateurs, and real estate: An anchoring-and-adjustment perspective on property pricing decisions. *Organizational Behavior and Human Decision Processes*, *39*, 84–97.

Norton, C. M. (1993). The social psychology of credit. *Credit World*, *82*, 18–22.

Norum, P. S. (2008). The role of time preference and credit card usage in compulsive buying behaviour. *International Journal of Consumer Studies*, *32*, 269–75.

Norvilitis, J. M., Merwin, M. M., Osberg, T. M., Roehling, P. V., Young, P., & Kamas, M. M. (2006). Personality factors, money attitudes, financial knowledge, and credit-card debt in college students. *Journal of Applied Social Psychology*, *36*, 1395–1413.

Nowak, M., Page, K., & Sigmund, K. (2000). Fairness versus reason in the ultimatum game. *Science*, *289*, 1773–5.

Nye, F. I. (1979). Choice, exchange, and the family. In W. R. Burr, R. Hill, F. I. Nye & I. L. Reiss (eds.), *Contemporary theories about the family* (vol. 2, pp. 1–41). New York: Free Press.

Nyman, C., & Reinikainen, L. (2007). Elusive independence in a context of gender equality in Sweden. In J. Stocks, C. Díaz-Martínez, & B. Halleröd (eds.), *Modern couples sharing money, sharing life* (pp. 41–71). Basingstoke: Palgrave Macmillan.

Nyman, C., Reinikainen, L., & Stocks, J. (2013). Reflections on a cross-national qualitative study of within-household finances. *Journal of Marriage and Family*, *75*, 640–50.

O'Curry, S., & Strahilevitz, M. (2001). Probability and mode of acquisition effects on choices between hedonic and utilitarian options. *Marketing Letters*, *12*, 37–49.

O'Guinn, T. C., & Faber, R. J. (1989). Compulsive buying: A phenomenological exploration. *Journal of Consumer Research*, *16*, 147–57.

Oakley, A. (1980). For love or money: The unspoken deal. *New Society*, *54*, 564–5.

Oberlechner, T. (2004). *The psychology of the foreign exchange market*. Chichester: Wiley.

Odean, T. (1998a). Are investors reluctant to realize their losses? *Journal of Finance*, *53*, 1775–98.

(1998b). Volume, volatility, price and profit when all traders are above average. *Journal of Finance*, 53, 1887–1934.

(1999). Do investors trade too much? *American Economic Review*, *89*, 1279–98.

Oishi, S., Kesebir, S., & Diener, E. (2011). Income inequality and happiness. *Psychological Science*, *22*, 1095–1100.

Oishi, S., Schimmack, U., & Diener, E. (2012). Progressive taxation and the subjective well-being of nations. *Psychological Science*, *23*, 86–92.

Olson, N. E. (2015). Procedural justice for all: A taxpayer rights analysis of IRS earned income credit compliance strategy. *Advances in Taxation*, *22*, 1–35.

Oosterbeek, H., Sloof, R., & van de Kuilen, G. (2004). Cultural differences in ultimatum game experiments: Evidence from a meta-analysis. *Experimental Economics*, *7*, 171–88.

Opaschowski, H. W. (1982). *Psychologie und Soziologie der Freizeit* [Psychology and sociology of free time]. Opladen: Leske und Budrich.

(2001). *Deutschland 2010: Wie wir morgen arbeiten und leben. Voraussagen der Wissenschaft zur Zukunft unserer Gesellschaft* [Germany 2010: How we will work and live tomorrow] (2nd edn). Hamburg: Germa Press.

Orviska, M., & Hudson, J. (2002). Tax evasion, civic duty and the law abiding citizen. *European Journal of Political Economy*, *19*, 83–102.

Osman, M. (2004). An evaluation of dual-process theories or reasoning. *Psychonomic Bulletin & Review*, *11*, 988–1010.

Ostaszewski, P., Green, L., & Myerson, J. (1998). Effects of inflation on the subjective value of delayed and probabilistic rewards. *Psychonomic Bulletin & Review*, *5*, 324–33.

Ottaviani, C., & Vandone, D. (2011). Impulsivity and household indebtedness: Evidence from real life. *Journal of Economic Psychology*, *32*, 754–61.

Otto, A. M., Schots, P. A., Westerman, J. A., & Webley, P. (2006). Children's use of saving strategies: An experimental approach. *Journal of Economic Psychology*, *27*, 57–72.

Owen, G. (2001). Game theory. In N. J. Smelser & P. B. Baltes (eds.), *International Encyclopedia of the Social & Behavioral Sciences* (pp. 5863–8). Oxford: Pergamon.

Owens, J., & Hamilton, S. (2004). Experience and innovations in other countries. In H. J. Aaron & J. Slemrod (eds.), *The crisis in tax administration* (pp. 347–88). Washington, DC: Brookings Institution Press.

Oxenfeldt, A. R. (1950). Consumer knowledge: Its measurement and extent. *Review of Economics and Statistics*, *32*, 300–14.

Pahl, J. (1989). *Money and marriage*. Houndmills: Macmillan.

(1995). His money, her money: Recent research on financial organisation in marriage. *Journal of Economic Psychology*, *16*, 361–76.

(2008). Family finances, individualisation, spending patterns and access to credit. *Journal of Socio-Economics*, *37*, 577–91.

Palan, K. M., & Wilkes, R. E. (1997). Adolescent–parent interaction in family decision making. *Journal of Consumer Research*, *24*, 159–69.

Park, C. G., & Hyun, J. K. (2003). Examining the determinants of tax compliance by experimental data: A case of Korea. *Journal of Policy Modeling*, *25*, 673–84.

Passauer, H. (1992). Zum Image von Männern und Frauen in Führungspositionen. Selbstbild und Fremdbild in den 1990ern [On the image of men and women in leadership positions] (unpublished thesis). University of Graz.

Pataki, S., Shapiro, C., & Clark, M. S. (1992). Acquiring distributive justice norms: Effects of age and relationship type. *Journal of Social and Personal Relationships*, *11*, 427–42.

Paul, K. I., & Moser, K. (2009a). Unemployment impairs mental health: Meta-analyses. *Journal of Vocational Behavior*, *74*, 264–82.

(2009b). Metaanalytische Moderatoranalysen zu den psychischen Auswirkungen der Arbeitslosigkeit – ein Überblick [Meta-analytic moderator analyses on psychological effects of unemployments – an overview]. In A. Hollederer (ed.), *Gesundheit von Arbeitslosen fördern: Ein Handbuch für Wissenschaft und Praxis* (pp. 39–61). Frankfurt am Main: Fachhochschulverlag.

Penz, E., & Kirchler, E. (2012). Sex-role specialisation in a transforming market: Empirical evidence from Vietnamese middle-class households. *Journal of Marcromarketing*, *32*, 61–73.

Penz, E., Meier-Pesti, K., & Kirchler, E. (2004). It's practical, but no more controllable: Social representations of the electronic purse in Austria. *Journal of Economic Psychology*, *25*, 771–87.

Peplau, L. A. (1983). Roles and gender. In H. H. Kelley, E. Berscheid, A. Christensen, J. H. Harvey, T. L. Huston, G. Levinger, E. McClintock, L. A. Peplau, & D. R. Peterson (eds.), *Close relationships* (pp. 220–64). New York: Freeman.

Perry, V. G. (2008). Is ignorance bliss? Consumer accuracy in judgments about credit ratings. *Journal of Consumer Affairs*, *42*, 189–205.

Peterlik, R.-U. (2009). Finanzielle Haushaltsentscheidungen in Vietnam – Anwendung und Adaptation der Wiener Tagebuchstudie [Financial decision-making in households in Vietnam: Application and adaptation of the Vienna Diary Study] (unpublished dissertation). University of Vienna.

Peters, E., Västfjäll, D., Gärling, T., & Slovic, P. (2006). Affect and decision making: A 'hot' topic. *Journal of Behavioral Decision Making*, *19*, 79–85.

Petersen, L. E., & Six, B. (2008). *Stereotype, Vorurteile und soziale Diskriminierung* [Stereotypes, prejudice and social discrimination]. Weinheim: Beltz.

Peterson, C., & Seligman, M. E. P. (2004). *Character strengths and virtues: A handbook and classification*. Oxford: Oxford University Press.

Petty, R. E., & Cacioppo, J. T. (1986). The elaboration likelihood model of persuasion. In L. Berkowitz (ed.), *Advances in experimental social psychology* (pp. 123–205). New York: Academic Press.

Petty, R. E., Wegener, D. T., & Fabrigar, L. R. (1997). Attitudes and attitude change. *Annual Review of Psychology*, *48*, 609–47.

Phillips, J., & Land, K. C. (2012). The link between unemployment and crime rate fluctuations: An analysis at the county, state, and national levels. *Social Science Research*, *41*, 681–94.

Pichevin, M.-F., Hurtig, M.-C., & Piolat, M. (1993). *Studies on the self and social cognition*. Singapore: World Scientific.

Pinner, W. (1997). *Die verrückte Börse: Eine Einführung in die Börsenpsychologie* [The crazy stock market: An introduction to the psychology of the stock market]. Düsseldorf: Econ.

Piñón, A., & Gärling, T. (2004). Effects of mood on adoption of loss frame in risky choice. *Göteborg Psychological Reports*, *34*, 1–11.

Pitters, J., & Oberlechner, T. (2014). The psychology of trading and investing. In H. K. Baker & V. Ricciardi (eds.), *Investor behavior: The psychology of financial planning and investing* (pp. 457–76). Hoboken, NJ: John Wiley & Sons.

Plassmann, H., O'Doherty, J., Shiv, B., & Rangel, A. (2008). Marketing actions can modulate neural representations of experienced pleasantness. *Proceedings of the National Academy of Sciences*, *105*, 1050–4.

Pollai, M., Hoelzl, E., & Possas, F. (2010). Consumption-related emotions over time: Fit between prediction and experience. *Marketing Letters*, *21*, 397–411.

Pollay, R. W. (1968). A model of family decision making. *British Journal of Marketing*, *2*, 206–16.

Pommerehne, W., & Weck-Hannemann, H. (1996). Tax rates, tax administration and income tax evasion in Switzerland. *Public Choice*, *88*, 161–70.

Ponthieux, S. (2012). *Intra-household sharing of resources: An exploration of the 'black box' with the 2010 EU-SILC module*. Brussels: Eurostat.

Porcano, T. M. (1988). Correlates of tax evasion. *Journal of Economic Psychology*, *9*, 47–67.

Porter, L. W., & Lawler, E. E. (1968). *Managerial attitudes and performance*. Homewood, IL: Irwin-Dorsey.

Prantl, N. (2005). Das Konzept Work-Life-Balance eingebettet in die beiden Hauptlebensbereiche 'Arbeit' und 'Freizeit' [The concept of work-life balance embedded in the two main areas of life 'work' and 'free time']. *Organisationsberatung, Supervision, Coaching*, *12*, 321–31.

Prelec, D., & Loewenstein, G. (1998). The red and the black: Mental accounting of savings and debt. *Marketing Science*, *17*, 4–28.

Prince, M. (1993). Women, men, and money styles. *Journal of Economic Psychology*, *14*, 175–82.

Prinz, A. (2004). Steuermoral und Religiösität in Ost- und Westdeutschland [Tax morale and religiosity in East and West Germany]. *Schmollers Jahrbuch, Zeitschrift für Wirtschafts- und Sozialwissenschaften*, *124*, 511–37.

Prinz, A., & Pawelzik, M. R. (2008). Neuroökonomik [Neuroeconomics]. In S. Gauggel & M. Herrmann (eds.), *Handbuch der Psychologie*, vol. 8, *Handbuch der Neuro- und Biopsychologie (*pp. 68–79). Göttingen: Hogrefe.

Pruckner, G. J., & Sausgruber, R. (2013). Honesty on the streets. A field study on newspaper purchasing. *Journal of the European Economic Association*, *11*, 661–79.

Pulford, B. D., & Colman, A. M. (2008). Size doesn't really matter. Ambiguity aversion in Ellsberg's urns with few balls. *Experimental Psychology*, *55*, 31–7.

Pulver, U. (1991). *Die Bausteine des Alltags: Zur Psychologie des menschlichen Arbeitens and Handelns* [The building blocks of everyday life: Towards a psychology of human work and action]. Heidelberg: Asanger.

Purkhardt, S. C. (2015). *Transforming social representations: A social psychology of common sense and science*. London: Psychology Press.

Raab, G., Elger, C. E., Neuner, M., & Weber, B. (2011). A neurological study of compulsive buying behavior. *Journal of Consumer Policy*, *34*, 401–13.

Raab, G., Neuner, M., Reisch, L. A., & Scherhorn, G. (2005). *Screeningverfahren zur Erhebung von kompensatorischem und süchtigem Kaufverhalten. Handanweisung* [Screening procedures to identify compensatory and addicted shopping behaviour]. Göttingen: Hogrefe.

Raijas, A. (2007). Joint purchase decisions: Experiences of Finnish families with children. Paper presented at 'Sociology of

Consumption', 8th Annual Conference of the European Sociological Association, Glasgow, September.

Rand, D. G., Greene, J. D., & Nowak, M. A. (2012). Spontaneous giving and calculated greed. *Nature*, *489*, 427–30.

Randow, G. von (1999). *Das Ziegenproblem: Denken in Wahrscheinlichkeiten* [The goat problem: Thinking in probabilities]. Reinbek bei Hamburg: Rowohlt.

Ranyard, R. (ed.) (2017). *Economic psychology*. Chichester: Wiley.

Ranyard, R., Burgoyne, C., Saldanha, G., & Routh, D. (2003). *Living with the euro but thinking in punts? A preliminary report of experiences in the Republic of Ireland*. Paper presented at the IAREP (International Association for Research in Economic Psychology) Euro-Workshop, Vienna, July.

Ranyard, R., & Craig, G. (1993). Estimating the duration of a flexible loan: The effect of supplementary information. *Journal of Economic Psychology*, *14*, 317–35.

Ranyard, R., Hinkley, L., & Williamson, J. (2001). Risk management in consumers' credit decision making. *Zeitschrift für Sozialpsychologie*, *32*, 152–61.

Ranyard, R., & McHugh, S. (2012). Bounded rationality in credit consumers' payment protection insurance decisions: The effect of relative cost and level of cover. *Journal of Risk Research*, *15*, 937–50.

Rao, A. R., & Monroe, K. B. (1989). The effect of price, brand name, and store name on buyers' perceptions of product quality – an integrative review. *Journal of Marketing Research*, *26*, 351–7.

Rapoport, A., & Chammah, A. M. (1965). *Prisoner's dilemma: A study in conflict and cooperation*. Ann Arbor: University of Michigan Press.

Rath, T., & Harter, J. (2010). *Wellbeing: The five essential elements*. New York: Gallup Press.

Ratliff, K., & Oishi, S. (2013). Gender differences in implicit self-esteem following a romantic partner's success or failure. *Journal of Personality and Social Psychology*, *105*, 688–702.

Rauch, A., & Frese, M. (2007). Let's put the person back into entrepreneurship research: A meta-analysis and the relationship between business owner's personality traits, business creation, and success. *European Journal of Work and Organizational Psychology*, *16*, 353–85.

Read, D., & Loewenstein, G. (1995). Diversification bias: Explaining the discrepancy in variety seeking between combined and separated choices. *Journal of Experimental Psychology: Applied*, *1*, 34–49.

Read, D., Loewenstein, G., & Rabin, M. (1999). Choice bracketing. *Journal of Risk and Uncertainty*, *19*, 171–97.

Reber, A. S. (1993). *Implicit learning and tacit knowledge*. Oxford: Oxford University Press.

Reekie, G. (1992). Changes in the Adam less Eden: The spatial and sexual transformation of a Brisbane department store 1930–90. In R. Shields (ed.), *Lifestyle shopping: The subject of consumption* (pp. 170–94). London: Routledge.

Rehn, M. L. (1981). Die Theorie der objektiven Selbstaufmerksamkeit and ihre Anwendung auf eine neue Methode der Befindensmessung: Das Tagebuch [The theory of objective self-awareness and its application for a new method of measuring findings: The diary] (unpublished thesis). University of Erlangen-Nuremberg.

Reimer, T., & Hoffrage, U. (2006). The ecological rationality of simple group heuristics: Effects of group member strategies on decision accuracy. *Theory and Decision*, *60*, 403–38.

Reimer, T., Hoffrage, U., & Katsikopoulos, K. (2007). Entscheidungsheuristiken in Gruppen [Decision-making heuristics in groups]. *NeuroPsychoEconomics*, *2*, 7–29.

Reisch, L. A., & Sunstein, C. R. (2016). Do Europeans like nudges? *Judgement and Decision Making*, *11*, 310–25.

Rieck, C. (2008). *Spieltheorie: Eine Einführung* [Game theory: An introduction] (8th edn). Eschborn: Christian Rieck.

Riegel, K. (2007). *Ekonomická psychologie* [Economic psychology]. Prague: Vydala Grada.

Rizavi, S. S., & Sofer, C. (2010). *Household division of labor: Is there any escape from traditional gender roles?* (Working Paper CES 10009). Paris: Centre d'Economie de la Sorbonne.

Robbins, L. (1932). *An essay on the nature and significance of economic science*. London: Macmillan.

Robbins, S. P. (1993). *Organizational behavior: Concepts, controversies, and applications* (6th edn). Englewood Cliffs, NJ: Prentice Hall.

Roberts, M. L., Hite, P. A., & Bradley, C. F. (1994). Understanding attitudes toward progressive taxation. *Public Opinion Quarterly*, *58*, 165–90.

Robinson, J. P., Yerby, P., Fieweger, J., & Somerick, N. (1977). Sex-role differences in time use. *Sex Roles*, *3*, 443–58.

Robinson, M. D., & Clore, G. L. (2001). Simulation, scenarios, and emotional appraisal: Testing the convergence of real and imagined reactions to emotional stimuli. *Personality and Social Psychology Bulletin*, *27*, 1520–32.

Rode, C., Cosmides, L., Hell, W., & Tooby. J. (1999). When and why do people avoid unknown probabilities in decisions under uncertainty? Testing some predictions from optimal foraging theory. *Cognition*, *72*, 269–304.

Rodler, C., & Kirchler, E. (1998). *Economic decisions – tactics used to influence the partner: The Vienna diary study*. Paper presented at the SASE 10th International Conference on Socio-Economics, Vienna, July.

(2002). *Führung in Organisationen* [Leadership in organisations]. Vienna: WUV.

Rodler, C., Kirchler, E., & Hoelzl, E. (2001). Gender stereotypes of leaders: An analysis of the contents of obituaries from 1974 to 1998. *Sex Roles*, *45*, 827–43.

Roethel, C. (2003). Die Qual der Wahl: Entscheidungen rechtzeitig treffen [The agony of choice: Making decisions at the right time]. *Psychologie Heute*, *6*, 32–7.

Rojas, M. (2007). Heterogeneity in the relationship between income and happiness: A conceptual-referent-theory explanation. *Journal of Economic Psychology*, *28*, 1–14.

Roland-Lévy, C. (2002). Passage du franc à l'euro: Représentation sociale et attitude [Change from franc to euro: Social representations and attitudes]. *Cahiers Internationaux de Psychologie Sociale*, *55*, 39–48.

Roland-Lévy, C., & Adair, P. (1998). *Psychologie économique: Théories et applications* [Economic psychology: Theories and applications]. Paris: Economica.

Roland-Lévy, C., Pappalardo Boumelki, F.-E., & Guillet, E. (2010). Representations of the financial crisis: Effect on social representations of savings and credit. *Journal of Socio-Economics*, *39*, 142–9.

Roos, V., Chiroro, P., van Coppenhagen, C., & Smith, I. E. (2005). Money adventures: Introducing economic concepts to preschool children in the South African context. *Journal of Economic Psychology*, *26*, 243–54.

Rosa, H. (2003). Social acceleration: Ethical and political consequences of a desynchronized high-speed society. *Constellations: An International Journal of Critical and Democratic Theory*, *10*, 3–52.

(2013). *Social acceleration: A new theory of modernity*. New York: Columbia University Press.

Rosette, A. S., & Tost, L. P. (2010). Agentic women and communal leadership: How role prescriptions confer advantage to top women leaders. *Journal of Applied Psychology*, *95*, 221–35.

Ross, L. (1977). The intuitive psychologist and his shortcomings: Distortion in the attribution process. In L. Berkowitz (ed.), *Advances in experimental social psychology* (vol. 10, pp. 174–221). New York: Academic Press.

Ross, L., & Nisbett, R. (1991). *The person and the situation*. New York: McGraw-Hill.

Rosso, B. D., Dekas, K. H., & Wrzesniewski, A. (2010). On the meaning of work: A theoretical integration and review. *Research in Organizational Behavior*, *30*, 91–127.

Rost, K., & Osterloh, M. (2008). Unsichtbare Hand des Marktes oder unsichtbares Handschütteln? Wachstum der Managerlöhne in der Schweiz [Invisible hand of the market or invisible handshakes? Salary growth for top managers in Switzerland]. *Die Unternehmung*, *3*, 274–304.

Roth, A. (1988). Laboratory experimentation in economics: A methodological overview. *Economic Journal*, 98, 974–1031.

Rötheli, T. F. (2010). Causes of the financial crisis: Risk misperception, policy mistakes, and banks' bounded rationality. *Journal of Socio-Economics*, *39*, 119–26.

Rothstein, B. (2000). Trust, social dilemmas, and collective memories: On the rise and decline of the Swedish model. *Journal of Theoretical Politics*, *12*, 477–99.

Rottenstreich, Y., & Hsee, C. K. (2001). Money, kisses, and electric shocks: On the affective psychology of risk. *Psychological Science*, *12*, 185–90.

Rotter, J. B., Chance, F. E., & Phares, E. J. (1972). *Applications of a social learning theory of personality*. New York: Holt, Rinehart & Winston.

Rousseau, D. (1995). *Psychological contracts in organization: Understanding written and unwritten agreements*. Thousand Oaks, CA: Sage.

Routh, D. A., & Burgoyne, C. B. (1998). Being in two minds about a single currency: A UK perspective on the euro. *Journal of Economic Psychology*, *19*, 741–54.

Rumiati, R., & Bonini, N. (1996). *Le decisioni degli esperti* [The decisions of experts]. Bologna: II Mulino.

Rumiati, R., & Lotto, L. (1996). Varieties of money. Experts' and non-experts' typicality judgments. *Journal of Economic Psychology*, *17*, 403–13.

Runyan, R. C., Huddleston, P., & Swinney J. (2006). Entrepreneurial orientation and social capital as small firm strategies: A study of gender differences from a resource-based view. *International Entrepreneurship and Management Journal*, *2*, 455–77.

Ryan, M. K., Haslam, S. A., Hersby, M. D., & Bongiorno, R. (2011). Think crisis – think female: The glass cliff and contextual variation in the think manager – think male stereotype. *Journal of Applied Psychology*, *96*, 470–84.

Ryan, R. M., & Deci, E. L. (2000). Self-determination theory and the facilitation of intrinsic motivation, social development, and well-being. *American Psychologist*, *55*, 68–78.

Rynes, S. L., Gerhart, B., & Parks, L. (2005). Personnel psychology: Performance evaluation and pay for performance. *Annual Review of Psychology*, *56*, 571–600.

Sachverständigenrat (2009). *Die Zukunft nicht aufs Spiel setzen. Jahresgutachten 2009/10* [Not to risk the future. Yearly Report 2009/10]. Wiesbaden: Sachverständigenrat zur Begutachtung der gesamtwirtschaftlichen Entwicklung, Statistisches Bundesamt.

(2015). *Zukunftsfähigkeit in den Mittelpunkt. Jahresgutachten 2015/16* [Future competence in focus. Yearly Report 2015/16]. Wiesbaden: Sachverständigenrat zur Begutachtung der gesamtwirtschaftlichen Entwicklung, Statistisches Bundesamt.

Sakurai, Y., & Braithwaite, V. (2003). Taxpayers' perceptions of practitioners: Finding one who is effective and does the right thing? *Journal of Business Ethics*, *46*, 375–87.

Salo, A. A., & Weber, M. (1995). Ambiguity aversion in first-price sealed-bid auctions. *Journal of Risk and Uncertainty*, *11*, 123–37.

Samuelson, P. A. (1938). The empirical implications of utility analysis. *Econometrica*, *6*, 344–56.

(1980). *Economics*. New York: McGraw-Hill.

Samuelson, P. A., & Nordhaus, W. D. (2007). *Volkswirtschaftslehre* [Economics] (18th edn). Landsberg am Lech: mi-Fachverlag.

Sanchez, P., & McCauley, D. (2006). Measuring and managing engagement in a cross-cultural workforce: New insights for global companies. *Global Business and Organizational Excellence*, *26*, 41–50.

Sandmo, A. (2003). Three decades of tax evasion: a perspective on the literature. Paper presented at the Skatteforum (The Research Forum on Taxation), Rosendal, Norway.

Sanfey, A. G. (2007). Decision neuroscience: New directions in studies of judgment and decision making. *Current Directions in Psychological Science*, *16*, 151–5.

Sanfey, A. G., Rilling, J. K., Aronson, J. A., Nystrom, L. E., & Cohen, J. D. (2003). The neural basis of economic decision-making in the ultimatum game. *Science*, *300*, 1755–8.

Saunders, E. M. (1993). Stock prices and Wall Street weather. *American Economic Review*, *83*, 1337–45.

Save the Children International Union (1933). *Children, young people and unemployment*. Genf: Eigenverlag.

Scanzoni, J. (1972). *Sexual bargaining: Power politics in the American marriage*. Englewood Cliffs, NJ: Prentice Hall.

Scanzoni, J., & Fox, G. L. (1980). Sex roles, family and society: The seventies and beyond. *Journal of Marriage and Family*, *42*, 743–56.

Scanzoni, J., & Polonko, K. (1980). A conceptual approach to explicit marital negotiation. *Journal of Marriage and Family*, *42*, 31–44.

Schachter, S., Hood, D. C., Andreassen, P., & Gerin, W. (1986). Aggregate variables in psychology and economics:

Dependence and the stock market. In B. Gilad & S. Kaish (eds.), *Handbook of behavioral economics* (vol. 3, pp. 237–71). London: Greenwich.

Schachter, S., Hood, D. C., Gerin, W., Andreassen, P., & Rennert, M. (1985). Some causes and consequences of dependence and independence in the stock market. *Journal of Economic Behavior and Organization*, *6*, 339–57.

Schaninger, C. M., & Buss, W. C. (1986). A longitudinal comparison of consumption and finance handling between happily married and divorced couples. *Journal of Marriage and Family*, *48*, 129–36.

Scharfstein, D. S., & Stein, J. C. (1990). Herd behavior and investment. *American Economic Review*, *80*, 465–79.

Schepanski, A., & Kelsey, D. (1990). Testing for framing effects in taxpayer compliance decisions. *Journal of the American Taxation Association*, *12*, 60–77.

Schepanski, A., & Shearer, T. (1995). A prospect theory account of the income tax withholding phenomenon. *Organizational Behavior and Human Decision Processes*, *63*, 174–86.

Scherhorn, G. (1990). The addictive trait in buying behaviour. *Journal of Consumer Policy*, *13*, 33–51.

Scherhorn, G., Reisch, L. A., & Raab, G. (1990). Addictive buying in West Germany: An empirical study. *Journal of Consumer Policy*, *13*, 355–87.

Schimmack, U., & Oishi, S. (2005). The influence of chronically and temporarily accessible information on life satisfaction judgments. *Journal of Personality and Social Psychology*, *89*, 395–406.

Schindler, R. M., & Kibarian, T. M. (1996). Increased consumer sales response through use of 99-ending prices. *Journal of Retailing*, *72*, 187–99.

(2001). Image communicated by the use of 99 endings in advertised prices. *Journal of Advertising*, *30*, 95–9.

Schindler, R. M., & Kirby, P. N. (1997). Patterns of rightmost digits used in advertised prices: Implications for nine-ending effects. *Journal of Consumer Research*, *24*, 192–201.

Schmale, H. (1983). *Psychologie der Arbeit* [Psychology of work]. Stuttgart: Klett-Cotta.

Schmidt, U., Starmer, C., & Sugden, R. (2008). Third-generation prospect theory. *Journal of Risk and Uncertainty*, *36*, 203–23.

Schmitt-Rodermund, E. (2005). Wer wird Unternehmer? Persönlichkeit, Erziehungsstil sowie frühe Interessen und Fähigkeiten als Vorläufer für unternehmerische Aktivität im Erwachsenenalter [Who becomes an entrepreneur? Personality, parenting style, and early interests and skills as precursors of adult entrepreneurial activity]. *Wirtschaftspsychologie*, *2*, 8–23.

Schmölders, G. (1959). Fiscal psychology: A new branch of public finance. *National Tax Journal*, *12*, 340–5.

(1960). *Das Irrationale in der öffentlichen Finanzwirtschaft* [The irrational in the public financial economy]. Frankfurt am Main: Suhrkamp.

(1966). *Psychologie des Geldes* [Psychology of money]. Reinbeck bei Hamburg: Rowohlt.

(1975). *Einführung in die Geld- und Finanzpsychologie* [Introduction to the psychology of money and finance]. Darmstadt: Wissenschaftliche Buchgesellschaft.

(1978). *Verhaltensforschung im Wirtschaftsleben* [Behavioural research in economic life]. Hamburg: Rowohlt.

Schneider, F. (2003). Zunehmende Schattenwirtschaft in Deutschland: Eine wirtschafts- und staatspolitische Herausforderung [The growing shadow economy in Germany: A challenge for economic and state policy]. *Vierteljahreshefte zur Wirtschaftsforschung*, *72*, 148–59.

(2007). *Size and development of the shadow economy in Germany and Austria: Some preliminary findings* (Working Paper 2007–15). Basel: Center for Research in Economics, Management and the Arts.

(2012). Tax evasion in Europe. *Cesifo Forum*, *13*, 3–12.

(2015). *Size and development of the shadow economy of 31 European and 5 other OECD countries from 2003 to 2015: Different developments*. Linz: Department of Economics, Johannes Kepler University Linz. Retrieved from www.econ.jku.at/members/Schneider/files/publications/2015/ShadEcEurope31.pdf (accessed 13 July 2016).

Schneider, F., & Buehn, A. (2013). *Shadow economies in highly developed OECD countries: What are the driving forces?* (Working Paper 1317). Linz: Department of Economics, Johannes Kepler University Linz.

Schneider, F., & Klinglmair, R. (2004). *Shadow economics around the world: What do we know?* (Working Paper 1167). Munich: Center for Economic Studies and Ifo Institute for Economic Research Cesifo.

Schneider, H., Schönenberg, I., & Ferié, F. (2013). The distribution of influence in purchase decisions by male homosexual couples. *Journal of Consumer Behavior*, *12*, 345–57.

Schneider, W., & Shiffrin, R. M. (1977). Controlled and automatic human information processing: I. Detection, search, and attention. *Psychological Review*, *84*, 1–66.

Schöny, W., Grausgruber, A., & Sommereder, M. (1988). Epidemiologische Suizidraten in Oberösterreich [Epidemiological suicide rates in Upper Austria]. *Gemeindepsychiatrie*, *9*, 53–61.

SCHUFA (2014). *SCHUFA Kredit-Kompass 2014* [SCHUFA Credit compass 2014]. Wiesbaden: SCHUFA Holding AG.

Schultz-Gambard, J., & Balz, H. J. (1988). Schicksal arbeitslos: Ein Überblick über die Ergebnisse angewandt-sozialpsychologischer Forschung zu den Folgen und Einflussfaktoren bei Arbeitslosigkeit [Unemployment as fate: An overview of results from applied psychology on the consequences and determinants of unemployment]. *Gruppendynamik*, *19*, 239–73.

Schulze, H., Spiller, A., Böhm, J., & de Witte, T. (2008). Ist Geiz wirklich geil? Preis–Qualitäts-Relationen von Hersteller- und Handelsmarken im Lebensmittelmarkt [Is greed really sexy? Price–quality relations of manufacturer and trade brands on the market for food]. *Agrarwirtschaft*, *57*, 299–310.

Schulz-Hardt, S., Vogelgesang, F., & Mojzisch, A. (2007). Finanzpsychologie [Financial psychology]. In K. Moser (ed.), *Wirtschaftspsychologie* (pp. 193–219). Heidelberg: Springer.

Schumacher, E. (1986). *Arbeitslosigkeit und psychische Gesundheit: Ergebnisse der Forschung* [Unemployment and mental health: Results from research]. Munich: Profil.

Schumacher, J., Klaiberg, A., & Brähler, E. (eds.) (2003). *Diagnostische Verfahren zu Lebensqualität and Wohlbefinden* [Diagnostic procedures for quality of life and well-being]. Göttingen: Hogrefe.

Schütz, A. (1999). It was your fault! Self-serving biases in autobiographical accounts of conflicts in married couples. *Journal of Social and Personal Relationships*, *16*, 193–208.

Schwartz, H. (2008). *A guide to behavioral economics*. Alexandria, VA: Higher Education Publications.

Schwartz, R., & Orleans, S. (1967). On legal sanctions. *University of Chicago Law Review*, *34*, 274–300.

Schwarz, N. (1987). *Stimmung als Information: Untersuchungen zum Einfluss von Stimmungen auf die Bewertung des eigenen Lebens* [Mood as information: Investigations of the influence of moods on evaluations of one's own life]. Berlin: Springer.

(1990). Feelings as information: Informational and motivational foundations of affective states. In E. T. Higgins & R. Sorrentino (eds.), *Handbook of motivation and cognition: Foundations of social behaviour* (vol. 2, pp. 53–92). New York: Guilford Press.

(1996). Cognition and communication. *Judgment biases, research methods, and the logic of conversation*. Mahwah, NJ: Lawrence Erlbaum Associates.

(1998). Warmer and more social: Recent developments in cognitive social psychology. *Annual Review of Sociology*, *24*, 239–64.

(1999). Self-reports: How the questions shape the answers. *American Psychologist*, *54*, 93–105.

(2001). Feelings as information: Implications for affective influences on information processing. In L. L. Martin & G. L. Clore (eds.), *Theories of mood and cognition: A user's guidebook* (pp. 159–76). Hillsdale, NJ: Erlbaum.

Schwarz, N., & Clore, G. L. (1983). Mood, misattribution, and judgments of well-being: Informative and directive functions of affective states. *Journal of Personality and Social Psychology*, *45*, 513–23.

Schwarz, N., & Hippler, H. J. (1987). What response scales may tell your respondents. In H. J. Hippler, N. Schwarz, & S. Sudman (eds.), *Social information processing and survey methodology* (pp. 163–78). New York: Springer.

Schwarz, N., & Scheuring, B. (1988). Judgments of relationship satisfaction: Inter- and intraindividual comparisons as a function of questionnaire structure. *European Journal of Social Psychology*, *18*, 485–96.

Schwarz, N., Strack, F., Kommer, D., & Wagner, D. (1987). Soccer, rooms, and the quality of your life: Mood effects on judgments of satisfaction with life in general and with specific domains. *European Journal of Social Psychology*, *17*, 69–79.

Schwarz, N., Wänke, M., & Bless, H. (1994). Subjective assessments and evaluations of change: Some lessons from social cognition research. In W. Stroebe & M. Hewstone (eds.), *European review of social psychology* (vol. 5, pp. 181–210). Chichester: Wiley.

Scitovsky, T. (1976). *The joyless economy: An inquiry into human satisfaction and dissatisfaction*. Oxford: Oxford University Press.

Sedlacek, T. (2011). *Economics of good and evil: The quest for economic meaning from Gilgamesh to Wall Street*. Oxford: Oxford University Press.

Seidl, C., & Traub, S. (2001). Taxpayers' attitudes, behavior, and perception of fairness. *Pacific Economic Review*, *6*, 255–67.

(2002). Die Akzeptanz des deutschen Steuersystems: Eine demoskopische Untersuchung [Acceptance of the German tax system: A demoscopic investigation]. In E. Theurl & E. Thöni (eds.), *Zukunftsperspektiven der Finanzierung öffentlicher Aufgaben* (pp. 7–27). Vienna: Böhlau.

Seldon, A. (ed.) (1979). *Tax avoison: The economic, legal and moral inter-relationships between avoidance and evasion*. London: Institute of Economic Affairs.

Seligman, M. E. P. (1975). *Helplessness: On depression, development, and death*. San Francisco: Freeman.

(2011). *Flourish: A visionary new understanding of happiness and well-being*. New York: The Free Press.

Sent, E.-M. (2004). Behavioral economics: How psychology made its (limited) way back into economics. *History of Political Economy*, *36*, 735–60.

Servon, L. J., & Kaestner, R. (2008). Consumer financial literacy and the impact of online banking on the financial behavior of lower-income bank customers. *Journal of Consumer Affairs*, *42*, 271–305.

Sevilla-Sanz, A., Gimenez-Nadal, J. I., & Fernandez, C. (2010). Gender roles and the division of unpaid work in Spanish households. *Feminist Economics*, *16*, 137–84.

Seymour, D., & Lessne, G. (1984). Spousal conflict arousal: Scale development. *Journal of Consumer Research*, *11*, 810–21.

Shafir, E., Diamond, P., & Tversky, A. (1997). Money illusion. *Quarterly Journal of Economics*, *112*, 341–74.

Shamir, J. (1985). Consumers' subjective perception of price in times of inflation. *Journal of Economic Psychology*, *6*, 383–98.

Shane, S., & Venkataraman, S. (2000). The promise of entrepreneurship as a field of research. *Academy of Management Review*, *25*, 217–26.

Shefrin, H., & Statman, M. (1985). The disposition to sell winners too early and ride loosers too long: Theory and evidence. *Journal of Finance*, *60*, 777–90.

Sher, L. (2005). Alcohol use and suicide rates. *Medical Hypotheses*, *65*, 1010–12.

Sherif, M., & Hovland, C. I. (1961). *Social judgment: Assimilation and contrast effects in communication and attitude change*. New Haven, CT: Yale University Press.

Sheth, J. N. (1974). A theory of family buying decisions. In J. N. Sheth (ed.), *Models of buyer behavior: Conceptual, quantitative, and empirical* (pp. 37–55). New York: Harper and Row.

Shiller, R. J. (2000). *Irrational exuberance*. Princeton, NJ: Princeton University Press.

(2008). *The sub-prime solution*. Princeton, NJ: Princeton University Press.

(2015). *Irrational exuberance* (3rd revised edn). Princeton, NJ: Princeton University Press.

Shiloh, S., Gerad, L., & Goldman, B. (2006). Patients' information needs and decision-making processes: What can be learned from genetic counselees? *Health Psychology*, *25*, 211–19.

Shim, S., Barber, B. L., Card, N. A., Xiao, J. J., & Serido, J. (2010). Financial socialization of first-year college students: The roles of parents, work, and education. *Journal of Youth and Adolescence*, *39*, 1457–70.

Shiv, B., Carmon, Z., & Ariely, D. (2005). Placebo effects of marketing actions: Consumers may get what they pay for. *Journal of Marketing Research*, *42*, 383–93.

Shleifer, A. (2000). *Inefficient markets: An introduction to behavioral finance*. Oxford: Oxford University Press.

Shleifer, A., & Vishny, R. (1997). The limits of arbitrage. *Journal of Finance*, *52*, 35–55.

Shore, T. H., & Tashchian, A. (2006). Effects of internal and external pay comparisons on work attitudes. *Journal of Applied Social Psychology*, *36*, 2578–98.

Shu, L. L., Mazar, N., Gino, F., Ariely, D., & Bazerman, M. H. (2012). Signing at the beginning makes ethics salient and decreases dishonest self-reports in comparison to signing at the end. *Proceedings of the National Academy of Sciences*, *109*, 15197–200.

Shubik, M. (1971). The dollar auction game: A paradox in non-cooperative behavior and escalation. *Journal of Conflict Resolution*, *15*, 109–11.

Sias, R. W. (2004). Institutional herding. *Review of Financial Studies*, *17*, 165–206.

Sierminska, E. (2015). Does it pay to be beautiful? *IZA World of Labor*, *161*, 1–10.

Sillamaa, M. A. (1999). Taxpayer behavior in response to taxation: Comment and new experimental evidence. *Journal of Accounting and Public Policy*, *18*, 165–77.

Silver, R., & Wortman, C. (1980). Coping with undesirable life events. In J. Garber & M. E. P. Seligman (eds.), *Human helplessness: Theory and applications* (pp. 279–340). New York: Academic Press.

Simmel, G. (1923/1996). Faithfulness and gratitude (trans. K. H. Wolff). In A. E. Komter (ed.), *The gift: An interdisciplinary perspective* (pp. 39–48). Amsterdam: Amsterdam University Press. (Reprinted from *The sociology of Georg Simmel*, ed. K. H. Wolff (pp. 379–95), New York: The Free Press, 1950.)

Simon, H. A. (1957). *Models of man*. New York: Wiley.

(1992). What is an 'explanation' of behaviour? *Psychological Science*, *3*, 150–61.

Simonson, I. (1990). The effect of purchase quantity and timing on variety-seeking behavior. *Journal of Marketing Research*, *27*, 150–62.

Simpson, S. S. (2002). *Corporate crime, law, and social control*. Cambridge: Cambridge University Press.

Skinner, B. F. (1953). *Science and human behavior*. New York: Macmillan.

Skolka, J. (1985). Berufsarbeit und Eigenleistungen [Professional work and individual contributions]. In J. Skolka (ed.), *Die andere Wirtschaft* (pp. 27–38). Vienna: Signum.

Slemrod, J. (1985). An empirical test for tax evasion. *Review of Economics and Statistics*, *67*, 232–8.

(ed.) (1992). *Why people pay taxes: Tax compliance and enforcement*. Ann Arbor: University of Michigan Press.

Slemrod, J., Blumenthal, M., & Christian, C. (2001). Taxpayer response to an increased probability of audit: Evidence from a controlled experiment in Minnesota. *Journal of Public Economics*, *79*, 455–83.

Sloman, S. A. (1996). The empirical case for two systems of reasoning. *Psychological Bulletin*, *119*, 3–22.

Sloterdijk, P. (2010). *Die nehmende Hand und die gebende Seite* [The hand that takes and the side that gives]. Berlin: Suhrkamp.

Slovic, P. (1995). The construction of preference. *American Psychologist*, *50*, 364–71.

Slovic, P., Finucane, M. L., Peters, E., & MacGregor, D. G. (2004). Risk as analysis and risk as feelings: Some thoughts about affect, reason, risk, and rationality. *Risk Analysis*, *24*, 311–22.

Slovic, P., Malmfors, T., Krewski, D., Mertz, C. K., Neil, N., & Bartlett, S. (1995). Intuitive toxicology. II. Expert and lay judgments of chemical risks in Canada. *Risk Analysis*, *15*, 661–75.

Smith, A. (1759/2000). *A theory of moral sentiments*. Amherst, NY: Prometheus Books.

(1776/1970). *The wealth of nations*. Harmondsworth: Penguin.

Smith, E. R., & DeCoster, J. (2000). Dual-process models in social and cognitive psychology: Conceptual integration and links to underlying memory systems. *Personality and Social Psychology Review*, *4*, 108–31.

Smith, P. (1994). Assessing the size of the underground economy: The Canadian statistical perspectives. (Statistics Canada, Catalogue no. 13–604-MIB no. 28). *Canadian Economic Observer*, May, 1–25.

Smith, R. E., Leffingwell, T. R., & Ptacek, J. T. (1999). Can people remember how they coped? Factors associated with discordance between same-day and retrospective reports. *Journal of Personality and Social Psychology*, *76*, 1050–61.

Smith, V. L. (2008). *Rationality in economics: Constructivist and ecological forms*. Cambridge: Cambridge University Press.

Smith, V. L., Suchanek, G., & Williams, A. (1988). Bubbles, crashes and endogenous expectations in experimental spot asset markets. *Econometrics*, *56*, 1119–51.

Smith, V. L., & Williams, A. W. (1993). Experimentelle Marktwirtschaft [Experimental market economy]. *Spektrum der Wissenschaft*, *2*, 68–74.

Snelders, H. M. J., Hussein, G., Lea, S. E. G., & Webley, P. (1992). The polymorphous concept of money. *Journal of Economic Psychology*, *13*, 71–92.

Soelberg, P. O. (1967). Unprogrammed decision making. *Industrial Management Review*, *8*, 19–29.

Solnick, S. J., & Hemenway, D. (1998). Is more always better? A survey on positional concerns. *Journal of Economic Behavior & Organization*, *37*, 373–83.

Solomon, M. R. (2011). *Consumer behavior: Buying, having, and being* (9th edn). Boston, MA: Pearson.

Soman, D. (2001). The mental accounting of sunk time costs: Why time is not like money. *Journal of Behavioral Desicion Making*, *14*, 169–85.

Sonnenberg, S. J. (2008). Household financial organisation and discursive practice: Managing money and identity. *Journal of Socio-Economics*, *37*, 533–51.

Sonnentag, S. (2012). Psychological detachment from work during leisure time: The benefits of mentally disengaging from work. *Current Directions in Psychological Science*, *21*, 114–18.

Soster, R. L., Gershoff, A. D., & Bearden, W. O. (2014). The bottom dollar effect: The influence of spending to zero on pain of payment and satisfaction. *Journal of Consumer Research*, *41*, 656–77.

Soutaris, V., Zerbinati, S., & Al-Laham, A. (2007). Do entrepreneurship programmes raise entrepreneurial intention of science and engineering students? The effect of learning, inspiration and resources. *Journal of Business Venturing*, *22*, 566–91.

Spectra (2003). *Euro: Das Preisgefühl will und will nicht besser werden* [Euro: The intuition for prices is still not getting better] (Spectra Aktuell 01/03). Linz: Spectra.

Spicer, M. W., & Lundstedt, S. B. (1976). Understanding tax evasion. *Public Finance*, *31*, 295–305.

Spicer, M. W., & Thomas, J. E. (1982). Audit probabilities and tax evasion decision: An experimental approach. *Journal of Economic Psychology*, *2*, 241–5.

Spiro, R. L. (1983). Persuasion in family decision-making. *Journal of Consumer Research*, *9*, 393–402.

Srinivasan, T. N. (1973). Tax evasion: A model. *Journal of Public Economics*, *2*, 339–46.

Srivastava, J., & Raghubir, P. (2002). Debiasing using decomposition: The case of memory-based credit card expense estimates. *Journal of Consumer Psychology*, *12*, 253–64.

Stanovich, K. E. (1999). *Who is rational? Studies of individual differences in reasoning*. Mahweh, NJ: Erlbaum.

(2004). *The robot's rebellion: Finding meaning in the age of Darwin*. Chicago, IL: University of Chicago Press.

Stanovnik, T. (1992). Perception of poverty and income satisfaction: An empirical analysis of Slovene households. *Journal of Economic Psychology*, *13*, 57–69.

Stavrova, O., Schlösser, T., & Fetchenhauer, D. (2011). Are the unemployed equally unhappy all around the world? The role of the social norms to work and welfare state provision in 28 OECD countries. *Journal of Economic Psychology*, *32*, 159–71.

Steenkamp, J.-B. E. M. (1988). The relationship between price and quality in the marketplace. *De Economist*, *136*, 491–507.

Steil, J. M. (1994). Equality and entitlement in marriage: Benefits and barriers. In M. J. Lerner & G. Mikula (eds.), *Entitlement and the affectional bond* (pp. 229–58). New York: Plenum Press.

Stengel, M. (1988). Freizeit: Zu einer Motivationspsychologie des Freizeitverhaltens [Leisure: The motivational psychology of leisure time behaviour]. In D. Frey, C. Graf Hoyos & D. Stahlberg (eds.), *Angewandte Psychologie* (pp. 561–84). Munich: Psychologie Verlags Union.

Stephan, E. R., & Kiell, G. (1998). Urteilsverzerrungen bei professionellen Akteuren im Finanzmarkt [Judgment distortions among professional actors on the financial market]. Lecture at the 41st Congress of the German Psychological Society, Dresden, September.

Stewart, W. H., & Roth, P. L. (2001). Risk propensity differences between entrepreneurs and managers – a meta-analytic review. *Journal of Applied Psychology*, *86*, 145–53.

Steyrer, J. (1995). *Charisma in Organisationen: Sozial-kognitive und psychodynamisch-interaktive Aspekte von Führung* [Charisma in organisations: Social-cognitive and psychodynamic-interactive aspects of leadership]. Frankfurt am Main: Campus.

Stiving, M., & Winer, R. S. (1997). An empirical analysis of price endings with scanner data. *Journal of Consumer Research*, *24*, 57–67.

Stocks, J., Díaz-Martínez, C., & Halleröd, B. (eds.) (2007). *Modern couples sharing money, sharing life*. Basingstoke: Palgrave Macmillan.

Stone, A. A., Schwartz, J. E., Broderick, J. A., & Deaton, A. (2010). A snapshot of the age distribution of psychological well-being in the United States. *Proceedings of the National Academy of Sciences*, *107*, 9985–90.

Strack, F., & Deutsch, R. (2004). Reflective and impulsive determinants of social behavior. *Personality and Social Psychology Review*, *8*, 220–47.

Strack, F., Martin, L. L., & Schwarz, N. (1988). Priming and communication: Social determinants of information use in judgments of life satisfaction. *European Journal of Social Psychology*, *18*, 429–42.

Strack, F., & Mussweiler, T. (1997). Explaining the enigmatic anchoring effect: Mechanisms of selective accessibility. *Journal of Personality and Social Psychology*, *73*, 437–46.

Strack, F., Werth, L., & Deutsch, R. (2006). Reflective and impulsive determinants of consumer behavior. *Journal of Consumer Psychology*, *16*, 205–16.

Strümpel, B. (1969). The contribution of survey research to public finance. In A. T. Peacock (ed.), *Quantitative analysis in public finance* (pp. 14–32). New York: Praeger.

Strümpel, B., & Katona, G. (1983). Psychologie gesamtwirtschaftlicher Prozesse [Psychology of macroeconomic processes]. In M. Irle & W. Sussmann (eds.), *Handbuch der Psychologie: Marktpsychologie: Marktpsychologie als Sozialwissenschaft* (vol. 1, pp. 225–81). Göttingen: Hogrefe.

Strümpel, B., Schmiedeskamp, J., & Schwartz, M. S. (1973). The function of consumer attitude data beyond econometric forecasts. In L. Mandell, G. Katona, J. N. Morgan, & J. Schmiedeskamp (eds.), *Surveys of consumers, 1971–72: Contributions to behavioral economics* (pp. 263–88). Ann Arbor: University of Michigan, Institute for Social Research.

Strzysch, M., & Weiß, J. (eds.) (1998). *Meyers großes Taschenlexikon in 24 Bänden* [Meyer's large paperback encyclopedia in 24 volumes] (vol. 24). Mannheim: B.I.-Taschenbuchverlag.

Stutzer, A. (2003). *Eine ökonomische Analyse menschlichen Wohlbefindens* [An economic analysis of human well-being]. Aachen: Shaker.

Su, C., Fern, E. F., & Ye, K. (2003). A temporal dynamic model of spousal family purchase-decision behaviour. *Journal of Marketing Research*, *40*, 268–81.

Su, C., Zhou, K. Z., Zhou, N., & Li, J. J. (2008). Harmonizing conflict in husband–wife purchase decision making: Perceived fairness and spousal influence dynamics. *Academy of Marketing Science Journal*, *36*, 378–94.

Sung, S., & Bennett, F. (2007). Dealing with money in low-moderate income couples: Insights from individual interviews. *Social Policy Review*, *19*, 151–73.

Sunstein, C. R. (2014). *Why nudge: The politics of libertarian paternalism*. New Haven, CT: Yale University Press.

(2016a). The council of psychological advisers. *Annual Review of Psychology*, *67*, 713–37.

(2016b). *The ethics of influence: Government in the age of behavioral science*. Cambridge: Cambridge University Press.

Surowiecki, J. (2004). *The wisdom of crowds: Why the many are smarter than the few and how collective wisdom shapes business, economies, societies, and nations*. London: Little Brown.

Sussman, A. B., & Alter, A. L. (2012). The exception is the rule: Underestimating and overspending on exceptional expenses. *Journal of Consumer Research*, *39*, 800–14.

Sussman, A. B., & Olivola, C. Y. (2011). Axe the tax: Taxes are disliked more than equivalent costs. *Journal of Marketing Research*, *48*, 91–101.

Sutter, M., & Kocher, M. (2007). Trust and trustworthiness across different age groups. *Games and Economic Behavior, 59*, 364–82.

Sutter, M., & Weck-Hannemann, H. (2003). Taxation and the veil of ignorance: A real effort experiment on the Laffer curve. *Public Choice, 115*, 217–40.

Svedsäter, H., Gamble, A., & Gärling, T. (2007). Money illusion in intuitive financial judgments: Influences of nominal representation of share prices. *Journal of Socio-Economics, 36*, 698–712.

Svenson, O. (1981). Are we all less risky and more skillful than our fellow drivers? *Acta Psychologica, 47*,143–8.

Svenson, O., & Nilsson, G. (1986). Mental economics: Subjective representations of factors related to expected inflation. *Journal of Economic Psychology, 7*, 327–49.

Svorencik, A. (2015). *The experimental turn in economics: A history of experimental economics* (Utrecht School of Economics Dissertation Series 029). Utrecht University.

Swedberg, R. (1991). Major traditions of economic sociology. *Annual Review of Sociology, 17*, 251–76.

Sweet, E., Nandi, A., Adam, E. K., & McDade, T. W. (2013). The high price of debt: Household financial debt and its impact on mental and physical health. *Social Science and Medicine, 91*, 94–100.

Swenson, C. (1988). Taxpayer behavior in response to taxation: An experimental analysis. *Journal of Accounting and Public Policy, 7*, 1–28.

Szinovacz, M. E. (1987). Family power. In M. B. Sussman & S. K. Steinmetz (eds.), *Handbook of marriage and the family* (pp. 651–93). New York: Plenum.

Szybillo, G. J., & Sosanie, A. K. (1977). Family decision making: Husband, wife and children. *Advances in Consumer Research, 4*, 46–9.

Szybillo, G. J., Sosanie, A. K., & Tenenbein, A. (1977). Should children be seen but not heard? *Journal of Advertising Research, 17*, 7–13.

Tajfel, H. (1978). *Differentiation between social groups: Studies in the social psychology of intergroup relations*. London: Academic Press.

(1981). *Human groups and social categories*. Cambridge: Cambridge University Press.

Tajfel, H., & Turner, J. C. (1979). An integrative theory of intergroup conflict. In W. G. Austin & S. Worchel (eds.), *The social psychology of intergroup relations* (pp. 33–47). Monterey, CA: Brooks/Cole.

Tang, J., Tang, Z., & Lohrke, F. T. (2008). Developing an entrepreneurial typology: The roles of entrepreneurial alertness and attributional style. *International Entrepreneurial Management Journal, 4*, 273–94.

Tang, T., Tang, D., & Luna-Arocas, R. (2005). Money profiles: The love of money, attitudes and needs. *Personnel Review, 34*, 603–18.

Tansuhaj, P. S., & Foxman, E. R. (1990). The use of triad data to study family puchase decisions. *Advances in Consumer Research, 17*, 523–5.

Tarde, G. (1902). *La psychologie économique* [Economic psychology]. Paris: Alcan.

Tellegen, A., Lykken, D., Bouchard, T., Wilcox, K., Segal, N., & Rich, S. (1988). Personality similarity in twins reared apart and together. *Journal of Personality and Social Psychology, 54*, 1031–9.

Tellis, G. J., & Wernerfelt, B. (1987). Competitive price and quality under asymmetric information. *Marketing Science, 6*, 240–53.

Thaler, R. H. (1980). Toward a positive theory of consumer choice. *Journal of Economic Behavior and Organization, 1*, 39–60.

(1985). Mental accounting and consumer choice. *Marketing Science, 4*, 199–214.

(1992). *The winner's curse: Paradoxes and anomalies of economic life*. New York: Macmillan.

(1999). Mental accounting matters. *Journal of Behavioral Decision Making, 12*, 183–206.

(2015). *Misbehaving: The making of behavioral economics*. New York: W. W. Norton.

(2015). The power of nudges, for good and bad. *The New York Times*, 31 October. Retrieved from www.nytimes.com/2015/11/01/upshot/the-power-of-nudges-for-good-and-bad.html (accessed 18 December 2016).

Thaler, R. H., & Johnson E. (1990). Gambling with the house money and trying to break even: The effects of prior outcomes on risky choice. *Management Science, 36*, 643–60.

Thaler, R. H., & Shefrin, H. M. (1981). An economic theory of self-control. *Journal of Political Economy, 89*, 392–406.

Thaler, R. H., & Sunstein, C. R. (2008). *Nudge: Improving decisions about health, wealth, and happiness*. New Haven, CT: Yale University Press.

Thibaut, J., & Kelley, H. H. (1959). *The social psychology of groups*. New York: Wiley.

Thierry, H. (1992). Pay and payment systems. In J. F. Hartley & G. M. Stephenson (eds.), *Employment relations* (pp. 136–60). Oxford: Blackwell.

Thomas, B., & Madigan, B. (1974). Strategy and job choice after redundancy: A case study in the aircraft industry. *Sociological Review, 22*, 83–102.

Thomas, K. D. (2013). Presumptive collection: A prospect theory approach to increasing small business tax compliance. *Tax Law Review, 67*, 111–68.

Thorndike, E. L. (1927). The law of effect. *American Journal of Psychology, 39*, 212–22.

Tichenor, V. J. (1999). Status and income as gendered resources: The case of marital power. *Journal of Marriage and Family, 61*, 638–50.

(2005). *Earning more and getting less: Why successful wives can't buy equality*. New Brunswick, NJ: Rutgers University Press.

Toates, F. (2006). A model of the hierarchy of behavior, cognition and consciousness. *Consciousness and Cognition, 15*, 75–118.

Todd, P., & Gigerenzer, G. (2000). Précis of simple heuristics that make us smart. *Behavioral and Brain Science, 23*, 727–80.

Torgler, B. (2002). Speaking to theorists and searching for facts: Tax morale and tax compliance in experiments. *Journal of Economic Surveys, 16*, 657–83.

(2007). *Tax compliance and tax morale: A theoretical and empirical analysis*. Cheltenham: Edward Elgar.

Torgler, B., & Schneider, F. (2009). The impact of tax morale and institutional quality on shadow economy. *Journal of Economic Psychology, 30*, 228–45.

Traut-Mattausch, E., Greitemeyer, T., Frey, D., & Schulz-Hardt, S. (2007). Illusory price increases after the euro changeover in

Germany: An expectancy-consistent bias. *Journal of Consumer Policy*, *30*, 421–34.

Traut-Mattausch, E., Schulz-Hardt, S., Greitemeyer, T., & Frey, D. (2004). Expectancy confirmation in spite of disconfirming evidence: The case of price increases due to the introduction of the euro. *European Journal of Social Psychology*, *34*, 739–60.

Trevelyan, R. (2011). Self-regulation and effort in entrepreneurial tasks. *International Journal of Entrepreneurial Behaviour and Research*, *17*, 39–63.

Treynor, J. L. (1987). Market efficiency and the bean jar experiment. *Financial Analysts Journal*, *43*, 50–3.

Trivedi, V. U., Shehata, M., & Lynn, B. (2003). Impact of personal and situational factors on taxpayer compliance: An experimental analysis. *Journal of Business. Ethics*, *47*, 175–97.

Trivedi, V. U., Shehata, M., & Mestelman, S. (2005). Attitudes, incentives, and tax compliance. *Canadian Tax Journal*, *53*, 29–61.

Tucker, A. W. (1950). A two-person dilemma. Mimeo, Stanford University. Published under the heading 'On jargon: the prisoner's dilemma.' *UMAP Journal*, *1*, 1980, p. 101.

Turner, J. C., Hogg, M. A., Oakes, P. J., Reicher, S. D., & Wetherell, M. (1987). *Rediscovering the social group: A self-categorization theory*. Oxford: Basil Blackwell.

Tversky, A. (1972). Elimination by aspects: A theory of choice. *Psychological Review*, *79*, 281–99.

(1973). Inductive inference: Judgment under uncertainty. In G. J. Dalenoort (ed.), *Process models for psychology*. Rotterdam: Rotterdam University Press.

(1977). Features of similarity. *Psychological Review*, *84*, 327–52.

Tversky, A., & Kahneman, D. (1974). Judgment under uncertainty: Heuristics and biases. *Science*, *185*, 1124–31.

(1981). The framing of decisions and the psychology of choice. *Science*, *211*, 453–8.

(1983). Extensional versus intuitive reasoning: The conjunction fallacy in probability judgment. *Psychological Review*, *90*, 293–315.

(1991). Loss aversion in riskless choice: A reference-dependent model. *Quarterly Journal of Economics*, *106*, 1039–61.

(1992). Advances in prospect theory: Cumulative representation of uncertainty. *Journal of Risk and Uncertainty*, *5*, 297–323.

Tybout, A. M., & Artz, N. (1994). Consumer psychology. *Annual Review of Psychology*, *45*, 131–69.

Tyler, T. R. (2003). Trust within organisations. *Personnel Review*, *32*, 556–68.

Tyler, T. R., Goff, P. A., & MacCoun, R. J. (2015). The impact of psychological science on policing in the United States: Procedural justice, legitimacy, and effective law enforcement. *Psychological Science in the Public Interest*, *16*, 75–109.

Tyszka, T. (1994). Cognitive representation of economics. Paper presented at the IAREP/SABE conference, Rotterdam, July.

Tyszka, T., & Sokolowska, J. (1992). Perception and judgments of the economic system. *Journal of Economic Psychology*, *13*, 421–48.

Tyszka, T., & Zaleskiewicz, T. (2006). When does information about probability count in choices under risk? *Risk Analysis*, *26*, 1623–36.

Ulich, E., & Ulich, H. (1977). Über einige Zusammenhänge zwischen Arbeitsgestaltung und Freizeitverhalten [On a few associations between the organisation of work and free time behaviour]. In T. Leuenberger & K.-H. Ruffmann (eds.), *Bürokratie – Motor oder Bremse der Entwicklung* (pp. 209–27). Berne: Lang.

Unrein, H. (1978). *Arbeitslosigkeit: Fakten, Aspekte, Wirkungen* [Unemployment: Facts, aspects, effects]. Cologne: Wissenschaft und Politik.

US Bureau of Economic Analysis (2017). Real gross domestic product per capita [A939RX0Q048SBEA]. Retrieved from FRED, Federal Reserve Bank of St. Louis; https://fred.stlouisfed.org/series/A939RX0Q048SBEA (accessed 3 January 2017).

Uysal, S. D., & Pohlmeier, W. (2011). Unemployment duration and personality. *Journal of Economic Psychology*, *32*, 980–92.

van de Braak, H. (1983). Taxation and tax resistance. *Journal of Economic Psychology*, *3*, 95–111.

van der Heijden, J., & Kosters, M. (2015*). From mechanism to virtue: Evaluating nudge-theory* (RegNet Working Paper 80). Regulatory Institutions Network, Australian National University, Canberra.

Van Dijk, E., & Zeelenberg, M. (2003). The discounting of ambiguous information in economic decision making. *Journal of Behavioral Decision Making*, *16*, 341–52.

Van Everdingen, Y. M., & van Raaij, W. F. (1998). The Dutch people and the euro: A structural equations analysis relating national identity and economic expectations to attitude towards the euro. *Journal of Economic Psychology*, *19*, 721–40.

Van Lange, P. A. M., & Joireman, J. A. (2008). How can we promote behavior that serves all of us in the future? *Social Issues and Policy Review*, *2*, 127–57.

van Raaij, W. F. (1981). Economic psychology. *Journal of Economic Psychology*, *1*, 1–24.

(2016). *Understanding consumer financial behavior*. Basingstoke: Palgrave Macmillan.

van Raaij, W. F., & van Rijen, C. (2003). *Money illusion and euro pricing*. Paper presented at the IAREP (International Association for Research in Economic Psychology) Euro-Workshop, Vienna, July.

van Raaij, W. F., van Veldhoven, G. M., & Wärneryd, K.-E. (eds.) (1988). *Handbook of economic psychology*. Dordrecht: Kluwer.

Van Rooij, M. C., Lusardi, A., & Alessie, R. J. (2011). Financial literacy and retirement planning in the Netherlands. *Journal of Economic Psychology*, *32*, 593–608.

Vanek, J. (1974). Time spent in housework. *Scientific American*, *231*, 116–20.

Västfjäll, D., Gärling, T., & Kleiner, M. (2004). Preference for mood, emotional reaction, and anticipated emotional reaction. *Scandinavian Journal of Psychology*, *45*, 25–34.

Vaughn, R. (1980). How advertising works: A planning model. *Journal of Advertising Research*, *20*, 27–33.

Vázquez, J. (2013). Happiness among the garbage: Differences in overall happiness among trash pickers in León (Nicaragua). *Journal of Positive Psychology*, *8*, 1–11.

Veblen, T. (1899). *The theory of the leisure class: An economic study in the evolution of institutions*. New York: Macmillan.

Veenhoven, R. (1984). *Conditions of happiness*. Dordrecht: R. Reidel.

(1991). Is happiness relative? *Social Indicators Research*, *24*, 1–34.
(1994). Is happiness a trait? Tests of the theory that a better society does not make people any happier. *Social Indicators Research*, *32*, 101–60.
(2000). The four qualities of life: Ordering concepts and measures of the good life. *Journal of Happiness Studies*, *1*, 1–39.
(2016a). Average happiness in 159 nations 2005–2014. World Database of Happiness, Erasmus University Rotterdam. Retrieved from http://worlddatabaseofhappiness.eur.nl/hap_nat/findingreports/RankReport_AverageHappiness.php (accessed 29 July 2016).
(2016b). *Happy life years in 159 nations 2005–2014*. World Database of Happiness, Erasmus University Rotterdam. Retrieved from http://worlddatabaseofhappiness.eur.nl/hap_nat/findingreports/RankReport_HappyLifeYears.php (accessed 21 June 2016).
(2017). *Distributional findings on happiness in United States (US)*, World Database of Happiness, Erasmus University Rotterdam. Retrieved from http://worlddatabaseofhappiness.eur.nl (accessed 4 January 2017).
Veit, O. (1927). Grundlagen der Steuermoral [Foundations of tax morale]. *Zeitschrift für die gesamte Staatswissenschaft*, *83*, 317–44.
Venkataraman, S. (1997). The distinctive domain of entrepreneurship research: An editor's perspective. In J. Katz & R. Brockhaus (eds.), *Advances in entrepreneurship, firm emergence, and growth* (vol. 3, pp. 119–38). Greenwich, CT: JAI Press.
Vergès, P. (1987). A social & cognitive approach to economic representations. In W. Doise & S. Moscovici (eds.), *Current issues in European social psychology* (pp. 271–304). Cambridge: Cambridge University Press.
Vergès, P., Tyszka, T., & Vergès, P. (1994). Representations of economics by French and Polish students. Paper presented at the IAREP/SABE conference, Rotterdam, July.
Vershofen, W. (1940). *Handbuch der Verbrauchsforschung* [Handbook of consumer research]. Berlin: Heymann.
Vetter, A. (1966). *Anthropologie der Person* [Anthropology of the person]. Freiburg: Alber.
Viaud, J., & Roland-Lévy, C. (2000). A positional and representational analysis of consumption. Households when facing debt and credit. *Journal of Economic Psychology*, *21*, 411–32.
Vigderhous, G., & Fishman, G. (1978). The impact of unemployment and familial integration on changing suicide rates in the USA, 1920–1969. *Social Psychiatry*, *13*, 239–48.
Vlek, C., & Stallen, P. J. (1981). Judging risks and benefits in the small and in the large. *Organizational Behavior and Human Performance*, *28*, 235–71.
Vogel, J. (1974). Taxation and public opinion in Sweden: An interpretation of recent survey data. *National Tax Journal*, *27*, 78–85.
Vogel, L., Menz, J.-O., & Fritsche, U. (2009). Prospect theory and inflation perceptions – an empirical assessment (DEP Discussion Papers Macroeconomics and Finance Series 3/2009). University of Hamburg, Department of Economics and Politics.
Vogler, C. (1998). Money in the household: Some underlying issues of power. *Sociological Review*, *46*, 687–713.
Vogler, C., Brockmann, M., & Wiggins, R. D. (2006). Intimate relationships and changing patterns of money management at the beginning of the twenty-first century. *British Journal of Sociology*, *57*, 455–82.
(2008). Managing money in new heterosexual forms of intimate relationships. *Journal of Socio-Economics*, *37*, 552–76.
Vogler, C., Lyonette, C., & Wiggins, R. D. (2008). Money, power and spending decisions in intimate relationships. *Sociological Review*, *56*, 117–43.
Vogler, C., & Pahl, J. (1994). Money, power and inequality within marriage. *Sociological Review*, *42*, 263–88.
Vogt, C. (2000). The evolution of cooperation in prisoner's dilemma with an endogenous learning mutant. *Journal of Economic Behavior and Organization*, *42*, 347–73.
(2001). Kooperation im Gefangenen Dilemma durch endogenes Lernen [Cooperation in the prisoner's dilemma through edogenous learning] (Unpublished dissertation). University of Magdeburg.
Vohs, K. D. (2015). Money priming can change people's thoughts, feelings, motivations, and behaviors: An update on 10 years of experiments. *Journal of Experimental Psychology: General*, *144*, e86–e93.
Völckner, F., & Hofmann, J. (2007). The price-perceived quality relationship: A meta-analytic review and assessment of its determinants. *Marketing Letters*, *18*, 181–96.
Volkmann, J. (1951). Scales of judgement and their implications for social psychology. In J. H. Rohrer & M. Sherif (eds.), *Social psychology at the crossroads* (pp. 273–96). New York: Harper.
Von Neumann, J., & Morgenstern, C. (1944). *Theory of games and economic behavior*. Princeton, NJ: Princeton University Press.
von Rosenstiel, L. (1992). *Grundlagen der Organisationspsychologie* [Fundamental principles of organisational psychology]. Stuttgart: Schäffer-Poeschel.
von Rosenstiel, L., & Ewald, G. (1979). *Marktpsychologie* [Market psychology] (vol. 1). Stuttgart: Kohlhammer.
Voß, G. G., & Pongratz, H. J. (1998). Der Arbeitskraftunternehmer. Eine neue Grundform der Ware Arbeitskraft? [The workforce entrepreneur. A new basic form of labour power as a commodity]. *Kölner Zeitschrift für Soziologie und Sozialpsychologie*, *50*, 131–58.
Vroom, V. H. (1964). *Work and motivation* (3rd edn). New York: Wiley.
Wacker, A. (1983). *Arbeitslosigkeit: Soziale und psychische Folgen* [Unemployment: Social and mental consequences]. Frankfurt am Main: Europäische Verlagsgesellschaft.
Wagner, R. (1999). Attributionsmuster und Arbeitslosigkeit – eine Längsschnittstudie über die Entwicklung von Attributionsmustern und deren psychischen Konsequenzen während der Arbeitsplatzunsicherheit und der anhaltenden Arbeitslosigkeit [Patterns of attribution and unemployment] (unpublished dissertation). University of Vienna.
Wagner, W., Duveen, G., Farr, R., Jovchelovitch, S., Lorenzi-Cioldi, F., Marková, I., & Rose, D. (1999). Theory and method of social representations. *Asian Journal of Social Psychology*, *2*, 95–125.
Wagner, W., Kirchler, E., & Brandstätter, H. (1984). Marital relationships and purchasing decisions. To buy or not to buy, that's the question? *Journal of Economic Psychology*, *5*, 139–57.

Wahl, I., Kastlunger, B., & Kirchler, E. (2010). Trust in authorities and power to enforce tax compliance: An empirical analysis of the 'slippery slope framework'. *Law and Policy*, *32*, 383–406.

Wahl, I., Pollai, M, & Kirchler, E. (2013). Status, identification and in-group favouritism of the unemployed compared to other social categories. *Journal of Socio-Economics*, *43*, 37–43.

Wainer, H. A., & Rubin, I. M. (1969). Motivation of research and development entrepreneurs: Determinants of company success. *Journal of Applied Psychology*, *53*, 178–84.

Wakker, P. P. (2010). *Prospect theory: For risk and ambiguity*. Cambridge: Cambridge University Press.

Walbran, B., MacMahon, B., & Bailey, A. E. (1965). Suicide and unemployment in Pennsylvania, 1955–1961. *Archiv of Environment Health*, *10*, 11–15.

Walenta, C., & Kirchler, E. (2011). *Führung* [Leadership]. Vienna: Facultas.wuv.

Walker, C. M. (1996). Financial management, coping and debt in households under financial strain. *Journal of Economic Psychology*, *17*, 789–807.

Walster [Hatfield], E., Walster, G. W., & Berscheid, E. (1978). *Equity: Theory and research*. Boston, MA: Allyn and Bacon.

Wanberg, C. R., Glomb, T. M., Song, Z., & Sorenson, S. (2005). Job-search persistence during unemployment: A 10-wave longitudinal study. *Journal of Applied Psychology*, *3*, 411–30.

Wanberg, C. R., Kanfer, R., & Rotundo, M. (1999). Unemployed individuals: Motives, job-search competencies, and job-search constraints as predictors of job seeking and reemployment. *Journal of Applied Psychology*, *84*, 897–910.

Wanberg, C. R., Song, Z., & Hough, L. M. (2002). Predictive validity of a multidisciplinary model of reemployment success. *Journal of Applied Psychology*, *87*, 1100–20.

Wanberg, C. R., Watt, J. D., & Rumsey, D. J. (1996). Individuals without jobs: An empirical study of job-seeking behavior and reemployment. *Journal of Applied Psychology*, *81*, 76–87.

Wang, J., & Xiao, J. J. (2009). Buying behavior, social support and credit card indebtedness of college students. *International Journal of Consumer Studies*, *33*, 2–10.

Wang, X. T. (1996). Domain-specific rationality in human choices: Violations of utility axioms and social contexts. *Cognition*, *60*, 31–63.

Ward, S., & Wackman, D. B. (1973). Children's purchase influence attempts and parental yielding. In H. H. Kassajian & T. S. Robertson (eds.), *Perspectives in consumer behavior* (pp. 369–74). Glenview, IL: Scott, Foresman.

Wärneryd, K.-E. (1988a). Economic psychology as a field of study. In W. F. van Raaij, G. M. Van Veldhoven, & K.-E. Wärneryd (eds.), *Handbook of economic psychology* (pp. 2–41). Dordrecht: Kluwer.

(1988b). The psychology of innovative entrepreneurship. In W. F. van Raaij, G. M. van Veldhoven, & K.-E. Wämeryd (eds.), *Handbook of economic psychology* (pp. 404–47). Dordrecht: Kluwer.

(1993). Psychology + economics = economic psychology? (unpublished paper). Stockholm School of Economics.

(1999). *The psychology of saving: A study on economic psychology*. Cheltenham: Edward Elgar.

(2001). *Stock-market psychology: How people value and trade stocks*. Cheltenham: Edward Elgar.

Wärneryd, K.-E., & Walerud, B. (1982). Taxes and economic behavior: Some interview data on tax cheating in Sweden. *Journal of Economic Psychology*, *2*, 187–211.

Warr, P. B. (1983). Job loss, unemployment and psychological well-being. In V. Allen & E. van de Vliert (eds.), *Role transitions* (pp. 263–85). New York: Plenum Press.

Warr, P. B., & Payne, R. L. (1983). Social class and reported changes in behavior after job loss. *Journal of Applied Social Psychology*, *13*, 206–22.

Waters, L. E., & Moore, K. A. (2001). Coping with economic deprivation during unemployment. *Journal of Economical Psychology*, *22*, 461–82.

Weber, M. (1968). *Soziologie – weltgeschichtliche Analysen – Politik* [Sociology – analyses of world history – politics]. Stuttgart: Kröner.

(1993). Ambiguitätseffekte in experimentellen Märkten [Ambiguity effects in experimental markets]. In Rheinisch-Westfälische Akademie der Wissenschaften (ed.), *Vorträge N 397* (pp. 33–47). Opladen: Westdeutscher Verlag.

Weber, M., & Camerer, C. F. (1998). The disposition effect in securities trading: An experimental analysis. *Journal of Economic Behavior & Organization*, *33*, 167–84.

Webley, P. (2004). Tax compliance by businesses. In H. Sjögren & G. Skogh (eds.), *New perspectives on economic crime* (pp. 95–126). Cheltenham: Edward Elgar.

Webley, P., & Lea, S. E. G. (1993). The partial unacceptability of money in repayment for neighborly help. *Human Relations*, *46*, 65–76.

Webley, P., Lea, S. E. G., & Portalska, R. (1983). The unacceptability of money as a gift. *Journal of Economic Psychology*, *4*, 223–38.

Webley, P., Robben, H. S. J., Elffers, H., & Hessing, D. J. (1991). *Tax evasion: An experimental approach*. Cambridge: Cambridge University Press.

Weck, H., Pommerehne, W. W., & Frey, B. S. (1984). *Schattenwirtschaft* [The shadow economy] (WiSt Taschenbücher). Munich: Vahlen.

Weck-Hannemann, H., & Pommerehne, W. (1989). Einkommenssteuerhinterziehung in der Schweiz: Eine empirische Analyse [Income tax evasion in Switzerland: An empirical analysis]. *Schweizerische Zeitschrift für Volkswirtschaft und Statistik*, *125*, 515–56.

Wedel, M., & Leeflang, P. S. H. (1998). A model for the effects of psychological pricing in Gabor-Granger price studies. *Journal of Economic Psychology*, *19*, 237–60.

Weibel, A., & Bernhard, U. (2006). Verdienen Topmanager zu viel? [Do top executives earn too much?]. *Zeitschrift für Organisation*, *2*, 75–80.

Weilbacher, W. M. (2001). Point of view: Does advertising cause a 'hierarchy of effects'? *Journal of Advertising Research*, *41*, 19–26.

Weinert, A. B. (1998). *Organisationspsychologie: Ein Lehrbuch* [Organisational psychology: A textbook] (4th edn). Weinheim: Psychologie Verlags Union.

Weinstein, N. D. (1984). Why it won't happen to me: Perceptions of risk factors and susceptibility. *Health Psychology*, *2*, 431–57.

West, C., & Zimmerman, D. H. (1987). Doing gender. *Gender and Society*, *1*, 125–51.

Wiendieck, G. (1990). Börse als vernachlässigter Bereich der Wirtschaftspsychologie [The stock market as a neglected area of economic psychology]. In P. Maas & J. Weibler (eds.), *Börse und Psychologie* (pp. 38–57). Cologne: Deutscher Institutsverlag.

Williams, C. C. (2007). *Rethinking the future of work: Directions and visions*. Basingstoke: Palgrave Macmillan.

Williamson, J., Ranyard, R., & Cuthbert, L. (2000). A conversation-based process tracing method for use with naturalistic decisions: An evaluation study. *British Journal of Psychology, 91*, 203–21.

Williamson, M. R., & Wearing, A. J. (1996). Lay people's cognitive models of the economy. *Journal of Economic Psychology, 17*, 3–38.

Wilson, F., & Stocks, J. (2007). The meaning of breadwinning in dual-earner couples. In J. Stocks, C. Díaz-Martínez, & B. Halleröd (eds.), *Modern couples sharing money, sharing life* (pp. 72–99). Basingstoke: Palgrave Macmillan.

Wilson, J. L. F., & Sheffrin, S. (2005). Understanding surveys of taxpayer honesty. *Finanzarchiv, 61*, 256.

Wilson, T. D. (2002). *Strangers to ourselves*. Cambridge, MA: Belknap.

Wilson, T. D., & Gilbert, D. T. (2003). Affective forecasting. *Advances in Experimental Social Psychology, 35*, 345–411.

Winder, K. (2009). Flexible scheduling and the gender wage gap. *The B. E. Journal of Economic Analysis and Policy, 9*, Article 30 [no pagination].

Winer, R. S. (1986). A reference price model of brand choice for frequently purchased products. *Journal of Consumer Research, 13*, 250–6.

Winkelmann, P. (2008). *Marketing und Vertrieb* [Marketing and distribution] (6th edn). Munich: Oldenbourg.

Winter-Ebmer, R., & Zweimüller, J. (1991). Sind Schulungsmaßnahmen ein wirkungsvolles Mittel zur Bekämpfung individueller Arbeitslosigkeit? [Are training programs an effective means of fighting individual unemployment?]. *Wirtschaftspolitische Blätter, 5–6*, 695–700.

Wiswede, G. (1991). *Einführung in die Wirtschaftspsychologie* [Introduction to economic psychology]. Munich: UTB.

(2007). *Einführung in die Wirtschaftspsychologie* [Introduction to economic psychology] (4th edn). Munich: UTB.

Witte, E., & Raphael, C. (2004). Der Euro, der junge Konsument und die wirtschaftliche Entwicklung [The euro, young consumers and economic development]. *Wirtschaftspsychologie, 6*, 71–4.

Wood, G. (1978). The knew-it-all-along effect. *Journal of Experimental Psychology: Human Perception and Performance, 4*, 345–53.

Woll, A. (1981). *Allgemeine Volkswirtschaftslehre* [General economics]. Munich: Vahlen.

World Bank Group (2016). GDP per capita (current US$). Retrieved from http://data.worldbank.org/indicator/NY.GDP.PCAP.CD (accessed 21 June 2016).

Wu, G., Zhang, J., & Gonzalez, R. (2004). Decision under risk. In N. Harvey & D. Koehler (eds.), *Blackwell handbook of judgment and decision making* (pp. 399–423). Malden, MA: Blackwell.

Wyer, R. S., & Carlston, D. (1979). *Social cognition, inference and attribution*. Hillsdale, NJ: Erlbaum.

Yamauchi, K., & Templer, D. (1982). The development of a money attitudes scale. *Journal of Personality Assessment, 46*, 522–8.

Yang, X., Zafar, U. A., Morry, G., Kuan, H. N., Wan, L. T., & Chai, Y. W. T. (2006). Spousal influence in Singaporean family purchase decision-making process. *Asia Pacific Journal of Marketing and Logistics, 18*, 201–22.

Yap, S. C. Y., Anusic, I., & Lucas, E. L. (2012). Does personality moderate reaction and adaption to major life events? Evidence from the British Household Panel Survey. *Journal of Research in Personality, 46*, 477–88.

Yap, S. C., Wortman, J., Anusic, I., Baker, S. G., Scherer, L. D., Donnellan, M. B., & Lucas, R. E. (2016). The effect of mood on judgments of subjective well-being: Nine tests of the judgment model. *Journal of Personality and Social Psychology* [advance online publication]. doi: 10.1037/pspp0000115.

Yavas, A., Senfton, M., & Katok, E. (2002). Implementation by iterative dominance and backward induction: An experimental comparison. *Journal of Economic Theory, 104*, 89–103.

Yavas, U., Babakus, E., & Delener, N. (1994). Family purchasing roles in Saudi Arabia: Perspectives from Saudi wives. *Journal of Business Research, 31*, 75–86.

Zapf, W. (2000). Social reporting in the 1970s and in the 1990s. *Social Indicators Research, 51*, 1–15.

Zapf, W., Schupp, J., & Habich, R. (eds.) (1996). *Lebenslagen im Wandel: Sozialberichterstattung im Längsschnitt* [Changing living conditions: Longitudinal social reporting]. Frankfurt am Main: Campus.

Zaugg, R. J. (2006). *Work–life balance: Ansatzpunkte für den Ausgleich zwischen Erwerbs- und Privatleben aus individueller, organisationaler und gesellschaftlicher Sicht* [Work-life balance: Starting points for the adjustment between professional life and private life from an individual, organisational and societal perspective] (Discussion Paper 9). Lahr: Wissenschaftliche Hochschule Lahr WHL.

Zawadski, B., & Lazarsfeld, P. (1935). Psychological consequences of unemployment. *Journal of Social Psychology, 6*, 224–51.

Zeelenberg, M. (1999). Anticipated regret, expected feedback and behavioral decision-making. *Journal of Behavioral Decision Making, 12*, 93–106.

Zeelenberg, M., & Pieters, R. (2007). A theory of regret regulation 1.0. *Journal of Consumer Psychology, 17*, 3–18.

Zeelenberg, M., & van Dijk, E. (1997). A reverse sunk cost effect in risky decision making: Sometimes we have too much invested to gamble. *Journal of Economic Psychology, 18*, 677–91.

Zhao, H., & Seibert, S. E. (2006). The big five personality dimensions and entrepreneurial status: A meta-analytical review. *Journal of Applied Psychology, 91*, 259–71.

Zikic, J., & Klehe, U. C. (2006). Job loss as a blessing in disguise: The role of career exploration and career planning in predicting reemployment quality. *Journal of Vocational Behavior, 69*, 391–409.

INDEX